Creation and Humanity

The Sources of Christian Theology
Editorial Board

Dr. Timothy F. George, Beeson Divinity School,
Samford University, Birmingham, Alabama

Dr. Lois Malcolm, Luther Seminary, St. Paul, Minnesota

Dr. John A. McGuckin, Union Theological Seminary, New York

Dr. Joseph P. Wawrykow, University of Notre Dame,
Notre Dame, Indiana

Creation and Humanity

The Sources of Christian Theology

Edited by Ian A. McFarland

WESTMINSTER
JOHN KNOX PRESS
LOUISVILLE · KENTUCKY

© 2009 Westminster John Knox Press

1st edition

Published by Westminster John Knox Press
Louisville, Kentucky

09 10 11 12 13 14 15 16 17 18—10 9 8 7 6 5 4 3 2 1

All rights reserved. No part of this book may be reproduced or transmitted in any form or by any means, electronic or mechanical, including photocopying, recording, or by any information storage or retrieval system, without permission in writing from the publisher. For information, address Westminster John Knox Press, 100 Witherspoon Street, Louisville, Kentucky 40202-1396. Or contact us online at www.wjkbooks.com.

Scripture quotations from the New Revised Standard Version of the Bible are copyright © 1989 by the Division of Christian Education of the National Council of the Churches of Christ in the U.S.A. and are used by permission.

Every effort has been made to determine whether texts are under copyright. If through an oversight any copyrighted material has been used without permission, and the publisher is notified of this, acknowledgment will be made in future printings.

See "Permissions," pp. 451–52, for additional permission information.

Book design by Drew Stevens
Cover design by Eric Walljasper, Minneapolis, MN

Library of Congress Cataloging-in-Publication Data

Creation and humanity : the sources of Christian theology / edited by Ian A. McFarland.
    p. cm. — (The sources of Christian theology)
  Includes bibliographical references (p.   ).
  ISBN 978-0-664-23135-4 (alk. paper)
 1. Creation. 2. Theological anthropology—Christianity. 3. Good and evil—Religious aspects—Christianity. 4. Providence and government of God—Christianity. I. McFarland, Ian A. (Ian Alexander), 1963–
  BT695.C677 2009
  230—dc22

2009001907

PRINTED IN THE UNITED STATES OF AMERICA

∞ The paper used in this publication meets the minimum requirements of the American National Standard for Information Sciences—Permanence of Paper for Printed Library Materials, ANSI Z39.48-1992.

Westminster John Knox Press advocates the responsible use of our natural resources. The text paper of this book is made from 30% postconsumer waste.

Contents

Series Introduction	vii
Acknowledgments	ix
A Note on the Selection and Arrangement of Texts	xi
Introduction	xiii
Abbreviations	xxxiii

Chapter 1. God as Creator — 1
- 1: Justin Martyr, *First Apology* — 3
- 2: Theophilus of Antioch, *To Autolycus*, Book 2 — 4
- 3: Origen of Alexandria, *On First Principles*, Book 1 — 7
- 4: Augustine, *Confessions*, Book 11 — 9
- 5: Bonaventure, *Breviloquium*, 2 — 16
- 6: Thomas Aquinas, *Summa contra Gentiles*, 2:17–19, 38 — 24
- 7: Friedrich Schleiermacher, *Christian Faith*, §§40–41 — 30
- 8: Regin Prenter, "The Biblical Witness Concerning Creation" — 39
- 9: David Kelsey, "The Doctrine of Creation from Nothing" — 47
- 10: Jürgen Moltmann, "Creation Out of Nothing" — 65
- 11: Catherine Keller, "The Pluri-Singularity of Creation" — 72
- 12: Dimitru Staniloae, "Creation 'Ex Nihilo' in Time" — 86

Chapter 2. The Creature — 95
- 1: Irenaeus of Lyons, *Against Heresies*, Book 5 — 97
- 2: Gregory of Nyssa, *On the Making of Humankind* — 104
- 3: John Chrysostom, *Homilies Concerning the Statues* — 118
- 4: Maximus the Confessor, *Difficulty* 41 — 123
- 5: Thomas Aquinas, *Summa Theologiae*, 1.93 — 129
- 6: Sojourner Truth, "Ar'n't I a Woman?" — 137
- 7: Karl Barth, "The Basic Form of Humanity" — 138
- 8: Hans Urs von Balthasar, "Woman as Answer" — 148
- 9: Rosemary Radford Ruether, "Toward a Feminist Anthropology beyond Liberalism and Romanticism" — 156
- 10: John Zizioulas, "From Biological to Ecclesial Existence: The Ecclesiological Significance of the Person" — 161
- 11: Mary McClintock Fulkerson, "Contesting the Gendered Subject: A Feminist Account of the *Imago Dei*" — 173

Chapter 3: Evil and Sin — 191

  1: Origen of Alexandria, *On First Principles*, Book 1 — 193
  2: Athanasius, *Against the Heathen* — 200
  3: Augustine of Hippo, *The City of God*, Book 14 — 204
  4: Thomas Aquinas, *On Evil*, Quest 3 — 215
  5: John Calvin, *Institutes of the Christian Religion*, Book 2, Chapter 1 — 230
  6: Teresa of Avila, *The Interior Castle*, 1 — 239
  7: Friedrich Schleiermacher, *Christian Faith*, §§69, 71–72.2 — 247
  8: Walter Rauschenbusch, "The Kingdom of Evil" — 262
  9: Karl Barth, "The Reality of Nothingness" — 269
  10: Reinhold Niebuhr, "Sin and Man's Responsibility" — 281
  11: Valerie Saiving, "The Human Situation: A Feminine View" — 289
  12: James H. Cone, "God and Black Suffering" — 304
  13: David Ray Griffin, "The Furies and the Goodness of God" — 315
  14: Stephen G. Ray Jr., "Redeeming Sin-Talk" — 325
  15: Rowan Williams, "Against Symbols" — 334

Chapter 4: Providence — 339

  1: Irenaeus of Lyons, *Against Heresies*, Book 3 — 341
  2: Augustine of Hippo, *On the Holy Trinity*, Book 3 — 344
  3: Thomas Aquinas, *Summa Theologiae*, 1.22, 103 — 353
  4: Julian of Norwich, *Showings* (Long Text) — 362
  5: John Calvin, *Institutes of the Christian Religion*, Book 1, Chapter 16 — 367
  6: Friedrich Schleiermacher, *Christian Faith*, §§46–47 — 374
  7: Karl Barth, "The Christian Belief in Providence" — 391
  8: Pierre Teilhard de Chardin, *The Future of Man* — 399
  9: John B. Cobb Jr. and David Ray Griffin, "Why an Evolutionary Process?" — 406
  10: Grace Jantzen, "Action and Embodiment" — 411
  11: Wolfhart Pannenberg, "The Doctrine of Creation in an Age of Scientific Cosmology" — 419
  12: Arthur Peacocke, "God's Interaction with the World" — 429
  13: Kathryn Tanner, "Is God in Charge?" — 435

Permissions — 451
Suggestions for Further Reading — 453
Index — 457

Series Introduction

The Sources of Christian Theology is a series of books to provide resources for the study of major Christian doctrines.

The books are edited by expert scholars who provide an extended introductory discussion of the important dimensions of the doctrine. The main focus of each volume is on selections of source materials. These are drawn from major Christian theologians and documents that convey essential elements of theological formulations about each doctrine. The editor provides context and backgrounds in short introductory materials prior to the selections. A bibliography for further study is included.

There is no substitute in theological study for a return to the "sources." This series provides a wide array of source materials from the early church period to the present time. The selections represent the best Christian theological thinking and display the range of ways in which Christian persons have thought about the issues posed by the major aspects of Christian faith.

We hope that those interested in the study of Christian theology will find these volumes rich and valuable resources. They embody the efforts of Christian thinkers to move from "faith" to "understanding."

Donald K. McKim
Westminster John Knox Press

Acknowledgments

Putting together an anthology is a tricky business, even in an age when electronic communication and text transfer help to ease the burden of obtaining permissions and uploading individual extracts. I am grateful, first of all, to Don McKim for inviting me to work on this project. Thanks, too, go to Dilu Nicholas and Julie Tonini at Westminster John Knox Press for keeping permissions organized and paying the bills. My research assistants, Vance West and John Penniman, did yeoman service in doggedly tracking down the holders of copyright, and John's perseverance with the scanner was invaluable in getting the various selections into electronic format. Finally, I owe a large debt to my former colleague, David Fergusson, now Professor of Divinity at the University of Edinburgh, whose own careful thinking on the doctrine of creation has deeply shaped my engagement with the topic.

A Note on the Selection and Arrangement of Texts

The enormous quantity and breadth of material Christians have written on the doctrine of creation makes it a foregone conclusion that any anthology will be selective. This volume is no exception, as is especially evident in the lack of attention given to the nonhuman creation (including angels and demons as well as animals, plants, and the inorganic realm). While this is at least partly a function of the strongly anthropocentric character of Christian reflection on creation, other relevant questions (e.g., the relationship between nature and grace, the world as the theater of divine glory) also receive short shrift. My only defense is that some such omissions are unavoidable in a volume of this size; my hope is that the quality of material included is sufficient to leave the reader with a text that is useful, if by no means complete.

Perhaps even more problematic than the necessarily limited number of topics covered, however, is the choice of theological voices represented in the readings. Thomas Aquinas appears in all four sections, but he is hardly the only theologian who might have done so. Origen, Augustine, Calvin, and Schleiermacher (to name only a few) are given more limited exposure, though they are no less comprehensive in their theological vision. And figures as influential as John of Damascus, Luther, Wesley, and Rahner appear nowhere at all. With such an embarrassment of theological riches available, the inclusion of comparatively minor figures like Theophilus of Antioch, Sojourner Truth, and Regin Prenter, as well as a host of contemporary writers whose impact on the tradition cannot yet be assessed with any degree of certainty, may seem questionable, to say the least. Some explanation is therefore in order.

My aim in selecting texts has been first and foremost to provide as broad a range as possible of significantly different approaches to key issues within the doctrine of creation. Second I have thought it important to include within each section influential voices from the premodern period, as a means both of highlighting the diversity of perspectives within "mainline" Christian theology and of helping the reader see the way in which particular themes are (or are not) developed within the tradition. Third, I have sought to be inclusive of as broad as possible a range of confessional traditions, as well as voices of those who, by reason of gender or ethnicity, have largely been excluded from theological conversation in the past. Finally, in order to allow readers to enter more fully into the texture of individual writers' thought, I have opted for a comparatively small number of longer readings rather than a more extensive list of shorter excerpts.

Needless to say, these criteria often work against one another, thereby complicating the selection process. I have been greatly assisted by many (including especially the series editors) in helping to overcome some of my own prejudices and blind spots.

Within each of the main sections, readings are arranged in chronological order to help the reader to track some of the ways that Christian reflection on each of the book's four main subtopics has developed over time. An effort has been made to cover the same basic chronological periods (i.e., patristic, medieval-Reformation, and modern) in each section in order to give a sense of major turning points in the history of Christian reflection on creation. The balance of readings, however, has been weighted toward the modern period in order to communicate a sense of the range of options currently "in play" in contemporary theology. In addition, each text is accompanied by a brief introduction to help orient the reader to the character and context of the author (n.b., for authors appearing more than once, biographical information is given with the first entry only), and to summarize the significance of the selection for Christian theology.

With respect to the presentation of individual selections, all footnotes present in the original published version of a text have been retained, but the desire to avoid an overly technical apparatus in a student anthology has led me to be more selective with respect to the inclusion of explanatory footnotes added by editors to pre-twentieth-century selections. Furthermore, both original and editorial footnotes have been revised where necessary to ensure consistency in referencing conventions across the volume. These revisions include the following:

1. Using standard academic (i.e., *Chicago Manual of Style*) format for citation of monographs and articles
2. Employing abbreviations for frequently cited texts (see p. xxxiii below)
3. Using Arabic numerals only when referencing premodern texts (e.g., *Against Heresies* 3.20.3 means book 3, chapter 20, section 3; *The City of God* 5.6–9 means book 5, chapters 6–9; *Summa Theologiae* 1.93.2–4 means part 1, question 93, articles 2–4, and so forth)
4. Standardizing translation of foreign-language titles (e.g., Gregory of Nyssa's treatise on human creation is always referred to as *On the Making of Humankind*)
5. Including reference to an English translation (ET), where available, whenever a foreign-language text is cited

Finally, I have tried to update archaic language from older translations with a more contemporary idiom.

Introduction

In everyday speech *creation* is synonymous with "the world" or "the universe." This usage hides the fact that unlike these other terms *creation* implicitly refers to an act of creating and, more specifically, to an agent who creates. Within Christian circles these implicit features tend to be much more to the fore, so that creation is understood as the intentional project of a creator God; but even here the focus tends to be limited to the question of how things began. Considered in the context of Christian doctrine as a whole, however, the topic of creation extends well beyond the world's origin. Because for Christians the God who creates "in the beginning" does not withdraw from the scene and leave the world to its own devices, the doctrine of creation properly refers to *the totality of God's relations to everything that is not God*. As such, creation is not just about what happened once upon a time; it includes the many dimensions of how God continues to interact with what God has made.

Fortunately, the history of reflection on the doctrine of creation in the Christian tradition suggests ways of dividing up this topic that help to shape theological reflection on the broad range of subject matter it includes. I have chosen four subdivisions, which correspond to the chapters of this book:

1. *God as Creator*: God in distinction from everything that is not God
2. *The Creature*: that which is not God but is *from* God
3. *Evil and Sin*: that which is not God and is *not from* God
4. *Providence*: God's direction of everything that is not God to its divinely intended end

These four chapters are far from being self-contained. Each of the texts in this volume bears witness to the ways in which these subdivisions naturally bleed into one another: for example, to speak of God as creator already raises the question of what it is that God creates; the experience of creation invariably runs up against the fact of sin; talk of sin raises questions of providence; and talk about providence is inseparable from some account of how God is distinguished from the world. Nevertheless, these subdivisions do reflect distinct questions that arise in connection with the doctrine of creation, and their sequence follows in a rough fashion the narrative order of the Christian story: God creates (1) a world (2) that, though threatened by destruction (3), remains under God's protective guidance (4).

God as Creator

The affirmation of God as creator is an ancient feature of Christian faith. The first article of the Apostles' Creed (whose origins can be traced back to the second century) reads, "I believe in God, the Father almighty, creator of heaven and earth."[1] Several points are worth noting in this deceptively simple proposition. First, the confession of God as creator is explicitly described as a matter of *faith* (see Heb. 11:3). There is no suggestion here that belief in creation is self-evident, or that it is somehow easier to accept than the subsequent articles on the resurrection or the forgiveness of sins. Indeed, no less a figure than Martin Luther argued that it was actually *more* difficult to believe in creation than in the incarnation![2] If the language of the creed is taken seriously, creation is not a place where Christian doctrine swerves closer to the domains of philosophy or science than elsewhere. As will become apparent from many of the texts included in this volume, this is not to deny that scientific views about the origin of the world may have significant implications for Christian claims about creation; but it is to reject the view that the doctrine of creation is best understood as a theory about the world's origin.

In fact, the language of the creed suggests that the doctrine of creation is primarily a claim about the identity of God and only derivatively about the origin of the world. Specifically (and this is the second main point to note about the phrasing of the creed), God's status as creator is a function of God's identity as "the Father almighty." Creation is a work God performs. As such, it is rooted in the kind of divinity God is. In other words, what God *does* in making the world is rooted in who God *is* apart from this making. The creed identifies two elements of this divine "who." First, God is *Father*.[3] This term distinguishes the Christian creator from every interpretation of deity as an abstract and impersonal power. The Father is the God proclaimed by Jesus as the one who is faithful and who, more importantly, demonstrates this faithfulness by raising Jesus from the dead (Acts 13:26–33). To name God as Father is therefore to identify him as trustworthy and good.

Furthermore, to identify God as Father is also to say something about the nature of this goodness. As Christians reflected further on the implications of their belief that Jesus' resurrection was decisive for understanding

---

1. Although the Old Roman Creed, from which the later Apostles' Creed derived, lacked the words "creator of heaven and earth," they were arguably superfluous, since "where the term 'Father' was used" in the late second century "the reference was to God in His capacity as Father and creator of the universe." J. N. D. Kelly, *Early Christian Creeds*, 3rd ed. (New York: Continuum, 2006), 136; cf. 372.

2. Martin Luther, *WA*, vol. 39/II, 340.

3. The creedal language for the divine persons is thoroughly patriarchal and, as such, problematic for contemporary proclamation of the Christian gospel. The difficulties in finding an acceptable alternative have been well rehearsed in the literature, and the prospects for ecumenical consensus are not promising. Throughout this text I will endeavor to make use of inclusive language for God wherever possible, but I will retain the traditional terminology for the divine persons as a means of conversing with and making sense of the tradition.

who God is, they concluded that "Father" was not simply a title God took on in the first century in claiming Jesus as Son but was rather intrinsic to the divine identity from all eternity: God is Father because God is eternally in relationship with the Son and thus eternally faithful—even apart from creation. At the same time, the confession of God's eternal relationality allows the work of creation to be seen as fundamentally consistent with God's character. God does not create because God is lonely or incomplete; but neither is creation arbitrary or capricious. On the contrary, the fact that God is eternally Father allows the work of creation to be seen as an outward extension of God's own intradivine love that is as natural as it is gracious. Thus, while for God to be Father is not the same as for God to be creator, it is the ground of God's creating work.

The second element of the divine "who" that the creed identifies is God's being "almighty." The Latin word this translates is *omnipotens*, from which the English word *omnipotent*, or all-powerful, derives. Behind both terms is the biblical Greek title *pantocrator* (Rev. 1:8; 4:8; 11:17 and passim), which literally means "all-ruler." This term is more precise than *omnipotent*, because rather than raise the specter of a divinity who is simply identified with power in the abstract, it points specifically to God's concrete lordship over what is: God is not rightly conceived as an arbitrary deity who can do anything but rather as the sovereign Lord who has made and remains unswervingly and indefeasibly committed to this world and its myriad creatures across time and space. To confess God as almighty is thus not to say that only God has power; it is instead to identify God as the one who is the ground of all creaturely empowerment. In short, it is precisely *as* "Father"—the one who eternally loves the Son in the power of the Holy Spirit—that God *is* "almighty," so that God's power as creator is properly understood in the context of loving relationship rather than tyrannical rule.

Granted this underlying characterization of the creator, however, what is the significance of the work of creation itself? Though the creation story of Genesis 1 is generally taken as a classic proof text for the doctrine of creation, its implications for a theology of creation are not as straightforward as they might first appear. In this text God's relationship to the world is characterized in Hebrew by the verb *bara'*, which is normally translated "to create." Much is often made of the fact that in the Hebrew Scriptures this verb is predicated only of God, and while it is important not to overstate the significance of this point (since in vv. 7, 16, and 25 of this chapter God's creating activity is described using the verb *'asah*, which is not restricted to the deity), it does suggest that God stands in a unique relationship to the world as a whole that has no exact parallel in any relationship that exists between creatures. Yet what is the nature of this relationship? What does it mean to say that God "creates"? Does talk of creation imply that the world had a beginning in time, or might the world be eternal? Does the characterization of God as creator mean that God is the only power responsible for the world's existence, or did God work on, with, or against other primordial entities to bring the cosmos into being?

The evidence within Genesis 1 is ambiguous. Most English versions follow the lead of the earliest surviving translation of the Hebrew, the Greek Septuagint, by rendering the first three verses of Genesis as a series of separate sentences. The King James Version is typical:

> In the beginning God created the heaven and the earth.
> And the earth was without form, and void; and darkness *was* upon the face of the deep. And the Spirit of God moved upon the face of the waters.
> And God said, Let there be light: and there was light.
> (Gen. 1:1–3 KJV)

Against this tradition, however, many modern scholars (following the lead of medieval Jewish exegetes) have concluded that the first words of the Hebrew text are better rendered as a dependent clause, with the result that these same three verses are properly read as just one sentence:

> When God began to create heaven and earth—the world being then a formless waste, with darkness over the deep and only an awesome wind sweeping over the face of the waters—God said, "Let there be light"; and there was light.[4]

This latter reading seems to presuppose a chaos of some sort that preexists God's creative activity: a windswept, watery deep engulfing a formless world. Though this swirling "deep" is not personified in the narrative, it is hard to avoid the impression that it is in some sense resistant to change (cf. Job 26:12–13; Ps. 74:14; 89:10; Isa. 51:9, where the imagery of God combating hostile marine powers is much more explicit). It is in any case evidently already present as the raw material for God's creative activity, and a number of recent writers on creation (including Catherine Keller; see pp. 72–86 below) have argued that Christians need to take this dimension of the biblical witness on creation far more seriously than the majority of theologians down through the centuries have been inclined to do.

For most of the history of the church, however, there was virtual consensus on the character of God's creative work that left no room for the questions raised by contemporary exegesis. The exegetical difficulties of Genesis 1 could be alleviated (if not fully resolved) by reference to John 1:1–3, where the grammar of "the beginning" was unambiguous and included no mention of any reality other than God:

> In the beginning was the Word, and the Word was with God, and the Word was God. He was in the beginning with God. All things came into being through him, and without him not one thing came into being.[5]

---

4. E. A. Speiser, *Genesis* (Garden City, NY: Doubleday, 1964), 3 [translation slightly altered]; cf. the commentary on p. 12. This phrasing is followed by the translators of the NRSV, though they begin a new sentence with v. 3.

5. All further biblical translations are taken from the NRSV, unless otherwise indicated.

In light of these passages—and over against cosmologies in which matter was held to be eternal—the overwhelming majority of Christians since the late second century have maintained that the world had a definite beginning, with creation as the first act in an ongoing story that would conclude with the Last Judgment. This perspective not only fit with the broadly narrative shape of the emerging Christian canon, with its movement from origin through crisis to consummation; it also reflected the theological conviction that a world that had always existed would be equiprimordial with God and therefore (seemingly) either not fully subject to God's lordship or not clearly distinguished from God. The vast majority of Christians believed that avoiding these two conclusions required affirming that there was a cosmic "zero hour" when the world first came into being.

Similar considerations led to the denial that the creation of the world involved any other realities apart from God alone. Again, the opening verses of the Fourth Gospel (see also 1 Cor. 8:6), where there is no mention of any watery deep or formless void, are strongly suggestive. Other cosmologies might imagine God working with preexisting matter or struggling with various supernatural powers, but for Christians creation was the work of God alone (see Isa. 44:24), who brought all things into existence by the gracious and irresistible power of the divine Word (see Ps. 33:8–9). To invoke any other factor as ingredient to creation seemed necessarily to compromise divine sovereignty. How could God truly be "almighty" if God had to reckon with other forces when bringing the world into being? Wouldn't such forces invariably constrain God's capacity to realize the world God intended?

In order to secure God's sole creative agency against every possible qualification, the early church had by the end of the second century settled on the doctrine of "creation from nothing" (*creatio ex nihilo*). The point of this phrase was not to provide a summary description of the work of creation (as though "nothing" were itself a kind of stuff out of which God made the world), but precisely to insist that God's creation of the world had no parallel with any process of making within the created order. Perhaps the most natural model of creaturely making is that of deliberate shaping or fashioning, in which an agent crafts something from substances that lie to hand (e.g., a potter shaping clay). Such making requires as raw material some preexisting stuff, which serves as both the ground and limit for whatever is made. In declaring that God created "from nothing" Christians wanted to insist that God's creative activity had no ground or limit other than God's own will: in contrast to all human creation "from" something that exists alongside the artisan, in the divine work of creation God is the only precondition for what is created.

Yet in affirming that God was the only precondition for creation, Christians did not want to suggest that creation was somehow part of God. Thus, in addition to ruling out models of making as manufacture, the doctrine of creation from nothing was also designed to exclude processes in which the thing made is substantially continuous with the maker, like the experience of giving birth or the emanation of light from fire or a stream from a spring. To say that the world is created from nothing is to affirm that God is the agent but not the substance of creation: although creation is from God, it is not in any sense divine. This radical distinction between creator and creation seemed consistent with the biblical depiction of God's creating by a word of command, as well as with the biblical writers' emphasis on the consistently personal character of God's ongoing interactions with creation. Furthermore, it echoes the frequent reminders of God's essential incomparability with the created order (see Num. 23:19; 1 Sam. 15:29; Isa. 55:9; Mark 10:18; cf. Exod. 33:20).

In this way, the doctrine of creation from nothing implies a radical form of divine transcendence that gives further specification to the confession of God as "almighty." As the one and only condition of creation's existence, God stands apart from and over the world: every creature is in every respect absolutely dependent on God for its existence, but God is completely independent of the creation. This radical vision of divine transcendence has been called into question (especially, though not exclusively, by process theologians influenced by the philosophy of Alfred North Whitehead) both on the basis of exegetical arguments like those described above and on the grounds that it promotes an arbitrary and authoritarian model of God that is inconsistent with Christian convictions regarding the freedom and integrity of creation. Nevertheless, the idea of God's radical otherness with respect to the world continues to enjoy strong support as the best means of doing justice to the Christian belief that because the creation is entirely and exclusively gift, its form is not determined or constrained by any reality other than God.

The Creature
Granted God's identity as creator, it is only natural to ask what it is God has created. The Apostles' Creed answers this question with "heaven and earth," a phrase that echoes the language of Genesis 1:1 and is clearly meant to include the whole cosmos (cf. Rev. 4:11). The fourth-century Nicene Creed stresses the all-inclusive character of God's creative work by adding "of all that is, visible and invisible," thereby affirming that God's creative work includes not only the material universe that we see but also the invisible realm of spiritual beings like angels and demons. In a more contemporary idiom the doctrine of creation affirms that God's creative work covers the whole of the space-time continuum, including both all those creatures that have ceased to exist and those that have yet to be. Because it is unilaterally dependent on God, all creation is contingent: neither creation as a whole nor any single creature within it exists by necessity. Yet because everything that exists, living or nonliving, great or small, has been created by God, its

contingency does not speak against its intrinsic value. On the contrary, every creature, as creature, is the object of God's love and is consequently "very good" (Gen. 1:31).

Crucially, this foundational affirmation of the goodness of creation is coupled with an insistence that to be a creature is to be radically other than God. In the previous section this distinction was considered from the side of the creator; now it needs to be developed from the side of the creature. Here its primary implication is a refusal to regard any creature as worthy of worship: because the creature is other than God, it is not to be worshiped as God (Deut. 4:19; 17:2–5). While this exclusivity is often contrasted unfavorably with religious traditions that do not distinguish between the natural world and the divine in this way, it does not in any way constitute a denigration of nature. On the contrary, when read in the context of belief in creation's essential goodness, it means that a creature's value is not dependent on its being divine. Rather, its worth is simply a corollary of its existence, since that fact alone confirms its status as a creature of God. In short, every creature is good simply because it *is*.

This same line of reasoning dictates that a creature's attributes are no more divine than the creature itself and thereby implies that the absolute distinction between creator and creation posited by the doctrine of *creatio ex nihilo* not only rules out worship of the creature but also excludes every attempt to depict God in creaturely form. Because God transcends the categories of time and space within which creatures live, move, and have their being, any attempt at a physical depiction of God will necessarily be false to the divine reality and is therefore prohibited (Exod. 20:4; Deut. 5:8; cf. 4:15–18; Acts 17:19; Rom. 1:23). Even talking about God in creaturely terms is problematic, because God's very name—"I AM WHO I AM" (Exod. 3:14)—amounts to a declaration that the divine freedom precludes God being represented verbally any more than visually.

Again, these conclusions should not be taken to imply a negative assessment of creaturehood. They are more profitably seen as affirming that creation has its own integrity as a reality that, though from God, is distinct from God. To be a creature is not to be a more or less ample fragment of divinity, but to be something genuinely different from God—and something that is good precisely in that difference. And because the whole of the created order in its goodness displays and bears witness to God's glory (Ps. 19:1–4; cf. Matt. 6:28–29), none of it is to be taken for granted, let alone despised. The fact that the culmination of the creation narrative of Genesis 1 is the sabbath, in which God takes satisfaction in the completion—and, by implication, in the completeness—of "all the work that [God] had done" (Gen. 2:2), sets the tone for the high regard in which the created order in its totality is to be held. A continuing tradition of sabbath rest is enjoined not only for people but also for the animals that serve them (Deut. 5:14; cf. 25:4), and, on a more extended timescale, for the land itself

(Lev. 25:3-5). Nor is the respect due to the created order limited to those segments of direct benefit to humanity. The closing chapters of the book of Job highlight God's concern for wild animals whose flourishing is of no practical value whatever (38:39-39:30), including monsters whose very existence seems to threaten human beings (40:15-41:34).

Yet as much as it is true that the whole of creation is destined for redemption and renewal (Isa. 11:6-9; 65:25; Rom. 8:21; Rev. 21:5; cf. Col. 1:20), humankind is the focus of God's creative work in the Bible. Human beings stand at the center of the otherwise quite different creation stories of Genesis 1 and 2. They alone are singled out for the exercise of dominion over other animals (Gen. 1:28; cf. 2:15, 19; 9:2), and the redemption of the rest of creation seemingly waits on their vindication as children of God (Rom. 8:19). If with respect to the basic features of their biology human beings are indistinguishable from beasts of the field (Eccl. 3:18-21; cf. Job 14:1), there remains a conviction that God has nevertheless set them apart:

> . . . you have made them a little lower than God,
> and crowned them with glory and honor.
> You have given them dominion over the works of your hands;
> you have put all things under their feet.
>
> (Ps. 8:5-6)

Even the angels seem to be in an inferior position by comparison with what God has done for human beings (1 Pet. 1:12).

The Bible's preoccupation with humankind has given the doctrine of human being (or theological anthropology) a central place in Christian reflection on creation, with particular attention given to the question of what makes human beings distinctive among God's creatures. This strongly anthropocentric perspective has been seen by some as an important source for the continuing legacy of disregard for the well-being of the natural environment in historically Christian societies.[6] While more recent theologies of creation have sought to correct the theological tradition's nearly exclusive preoccupation with humankind, it is undeniable that the overwhelming bulk of Christian reflection on what it means to be a creature has centered on the status of human beings. In order to represent the tradition fairly, this anthology has followed suit. While some of the implications of this persistent focus on humanity remain troubling, it is important to note that the results of theological reflection on humankind often lead to conclusions whose significance for the theology of creation is not limited to *Homo sapiens*, even if humanity serves as the starting point.

From the second century onward, theologians have fastened on to the biblical claim that human beings were created "in the image of God" (Gen.

---

6. Classically, in Lynn White Jr., "The Historical Roots of Our Ecologic Crisis," *Science* 155 (1967): 1203-7. For a more balanced assessment see H. Paul Santmire, *The Travail of Nature: The Ambiguous Ecological Promise of Christian Theology* (Philadelphia: Fortress Press, 1985).

1:27) as the decisive clue to understanding how humankind is related both to the rest of the created order and to God. Consensus on the central importance of this phrase, however, has not translated into agreement regarding its content. Some, noting that God's intention to create human beings in the divine image is correlated with their being assigned dominion over the other animals (Gen. 1:26), have interpreted the divine image *functionally*: human beings bear God's image in that they rule over creation on God's behalf. More recently, others have argued that the parallelism between "in the image of God [God] created them" and "male and female [God] created them" in Gen. 1:27 implies that the divine image should be understood *relationally*: the image of the triune God is found in those patterns of human mutuality typified by the loving union of man and woman in marriage. The most widely held position, however, has interpreted the divine image *noetically*, as referring to some mental capacity (e.g., reason, freedom, or self-consciousness) that so reflects divinity as to elevate humanity above all other earthly creatures.

Serious objections can be raised against each of these positions. Humanity's dominion is more naturally read as a consequence of creation in the divine image than as its content. And given that sexual dimorphism is not unique to humankind, the juxtaposition of "male and female" with "the image of God" seems better explained as affirming that both men and women are created in God's image than as identifying the image with sexual difference. Finally, the various noetic approaches, for all their popularity, lack any clear biblical warrant and accord ill with the principle that no creaturely attribute, however exalted, is ontologically more divine than any other. Nevertheless, all three approaches do attempt to make sense of the way that humanity appears in the Bible as the fulcrum of the relationship between creator and creation, thereby providing a useful reference point for identifying key features of that broader relationship.

Two such features in particular deserve mention. First, human beings' status as creatures means that they are inescapably connected to other creatures. The creation stories themselves point to this ontological link: in Genesis 1 humankind is created on the same day as the other land animals (vv. 24–27) and is together with them given the plants for food (vv. 29–30); and Genesis 2 suggests an even closer kinship by noting that animals and human beings alike were formed by God from the ground (cf. vv. 7 and 19). Thus, although the bulk of traditional theological anthropologies have focused on humanity's noetic capacities as a decisive point of contact with the heavenly realm, the body could never be completely ignored, especially given the importance of bodily resurrection as a central feature of the Christian hope. Thus, if the kinship with the rest of the material order to which the body bears witness was often a source of embarrassment for theologians, it explains Paul's view that humanity's longing for bodily redemption is shared by the whole creation (Rom. 8:19–23)—as well as suggesting that modern science's claim of a common ancestry for all living things has more resonance with the biblical witness than its religious critics recognize.

A second feature of Christian belief regarding the character of created existence follows directly on the first. If creatures are decisively other than God, the fact that they are from God means that they are bound to God as inescapably as they are bound to one another. In other words, to be *from* God as a creature is also in some way (which differs for every type of creature) to be *for* God, in the sense of having a purpose under God. Since God stands in no need of the creature, moreover, this purpose can only be understood in terms of the continuous flourishing of creation itself as a theater of God's glory. It follows that the world of created "nature" is not a self-contained entity that flows along independently of the realm of divine "grace." Instead—and in line with the venerable principle that grace completes rather than subverts nature (*gratia non tollit naturam sed perficit*)—to be from God is to have an integrity over against God as a distinct "nature," the proper destiny of which is not to be drawn out of itself to some "supernatural" plane but to be most truly the nature it was created to be.

Needless to say, the claim that the creature is made to fulfill its nature raises all manner of questions about how concretely any given nature is properly fulfilled. The debates in theological anthropology over the meaning of the divine image exemplify the difficulties associated with defining the natural that shape, for example, contemporary disagreements among Christians over homosexuality. Yet the problems associated with particular cases do not detract from the central point that *natural* does not refer to a form of existence that is apart from (let alone against) God. For creation to be natural is simply for it to be what God made it to be: other than God, yet subsisting in this otherness with and by God's grace. Because God's grace is the sole condition of creation's coming into existence in the first place, nature's persistence in existence in distinction from God is inseparable from its being for God: it can be what it is only as God lets it be (cf. Gen. 1), but God has no other desire and aim than that it should be—not only having life, but having it abundantly (John 10:10).

Evil and Sin
Unfortunately, reflection on creation must reckon with the fact that all too often neither we nor our fellow creatures enjoy this promise of abundant life. The created order does not seem to be following a path to ever greater integrity under God. Quite the contrary, it seems to be subject to an inexorable process of death, decay, and dissolution. This dissonance between the promise and the experience of created existence is the basis of Christian reflection on evil, which can be understood broadly as that which impedes creatures' flourishing. Because the experience of evil seems so profoundly inconsistent with Christian belief in a creator God, theological reflection

on "the problem of evil" is sometimes described as *theodicy*, which refers to the justice of God's ways. The crux of the problem is simply stated: If God is both good ("Father") and sovereign ("almighty"), why don't creatures flourish? Why instead is creation "subjected to futility" (Rom. 8:20)? The very form of the question suggests three possible approaches to the problem, which we will examine in turn.

First, one might explain the experience of evil by questioning God's *goodness*. Clearly, if God is not good, then there is no inconsistency in God's allowing (or even deliberately fomenting) evil. The idea of an amoral (let alone immoral) God might seem to undermine the whole point of theodicy as an effort to vindicate God's righteousness. The book of Job, however, provides serious biblical support for this position, with its depiction of the innocent sufferer who refuses to mitigate God's responsibility for his torments, on the one hand, and of a God who refuses to be held morally accountable, on the other. These considerations notwithstanding, this approach has not commended itself to Christian theologians, for whom it has seemed incompatible with the divine commitment to overcome evil as revealed in the cross and resurrection of Jesus. It has, however, been developed with considerable moral power by some post-Holocaust Jewish thinkers as the most fitting response to divine inaction in the face of the Nazis' "final solution."[7]

A second possible approach to the problem of evil questions not God's goodness but rather God's *power*. This approach, too, has found few takers within the Christian tradition as a whole, because if God's power is limited, then God is unable to guarantee creaturely well-being in the face of every possible opposition, and the gospel promise that nothing can separate us from God's love (Rom. 8:38–39) is vitiated. In the twentieth century, however, process theologians have developed a comprehensive vision of God's relationship to the world that rejects the traditional understanding of divine omnipotence. Arguing that the idea of an almighty God is inconsistent not only with divine goodness but also with creaturely freedom, process thinkers conceive of God's creating by persuasion rather than by command: God always seeks to elicit the maximum degree of flourishing from any given state of affairs, but creatures retain the capacity to diverge from the paths God presents to them. From this perspective God always seeks to minimize evil (by continually providing entities the opportunity to maximize the good in any situation) but is incapable of preventing it. Though the logical consistency of process theodicy is undeniable, most theologians have judged that the revisions it demands to basic features of Christian belief in God's relation to the world are too severe for it to be accepted as a theologically satisfactory solution to the problem of evil.

---

7. See especially Arthur A. Cohen, *The Tremendum: A Theological Interpretation of the Holocaust* (New York: Crossroad, 1981), and Richard L. Rubenstein, *After Auschwitz: History, Theology, and Contemporary Judaism* (Baltimore: Johns Hopkins University Press, 1992).

The third and most popular way in which Christians have attempted to construct a plausible theodicy has been to question *the reality of evil*. This basic approach covers a range of quite different proposals. Some have taken the position that evil is simply an illusion, but this view (held by some Gnostic groups in the early Christian centuries and by the Church of Christ, Scientist in the present) has been rejected by the wider Christian tradition as incompatible with belief in the reality of the material environment within which pain and suffering are experienced. A less extreme variation views evil as a matter of divine pedagogy. According to this view, God uses pain and suffering in order to help perfect creatures, whether by correcting the sinful or spurring the virtuous on to new heights of righteousness. While this interpretation of suffering as a process of "soul-making" is not without biblical warrant (see, e.g., Deut. 28:58–59; Rom. 5:3–4; Heb. 12:6), it tends to be viewed as inadequate to serve as a comprehensive theodicy. Critics note that while some experiences of suffering may be an unavoidable concomitant of spiritual maturation (e.g., virtues like courage and generosity can only be cultivated where suffering and loss are a real possibility), to explain every instance of evil in these terms seems inconsistent with the way in which biblical stories from the exodus to Jesus' works of healing depict suffering as a violation of God's will.

The most common approach to evil in the tradition questions its reality in a different way, by defining evil as whatever is contrary to God's will. On this view, if (as the doctrine of *creatio ex nihilo* affirms) the existence of every creature is due solely to God's will, then it follows that evil—precisely as that which is *not* God's will—can have no proper existence. This is not to say that evil is merely a figment of the imagination, but rather to argue that the failure of creatures to flourish is the experience of a lack (or privation) of being. To cite a classic illustration of this point, the evil in a rotten apple is not the property of the apple as such; rather, the rottenness is present exclusively where the apple is not (i.e., where it is ceasing to be an apple and thus is falling into nonbeing). In this way, evil can be said to "exist" only in an improper sense: it is not an illusion, but neither can it be said to exist in the same way that God or God's creatures do. It has no genuine being of its own. Instead, it is parasitic on that which does exist—to the extent that if evil were to succeed in reducing all creation to nonexistence, it, too, would cease to "exist."

It is important to stress that this way of describing evil does not provide an explanation for *why* evil should exist. On the contrary, it implies that evil *cannot* be explained: as that which is not God's will, there simply is no ontological basis for its existence. Insofar as the explanation of evil as a privation of the good was developed in concert with a refusal to concede any qualification of God's goodness and sovereignty, however, this approach to theodicy tends to go with an insistence that evil is finally subject to God's sovereign will. In other words, although evil is in itself opposed to the good, it nevertheless serves the good—a theme present already in the Old Testament (see especially Gen. 50:20), but taking center stage in the Christian understanding of Christ's crucifixion and resurrection (Acts 3:17–18, 26). This is not to say that evil is "really" good for the one who suffers it (as in the soul-making theology discussed above), but it is to insist that God is both willing (as "Father") and able (as "almighty") to bring good out of evil.[8]

Nevertheless, this account falls short of explaining why God allows evil in the first place. The principle that evil is by definition opposed to God's will rules out the possibility that God actively wills evil as a means of securing the good. But how can evil come about at all if the almighty God does not will it? In line with the overall anthropocentrism of Christian reflection on creation, the most popular answer to this question has involved tracing all evil back to human choice. This strategy brings us no closer to an explanation of evil as such, since if every creature, together with the totality of its environment, is a product of God's will (and therefore entirely good in every dimension of its being), it is impossible to identify any reason for its turning against God. The ultimate cause of evil thus remains inexplicable. Nevertheless, the basic Christian conviction that some creatures—especially human beings—are responsible agents rightly held accountable for their deeds opens a space for reconciling the fact of evil with belief in creation's essential goodness: the fault lies not with God, but with human perversity.[9]

There are two obvious problems with this way of approaching the problem of evil. The first has to do with an inherent tension between belief in human responsibility and in divine sovereignty. Can an almighty God really be cleared of responsibility for actions of the human creature? As a means of addressing this concern, some theologians make a distinction between an "active" will by which God promotes the good and a merely "permissive" will by which God allows evil. Critics have questioned, however, whether this way of shielding God from moral accountability for evil is compatible with belief in creation from nothing, on the grounds that the category of permission implies a degree of independence of the creature from the creator that the *ex nihilo* appears to exclude.

The second problem has to do with the fact that alongside the many varieties of "moral evil" that are attributable to human wickedness (e.g., selfishness, deception, slander, neglect, exploitation, torture, war) there are

---

8. "The idea of the good creation ... is in no sense a denial of evil. Rather this conviction has been the sole condition for understanding evil as a *perversion* rather than a *necessity* of our existence, and so for understanding human life as redeemable." Langdon Gilkey, *Maker of Heaven and Earth: A Study of the Christian Doctrine of Creation* (Garden City, NY: Doubleday, 1959), 182–83.

9. Usually theologians have argued that human beings were tempted by the devil and thus did not simply originate evil themselves; but this elaboration fails to solve the problem on two counts. First, it does not explain why essentially good human beings would have listened to the voice of the tempter. Second, it only pushes the problem of evil's ultimate origins back a step: for if the devil was created good—as Christian doctrine insists he was—then why did *he* turn to evil?

the many instances of "natural evil" for which it is impossible to identify a malevolent human agent (e.g., freak accidents, disease, predation, natural disasters). Traditionally, this problem was overcome by means of the doctrine of the fall. According to this interpretation of human history, the primordial sin of disobedience to God's command committed by the first human couple brought in its wake a disruption of the whole natural order in addition to bequeathing to all subsequent human generations an inherent propensity to sinful behavior (see especially Gen. 2:16–17; 3:16–19, 22–24; cf. Rom. 5:12; 8:20–21). In this way, the blame for natural as well as moral evil could ultimately be laid at humanity's doorstep; this "fall" from a state of original righteousness explained why humankind was beset by the power of evil both without and within.

Yet the picture of natural history presented by modern science would seem to deal a fatal blow to this way of handling theodicy. All the evidence suggests that freak accidents, animal predation, debilitating diseases, and natural catastrophes were constitutive features of terrestrial life long before the relatively recent appearance of human beings, who would have been faced with such phenomena from the outset. Even within the sphere of moral evil, the idea that the transgression of Adam and Eve infected all later generations of humanity with the congenital guilt of "original sin" has been subject to severe criticism. Aside from the questions science raises about the historicity of the Genesis creation narratives, people have called into question the coherence of the idea of inherited sinfulness. How can human beings be viewed as responsible agents if their actions are inherently sinful, as the doctrine of original sin (at least in its Western, Augustinian version) demands? And what sense does it make to try to battle sin in society if all such efforts will themselves be tainted by sin? While these questions are not new, they have been raised with particular force in the modern period, further complicating theologians' attempts to provide a coherent account of evil.

However much they may make theologians uncomfortable, however, such questions serve a valuable function insofar as they destabilize any analysis of evil (whether in its "moral" or "natural" form) that underplays its lack of fit with the Christian doctrine of creation. A theology that can incorporate evil seamlessly into its account of God's relationship with the world arguably fails to do justice to evil's status as that which has no place in—and thus should not be part of—the creation. As the church's best thinkers have realized, the topic of evil and sin arises within theology as a surd: something that is not resolvable in terms of the fundamental topics of God, creation, nature, and grace that shape the Christian vision of what is ultimately real. A theologically credible interpretation of evil faces the task of explaining how it is possible to speak coherently of something other than God that is not from God. Similarly, an adequate account of sin must make some sense of the claim that creatures who are from God—and therefore good in every dimension of their being—nevertheless embrace evil, turning away from God and thereby undermining the very basis of their existence.

Given these conditions, it is not to be expected that any theological treatment of evil and sin will be finally or fully adequate. Instead, theologians find themselves challenged to pursue a balancing act, poised on a knife-edge between denying that evil is real (thereby failing to take seriously God's opposition to it) and ascribing it too much reality (so that it becomes either a creature in its own right or a second divine power alongside God). While it is very difficult for those committed to following this difficult path to avoid erring on one side or the other, the most successful move forward by focusing less on the irresolvable problem of evil's origin and more on the biblically much clearer question of how God responds to it. A theology that focuses on God's intractable opposition to evil and sin is in a good position neither to underestimate nor overestimate its significance as that which, in its very real resistance to God, is nevertheless ultimately subject to God.

Providence

The question of how God preserves and directs creation so that the flourishing of creatures is achieved in spite of the effects of sin and evil encompasses the fourth main subdivision of creation, the doctrine of providence. The topic of providence takes its name from the story of the binding of Isaac in Genesis 22. At the climactic point of the story, God intervenes to prevent Abraham from sacrificing his son, providing a ram instead and leading Abraham to name the place "'The Lord will provide'" (Gen. 22:14). The story encapsulates the essential features of what Christians mean when they speak of providence: God's eye is on all that happens to ensure that God's goal of creaturely flourishing is realized in spite of every seeming obstacle. In this way, the doctrine of providence can be seen as a natural extension of the doctrine of creation from nothing, insofar as it stresses both that the world is utterly dependent on God for its existence and that this dependence is a manifestation of God's gracious love.

Providence may thus be distinguished as that dimension of the doctrine of creation that is concerned with God's ongoing interaction with the creation between the time of its origin and its eschatological consummation. Traditionally, this relationship is understood as having three dimensions, named by the Latin terms *conservatio*, *concursus*, and *gubernatio*. *Conservatio* refers to the divine work of preservation and, along with the other two, can be seen as a corollary of the doctrine of creation from nothing: if God is the only basis for a creature's coming into being in the first place, then the creature's ongoing existence never has any basis but the gracious will of God. That a creature continues in existence rather than falling into nonbeing is, therefore, no less a matter of God's grace than its being called into existence. The doctrine of divine *concursus*, or accompaniment, pushes the logic of this position still further by emphasizing that God sustains every creature not only in the sheer fact of its existence but also in its various actions. As a creature rests, moves, feeds, thinks, speaks, or does anything else, it makes use of natural capacities that (precisely because they are natural) are also created by God and, therefore, function only when and as God wills.

Yet if the divine *concursus* is no less implicit in the doctrine of creation from nothing than that of *conservatio*, its implications are frequently seen as far more troubling. It is one thing to affirm that God preserves the world in its created state—seeing to it that

> "seedtime and harvest, cold and heat,
> summer and winter, day and night,
> shall not cease"
> (Gen. 8:22; cf. Matt. 5:45)

It is quite another to argue that every creaturely action within this system is itself a product of God's will. Critics charge that such a claim necessarily subverts creaturely agency in a way that robs creatures of their integrity as beings genuinely distinct from God. The same concerns surround the idea of *gubernatio*, or the divine direction of creation to the end God intends. If God's omnipotence means that creation will without fail reach the end God intends, doesn't that invariably undermine any meaningful notion of creaturely freedom? Doesn't the integrity of human beings as free and responsible agents presuppose the possibility that God's aims for creation may not be realized?

Of course, it is part and parcel of traditional belief that God's intention for creation is that it should find eternal affirmation in the life of God. Thus Paul is able to come to terms with creation's subjection to futility on the grounds that it was so subjected "in hope, that the creation itself will be set free from its bondage to decay and will obtain the freedom of the glory of the children of God" (Rom. 8:21). Yet the fact that God's aims are positive does not really meet the substance of the objections to the doctrines of *concursus* and *gubernatio* voiced especially in the modern period, according to which the concept of flourishing becomes vacuous in a situation where God's will shapes and ultimately overrules all creaturely activity. These objections may be summarized as the worry that any concept of providence that includes robust doctrines of *concursus* and *gubernatio* becomes indistinguishable from fatalism, or the belief that everything happens by necessity. In response to these concerns, some modern theologians have sought to modify traditional Christian convictions about the character of God's providential rule.

Once again, the suggestions of process theologians are perhaps the most far-reaching in their implications for the shape of Christian faith as a whole. As already noted, process thinkers reject the classical confession of God as almighty. Insofar as God stands in intimate relation to every creature and presents to every creature at every moment that which will maximize that creature's flourishing, the concepts of *concursus* and *gubernatio* are retained, since God can be said to be acting with each creature in order to guide it toward a given end. At the same time, because God's action is conceived as a matter of persuading or luring rather than command or control, the force of these concepts is attenuated in process perspective: creatures do not act without God, but they retain freedom over against God that precludes both that God is the immediate cause of all creaturely action and that God infallibly directs such action to a predetermined outcome.

The process approach trades on a fundamentally competitive vision of the relationship between the divine and creaturely action: the more the creature is responsible for a particular deed, the less God must be, and vice versa. Such a position entails a profound modification of the classical Christian understandings of God's relationship to the world. Over against a more theologically traditional vision of divine transcendence, according to which God is ontologically independent of the world, process thought presupposes an ontological interdependence of God and the world known as *panentheism*. In distinction from pantheists (for whom the world is simply a manifestation of divine being), panentheists hold that God and the world are distinct but correlative realities: God shapes the fundamental character of their relationship by the communication of novel possibilities of existence to other entities, but creatures have their own freedom that is independent of divine fiat. Moreover, the relationship between God and the world is such that the world in its freedom affects God no less profoundly than God affects the world.

Not all Christian panentheists identify themselves as process theologians. Some have proposed that the God-world relationship is best understood as analogous to that between the human mind and the body. Others conceive of God as the ultimate boundary condition of the physical universe, shaping the course of cosmic evolution by establishing conditions that constrain—without violating—the operation of natural laws in much the same way that a river channel constrains the flow of water without affecting the basic principles of fluid dynamics. According to still another approach, God establishes God's own identity as Lord in and through the totality of interactions with creatures that constitute world history. Each of these positions is characterized by divergent understandings of the precise character of God's relationship to the world, including significantly different levels of confidence regarding the ultimate vindication of God's will for creation.

Notwithstanding these differences, however, the various forms of panentheism are all motivated on the one hand by a desire to avoid the specter of a divine determinism, and on the other by a quest to develop a model of divine action in space and time that is consistent with the regular operation of the laws of nature. The panentheist claim is that if God's continuing, providential action in the world is to be consistent with the full range of human experience, it must be conceived in terms that honor the integrity of creation as that which is genuinely other than—and therefore enjoys relative autonomy with respect to—God. From this perspective for God to supervene on the creation by violating natural laws or turning the human will to achieve a particular end is to undermine the very possibility of speaking of God's being in relation to (and thus distinct from) creation. Instead, the whole affair verges on occasionalism, in which God's role as sole cause is stressed to such an extent that worldly events lose their integrity as genuinely creaturely happenings.

Defenders of a more traditional understanding of divine transcendence (and of correspondingly more robust interpretations of *concursus* and *gubernatio*) counter that the creation's genuine otherness from God does not require the degree of autonomy that panentheists suppose. They argue that the otherness of creatures rests precisely in their created status and that to worry about divine encroachment on creaturely integrity mistakenly puts God and creation on the same ontological level. If one of the things that God makes is creaturely freedom, to suppose that such freedom must or even can operate independently of God is to fail to take seriously God's status as creator, whose will is the ground of (and thus cannot by definition be in competition with) creaturely activity in all its various forms. Needless to say, while this way of interpreting divine providence has no difficulty in affirming that creation will achieve the end God intends, it has much more difficulty making sense of evil as a power that is genuinely opposed to these divine intentions and yet remains entirely under God.

The terms of this debate over the way God governs creation show why the doctrine of providence is a (if not the) crucial point of intersection between theology and the natural sciences. Far more than the doctrine of creation from nothing, the doctrine of providence forces the question of the interface between God and the world. Austin Farrer calls this the problem of the "causal joint": what mechanism can be invoked to square belief in God's direction of the course of natural history with the scientific principle that all observable changes in the universe are explicable in terms of the operation of regular, mathematically describable natural laws?[10] Nowhere is this tension more acute than when it comes to the question of biological evolution. Given the variety of interpretations of the Bible's first chapters that have been proposed over the centuries, the chief problem here is less the difference between the timescale of Genesis and that of evolutionary biology than the question of mechanism, since evolutionary theory dictates that the course of natural selection is random and the doctrine of providence requires that it assume a particular direction if God's purposes for creation are to be realized.

---

10. Austin Farrer, *Faith and Speculation: An Essay in Philosophical Theology* (London: Adam & Charles Black, 1967), 65.

The debate on this point is complicated by the fact that there is disagreement among evolutionary biologists themselves over the extent to which the course of evolution is indeed random, with some significant figures (e.g., Richard Dawkins, Simon Conway Morris) arguing that various environmental factors constrain the course of evolution down particular paths (so that, for example, the eventual emergence of intelligent life is highly probable, if not strictly necessary). Such biological theories allow for considerable common ground with theologians who posit that God exerts only partial control over creaturely events: God can be seen as establishing and (to the extent possible without violating creaturely integrity) fostering conditions overwhelmingly likely to issue in the evolution of human beings without directly intervening in a way that would violate natural laws—though such strategies are, of course, tied to the continued viability of a particular scientific understanding of evolution. Proponents of a stronger version of divine providence are not so tied to a particular mechanism (since the doctrine of *concursus* implies that God is active in every creaturely process, whatever its nature), but they are constrained to admit that concepts like "random" or "chance" are matters of creaturely rather than divine experience: a strict interpretation of *creatio ex nihilo* is simply not consistent with the idea that anything could truly be random for God.

However developed in detail, the doctrine of providence arguably serves as the hermeneutic for every theologian's understanding of creation and thus as a fitting capstone to any review of the doctrine as a whole. If creation is about the totality of God's relationship to what is not God, providence is the point where the shape of that relationship is displayed in such a way as to make clear exactly what it means to say that God "creates." Specifically, it is in the context of reflection on providence that the plausibility of the principle of creation from nothing—that God is the sole ground and condition for creation's existence—is put to the test. The degree to which this principle is affirmed will shape a theologian's options for addressing the problem of evil, since the constraints of logic dictate that the ability to mitigate God's responsibility for evil stands in inverse relation to the strength with which God's capacity to guarantee creation's final outcome is affirmed. Furthermore, insofar as any discussion of divine power and purpose carries definite implications for the consummation of God's creative work, consideration of providence naturally points beyond the past and present to incorporate reflection on some aspects of creation's future. Through this implicit reference to creation's end, the idea of providence naturally shades into the doctrine of the last things, or eschatology (a connection visible especially in the selection from Teilhard de Chardin in chapter 4), thereby encompassing the full sweep of God's work in the world.

As everywhere else in Christian theology, no doctrinal formulation is fully satisfactory. Individual positions tend to be developed as a means of countering particular claims or tendencies to which a given theologian objects, and they invariably raise questions and problems of their own. Even the limited selection of texts that follow give ample evidence of the range of positions that have found a hearing in the Christian tradition as the church has struggled to confess its faith both clearly and truly. In the confidence that the limits of human understanding do not limit the power of the Spirit, it is hoped that study of these texts will help the reader reckon with the strengths and weaknesses of the various options in order to find those ways of speaking that assist the church today to remain true to its confession of God as "creator of heaven and earth."

Abbreviations

The following abbreviations are used for texts frequently cited. In each case, citations are referenced by volume and page number (or, in the case of the *PG* and *PL*, volume and column number).

ANF   *The Ante-Nicene Fathers: Translations of the Writings of the Fathers down to A.D. 325.* 9 vols. Ed. Alexander Roberts, James Donaldson, et al. Edinburgh, 1885–1897.
BC   *Book of Concord: The Confessions of the Evangelical Lutheran Church.* Ed. Robert Kolb, Timothy Wengert, James Schaffer. Minneapolis, 2000.
BL   *Die Bekenntnisschriften der evangelische-lutherischen Kirche.* 5th ed. Göttingen, 1963.
CR   *Ioannis Calvini Opera quae supersunt omnia.* Ed. Guiliemus Baum, Eduardus Cunitz, Eduardus Reuss. *Corpus reformatorum,* vols. 29–87. Brunsvigae, 1863–1900.
FC   *The Fathers of the Church: A New Translation.* New York/Washington, 1947–.
LCC   *The Library of Christian Classics.* 26 vols. Ed. John Baillie, John T. McNeill, and Henry P. Van Dusen. Philadelphia, 1953–1966.
LCL   *Aristotle.* 23 vols. Ed. G. P. Goold. *Loeb Classical Library.* Cambridge, 1926–1991.
LW   *Luther's Works.* American ed. 55 vols. Ed. Jaroslav Pelikan. Philadelphia/St. Louis, 1955–1986.
NPNF[1] *A Select Library of the Nicene and Post-Nicene Fathers of the Christian Church.* First Series. 14 vols. Ed. Philip Schaff. Edinburgh, 1886–1889.
NPNF[2] *A Select Library of the Nicene and Post-Nicene Fathers of the Christian Church.* Second Series. 14 vols. Ed. Philip Schaff and Henry Wace. Edinburgh, 1890–1900.
PG   *Patrologiae Cursus Completus, Series Graeca.* 161 vols. Ed. J.-P. Migne. Paris, 1857–1866.
PL   *Patrologiae Cursus Completus, Series Latina.* 221 vols. Ed. J.-P. Migne. Paris, 1844–1855.
WA   *D. Martin Luthers Werke: kritische Gesamtausgabe.* Weimar, 1883–.

CHAPTER 1
God as Creator

SELECTION **1**

Justin Martyr

First Apology

Born and raised in Palestine, Justin (ca. 100-ca. 165) converted to Christianity as an adult and moved to Rome, where he taught the new faith privately as a professional philosopher. This choice of career reflects Justin's personal experience of Christianity as the fulfillment of a lifelong philosophical quest for truth and, more specifically, as the perfection of the wisdom of the pagan thinkers. In his written work Justin sought to defend the truth of Christianity to a non-Christian audience. The following excerpts reflect this fundamentally apologetic concern, as Justin identifies similarities between pagan philosophy and Christian teaching, the second excerpt in particular focusing on how Plato's *Timaeus* (especially 29D-30C; 48E-50C) echoes themes from the creation story in Genesis 1. This latter parallel is significant for its witness to early Christian interpretation of creation as the shaping of preexisting matter ("creation from chaos") rather than what would soon become the orthodox doctrine of creation from nothing.

From *Early Christian Fathers*, LCC 1:280-81.

Chapter 20

Both the Sibyl and Hystaspes said that there should be a dissolution by God of things corruptible. And the philosophers called Stoics teach that even God Himself shall be resolved into fire, and they say that the world is to be formed anew by this revolution; but we understand that God, the Creator of all things, is superior to the things that are to be changed. If, therefore, on some points we teach the same things as the poets and philosophers whom you honor, and on other points are fuller and more divine in our teaching, and if we alone afford proof of what we assert, why are we unjustly hated more than all others? For while we say that all things have been produced and arranged into a world by God, we shall seem to utter the doctrine of Plato; and while we say that there will be a burning up of all, we shall seem to utter the doctrine of the Stoics: and while we affirm that the souls of the wicked, being endowed with sensation even after death, are punished, and that those of the good being delivered from punishment spend a blessed existence, we shall seem to say the same things as the poets and philosophers; and while we maintain that men ought not to worship the works of their hands, we say the very things which have been said by the comic poet Menander, and other similar writers, for they have declared that the workman is greater than the work.

Chapter 59

And that you may learn that it was from our teachers—we mean the account given through the prophets—that Plato borrowed his statement that God, having altered matter which was shapeless, made the world, hear the very words spoken through Moses, who, as above shown, was the first prophet, and of greater antiquity than the Greek writers; and through whom the Spirit of prophecy, signifying how and from what materials God at first formed the world, spoke thus: "In the beginning God created the heaven and the earth. And the earth was invisible and unfurnished, and darkness was upon the face of the deep; and the Spirit of God moved over the waters. And God said, Let there be light; and it was so [Gen. 1:1–3]." So that both Plato and they who agree with him, and we ourselves, have learned, and you also can be convinced, that by the word of God the whole world was made out of the substance spoken of before by Moses. And that which the poets call Erebus [the underworld], we know was spoken of formerly by Moses [Deut. 32:22?].

SELECTION 2

Theophilus of Antioch

To Autolycus, Book 2

Little is known of Theophilus (died ca. 180) beyond the fact that he served as leader of the church in Antioch in the latter half of the second century. Like Justin, he is known primarily as an apologist, and the text *To Autolycus* is a justification of Christian belief addressed to a pagan skeptic. The following excerpt is significant for being the earliest explicit statement of the doctrine of creation from nothing (*creatio ex nihilo*). Unlike Justin, who saw no problem in affirming creation from preexisting matter, Theophilus argues that God's absolute sovereignty forbids the supposition that matter existed eternally alongside God. It follows that God creates the world not from unformed matter but from "nothing." Moreover, because Theophilus stresses that the account in Genesis is the product of divine revelation, he tends to highlight more than Justin the differences between Christian and pagan accounts of the world's origin (though Theophilus refers to the poet Hesiod rather than the philosopher Plato).

From *Fathers of the Second Century*, ANF 2:97–100.

Chapter 9

But men of God carrying in them a holy spirit and becoming prophets, being inspired and made wise by God, became God-taught, and holy, and righteous. Wherefore they were also deemed worthy of receiving this reward, that they should become instruments of God, and contain the wisdom that is from Him, through which wisdom they uttered both what regarded the creation of the world and all other things. For they predicted also pestilences, and famines, and wars. And there was not one or two, but many, at various times and seasons among the Hebrews; and also among the Greeks there was the Sibyl; and they all have spoken things consistent and harmonious with each other, both what happened before them and what happened in their own time, and what things are now being fulfilled in our own day: wherefore we are persuaded also concerning the future things that they will fall out, as also the first have been accomplished.

Chapter 10
And first, they taught us with one consent that God made all things out of nothing; for nothing was coeval with God: but He being His own place, and wanting nothing, and existing before the ages, willed to make man by whom He might be known; for him, therefore, He prepared the world. For he that is created is also needy; but he that is uncreated stands in need of nothing. God, then, having His own Word internal within His own bowels, begat Him, emitting Him along with His own Wisdom before all things. He had this Word as a helper in the things that were created by Him, and by Him He made all things. He is called "governing principle," because He rules, and is Lord of all things fashioned by Him. He, then, being Spirit of God, and governing principle, and wisdom, and power of the highest, came down upon the prophets, and through them spoke of the creation of the world and of all other things. For the prophets were not when the world came into existence, but the wisdom of God which was in Him, and His holy Word which was always present with Him. Wherefore He speaks thus by the prophet Solomon: "When He prepared the heavens I was there, and when He appointed the foundations of the earth I was by Him as one brought up with Him" [Prov. 8:27]. And Moses, who lived many years before Solomon, or, rather, the Word of God by him as by an instrument, says, "In the beginning God created the heaven and the earth" [Gen. 1:1]. First he named the "beginning," and "creation," then he thus introduced God; for not lightly and on slight occasion is it right to name God. For the divine wisdom foreknew that some would trifle and name a multitude of gods that do not exist. In order, therefore, that the living God might be known by His works, and that [it might be known that] by His Word God created the heavens and the earth, and all that is therein, he said, "In the beginning God created the heavens and the earth." Then having spoken of their creation, he explains to us: "And the earth was without form, and void, and darkness was upon the face of the deep; and the Spirit of God moved upon the water" [Gen. 1:2]. This, sacred Scripture teaches at the outset, to show that matter, from which God made and fashioned the world, was in some manner created, being produced by God. . . .

Chapter 12

Of the six days' work [of creation] no man can give a worthy explanation and description of all its parts, not though he had ten thousand tongues and ten thousand mouths; nay, though he were to live ten thousand years, sojourning in this life, not even so could he utter anything worthy of these things, on account of the exceeding greatness and riches of the wisdom of God which there is in the six days' work above narrated. Many writers indeed have imitated [the narration], and essayed to give an explanation of these things; yet, though they thence derived some suggestions, both concerning the creation of the world and the nature of man, they have emitted no slightest spark of truth. And the utterances of the philosophers, and writers, and poets have an appearance of trustworthiness, on account of the beauty of their diction; but their discourse is proved to be foolish and idle, because the multitude of their nonsensical frivolities is very great; and not a stray morsel of truth is found in them. For even if any truth seems to have been uttered by them, it has a mixture of error. And as a deleterious drug, when mixed with honey or wine, or some other thing, makes the whole [mixture] hurtful and profitless; so also eloquence is in their case found to be labor in vain; yea, rather an injurious thing to those who credit it. Moreover, [they spoke] concerning the seventh day, which all men acknowledge; but the most know not that what among the Hebrews is called the "Sabbath," is translated into Greek the "Seventh," a name which is adopted by every nation, although they know not the reason of the appellation. And as for what the poet Hesiod says of Erebus as well as the earth being produced from chaos, and of love which lords it over his [Hesiod's] gods and men, his dictum is shown to be idle and frigid, and quite foreign to the truth. For it is not meet that God be conquered by pleasure; since even men of temperance abstain from all base pleasure and wicked lust.

Chapter 13

Moreover, his [Hesiod's] human, and mean, and very weak conception, so far as regards God, is discovered in his beginning to relate the creation of all things from the earthly things here below. For man, being below, begins to build from the earth, and cannot in order make the roof, unless he has first laid the foundation. But the power of God is shown in this, that, first of all, He creates out of nothing, according to His will, the things that are made. "For the things which are impossible with men are possible with God" [Luke 18:27]. Wherefore, also, the prophet mentioned that the creation of the heavens first of all took place, as a kind of roof, saying: "At the first God created the heavens"—that is, that by means of the "first" principle the heavens were made, as we have already shown. And by "earth" he means the ground and foundation, as by "the deep" he means the multitude of waters; and "darkness" he speaks of, on account of the heaven which God made covering the waters and the earth like a lid. And by the Spirit which is borne above the waters, he means that which God gave for animating the creation, as he gave life to man, mixing what is fine with what is fine. For the Spirit is fine, and the water is fine, that the Spirit may nourish the water, and the water penetrating everywhere along with the Spirit, may nourish creation. For the Spirit being one, and holding the place of light, was between the water and the heaven, in order that the darkness might not in any way communicate with the heaven, which was nearer God, before God said, "Let there be light." The heaven, therefore, being like a dome-shaped covering, comprehended matter, which was like a clod. And so another prophet, Isaiah by name, spoke in these words: "It is God who made the heavens as a vault, and stretched them as a tent to dwell in" [Isa. 40:22]. The command, then, of God, that is, His Word, shining as a lamp in an enclosed chamber, lit up all that was under heaven, when He had made light apart from the world. And the light God called Day, and the darkness Night. Since man would not have been able to call the light Day, or the darkness Night, nor, indeed, to have given names to the other things, had not he received the nomenclature from God, who made the things themselves. In the very beginning, therefore, of the history and genesis of the world, the holy Scripture spoke not concerning this firmament [which we see], but concerning another heaven, which is to us invisible, after which this heaven which we see has been called "firmament," and to which half the water was taken up that it might serve for rains, and showers, and dews to mankind. And half the water was left on earth for rivers, and fountains, and seas. The water, then, covering all the earth, and specially its hollow places, God, through His Word, next caused the waters to be gathered into one collection, and the dry land to become visible, which formerly had been invisible. The earth thus becoming visible was yet without form. God therefore formed and adorned it with all kinds of herbs, and seeds and plants.

SELECTION 3

Origen of Alexandria

On First Principles, Book 1

Origen of Alexandria (ca. 185–ca. 254) was probably the most brilliant and certainly the most influential theologian of the period before the Council of Nicaea, known and respected for his learning by Christians and non-Christians alike. His *Hexapla*, a critical edition of six versions of the Old Testament arranged in parallel columns, was a wonder of the age. Origen supplemented this study of the biblical text with an enormous volume of biblical commentaries and sermons, characterized by a consistent use of allegorical interpretation as a means of accounting for apparent discrepancies in the biblical narrative. His exegesis dominated Greek reading of the Bible throughout the patristic period, and, thanks to its appropriation by Jerome, was also influential on the Latin church. He died as a consequence of imprisonment and torture during the Decian persecution of 250–251.

Though books on the Bible constitute the vast majority of Origen's works, he is probably best known for his comparatively early treatise *On First Principles*, from which the following extract is taken. In this work Origen proposes a systematic Christian cosmology in opposition to the dualism of Gnostic Christians. In line with this aim, his worldview is centered in a strict monotheism that affirms the biblical God as the sole source of all being. In working out the implications of this basic vision, however, Origen made a number of speculative moves that proved controversial at the time, eventually leading to his posthumous condemnation at the Second Council of Constantinople in 553. Thus, in the following excerpt (which survives in only one manuscript in Latin translation, the accuracy of which is open to some question) Origen appears to argue that the confession of God as eternal and unchanging demands that creation also be thought of as eternal rather than having a temporal beginning, since otherwise it would follow that God's will was not immutable, as the doctrine of God's eternal perfection seemed to demand.

From Origen of Alexandria, *On First Principles* (London: SPCK, 1936), 41–43.

3. This blessed and ruling power, therefore, that is, the power that exercises control of all things, we call the Trinity. This is the good God and Kindly Father of all, at once beneficent power and creative power, that is, the power that does good and creates and providentially sustains. And it is absurd and impious to suppose that these powers of God have been at any time in abeyance for a single moment. Indeed, it is unlawful even to entertain the least suspicion that these powers, through which chiefly we gain a worthy notion of God, should at any time have ceased from performing works worthy of themselves and have become inactive. For we can neither suppose that these powers which are in God, nay, which are God, could have been thwarted from without, nor on the other hand, when nothing stood in their way, can we believe that they were reluctant to act and perform works worthy of themselves or that they feigned impotence. We can therefore imagine no moment whatever when that power was not engaged in acts of well-doing. Whence it follows that there always existed objects for this well-doing, namely, God's works or creatures, and that God, in the power of his providence, was always dispensing his blessings among them by doing them good in accordance with their condition and deserts. It follows plainly from this, that at no time whatever was God not Creator, nor Benefactor, nor Providence.

4. Yet in this matter human intelligence is feeble and limited, when it tries to understand how during the whole of God's existence his creatures have

existed also, and how those things, which we must undoubtedly believe to have been created and made by God have subsisted, if we may say so, without a beginning. Since then there is this conflict in our human thoughts and reasonings, and the soundest arguments on either side oppose and rebut one another, each bending the mind of the thinker into its own direction, this truth, which can be confessed without any risk to piety, presents itself as appropriate to the small and narrow capacity of our mind, namely, that God the Father always existed, and that he always had an only-begotten Son, who at the same time . . . is called Wisdom. This is that Wisdom in whom God delighted when the world was finished [Prov. 8:30], in order that we might understand from this that God ever rejoices. In this Wisdom, therefore, who ever existed with the Father, the Creation was always present in form and outline, and there was never a time when the pre-figuration of those things which hereafter were to be did not exist in Wisdom.

5. It is probably in this way that, so far as our weakness allows, we shall maintain a reverent belief about God, neither asserting that his creatures were unbegotten and coeternal with him nor on the other hand that he turned to the work of creation to do good when he had done nothing good before. For the saying that is written, "In wisdom hast thou made all things" [Ps. 104], is a true one. And certainly if "all things have been made in wisdom," then since Wisdom has always existed, there have always existed in Wisdom, by a pre-figuration and pre-formation, those things which afterwards have received substantial existence. This is, I believe, the thought and meaning of Solomon when he says in Ecclesiastes: "What is it that hath been made? The same that is to be. And what is it that hath been created? The same that is destined to be created. And there is nothing fresh under the sun. If one should speak of anything and say, Behold, this is new: it already hath been, in the ages that were before us" [Eccl. 1:9–10]. If then particular things, which are "under the sun" have already existed in the ages which were before us—since "there is nothing fresh under the sun"—then undoubtedly all genera and species have forever existed, and possibly even individual things; but either way, the fact is made clear that God did not begin at a certain time to be Creator, when he had not been such before.

SELECTION 4

Augustine

Confessions, Book 11

Though many of his teachings are regarded with some misgiving by Orthodox theologians, the influence of Augustine of Hippo (354–430) on Western Christianity, both Catholic and

Protestant, is without equal. Born in Africa to a pagan father and a Christian mother and famously converting to Christianity as an adult, his many treatises, sermons, and letters cover the full gamut of theological topics and profoundly shaped subsequent discussion on subjects as varied as the Trinity, sin, the church, and human freedom. He was also fascinated by the theme of creation, which he revisited again and again in the course of his lengthy career in a series of commentaries on the first chapters of Genesis, ranging from the early *On Genesis against the Manichees* (389) to the magisterial *Literal Interpretation of Genesis* (415). Yet probably the most famous treatment of the subject comes in the later chapters of his *Confessions* (397), from which the following extract is taken.

Augustine reports that an important factor in his conversion to Christianity was the discovery that what he had regarded as absurdities in the biblical narrative could be resolved by recourse to Origen's style of allegorical interpretation. In the following selections, however, he rejects Origen's idea of an eternal creation and argues that the universe had a temporal beginning. Origen had worried that ascribing a beginning to creation implied change in God, but Augustine counters that the idea of change only makes sense within the context of time—and that a God who creates ex nihilo is no more subject to time than to any other external factor. Indeed, Augustine argues that God's eternity implies that time itself is a creature, since it is an integral part of the transience that distinguishes creaturely existence from that of the Creator.

From *Confessions and Enchiridion*, LCC 7:247–55, 268.

Chapter 4
Look around; there are the heaven and the earth. They cry aloud that they were made, for they change and vary. Whatever there is that has not been made, and yet has being, has nothing in it that was not there before. This having something not already existent is what it means to be changed and varied. Heaven and earth thus speak plainly that they did not make themselves: "We are, because we have been made; we did not exist before we came to be so that we could have made ourselves!" And the voice with which they speak is simply their visible presence. It was you, O Lord, who made these things.

You are beautiful; thus they are beautiful. You are good; thus they are good. You are; thus they are. But they are not as beautiful, nor as good, nor as truly real as you their Creator are. Compared with you, they are neither beautiful nor good, nor do they even exist. These things we know, thanks be to you. Yet our knowledge is ignorance when it is compared with your knowledge.

Chapter 5
But *how* did you make the heaven and the earth, and what was the tool of such a mighty work as yours? For it was not like a human worker fashion-

ing body from body, according to the fancy of his mind, able somehow or other to impose on it a form which the mind perceived in itself by its inner eye (yet how should even he be able to do this, if you had not made that mind?). He imposes the form on something already existing and having some sort of being, such as clay, or stone or wood or gold or such like (and where would these things come from if you had not furnished them?). For you made his body for the artisan, and you made the mind which directs the limbs; you made the matter from which he makes anything; you created the capacity by which he understands his art and sees within his mind what he may do with the things before him; you gave him his bodily sense by which, as if he had an interpreter, he may communicate from mind to matter what he proposes to do and report back to his mind what has been done, that the mind may consult with the Truth which presides over it as to whether what is done is well done. All these things praise thee, the Creator of them all. But how did you make them? How, O God, did you make the heaven and earth? For truly, neither in heaven nor on earth did you make heaven and earth—nor in the air nor in the waters, since all of these also belong to the heaven and the earth. Nowhere in the whole world did you make the whole world, because there was no place where it could be made before it was made. And you did not hold anything in your hand from which to fashion the heaven and the earth,[1] for where could you have gotten what you had not made in order to make something with it? Is there, indeed, anything at all except because you are? Thus you spoke and they were made,[2] and by your Word you made them all.

Chapter 6

But how did you speak? Was it in the same manner in which the voice came from the cloud saying, "This is my beloved Son"?[3] For that voice sounded forth and died away; it began and ended. The syllables sounded and passed away, the second after the first, the third after the second, and thence in order, till the very last after all the rest; and silence after the last. From this it is clear and plain that it was the action of a creature, itself in time, which sounded that voice, obeying your eternal will. And what these words were which were formed at that time the outer ear conveyed to the conscious mind, whose inner ear lay attentively open to your eternal Word. But it compared those words which sounded in time with your eternal Word sounding in silence and said: "This is different; quite different! These words are far below me; they are not even real, for they fly away and pass, but the Word of my God remains above me forever." If, then, in words that sound and fade away you said that heaven and earth should be made, and thus *made* heaven and earth,

---

1. Contrast the notion of creation in Plato's *Timaeus* as appropriated by Justin Martyr in his *First Apology* [see pp. 3–4].
2. Cf. Ps. 33:9.
3. Matt. 3:17.

then there was already some kind of corporeal creature before heaven and earth by whose motions in time that voice might have had its occurrence in time. But there was nothing corporeal before the heaven and the earth; or if there was, then it is certain that already, without a time-bound voice, you had created whatever it was out of which you made the time-bound voice by which you said, "Let the heaven and the earth be made!" For whatever it was out of which such a voice was made simply did not exist at all until it was made by you. Was it decreed by your Word that a body might be made from which such words might come?

Chapter 7

You call us, then, to understand the Word—the God who is God with you—which is spoken eternally and by which all things are spoken eternally. For what was first spoken was not finished, and then something else spoken until the whole series was spoken; but all things at the same time and forever. For, otherwise, we should have time and change and not a true eternity, nor a true immortality. This I know, O my God, and I give thanks. I know, I confess to you, O Lord, and whoever is not ungrateful for certain truths knows and blesses thee along with me. We know, O Lord, this much we know: that in the same proportion as anything is not what it was, and is what it was not, in that very same proportion it passes away or comes to be. But there is nothing in your Word that passes away or returns to its place; for it is truly immortal and eternal. And, therefore, to the Word coeternal with you, at the same time and always you say all that you say. And whatever you say shall be made is made, and you make nothing otherwise than by speaking. Still, not all the things that you make by speaking are made at the same time and always.

Chapter 8

Why is this, I ask you, O Lord my God? I see it after a fashion, but I do not know how to express it, unless I say that everything that begins to be and then ceases to be begins and ceases when it is known in your eternal Reason that it ought to begin or cease—in your eternal Reason where nothing begins or ceases. And this is your Word, which is also "the Beginning," because it also speaks to us.[4] Thus, in the gospel, he spoke through the flesh; and this sounded in the outward ears of men so that it might be believed and sought for within, and so that it might be found in the eternal Truth, in which the good and only Master teaches all his disciples. There, O Lord, I hear your voice, the voice of one speaking to me, since he who teaches us speaks to us. But he that does not teach us does not really speak to us even when he speaks. Yet who is it that teaches us unless it be the Truth immutable? For even when we are instructed by means of the

---

4. Cf. the Vulgate of John 8:25.

mutable creation, we are thereby led to the Truth immutable. There we learn truly as we stand and hear him, and we rejoice greatly "because of the bridegroom's voice,"[5] restoring us to the source whence our being comes. And therefore, unless the Beginning remained immutable, there would then not be a place to which we might return when we had wandered away. But when we return from error, it is through our gaining knowledge that we return. In order for us to gain knowledge he teaches us, since he is the Beginning, and speaks to us.

Chapter 9

In this Beginning, O God, you made heaven and earth—through your Word, your Son, your Power, your Wisdom, your Truth: all wondrously speaking and wondrously creating. Who can comprehend such things and who can tell of it? What is it that shines through me and strikes my heart without injury, so that I both shudder and burn? I shudder because I am unlike it; I burn because I am like it. It is Wisdom itself that shines through me, clearing away my fog, which so readily overwhelms me so that I faint in it, in the darkness and burden of my punishment. For my strength is brought down in neediness, so that I cannot endure even my blessings until you, O Lord, who has been gracious to all my iniquities, also heal all my infirmities—for it is you who "shalt redeem my life from corruption, and crown me with loving-kindness and tender mercy, and shalt satisfy my desire with good things so that my youth shall be renewed like the eagle's."[6] For by this hope we are saved, and through patience we await your promises. Let him that is able hear you speaking to his inner mind. I will cry out with confidence because of your own oracle, "How wonderful are thy works, O Lord; in wisdom thou hast made them all."[7] And this Wisdom is the Beginning, and in that Beginning you made heaven and earth.

Chapter 10

Now, are not those still full of their old carnal nature[8] who ask us: "What was God doing *before* he made heaven and earth? For if he was idle," they say, "and doing nothing, then why did he not continue in that state forever—doing nothing, as he had always done? If any new motion has arisen in God, and a new will to form a creature, which he had never before formed, how can that be a true eternity in which an act of will occurs that was not there before? For the will of God is not a created thing, but comes

---

5. Cf. John 3:29.
6. Cf. Ps. 103:4, 5 (mixed text).
7. Ps. 104:24.
8. *Pleni vetustatis suae.* In *Sermon* 267.2 (*PL* 38.1230), Augustine has a similar usage. Speaking of those who pour new wine into old containers, he says, *Carnalitas vetustas est, gratia novitas est* ("Carnality is the old nature; grace is the new"); cf. Matt. 9:17.

before the creation—and this is true because nothing could be created unless the will of the Creator came before it. The will of God, therefore, pertains to his very Essence. Yet if anything has arisen in the Essence of God that was not there before, then that Essence cannot truly be called eternal. But if it was the eternal will of God that the creation should come to be, why, then, is not the creation itself also from eternity?"[9]

Chapter 11

Those who say these things do not yet understand you, O Wisdom of God, O Light of souls. They do not yet understand how the things are made that are made by and in you. They endeavor to comprehend eternal things, but their heart still flies about in the past and future motions of created things, and is still unstable. Who shall hold it and fix it so that it may come to rest for a little; and then, by degrees, glimpse the glory of that eternity which abides forever; and then, comparing eternity with the temporal process in which nothing abides, they may see that they are incommensurable? They would see that a long time does not become long, except from the many separate events that occur in its passage, which cannot be simultaneous. In the Eternal, on the other hand, nothing passes away, but the whole is simultaneously present. But no temporal process is wholly simultaneous. Therefore, let it[10] see that all time past is forced to move on by the incoming future; that all the future follows from the past; and that all, past and future, is created and issues out of that which is forever present. Who will hold the heart of man that it may stand still and see how the eternity which always stands still is itself neither future nor past but expresses itself in the times that are future and past? Can my hand do this, or can the hand of my mouth bring about so difficult a thing even by persuasion?

Chapter 12

How, then, shall I respond to him who asks, "What was God doing *before* he made heaven and earth?" I do not answer, as a certain one is reported to have done facetiously (shrugging off the force of the question). "He was preparing hell," he said, "for those who pry too deep." It is one thing to see the answer; it is another to laugh at the questioner—and for myself I do not answer these things thus. More willingly would I have answered, "I do not know what I do not know," than cause one who asked a deep question to be ridiculed—and by such tactics gain praise for a worthless answer. Rather, I say that you, our God, are the Creator of every creature. And if in the term "heaven and earth" every creature is included, I make bold to say

---

9. The notion of the eternity of this world was widely held in Greek philosophy, in different versions, and was incorporated into the Manichean rejection of the Christian doctrine of *creatio ex nihilo* which Augustine is citing here. He returns to the question, and his answer to it, again in *City of God* 11.4–8.

10. The unstable "heart" of those who confuse time and eternity.

further: "Before God made heaven and earth, he did not make anything at all. For if he did, what did he make unless it were a creature?" I do indeed wish that I knew all that I desire to know to my profit as surely as I know that no creature was made before any creature was made.

Chapter 13
But if the roving thought of someone should wander over the images of past time, and wonder that you, the Almighty God, the All-creating and All-sustaining, the Architect of heaven and earth, did for ages unnumbered abstain from so great a work before you actually did it, let him awake and consider that he wonders at illusions. For in what temporal medium could the unnumbered ages that you did not make pass by, since you are the Author and Creator of all the ages? Or what periods of time would those be that were not made by you? Or how could they have already passed away if they had not already been? Since, therefore, you are the Creator of all times, if there was any time *before* you made heaven and earth, why is it said that you were abstaining from working? For you made that very time itself, and periods could not pass by *before* you made the whole temporal procession. But if there was no time *before* heaven and earth, how, then, can it be asked, "What were you doing then?" For there was no "then" when there was no time.

Nor do you precede any given period of time by another period of time. Otherwise you would not precede all periods of time. In the eminence of your ever-present eternity, you precede all times past, and extend beyond all future times, for they are still to come—and when they have come, they will be past. But "You are always the Same and your years shall have no end."[11] Your years neither go nor come; but ours both go and come in order that all separate moments may come to pass. All your years stand together as one, since they are abiding. Nor do your years past exclude the years to come because your years do not pass away. All these years of ours shall be with you, when all of them shall have ceased to be. Your years are but a day, and your day is not recurrent, but always today. Your "today" does not yield to tomorrow and does not follow yesterday. Your "today" is eternity. Therefore, you generated the Coeternal, to whom you said, "This day I have begotten you."[12] You made all time and you are before all times, and there was never a time when there was no time.

Chapter 14
There was no time, therefore, when you had not made anything, because you made time itself. And there are no times that are coeternal with you, because you abide forever; but if times should abide, they would not be

---
11. Cf. Ps. 102:27.
12. Ps. 2:7.

times. For what is time? Who can easily and briefly explain it? Who can even comprehend it in thought or put the answer into words? Yet is it not true that in conversation we refer to nothing more familiarly or knowingly than time? And surely we understand it when we speak of it; we understand it also when we hear another speak of it. What, then, is time? If no one asks me, I know what it is. If I wish to explain it to him who asks me, I do not know. Yet I say with confidence that I know that if nothing passed away, there would be no past time; and if nothing were still coming, there would be no future time; and if there were nothing at all, there would be no present time. But, then, how is it that there are the two times, past and future, when even the past is now no longer and the future is now not yet? But if the present were always present, and did not pass into past time, it obviously would not be time but eternity. If, then, time present—if it be time—comes into existence only because it passes into time past, how can we say that even this *is*, since the cause of its being is that it will cease to be? Thus, can we not truly say that time *is* only as it tends toward nonbeing? . . .

Chapter 30
And I will be immovable and fixed in you, and your truth will be my mold. And I shall not have to endure the questions of those men who, as if in a morbid disease, thirst for more than they can hold and say, "What did God make before he made heaven and earth?" or, "How did it come into his mind to make something when he had never before made anything?" Grant them, O Lord, to consider well what they are saying; and grant them to see that where there is no time they cannot say "never." When, therefore, he is said "never to have made" something, what is this but to say that it was made in no time at all? Let them therefore see that there could be no time without a created world, and let them cease to speak vanity of this kind. Let them also be stretched out to those things which are before them, and understand that you, the eternal Creator of all times, are before all times and that no times are coeternal with you; nor is any creature, even if there is a creature "above time."

SELECTION 5

Bonaventure

Breviloquium, 2

Known as the Seraphic Doctor, Bonaventure (1221–1274) was the leading medieval theologian of the Franciscan order in much the same way that his contemporary, Thomas Aquinas, was among the Dominicans. Much more than Aquinas, however, Bonaventure has a reputation for theological conservatism, holding fast to the more traditional forms of Augustinian thought in the face of the new theological currents initiated by the reintroduction of Aristotle to Europe during the thirteenth century. Yet as the following selection demonstrates, he was perfectly willing to follow Augustine and other earlier theologians in allowing for flexibility in interpreting the creation narrative of Genesis 1 in the effort to reconcile the biblical witness with commonly accepted scientific knowledge.

As its title suggests, the *Breviloquium* is a summary of the main points of Christian doctrine, which Bonaventure had treated at greater length in his massive *Commentary* on the *Sentences* of Peter Lombard. In the five chapters excerpted here, he begins by listing the theological errors that the doctrine of creation from nothing is designed to exclude before going on to explain the logic behind the order of the creation narrative (which corresponds well with contemporary critical views on the parallelism between days 1–3 and 4–6). In chapters 3–4 he gives a largely "scientific" account of the structure and dynamics of the physical universe as it was understood in his day—an account whose loose fit with Genesis 1 is then explained in chapter 5 in terms of the hermeneutical principle that the Bible's primary purpose is to communicate God's work of redemption and not to provide a technical scientific description of the world.

From *The Works of Bonaventure* (Paterson, NJ: St. Anthony Guild Press, 1963), 2:69–85.

Chapter 1: On the Creation of the Universe

1. Having summarily considered the Trinity of God, it is proper to speak next of creation. Briefly, the following must be held. The entire fabric of the universe was brought into existence in time and out of nothingness, by one first Principle, single and supreme, whose power, though immeasurable, "has disposed all things by measure and number and weight" [Wis. 11:20].

2. In general, then, concerning the production of creatures, the foregoing must be held, to build up a true concept and avoid error. By saying IN TIME, we exclude the false theory of an eternal universe. By saying OUT OF NOTHINGNESS, we exclude the false theory of an eternal material principle. By saying ONE PRINCIPLE, we exclude the Manichean error of the plurality of principles. By saying SINGLE AND SUPREME, we exclude the error of those who hold that God produced the inferior creatures through the ministry of the spirits. And by adding measure and number and weight, we indicate that the creature is an effect of the creating Trinity in virtue of a triple causality: efficient, through which they are given unity, mode, and measure; exemplary, through which they are given truth, species, and number; final, through which they are given goodness, order, and weight. These, as traces of the Creator, are present in all creatures, whether material or spiritual or composites of both.

3. This should be understood as follows. For the sake of perfect order and repose in things, all must be led back to the one Principle, who necessarily

must be first in order to procure repose for other beings, and most perfect in order to procure additional perfections for them. Now, a first principle in whom there is repose can be nothing else but one: hence, if He creates a world, He must bring it forth out of nothingness, since He cannot possibly make it of His own substance. Moreover, creation out of nothingness implies, on the part of the creature, a state of being subsequent upon a state of non-being, and, on the part of the Principle, a boundless productive power, which is found in God alone: necessarily, then, the universe must be created in time by this same boundless power acting in itself and without intermediary.

4. The utterly perfect Principle from whom flows the perfection of all things must act by His own power and law, and for Himself as an end; for in His action He needs none but Himself. Hence, He must be the threefold cause of all creatures: efficient, exemplary, and final. As a result, every creature must bear the same threefold reference to the first Cause: for every one exists by virtue of the efficient cause, is patterned after the exemplary cause, and ordained toward the final cause. For this reason, every creature is one, true, and good; has mode, species, and order; and has measure, distinct existence [number], and weight—for weight is defined as an orderly tendency. All this applies to every creature in general, whether material, spiritual, or composite, as is human nature.

Chapter 2: On the Actual Production of Physical Nature
1. We shall consider physical nature as regards its actual production, its essence, and its operation.

Concerning production, we must specifically hold that physical nature was brought into existence in six days. "In the beginning," before any day, "God created the heavens and the earth" [Gen. 1:1]. On the first day, light was made; on the second, "the firmament in the midst of the waters" [Gen. 1:6]; on the third, the waters were separated from the land and "gathered into one place" [Gen. 1:9]; on the fourth, the heavens were adorned with lights; on the fifth, the air and the water were furnished with birds and fishes; on the sixth, the earth was completed with animals and men. On the seventh day, God rested; rested not from activity and work—He continues to act to this very hour—but from creating any new nature, since all things had been created either in their prototypes, as those things that multiply by generation, or in their seminal principle, as other things that are brought about in a different way.

2. This should be understood as follows. Since all things flow from the first and utterly perfect Principle, who is omnipotent, all-wise, and all-beneficent, their production must reflect the same three attributes or perfections. Therefore, the divine operation which built the fabric of the universe was threefold: creation, properly reflecting omnipotence; division, reflecting wisdom; and provision, reflecting a most generous bounty.

Because creation is out of nothingness, the creative act, foundation of all times and things, came about in the beginning, before any day.

3. Now, since there is a threefold qualitative distinction between cosmic substance, the act of dividing extended over three days. There is a distinction between the luminous, the translucent, and the opaque natures, and this was brought about on the first day through the separation of light from darkness. There is a distinction between one translucent nature and the other, and this was brought about on the second day through the separation of the waters. And there is a distinction between translucent and opaque natures, and this was brought about on the third day through the separation of water from land. Later, we shall see how, through these separations, we are given to understand implicitly the division of the heavenly bodies and of the elements. That is why the division was fittingly accomplished in three days.

4. Since provision parallels division, it also was brought about in three days. For there is a provisioning of the luminous nature, and this occurred on the fourth day through the forming of the stars, the sun, and the moon. There is a provisioning of the translucent nature, and this occurred on the fifth day, when fish and bird were made from the waters to people the water and the air. And there is a provisioning of the opaque nature, that is, of the land, and this occurred on the sixth day when the mammals and reptiles were made, and finally, as the crown of all, man.

5. God could have brought all this about in a single instant. He chose instead to act through time, and step by step, and this for three reasons. First, there was to be a distinct and clear manifestation of power, wisdom, and goodness; second, there was to be fitting correspondence between the days or times and the operations; third, the succession of days was to prefigure all future ages, in the same way as, at creation, the seeds of all future beings were planted. So the distinction of the future times—explained above where we spoke of the seven ages of history—stemmed, as if from seeds, from the distinction of the seven days. That is why, to the six days of work, there is added one of rest: a day to which no dusk is ascribed—not that this day was not followed by night, but because it was to prefigure the repose of souls that shall have no end.

Now, if it should be said, in opposition, that all things were made at once, this is simply considering the seven days from the viewpoint of angels. At any rate, the first manner of speaking is more in keeping with the Scriptures and the opinions of the saints, both before and after blessed Augustine.

Chapter 3: On the Essence of Physical Nature

1. Concerning the essence of physical nature, the following must be held. The entire fabric of the physical world consists in the heavenly and the elemental natures. Heavenly nature comprises three main heavens: the empyrean heaven, the crystalline heaven, and the firmament. Beneath the firmament, which is the heaven of stars, are the seven spheres of the

planets: Saturn, Jupiter, Mars, the Sun, Venus, Mercury, and the Moon. Elemental nature is divided into four spheres: Fire, Air, Water, and Earth.

Thus, ranging from the highest heaven down to the center, the earth, there are ten heavenly and four elemental spheres, which make up in a distinct, perfect, and orderly fashion the whole physical cosmos.

2. This should be understood as follows. If physical nature was to be complete in itself, reflecting also the manifold wisdom of the first Principle, there had to be a multiplicity of forms, such as appears in minerals, plants, and animals. Therefore, some simple essences had to be first established, the various combinations of which would result in this multiplicity. Such simple essence is the nature that is subject to opposition; and this is elemental nature. There had to be also a nature that, in compounds, would adjust the opposition between the elements. Such nature, itself free from opposition, is that of light and of the supercelestial bodies.

3. Since there is no compounding without active and passive opposition, the opposition in the elements had to be twofold: one, between the active qualities, that is, hot and cold; two, between the passive qualities, that is, wet and dry. Now, any element is both active and passive, and thus has two qualities, one active and the other passive, of which, however, one is always principal and characteristic. That is why there are only four elements, corresponding to the four said qualities in their four combinations.

4. Now, heavenly nature can be motionless and uniform, and such is the empyrean, for it is pure light. It can be mobile and multiform, and such is the firmament. It can be mobile and uniform, and such is the crystalline heaven, between the empyrean and the stellar. The fourth combination—the motionless and multiform—cannot exist because multiplicity of form leads to varied movements, and not to uniform repose.

5. Thus, there are three heavens. The first, the empyrean, is luminous throughout; the second, the crystalline, is translucent throughout; the third, the firmament, is a combination of the first two. There being three incorruptible heavens and four variable elements, God designed the seven spheres of the planets for the sake of due connection, concordance, and correspondence. The planets, through their varied movements and incorruptible forms, act as a bond or junction between the inferior elemental spheres and the superior heavenly spheres. Thus, they perfect and complete the universe. The universe itself is organized in numerical proportions. It is made up of the ten heavenly and the four elemental spheres. These make the universe so beautiful in its proportions, so complete and orderly, that in its own way it offers an image of its Principle.

Chapter 4: On the Action and Influence of Physical Nature
1. As regards the influence of physical nature, the following must be held. The heavens influence the earth and the elements by dividing time into days, months, and years. Indeed, the Scriptures say that the heavens should

"serve as signs and for the fixing of seasons, days and years" [Gen. 1:14]. The heavens also influence the efficient production of things that can be generated and corrupted, that is, of mineral, vegetal, and sentient beings, and of the human body. Yet they enter into the determination of times and the course of events in such a way that they can never be taken as sure signs of future contingent events, nor can they affect free will through the power of the constellations, which some philosophers call fate.

2. This should be understood as follows. The heavenly bodies, so close to the first Principle, have light, motion, heat, and power: light by reason of their form and species; motion, by reason of the influence upon them of a superior agent; heat, by reason of their influence upon an inferior passive element; power, in all the aforementioned ways. This being so, the heavenly bodies, through their light and motion, determine the divisions of time. The day is measured by sunlight and by the heavenly movements; the month, by the course of the moon along its elliptic path; the years, by the course of the sun along the same path; and the seasons, by the various motions of the planets, their separation and conjunction, their ascent and descent; their regression and state, for it is these things which cause seasonal variations.

3. As the heavenly bodies prompt, promote, and harmonize through power and heat, they influence the production of those things that are generated from the elements. By a process of conciliation remote from equalization, they influence minerals; by a process of conciliation and to some extent equalization, they influence plants; by a process of conciliation that is largely equalization, they influence sentient beings; finally, by a process of conciliation that is full equalization, they influence the human body, which is fitted to receive the most noble form, the soul. All sentient bodily beings are ordained toward this object and this end: this form fully existing, alive, sensitive, and intellective, by which the sensitive bodily nature of man is to be returned, as in an intelligible circle, to its first Principle in whom it will be completed and beatified.

4. And because the soul tends to its end through free will, by reason of this freedom it is superior to any physical power. That is why all things are subservient to the soul, whose essential nature it is to be under none but God—not fate or any power deriving from the position of the stars.

5. Hence, it is undubitably true that we human beings are the end of all existing things. All material things are made to serve man, and to enkindle in him the fire of love and praise for the Maker of the universe through whose providence all is governed. Therefore, the fabric of his sensitive body is like a house made for man by the supreme Architect to serve until such time as he may come to the "house not made by human hands, . . . in the heavens" [2 Cor. 5:1]. Just as the soul, by reason of the body and to gain merit, now lives on earth, so will the body, by reason of the soul and to gain reward, some day live in heaven.

Chapter 5: On How These Things Are Described in Holy Scripture

1. It should be clear from what has been said that orderliness exists not only in the way God created things in time and arranged them in space, but also in the way He governs them in their interrelationship. It should be clear, too, that there is order in the way the Scriptures tell us all that we need to know. They do not, however, explicitly describe the different spheres of the heavens and of the elements; they say little or nothing about the motions and effects of the heavenly bodies, or the combinations of the elements and their compounds; and what is more, they say nothing explicitly about the creation of the heavenly spirits in the account of how the present universe was made.

2. This should be understood as follows. The first Principle opens Himself to our mind through the Scriptures and through creatures. In the book of creatures, He manifests Himself as the effective Principle, and in the book of Scriptures, as the redemptive Principle. Now, the redemptive Principle cannot be known unless the effective Principle also is known. So Scripture, though mainly concerned with the work of redemption, must also deal with the work of creation, as that leads to the knowledge of the first, the effective and redemptive Principle. Hence, this knowledge is both lofty and salutary: lofty, because it is concerned with the effective Principle, the Creator; and salutary, because it is concerned with the redemptive Principle, Christ the Saviour and Mediator.

3. Again, because this knowledge is lofty as it concerns the first Principle and the supreme Being, it does not lower itself to describing the specific beings of nature, or their motions, powers, and differences. It remains on the general level whereon specific beings are only implied, describing the creation of the world in a general manner, as regards the disposition and effect of luminous, translucent, and opaque natures.

4. Because in the first Principle, who is the object of Scripture, there is the order of nature by virtue of His existence, the order of wisdom by virtue of His providence, and the order of goodness by virtue of His operation; and because the order of nature indicates simultaneous existence and equality, the order of wisdom, priority and posteriority, and the order of operation, superiority and subordination: therefore, to indicate the order of nature, Scripture makes clear how God was to operate. In the beginning, before time was, the luminous, translucent, and opaque natures were brought from non-being into being. This is implied in the words: "In the beginning God created the heavens and the earth, . . . and the spirit of God was stirring above the waters" [Gen. 1:1-2]. Here, the word "heavens" implies the luminous nature, the word "earth," opaque nature, and the word "*waters*," the transparent or translucent nature, whether subject to opposition or elevated above it. Here, also, is implied the eternal Trinity, that is, the Father under the term "God creating," the Son under the term "the Beginning," and the Holy Spirit under the term "the Spirit of God."

It is in this sense that the words "He that liveth forever created all things together" [Sir. 18:1] are to be understood; not as meaning, what poets have fantasied, that He created all in utter chaos, for He so created the threefold nature that the first would be on high, the intermediate in the middle, and the last below; nor as meaning that all three natures were in a state of complete distinctness, for while the heavens were perfect, the earth was still unorganized, and the intermediate nature, holding the middle place, had not yet been brought unto a state of perfect separateness.

5. To indicate the order of wisdom in disposing, Scripture shows that the threefold nature was not divided and furnished in a single operation. To correspond to the trineness of created nature, separation also took three days, and furnishing, another three. Thus, as God in the beginning, before the dawn of time, created a triple nature all at once, even so, when time began its course, he used a triple measure of duration, as it were a triple day, to make a triple division in the triple created nature; and He used another triple day to provide the triply distinct nature with a triple furnishing.

6. To indicate the ORDER OF GOODNESS in operating, Scripture shows that the three natures were established in the world according to the norm of superior and inferior, as the dignity and influence of each required.

Because luminous nature is the brightest, its place is the upper sphere. Opaque nature, having the least splendor, belongs in the lower. Translucent nature, being intermediate, belongs in the middle place. Now, both heavenly and elemental natures have something of translucency and transparency; and luminosity also is shared by both. Therefore, it is rightly said that the firmament was established "between the waters" [Gen. 1:6]. This does not mean that the waters above the firmament are fluid, cold, heavy, corruptible: on the contrary, they are subtle, incorruptible, transparent, so sublime as to be free from all opposition. Thus, because of the nobility of their formal constitution, they are of heavenly nature and are to be placed among heavenly things.

7. They are to be placed there also by reason of their power and influence. All physical action of inferior beings receives its rule, origin, and energy from the heavenly nature. Now, there are two active qualities, hot and cold. The heaven of the stars, by reason of its luminosity, is the chief agent of warmth, while another, the crystalline heaven, is the chief agent of cold. And as the heaven of stars is not formally hot, although it acts to produce heat, so the heaven that is called liquid or crystalline is not, in nature, cold. Hence, what the inspired writers say about the waters being put there as a shield against the heat of the higher bodies, and other like statements, are to be taken, not as formal affirmations of essence, but rather as pertaining to efficacy and influence.

And so the establishing of creation in the aforesaid order accords with the order both of creating Wisdom and of divine Scripture, which is lofty knowledge.

8. Again, because it is salutary knowledge, Scripture does not specify the work of creation except for the sake of the work of reparation. And because the angels were so created that, once fallen, they were beyond redeeming, as will be seen later nothing is said explicitly and literally about their creation and fall, since no reparation was to follow.

9. Yet, because complete silence concerning the creation of the loftiest creatures would have been inconsistent with the loftiness of Scripture, therefore the sacred writings so describe the creation of things as to impart a lofty and salutary knowledge, but in such a way that the literal account of the whole creation is applied symbolically, in a spiritual sense, to the hierarchies of the angels and of the Church. Hence, in the three natures first to be produced, heaven, according to this spiritual reading, refers to the angelic hierarchy, earth to the ecclesiastical, and water to grace, through which both are refreshed.

10. Again, the seven days mean the seven states of the Church through the succession of the seven ages. The same series of seven also means the seven illuminations through which the angels rise from the creature to God. Thus, the foregoing reveals the sufficiency and truth of the Scriptures, according to the various opinions of the saints; that is, Augustine and others. Rightly understood, these opinions are not contradictory, but true.

SELECTION 6

Thomas Aquinas

Summa contra Gentiles,
2.17–19, 38

The Dominican Thomas Aquinas (ca. 1225–1274) is widely recognized as among the greatest theologians of the western Middle Ages, and his theology has retained a central place in Catholic teaching. While no less profoundly shaped by the thought of Augustine than Bonaventure, Aquinas was also deeply impressed by the intellectual power of Aristotle, whose thought was being reintroduced to Europe in the thirteenth century by way of Arabic translations and commentaries. Though Aquinas's work is often described as a synthesis of Aristotelian and Christian thought, he was far from treating the two as equally authoritative. It would be more accurate to say that Aquinas, convinced that the unity of God implied that the truths of reason could not conflict with the truths of revelation, sought to show that the best insights of Aristotelian philosophy were fully consistent with the faith of the church.

The following selection on the logic of creation from nothing comes from the first of Aquinas's great compendia of Christian doctrine, the *Summa con-*

tra Gentiles (1258–1264).[1] Thomas begins by arguing that since creation involves no preexisting substance, it cannot be characterized as or understood to entail any sort of change or movement. On this basis he defines creation as a "kind of relation"—specifically a relation of unilateral dependence of the creature on God—rather than a process of change or succession. He then goes on to argue that this understanding of creation is equally consistent with the universe having a temporal beginning and with its being eternal. Thus, though Thomas ultimately maintains that the eternity of the world is not consistent with Christian faith, he argues his case on the basis of what is fitting or becoming to God (since "God's might and goodness are especially made manifest in that things other than Himself were not always") rather than on grounds of logical necessity.

From *The Summa contra Gentiles of Saint Thomas Aquinas: The Second Book*
(London: Burns, Oates, & Washbourne, 1923), 25–29, 82–85.

Chapter 17: That Creation Is Neither Movement nor Change

Having proved the foregoing, it is evident that God's action, which is without prejacent matter and is called *creation*, is neither movement nor change, properly speaking. For all movement or change is "the action of that which is in potentiality as such."[2] Now in this action there preexists nothing in potentiality to receive the action, as we have proved.[3] Therefore it is neither movement nor change.

Again. The extremes of a movement or change are included in the same order: either because they come under one genus, as contraries, for instance in the movement of growth and alteration, and when a thing is carried from one place to another; or because they have one potentiality of matter in common, as privation and form in generation and corruption. But neither of these applies to creation: for it admits of no potentiality, nor of anything of the same genus that may be presupposed to creation, as we have proved.[4] Therefore there is neither movement nor change therein.

Further. In every change or movement there must be "something that is conditioned otherwise now and before: since the very name of change shows this."[5] But when the whole substance of a thing is brought into being, there can be no same thing that is conditioned in one way and in another, for it would not be produced, but presupposed to production. Therefore creation is not a change.

---

1. Some early manuscripts of the text give the different title of *Book on the Truth of the Catholic Faith against the Errors of the Infidels*, suggesting a more limited scope that in the opinion of many is more in keeping with the character of the text.
2. Aristotle, *Physics*, 3.1.6; ET, *LCL* 4:195.
3. See *Summa contra Gentiles*, 2.16.
4. Ibid.
5. Aristotle, *Physics*, 5.1.7; ET, *LCL* 5:15.

Further. Movement and change must needs precede that which is made by change or movement: because *having been made* is the beginning of rest and the term of movement. Wherefore all change must be movement or the term of a movement that is successive. For this reason, what is being made, is not: for as long as movement lasts, something is being made and is not: whereas in the term itself of movement, wherein rest begins, no longer is a thing being made, but it has been made. Now in creation this is impossible: for if creation preceded as movement or change, it would necessarily presuppose a subject, and this is contrary to the nature of creation. Therefore creation is neither movement nor change.

Chapter 18: How to Solve the Objections against Creation

From this we may see the vacuity of those who gainsay creation by arguments taken from the nature of movement and change: such as that creation must needs, like other movements and changes, take place in some subject, and that it implies the transmutation of non-being into being, like that of fire into air.

For creation is not a change, but the very dependence of created being on the principle whereby it is produced. Hence it is a kind of relation. Wherefore nothing prevents its being in the creature as its subject. Nevertheless creation would seem to be a kind of change according only to our way of understanding: in so far, to wit, as our intellect grasps one and the same thing as previously non-existent, and as afterwards existing.

It is clear however that if creation is a relation, it is a thing: and neither is it uncreated, nor is it created by another relation. For since a created effect depends really on its creator, this relation must needs be some thing. Now every thing is brought into being by God.[6] Therefore it receives its being from God. And yet it is not created by a different creation from the first creature which is stated to be created thereby. Because accidents and forms, just as they are not *per se*, so neither are they created *per se*, since creation is the production of a being, but just as they are in another, so are they created when other things are created.

Moreover. A relation is not referred through another relation,—for in that case one would go on to infinity,—but is referred by itself, because it is essentially a relation. Therefore there is no need for another creation whereby creation itself is created, so that one would go on to infinity.

Chapter 19: That in Creation There Is No Succession

It is also clear from the foregoing that all creation is without succession.

For succession is proper to movement: while creation is not a movement nor the term of a movement, as change is.[7] Therefore there is no succession therein.

---

6. See *Summa contra Gentiles*, 2.15.
7. See ch. 17 above.

Again. In every successive movement there is some mean between its extremes: for "a mean is that which a continuously moved thing reaches first before reaching the term."[8] Now between being and non-being which are as the extremes of creation, no mean is possible. Therefore there is no succession therein.

Moreover. In every making wherein there is succession, a thing is becoming before it has been made, as is proved in *Physics* 6.[9] Now this cannot happen in creation. Because the becoming which would precede being made, would need a subject. And this could not be the creature itself whose creation is in question, since it is not before it is made. Nor would it be in the maker, because to be moved is the act not of the mover, but of the thing moved.[10] It follows that becoming would have for its subject some pre-existing matter of the thing made. But this is incompatible with creation.[11] Therefore there can be no succession in creation.

Further. Every making that proceeds by succession must needs take time: since before and after in movement are reckoned by time.[12] Now time, movement, and the thing subject to movement are all simultaneously divided.[13] This is evident in local movement: for that which is moved with regularity passes through half a magnitude in half the time. Now the division in forms that corresponds to division of time is according to intensity and remissness: thus if a thing is heated to such a degree in so much time, it is heated to a less degree in less time. Accordingly succession in any movement or making is possible according as the thing in respect of which there is motion is divisible: either according to quantity, as in local movement and increase; or according to intensity and remission, as in alteration. Now the latter occurs in two ways. First, because the form which is the term of movement is divisible in respect of intensity and remission, as when a thing is in motion towards whiteness: secondly, because such a division happens in dispositions to such a form; thus the becoming of fire is successive on account of the previous alteration as regards the dispositions to the form. But the substantial being itself of a creature is not divisible in this way, for "substance cannot be more or less."[14] Nor do any dispositions precede creation, since there is no pre-existing matter, for disposition is on the part of matter. It follows therefore that there cannot be succession in creation.

Further. Succession in the making of things results from a defect of the matter, that is not suitably disposed from the beginning for the reception of the form: wherefore, when the matter is already perfectly disposed for

---

8. Aristotle, *Physics*, 5.3.2; ET, *LCL* 5:37.
9. Aristotle, *Physics*, 6.6.10; ET, *LCL* 5:155.
10. See Aristotle, *Physics*, 3.3.1; ET, *LCL* 4:208–9.
11. See *Summa contra Gentiles*, 2.21.
12. See Aristotle, *Physics*, 4.11.5; ET, *LCL* 4:386–87.
13. See Aristotle, *Physics*, 6.4.6; ET, *LCL* 5:131–32.
14. Aristotle, *Categories*, 5.20; ET, *LCL* 1:31.

the form, it receives it in an instant. For this reason, since a diaphanous body is always in the last disposition for light, it is actually illumined as soon as the luminous body is present: nor does any movement precede on the part of the illuminable body, but only local movement on the part of the illuminant, which becomes present. But in creation nothing is required beforehand on the part of matter: nor does the agent lack anything for His action, that may afterwards accrue to Him through movement, since He is utterly immovable, as we have shown in the First Book of this Work.[15] It follows therefore that creation is instantaneous. Hence in the same instant a thing is being created and is created, just as in the same instant a thing is being illumined and is illumined.

Hence divine Scripture declares that the creation of things took place in an indivisible instant, when it says: "In the beginning God created heaven and earth" [Gen. 1:1]: which beginning Basil expounds as "the beginning of time,"[16] and this must be indivisible. . . .

Chapter 38: Arguments by Which Some Endeavour to Prove That the World Is Not Eternal

Now there are some arguments brought forward by certain people to prove that the world was not always: they are taken from the following.

For it has been proved that God is the cause of all things. But a cause must precede in duration the things made by its action.

Again. Since all being is created by God, it cannot said to be made from some being, so that it must be made from nothing, and consequently has being after non-being.

Also, because it is not possible to pass by an infinite number of things. Now if the world were always, an infinite number of things would have now been passed by: since what is past, is passed by, and if the world was always, there is an infinite number of days or an infinite number of solar revolutions.

Further. It follows that an addition is made to the infinite, since every day something is added to the past days or revolutions.

Moreover. It follows that it is possible to go on to infinity in efficient causes, if there was always generation; and we are bound to admit this latter if the world was always: because the son's cause is his father, and another man is the latter's father, and so on indefinitely.

Again. It will follow that there is an infinite number of things: namely the immortal souls of an infinite number of men.

Now since these arguments do not conclude of absolute necessity, although they are not devoid of probability, it is enough merely to touch upon them, lest the Catholic faith seem to be founded on empty reason-

---

15. See *Summa contra Gentiles*, 1.13.
16. Basil of Caesarea, *Hexameron*, 1.5 (*PG* 29b.13C; ET, *NPNF*[2], 55).

ings, and not, as it is, on the most solid teaching of God. Wherefore it seems right that we should indicate how those arguments are met by those who asserted the eternity of the world.

For the first statement that an agent necessarily precedes the effect brought about by its operation, is true of those things which act by movement, because the effect is not until the movement is ended, and the agent must necessarily exist even when the movement begins. On the other hand in those things which act instantaneously, this is not necessary: thus as soon as the sun reaches the point of the East, it enlightens our hemisphere.

Also, that which is said in the second place is of no avail. For in order to contradict the statement, "Something is made from something," if this be not granted, we must say "Something is not made from something," and not, "Something is made from nothing," except in the sense of the former: whence we cannot conclude that it is made after not being.

Again, the third argument is not cogent. For though the infinite in act be impossible, it is not impossible in succession, since any given infinite taken in this sense is finite. Hence each of the preceding revolutions could be passed by, since it was finite. But in all of them together, if the world had been always, there would be no first revolution. Wherefore there would be no passing through them, because this always requires two extremes.

Again, the fourth argument put forward is weak. For nothing hinders the infinite receiving an addition on the side on which it is finite. Now supposing time to be eternal, it follows that it is infinite anteriorly but finite posteriorly, since the present is the term of the past.

Nor is the argument cogent which is given in the fifth place. For it is impossible, according to philosophers, to have an infinite number of active causes which act together simultaneously: because the effect would have to depend on an infinite number of simultaneous actions. Such are causes that are *per se* infinite, because their infinity is required for their effect. On the other hand in causes that do not act simultaneously, this is not impossible, according to those who assert that generation has always been. And this infinity is accidental to the causes, for it is accidental to the father of Socrates that he is another man's son or not. Whereas it is not accidental to the stick forasmuch as it moves the stone, that it be moved by the hand, since it moves forasmuch as it is moved.

The objection taken from souls is more difficult. And yet the argument is not of much use, since it takes many things for granted.[17] For some of those who maintained the eternity of the world, asserted that human souls do not survive the body. Some said that of all souls there survives only the separate intellect, or the active intellect according to some, or even the passive intellect according to others. Some have held a kind of rotation

---

17. See *Summa contra Gentiles*, 2.81.

in souls, saying that the same souls after several centuries return to bodies. And some do not consider it incongruous that there should be things actually infinite in those which have no order.

Nevertheless one may proceed to prove this more efficiently from the end of the divine will, as we have indicated above.[18] For the end of God's will in the production of things, is His goodness as manifested in His effects. Now God's might and goodness are especially made manifest in that things other than Himself were not always. For the fact that they have not always been clearly shows that other things beside Himself have their being from Him. It also shows that He does not act by a necessity of His nature, and that His power is infinite in acting. Therefore it was most becoming to the goodness of God, that He should give His creatures a beginning of their duration.

From what has been said we are able to avoid the various errors of the pagan philosophers. Some of whom asserted the eternity of the world; others asserted that the matter of the world is eternal, out of which at a certain time the world began to be formed; either by chance; or by some intellect; or else by attraction and repulsion. For all these suppose something eternal beside God: which is incompatible with the Catholic faith.

SELECTION 7

Friedrich Schleiermacher

Christian Faith, §§40–41

Known as the father of liberal theology, Friedrich Daniel Ernst Schleiermacher (1768–1834) is widely regarded as the most influential theologian of the nineteenth century. In his monumental treatise *Christian Faith* Schleiermacher sought to reclaim the academic credibility of theology in the wake of the criticism to which it had been subjected by rationalist thinkers of the Enlightenment. He began by arguing that religion needed to be reconceived as a matter neither of knowing (science) nor of doing (ethics) but rather of feeling, a more fundamental experience of "absolute dependence" (*schlechthinnige Abhängigkeit*) that defined for Schleiermacher the essence of the human encounter with God. Theology, in turn, was to be understood as the systematic reflection on this feeling of absolute dependence as it has been shaped by the particular historical events that constitute a given religious tradition. Thus, Schleiermacher maintains that the distinguishing mark of specifically Christian theology is "that in it everything is related to the redemption accomplished by Jesus of Nazareth" (*Christian Faith*, sec. 11).

---

18. See ibid., 2.35.

The following selection from *Christian Faith* shows how this overall approach to theology shapes Schleiermacher's interpretation of the doctrine of creation. Because the proper subject of doctrine is exclusively the articulation of religious feeling, Schleiermacher eschews any interpretation of creation as a scientific explanation of the origin of the world. Indeed, because it is to be understood exclusively in terms of the Christian's feeling of absolute dependence, he argues that the doctrine of creation deals only incidentally with questions of origin, except insofar as to exclude the idea that anything originated independently of God (since this would contradict the feeling of absolute dependence on God). The idea of creation ex nihilo is to be interpreted in this purely negative sense; indeed, because the point of the doctrine of creation is to subsume all reality under the experience of absolute dependence on God, Schleiermacher expresses sympathy with Origen's doctrine of eternal creation on the grounds that the alternative suggests change in God and thereby makes God subject to time. This move provides the basis for the criticism that Schleiermacher's method leads him to collapse the doctrine of creation into that of preservation in a manner inconsistent with the Bible.

From *Christian Faith,* trans. Terrence N. Tice, Catherine L. Kelsey, and Edwina Lawler (Louisville, KY: Westminster John Knox Press, forthcoming).

§40
Every notion concerning the origin of the world by which anything whatsoever is excluded from having been originated by God or by which even God is placed under those definitions and those contrasts that have originated only in the world and through the world contradicts the religious self-consciousness that comprises the basis here.

Acts 17:24, Rom. 1:19–20, Heb. 11:3.

1. The New Testament passages just cited take the lead in our dismissing every more closely defined notion of creation. Even the expression *hrēmati*[1] is only a negative factor for any closer definition, namely to exclude any notion of any sort of instrument or means. It is also possible to say, in agreement with this expression and with equal correctness, that the world itself, viewed as having come into being through speaking, is that which has been spoken by God.[2] On this ground, moreover, we may be satisfied to set forth those negative characteristics as rules of judgment for whatever has intruded in faith-doctrine, but by our own conviction unjustifiably, as a closer definition of this concept. This is so, for since our immediate self-consciousnes represents finite being only in the identity of

---

1. Ed. note: "by the word" (Heb. 11:3).

2. Luther, *On Genesis* (1535), on Gen. 1:5 in I, §51: "What else, then, is the entire creation than a word of God said and expressed by God, . . . thus so that creating is no more difficult for God than naming it is for us." Ed. note: cf. also *LW* 1:22.

origination and continuation, we find in that self-consciousness neither occasion for explication of origination by itself alone nor any lead toward it; thus, by virtue of that self-consciousness, we also can take no special part in such an explication.

The further development of the doctrine of creation in dogmatics comes from a time when people wanted to draw even the material for natural sciences from Scripture and when the features that belong to all the more advanced sciences still lay latent in theology itself. Hence, it belongs to the subsequent total separation of the two fields of inquiry that we now leave this subject to natural science investigations that go back in time and space, whether they can lead us up to the formative powers and masses of world bodies or take us still further. Moreover, it also belongs to this total separation that, given the above presupposition, we calmly await the results of these investigations. We do so, in that every scientific endeavor that works with the concepts "God" and "world" without being dependent on any Christian faith-doctrine, or thereby becoming so, must be bounded by the same definitions of them if these two concepts are not to cease being two different ones.

2. Now, we acknowledge that the New Testament passages offer no material whatsoever toward any further development of the doctrine of creation. We also acknowledge that even when inquiries into faith-doctrine were caught up in that confusion of their task with that of philosophers to which we have adverted, they still always referred back to Scripture. Accordingly, we have, first of all, to look at the Mosaic narrative and at Old Testament passages that are, to a certain extent, collectively dependent on it. Now, it is undeniable that the Reformers took that narrative to be an actual historical account.[3] Yet, what Luther says is primarily directed against allegorical explanation, and Calvin's outlook forthwith excludes any use of this creation narrative toward formation of an actual theory. It is in every way advantageous for this subject that nothing from this material has gained entry into the creedal symbols, especially since the difference between the two narratives in Genesis is so significant—if one does not want forcibly to regard the second one as a recapitulating continuation of the first—that one can hardly attribute a genuinely historical character to them.

Suppose that we then add to all these considerations the fact that in those Old Testament passages which mention creation, in part the same simplicity prevails as in the New Testament passages that do so,[4] and in part the Mosaic statements do indeed underlie them but are nonethe-

---

3. (1) Luther, *On Genesis* (1535) on Gen. 1:3 [ET, *LW* 1:19]: "For Moses wrote a history and told of things that had happened." (2) Calvin, *Institutes* (1559) 1.14.3 [ET, *LCC* 20:162.]: "To be sure, Moses, accommodating himself to the rudeness of the common folk, mentions in the history of the creation no words of God other than those which show themselves to our own eyes."

4. Isa. 45:18 and Jer. 10:12.

less very liberally handled.⁵ Let us also add the observations that a purely didactic use of this account never appeared and that Philo, who thoroughly rejected interpreting the "six days" of creation in the literal sense, would surely have had predecessors. On these grounds, we can rather securely conclude, first, that the literal account was never generally held to at that time but that a dim but healthy feeling has always lingered to the effect that this old monument should not be treated in accordance with our notions of history. Hence, we have no reason to maintain a stricter historical appreciation of it than the Jewish people itself did in its best times.

Suppose that it were granted, however, that people were fully justified in assuming that the Mosaic description was an historical account communicated in an extraordinary way. The only implication would be that in this way we would have attained a natural scientific insight not to be gained differently; yet, in accordance with our usage of the term, in no fashion would the particular aspects of that insight be "faith-doctrines" on that account, since our feeling of absolute dependence would obtain neither a new content nor a different formation nor any sort of closer definition thereby. Hence, not even a commentative interpretation of that insight nor any assessment of such interpretations can be a task for dogmatics in any way whatsoever.

3. As concerns the various definitions that have been proposed, it is quite clear that our feeling of absolute dependence could not be referred to the general constitution of all finite being if anything within it were, or ever had been, independent of God. It is also just as certain, however, that if within all finite being, as such, there were anything at all that would have entered into it at its origination that could be viewed as independent of God, then because precisely this thing would also have to exist in us,⁶ the feeling of absolute dependence could itself have no truth in it, even in relation to ourselves. Suppose, on the other hand, that God were imagined to be limited in any way as the one creating, thus similar in God's own activity to that which is nonetheless to be absolutely dependent on God. Then the feeling that gives evidence of this dependence likewise could not be true, in that this likeness and dependence would cancel each other out and thus finite being, inasmuch as it would be like God, could not be absolutely dependent on God.

Except under one of these two forms, however, a contradiction between any theory of creation whatsoever and the general foundation contained in our religious self-consciousness is inconceivable. With the Christian characteristic of our religious self-consciousness, however, given that this characteristic already presupposes an actual experience, a doctrine of sheer

---

5. Ps. 33:6–9, Ps. 104, and Job 38:4ff.

6. Ed. note: Here the assumption is that everything in nature is interconnected; thus, if anything in it were independent of God, our own dependence would be compromised too.

creation also cannot stand in contradiction, because that doctrine, as such, does not take the continuation of that creation into consideration. Thus, Christian piety can have no interest in these investigations other than to steer clear of these two shoals. Now, whether pursuing this interest is easy or whether here too whoever wants to avoid the one shoal all too readily steers close to the other shoal have both to be discovered based on a closer observation of additional items that are accepted in faith-doctrine.[7]

§41

If the concept of creation is to be further explicated, the origination of the world must indeed be traced back entirely to divine activity, yet not in such a way that this is defined after the manner of human activity. Moreover, the origination of the world is to be represented as that realization of time which conditions all change, yet not in such a way that divine activity would itself become a temporal activity....

1. The expression "out of nothing" denies that before the origination of the world anything at all would have been in existence besides God, anything that would have entered as material into forming the world. Indisputably, moreover, the assumption that there would have been any material at hand independent of divine activity would destroy the feeling of absolute dependence and would present the real world as a mixture made up of what existed by God and of what did not exist by God.[8] Now, however, this formula undeniably recalls the Aristotelian category *ex ou*[9] and imitates it. In this way, it is reminiscent, on the one hand, of the human way of forming, which gives form to some material already present, and, on the

---

7. Ed. note: In earlier propositions, all introductory, Schleiermacher developed a conceptual framework for what this final paragraph points to, as well as for what is to follow in the rest of Part One. Thus, in §§30–31 he stated that reflections on the "direct description" of the "religious affective states," or "dispositions," that constitute this religious self-consciousness have always come in three forms. "In every instance," the "basis" for all three forms of reflection lies in these religious states. Whether the form may primarily concern (1) "descriptions of situations in human life" or (2) "concepts regarding divine attributes" or (3) "assertions regarding the constitution of the world" (cf. also §35), their presentation throughout is to be interdependent (cf. §19 and §28). Also, every doctrinal proposition, each proposition being both "ecclesial" and "scientific" (cf. §§2–17), strictly refers to "divine revelation" as expressed in "the redemption accomplished in Jesus of Nazareth" (§§11, 13–14); thereby they are all meant to represent the highest of the monotheistic modes of life or religious community (cf. §§7–12). These doctrines are all to be systematically arranged (§§20–21), to present in Evangelical perspective faith-doctrine for a united (Lutheran-Reformed, Protestant) church (§§22–25). They exclude Christian ethics only for reasons based on tradition and convenience, not for any essential reason (§26). They "appeal" to Scripture and to confessional writings, but they do not use either source as proof-texts (§27).

8. Ed. note: Cf. §§38–39. The doctrines of creation and preservation must be understood and explicated in such a way that "the original expression" can be fully presented based on either doctrine (§38). "The doctrine of creation is to be explicated, first and foremost, with a view to warding off anything alien, so that nothing of the way in which the question of how the world has originated is answered elsewhere will slip into our sphere and contradict the pure expression of the feeling of absolute dependence. In contrast, the doctrine of preservation is to be explicated, first and foremost, so as fully to present that basic feeling itself" (§39).

9. Ed. note: "out of what is not."

other hand, of how nature proceeds to assemble bodies out of a number of elements. Inasmuch as all that is already in the course of nature is then strictly distinguished from the initial arising of it and likewise inasmuch as the creation is raised above its sheer formation, the expression "out of nothing" is also beyond reproach.

Yet . . . a pre-existence of forms before things appear can be concealed behind one's negation of matter—not outside God, of course, but in God. In itself, this position too would seem to bear no risk. However, in that the two members of this contrast, matter and form, still do not then relate in the same way to God, God is drawn away from a status of indifference with respect to that contrast and is thus to a certain degree placed under it. Of course, it is also true that the forms' being in God before things exist, viewed as already nevertheless relating to existing things, can be called a "being prepared" for them. Doing this, however, immediately violates the other rule. . . . This is so, for then God would no longer be thought to exist beyond all God's engagement with time if there were two divine activities that, as preparation and creation, could be conceived as occurring only in a distinct temporal sequence. In his fashion, most dryly and impartially, Anselm expresses this sort of temporal similarity.[10] Hilary wanted to cancel out all temporal distinctions whatsoever; yet, he succeeded in this only with respect to what now still arises, albeit in its particularity, in time, but not with respect to the original creation, for one cannot say of this creation that it would have been made in God's foreknowing *efficacious action* already before it came into being.[11]

Here it can be remarked only incidentally that the expression "out of nothing" has also frequently come up in order to distinguish the creation of the world from the generation of the Son.[12] Now, if the generation of the Son were generally acknowledged to be an eternal one and the creation of the world were likewise generally acknowledged to be a temporal one, then it would not be necessary to set forth yet another distinction; or, even if people were in complete agreement only in this domain on the distinction

---

10. *Zeitgleichheit.* Ed. note: Anselm asserted that "before" things were made there was "nothing," except that there was already a "pattern" or "form" in the Maker's reason, hence the temporal similarity just mentioned between the "beforehand" and the act of creation itself. Hilary of Poitiers had held that all things were originally made simultaneously, without even an instant's distinction in time.

11. Hilary of Poitiers, *On the Trinity* 12.39: "It was present with God when the heavens were prepared. Is the preparation of the heavens a matter of time for God, so that a sudden movement of thought crept into his understanding, as if it had been previously inactive and dull, and in a human way God searched for material and instruments for the building of the world? . . . The things that shall be although they are yet to be insofar as God is concerned, for whom there is nothing new and unexpected in things to be created, since it belongs to the dispensation of time for them to be created, and they have already been created in the activity of the divine power that foresees the future." Ed. note: *PL* 10.457; ET, *FC* 25:327–28.

12. Augustine, *Confessions* 12.7: "Thou didst not make heaven and earth out of Thyself; otherwise, it would have been equal to Thy only begotten Son. . . . And, apart from Thee, there was nothing else from which Thou mightest make them. . . . Therefore, Thou hast made heaven and earth out of nothing." Ed. note: *PL* 32.828; ET, *FC* 21:372–73.

between acts of generation and creation, it would not be necessary to make any distinction beyond that one. Yet, even in this respect the expression "out of nothing" is not necessary for this purpose, in that even if one does not identify "Word" and "Son" at all, the expression "are made by God's Word"[13] already adequately safeguards against any confusion between "Word" and "Son" even if one does not call special attention to the distinction between "creation" and "generation."[14]

2. Now, suppose that, as is indicated above, we separate out the initial origination[15] so strictly that we already reckon everything that is not absolutely primitive to the course of nature, which is involved in a process of development, and thus place it all under the concept of "preservation." Then the question as to whether the creation itself occupied a period of time would already be settled in the negative. The distinction between a first and second creation or between an indirect and a direct creation would always revert either, in general terms, to a becoming of what is complex out of what is simple[16] or to a becoming of what is organic out of what is elemental.[17] Here however, to let another creation enter in means either, in turn, to lift the distinction between creation and preservation entirely or to presuppose different "matter" in each case, without all the forces that are inherent in it; and the latter is a completely empty thought. If, instead, one first imagines "matter" even in the case of creation—even though one might just as well imagine "forces" instead—from that point on, being that is alive and in motion must have persisted and developed further. Otherwise, creation of sheer matter would also have been simply a preparation, an external, material creation corresponding to that internal, formal creation we have already noted here. Hence, we have no recourse but to refer these definitions back to a time when people could take pleasure in such abstractions, because then the question of a dynamic outlook regarding nature had not yet arisen.[18]

---

13. Luther, *Psalm 90*: "For this all things are made by God's Word, so that they may more reasonably be called born than created or renewed, for no instrument or means was attached thereto." Ed. note: cf. also *LW* 13:92.

14. Ed. note: the words used here and just above are *Schaffen* and *Erzeugen*.

15. *Erste Entstehung*. Ed. note: Here this act corresponds to that of "creation" (*Schöpfung*), strictly comprising only that which is "absolutely primitive" (*alles schlechthin Primitive*).

16. Hippolytus, *Fragments in Genesis*: "On the first day God created as much as God wanted from that which did not exist. On the other days God created not from that which did not exist but from those things created on the first day, changing course as God wanted." Ed. note: PG 10.585–86.

17. John of Damascus, *An Exact Exposition of the Orthodox Faith* 2.5: "Some [things], such as heaven, earth, air, fire and water, [he made] from no pre-existing matter, and others, such as animals, plants and seeds, he made from those things which had their existence directly from him." Ed. note: PG 94.880; ET, FC 37:210.

18. Ed. note: Schleiermacher, in contrast, could and did regularly think at least of Newtonian "forces" (*Kräfte*) in general and, in biology and psychology, of vital, organic, developmental forces; and he could and did think of all these forces as inherent in all created being. This outlook was of great assistance to him in his also thinking of how enactment of "the divine causality" was possible in the nature of human beings, as under conditions of "the world" in general, this as an expression of "the one eternal divine decree" of creation and of its special fulfillment in redemption.

Another question that also does not at all belong within the domain of faith-doctrine concerns the relationship of the world's creation to time. It is this: whether there was any time before the world was created or whether time would have begun only along with the world. Suppose, however, that we take "world" only in the broadest sense. In that sense we cannot affirm that there was any time before the world was created, because such a time could have referred only to God and therefore God would be displaced into time. With its *quando ipsi visum*[19] the *Belgic Confession* plainly falls into this mistake, however, and we must again refer back to Augustine's formula in opposition to it.[20]

In fine, the controversy over a temporal versus eternal creation of the world, which can be referred back to the question as to whether a being of God can or must be imagined without creatures, is in any case of no concern whatsoever to what the feeling of absolute dependence immediately contains, and therefore it is, in and of itself, a matter of indifference how the controversy will be decided. Only to that extent need we be aware that one must combine with the notion of a creation in time that of a beginning of divine activity outward or that of a beginning of divine dominion, as Origen presented the matter.[21] In the latter case, God would thereby be placed within the sphere of change, thus displaced into being temporally. Consequently, the contrast between God and finite being would be diminished, and in this way the purity of the feeling of dependence would then indeed be endangered. Although Augustine,[22] in order to avoid such a danger, sets forth only a single act of the divine will with respect to the earlier non-being of things and the later being of things, this move is hardly a satisfactory solution either. In that case, an equally effective divine act of will that the world not exist earlier would belong to this one. Thus, one would have to assume that the world would have come into being earlier without this particular act of divine will, consequently that a

---

19. Ed. note: "as it seemed good to him."
20. Ed. note: Augustine, *On Genesis Against the Manichees* (391) I.2: "Hence, we cannot say that there was a time before God made anything." *PL* 34.175; ET, *FC* 84:50.
21. Ed. note: Notably, though perhaps dubiously attributed to Origen is the thesis that Almighty God was always accompanied by the world, which he eternally created, and that God was also finite, not infinite, else God could not have had thought even of Godself. [See pp. 7–9 above.]
22. Augustine, *The City of God* 11.4.2: "There are those who say that the universe was indeed created by God, denying a temporal but admitting a creational beginning, as though, in some hardly comprehensible way, the world was made, but made from all eternity. Their purpose seems to be to save God from the charge of arbitrary rashness. They would not have us believe that a completely new idea of creating the world suddenly occurred to God or that a change of mind took place in God, in whom there can be no change," etc. *Ibid.* 11.15: "But when I consider what God could be the Lord of if there was not always some creature, I shrink from making any assertion." *Ibid.* 11.17: "but by one and the same eternal and unchangeable will he effected regarding the things he created both that formerly, so long as they were not they should not be, and that subsequently, when they began to be, they should come into existence." *Ibid.* 11.6: "then assuredly the world was made not in time but simultaneously with time." [See pp. 9–16 above.]

capacity to move into existence would have been present independent of God. Suppose, however, that this same single divine will were also an ineffective will during the non-being of things, in that God no more blocked than brought about anything. Then what would still remain is the transition from non-action into action—even if one expresses this transition differently as one from willing into efficacious action[23]—against which it may be said that it is impossible to imagine how the notion that God does not exist apart from what is absolutely dependent on God should be able to weaken or confuse religious self-consciousness in any way. The same observation applies, then, to another approach not to be dealt with here at all, namely the referring of the word by which God is said to have created the world back to that Word which was "eternally with God," for this claim can never be properly clarified[24] unless the creating by the eternal Word was also eternal.

Postscript

To these considerations can be added the claim that God created[25] the world by a *free* decree. Now, it is self-evident that one on whom everything is dependent is absolutely free. Yet, suppose that by "free decree" one is thinking of a prior deliberation from which a choice follows. Alternatively, suppose that one expresses that "freedom" in such a way that God could just as well not have created the world, because one opines that the only options are either that it was possible for God not to have created or that God would have had to create the world. In this way, one would already have been thinking of freedom only in contrast with necessity and thus, in that one was ascribing such a freedom to God, have displaced God into the domain of contrasts.[26]

---

23. [In Latin:] "Let us add that God willed it from eternity, for whatever God wills he has willed it from eternity. What he had already willed from eternity was finally done at some time. [In German:] Thus he did work and was active in such a way that the world came into being." Friedrich Nathanael Morus, *Commentarius exegetico-historicus in suam theologiae christianae epitomen*, ed. K. A. Hempel (Leipzig, 1797–1798), Tom I, 292.

24. Cf. Martin Luther, *Sämtliche Schriften* (Walch, 1740), 1:23–28; 3:26–40. Ed. note: ET, *LW* 1:17–18 (the entire passage is on 16–19, corresponding exactly to Walch, 23–29).

25. Ed. note: Here, as above, the verb form "create, created" translates *schaffen, geschafft* (which can also mean "make, made"). Schleiermacher does not use the verb *schöpfen* in this doctrinal discussion, only the noun *Schöpfung* (or the "creation"—except when it is noted that he uses *Schaffen* to refer to the process rather than the product).

26. Ed. note: The real, organic world, for Schleiermacher, was always defined in part by the existence of contrasts within it, none of them absolute (as is possible in the logic of mathematics). As infinite—not caught up in finitude—"God" is different, wholly other, in not admitting of internal contrast, by definition. . . . In the strictly theological domain, God is viewed in the same way, though now always within the divine "economy"—i.e. engagement in and with the world—not *in se*, not in Godself apart from that economy. Of God *in se* the only thing that can be said with perfect confidence is: "God is love" (see §167).

SELECTION 8

Regin Prenter

"The Biblical Witness Concerning Creation"

In this selection from his treatise *Creation and Redemption*, Danish Lutheran theologian Regin Prenter (1907–1990) argues that the doctrine of creation be understood as the narrative of God's ongoing struggle against the forces of chaos. Prenter contends that this kind of dualistic framework is presupposed in a wide variety of biblical texts describing the work of creation (including Gen. 1, with its reference to the watery "deep"), but he also insists that it is vital to securing the unity of God against those who would separate creation and redemption into distinct and even contrary processes.[1] Against such perspectives, Prenter argues that the Bible consistently links the themes of creation and redemption as different aspects of a single divine struggle against the power of death, leading him to interpret creation as an ongoing process (*creatio continua*) rather than a one-time event in the past.

Moreover, Prenter maintains that this insistence on a *narrative* dualism as the most appropriate framework for telling the Christian story does not commit him to an *ontological* dualism that posits evil or chaos as an ultimate principle equiprimordial with God. Indeed, he argues that Christians should be agnostic about questions of the origin of the world, since the "concern of the Old Testament is not to explain how the world came into existence; its concern is that the life of the world may be preserved." In this way, he avers that the doctrine of creation is properly interpreted as part of the good news of God's defeat of sin, death, and the devil and (like Schleiermacher) denies that it is to be seen as a source of scientific or metaphysical knowledge.

From *Creation and Redemption* (Philadelphia: Fortress Press, 1967), 193–202.

The biblical witness understands creation dualistically as God's struggle against all forces of destruction, historically as a continuous and therefore present reality, and eschatologically as an organic part of his work of redemption and consummation. The biblical witness thus distinguishes itself from all cosmological-metaphysical speculations regarding the origin of the world and evil.

1. Prenter mentions Marcion and the Gnostics, who actually viewed the Redeemer and the Creator as different beings, but it is likely that he also has in view modern theologians like Rudolf Bultmann, whose focus on the individual decision to accept the gospel led him to minimize the significance of the doctrine of creation for Christian faith.

The biblical witness concerning the God of creation meets us especially in the Old Testament, since ... creation is the ultimate ground of the establishment of the covenant. The most prominent feature of this witness is that it possesses no direct cosmological interest. The concern of the Old Testament is not to explain how the world came into existence; its concern is that the life of the world may be preserved. The Old Testament ideas concerning creation are not philosophical but cultic. The strongest Old Testament witnesses concerning the miracle of creation are found in hymns which originally were of cultic nature, for example, the so-called enthronement psalms (Ps. 95:3–6; 96:4–10; 100:3). And in Old Testament scholarship there is currently a discussion going on concerning the extent to which the classic account of creation in Gen. 1:1–2:4 may not also be a cultic passage. There are even those who have contended that the six-day scheme of this account harks back to its having been a ritual for a festival week, the first day of which was celebrated as a new year festival with Yahweh ascending his throne, and the six subsequent days corresponding to the different days in the creation story, being a celebration of his work of creation with its triumph over the powers of chaos. This theory runs into several difficulties and is hardly tenable, but it is significant that the suggestion could be made at all. If the creation story in Gen. 1 is to be understood in harmony with the rest of the Old Testament witness concerning creation—and not contrary to it, as has been common in dogmatics—then we must also in the interpretation of this account observe the close connection between creation and cult.

In the cultic interpretation, which also underlies the original Old Testament cult, creation and cult belong together. In primitive cult, such as the Canaanitish, creation is a drama in which the members of the cult participate. Through the cult both the god and the participants in the cult are strengthened. As the content of the myth is dramatically enacted, the power which upholds the life of the community is renewed and the powers of chaos are again overcome as at the origin of the community. The primitive cult is the experience of creation in the form of holy drama.

This cultic idea, which can be traced in the cultic poetry of the Old Testament, is related to this primitive view which, of course, gradually gave way in postexilic religion to domination by law and eschatology. If, however, we are to understand the Old Testament witness concerning creation, we must hear it in the context where it originally belonged; otherwise we misunderstand it. The difficulty connected with the incorporation of this witness into a Christian context is another question, one which we must raise in due time. We must first understand the Old Testament witness concerning creation as that witness understands itself.

Following is a presentation of some of the main characteristics of this cultic conception of the creation.[2] In the first place, creation is viewed

---

2. Cf. Johannes Pedersen, *Israel* (London: Oxford, 1926), 1–2:470 ff.; 3–4:428 ff.

against a dualistic background. It is God's struggle against death in order that life may be preserved. Creation takes place as God overcomes the powers of chaos, death, and destruction. In the old creation hymns this struggle is presented in mythological form. In the creation story in Gen. 1:1–2:4 the mythological element is recessive. The world of chaos which is overcome by God's creative power is the water, the abyss which in the creation hymns is sometimes represented as a mythological being, the dragon, Leviathan, or Rahab. As God overcomes the powers of chaos, life comes forth. The water which is conquered becomes fruitful springs and rain.

In the second place, creation is a present activity. Indeed there is an initial creation in time, in harmony with the historical view which characterizes all of the material of the Old Testament and which has its basis in the origin of the people through their liberation from Egypt. In that sense creation is also in the Old Testament a *creatio ex nihilo*, though the expression does not appear in the Old Testament writings proper. But that which took place in the beginning continues to take place. Creation is God's continually ongoing struggle against the powers of destruction. In the cultic hymns the renewal of the creation is something which is experienced in the present (Ps. 96:11–13).

In the third place, creation is a unity of nature and culture. Our modern separation between the world of nature, which operates according to mechanical laws, and the world of culture, which is the product of man's creativity, is foreign to the Old Testament. That world which comes into being through God's creative act is not merely the raw material for man's creativity; but man and his work are, as such, involved in the act of creation, as stated in the creation hymn: "Man goes forth to his work and to his labor until the evening" (Ps. 104:23). Creation is the establishment of order and law (Ps. 74:17; 148:6). The world which thus comes into being is the earth (*'erets*), the populated and cultivated land, the world of culture as over against the wilderness, which is the abode of demons, where the curse reigns, the land which threatens to destroy life (Ps. 65:10–13; 89:11–12; Isa. 45:18).

In the fourth place, as the unity of nature and culture creation is *history*. The creation of the people's earth, its land, is the creation of the people itself. Therefore the creation of the world in the beginning, the creation of the people through their liberation from Egypt, and the experience of the miracle of creation in the present are in a unique manner united in the descriptions of the creation. These three elements constitute one connected act of God, one history. It is this historical view of creation which prevents creation and the God of creation in Israel from ever disintegrating into the unhistorical nature myth of some fertility cult. The dragon which is overcome in the creation struggle corresponds to the historical Egypt, and Egypt is called Rahab (Isa. 30:7. Cf. Ps. 87:4; Job 26:12). It is the same arm of Yahweh and the same miracle which are at work in the creation in the beginning and in the people's journey through the Red Sea

(Isa. 51:9–10). And as the creation was re-enacted in the people's release from Egypt, so it repeated itself also in their return from Babylon. Therefore Deutero-Isaiah is full of the creation theology of the enthronement hymns. The Exile is a return to the wilderness existence; the banished people are in the wilderness. But now the miracle of creation will be repeated for them (Isa. 43:14–21).[3]

This unity between the creation of the world in the beginning, the creation of the people through their deliverance from Egypt, the reenactment of creation in the cult, and the peoples' return from Babylon—this unity finds its particular expression in the great spring festival of the Passover, in which earlier harvest festivals are indissolubly merged with a feast in memory of the deliverance from Egypt.[4] In the Passover, the most important festival of the Israelites. cultic and historical ideas of creation are fused into one—the characteristic which distinguishes the Israelitic religion from the Canaanitic cults which lack the historical element.[5]

And this brings us to the New Testament witness concerning the God of creation. On the one hand, it presupposes the Old Testament witness concerning creation; the apostolic message is, of course, the fulfillment of the prophetic. In the preaching of Jesus the clearest reference is the passage in the Sermon on the Mount (Matt. 6:25–33) where he warns against anxiety and refers to the Creator who provides for the birds and the flowers, and therefore also for man. Here, as in the Old Testament, creation is understood as a present reality, and not as a past event explaining the origin of the world. The same is true in the case of Acts 14:15–17, Paul's sermon at Lystra. God is here proclaimed as the Creator, the "living God who made the heaven and the earth and the sea and all that is in them," who did not "leave himself without witness, for he did good and gave you from heaven rains and fruitful seasons, satisfying your hearts with food and gladness."[6]

---

3. Cf. Sigmund Mowinckel, *He That Cometh* (New York: Abingdon, 1956), 96 ff.

4. This understanding of creation as salvation history results in an ever stronger emphasis upon the divine word as the agent of creation, as we know from Gen. 1:1 ff; Ps. 33:6, 148:5; Job 38:11, and especially Deutero-Isaiah 41:4; 44:26–28; 45:1–2; and 48:13. The idea of the *word* as the agent of creation modifies the mythological description. It is the Lord's audible word before which the powers of destruction must give way (Ps. 29:8).

5. This connection between the cultic and the historical makes it impossible to imagine that the background of the Israelite enthronement hymns could be purely cultic myths about a dying and resurrected deity. Johannes Pedersen emphatically denies the possibility of an ideology concerning a renewed deity on Israelite soil. He contends that the idea of world renewal in the Israelitic cult may for that very reason have been weakened: "But Yahweh's occupation of the throne was not a regeneration of Yahweh, but a renewal of the covenant and the promise of power for Israel. Hence, it is questionable whether we may assume that there was a real regeneration of the world in the cult, or whether the regeneration of the world did not rather consist in a mere glorification of Yahweh's creative work in primeval ages and an assurance of his constant maintenance of the order of the universe, as denoted by the fact that he 'judges'" (Pedersen, *Israel* 3–4:444. Cf. Mowinckel, *He That Cometh*, 80 ff.).

6. In these passages we meet an Old Testament ethos in contradistinction to the Hellenistic dualism which views the material world as non-being and therefore evil. The biblical doctrine of creation's refutation of this Hellenistic dualism is indicated in Mark 7:18–19; Rom. 14:14; and 1 Tim. 4:1–4.

On the other hand, the New Testament places the main accent elsewhere. The apostolic message is eschatological; it points forward to Christ's second coming. The creature is subject to perishableness and awaits with longing the new creation (Rom. 8:20-22). As God did his mighty works and overcame his enemies both through his initial creative act and through the liberation of his people from Egypt, so he also acts now in the final decisive struggle which is to usher in the new age. The drama opened with the coming of Jesus Christ and with his death and resurrection, and it will end with his second coming. (We have already observed that in the message of Deutero-Isaiah the historical content of the idea of creation has eschatological implications. We can already detect the eschatological element in the Passover and in Israel's cult generally. The expectation of the renewal of creation in the cult is organically one with the expectation of God's historical deliverance of his people from their various afflictions. It is therefore not always easy to determine whether a given Old Testament psalm is cultic or historical, since there is always a connection between the cultic and the historical. And it is this connection which explains eschatology's origin in the cult and which explains the prosperity of eschatology after the real cult religion had fallen into decay.)

In the New Testament the word "creation" is especially associated with eschatological consummation.[7] The resurrection is the center of this new creation. As attested by the Old Testament royal psalms, the reign of Jesus Christ means that he is lord over his enemies. Through this reign the reign of Yahweh is also realized together with his victory over the powers of destruction, victory won through his act of creation. In the same way Jesus the Messiah is to be king by putting all of his enemies under his feet and by destroying the last enemy, which is death. Then comes the resurrection, the time of the new creation (1 Cor. 15:20-28). And this new creation through Jesus Christ, just like the creation in the Old Testament, is viewed against a dualistic background. Jesus Christ ushers in the new age through a decisive battle against and victory over the powers of destruction. The kingdom of God comes when Jesus the stronger one enters the house of the strong one and lays it waste. This he does through the miracles, particularly the miracle of driving out demons. Here we see the triumph of the new creation (Matt. 12:25-30; Col. 2:15; Rom. 8:38-39).

But the important thing in the New Testament's eschatological witness concerning creation is that this second creation, the redemption, is connected with the first creation, just as in the Old Testament the first creation, the deliverance from Egypt, the creation's renewal at the Passover and New Year festivals, deliverance from the enemy in all manner of

---

7. *Paliggenesia*, the new creation, or the new birth, is in Matt. 19:28 identified with the second coming. In the same way Paul speaks in Gal. 6:15 and 2 Cor. 5:17 about the fellowship with Christ in the new age as a new creation, *kaine ktisis*. And Ephesians refers to the creation of the new man in Christ (2:15; 4:24; cf. Col. 3:10).

situations, and the liberation from the Babylonian captivity are connected with one another. It is the same God whose mighty arm is at work in all of these events. It is the same creative work which is being carried forward. Thus, the redemption, the new creation, is actually the consummation of the creation of the world and of Israel. In this second creation, therefore, God's kingly rule over the world, referred to in the enthronement psalms, is finally realized. Israel becomes the new Israel which embraces all peoples and tongues.[8]

This unity of creation and redemption—which decisively sets the biblical message of salvation apart from all dualistic religions which view salvation as release from the created world rather than a restoration of the world—is most clearly expressed in that which is the most distinctive feature of the New Testament witness concerning creation, namely, that Christ is declared to be the agent both of the first and the second creation. Christ is the creative word through which God created all things in the beginning (John 1:1-18; I Cor. 8:6; Col. 1:16-17; Heb. 1:2).

We shall deal with the idea of the pre-existence of Christ later in connection with our discussion of Christology. Here we shall merely emphasize that this idea calls attention in a most powerful way to the unity of creation and redemption. And in the ancient church, when gnosticism and Marcionism wanted to separate the evil demiurge from the redeeming Christ, this idea of the unity of creation and redemption was of enormous significance in maintaining the reality and the goodness of the first creation. Everything has been created not only *for* Christ, but also *by* him. Therefore Christ the Redeemer came not to a strange world, but to his own (John 1:11). But the idea of Christ as Creator is meaningful even now. It means that the Creator is revealed through Christ. The hidden will of the Creator, which we meet in the Creator's work, and which we cannot know, is clearly revealed in Christ. God's purpose in his hidden creative will is the same as in his revealed saving will. Hence, we cannot place creation and salvation in opposition to one another and in the fashion of Marcionism think of salvation as something which tears us out of our creaturely existence. Salvation is not something "supernatural." And when we hold fast to the biblical description of creation as a present reality, the thought of Christ's pre-existence and creative work assumes tremendous actuality.[9] It means that Christ is not merely a religious object, but the world ruler who sits on the right hand of the Father, as the king in Psalm 110. And it means, further, that when we are unable to see God's hidden will in that which transpires in nature and in history, then faith clings to the fact that God's hidden creative will is identical with his saving will revealed in Christ, for

---

8. From the two—Israel and the heathen—God created one new man (Eph. 2:15).

9. The New Testament witness concerning Christ as the agent of creation does not overlook this fact, namely, that creation is something in the present. It says not only that all things were made by him, but also that all things exist—now, in this moment—through him. 1 Cor. 8:6; Col. 1:17.

"in him all things hold together" (Col. 1:17). But it also means that Christ is the lord of history. The course of world history, including the history of religion, is no fortuity, though we may not with our minds be able to discover any plan. Faith holds fast to the conviction that Christ at the right hand of the Father, as the ascended and preexistent Christ, is the lord of history—that the hidden and inscrutable will which we meet in the events of history is the same revealed will which speaks to us in the gospel message of salvation, and that it speaks with the same purpose.[10]

This twofold biblical witness concerning creation—the Old Testament historical-cultic and the New Testament messianic-eschatological—is the background of all Christian proclamation concerning the God of creation. This witness stands in sharp contrast to philosophical ideas of creation, which in the form of natural theology have too often influenced Christian thought on creation. The biblical witness concerning creation accounts for the origin of the world as little as it does for the origin of evil. Neither science nor the Christian faith in creation can solve these two metaphysical problems.

That kind of solution is made impossible by the dualistic perspective from which creation must be viewed. Creation as well as redemption is a struggle against the enemies of God. The fear of a metaphysical Manichaeism which operates with the idea of two eternally equal principles—one evil and one good—must not be permitted to minimize this dualistic perspective of the biblical idea of creation. When it is remembered that neither the origin of the world nor the origin of evil can nor need be explained, it also becomes unnecessary for either theology or preaching to choose between a metaphysical monism and a metaphysical dualism. The biblical witness and Christian preaching do not go back to a condition prior to creation, where nothing existed except God himself, who out of this nothing first created matter (*creatio prima*) and then (*creatio secunda*) out of this matter created the world—as is maintained in Thomism and orthodoxy. When we speak of creation as a *creatio ex nihilo*, *nihil*, is not, then, an empty nothingness which we may be able to imagine through a deduction from empirical reality; but it is that unfathomable abyss which surrounded God prior to creation and which the human understanding neither can nor ought penetrate. An attempt to go back beyond the beginning of creation is a *theologia gloriae*. It is a speculation concerning God's eternal majesty, which has no place in faith and preaching.

The dualistic perspective, then, means also that creation has not ceased, but is continually taking place. It is a *creatio continua*. A sharp differentiation between creation and preservation has no basis in the biblical witness concerning creation, neither in the Old Testament nor in the New. Such

---

10. This reference to Christ as Creator is the basis of the Lutheran idea of the so-called two kingdoms—the secular and the spiritual—in both of which God works toward the same goal.

differentiation is based on the notion that a metaphysical-cosmological idea of creation is to be combined with a biblical idea of providence. According to this notion creation stands for a metaphysically explained origin of the world, and preservation stands for God's present creative work through which he provides for his children. But such differentiation is artificial and factually unwarranted. It presupposes a conception of creation according to which the world is thought to have existence independent of God's continued creativity. But this is an altogether unbiblical idea.[11] Since the work of creation has not ceased, there is no final knowledge concerning God's creative work. Man is not a spectator of the work of creation, but a coworker in creation. Man may know God's handiwork in part. All human knowledge is knowledge of what God has already made. But God's creative work goes beyond what man can know. Therefore man cannot know God's creative work objectively; he can only worship and praise since he receives life and salvation from the Creator's bountiful hand.

This brings us to the third and most important point in the Christian idea of creation: Creation and redemption belong together. Creation is the beginning of redemption, and redemption is the consummation of creation. This is because we do not know God's perfect creation. We know God's creative work only as it unfolds itself in that world in which the rebellion of the fall is constantly challenging God's creative victory. We are not able to explain how God's struggle against and victory over the powers of chaos in the first creation could be followed by a new rebellion on the part of the very powers which had just been vanquished and which in the beginning had wanted to lay God's work of creation waste. We know only that in the world in which we live God's creative will is at the same time his redemptive will. As God through his unceasing struggle against the powers of chaos carries his work of creation forward, he is also active in the special covenant or salvation history subduing the rebellious powers of destruction, which are at work after (and through the agency of) the first creation. And these two activities, creation and redemption, go hand in hand from the very beginning. Both are a struggle against the same enemy with the same end in view: the final consummation of God's creative work and the final destruction of all the powers of chaos.

In the proclamation of redemption there will therefore always be a strong affirmation of creation. Christian proclamation repudiates all dualism and contempt for the world, and praises and glorifies the earth with its flowers and animals, its work and its love. But in the proclamation of creation there is also an affirmation of redemption, as Paul expresses it, a longing for redemption: "The whole creation has been groaning in travail

---

11. "When thou hidest thy face, they are dismayed; when thou takest away their breath, they die and return to their dust. When thou sendest forth thy Spirit, they are created; and thou renewest the face of the ground" (Ps. 104:29–30). This represents biblical thinking regarding the creation. Creation and preservation are here conceived of as belonging together.

together until now" (Rom. 8:22). This must be taken with absolute seriousness in opposition to all superficial optimism regarding culture. The Bible's great and joyous affirmation of God's entire creation does not mean that it has a superficially romantic view of life.

These three characteristics of the biblical witness concerning creation, then, are not fortuitous temporal-historical peculiarities which may be ignored. They constitute a necessary part of the message concerning Jesus Christ the living lord of the church, proclaimed and mediated through word and sacrament. That is, he is proclaimed and attested in the church as the very lord and king of creation, redemption, and consummation—the covenant lord and king.

SELECTION 9

David Kelsey

"The Doctrine of Creation from Nothing"

A long-time professor of theology at the Yale Divinity School, David Kelsey (1932-) gives in the following essay one of the most careful analyses of the logic of *creatio ex nihilo* in the modern period. His analysis falls into two parts. First, he argues that the doctrine, as traditionally interpreted, commits its adherents to (1) a set of metaphysical claims about the relationship between God and the world (e.g., that the world is contingent and absolutely dependent on God); (2) a set of attitudes toward the world (e.g., respect toward the various creatures God has made); and (3) a historical claim that the world originated at a certain temporal point (what contemporary cosmologists call $t = 0$). In this way, Kelsey contends that an adequate account of creation from nothing must be distinguished both from fundamentalist reductions of the doctrine to a set of factual claims and from the equally one-sided attempts of liberals like Schleiermacher to equate it entirely to a set of attitudes or feelings. Perhaps still more significantly, he notes that while the various components are clearly related in Christian experience, they are logically independent of one another and, still more specifically, that Christian metaphysical convictions about the world's contingency and dependence on God hold irrespective of whether or not the universe had a beginning in time.

Having outlined what he sees as the three essential components of the doctrine, Kelsey proceeds to reflect on the warrants used to support it and, correspondingly, the kinds of experiences that might lead Christians to reject it. He notes that the warrants used to support the doctrine in the tradition are complex, ranging from historical claims about what the church has uniformly taught to empirical claims about the correspondence between the doctrine and the best current scientific accounts of the world, pointing out that both these warrants are potentially subject to falsification. But he also argues that the doctrine could be invalidated by lack of "fit" with the attitudes Christians hold toward the world, suggesting that sufficiently severe existential shock (e.g., widespread experience of radical evil or of unrelieved suffering) might render the doctrine incredible on very different—but no less conclusive—grounds than scientific data.

> From *Evolution and Creation*, ed. Ernan McMullin (Notre Dame, IN: University of Notre Dame Press, 1985), 176–92, 195–96.

Most Christian communities affirm the creation of the world by God from nothing. . . . As we shall see, while Christians have always affirmed that the world was created, they have not always affirmed that it is God's *creatio ex nihilo*. What is being said when the doctrine of *creatio ex nihilo* is affirmed? In particular, what is the force of the phrase *ex nihilo*? In order to get at this topic, it will be useful to ask two questions of the doctrine. (1) What is its scope? That is, in affirming the doctrine what sorts of things does one express or claim? (2) What warrants the doctrine theologically? That is, what considerations lead Christian communities to affirm the doctrine? And under what conditions would these affirmations fail as Christian doctrine?

1. Scope

In affirming the doctrine of creation what sorts of things is one saying? One is doing at least the following: claiming that a peculiar relationship obtains between God and all that is not God; making certain performative utterances; and perhaps making the claim that a singular event occurred.

God's World-Relatedness

The most obvious thing done in affirming the doctrine of creation is to claim that God is related to the world in a peculiar way. Its peculiarity consists in its being unique and free. To affirm this is to make three interrelated claims.

(1) To affirm that God "creates" the world "from nothing" is to claim that God is related to all that is not God in a continuously active "productive" way. Anselm brings this out in his *Monologion* when he gives a classic analysis of the phrase 'from nothing' (chap. 8). It could, he says, be understood in any of three ways. (a) It might mean "nothing was created at all." But that is unintelligible as a formulation of a claim about, precisely, the creation of the actual world. (b) "Created from nothing" might mean that the world was created from nothing itself (*de nihilo ipso*), as though "nothing" were somehow an existent substance from which something could be created.

But this is self contradictory. (c) "Created from nothing" means instead: "Created, but not from *anything.*" This is, admittedly, a peculiar way to describe a relationship. It says two things at once. It claims that the world ("all that is not God") is passively related to God in a relationship of absolute dependence for its existence. And it claims that God actively relates to the world in a way that actualizes it. This relationship of active productivity in which God stands to the world is one that obtains continuously as long as there is a world. God's creativity is continuous, coterminal with the world. God's world-relatedness is more properly a continuing relating.

(2) Anselm's analysis brings out a second claim. God's relation to the world is strictly unique. Anselm points out (chap. 11) that to say that God creates the world but "not from anything" is to say that divine creating is not like any productive, generative, shaping, or making relationships we know of between an agent and a patient. All such analogies presuppose something that, as patient, undergoes the production, generation, shaping, or making. But that is precisely what the phrase *ex nihilo* excludes in regard to the Creator-creation relationship. Thus in claiming that God stands in a peculiar relationship with the world, the doctrine of creation from nothing employs an analogy for that relationship and then qualifies the applicability of the analogy very severely. It suggests that the relation is more like one broad class of relationships than it is like others. It is not like a logical relation (as though the world were deduced from God), or like a spatiotemporal relation (as though God were X billion light years away from the world). It is more like the relationship one has to an object by virtue of one's intentional acts of shaping and making it. Nonetheless, this likeness is very limited. In particular, God's "productive" and "casual" relation with the world is strictly unique, and so we are bereft of analogies by which to suggest how God is "creative."

(3) Anselm's discussion illustrates a third claim about God's world-relatedness made in affirmations of the traditional doctrine of creation from nothing. To say that God creates the world, but not from anything, is to insist that God's world-relating is not necessitated by any reality other than God. God's world-relating is not restricted or required by the nature of anything that is real apart from creation and out of which God creates. In that sense God's world-relating is free.

World's God-Relatedness

To affirm the doctrine of creation from nothing is to do two broad kinds of things in regard to the world (i.e., "all that is not God"). As Donald Evans showed in exhaustive detail in *The Logic of Self Involvement*,[1] it is at once to commit oneself to a number of attitudes and interests in regard to the world and to make certain truth claims about the world. Evans brings

---

1. Donald Evans, *The Logic of Self Involvement* (London: SCM Press, 1963).

this out by adapting J. L. Austin's analysis of the performative force of our utterances, that is, what we do in what we say. To affirm the doctrine of creation is undoubtedly to use language to make claims (in this case about the world) that invite assessment of their truth and falsity. But it is also and at the same time to use language to imply that one has certain attitudes and that one holds certain intentions or commitments to behave in certain ways (again, in this case in regard to the world). The relation between these two sides of affirmation of the doctrine of creation (between truth-claiming and existential self-involvingness) is probably the root of most of the difficulties besetting efforts to give a perspicuous account of the meaning of the doctrine. If the existentially self-involving force of affirming the doctrine is stressed exclusively and the fact-claiming ignored or "translated" wholly into the former, then the doctrine ceases entirely to make any serious claim on anyone's credence and is reduced to being an expression of feelings that could equally well be expressed in many other ways. It is trivialized. If the existentially self-involving force of affirming the doctrine is ignored and the truth-claiming alone expressed, the claims by themselves seem so vast and, perhaps, vague that it is difficult to see what of importance is at stake in making them. No consequences for anything else one believes to be true or for the shape of one's life would flow from them. That would be particularly troubling at the point of apparent incongruence between the theological truth-claim about the "goodness" of creation and the manifest fact of evil in the world. We cannot hope to explore thoroughly these two aspects of the doctrine. The most we can do is outline major features of each and explore the main ways in which they are interrelated.

(1) To affirm the doctrine of creation is to make at least two major kinds of claims about all that is not God. First, it is to claim that the world is intelligible, and that in two distinguishable senses. It is intelligible in the sense that for all its variegation and changeability it exhibits regularities that can be discovered to an end. The world can be understood in terms of God's purposes for it in creating it. This is tied up with the claim that the freedom of God's active relating to the world finds better analogues in the relationships between persons and artifacts constituted by purposeful human productive actions than in those provided by logical, spatial, or nonpersonal causal relationships.

Second, to affirm the doctrine of creation is to claim that the world is genuinely other than God. Given major themes in the Christian understanding of God which are logically independent of the doctrine of creation, that has several implications. It means that our experience of the world as a plurality of variously powerful particulars, complexly interrelated and often conflicting, is no illusion. Such experience is not a misapprehension of a deeper underlying divine unity. The world's diversity is irreducibly real in its own way. Furthermore, given that the creator is good, these concrete particulars are good precisely in their particularity and in the conditions that in fact characterize particularity in this world. To be material, temporal, and genuinely separate from one another is good. Furthermore, such a world cannot be described as a kind of reality somehow antithetical to God. All that is other than God is genuinely other than God, but not antithetical to God; it is simply different from God.

Can the nature of the difference be conceptualized? Trying to do so has led to a third implication. Given that the hallmark of divine reality is "necessary existence," the most general characteristic of all that is not God has been said to be "contingent existence."[2] The claim here is that all that is not God stands constantly in a relation to God of dependence on God's continuing productive activity for its very existence. It is precisely that God-relatedness that constitutes it as creature.

What sorts of claims are these? As we shall see, these doctrinal claims seem logically tied to a large range of attitudes, intentions, and dispositions that shape the personal identities and the behavior of those who affirm the doctrine. But it seems clear that these claims cannot be reduced to or translated without remainder into expressions of those practical commitments. In some way these are truth claims. Moreover, they are important truth claims because they are presuppositions of the Christian enterprise in its practical aspects. It is very difficult to make the case that they are in any direct way grounded in or inferred from experience. Perhaps it would be possible, though difficult, to specify conditions under which experience would tend to disconfirm the claim that the world is teleologically intelligible. It is notoriously difficult to say how we would experience the world differently were it not "contingent" on God for its existence. These claims seem rather to be claims about absolutely general features of the world, so general that they are the conditions of any experience of any part of it rather than claims somehow "based" on experience. They are metaphysical claims. To believe them is to hold metaphysical beliefs.

(2) To affirm the doctrine of creation from nothing is to take on oneself a range of attitudes toward, and intentions to behave in certain ways in, the world. To affirm it is a self-involving utterance. Thus, in affirming the doctrine of creation one not only claims that the world is intelligible but also implies that one has and cultivates the disposition actively not only to pay attention to it in delight but also to understand it. More particularly, it implies that one is disposed to think about it and to act in it in ways that

---

2. The notion of "necessary existence" is undoubtedly problematic and so is the contrast "necessary existence/contingent existence." In certain kinds of neo-Thomism a great deal of effort was made to giving precise ontological content to both of them. But the notions are not the invention of that intellectual tradition, and that particular kind of ontology is not identical with the Christian doctrinal point being made. The latter, it may be suspected, profits from a certain creative ambiguity. Cf. Etienne Gilson, *The Spirit of Medieval Philosophy* (New York: Charles Scribner's Sons, 1940), chapters 3–5 for a good example of the neo-Thomism referred to.

are appropriate to the ends to which it is ordered. In traditional Christian language it would have been said that the ultimate end to which creation is ordered is the glorification of God. Hence one implies intentions to construe the world and act in the world in ways that express God's glory. In traditional language it would have been said that the proximate end to which the creation is ordered is the realization of the well-being of the several kinds of creatures in their particularity, since it is precisely their well-being that most fully expresses in a creaturely mode the glory of God. Hence, in affirming the doctrine of creation one implies that one has taken on oneself intentions to act in creation in ways that nurture and preserve the well-being of the several kinds of creatures. Of course, it has also been the case that having intentions to act in the world in generally the same kinds of way has not kept Christians from disagreeing strongly about just what specific actions are in fact the appropriate enactments of intentions to nurture and preserve the well-being of the several kinds of creatures.

In affirming the doctrine of creation one not only claims that the world genuinely is other than God but also implies one has the attitude of respect rather than reverence toward all that is not God. Reverence is an attitude appropriate to what is divine. Creation is other than God. There is no aspect or component of creatures that is unqualifiedly "divine." They are utterly secular, deserving respect as God's creatures but not reverence. This has important negative implications regarding all claims, religious or other, that the way by which human beings may find release from suffering and realize happiness is to recognize and seek union with the divine dimension ingredient in themselves and in all nature.

In affirming the doctrine of creation one not only claims that the physical particularity, variety, and variability that characterize all that is not God is not evil, but one also implies that one has the attitude of gratitude for it. One has toward it the attitude that is appropriate to have toward a gift. The combination of reverence and gratitude is a specific kind of wonder or awe that is appropriate to something that is in some deep way mysterious. Not that the world is claimed to be mysterious in the sense of being unintelligible. On the contrary, to affirm the doctrine of creation is to claim that the world is intelligible. Rather, it is an awe that is appropriate to grace, to that which is given for the well-being of the recipient and is neither earned by the recipient nor compelled by the circumstances of the giver.

Creation as Event

For the overwhelming majority of Christians until at least the eighteenth century, and for very many even up to the present, to affirm the doctrine of creation from nothing has been to make a claim about the occurrence of a singular event in the more or less distant past in which the world originated. It is a claim about cosmogony and not only about cosmology, about the historical genesis of the universe and not merely about the universe's intelligible unity in its continuing relation of dependence on God. The history of Christian theological reflection on the topic of creation is a story of shifting relations between cosmogonic and cosmological claims. In the very earliest period affirmation of the doctrine invoked claiming both that the world stood in continuing dependency relation to God and that the world originated in a singular event. And the two claims were not clearly differentiated.[3] As we shall see in the next section, polemical considerations led to an emphasis on the interpretation of creation as an event.

It has been a matter of controversy just how this interpretation should be expressed. Until the early twentieth century it would have been common to say that what was being asserted was that the world had a "beginning in time." But that phrase is open to misunderstanding. Augustine, the most influential writer on this topic from the fourth to at least the sixteenth centuries, argued that time itself must be said to come into existence through this singular event. There would thus have been a first moment of time, the moment of the singular event of creation. However, under the impact of Newton's mechanics theological formulations began to change in the seventeenth century. In the new framework space and time are absolute and without beginning, though of themselves without content. God's creative act could thus be thought of as the introjecting (as it were) of matter into the previously empty framework of space and time. A "beginning in time" would then be a first moment for the material world in time but not a first moment of time.

A second ambiguity came to light more recently. To say that the world had a beginning in time was traditionally thought to be equivalent to saying that the world's temporal duration had been finite. Discussions of this topic before the present century shared the assumption that time is a single well-defined framework and that it is indifferent which sort of motion be chosen as the basis for its measurement. One of the implications of Einstein's theory of relativity, one that was not immediately noted, is that time is not a single unique framework and that it does make a difference what type of motion is chosen for its measurement. There is thus an ineliminable element of conventionality about assertions regarding the passage of time. It may after all not then be a matter of fact as to whether the lapse of time since the creation-event comes out as finite or as infinite. It depends on whether the basis of the measure is a cyclical (countable) process, such as atomic vibrations, or a continuous one, such as the expansion of the universe itself. The former could give a finite measure, whereas the latter could come out as infinite.[4] This unexpected conventionality makes it even

---

3. Cf. Jaroslav Pelikan, "Creation and Causality in the History of Christian Thought," in *Issues in Evolution*, vol. 3 of *Evolution after Darwin*, vol. 3, ed. Sol Tax and Charles Callender (Chicago: University of Chicago Press, 1960), 29–41.

4. Ernan McMullin, "How Should Cosmology Relate to Theology?" in *The Sciences and Theology in the Twentieth Century*, ed. A. R. Peacocke (Notre Dame, IN: University of None Dame Press, 1981), 35.

more difficult to formulate clearly what the implications of the doctrine of creation are for the notion of a "beginning in time."

Interrelations

We have seen that the scope of the Christian doctrine of creation includes three kinds of truth claims (about God's continuing relatedness to the world, about the world's continuing relatedness to God, and about the occurrence of a singular event) and several kinds of performative, self-involving force (implying attitudes, intentions, and dispositions at the very least). Are there logical relationships among any or all of these?

Given the central task of Christian theology, what is centrally important in the affirmation of the doctrine of creation is expressed in the various types of self-involving force. It is the attitudes, intentions, dispositions, and the like that are expressed in that fashion that shape the specific forms of human identity, personal and communal, which Christian doctrine seeks critically to describe. Clearly, the beliefs stated in the truth-claims that are made in affirming the creed are also essential to that which doctrine critically describes. But how are they related to affirmations of doctrine as self-involving performative utterances?

How are such attitudes as respect and gratitude for the world and intentions such as the intention to care for the well-being of fellow creatures related to the claim that the world stands in a relation of dependency on God? They are not implied by the claim. There would be no inconsistency in making the claim and holding contrary attitudes and dispositions. Nor would there be any inconsistency if one added the claim that the God on whom the world depends loves the world. One might still quite consistently believe the loving God is nonetheless unlovable and hold contrary attitudes to the world, disrespect, say, or disinterest. Nor does personal avowal of the attitudes and intentions necessarily imply a claim about the world's God-relatedness. One could consistently avow the attitudes and claims, affirm the world lovable, and yet deny that the world is God-related. Nonetheless, it is clear that Christian doctrines of creation from nothing insist that the truth-claiming and the performative force of what is done in affirming the doctrine are not accidentally and arbitrarily held together. How is their inseparability to be understood?

Donald Evans has made the suggestion that the doctrine of creation, taken as a complex whole, may be understood as an elaborated "parabolic onlook."[5] It is an "onlook" in that it has the same logical form as such familiar expressions as: "I look on Harry as my brother" and "I look on the State as my father." Such expressions have the form "I look on x as y." In each case there is implied both *a similarity of attitude* and *a similarity of fact* that makes the similar attitudes appropriate. What is said is, "X is such

---

5. Evans, *The Logic of Self-Involvement*, 124–235; 220–28.

that (implied truth-claim) the *attitude* appropriate to *y* is similar to the attitude appropriate to *x*." The onlook expressed by the doctrine of creation is "parabolic" in the sense that the attitude known to be appropriate to *y* is a parable or analogue for the attitude to *x*.

Not all expressions of the form "I look on *x* as *y*" are parabolic. But the ones involved in affirming the doctrine of creation seem to be. Thus, as we have seen, the doctrine framed in the form "I look on the world as something made freely and in love as a gift" implies that I have toward the world attitudes and intentions appropriate to a gift made for us. But the addition "but not made from anything" reminds one that one has no adequate analogue for the "making" or the "giving." The relation between the attitude one has toward an ordinary gift and that about the gift in virtue of which the attitude is appropriate is only a parable for the relation between the attitude the believer has toward the world and that about the world (i.e., its God-relatedness) that makes the attitude appropriate. In affirming the doctrine of creation one is not justifying certain implied attitudes, intentions, dispositions, and the like by inferring them from claimed truths. Nor is one founding the truth-claims by showing them to be the necessary formal conditions for the attitudes and such. One is simply expressing the interconnected beliefs, on the one side, and attitudes, intentions, and dispositions, on the other, which together are constituent of Christian forms of life.

The same analysis can be made of the relation between the attitudes and intentions implied in affirming the doctrine of creation from nothing and the truth-claim (made in the same affirmation) that the world originated in a singular event in the past. In general, whereas the claim about the world's dependency relation on God is a metaphysical claim, the claim about the world's absolute origination is a historical claim. Two points need to be made about the role of this historical claim within the inner logic of the doctrine of creation. The first is that making the claim does not involve the introduction of any new parables into expression of the onlook. Both the claim that the world stands constantly and universally in a dependency relation on God and the claim that the world as it is is the end result of a long history originating in a singular event "caused" by God are formulations of the "such that" about the world that makes certain attitudes and intentions toward it appropriate. The second point is that the historical claim implies no additional attitudes or intentions not also implied by the metaphysical claim. Nor does it rule out any attitudes or intentions that might be made along with making the metaphysical claim were the latter made alone.

Finally, in affirming the doctrine of creation from nothing how are the metaphysical and the historical truth-claims related to each other? Let us give the question an edge: Could one retain the claim about the dependency relation (metaphysical) and abandon the claim about an originating event (historical), without either internal inconsistency in one's theology or an unwarranted revision of the meaning of the metaphysical claim itself? The answer seems to be Yes.

The claim that the world has its absolute origination in a singular event in the past might imply that the world ever since stands constantly in a dependency relationship on God. That this is so in the Christian framework is reflected in the history of Christian doctrine. When the claim about "creation" has been identified with a claim about an originating event, it is always insisted that its necessary corollary is a doctrine of preservation (the metaphysical claim).[6]

But the claim that the world stands in a dependency relation on God does not necessarily imply the claim that there was an originating event. The lapse of time during which the world has stood in this relation might be infinite. The added qualification *ex nihilo* does not contradict this. As we have seen, its force is to qualify the adequacy of every analogy for divine creativity. It does not bear on the question whether duration of the world's God-relatedness is finite or infinite.

Hence, the historical claim is logically detachable from the metaphysical claim and could be dropped without introducing incoherence into the doctrine or tacitly altering the meaning of the metaphysical claim. This point is implicit in the history of the doctrine in debates about whether the "eternity" of the world could be proved. Medieval debates were sparked by recovery in the thirteenth century of Aristotle's texts in which the "eternity" of the world was taught. Christian theologians would all have agreed that biblical revelation veridically teaches the cosmological claim that the world had a "beginning in time." Some theologians, like Bonaventure, thought that Scripture's claim could be demonstrated philosophically and Aristotle's claim disproven. Others were in the awkward position of holding that Aristotle's demonstration was valid but has to be superseded by revelation's claim. Others, like Thomas Aquinas, thought that it could be shown philosophically that neither position could be demonstrated. What is noteworthy here is that the claim about an absolute origination of the world was included in the doctrine of creation by all these theologians solely on the grounds that, in their view, it is taught by Scripture. Debates about the validity of the contrary view, that the world is eternal, were conducted entirely as philosophical arguments. Nobody argued that any other part of the doctrine, or any other Christian doctrine, would be undercut were Aristotle's view to be validated. The only theological issue at stake, and it is not unimportant, was faithfulness to biblical revelation.

2. Theological Warrants

There are at least two kinds of assessment that must be made of every Christian doctrinal proposal: Is it properly "Christian," that is, is it the sort

---

6. Cf. Pelikan, "Creation and Causality," 36.

of proposal that a Christian community ought in all self-consistency to adopt to guide its life and thought? And, in any case, is it true? Obviously, one may not simply assume that in every case an affirmative answer to one of these questions implies an affirmative answer to the other. The matter would have to be examined case by case, however much one might trust that in fact what is properly "Christian" will turn out to be true as well and vice versa. In this section we will continue to confine ourselves to the inner logic of Christian doctrine and ask only: By what sorts of appeals have Christians warranted the doctrine of creation from nothing as the doctrine Christians ought to affirm? So far as Christian theology is concerned, what are its warrants?

As the doctrine was slowly being worked out into its classical formulations during the first five centuries of Christian thought, it would have been said that the decisive appeal was to the biblical writings which teach divinely revealed truth. Two comments need to be made about this. Their joint consequence, I hope to show, is that what have warranted the doctrine's Christian appropriateness are considerations that go well beyond anything a simple appeal to Scripture alone could provide and that leave the doctrine open to several kinds of possible failures.

First, appeal was made to Scripture interpreted according to credal formulae. It is commonly accepted that credal formulae are very ancient in the life of the Christian movement. There probably were credal formulae that antedated the writing of the New Testament texts and are quoted in them. They were used in the context of acts of worship performed to glorify God. They functioned, among other things, to describe who God is. They did not characteristically make claims that God does various things. Rather, they expressed trust in God ("We believe in one God") who does thus and so ("maker of heaven and earth"). It is as though the mention of things God does came in answer to the unstated question Who is the One you worship? They served to sum up the Christian understanding of God. When interpretation of Scripture is guided by such credal formulae, the description of God given by the formulae serves as something like a rule by which to unify the otherwise very diverse materials in the Bible: construe it all as in one way or another contributing to a description of the self-same God. Accordingly, some of the earliest formulations of Christian claims about creation (e.g., in sermons in Acts 14:15 and 17:24–28 and, arguably at least from its structure, Justin Martyr's mixture of Scripture and Platonic doctrine very early in the second century) are more about God and God's world-relatedness than about the world and its God-relatedness. It is not accidental that they are claims about creation but not claims of *creatio ex nihilo*.

Moreover, when interpretation of the Bible is governed by credal formulae, Scripture tends to be construed as a call to a distinctive way of being human and of living a human life. Credal formulae not only describe who

God is, but they also describe who we are: we are the people whose lives are given distinctive shape by our response to this God's presence. Interpreted in the light of such formulae, Scripture's description of God's world-relatedness is seen not so much as the basis for a cosmology as the basis for an account of the forms of life that are appropriate responses to God. Accordingly, the Christian doctrine of creation, insofar as it is addressed to Christian communities themselves, is ordered to the practical matter of helping the community to be true to its own identity. Undoubtedly, then, the "Christianness" of the doctrine of creation was warranted by appeal to Scripture. But the interpretation of Scripture was itself "ruled" by credal expressions. Insofar as that was the case, the doctrine had as its audience the Christian communities themselves, and its aim was to guide reflection on the nature of Christian identity by elaborating some claims about the One to whom Christian life is a response.

In fact, the doctrine of creation from nothing was never merely a restatement of cosmologies found in the Bible. Nor, I think, can it be otherwise today. Theologians appeal to biblical texts interpreted in the light of modern critical scholarship. This reveals a diversity among the canonical texts but provides no basis for deciding which to make normative. While there are one, perhaps two, New Testament texts that imply creation from nothing (Rom. 4:17; perhaps Heb. 11:3), the text traditionally made central because of its place in the most extensive creation narratives, namely Gen. 1:1-2, does not clearly imply creation from nothing. Genesis 1:1 may equally well be translated in either of two ways: (a) "In the beginning God created the heaven and the earth." When translated that way, verse 2 reports the immediate effect of God's creativity: "And the earth was without form and void and darkness was upon the face of the deep." Or (b), "When God set about to create heaven." When translated this way, verse 2 comes in as a parenthesis—describing what the conditions were when God began to create, namely, "the world being then a formless waste, with darkness over the seas and only an awesome wind sweeping over the water" (Speiser). The first translation arguably at least implies creation from nothing. The second—and now very widely adopted—translation clearly contradicts it: God begins, not with nothing, but with formless waste. The exegetical controversy about this text is unresolved and perhaps unresolvable.[7] This would frustrate any effort to warrant the Christian appropriateness of the doctrine of creation from nothing by direct appeal only to biblical texts interpreted in the light of critical scholarship. The doctrine can no more

---

7. E. A. Speiser, *Genesis* (Garden City, NY: Doubleday, 1964), 3. Speiser discusses the problems confronting translator and interpreter on pp. 8-13. That Genesis 1 must be translated in a way that expresses precisely the *ex nihilo* clause is argued, *contra* Speiser, on form-critical and internal theological consistency grounds by Brevard Childs, *Myth and Reality in the Old Testament* (London: SCM Press, 1960), 30-42, and by Gerhard von Rad, *The Problem of the Hexateuch and Other Essays* (Edinburgh: Oliver & Boyd, 1966), 131-44.

be treated today as an elaboration of biblical cosmology than it ever was. If Christian communities are going to continue to affirm it, it must be on other and more complex grounds having to do with its ties to the description of the One the communities worship and to the corporate identity shaped in them by worshipping that One.

The second point that needs to be made is that the doctrine of creation from nothing was formulated in polemical contexts. Its purpose was not only to guide faithful Christian communities. It was also designed to refute non-Christian religious and philosophical movements and to correct Christian communities who were deemed to have become confused by those non-Christian movements. The *ex nihilo* clause was a defense against teaching that was attractive to some Christians but was also—as the polemic was designed to show—implicitly contrary to the communities' understanding of God and of themselves as expressed in their credal formulae.

Some pagan thinkers, for example, held that matter is coeternal with the world. The eternity of matter appeared to be compatible with credal formulae and with the teaching of some Christian thinkers like Justin Martyr, for whom the doctrine of creation says only that God made the world. That is compatible with the view that God made it "out of" matter coeternal with God. However, to other early Christian thinkers like Theophilus of Antioch (c. 175 AD), who seems to have been the first of the Fathers to insist on the *ex nihilo* clause,[8] the eternity of matter implicitly contradicts the description of God given in credal formulae. To affirm the coeternity of God and matter seems to posit two ultimate principles of reality in contradiction to the credal ascription of absoluteness to One alone. In order to make it clear that Christians' description of God excludes the eternity of matter and hence a second ultimate principle, the *ex nihilo* clause began to be added to the claim about God's world-relatedness: God is actively related to the world, producing it, but not *from* anything.

A second example: by the early third century some Christian spokespersons[9] developed theologies that assumed a sharp antithesis between spirit and matter. What is spiritual was assumed to be akin to God, and what is material was assumed to be antithetical to God. This dualism was reflected in their contrast between the Savior God and the Creator. The high God who alone deserves our worship is pure spirit and can have no positive relation to matter. The world of material things cannot be coeternal with the high God. Nor can it have been created by the high God. Its creator must

---

8. Cf. Pelikan, "Creation and Causality," 34.

9. The usual generic name for these movements has been "Gnostic." However, there are so many differences among these movements that it is far from clear that any such common term is useful. It seems, for example, to have been quite possible for some "Gnostics" to hold a doctrine of *creatio ex nihilo*. Clearly, rejection of the doctrine of creation is not itself a characteristic helping to define a "Gnostic." See Gerhard May, *Schopfung aus Dem Nichts* (Berlin: Walter de Gruyter, 1978). I am indebted to Professor Robert Wilken for this reference.

therefore be a being lesser both in power and goodness. We are spiritual beings, akin to the high God, exiled in this material world but saved from it by the high God. Against this the doctrine that the material world was created by God *ex nihilo* was formulated to insist that materiality is itself God's good gift and that material things are good precisely in their materiality and not somehow in spite of it. The *ex nihilo* clause was designed in part to point out that the Savior/Creator dualism implicitly contradicts the description given by credal formulae of the God Christians worship.

Thus in different polemical contexts the *ex nihilo* clause had the force of rejecting different teachings taken to be contradictory of Christian understanding of who God is and who Christian communities are. When efforts were made to warrant the clause's Christian appropriateness, it became necessary to move beyond appeal to Scripture in at least three ways. Each of these ways brings with it a way in which the doctrine of creation from nothing might fail.

For one thing, some proponents of the views being rebutted themselves appealed to Christian Scripture to warrant their views. For example, those who contrasted the Savior to the Creator accepted only the "apostolic witness" of the New Testament as authentic Christian Scripture and contrasted the God it described as Savior with the God described in Hebrew Scripture as the Creator. Clearly this controversy could not be adjudicated by simple appeal to Scripture. Now the issue is: What counts as authentic Christian Scripture and how is its interpretation certified? One way to answer this question was to appeal to institutional teaching authority in the Christian communities. Irenaeus provides a classic example of this. Writing in the early third century against a variety of thinkers whom he calls "Gnostics" and who reflect the dualistic views we have noted, Irenaeus claims that the Christian appropriateness of his formulations is warranted by the universal teaching of bishops in the churches.[10] Christ had entrusted right teaching to the apostles. They established bishops in each church to whom this teaching was entrusted, and they handed it down from generation to generation. Unbroken succession of the office of bishop in the church constitutes an institutional teaching authority by which to settle such questions as what counts as Christian Scripture and how it is properly to be interpreted.

In general this kind of appeal is vulnerable to historical disconfirmation. It rests on a picture of Christian beginnings as characterized by a high degree of uniformity in faith and practice among widely scattered communities. Modern historical research tends to invalidate that picture.[11] If the "Christianness" of the doctrine of *creatio ex nihilo* were largely established

---

10. Irenaeus, *Against Heresies*, 3.2.2; 3.3.3; 3.4.1.
11. See Robert Wilken, *The Myth of Christian Beginnings* (Notre Dame, IN: University of Notre Dame Press, 1980), for an excellent discussion of this point.

by an appeal specifically to the Christian canon of Scripture, and if the decision about which texts belong in the canon and the determination of how the canon is to be interpreted as a whole were warranted by appeal to belief and practice allegedly universal in the earliest period of the Church, then historical research could deprive the doctrine of this warrant.

The "Christianness" of the *ex nihilo* clause has also been at least partly warranted by a quite different kind of extrabiblical appeal. When Theophilus of Antioch stressed "*ex nihilo*" in the second century to reject the doctrine of the eternity of matter, he urged its Christian appropriateness by claiming that the prophets had taught it "with one consent."[12] This involved a subtle but very important shift in the way Scripture was construed. He takes Scripture to speak, not so much of God and God's world-relatedness (as credal formulae tend to do), but of the world and its God-relatedness. More exactly, focus is shifted from Scripture's witness to God to Scripture's cosmogony. As Jaroslav Pelikan has shown, throughout the development of the doctrine of creation it has been acknowledged that in the biblical stories "creation" may refer either to a relation between God and the world, or to an event of absolute world-origination, or to both. But during much of that history the stress has fallen so strongly on the originating event that the *ex nihilo* clause often came to be identified with that claim. That tendency seems to have begun with Theophilus. Its Christian appropriateness was partly warranted by appeal to biblical creation stories construed mainly as revealed information about the absolutely originating event.

That put the doctrine of creation from nothing on a logical par with nontheological cosmological and, especially, cosmogonic doctrines. That, in turn, suggested another strategy for warranting the doctrine's Christianness. If God created the world, then whatever truth we can discover about the world by whatever means is true because God created the world that way. Accordingly, one way to show the Christian appropriateness of a doctrine is to show that it comports well with the best understanding we have of the world. By the late fourth century Augustine had followed this strategy in the doctrine of creation in a way that was enormously influential on the subsequent development of the doctrine. For him the polemical target of the doctrine was the Manichean dualist cosmogony. According to it our world is marked by discord because it originated in cosmic strife between the Father of Light and the Archons of Darkness. Central to the Manicheans' cosmology was a commitment to rationality. They ridiculed Genesis' creation stories as irrational. Augustine's formulation of the doctrine of creation has as part of its background his earlier attraction to the Manichean's cosmology and his own commitment to "rationality." Accordingly, in his commentary on Genesis, *Literal Interpretation of Genesis*, he

12. See Pelikan, "Creation and Causality," 34ff., for the following discussion.

attempted to show the consistency of the biblical cosmology with the best "scientific knowledge" of his time. His own theory of knowledge led him to stress the literal meaning of the biblical text.

A major problem arose, however, whenever the literal meaning of the text conflicted with claims about the physical universe that were widely accepted as "demonstrated." Augustine concluded that formulation of claims about creation must be answerable to those "scientific" claims. Where there is such a conflict, it is a sign that the text should be interpreted allegorically rather than literally.[13] Thus there is a criterion other than the biblical texts by which a doctrine is to be warranted. On this strategy any warranting of the Christian appropriateness of the doctrine of creation from nothing must include reference to demonstrated truth, at least by exhibiting the consonance of the doctrine and that truth.

This way of warranting the doctrine of creation opens it to a corresponding way in which it might fail. It might be shown not to be cogent as a cosmogony. This could happen in a couple of ways. Analysis might show that its key concepts are too vague or confused to be useful. And it might show that inferences from one proposition within the doctrine to the next are illegitimate. Although one could not specify in advance when this would happen, presumably there would come a point when conceptual confusion and incoherence would lead to abandonment of this way of talking. The doctrine would then have failed.

Even if the doctrine survived such analysis, it might fail by being shown to be in severe tension with our best scientific understanding of the origins of the universe. If the Christianness of the doctrine is partly warranted by extrabiblical truth, then scientific enquiry into the origins of the physical universe might disconfirm rather than confirm the doctrine. A case in point: it seems to be held in some quarters that the big bang model of the origin of the physical universe tends to confirm the theological doctrine.[14] That is highly problematic, both theologically and scientifically.[15] Whatever else the model claims, it does not claim that the universe was brought into being in a single event by God, which is what the doctrine claims. It cannot be claimed that the big bang model supports the doctrine of creation. Nonetheless, as Ernan McMullin puts it, "If the universe began in time through the act of the creator, from our vantage point it would

---

13. Augustine, *Literal Interpretation of Genesis* 2.9 (*PL* 34.270–71).

14. See an allocution by Pope Pius XII, *Bulletin of the Atomic Scientists* 8 (1952): 143–46, and, perhaps, Robert Jastrow in his popular book *Until the Sun Dies* (New York: Norton, 1977). Jastrow is not terribly precise in his expression of his views, but it seems a possible and not unfair reading of him.

15. Central among the scientific problems with this influence is that there seems to be nothing in the Big Bang model that could rule out the possibility that the Big Bang itself was preceded by a "different" universe, all traces of which might have been obliterated by the Big Bang, but which nonetheless would have been the "material" for the next stage. Which is to say that it is far from clear that one can fairly infer from the Big Bang an absolute beginning in time.

look something *like* the big bang cosmologists are now talking about."[16] But now suppose that new discoveries lead to the abandonment of the big bang model and the adoption in its place of a very different model according to which the notion of a singular originating event is unintelligible. If the big bang model could not confirm the theological doctrine of creation, the new model could not disconfirm it. However, would not the apparent dissonance between the two tend to be abandonment of the theological claims about an absolute originating event? Probably it would.

It would probably result in abandonment of the theological claim about creation as a singular *event*, but it would probably not lead to an abandonment of the *doctrine* of creation from nothing. As we have taken pains to show, the doctrine as a complex whole is not simply a reformulation of biblical cosmology. The claim about an originating event is, in the light of critical scholarship, only tenuously rooted in Scripture. Furthermore, as we argued in part 1, although making truth-claims about the world is an irreducible and essential part of what is done in affirming the doctrine, the particular claim about an originating event is not logically indispensable. It could be dropped without introducing incoherence into the doctrine and without altering what is done by and to Christian communities in their affirming the doctrine.

In addition to appeals to institutional teaching authority in the Church and to our best scientific knowledge about the world, efforts to warrant the Christian appropriateness of the doctrine of creation from nothing have involved a third kind of extrabiblical appeal. It has been very powerful in the history of Christian theology, I believe, but this is admittedly very difficult to document. It is in a way an appeal to Christians' experience of the world. More particularly, it is an appeal to the wonder, gratitude, and sense of radical contingency with which Christians experience the world. It is an appeal to their experience of the world as grace. This is, not a substitute for appeal to Scripture, but rather an indirect appeal to Scripture. Experience is always conceptually shaped. When biblical writings are genuinely appropriated personally, their concepts, images, and narratives can shape the attitudes, dispositions, beliefs, etc., that comprise the personal identities of the persons who appropriate them. A community whose identity is decisively shaped by biblical narratives and the images and concepts they employ is a community of persons who experience the material context of life in a distinctive way, namely, as gift at once mysterious and loving. Put abstractly, refutation of what are deemed profoundly misleading doctrinal formulations then goes like this: Are not these formulations incoherent with our credal expressions' description of our own corporate identity? These misguided formulations would imply fear and loathing of material things, but our actual experience of material things is one of wonder and gratitude. Thus, for example,

---

16. McMullin, "How Should Cosmology Relate to Theology," 39; emphasis added.

the Christian appropriateness of laying stress on the goodness of matter is directly warranted by appeal to its coherence with that experience of wonder and gratitude and indirectly warranted by appeal to biblical writings that, when personally appropriated, shape that experience.[17]

This brings with it another and perhaps decisive way in which the doctrine might fail. I have adopted the suggestion that the doctrine of creation from nothing is, as a complex whole, the expression of an onlook, at once an avowal of attitudes and intentions to God and world and claims that God and world are such that these attitudes and intentions are appropriate. The theological doctrine is ordered to practical matters: elucidation of the attitudes, intentions, and the like that comprise Christian personal identity, communal and individual. The doctrine's logic reflects this. The truth-claiming done in affirming the doctrine is not reducible to the self-involving performative force of affirming the doctrine. It is nonetheless limited to the claims that elucidate certain attitudes and intentions by clarifying what it is in the nature of things that makes them appropriate. It is the self-involving and performative force of affirmation of the doctrine that is theologically central.

Now a self-involving performative utterance may fail, not by being falsified by evidence, but—to use the quasi-technical term J. L. Austin employed when he drew attention to these matters—by being infelicitous. It may suffer "infelicity" if I am insincere, lacking the attitude or intention I express. Or it may suffer "infelicity" if what I involve myself in is a promise and, however sincere I may be, I am unable to carry it out. Clearly, then, if the community that uses the doctrine to help elucidate its credal expression of its own self-identity lacks deep dispositions toward the relevant attitudes and intentions (say, gratitude or a commitment to care for the well-being of creatures), then its doctrine of creation fails by "infelicity." Affirming the doctrine would no longer be an authentic expression of the truth of the community.

This might come about as a result of a deep revulsion at moral horrors like the Holocaust or revulsion at physical suffering caused by persistent starvation and disease. Such revulsion might make it impossible to have or to enact the dispositions that are central to the way Christian communities are "set" in the world and are elucidated in the doctrine of creation. They might lead people to adopt a quite different personal "set" than the Christian ones. And that, of course, would be a matter of conversion to another way of being set into the world, perhaps a conversion to another religion. That surely is one decisive and fatal way in which the doctrine of creation from nothing could fail: that it should simply cease in fact to express the most basic way a community of persons is set into the world. Then its affirmation could not be anyone's self-involving utterance by which the

---

17. The philosophical theologian Austin Farrer explicitly set out to evoke just this way of "experiencing" the world as the precondition for being able to make his speculative theology credible. See *Finite and Infinite* (London: Dacre Press, 1943).

deepest of dispositions are taken on and personal identity is shaped. Then the affirmation of the doctrine would indeed be null and void, and our lives a kind of personal chaos over which it would only be right that there should brood a deep silence.

SELECTION **10**

Jürgen Moltmann

"Creation Out of Nothing"

Jürgen Moltmann (1926–) has been one of the most influential German theologians of the postwar generation, addressing the full gamut of doctrinal topics. Beginning with the publication of his *Theology of Hope* in 1964, Moltmann has sought to write his theology from a consistently eschatological perspective, viewing history as the place where God's promises to be present with and for his creation are fulfilled. In his later *The Crucified God* he developed this theme in terms of a Trinitarian theology built around the idea of a radical divine solidarity with the world that reaches its climax in the cross, where God experiences physical death as part of God's own intra-Trinitarian life.

The following excerpt, taken from *God in Creation*, the second in Moltmann's five-volume *Messianic Theology*, applies the Trinitarian dynamic of divine solidarity with the world to the doctrine of creation from nothing. Drawing on the Jewish kabbalistic doctrine of divine contraction or self-limitation (*zimsum*), Moltmann attempts to link creation and crucifixion as part of the same overall pattern of divine willingness to suffer in order that creation may flourish. He argues that the "nothing" of creation is best interpreted as a space that God—who otherwise fills all things—makes within the divine self for creation to be. In this way, the presupposition of "initial creation" becomes a form of divine self-humiliation that parallels the inauguration of the "new creation" in the cross of Christ. While the symmetry of Moltmann's vision is compelling and reflects genuine biblical themes of continuity between creation and resurrection (see Rom. 4:17), it has also been criticized for depicting a false opposition between Creator and creation, in which God needs to be absent in order for creatures to be able to be present.

From *God in Creation: A New Theology of Creation and the Spirit of God*
(New York: Harper & Row, 1991), 86–93.

The creation of the world is founded on God's determination that he will be the Creator. Before God issues creatively out of himself, he acts inwardly on himself, resolving for himself, committing himself, determining himself. Let me go a little more deeply into this idea with the help of the Jewish kabbalistic doctrine of God's "self-limitation" (*zimsum*).[1] This may help us to deepen the interpretation of the doctrine of the *creatio ex nihilo*. But we shall take up and employ the doctrine about God's self-limitation, and about Nothingness, in the messianic light of faith in the crucified Son of God.

Ever since Augustine, Christian theology has called God's work of creation an act of God outwards: *operatio Dei ad extra, opus trinitatis ad extra, actio Dei externa*. It distinguished this from an act of God inwards, which takes place in the divine relationships within the Trinity. Theologians have made this distinction between God's "inward" and his "outward" aspect so much as matter of course that no one has even asked the critical question: can the omnipotent God have an "outward" aspect at all? If we assume an *extra Deum*, does this not set God a limit? And who can set limits to God? If there were a realm outside God, God would not be omnipresent. This space "outside" God would have to be co-eternal with God. But an "outside God" of this kind would then have to be "counter" to God.

However, there is in fact one possible way of conceiving an *extra Deum*. But it is only the assumption of a self-limitation by God himself preceding his creation which can be reconciled with God's divinity without contradiction. In order to create a world "outside" himself, the infinite God must have made room beforehand for a finitude in himself. It is only a withdrawal by God into himself that can free the space into which God can act creatively. The *nihil* for his *creatio ex nihilo* only comes into being because—and in as far as—the omnipotent and omnipresent God withdraws his presence and restricts his power.

It was Isaac Luria who first of all developed these ideas in his doctrine of *zimsum*.[2] *Zimsum* means concentration and contraction, and signifies a withdrawing of oneself into oneself. Luria was taking up the ancient Jewish doctrine of the Shekinah, according to which the infinite God can so contract his presence that he dwells in the temple. But Luria applied it to God and creation. The existence of a world outside God is made possible by an inversion of God. This sets free a kind of "mystical primordial space" into which God—issuing out of himself—can enter and in which he can manifest himself. "Where God withdraws himself from himself to himself, he can call something forth which is not divine essence or divine being."[3] The Creator is not an "unmoved mover" of the universe. On the contrary, creation is

---

1. I am here developing ideas which I have already put forward in *The Trinity and the Kingdom: The Doctrine of God* (New York: Harper & Row, 1981), 109ff.
2. G. Scholem, "Schöpfung aus Nichts und Selbstverschränkung Gottes," in *Eranos Jahrbuch* 25 (1956): 115ff. The *zimsum* idea also plays a leading part in the Yiddish novels of Isaak Bashevis Singer, especially in *The Slave* (ET New York, 1962/London, 1963). He uses it in the form of the biblical metaphor: "God hides his face."
3. Scholem, "Schöpfung," 117.

preceded by this self-movement on God's part, a movement which allows creation the space for its own being. God withdraws into himself in order to go out of himself. He "creates" the preconditions for the existence of his creation by withdrawing his presence and his power. "In the self-limitation of the divine Being which, instead of acting outwardly in its initial act, turns inwards towards itself, Nothingness emerges. Here we have an act in which Nothingness is called forth."[4] It is the affirmative force of God's self-negation which becomes the creative force in creation and salvation.

The kabbalistic doctrine of the self-limitation of God has also found a place in Christian theology. Nicholas of Cusa, J. G. Hamann, Friedrich Oetinger, F. W. J. Schelling, A. von Oettingen, Emil Brunner and others all saw that when God permitted creation, this was the first act in the divine self-humiliation which reached its profoundest point in the cross of Christ.[5] Let us take up the idea at this point and think it through further.

1. God makes room for his creation by withdrawing his presence. What comes into being is a *nihil* which does not contain the negation of creaturely being (since creation is not yet existent), but which represents the partial negation of the divine Being, inasmuch as God is not yet Creator. The space which comes into being and is set free by God's self-limitation is a literally God-forsaken space.[6] The *nihil* in which God creates his creation is God-forsakenness, hell, absolute death; and it is against the threat of this that he maintains his creation in life. Admittedly the *nihil* only acquires this menacing character through the self-isolation of created beings to which we give the name of sin and godlessness. Creation is therefore threatened, not merely by its own non-being, but also by the non-being of God its Creator—that is to say, by Nothingness itself. The character of the negative that threatens it goes beyond creation itself. This is what constitutes its demonic power. Nothingness contradicts, not merely creation but God too, since he is creation's Creator. Its negations lead into that primordial space which God freed within himself before creation. As a self-limitation that makes creation possible, the *nihil* does not yet have this annihilating character; for it was conceded in order to make an independent creation "outside" God possible. But this implies the possibility of the annihilating Nothingness. It emerges from this that in a doctrine of Nothingness, a

---

4. Ibid., 118.

5. E. Brunner, *Dogmatics* II (Philadelphia: Westminster, 1952), 19: "This, however, means that God does not wish to occupy the whole of Space Himself, but that He wills to make room for other forms of existence. In doing so He limits Himself.... The *kenosis*, which reaches its paradoxical climax in the Cross of Christ, begins with the creation of the world." Cf. here G. Hendry, "Nothing," in *Theology Today* 39 (1982): 286ff.

6. Cf. in contrast K. Barth, *Church Dogmatics* III/3, ed. G. W. Bromiley and T. F. Torrance (Edinburgh: T & T Clark, 1960), §50: "God and Nothingness," 289–368. In his doctrine of creation Barth does not go beyond the Platonic definition of nothingness. However, in his doctrine of election (*Church Dogmatics* II/2) he develops insights into the annihilating nothingness drawn from the theology of the cross which lend theological depth to the Platonic Non-Being. For Barth's interpretation, cf. W. Krötke, *Sünde und Nichtiges bei Karl Barth*, 2nd ed. (Neukirchen, 1983).

distinction has to be made between the non-being of a creature, the non-being of creation, and the non-being of the Creator. It is only in connection with the last of these that we can talk about Nothingness.

2. God "withdraws himself from himself to himself" in order to make creation possible. His creative activity outwards is preceded by this humble divine self-restriction. In this sense God's self-humiliation does not begin merely with creation, inasmuch as God commits himself to this world: it begins beforehand, and is the presupposition that makes creation possible. God's creative love is grounded in his humble, self-humiliating love. This self-restricting love is the beginning of that self-emptying of God which Philippians 2 sees as the divine mystery of the Messiah. Even in order to create heaven and earth, God emptied himself of his all-plenishing omnipotence, and as Creator took upon himself the form of a servant.

This points to a necessary correction in the interpretation of creation: God does not create merely by calling something into existence, or by setting something afoot. In a more profound sense he "creates" by letting-be, by making room, and by withdrawing himself. The creative making is expressed in masculine metaphors. But the creative letting-be is better brought out through motherly categories.

3. If God is creatively active into that "primordial space" which he himself has ceded and conceded, does he then create "outwards"? Of course it is only through the yielding up of the *nihil* that a *creatio ex nihilo* is conceivable at all. But if creation *ad extra* takes place in the space freed by God himself, then in this case the reality outside God still remains in the God who has yielded up that "outwards" in himself. Without the difference between Creator and creature, creation cannot be conceived of at all; but this difference is embraced and comprehended by the greater truth which is what the creation narrative really comes down to, because it is the truth from which it springs: the truth that God is all in all. This does not imply a pantheistic dissolution of creation in God; it means the final form which creation is to find in God. Then the initial self-limitation of God's which makes creation possible assumes the glorifying, derestricted boundlessness in which the whole creation is transfigured. In Dante's words:

His glory, in whose being all things move, pervades Creation....[7]

The movement from God's initial self-limitation to his eschatological delimitation in respect of his creation can best be grasped if we compare the process of the original creation with the process of the new creation. According to the tradition of the Priestly Writing, creation in the beginning is a creation through the word. As such it is for the Creator effortless. It is not from *the labor* of his creative work that the Creator rests on the sabbath. But the divine creation of salvation in the midst of humanity's history of

---

7. Dante Alighieri, *Paradiso* 1.1–2.

disaster looks very different; for this is anything but effortless. Talking about the obliteration of the sins of God's people, Isa. 43.24f. says: "You have burdened me with your sins, you have wearied me with your iniquities. But I will blot out your transgressions for my own sake and I will not remember your sins." The Chosen One who, according to Isaiah 53, will bring salvation to the lost, is called *'ebed Yahweh*, the Servant of God. His soul has "travailed" (Isa. 53.11). He carries sins and sicknesses like a man who carries a heavy load (Isa. 53.4). That is why and that is how he is going to be victorious (Isa. 53.11,12). In the hymn in Philippians 2, the mystery of the Messiah is seen as his emptying of himself and humbling of himself in "the form of a servant." The new creation of salvation comes into being out of God's "labor and travail."[8] Through his self-emptying he creates liberation, through his self-humiliation he exalts, and through his vicarious suffering the redemption of sinners is achieved. It is these "works" that John means when he passes down to us as Jesus' last word on the cross: "It is finished" (John 19.30). Even the vital energies of the Holy Spirit always operate only in "the fellowship of Christ's sufferings," according to Paul (Phil. 3.10). It is in the fellowship of Christ's sufferings that the powers of the resurrection and the new creation are experienced and are efficacious (II Cor. 4.7ff.; 6.4ff.). This power is perfected in the weak (II Cor. 12.9). The new creation of heaven and earth is destined finally to emerge from the history of God's suffering, and to have this suffering at its centre. This new creation is to be the kingdom of the crucified Christ: "Worthy is the Lamb that was slain, to receive power and riches and wisdom and strength and honour and glory and blessing" (Rev. 5.12; also 7.14ff.; 11.15; 12.10f; 21.23). It is from the apotheosis of the Lamb that the kingdom of glory comes into being, as we see in the picture of the mystic Lamb which is to be found in the domes or apses of many Christian churches. The crucified one becomes the foundation and centre of the kingdom of glory which renews heaven and earth—the kingdom which already begins with his resurrection and glorification.

If we compare the processes of creation as they are described, we can see *initial creation* as the divine creation that is without any prior conditions: *creatio ex nihilo*; while *creation in history* is the laborious creation of salvation out of the overcoming of disaster. The *eschatological creation* of the kingdom of glory, finally, proceeds from the vanquishing of sin and death, that is to say, the annihilating Nothingness. God overcomes sin and the death of his creatures by taking their destiny on himself; and he overcomes in his own eternal Being the Nothingness which lies heavy over sin and death.

---

8. Cf. here J. Moltmann, "Justification and New Creation," in *The Future of Creation* (Philadelphia: Fortress, 1979), 149ff. Grace is really already to be found in the divine *preservation* of the creature who closes himself against God. Theological tradition has already given expression to this through the distinction between *paresis* and *aphesis hamartion* [binding and loosing of sins]. But if there is grace even in the preservation of the world, then there must also be grace in the creation of the world, from the very beginning.

If God's creativity goes back to a creative resolve, this already implies the Creator's openness for redeeming suffering and his readiness for his own self-humiliation. Because of the self-isolation of his creatures through sin and the consequence of sin, death, God's adherence to his resolve *to create* also means a resolve *to save*. *Creatio ex nihilo* in the beginning is the preparation and promise of the redeeming *annihilatio nihili*, from which the eternal being of creation proceeds. The creation of the world is itself a promise of resurrection, and the overcoming of death in the victory of eternal life (I Cor. 15.26, 55–57). So the resurrection and the kingdom of glory are the fulfillment of the promise which creation itself represents.

This brings us to a final interpretation of the statement about the *creatio ex nihilo*, from the standpoint of the cross of Christ. If God creates his creation out of nothing, if he affirms it and is faithful to it in spite of sin, and if he desires its salvation, then in the sending and surrender of his own Son he exposes himself to the annihilating Nothingness, so that he may overcome it in himself and through himself, and in that way give his creation existence, salvation and liberty. In this sense, by yielding up the Son to death in God-forsakenness on the cross, and by surrendering him to hell, the eternal God enters the Nothingness out of which he created the world. God enters that "primordial space" which he himself conceded through his initial self-limitation. He pervades the space of God-forsakenness with his presence. It is the presence of his self-humiliating, suffering love for his creation, in which he experiences death itself. That is why God's presence in the crucified Christ gives creation eternal life, and does not annihilate it. In the path of the Son into self-emptying and bondage, to the point of the death he died, and in the path of his exaltation and glorification by the whole creation, God becomes omnipresent. By entering into the God-forsakenness of sin and death (which is Nothingness), God overcomes it and makes it part of his eternal life: "If I make my bed in hell, thou art there" (Ps. 139.8).

In the light of the cross of Christ, *creatio ex nihilo* means forgiveness of sins through Christ's suffering, justification of the godless through Christ's death, and the resurrection of the dead and eternal life through the lordship of the Lamb.

In the light of creation, the cross of Christ means the true consolidation of the universe. Because from the very beginning the Creator is prepared to suffer in this way for his creation, his creation endures to eternity. The cross is the mystery of creation and the promise of its future.

Does the resurrection of the crucified Christ also bring the Nothingness of world history into the light of the resurrection? Here the experiences of Auschwitz and Hiroshima raise questions for which no answers are endurable, because the questions are fundamentally protests. Even Hegel found that there was a Negative which could not "be turned to good" in any dialectic. He therefore left the "unresolved contradiction"—the Peloponnesian and the Thirty Years' War, and other mass annihilations—out of his dialectic altogether. Ernst Bloch too was able to see nothing in the incinerators of Maidanek except the hard, meaningless, annihilating Nothingness: 'There is undoubtedly a grain of wheat that dies without bringing any fruit, a grain of wheat that is trampled into the ground, without there being truly—let alone necessarily—any positive negation of this negation afterwards.'[9] Only the militant hope that is associated with objectively real possibilities, he believes, can keep at bay the fields of annihilating Nothingness; but even the passion for life cannot completely do away with the death that is utterly meaningless. This idea of the negative is really Manichaean. It can do no more than "keep Nothingness at bay." It cannot abolish or overcome it.

Is Christian faith in the resurrection in a position to go any further than this? Certainly not in the practical struggle against war and mass annihilation. But where it can go further is in its hope in the God who raises the dead. Belief in the resurrection looks towards God at the very point where humanly speaking there is nothing to hope for and nothing to be done. This was already the situation in Israel's resurrection faith. In "the valley full of dry bones" Ezekiel heard "the word of the Lord": "Behold I will cause breath to enter you and you shall live" (Ezek. 37.1ff.). Even the resurrection of Christ after his execution was not for Christians a potentiality for Being which was still inherent in his Non-being. It was the miracle of God's new creation. The hope of resurrection therefore brings even the Nothingness of world history into the light of the new creation.

Does this have practical consequences? It does not lead to the kind of optimism that overlooks the negative. But it does offer the strength to hold fast to what is dead, and to remain mindful of those who have died. The hope of resurrection brings the living and the dead into a single fellowship of hope. In this fellowship death is not suppressed, nor are the dead given over to oblivion. The messianic community of the church of the risen Christ has always be understood as a community of the living *and the dead* (Rom. 4.7–9; Luke 20.38). This hope, which binds the living and the dead together, can be expressed in negative terms: "Even the dead will not be safe from the enemy once he is victorious."[10] But the protest against senseless murder, with which no one can come to terms, can only retain its staying power if it is borne up by a hope for the victims of that senseless murder. The protest against the annihilating Nothingness must not lead to the suppression and forgetfulness of the annihilated; and equally, hope for the annihilated must not permit us to come to terms with their annihilation. The first is obviously the danger for revolutionaries; the second is the danger of the religious.

---

9. This is the main problem in E. Bloch, *Philosophische Grundfragen. Zur Ontologie des Noch-Nicht Seins* (Frankfurt, 1961), 1: esp. 60ff. For criticism cf. Moltmann, *Theologie der Hoffnung*, 3rd ed. (Munich, 1965), Anhang: "Das Prinzip Hoffnung" und die "Theologie der Hoffnung," 313ff., esp. 326ff. (appendix not in ET).

10. W. Benjamin, *Illuminationen* (Frankfurt, 1961), 270–71.

Will the eschatological Nothingness be brought into the light of the new creation as well, through the raising of the crucified Christ? This question hangs together with the previous one, because experience of the Nothingness of world history is a foretaste of the apocalyptic annihilation of the world. This makes it a difficult question to answer, because the apocalyptic situation which we call "the end of the world" has not yet come about, although human beings have at their disposal all the necessary means for destroying "their world," at least, and all life on earth. But the answer cannot be any different from the answer to the previous question. Even "the end of the world" can set no limits to the God who created the world out of nothing, the God who in his Son exposed his own self to annihilating Nothingness on the cross, in order to gather that Nothingness into his eternal being. And this is true whether the end of the world is brought about by natural catastrophe or human crime. How should the Creator-out-of-nothing be diverted from his intention and his love through any devastations in what he has created? Anyone who expects "the end of the world" is denying the world's Creator, whatever may prompt his apocalyptic anxiety. Faith in God the Creator cannot be reconciled with the apocalyptic expectation of a total *annihilatio mundi*.[11] What accords with this faith is the expectation and active anticipation of the *transformatio mundi*. The expectation of "the end of the world" is a vulgar error. Like the expectation of the *annihilatio mundi*, it is gnostic in origin, not biblical. It is the means by which many people would like God to win acceptance at the world's expense. But eschatology is nothing other than faith in the Creator with its eyes turned towards the future. Anyone who believes in the God who created being out of nothing, also believes in the God who gives life to the dead. This means that he hopes for the new creation of heaven and earth. His faith makes him prepared to withstand annihilation, even when there is nothing left to hope for, humanly speaking. His hope in God commits him to faithfulness to the earth.

SELECTION 11

Catherine Keller

"The Pluri-Singularity of Creation"

Catherine Keller (1953–) is a feminist theologian who teaches at the Divinity School of Drew University. In her book *Face of the Deep: A Theology of Becoming* she analyzes the peculiar

---

11. K. Stock, *Annihilatio mundi. Johann Gerhards Eschatologie der Welt* (Munich, 1971).

grammar of the opening verses of Genesis to argue that the watery "deep" (*tehom* in Hebrew) is present alongside God "in the beginning" in a way that challenges the traditional Christian picture of creation as the absolutely unconditioned work of a completely self-sufficient deity. In its stead she proposes what she calls a "tehomic theology" that interprets creation as the process of the emergence of order from chaos: God is not the sole origin of all that is, but rather the one who elicits structure, complexity, and particularity from a primordial flux. In this way, she seeks to replace the doctrine of creation from nothing (*creatio ex nihilo*) with an alternative model of "creation from the depths" (*creatio ex profundis*).

The following selection from this work draws on a range of material ranging from medieval Jewish mysticism to postmodern critical theory to probe the textual instabilities that Keller believes render the conventional Christian reading of Genesis 1 untenable. While her reading cuts against traditional theologies of creation, the fact that her argument is ultimately rooted in the grammar of the Hebrew text suggests a relatively high view of scriptural authority. Moreover, though she protests against the picture of God as an all-sufficient divine singularity, she is far from denying the need for a Creator, since particular creatures only issue from the creativity inherent in the "the chaotic buzz and plenum" of the deep through an agent's decision to actualize certain possibilities over others. Nevertheless, because this work is a function of the agent's inherent relation to—and corresponding dependence on—the larger creative matrix, Keller's God remains just one factor within the world rather than its sovereign source.

From Catherine Keller, *Face of the Deep: A Theology of Becoming*
(London: Routledge, 2003), 172–82.

Created God—*bara elohim*

We want a principle, a system, an integration, and we want elements, atoms, number. We want them, and we make them A single God, and identifiable individuals.

(Michel Serres, *Genesis*[1])

If we do not rethink and rebuild the whole scene of representation, the angels will never find a home, never stay anywhere.

(Luce Irigaray, "Belief Itself"[2])

I. God Creates

God. *Gott*. Its consonants grind like teeth. G-d. Who, saying this name, does not take it in vain? I have hardly been able to write it, to subject it to sentences that start "God is," "God does." As though "God" identifies

---

1. Michel Serres, *Genesis* (Ann Arbor: University of Michigan Press, 1995), 2–3.
2. Luce Irigaray, "Belief Itself," in *Sexes and Genealogies* (New York: Columbia University Press, 1993), 42.

something, some One, rather than, as Meister Eckhart insists, "a non-God, a nonspirit, a nonperson, a nonimage."[3] As though the holy monosyllable might—after dying so many modern deaths, after performing so many gender tricks (the wishful She, the hiccupping S/He, the blustering He) pull off some liberating new feat of representation. But if we delete the *theos* from theology, what does it leave? A logos alone, a regime of secular monologoi, from which mystery, prophecy and the love that is stronger than death have evaporated? An elite post-theism, which shuns all theologies of social and symbolic struggle?

So I can no longer continue to elude the question: from the topos of the deep, does one confess "God the Creator of Heaven and Earth"? Clearly a tehomic theology does not use "God" as the founding word, "God creates" as its original act and fact. If the *bet* of *bereshit* offered an alternative starting point, a grammatical shelter for uncertain beginnings, does its offbeat opening perhaps also relocate the identifiable subject of theology? In this almost kabbalistic hope, the present chapter sounds out the singular plurality of the next phrase of Genesis. *Bara elohim.*

II. The Elohimic Multiple

Retreat momentarily to the desert, to the beginnings of monotheism, which among the Hebrews was gestating slowly, nomadically, uncertainly, amidst a universe of erotic and combative divine multiplicities. Here the god-word still breathes. Whisper: *Elohim*—a flux of syllables, labial, multiple. Its ending marks it stubbornly as a plural form of "*eloh*"; here (but not always) it takes the single verb form: *bara*. "*Theos*," "*deus*," "God" obliterate the traces of this singular Elohimic plural—or rather, of its theological significance. It/they/s/he is hard to identify (let alone to preach). Elohim, like Allah, derives by way of the little used Eloah from the common Semitic term *il* or *el*, both of which occur in the Bible infrequently except "in the purely poetic books of Psalms and Job." This Elohimic tree of names is far wider than YHWH, "the special covenant name of the Israelite national God."[4] Elohim is "an appellative, that is, it can be used of any deity. It is not a personal name, such as Yahweh, el Shaddai, Marduk or Chemosh."[5] Elohim, however, is a common name for the object of the Bible's personal monotheism.

What shall we make of its impersonal plurality? Amidst all the "careful defining, separating and opposing" that accompanies God-naming, this is a "curious slippage," suggest Danna Fewell and David Gunn. "God 'himself' is unsure whether he is plural or singular, echoing the narrator's grammati-

---

3. Meister Eckhart, Sermon 83: *Renovamini spiritu* (Eph. 4:23). "So be silent," says Eckhart (speaking right to me and fellow theologians), "and do not chatter about God; for when you do chatter about him you are telling lies and sinning." *German Works. Meister Eckhart: The Essential Sermons, Commentaries, Treatises, and Defense* (Mahwah, NJ: Paulist Press, 1981), 207–8.
4. Walther Eichrodt, *Theology of the Old Testament* (Philadelphia: Westminster Press, 1961), 178.
5. Gordon Wehram, *Biblical Commentary on Genesis* (Waco, TX: Word Books, 1987), 15.

cal confusion of a plural name (*elohim*, which may or may not be a proper noun!) and a singular verb."[6] Most biblical commentators would manfully protest that the plural form is "used to denote plenitude of might."[7] They read Elohim as an "abstract plural," or "plural of intensity," suited to the task of summing up the whole of divine power in a personal unity." "Yahweh is not just one individual '*el*,' but '*elohim*,' the sum of all gods, i.e., Godhead pure and simple, and as such, for Israel at any rate, he rules out all other deities." Thus Walther Eichrodt argues that far from preserving any lingering plurality of gods, the writer of Genesis 1 is said to use the term for the Creator God in order "to protect his cosmogony from any trace of polytheistic thought and at the same time describe the Creator God as the absolute Ruler and the only Being whose will carries any weight."[8] Certainly it is this dominological explanation that has carried weight: the plural signifies all the prior gods YHWH has replaced (or swallowed?); the plural beefs up His Oneness. Thus the exclusive use of the verb *bara* to "designate divine creative activity" can further intensify His singularity: the verb alone is thus expected to carry "the idea both of complete effortlessness and *creatio ex nihilo*."[9] Pure and simple. Theologians, in the meantime, simply skirt this God(s)-talk (as another obsolescent Hebraicism), except perhaps to find Old Testament traces of the Christian trinity.

Registered in the theogram of the plural Elohim, however, there remain traces of another interpretation—not of a polytheistic reading but of one which took the residual multiplicity with theological seriousness. Medieval rabbinic commentators were fascinated by the plural form of Elohim. For example, Abraham Ibn Ezra, born in Spain in 1089, poet, grammarian, philosopher and exegete, held that "the noun is plural because its sense makes reference to *the angels*."[10] In verse 20 of the first Genesis narrative, at the moment of the creation of the humans, the plural subjectivity of Elohim gets dramatically reinforced: "let us create. . . ." The verb *bara* is

---

6. Fewell and Gunn transcribe thus: "Then God(s) [or 'divinity'] said [sing.] 'let us make humankind in our image, after our likeness.' . . . So God(s) created [sing.] humankind in his own image, in the image of God(s) he created him, male and female he created them. . . .'" Significantly, they add: "the slippage extends from the God(s) to the human(s) created in his/their image. When humankind is one (him/it) it is also plural—male and female (them)." Dana Nolan Fewell and David M. Gunn, *Gender, Power, & Promise: The Subject of the Bible's First Story* (Nashville: Abingdon Press, 1993), 23.

7. According to a standard Jewish commentary on verse 1, "Elohim is the general designation of the Divine Being in the Bible, as the fountain and source of all things. *Elohim* is a plural form, which is often used in Hebrew to denote plenitude of might. Here it indicates that God comprehends and unifies all the forces of eternity and infinity." Thus it can say of "created" that "the Hebrew word is in the singular, thus precluding the idea that its subject, Elohim, is to be understood in a plural sense." *The Pentateuch and Haftorahs: Hebrew Text with English Translation and Commentary*, ed. J. H. Hertz (London: Soncino Press, 1988), 2.

8. Eichrodt, *Theology*, 186.

9. Gerhard von Rad, *Genesis: A Commentary* (Philadelphia: Westminster Press, 1961), 47.

10. Ibn Ezra's Commentary on the Pentateuch, along with other medieval commentaries, becomes a key resource for Samuelson's Jewish philosophical reading of "creation." Norbert Samuelson, *Judaism and the Doctrine of Creation* (Cambridge: Cambridge University Press, 1994), 137.

here for the first time repeated.[11] But here the plural *Elohim* takes the *plural* verb form. Scholars generally acknowledge a background reference to a divine court or heavenly counsel. Rashi, intriguingly, had found evidence here of "the humility of God." "Since Man was to be in the likeness of the angels and they would be jealous of Him, He *consulted* them (*nimlakh*) ... He *asked permission* of His court" (my emphases). The role of the angels, comments Avivah Gottlieb Zornberg of Rashi's interpretation, "is to suggest a 'many-ness' of viewpoints, a spectrum of opinions, that God has to convince, placate, ultimately to 'receive permission.'"[12] According to Rashi the text itself risks heresy by drawing on the plural verb, with all its pagan reverberations: "In spite of the license given to heretics by this formulation, the text does not restrain itself from teaching the virtue of humility: the great one should consult with, request permission from, the small one. For if the text had said, 'Let Me make man,' we would not have learned He spoke with His angelic court, but merely with Himself." This startling bit of hermeneutical democratization itself "risks heresy" to encounter the simple unity of the Aristotelian-Christian God, even as it challenges the dominological tendency of all monotheism.

These grammatalogical angels raise untoward questions. "The angel of the Lord" pops up at regular intervals in the Hebrew Bible, but is notoriously prone to merge with YHWH himself, so that "YHWH" and "the angel of YHWH" can be used quite interchangeably. The questions become thornier when with Ibn Ezra we spy the angels already inhabiting the first "Elohim created."[13] If the angels are themselves part of the Creator—part of the name Elohim—then how could they have *been* created? Is the Creator a committee? Protestantism has had little patience with this divine complexity. Holy wing of western modernity and hatchery of biblical scholarship, it has rightly suspected these hazy plurals of all manner of vestigial polytheism. Thus it phased out angelology, sophialogy, hagiography and Mariology, condensing the tiered multiplicities preserved in Judaism and Catholicism into "God." And Christ: the one Son of God, eclipsing many biblical "*beni Elohim*." And oh yes, the Holy Ghost (though that winged one has always threatened to fly the coop, as the chaotic activity of *ruach elohim* goes to show).[14]

Even though angels were discredited in modernity and downplayed in its religious institutions, popular culture can't get, or see, enough of them.

---

11. The rare *bara* also occurs in Genesis 32 and 1 Samuel 28:13.

12. Avivah Gottlieb Zornberg, *The Beginnings of Desire: Reflections on Genesis* (New York: Doubleday, 1995), 4–5.

13. Ibn Ezra differs, for instance, from Rashi, who has the angels created on the second day. Zornberg, *Beginnings of Desire*, 5.

14. Eichrodt notes in connection with the plural of *elohim* that the angels are called *bene elohim* ("sons of God") in Genesis 6:2, 4; Job 1:6, etc., in which *bene* "is not to be taken in a genealogical sense, but as an expression connoting 'congruence' or 'belonging together.' Analogous is the use of *ruach elohim* to mean the 'spirit of divinity'" (Genesis 41:38–39). Eichrodt, *Theology*, 186, n. 2.

The rosy Victorian sentiment for bare bottomed as well as diaphanously gowned androgyne guardian angels has yielded to their blockbuster status, starring recently, for example, John Travolta in *Michael*, Michael Landes [sic] in *Highway to Heaven*, and, weekly, Della Reed [sic] in *Touched by an Angel*. Such angelic luminaries, poignant in their in-between condition, sometimes yearning for human flesh and passion (as portrayed sensitively in *Angels over Berlin*), are conventionally imagined as emissaries, lieutenants or mediators, winging down from the Father enthroned above. But not always. The angelic multiplicity of *God him/her/it/themself* may appear even in a severely monotheist (and highbrow) setting. I am thinking of the sextet of three male and three female solo voices who perform together the voice of God in Arnold Schonberg's haunting *Moses und Aaron*: an atonal, bi-gendered pluri-singularity of Elohim.

In his philosophical reading of the Jewish creation tradition, Norbert Samuelson insists on the plurality of entities—not just angels but "thrones," *hochmah* or *torah, tohu, bohu, tehom, mayim*—variously presupposed in the reality *before* the creation. "This pre-creation universe is populated by things named in the Genesis account, as well as other entities not explicitly named."[15] He draws upon the angelological rejection of the *ex nihilo* formula. "The verb '*bara*,'" had claimed Ibn Ezra, "is singular because its referent is the Holy One." Ibn Ezra "rejects the claim that *BARA* must mean bringing something into existence out of nothing" (ibid., p. 137). To reread the verb—*verbum*, Word as event rather than subject or object—means, it would seem, to revise the doctrine of creation. But in Jewish thought, unlike Christian, the question of the *ex nihilo* had not been nailed shut.[16] Samuelson contrasts Ibn Ezra's reading of the creation to that of the slightly later Nachmanides, for whom the universe before creation was nothing except "space predisposed to be made into something." Yet such a predisposition belies simple nothingness. Nachmanides interprets Elohim as the "power of the powers of everything." Samuelson reads the latter not as a unifying omnipotence but as a depersonfication of Ibn Ezra's angels. They morph into "the first form and matter whose combination produces

---

15. Samuelson, *Judaism*, 133.

16. The Midrash Rabbah: Genesis early opposed any notion of a preexistent chaos, redolent as it still was of an animate or pagan Others. While the *ex nihilo* position took hold in Judaism as a reaction against Gnosticism (and no doubt a determination not to be out-maneuvered by the Christian God's omnipotence), rabbinic teachings—reacting in part against the style of hellenistic exegesis consolidated in the church—did not take the form of doctrinal exposition. Likening the notion of creation from chaos to that of a monarch building a "palace on a site of sewers, dunghills, and garbage" and so discrediting it, the text has R. Huna argue: "If the matter were not written, it would be impossible to say it, viz., GOD CREATED HEAVEN AND EARTH; out of what? Out of NOW THE EARTH WAS TOHU AND BOHU(1.2)." Chap. 5.1, 2–3. "Three cosmological traditions can be distinguished among the rabbinic texts, according to creation from an eternal matter, creation *ex nihilo*, and emanation theory." Tamar Rudavshy, *Time Matters: Time, Creation and Cosmology in Medieval Jewish Philosophy* (Albany: State University of New York Press, 2000), 5. Cf. also Samuelson's analysis of the multiple Hebrew and Latin variations on the theme of "out of nothing." *Judaism*, 101 ff.

the four primary elements of earth, water, air, and fire."[17] Venturing his own analogue to the medieval philosophical commentaries on the *Genesis Rabbah*, Samuelson refutes the legitimacy of deriving the *ex nihilo* from either the Hebrew or rabbinic heritage. He links the precreation "space" and its medieval "elements" with the material of energies of contemporary physics.[18]

These Jewish cosmological alternatives hold open a differential conception of the deity. "Even 'in the beginning' there is God and not-God, thus enabling God, as concept, to be."[19] The not-God within God reinscribes at the same time the many within the one—a move that should not be altogether alien to Christian Trinitarians. Does the angelic plurisingularity return today to question the concept of any single, separable individuals— a question readily metabolized in the indeterminacies, multiplicities and infinities of recent science and philosophy?

III. The Angelic Swarm

Let us not, however, too quickly subsume the old angels under a newer science. It could go the other way. For instance, in the form of a dialog between leading Continental philosophers of science, Bruno Latour attempts to tease out Michel Serres' hermeneutic of chaotic multiples. Serres offers in response a figuration that emerges "at the beginning of the Christian era, taking into account Semitic influences—that of the *multiplicity of angels*." He refers to paintings behind the altars of Rome, "whose backgrounds are filled with wings."[20] Serres opposes this image to that of a conventional Creator, "a single god who is a producer, a radiating source of life like a sun, or a story of the origin of time." He paints a hermeneutical vista "like a heaven filled with angels, obscuring God somewhat." This unscientific epiphany of angels understandably perturbs Latour: "this is not going to clarify things for the public." Besides, he snaps, delivering the *coup de grâce*: "it's not important—this is a theological quarrel!" Serres perversely pursues this insignificance: "They are restless, unsystematic (which you find suspect), troublemakers, boisterous, always transmitting,

---

17. Samuelson, *Judaism*, 141.

18. Ibid., 206–40. Finding in contemporary astrophysics a more radical notion of creation from nothing than in "the Jewish dogma of creation," he suggests that while there is extensive congruence between the classic Jewish teaching and physics, the latter "fails to capture the sense in which this nothing is a motion towards something." Ibid., 240. According to Nobel winner Ilya Prigogine, Big Bang theorists overreach their own data when they imply a creation from nothing. He argues for the possibility of "an irreversible process transforming gravitation into matter," claiming that the Minkowsky vacuum, the starting point for such transformation, "does not *describe creation ex nihilo*." There would for him be no basis for inferring that there was a time before any temporality. Ilya Prigogine, *The End of Certainty: Time, Chaos, and the New Laws of Nature* (New York: Free Press, 1997), 179.

19. Stephen Moore, in personal correspondence, February 2002.

20. Michel Serres with Bruno Latour, *Conversations on Science, Culture, and Time* (Ann Arbor: Michigan University Press, 1995), 118.

not easily classifiable, since they fluctuate. Making noise, carrying messages, playing music, tracing paths, changing paths... Hiding God, revealing God." Now he is on a theological roll, embarrassing Latour further: "This is the transcendental I'm talking about—*the archangelic space-time, the enormous cloud, without clear edges, of angels who pass, a great turbulence of passages. A swarm.* Perhaps what I was writing all along was an angelology" (ibid., p. 118; my emphasis).

The cloud of angels conceals and reveals Serres' philosophy of "the multiple." In distinction from hermeneutics, the angels do not *bring* messages but as the multiple embody them. "The angels are the messages; their very body is a message." Therefore "what differentiates angels from Hermes is their multiplicity, their cloud, their whirlwinds. I was about to say their chaos, since their collectivity is similar to it. In the reredos in Rome sometimes there are ninety-seven of them, sometimes thirty-two, sometimes twelve—why these numbers? Pure multiplicity" (ibid., p. 119). One sees with new eyes the swarms of angels churning turbulently over the surfaces of Christian art: for instance, El Greco's late *Annunciation*, through whose dramatic chiaroscuro cherub heads proliferate like clusters of grapes, or bubbles, uncannily indistinct for their period, anticipated a much later expressionism—overwhelming the tightened counterreformation boundaries between the heavenly and earthly spheres; and in the process subverting the canon of representation.

Does this indeterminate multiplicity of angels, cherubs, hosts, perhaps hint at a resignification of the divine it/her/him/theirself? With a tehomic hermeneutic, we read Job's whirlwind, with its chaotic swarms of star, angel and beast, as a midrash on the Genesis creation: the angels of Job, *beni elohim*, echoed the rush and grammar of *ruach elohim*. Might we now begin to reinterpret the "Elohim created" of Genesis 1.1 from the perspective of the verse of chaos? As early as Deleuze and Guattari to philosophize a "positive chaos" from new developments in science, Serres, in his *Genesis*, had written: "Sea, forest, rumor, noise, society, life, works and days, all common multiples; we can hardly say they are objects, yet they require a new way of thinking. I'm trying to think *the multiple as such*."[21]

The multiple as such. Both angels and primal elements can thus be read amidst its uncountable swarms: "The increasing deluge, fire, multiplicity always returns. Forest, sea, fire, deluge, figures of the crowd" (ibid., p. 56). Yet when our thought habits press toward unity and division, the multiple is reduced to an aggregate of ones, contained within, adding up or reducing down to a single One: "We want them, and we make them. A single God, and identifiable individuals" (ibid., p. 2f.). But these sub- and superunities keep dissolving as we approach them. "We've never hit upon truly atomic, ultimate, indivisible terms that were not themselves, once again,

---

21. Serres, *Genesis*, 6; my emphasis.

composite... The bottom always falls out of the quest for the elementary" (ibid., p. 3). The elementary bottoms into the elemental. Simplicity drops into a bottomless complexity. Does the vilified and nilified chaos of Genesis name that very fall? Is the *ex nihilo* the false bottom of theology? At any rate, a tehomic quasi-midrash may now be able to reconcile the two readings suggested by Samuelson of the Elohimic multiple: as angels and as energies.

IV. Divining the Multiple

If Elohim bottoms into the "power of the powers" of the Nachmaniean elements, its deity would not fall far from Moltmann's "Spirit of life," Pannenberg's divine "field of force," or Cobb's "creative transformation."[22] What if we read "God" not as the separate One—marketed as the only alternative to an older aggregate of separate Ones but as a distinctive plurisingularity of the text? Such a divine plurisingularity will bear little resemblance to the standard theology of Genesis 1.1, such as: "we are given the barest statement of a sequence of facts resulting from the fiat of the supreme and absolute master of the universe."[23] In itself, however, the text portrays no "absolute mastery." It can just as well suggest an elemental power of creativity, articulate, humble, kenotic, almost democratic, in its delegations; and effusive in its delights.

In further exegetical attestation of this elemental Elohimic multiple, Lynn Bechtel translates "Elohim" as "differentiated unity," appropriate to a "group-orientation" where individuality comes only embedded in collectivity and nature.[24] Within this differential-relational orientation, the "days" of creation would read out as a nonlinear series, rather like Serres' fractal model of time, full of folds, recapitulations and bifurcations: "Basic time, close to chaos, is made up of jolts, of fluctuations, it is not integratable, it cannot congeal either in mass or in class, it can't freeze."[25] The prehuman species would multiply in co-creative collectives; their "swarming" life iterates, amplifies, embodies the angelic host. Creation takes place

---

22. "As a field of force, the creative working of the Spirit of God is linked to time and space in its sphere of operations," suggests Pannenberg. Yet in order to preserve the purity of origin, he separates this pneumatological and eschatological function of the Holy Spirit from the "creative speaking of God by which the dynamic of his Spirit becomes the origin of the specific creaturely reality." Wolfhart Pannenberg, *Systematic Theology*, vol. 2 (Grand Rapids: Wm. B. Eerdmans Publishing Co., 1994), 110. Pannenberg deploys modern energy physics to reinterpret the creativity of the Spirit as involving "an element of indeterminacy," and of "the event of information" as constituting the transition to an independent form of "creaturely operation." Yet (unlike Samuelson, for instance, let alone process theologians, who similarly draw upon astrophysics at the heart of their theology) he means thereby to vouchsafe the *ex nihilo* formula.

23. E. A. Speiser, *Genesis* (Garden City, NY: Doubleday, 1964), 8–9.

24. Lynn Bechtel, unpublished manuscript, "Genesis 1:1–2:4a Revisited: The Perpetuation of What Is," 6.

25. Serres, *Genesis*, 100.

within a fluid interdimensionality; indeed within something like the viscous, insubstantial interdependence of what Serres calls "*relational bodies*." Always already taking body, the creation opens the concept of the incarnation beyond its singularity.

A multiplicity of differences-in-relation, the multiple that as such is the relational, might even thaw open the logic of the Christian trinity. For the most part, its three "persons" sit awkwardly frozen in an exceptionalism that only proves the rule of the One. So first Christianity would have to withdraw from Judaism the stereotype of a legalistic, simplistic monotheism. Judaism has served as foil for the trinitarian dimensionality of its Christian successor. Yet quite apart from the ambiguous status of the (non)creatures of verse 2, the canonic, apocalyptic, midrashic and mystical forms of Judaism have bred magnificent throngs of divine beings: angels, shekhinah, *beni elohim*, thrones, word, torah, hochma/sophia, spirit(s), sephiroth.[26] Crowding and complicating the hermeneutical time-space, the turbulent swarm of godhood has always transgressed any possible boundaries between the One Original Creator and the many derivative creatures. In this beginning, we hear not just anyone. And not just the One. We hear *the Manyone*. A countless divinity. But the *subject* of creation?

V.

> With the Beginning
> the Concealed One who is not known created the palace.
> This palace is called *Elohim*.
> The secret is:
> "With Beginning,   created *Elohim*."
> (Genesis 1.1)
>   (Zohar[27])

Please read the above blank. The subject of the sentence of creation has been deliberately deleted. Or rather, the kabbalist has pried open a fissure left by the grammar of *bereshit*, exploiting the Hebrew placement of the verb *bara* before *Elohim*, its ostensible subject. So Moses de Leon changes the subject.[28] Elohim has been rewritten as the object rather than the subject of the act of creation! Nothing fills the gap: it gapes, unspeakably, ungrammatically. Centuries before the deconstruction of "the subject," the western hypersubject, the subject of subjects, quietly drops out. There is

---

26. I and III Enoch are especially rich in angelology.
27. *Zohar: The Book of Enlightenment* (Mahwah, NJ: Paulist Press, 1983), 50.
28. We are indebted to Mary McClintock Fulkerson's *Changing the Subject: Women's Discourses and Feminist Theology* (Minneapolis: Fortress Press, 1994) for this bottomless pun, as well as for the theological and indeed feminist reverberations (the latter inaudible) within de Leon or other medieval mystical writings of a challenge to the western Christian subject-structure.

no innocence of intention here. The "secret" message is urgently doubled: *Elohim* now signifies a created place, a *palace* (= *binah*, womb)—not "the Creator."[29]

In a certain sense we have seen Elohim deconstructing its own unity from the beginning. For the very ideal of a subject as singular, substantial self-identity belongs to a "scene of representation" foreign to Hebrew discourse. Might we thus imagine that *Zohar*, a text vying with the medieval scholastic tradition, wants to undermine the changeless Subject of western substance metaphysics—that singular One = One of the grammar by which the western subject sentenced its world? At any rate the *Zohar* has with uncanny prescience (in both senses) dislodged the original dominology, or the dominant origin, of western religion. But the secret leaks: the creator is not a subject; the subject is not a creator; the creation has no substantial subject.

Writing Elohim as *effect* of creation, the *Zohar* does not deny the proposition that "God creates"; it deconstructs its propositionality. No more does a theology of becoming deny that it is appropriate to worship God as the Creator. Of course I cannot appropriate mystical Judaism (with its textual discipline, specular experience, minority-within-minority cabal, let alone its ethnically distinct patrilineage of interpreters). But I can recognize a kindred attempt to free "God's creation" from cliché. Divinity cascades through kabbalistic iconography into a bi-gendered plurality of ten sephiroth. In its exorbitant hermeneutics, wombs appear, *binah*, among the divine names, secreting innumerable, carefully numbered emanations. Language branches (its graphic trees anticipating fractal scaling) into the multiplicity of names. We encountered *bet* as the first place—crown, *keter*, sephirah of nothingness; and Wisdom, concealed here also "with the beginning" as the sephirah *hochmah*.[30] Elohim in the *Zohar* signifies Binah (understanding), the third Sephira, "the womb, the Divine Mother . . . Created being has its source in Her; She is called 'the totality of all individuation' and 'the world that is coming,' constantly coming and flowing."[31]

Does the divine Manyone come again—with flowing anachronism—in the morphology of a famous recent differentiation of "woman" as "neither one nor two, but many"? Such a theology, neither monistic nor dualistic, prepares a pluralism not of many separate ones but of plurisingularities, of

---

29. Daniel Chanan Matt offers these helpful notes on the above text from the *Zohar*: "*The secret is*: The Zohar offers its mystical reading of the first words of Genesis. The . . . subject of the verse, Elohim, "God," follows the verb, "created." The Zohar insists on reading the words in the exact order they appear and thereby transforms Elohim into the object; cf. Megilla 9a. This means that there is now no subject, but that is perfect because the true subject of emanation cannot be named. For the Zohar the words no longer mean: 'In the Beginning God created,' but rather: "With Beginning by means of the point of Wisdom the Ineffable Source created *Elohim* the palace of *Binah*." Notes to 50, 210.

30. *Zohar*, 34.

31. Ibid. "*Elohim*: a divine name meaning 'God' or 'gods.' Here the name signifies Binah, the Divine Mother who gives birth to the seven lower sephirot; cf. *Zohar* 1.3b, 15b." *Zohar*, 210.

interdependent individuations, constantly coming, flowing, *through* one another. Of course borrowed bits of kabbalistic imagery will offer no solution to the problems of feminist theology: *Binah* even as Elohim is not the first or even second manifestation, both of which tend to masculinity. As in most mystical counterdiscourses, the disruption of the patriarchal imaginary by strangely sexed or unsexed icons still privileges a phallic, if feminized, subject-position. "The secret of redemption consists of the female becoming the corona of the male organ."[32] In case Jewish feminist warnings did not already forestall ms/appropriations, Elliot Wolfson's meticulous divulgence of the "secret" of masculine kabbalistic androgyny effectively chills misplaced enthusiasms.[33] But a tehomic theology does not aspire to a new feminist purity, free of patriarchal residues, numb to such heuristically queer, infinitely multiplicative, experiments.

The recapitulative flow of a becoming-feminism depends upon the emancipatory force of sheer plurality. As Judith Butler puts it: "If the regulative fictions of sex and gender are themselves multiply contested sites of meaning, then the very multiplicity of their construction holds out the possibility of a disruption of their univocal posturing."[34] The "univocal posturing" of the creator has always been gendered, as will be any protests against it. At the site of the sex/gender undecidabilities flocks a plurisingularity of contested meanings—angelic, abysmal, confrontive. They seem to be an elohimic subspecies of all that swarm "in the beginning." They will keep the blank open. They will keep the grammar of "God's creation" ambiguous.

VI. The Unruly Deep

It was always noticed how this name, whose true pronunciation is unknown, consists of pure breath ... while Elohim is the name of the divine effects.[35]

---

32. The Infinite, the *Eyn Sof* from which the gender binaries of the divine emanate, remains according to Elliot Wolfson "entirely masculine." Ultimately the female is subsumed in what he calls "the mythic complex of the androgynous phallus" (xiii). (But even the masculine deconstruction of the hermaphroditic, sliding masculinity need not close down the opening of sites of symbolic gender difference.) Elliot R. Wolfson, *Circle in the Square: Studies in the Use of Gender in Kabbalistic Symbolism* (Albany: State University of New York Press, 1995), 120–21.

33. Cf. Judith Plaskow, *Standing Again at Sinai: Judaism from a Feminist Perspective* (San Francisco: Harper & Row, 1990). For further discussion of Jewish feminist relations to mysticism, see ch. 14. For a discussion of parallel problems in Christianity, see Grace M. Jantzen, *Power, Gender and Christian Mysticism* (Cambridge: Cambridge University Press, 1995).

34. Judith Butler, *Gender Trouble: Feminism and the Subversion of Identity* (New York: Routledge, 1990), 32.

35. Friedrich Wilhelm Joseph von Schelling, *The Ages of the World* (New York: Columbia University Press, 1942), 52. Schelling was influenced by Kabbalah, both in its Jewish and its Christian modes. Moreover, he defends the importance of the Hebrew Torah as living text rather fiercely for his context: "But what particularly hinders teachers from reaching this whole is the almost improper disregard and neglect of the Old Testament in which they (not to speak of those who give it up altogether) only hold as essential what is repeated in the New Testament.... Only the singular lightning flashes that strike from the clouds of the Old Testament illuminate the darkness of primordial times, the first and the oldest reationships with the divine essence itself." Schelling, *The Ages of the World*, 51.

Schelling is here contrasting Elohim to YHWH, the four consonants that can be pronounced only in a rush of expiring air.[36] Could there be some linkage of this notion of Elohim as *effect* to the Elohimic womb-palace of the *Zohar*? If we read Elohim as *effect* of *bara* rather than as its *subject*, might we sneak in through the back door of "the palace"—to the doctrinal question of "God's creation"? Schelling represents the Romantic margin of German philosophy that found guidance in the Kabbalah and acknowledges a debt to the living Judaism. *Of Human Freedom* had invoked (simultaneously with his former room-mate Hegel, but far freer of system) the shocking idea of *God's own becoming*. God's genesis from—what? From "that within God which is not God himself, i.e., in that which is the basis of his existence."[37] The not-God within God? That basis (*Grund*) translates for him as "*das Grundlose*"—the "groundless ground" of both world and God. Its antecedent is the abyss of the kabbalistic *Eyn Sof* and its analog or influence of Boehme's divine *Ungrund*. Thus the radical imaginary of a divinity born from the dark depths—"all birth is a birth out of darkness into light"—required among philosophical Protestants the midwifery of Jewish mysticism.[38]

For Schelling the "groundless" is recognized by its character of "unruliness" and "depth": the precinct of the primal chaos. It is then the "depth" of God that gives birth to God: "*It is in the beginning in God, and is the God-begotten God himself.*"[39] The *bet* of beginning is the house of chaos: thus Elohim precipitates from this bottomless becoming. Becoming is not outside of God nor God outside of becoming. For Schelling "becoming" replaces the idea of "divine immanence" (which he considers too static, "a dead conceptual inclusion" of things in God). All that becomes is in God, but not as apples are in a basket; perhaps more as they grow in a tree. Because all that becomes, becomes *within* God—as *part* of God—God is also becoming. So a primal Other not separate from but within God—*différance* in precisely the sense of the originary non-origin—produces the elohimic effect within language.

To a theology of becoming, this radical genesis *divines* the potentiality of the tehom. Its creativity does not create by itself. By itself it *makes* no difference. Difference itself could remain wrapped in its bottomless layers churning in an eternal undecidability. We know this danger in ourselves.

---

36. I thank Rabbi Arthur Waskwo for first making me aware of this ancient reading of the unspeakable tetragrammaton as a set of consonants literally unpronounceable except as sheer breath.

37. Friedrich Wilhelm Joseph von Schelling, *Of Human Freedom* (Chicago: Open Court, 1936), 33.

38. The intuition of becoming-God echoes Eckhart's "birth of God from the soul." It nonetheless diverges from Eckhart's still more platonic self-identity of God. Cf. Aran Gare on Schelling, in *Process and Difference: Between Cosmological and Poststructuralist Postmodernisms* (Albany: State University of New York Press, 2002), 31–54. Schelling's figure of the God-begotten God, significantly, does not make reference to Christ.

39. Schelling, *Of Human Freedom*, 35.

Decision breaks like grace. The great cosmic decision has been traditionally, with justice, named *the creation*; its agency, *the creator*. That which divines the possible also limits the infinite to its multiplying finitudes. The scission, the cut, of the actual amidst the matrix of the possible makes *something*. It makes it not from nothing but from everything—from the unruly multiple. But "everything" in a state of potentiality is no thing. In this sense at least a tehomic theology can inhabit the *ex nihilo* formula. But it stresses not the empty abysm—the shadow of a lost foundation but the multiplicity of the no/thing, its chaotic buzz and plenum. Creation signifies not a zap in the void but a decision within a plenary of possibilities. Thus Nachmanides had translated *bara* as "to cut away" (*ligzor*). "The intelligent person will understand what I am alluding to," he winks.[40]

Surely that intelligent person can also name this selective wisdom, this divining difference, "creator of heaven and earth." The creator would be the agency of decision, thus at once of limitation and relation, by which creatures emerge from the creativity. But the creator remains always also in relation—on this the biblical tradition insists. Thus the creator also emerges from the dark depths—this the Bible has not explicated. Whitehead conceives the creator as "the outcome of creativity." Another philosophy of becoming, rendering Elohim as effect? Creativity "is" not creator. Nor is it creature. In the last chapter we drew "*différance*" and "creativity," philosophical first principles inherently resistant to their own status as Origin, into terminological confluence with the Deep. Indeed our Manyone *sounds* suspiciously related to Whitehead's definition of Creativity: "the many become one. . . ." But it is not the same. The many-becoming-one means in Whitehead the many-becoming-*many* ones. That creativity gives birth in the present text to the Manyone, in whom difference itself differentiates; who decides (as Barth stresses rightly) for the world; whose many ones in turn, for good and ill, make their own decisions, their own differences.

Only in relation to what we call *creation* can what we call *Creator* be signified, i.e., be imagined to exist. "It is as true to say that God creates the world, as that the world creates God."[41] In the reciprocity of influence, both arise as effects of the primal creativity. But Elohim then signifies the effect through whom all causes arise. The creativity is not a cause, not even the First Cause, but rather the condition that conditions all causal processes. The creativity itself does not become; it makes becoming possible. We imagine it therefore as the matrix of possibilities. In this tehomic matrix we are always beginning again. We decide; and we fall back into the undecidable. According to this imaginary of bottomless process, the divine decision is made not *for* us but *with and through* us. Amidst the

---

40. Rudavsky, *Time Matters*, 6.
41. Alfred North Whitehead, *Process and Reality: An Essay in Cosmology*, ed. David Ray Griffin and David Sherburne (New York: New Press, 1978 [1929]), 348.

chaosmic committee work of creation, what work remains for a creator to do—aside from its decisive delegations ("let the earth bring forth," etc.)? Can we say with process theology that the creator emits an eros, a "lure to novelty," an "initial aim"—the beginning condition, the "prevenient grace," to which every creature willy-nilly responds? The metaphor works best, I think, if held with hermeneutical lightness. Some respond more responsibly than others to the cosmic desire. Committees and democracies make a lot of messes. The creature either responds in creative sensitivity to its own context; or it blocks the flux of its own becoming.

In other words our responses become us. They generate our own plurisingular inter-subjectivities—out of the multiples of elemental energies, codes, socialities, ecologies that any moment constellate our cosmoi. Elohim would live among the effects: a becoming God, who inasmuch as we have language for it/them/her/him, is at minimum an irreducible effect of language. But not an effect *ex nihilo*. For this divinity arises out of those unruly depths, over which language catches its breath. The creator, creating, becomes. In singular plurality.

SELECTION **12**

Dimitru Staniloae

"Creation 'Ex Nihilo' in Time"

The Romanian priest Dumitru Staniloae (1903–1993) is recognized as one of the leading Orthodox theologians of the twentieth century. His discussion of creation from nothing reflects the emphasis in Orthodox thought on the importance of time as the means by which creation achieves the end for which it was initially intended by God. Correspondingly, the topic of the world's origin is linked closely with that of its deification, or eschatological destiny of life with God. Specifically, he argues that the doctrine of ex nihilo is inseparable from the belief that the world is moving toward a goal that transcends its own inherent possibilities. If the world is eternal, its possibilities are latent within it, and there can be no genuine movement, merely the aimless shifting of a timeless flux. Only insofar as the world has a cause outside itself, Staniloae contends, can it have a goal that is also outside itself—and therewith a basis for Christian hope.

This strong correlation between the origin and goal of the universe means that the beginning cannot really be separated from the subsequent history of God's dealings with the world. Insofar as God creates the universe as a whole, God also creates time as a whole, so that the "beginning" of Genesis 1 "implies the entire distance through time . . . which the created world must cover." This insistence that the scope of God's creative work includes the whole of time allows Staniloae to sit easily with the idea that new creaturely forms might emerge within time, though he emphasizes that all such forms are created with humanity in view, since it is only in ever-deepening dialogue with other personal beings that God's aims in bringing the creation into being are fully realized.

> From *The World: Creation and Deification*, vol. 2 of *The Experience of God: Orthodox Dogmatic Theology* (Brookline, MA: Holy Cross Orthodox Press, 2005), 7–18.

According to Christian faith the world and the human being have a beginning and will have an end, in their present form or in the form into which they can evolve by themselves. If they did not have a beginning, they would not be from nothing, and thus they would not be the exclusive work of the freedom and love of God, nor would they be destined for an existence within the fullness of God. Instead, the relative, imperfect form of the world would be the only and fatal essence of reality. Only if the world exists from nothing through the will of God can it be raised—after it has been prepared for in a certain way—to a plane of perfection in God, wise through his almighty will and his love. This beginning of the world and of the human being, and this end, which is not a total end, prove the love God has for both of them and give them a meaning.

A world existing from eternity in evolving forms, in essence identical with the present world, would itself be the absolute, that is, the only reality. But the absolute cannot bear the imprint of the meaningless or of limitations, an imprint that the present form of the world, regarded as the only reality, does contain in itself just as it contains those other and essentially identical limitations in which all things come together and fall apart. Even if there were an unknown higher meaning within this relativity, there would have to be someone who would be conscious of himself eternally and superior to this relativity. Moreover, if there is no one aware of such a meaning, a meaning of this kind does not even exist. Yet our consciousness, the highest form of existence in this world, begs for this world to be saved from its relativity; it must find its meaning on a plane of existence superior to itself.

However, if the one who created the world is not superior to it, he cannot save it. The salvation of the world by God presupposes its creation by God. If the world is created, it has a beginning. This truth can be demonstrated in another fashion.

The world has a beginning because its meaning is fulfilled in the human person. The human race also has a beginning because it moves toward an absolute and brings the world along with it. Humanity is not from eternity, for in such a case it would not be moving toward an absolute. In company with the world, it would contain the absolute in itself and would remain within it eternally. "Nothing of what is created has the final end in itself since it is not its own cause either, for otherwise it would be uncreated and without beginning and immovable, having nothing to move towards.... Nothing is an end in itself, for otherwise it would be inactive, since it possesses fullness within itself, and would always be the same and would not have its being from any other source. For what is an end in itself is also without a cause."[1]

According to our faith, the world and humanity are in motion because they are straining toward a perfect goal that they do not possess in themselves. As long as they are still in motion, they have not reached the perfect goal toward which they are straining. They sustain the motion because it was not they who provided themselves with it. Nor do they have perfection in themselves, but they have received the motion from the cause that brought them into existence. But that cause has not brought them into existence in the fullness within which it itself exists, for to have the infinite God create another infinite one besides himself would be a contradiction. Yet God does exert upon the world and upon humans the attraction of the fullness toward which they are striving and of which they will in the end partake, not by means of their own nature but by means of that communion in which humans will make themselves worthy to share through his free effort to advance toward it. This means that the eternal God takes up a position in connection with the temporary world and remains in connection with it. Hence, the state of becoming, or the temporary state in which creation is placed because of the "beginning" which has been given to it remains connected with eternity. God has come down to its temporal level without ceasing to remain always within the eternity toward which he wishes to raise the world.[2]

When the creative act is produced and creation appears, the expression "in the beginning" indicates the first union of the eternity of God with time. "In the beginning" means both the beginning of God's coming down to meet time and also the beginning of time, which takes its being through the creative power of the God who has thus come down; "in the beginning" is the first moment of the dialogue between the God who has come down to creation and the creation which is beginning along its path through time. Both St. Basil the Great and St. Gregory of Nyssa have noticed this, making use of Plato's remarkable notations concerning the expression *exaiphnes* (all at once, suddenly).[3] "For them [the fathers]

---

1. Maximus the Confessor, *Difficulties*, in *PG* 91.1072B–C.
2. This theme has been developed at length in Dumitru Staniloae, *Revelation and the Knowledge of the Triune God*, vol. 1 of *The Experience of God: Orthodox Dogmatic Theology* (Brookline, MA: Holy Cross Orthodox Press, 1994), 150–71.
3. Plato, *Parmenides* 156d–e: "... but this instant [*hē exaiphnēs hautē*], a strange nature, is something inserted between motion and rest, and it is in no time at all; but into it and from it what is moved changes to being at rest, and what is at rest to being moved." ET, R. E. Allen, *Plato's Parmenides* (Minneapolis, 1983), 43.

the 'in the beginning' of Genesis is 'suddenly' at the limit (in the geometric sense) of eternity and time, that is to say, as St. Basil very subtly showed, a kind of moment, atemporal in itself, whose creative explosion nevertheless gives rise to time: a point where, we might say, the divine will touches that which henceforward—as it passes from non-being to being—takes its beginning, and without ceasing to begin, becomes and endures."[4] Here is what St. Basil said:

> Perhaps these words "In the beginning God created" signify the rapid and imperceptible moment of creation. The beginning, in effect, is indivisible and instantaneous. The beginning of the road is not yet the road, and that of the house is not yet the house; so the beginning of time is not yet time and not even the least particle of it. If some objector tells us that the beginning is a time, he ought then, as he knows well, to submit it to the division of time—a beginning, a middle and an end. Now it is ridiculous to imagine a beginning of a beginning. Further, if we divide the beginning into two, we make two instead of one, or rather make several; we really make an infinity, for all that which is divided is divisible to the infinite. Thus then, if it is said, "In the beginning God created," it is to teach us that at the will of God the world arose in an atemporal manner (*achroos*).[5]

"In the beginning" [*par excellence*] suddenly the consent of the divine will which is above time meets the aspiration of the first moment of time, of the created existence in such a way that only the first one can be called "beginning." "[The Maker of the universe] needed *only the impulse of His will* [*tei rotei tou thelematos monei*] to bring the immensities of the visible world into being."[6] The "suddenly/all at once" of the world is the "all at once" of the divine will that the world should be. God produces in himself an "all at once" of his own will that gives rise to time, the time with which the world is linked. The "consent" of the divine will is God's acceptance of the relationship with time, and it is precisely through this that time receives existence. Through the "all at once" of the divine will the origin of time is posited in the divine will and time is seen to exist only through its relation with the will of God, which is above time. Time does not exist by itself from eternity apart from the divine will but takes its origin in the divine will in a "once for all/all at once" of the consent of this will.

Time does not only begin by virtue of the divine will; it also endures. God has not come down into relationship with time only to bring about its "beginning." There would be no point to bringing about that beginning on its own if time itself were not to be. For the "beginning" of time means the "beginning" of created things in their potentiality, as time does not exist where things are not in motion, and there would be no point

---

4. Olivier Clément, "Notes sur le temps (II)," in *Messager de l'Exarchat du Patriarche russe en Europe Occidentale* 7 (1957), 27:133–34.
5. Basil of Caesarea, *Hexameron* 1.6, in *PG* 29b.16C–17A; ET, *NPNF*[2], 8:55 [altered].
6. Basil, *Hexameron* 1.2, in *PG* 29b.8C; ET, *NPNF*[2], 8:53 [emphasis added].

to bringing created things into potential existence if that existence were to be only momentary. "Beginning" implies the entire distance through time (between the beginning and the end), which the created world must cover, as well as the will of God to be in continuous relationship with the world so as to bring it to the end willed by him. The divine act whereby the beginning of time or of the created world is willed implies in itself the willing of time or of the created world to its end as one whole, an "aeon" or "age." Moreover, this act of willing the beginning time, because it is the start of God's act of coming down into the world that is beginning, also implies that this coming down of God into relation with the entire movement of the world in time will be continuously maintained.

The time that follows upon the beginning, or the world that unfolds out of its potency, does not endure by itself any more than the "beginning" appears by itself. St. Basil says: "Since the beginning naturally precedes that which is derived from it, the writer, of necessity, when speaking to us of things which had their origin in time, puts at the head of his narrative these words: 'In the beginning God created.'"[7]

Just as the beginning of time or of the world does not spring forth from some impersonal power that exists by itself, but rather from the decision of the divine personal will that posits potentiality in the world, so neither does the unfolding of time or of the world come from a potency of its own but from the potentialities posited by God; moreover, this very development is willed and hence sustained in its continuation by the power of God. Each time a new order appears in existence, God says: "Let there be ...," thereby showing that he wants this newly created order to be and thus gives it a special power. Apart from the will and the power of God no new order would appear in existence or have its own place alongside all the others in the overall pattern.

An act of God posits within the already existing realities something that develops into new orders of existence. But in a certain sense all later realities have been foreseen in what was created in the beginning and, subsequently and more particularly, in the immediately preceding realities. Expressed in another way, what was created from the beginning was also created by God as capable of receiving the power through which new orders might appear. Therefore, everything comes forth from the will of God but his will also makes use of preceding realities. Or, to express it in yet another way, all things were created by God, but with a certain overall pattern and relationship among themselves. Thus, on the one hand all things can be said to have been created "in the beginning," while on the other hand creation can be said to come to a close with the creation of humanity. For creation does not reach its completion until, in humanity, God has revealed to it its meaning. Man appears only at the end because

---

7. Basil, *Hexameron* 1.4, in *PG* 29b.12C; ET, *NPNF*[2], 8:54.

he has need of all the things that have come before him, while all that has gone before man only finds its meaning in him. The successive appearance of other humans from the first human is no longer a creation like that in the beginning, for all remains on the same plane. On the other hand, however, each human soul is a new reality, for each human being is created within a real dialogue between God and the parents.

Nevertheless, even in the case of the first human, the human soul no longer comes forth from the potency formerly posited within the world "in the beginning," although like the other orders of existence, the soul too is foreseen from the "beginning" within both a command and a power of God. The soul is breathed by God himself,[8] that is, it is brought into existence out of nothing by a special act of God. For from the beginning God enters into a direct relation with the soul. The willed relation of God to the world or to time—a relation which founds their existence—means, in the case of human being, a dialogue with one who is a subject from the first moment, given that both God and human being are persons, while nature as a whole is brought into existence as an object or as a succession of objects, only through power. God creates this ensemble of objects, however, for the sake of a dialogue with humans. Otherwise, their creation would have no point. Thus in the human person the plane of the creation of nature is transcended for the act of creating the human soul belongs to another category. In the soul the direct relationship of God with the human person—a dialogical relationship and one that gives spiritual life—is manifested from the first moment as an act of breathing.

In the continuous dialogue with humans who have been brought successively into existence, the relationship of God with the world of time acquires its full meaning. The world is offered to the human person by God and to God by the human person. The world is seen by God in the human person and by the human person in dependence upon God. The extension of the existence of humans—in the form of an unending number of particular decisions of the will that confront the world as object and deal with their fellow human beings toward whom they live out an unconditioned responsibility—shows that humans do not exist through the prolonging of the activity of an indefinite and deeper force, but through the free will of God, which makes a continuous appeal to their wills. Moreover, the world too is willed by God as a reality that serves the existence of humans as partners in the dialogue with him, a dialogue of unconditioned responsibility among humans themselves and also toward God.

God creates the world and time, and he remains in connection with the world through his will for the sake of dialogue with conscious beings whom he wishes to lead into full communion with himself. To this end

---

8. The allusiveness of the Romanian text here cannot be reproduced in English: "the soul (*suflet*) is breathed (*suflat*) from God" [trans. note].

the world was made so that humans could make use of it in their growth into communion with God. The world was created with humanity in view. The world has developed through the guidance exercised by God over its component energies, until the moment when, through a special act of God (the "hand" of God), the biological organism was formed in which there appeared, through the "breath" of God, a rational soul in the image of God, a soul capable of dialogue with God, possessed of a yearning for ever deeper communion with him, and to this end, invested with the grace of God or set in relation to God from the beginning.

Just as the first moment of time has eternity as its basis, although not the eternity of an impersonal substratum but of the will of the God who is from eternity, so too every subsequent moment has as its basis the will of the eternal God who sustains the world in its development and calls humanity continually to a response, thereby making possible the watchful and intense existence of humans, that is, their responsible link with eternity.

The world is not opposed to eternity, as Origen held, nor is the world in itself a linear eternity. It has its origin in eternity, is sustained by eternity, and is destined to become everlasting in a kind of eternity that is not identical with that of God. For the world is not eternal through itself, but through God. St. Maximus the Confessor, distinguishing the "aeon" (*aion*) from eternity, holds the former to be eternity filled with the experiences of time or time filled with eternity. There exists a final aeon, in which all time is gathered together, just as there exists an initial aeon, which contains in God the possibilities that have been conceived of all things that will develop in time. The atemporal laws of creation, the ideas of time, are an aeon of this sort. The kind of life that belongs to the angels and the future life of humans and the world within that life of humans is a final aeon.[9] It is an aeonic eternity, not purely and simply the eternity of God. This eternity is for the sake of the world that is contained in God; it is given potentially in the "all at once/instantaneously," and passing through time, is gathered together again in the eschatological eternity. The initial aeon is not in motion. In itself the eschatological aeon possesses the experience of motion and even a kind of eternal stable movement around God (as, in the vision of Dionysius the Areopagite, the angels also possess it), for the creature who has reached its place in God deepens himself forever in the contemplation of and participation in the infinity of God, despite the fact that he is always immersed within this infinity. That potential "instantaneously/all at once" of the first day becomes a complete "all at once" of the endless eighth day; the issuing forth from eternity through creation comes to an end, after the movement through time, with the entry into eternity through resurrection.

---

9. Maximus, *Difficulties*, in *PG* 91.1164A-C, 1153A-C.

Lossky expresses this patristic concept as follows: "One must thus avoid the categories of time when one evokes eternity. If, however, the Bible uses them, it is to underline by means of a rich symbolism the positiveness of time, where ripen the encounters of God and man, its ontological autonomy as an adventure of human freedom, its possibility of transfiguration. The Fathers have well sensed this, and have guarded themselves against defining eternity *a contrario* from time. If the categories of time are movement, change, transition from one state to another, one cannot contrast them term for term with immobility, unchangeability, the invariability of a static eternity: that would be the eternity of Plato's intelligible world, not that of the living God. If God lives in eternity, this living eternity must go beyond the opposition of mobile time and immobile eternity."[10]

The fact that humanity, together with the world, feels totally dependent upon the will of God shows that humanity and the world do not have their source in a potency that is eternal of itself, and likewise that they are not from the being of God. The world is created by God out of nothing. The inner principles ("reasons") of the world that have been molded materially are created out of nothing but have as a model and are sustained by the eternal reasons (*logoi*) of the Logos. If the world had its origin from the being of God, it would be a partaker—by its very being—in his fullness, and humans who are linked with the world, would themselves also be eternal and equal with God; there would be no explanation for the responsibility humans have toward God nor for their thirst after an absolute that transcends the world. Nor does the world have its origin from an eternal substance that is co-existent with God, for then too the world would be equal with God in eternity and both God and the world would be reciprocally limited, neither God nor the world possessing the fullness. Hence, God would not have greater goodness than the world, and the world could not be saved from the absurdness of its relativity. Nor would an unconditioned human responsibility or any norm for such responsibility exist. Nor, again, could God imprint upon the world the form that he wished, or upon humanity a direction toward himself through the exercise of a responsibility. St. Athanasius wrote: "But others, including Plato, who is in such repute among the Greeks, argue that God has made the world out of matter previously existing and without beginning. For God could have made nothing, had not the material existed already; just as the wood must exist ready at hand for the carpenter, to enable him to work at all. But in so saying they know not that they are investing God with weakness. For if he is not himself the cause of the material, but makes things only of previously existing material, He proves to be weak, because unable to produce anything He makes without the material; just as it is without doubt a

---

10. Vladimir Lossky, *Orthodox Theology: An Introduction* (Crestwood, NY: St. Vladimir's Seminary Press, 1978), 62.

weakness of the carpenter not to be able to make anything required without his timber."[11]

The divine Spirit is able not only to produce modifications much greater than these upon the energy from which the forms of the world are made but also to produce this energy itself as an effect of his own spiritual energy, imprinting on it potentially the forms that will become actual in their own time, that is, so-called "reasons" (*logoi*) of things referred to by the holy fathers.[12]

---

11. Athanasius, *The Incarnation of the Word* 2.3.18–2.4.29, *Athanase d'Alexandrie. Sur l'Incarnation du Verbe*, ed. C. Kannengiesser, Sources Chrétiennes 199 (Paris), 264–66; ET, *NPNF*², 4:37.

12. Patrick McLaughlin, *The Church and Modern Science* (Dublin/London, 1957), 33, citing the address of Pius XII to the Pontifical Academy of Science, February 8, 1948.

CHAPTER 2
The Creature

SELECTION 1

Irenaeus of Lyons

Against Heresies, Book 5

Irenaeus (ca. 130–202) was raised a Christian in what is now Turkey, but he eventually settled in Lyons, where he succeeded to the episcopacy in about 180, most probably after his predecessor died in a local outbreak of anti-Christian persecution. His main work, *The Refutation and Overthrow of the Knowledge Falsely So Called* (more commonly known by the shorter title *Against Heresies*), has the distinction of being the first truly comprehensive exposition of Christian doctrine, though it is immediately concerned with the refutation of the teachings of Gnostic Christians (so called because they claimed a specially revealed knowledge— *gnosis* in Greek—superior to teachings of ordinary Christians). Irenaeus's Gnostic opponents had a very dim view of the material world, maintaining that it was a defective and ultimately hopeless form of existence from which believers sought to escape to an eternal, changeless realm of spirit. Against this position, Irenaeus insisted that the world of time and space was good and, as such, destined for ultimate glorification (*Haer.* 5.36).

Irenaeus's anthropology has a number of interesting features, including the belief that Adam and Eve were initially created as children (*Haer.* 4.37). Though he may have derived this opinion from Theophilus of Antioch (cf. *Autol.* 2.25), Irenaeus developed it in terms of his overall theology of the goodness of material existence by arguing that while God could have made humankind perfect from the beginning, human beings' dignity was better honored through the process of growing toward perfection through time by the exercise of their own abilities (*Haer.* 4.38). The following excerpt develops this theme further by arguing, first, that humankind's creation "in the image of God" (Gen. 1:27) includes the physical body no less than the rational soul, and, second, that human beings only fulfill their destiny when they grow from creation in God's image to achieve the divine likeness by cultivating the gift of the Holy Spirit.

From *The Apostolic Fathers with Justin Martyr and Irenaeus*, ANF 1:531–35.

Chapter 6

1. Now God shall be glorified in His handiwork, fitting it so as to be conformable to, and modeled after, His own Son. For by the hands of the Father, that is, by the Son and the Holy Spirit, the human being, and not [merely] a *part* of the human being, was made in the likeness of God. Now the soul and the spirit are certainly a part of the human being, but certainly not the [whole] human being; for the perfect human being consists

in the commingling and the union of the soul receiving the Spirit of the Father, and the admixture of that fleshly nature which was molded after the image of God. For this reason does the apostle declare, "We speak wisdom among them that are perfect" [1 Cor. 2:6], terming those persons "perfect" who have received the Spirit of God, and who through the Spirit of God do speak in all languages, as he used Himself also to speak. In like manner we do also hear many brethren in the Church, who possess prophetic gifts, and who through the Spirit speak all kinds of languages, and bring to light for the general benefit the hidden things of people, and declare the mysteries of God, whom also the apostle terms "spiritual," they being spiritual because they partake of the Spirit, and not because their flesh has been stripped off and taken away, and because they have become purely spiritual. For if any one take away the substance of flesh, that is, of the handiwork [of God], and understand that which is purely spiritual, such then would not be a spiritual human being but would be the spirit of a human being, or the Spirit of God. But when the spirit here blended with the soul is united to [God's] handiwork, the human being is rendered spiritual and perfect because of the outpouring of the Spirit, and this is the one who was made in the image and likeness of God. But if the Spirit be wanting to the soul, he who is such is indeed of an animal nature, and being left carnal, shall be an imperfect being, possessing indeed the image [of God] in his formation, but not receiving the similitude through the Spirit; and thus is this being imperfect. Thus also, if any one take away the image and set aside the handiwork, he cannot then understand this as being a human being, but as either some part of a human being, as I have already said, or as something else than a human being. For that flesh which has been molded is not a perfect human being in itself, but the human body, and part of a human being. Neither is the soul itself, considered apart by itself, the human being; but it is the human soul, and part of a human being. Neither is the spirit a human being, for it is called the spirit, and not a human being; but the commingling and union of all these constitutes the perfect human being. And for this cause does the apostle, explaining himself, make it clear that the saved human being is a complete as well as a spiritual human being; saying thus in the first Epistle to the Thessalonians, "Now the God of peace sanctify you perfect; and may your spirit, and soul, and body be preserved whole without complaint to the coming of the Lord Jesus Christ" [1 Thess. 5:23]. Now what was his object in praying that these three—that is, soul, body, and spirit—might be preserved to the coming of the Lord—unless he was aware of the [future] reintegration and union of the three, and [that they should be heirs of] one and the same salvation? For this cause also he declares that those are "the perfect" who present unto the Lord the three [component parts] without offence. Those, then, are the perfect who have had the Spirit of God remaining in them, and have preserved their souls and bodies blameless, holding fast the faith of

God, that is, that faith which is [directed] towards God, and maintaining righteous dealings with respect to their neighbors.

2. Whence also he says, that this handiwork is "the temple of God," thus declaring: "Know ye not that ye are the temple of God, and that the Spirit of God dwelleth in you? If any man, therefore, will defile the temple of God, him will God destroy: for the temple of God is holy, which [temple] ye are" [1 Cor. 3:16]. Here he manifestly declares the body to be the temple in which the Spirit dwells. As also the Lord speaks in reference to Himself, "Destroy this temple, and in three days I will raise it up. He spake this, however," it is said, "of the temple of His body" [John 2:19–21]. And not only does he acknowledge our bodies to be a temple, but even the temple of Christ, saying thus to the Corinthians, "Know ye not that your bodies are members of Christ? Shall I then take the members of Christ, and make them the members of a harlot?" [1 Cor. 6:15]. He speaks these things, not in reference to some other spiritual human being; for a being of such a nature could have nothing to do with a harlot: but he declares "our body," that is, the flesh which continues in sanctity and purity, to be "the members of Christ"; but that when it becomes one with a harlot, it becomes the members of a harlot. And for this reason he said, "If any man defile the temple of God, him will God destroy" [1 Cor. 3:17]. How then is it not the utmost blasphemy to allege, that the temple of God, in which the Spirit of the Father dwells, and the members of Christ, do not partake of salvation, but are reduced to perdition? Also, that our bodies are raised not from their own substance, but by the power of God, he says to the Corinthians, "Now the body is not for fornication, but for the Lord, and the Lord for the body. But God hath both raised up the Lord, and shall raise us up by His own power" [1 Cor. 6:13–14].

Chapter 7

1. In the same manner, therefore, as Christ did rise in the substance of flesh, and pointed out to His disciples the mark of the nails and the opening in His side (now these are the tokens of that flesh which rose from the dead), so "shall He also," it is said, "raise us up by His own power" [1 Cor. 6:14]. And again to the Romans he says, "But if the Spirit of Him that raised up Jesus from the dead dwell in you, He that raised up Christ from the dead shall also quicken your mortal bodies" [Rom. 8:11]. What, then, are mortal bodies? Can they be souls? Nay, for souls are incorporeal when put in comparison with mortal bodies; for God "breathed into the face of man the breath of life, and man became a living soul." Now the breath of life is an incorporeal thing. And certainly they cannot maintain that the very breath of life is mortal. Therefore David says, "My soul also shall live to Him" [Ps. 22:31, LXX], just as if its substance were immortal. Neither, on the other hand, can they say that the spirit is the mortal body. What therefore is there left to which we may apply the term "mortal body," unless

it be the thing that was molded, that is, the flesh, of which it is also said that God will vivify it? For this it is which dies and is decomposed, but not the soul or the spirit. For to die is to lose vital power, and to become henceforth breathless, inanimate, and devoid of motion, and to melt away into those [component parts] from which also it derived the commencement of [its] substance. But this event happens neither to the soul, for it is the breath of life; nor to the spirit, for the spirit is simple and not composite, so that it cannot be decomposed, and is itself the life of those who receive it. We must therefore conclude that it is in reference to the flesh that death is mentioned; which [flesh], after the soul's departure, becomes breathless and inanimate, and is decomposed gradually into the earth from which it was taken. This, then, is what is mortal. And it is this of which he also says, "He shall also quicken your mortal bodies." And therefore in reference to it he says, in the first [Epistle] to the Corinthians: "So also is the resurrection of the dead: it is sown in corruption, it rises in incorruption" [1 Cor. 15:42]. For he declares, "That which thou sowest cannot be quickened, unless first it die" [1 Cor. 15:36].

2. But what is that which, like a grain of wheat, is sown in the earth and decays, unless it be the bodies which are laid in the earth, into which seeds are also cast? And for this reason he said, "It is sown in dishonour, it rises in glory" [1 Cor. 15:43]. For what is more ignoble than dead flesh? Or, on the other hand, what is more glorious than the same when it arises and partakes of incorruption? "It is sown in weakness, it is raised in power" [1 Cor. 15:43] in its own weakness certainly, because since it is earth it goes to earth; but [it is quickened] by the power of God, who raises it from the dead. "It is sown an animal body, it rises a spiritual body" [1 Cor. 15:44]. He has taught, beyond all doubt, that such language was not used by him, either with reference to the soul or to the spirit, but to bodies that have become corpses. For these are animal bodies, that is, [bodies] which partake of life, which when they have lost, they succumb to death; then, rising through the Spirit's instrumentality, they become spiritual bodies, so that by the Spirit they possess a perpetual life. "For now," he says, "we know in part, and we prophesy in part, but then face to face" [1 Cor. 13:9–12]. And this it is which has been said also by Peter: "Whom having not seen, ye love; in whom now also, not seeing, ye believe; and believing, ye shall rejoice with joy unspeakable" [1 Pet. 1:8]. For our face shall see the face of the Lord and shall rejoice with joy unspeakable, that is to say, when it shall behold its own Delight.

Chapter 8

1. But we do now receive a certain portion of His Spirit, tending towards perfection, and preparing us for incorruption, being little by little accustomed to receive and bear God; which also the apostle terms "an earnest," that is, a part of the honor which has been promised us by God, where he

says in the Epistle to the Ephesians, "In which ye also, having heard the word of truth, the Gospel of your salvation, believing in which we have been sealed with the Holy Spirit of promise, which is the earnest of our inheritance" [Eph. 1:13]. This earnest, therefore, thus dwelling in us, renders us spiritual even now, and the mortal is swallowed up by immortality [2 Cor. 5:4]. "For ye," he declares, "are not in the flesh, but in the Spirit, if so be that the Spirit of God dwell in you" [Rom. 8:9]. This, however, does not take place by a casting away of the flesh, but by the impartation of the Spirit. For those to whom he was writing were not without flesh, but they were those who had received the Spirit of God, "by which we cry, Abba, Father" [Rom. 8:15]. If therefore, at the present time, having the earnest, we do cry, "Abba, Father," what shall it be when, on rising again, we behold Him face to face; when all the members shall burst out into a continuous hymn of triumph, glorifying Him who raised them from the dead, and gave the gift of eternal life? For if the earnest, gathering the individual into itself, does even now cause him to cry, "Abba, Father," what shall the complete grace of the Spirit effect, which shall be given to men by God? It will render us like unto Him, and accomplish the will of the Father; for it shall make human beings after the image and likeness of God.

2. Those persons, then, who possess the earnest of the Spirit, and who are not enslaved by the lusts of the flesh, but are subject to the Spirit, and who in all things walk according to the light of reason, does the apostle properly term "spiritual," because the Spirit of God dwells in them. Now, spiritual men shall not be incorporeal spirits; but our substance, that is, the union of flesh and spirit, receiving the Spirit of God, makes up the spiritual man. But those who do indeed reject the Spirit's counsel, and are the slaves of fleshly lusts, and lead lives contrary to reason, and who, without restraint, plunge headlong into their own desires, having no longing after the Divine Spirit, do live after the manner of swine and of dogs; these men, [I say], does the apostle very properly term "carnal," because they have no thought of anything else except carnal things.

3. For the same reason, too, do the prophets compare them to irrational animals, on account of the irrationality of their conduct, saying, "They have become as horses raging for the females; each one of them neighing after his neighbor's wife" [Jer. 5:3]. And again, "Man, when he was in honor, was made like unto cattle" [Ps. 49:20]. This denotes that, for his own fault, he is likened to cattle, by rivaling their irrational life. And we also, as the custom is, do designate men of this stamp as cattle and irrational beasts.

4. Now the law has figuratively predicted all these, delineating man by the [various] animals: whatsoever of these, says [the Scripture], have a double hoof and ruminate, it proclaims as clean; but whatsoever of them do not possess one or other of these [properties], it sets aside by themselves as unclean [Lev. 11:2; Deut. 14:3]. Who then are the clean? Those

who make their way by faith steadily towards the Father and the Son; for this is denoted by the steadiness of those which divide the hoof; and they meditate day and night upon the words of God [Ps. 1:2], that they may be adorned with good works: for this is the meaning of the ruminants. The unclean, however, are those which do neither divide the hoof nor ruminate; that is, those persons who have neither faith in God, nor do meditate on His words: and such is the abomination of the Gentiles. But as to those animals which do indeed chew the cud, but have not the double hoof, and are themselves unclean, we have in them a figurative description of the Jews, who certainly have the words of God in their mouth, but who do not fix their rooted steadfastness in the Father and in the Son; wherefore they are an unstable generation. For those animals which have the hoof all in one piece easily slip; but those which have it divided are more sure-footed, their cleft hoofs succeeding each other as they advance, and the one hoof supporting the other. In like manner, too, those are unclean which have the double hoof but do not ruminate: this is plainly an indication of all heretics, and of those who do not meditate on the words of God, neither are adorned with works of righteousness; to whom also the Lord says, "Why call ye Me Lord, Lord, and do not the things which I say to you?" [Luke 6:46]. For men of this stamp do indeed say that they believe in the Father and the Son, but they never meditate as they should upon the things of God, neither are they adorned with works of righteousness; but, as I have already observed, they have adopted the lives of swine and of dogs, giving themselves over to filthiness, to gluttony, and recklessness of all sorts. Justly, therefore, did the apostle call all such "carnal" and "animal" [1 Cor. 2:14; 3:1], who through their own unbelief and luxury do not receive the Divine Spirit, and in their various phases cast out from themselves the life-giving Word, and walk stupidly after their own lusts: the prophets, too, spoke of them as beasts of burden and wild beasts; custom likewise has viewed them in the light of cattle and irrational creatures; and the law has pronounced them unclean.

Chapter 9

1. Among the other [truths] proclaimed by the apostle, there is also this one, "That flesh and blood cannot inherit the kingdom of God" [1 Cor. 15:50]. This is [the passage] which is adduced by all the heretics in support of their folly, with an attempt to annoy us, and to point out that the handiwork of God is not saved. They do not take this fact into consideration, that there are three things out of which, as I have shown, the complete man is composed: flesh, soul, and spirit. One of these does indeed preserve and fashion [the individual]: this is the spirit; while as to another it is united and formed: that is the flesh; then [comes] that which is between these two: that is the soul, which sometimes indeed, when it follows the spirit, is raised up by it, but sometimes it sympathizes with the flesh, and falls into

carnal lusts. Those then, as many as they be, who have not that which saves and forms [us] into life [eternal], shall be, and shall be called, [mere] flesh and blood; for these are they who have not the Spirit of God in themselves. Wherefore people of this stamp are spoken of by the Lord as dead, "For," says He, "let the dead bury their dead" [Luke 10:60], because they have not the Spirit which quickens a person.

2. On the other hand, as many as fear God and trust in His Son's advent, and who through faith do establish the Spirit of God in their hearts, such people as these shall be properly called both "pure," and "spiritual," and "those living to God," because they possess the Spirit of the Father, who purifies a person, and raises him up to the life of God. For as the Lord has testified that "the flesh is weak," so [does He also say] that "the spirit is willing" [Matt. 26:41]. For this latter is capable of working out its own suggestions. If, therefore, any one admix the ready inclination of the Spirit to be, as it were, a stimulus to the infirmity of the flesh, it inevitably follows that what is strong will prevail over the weak, so that the weakness of the flesh will be absorbed by the strength of the Spirit; and that the person in whom this takes place cannot in that case be carnal, but spiritual, because of the fellowship of the Spirit. Thus it is, therefore, that the martyrs bear their witness, and despise death, not after the infirmity of the flesh, but because of the readiness of the Spirit. For when the infirmity of the flesh is absorbed, it exhibits the Spirit as powerful; and again, when the Spirit absorbs the weakness [of the flesh], it possesses the flesh as an inheritance in itself, and from both of these is formed a living human being—living, indeed, because he partakes of the Spirit, but human, because of the substance of flesh.

3. The flesh, therefore, when destitute of the Spirit of God, is dead, not having life, and cannot possess the kingdom of God: [it is as] irrational blood, like water poured out upon the ground. And therefore he says, "As is the earthy, such are they that are earthy" [1 Cor. 15:48]. But where the Spirit of the Father is, there is a living human being; [there is] the rational blood preserved by God for the avenging [of those that shed it]; [there is] the flesh possessed by the Spirit, forgetful indeed of what belongs to it, and adopting the quality of the Spirit, being made conformable to the Word of God. And on this account he (the apostle) declares, "As we have borne the image of him who is of the earth, we shall also bear the image of Him who is from heaven" [1 Cor. 15:49]. What, therefore, is the earthly? That which was fashioned. And what is the heavenly? The Spirit. As therefore he says, when we were destitute of the celestial Spirit, we walked in former times in the oldness of the flesh, not obeying God; so now let us, receiving the Spirit, walk in newness of life, obeying God. Inasmuch, therefore, as without the Spirit of God we cannot be saved, the apostle exhorts us through faith and chaste conversation to preserve the Spirit of God, lest, having become non-participators of the Divine Spirit, we lose the kingdom of

heaven; and he exclaims, that flesh in itself, and blood, cannot possess the kingdom of God.

4. If, however, we must speak strictly, [we would say that] the flesh does not inherit, but is inherited; as also the Lord declares, "Blessed are the meek, for they shall possess the earth by inheritance" [Matt. 5:5], as if in the [future] kingdom, the earth, from whence exists the substance of our flesh, is to be possessed by inheritance. This is the reason for His wishing the temple (i.e., the flesh) to be clean, that the Spirit of God may take delight therein, as a bridegroom with a bride. As, therefore, the bride cannot [be said] to wed, but to be wedded, when the bridegroom comes and takes her, so also the flesh cannot by itself possess the kingdom of God by inheritance; but it can be taken for an inheritance into the kingdom of God. For a living person inherits the goods of the deceased; and it is one thing to inherit, another to be inherited. The former rules, and exercises power over, and orders the things inherited at his will; but the latter things are in a state of subjection, are under order, and are ruled over by him who has obtained the inheritance. What, therefore, is it that lives? The Spirit of God, doubtless. What, again, are the possessions of the deceased? The various parts of the human being, surely, which rot in the earth. But these are inherited by the Spirit when they are translated into the kingdom of heaven. For this cause, too, did Christ die, that the Gospel covenant being manifested and known to the whole world, might in the first place set free His slaves; and then afterwards, as I have already shown, might constitute them heirs of His property, when the Spirit possesses them by inheritance. For he who lives inherits, but the flesh is inherited. In order that we may not lose life by losing that Spirit which possesses us, the apostle, exhorting us to the communion of the Spirit, has said, according to reason, in those words already quoted, "That flesh and blood cannot inherit the kingdom of God." It is just as if he were to say, "Do not err; for unless the Word of God dwell with, and the Spirit of the Father be in you, and if ye shall live frivolously and carelessly as if ye were this only, viz., mere flesh and blood, ye cannot inherit the kingdom of God."

SELECTION 2

Gregory of Nyssa

On the Making of Humankind

Gregory, Bishop of Nyssa (ca. 335–ca. 395), is the youngest of the three "Cappadocian fathers," alongside his brother, Basil of Caesarea, and their friend, Gregory of Nazianzus. Although probably best known for his role in helping to consolidate the Orthodox doctrine of the Trinity (he was present when the doctrine was given formal dogmatic definition at the First Council of Constantinople in 381) and for his defense of universal salvation (or *apokatastasis*), Gregory's writings span a broad range of topics in both Christian doctrine and spirituality. *On the Making of Humankind* was written as a supplement to his brother Basil's *Hexameron*, a treatise on Genesis 1 that had concluded with the creation of land animals.

Though Gregory remains firmly committed to the principle that body and soul are equally constitutive of human nature, his stress on the mind in general and freedom of the will in particular as central to humanity's creation in God's image (as well as his low estimation of the ultimate anthropological significance of sexual difference) bespeaks an anthropology much more one-sidedly noetic in orientation than that of Irenaeus. At the same time, he also argues that the creation of humankind in the image of God in Genesis 1 refers to the "entire plenitude of humanity" as conceived in the mind of God rather than to a particular feature of human nature as such. Thus, Gregory sees the fact that "mind is implanted alike in all" as a sign of this fundamental unity of the human species before God, and these two features of his anthropology combine to produce a very strong affirmation of human equality in spite of physical and cultural differences among individuals.

From *Gregory of Nyssa: Dogmatic Treatises, etc.*, NPNF[2] 5:404-9; 419-22.

Chapter 16

1. Let us now resume our consideration of the Divine word, "Let us make man in our image, after our likeness" [Gen. 1:26]. How mean and how unworthy of the majesty of humankind are the fancies of some heathen writers, who magnify humanity, as they supposed, by their comparison of it to this world! For they say that man is a little world, composed of the same elements with the universe. Those who bestow on human nature such praise as this by a high-sounding name, forget that they are dignifying man with the attributes of the gnat and the mouse: for they too are composed of these four elements, because assuredly about the animated nature of every existing thing we behold a part, greater or less, of those elements without which it is not natural that any sensitive being should exist. What great thing is there, then, in humanity's being accounted a representation and likeness of the world—of the heaven that passes away, of the earth that changes, of all things that they contain, which pass away with the departure of that which compasses them round?

2. In what then does the greatness of humanity consist, according to the doctrine of the Church? Not in likeness to the created world, but in being in the image of the nature of the Creator.

3. What therefore, you will perhaps say, is the definition of the image? How is the incorporeal likened to body? How is the temporal like the eternal? That which is mutable by change like to the immutable? That which is subject to passion and corruption to the impassible and incorruptible? That which constantly dwells with evil, and grows up with it, to that which is absolutely free from evil? There is a great difference between that which is conceived in the archetype, and a thing which has been made in its image: for the image is properly so called if it keeps its resemblance to the prototype; but if the imitation be perverted from its subject, the thing is something else, and no longer an image of the subject.

4. How then is a human being, this mortal, passible, short-lived creature, the image of that nature which is immortal, pure, and everlasting? The true answer to this question, indeed, perhaps only the very Truth knows: but this is what we, tracing out the truth so far as we are capable by conjectures and inferences, apprehend concerning the matter. Neither does the word of God lie when it says that humankind was made in the image of God, nor is the pitiable suffering of human nature like to the blessedness of the impassible Life: for if any one were to compare our nature with God, one of two things must needs be allowed in order that the definition of the likeness may be apprehended in both cases in the same terms: either that the Deity is passible, or that humanity is impassible; but if neither the Deity is passible nor our nature free from passion, what other account remains whereby we may say that the word of God speaks truly, which says that humankind was made in the image of God?

5. We must, then, take up once more the Holy Scripture itself, if we may perhaps find some guidance in the question by means of what is written. After saying, "Let us make man in our image," and for what purposes it was said "Let us make him," it adds this saying: "and God created man; in the image of God created He him; male and female created He them" [Gen. 1:27]. We have already said in what precedes, that this saying was uttered for the destruction of heretical impiety, in order that being instructed that the Only-begotten God made humankind in the image of God, we should in no wise distinguish the Godhead of the Father and the Son, since Holy Scripture gives to each equally the name of God: to Him Who made humankind, and to Him in Whose image humankind was made.

6. However, let us pass by our argument upon this point. Let us turn our inquiry to the question before us: how it is that while the Deity is in bliss, and humanity is in misery, the latter is yet in Scripture called "like" the former?

7. We must, then, examine the words carefully: for we find, if we do so, that that which was made "in the image" is one thing, and that which is now manifested in wretchedness is another. "God created man," it says; "in the image of God created He him" [Gen. 1:27]. There is an end of the creation of that which was made "in the image": then it makes a resump-

tion of the account of creation, and says, "male and female created He them" [Gen. 1:27]. I presume that every one knows that this is a departure from the Prototype: for "in Christ Jesus," as the apostle says, "there is neither male nor female" [Gal. 3:28]. Yet the phrase declares that man is thus divided.

8. Thus the creation of our nature is in a sense twofold: one made like to God, one divided according to this distinction: for something like this the passage darkly conveys by its arrangement, where it first says, "God created man, in the image of God created He him," and then, adding to what has been said, "male and female created He them,"—a thing which is alien from our conceptions of God.

9. I think that by these words Holy Scripture conveys to us a great and lofty doctrine; and the doctrine is this. While two natures—the Divine and incorporeal nature, and the irrational life of brutes—are separated from each other as extremes, human nature is the mean between them: for in the compound nature of humanity we may behold a part of each of the natures I have mentioned: of the Divine, the rational and intelligent element, which does not admit the distinction of male and female; of the irrational, our bodily form and structure, divided into male and female: for each of these elements is certainly to be found in all that partakes of human life. That the intellectual element, however, precedes the other, we learn as from one who gives in order an account of the making of humankind; and we learn also that humanity's community and kindred with the irrational is a provision for reproduction. For he says first that "God created man in the image of God" (showing by these words, as the Apostle says, that in such a being there is no male or female); then he adds the peculiar attributes of human nature, "male and female created He them."

10. What, then, do we learn from this? Let no one, I pray, be indignant if I bring from far an argument to bear upon the present subject. God is in His own nature all that which our mind can conceive of good; rather, transcending all good that we can conceive or comprehend. He creates humanity for no other reason than that He is good; and being such, and having this as His reason for entering upon the creation of our nature, He would not exhibit the power of His goodness in an imperfect form, giving our nature some one of the things at His disposal, and grudging it a share in another: but the perfect form of goodness is here to be seen by His both bringing human beings into being from nothing, and fully supplying them with all good gifts: but since the list of individual good gifts is a long one, it is out of the question to apprehend it numerically. The language of Scripture therefore expresses it concisely by a comprehensive phrase, in saying that humankind was made "in the image of God": for this is the same as to say that He made human nature participant in all good; for if the Deity is the fullness of good, and this is His image, then the image finds its resemblance to the Archetype in being filled with all good.

11. Thus there is in us the principle of all excellence, all virtue and wisdom, and every higher thing that we conceive: but pre-eminent among all is the fact that we are free from necessity, and not in bondage to any natural power, but have decision in our own power as we please; for virtue is a voluntary thing, subject to no dominion: that which is the result of compulsion and force cannot be virtue.

12. Now as the image bears in all points the semblance of the archetypal excellence, if it had not a difference in some respect, being absolutely without divergence it would no longer be a likeness, but will in that case manifestly be absolutely identical with the Prototype. What difference then do we discern between the Divine and that which has been made like to the Divine? We find it in the fact that the former is uncreated, while the latter has its being from creation: and this distinction of property brings with it a train of other properties; for it is very certainly acknowledged that the uncreated nature is also immutable, and always remains the same, while the created nature cannot exist without change; for its very passage from nonexistence to existence is a certain motion and change of the nonexistent transmuted by the Divine purpose into being.

13. As the Gospel calls the stamp upon the coin "the image of Caesar" [Matt. 22:20], whereby we learn that in that which was fashioned to resemble Caesar there was resemblance as to outward look, but difference as to material, so also in the present saying, when we consider the attributes contemplated both in the Divine and human nature, in which the likeness consists, to be in the place of the features, we find in what underlies them the difference which we behold in the uncreated and in the created nature.

14. Now as the former always remains the same, while that which came into being by creation had the beginning of its existence from change, and has a kindred connection with the like mutation, for this reason He Who, as the prophetical writing says, "knoweth all things before they be" [Sus. 42], following out, or rather perceiving beforehand by His power of foreknowledge what, in a state of independence and freedom, is the tendency of the motion of the human will, as He saw, I say, what would be, He devised for His image the distinction of male and female, which has no reference to the Divine Archetype, but, as we have said, is an approximation to the less rational nature.

15. The cause, indeed, of this device, only those can know who were eyewitnesses of the truth and ministers of the Word; but we, imagining the truth, as far as we can, by means of conjectures and similitudes, do not set forth that which occurs to our mind authoritatively, but will place it in the form of a theoretical speculation before our kindly hearers.

16. What is it then which we understand concerning these matters? In saying that "God created man" the text indicates, by the indefinite character of the term, all humankind; for was not Adam here named together

with the creation, as the history tells us in what follows? Yet the name given to the human being created is not the particular, but the general name [for humankind as such]: thus we are led by the employment of the general name of our nature to some such view as this: that in the Divine foreknowledge and power all humanity is included in the first creation; for it is fitting for God not to regard any of the things made by Him as indeterminate, but that each existing thing should have some limit and measure prescribed by the wisdom of its Maker.

17. Now just as any particular human being is limited by bodily dimensions, and the peculiar size which is conjoined with the superficies of the body is the measure of that being's separate existence, so I think that the entire plenitude of humanity was included by the God of all, by His power of foreknowledge, as it were in one body, and that this is what the text teaches us which says, "God created man, in the image of God created He him." For the image is not in part of our nature, nor is the grace in any one of the things found in that nature, but this power extends equally to all the race: and a sign of this is that mind is implanted alike in all: for all have the power of understanding and deliberating, and of all else whereby the Divine nature finds its image in that which was made according to it: the human being that was manifested at the first creation of the world, and the one that shall be after the consummation of all, are alike: they equally bear in themselves the Divine image.

18. For this reason the whole race was spoken of as one human being, namely, that to God's power nothing is either past or future, but even that which we expect is comprehended, equally with what is at present existing, by the all-sustaining energy. Our whole nature, then, extending from the first to the last, is, so to say, one image of Him Who is; but the distinction of kind in male and female was added to His work last as I suppose, for the reason which follows.

Chapter 17

1. It is better for us however, perhaps, rather to inquire, before investigating this point, the solution of the question put forward by our adversaries; for they say that before the sin there is no account of birth, or of travail, or of the desire that tends to procreation, but when they were banished from Paradise after their sin, and the woman was condemned by the sentence of travail, Adam thus entered with his consort upon the intercourse of married life, and then took place the beginning of procreation. If, then, marriage did not exist in Paradise, nor travail, nor birth, they say that it follows as a necessary conclusion that human souls would not have existed in plurality had not the grace of immortality fallen away to mortality, and marriage preserved our race by means of descendants, introducing the offspring of the departing to take their place, so that in a certain way the sin that entered into the world was profitable for human life: for the human

race would have remained in the pair of the first-formed, had not the fear of death impelled their nature to provide succession.

2. Now here again the true answer, whatever it may be, can be clear to those only who, like Paul, have been instructed in the mysteries of Paradise; but our answer is as follows. When the Sadducees once argued against the doctrine of the resurrection, and brought forward, to establish their own opinion, that woman of many marriages, who had been wife to seven brethren, and thereupon inquired whose wife she will be after the resurrection, our Lord answered their argument so as not only to instruct the Sadducees, but also to reveal to all that come after them the mystery of the resurrection-life: "for in the resurrection," He says, "they neither marry, nor are given in marriage neither can they die any more, for they are equal to the angels, and are the children of God, being the children of the resurrection" [Luke 20:35]. Now the resurrection promises us nothing else than the restoration of the fallen to their ancient state; for the grace we look for is a certain return to the first life, bringing back again to Paradise him who was cast out from it. If then the life of those restored is closely related to that of the angels, it is clear that the life before the transgression was a kind of angelic life, and hence also our return to the ancient condition of our life is compared to the angels. Yet while, as has been said, there is no marriage among them, the armies of the angels are in countless myriads; for so Daniel declared in his visions: so, in the same way, if there had not come upon us as the result of sin a change for the worse, and removal from equality with the angels, neither should we have needed marriage that we might multiply but whatever the mode of increase in the angelic nature is (unspeakable and inconceivable by human conjectures, except that it assuredly exists), it would have operated also in the case of men, who were "made a little lower than the angels," to increase mankind to the measure determined by its Maker.

3. But if any one finds a difficulty in an inquiry as to the manner of the generation of souls, had humankind not needed the assistance of marriage, we shall ask him in turn, what is the mode of the angelic existence, how they exist in countless myriads, being one essence, and at the same time numerically many; for we shall be giving a fit answer to one who raises the question how human beings would have been without marriage, if we say, "as the angels are without marriage;" for the fact that humanity was in a like condition with them before the transgression is shown by the restoration to that state.

4. Now that we have thus cleared up these matters, let us return to our former point: how it was that after the making of His image God contrived for His work the distinction of male and female. I say that the preliminary speculation we have completed is of service for determining this question, for He Who brought all things into being and fashioned Man as a whole by His own will to the Divine image, did not wait to see the number of souls made up to its proper fullness by the gradual additions of those coming

after; but while looking upon the nature of man in its entirety and fullness by the exercise of His foreknowledge, and bestowing upon it a lot exalted and equal to the angels, since He saw beforehand by His all-seeing power the failure of their will to keep a direct course to what is good, and its consequent declension from the angelic life, in order that the multitude of human souls might not be cut short by its fall from that mode by which the angels were increased and multiplied, for this reason, I say, He formed for our nature that contrivance for increase which befits those who had fallen into sin, implanting in mankind, instead of the angelic majesty of nature, that animal and irrational mode by which they now succeed one another.

5. Hence also, it seems to me, the great David pitying the misery of man mourns over his nature with such words as these, that, "man being in honor knew it not" (meaning by "honor" the equality with the angels), therefore, he says, "he is compared to the beasts that have no understanding, and made like unto them" [Ps. 49:13, LXX]. For he truly was made like the beasts, who received in his nature the present mode of transient generation, on account of his inclination to material things.

Chapter 18

1. For I think that from this beginning all our passions issue as from a spring, and pour their flood over man's life; and an evidence of my words is the kinship of passions which appears alike in ourselves and in the brutes; for it is not allowable to ascribe the first beginnings of our constitutional liability to passion to that human nature which was fashioned in the Divine likeness; but as brute life first entered into the world, and human beings, for the reason already mentioned, took something of their nature (I mean the mode of generation), they accordingly took at the same time a share of the other attributes contemplated in that nature; for the likeness of humanity to God is not found in anger, nor is pleasure a mark of the superior nature; cowardice also, and boldness, and the desire of gain, and the dislike of loss, and all the like, are far removed from that stamp which indicates Divinity.

2. These attributes, then, human nature took to itself from the side of the brutes; for those qualities with which brute life was armed for self-preservation, when transferred to human life, became passions; for the carnivorous animals are preserved by their anger, and those which breed largely by their love of pleasure; cowardice preserves the weak, fear that which is easily taken by more powerful animals, and greediness those of great bulk; and to miss anything that tends to pleasure is for the brutes a matter of pain. All these and the like affections entered man's composition by reason of the animal mode of generation.

3. I may be allowed to describe the human image by comparison with some wonderful piece of modeling. For, as one may see in models those carved shapes which the artificers of such things contrive for the wonder

of beholders, tracing out upon a single head two forms of faces; so human beings seem to me to bear a double likeness to opposite things—being molded in the Divine element of their mind to the Divine beauty, but bearing, in the passionate impulses that arise in them, a likeness to the brute nature; while often even their reason is rendered brutish, and obscures the better element by the worse through its inclination and disposition towards what is irrational; for whenever human beings drag down their mental energy to these affections, and force their reason to become the servant of their passions, there takes place a sort of conversion of the good stamp in them into the irrational image, their whole nature being traced anew after that [irrational] design, as their reason, so to say, cultivates the beginnings of their passions, and gradually multiplies them; for once it lends its cooperation to passion, it produces a plenteous and abundant crop of evils.

4. Thus our love of pleasure took its beginning from our being made like to the irrational creation, and was increased by the transgressions of human beings, becoming the parent of so many varieties of sins arising from pleasure as we cannot find among the irrational animals. Thus the rising of anger in us is indeed akin to the impulse of the brutes; but it grows by the alliance of thought: for thence come malignity, envy, deceit, conspiracy, hypocrisy; all these are the result of the evil husbandry of the mind; for if the passion were divested of the aid it receives from thought, the anger that is left behind is short-lived and not sustained, like a bubble, perishing straightway as soon as it comes into being. Thus the greediness of swine introduces covetousness, and the high spirit of the horse becomes the origin of pride; and all the particular forms that proceed from the want of reason in brute nature become vice by the evil use of the mind.

5. So, likewise, on the contrary, if reason instead assumes sway over such emotions, each of them is transmuted to a form of virtue; for anger produces courage, terror caution, fear obedience, hatred aversion from vice, the power of love the desire for what is truly beautiful; high spirit in our character raises our thought above the passions, and keeps it from bondage to what is base; yea, the great Apostle, even, praises such a form of mental elevation when he bids us constantly to "think those things that are above" [Col. 3:2]; and so we find that every such motion, when elevated by loftiness of mind, is conformed to the beauty of the Divine image.

6. But the other impulse is greater, as the tendency of sin is heavy and downward; for the ruling element of our soul is more inclined to be dragged downwards by the weight of the irrational nature than is the heavy and earthy element to be exalted by the loftiness of the intellect; hence the misery that encompasses us often causes the Divine gift to be forgotten, and spreads the passions of the flesh, like some ugly mask, over the beauty of the image.

7. Those, therefore, are in some sense excusable, who do not admit, when they look upon such cases, that the Divine form is there; yet we may

behold the Divine image in human beings by the medium of those who have ordered their lives aright. For if the person who is subject to passion, and carnal, makes it incredible that humanity was adorned, as it were, with Divine beauty, surely the person of lofty virtue and pure from pollution will confirm you in the better conception of human nature.

8. For instance (for it is better to make our argument clear by an illustration), one of those noted for wickedness—some Jeconiah, say, or some other of evil memory—has obliterated the beauty of his nature by the pollution of wickedness; yet in Moses and in people like him the form of the image was kept pure. Now where the beauty of the form has not been obscured, there is made plain the faithfulness of the saying that humankind is an image of God.

9. It may be, however, that some one feels shame at the fact that our life, like that of the brutes, is sustained by food, and for this reason deems humankind unworthy of being supposed to have been framed in the image of God; but he may expect that freedom from this function will one day be bestowed upon our nature in the life we look for; for, as the Apostle says, "the Kingdom of God is not meat and drink" [Rom. 14:17]; and the Lord declared that "man shall not live by bread alone, but by every word that proceedeth out of the mouth of God" [Matt. 4:4]. Further, as the resurrection holds forth to us a life equal with the angels, and with the angels there is no food, there is sufficient ground for believing that human beings, who will live in like fashion with the angels, will be released from such a function. . . .

Chapter 28

1. It is perhaps not beyond our present subject to discuss the question which has been raised in the churches touching soul and body. Some of those before our time who have dealt with the question of "principles" think it right to say that souls have a previous existence as a people in a society of their own, and that among them also there are standards of vice and of virtue, and that the soul there, which abides in goodness, remains without experience of conjunction with the body; but if it does depart from its communion with good, it falls down to this lower life, and so comes to be in a body. Others, on the contrary, marking the order of the making of man as stated by Moses, say, that the soul is second to the body in order of time, since God first took dust from the earth and formed man, and then animated the being thus formed by His breath [Gen. 2:7]: and by this argument they prove that the flesh is more noble than the soul; that which was previously formed than that which was afterwards infused into it: for they say that the soul was made for the body, that the thing formed might not be without breath and motion; and that everything that is made for something else is surely less precious than that for which it is made, as the Gospel tells us that "the soul is more than meat and the body than raiment" [Matt. 6:25], because the latter things exist for the sake of the

former—for the soul was not made for meat nor our bodies for raiment, but when the former things were already in being the latter were provided for their needs.

2. Since then the doctrine involved in both these theories is open to criticism—the doctrine alike of those who ascribe to souls a fabulous pre-existence in a special state, and of those who think they were created at a later time than the bodies, it is perhaps necessary to leave none of the statements contained in the doctrines without examination: yet to engage and wrestle with the doctrines on each side completely, and to reveal all the absurdities involved in the theories, would need a large expenditure both of argument and of time; we shall, however, briefly survey as best we can each of the views mentioned, and then resume our subject.

3. Those who stand by the former doctrine, and assert that the state of souls is prior to their life in the flesh, do not seem to me to be clear from the fabulous doctrines of the heathen which they hold on the subject of successive reincarnation: for if one should search carefully, he will find that their doctrine is of necessity brought down to this. They tell us that one of their sages said that he, being one and the same person, was born a man, and afterwards assumed the form of a woman, and flew about with the birds, and grew as a bush, and obtained the life of an aquatic creature; and he who said these things of himself did not, so far as I can judge, go far from the truth: for such doctrines as this of saying that one soul passed through so many changes are really fitting for the chatter of frogs or jackdaws, or the stupidity of fishes, or the insensibility of trees.

4. And of such absurdity the cause is this—the supposition of the pre-existence of souls for the first principle of such doctrine leads on the argument by consequence to the next and adjacent stage, until it astonishes us by reaching this point. For if the soul, being severed from the more exalted state by some wickedness after having once, as they say, tasted corporeal life, again becomes a man, and if the life in the flesh is, as may be presumed, acknowledged to be, in comparison with the eternal and incorporeal life, more subject to passion, it naturally follows that that which comes to be in a life such as to contain more occasions of sin, is both placed in a region of greater wickedness and rendered more subject to passion than before (now passion in the human soul is a conformity to the likeness of the irrational); and that being brought into close connection with this, it descends to the brute nature: and that when it has once set out on its way through wickedness, it does not cease its advance towards evil even when found in an irrational condition: for a halt in evil is the beginning of the impulse towards virtue, and in irrational creatures virtue does not exist. Thus it will of necessity be continually changed for the worse, always proceeding to what is more degraded and always finding out what is worse than the nature in which it is: and just as the sensible nature is lower than the rational, so too there is a descent from this to the insensible.

5. Now so far in its course their doctrine, even if it does overstep the bounds of truth, at all events derives one absurdity from another by a kind of logical sequence: but from this point onwards their teaching takes the form of incoherent fable. Strict inference points to the complete destruction of the soul; for that which has once fallen from the exalted state will be unable to halt at any measure of wickedness, but will pass by means of its relation with the passions from rational to irrational, and from the latter state will be transferred to the insensibility of plants; and on the insensible there borders, so to say, the inanimate; and on this again follows the non-existent, so that absolutely by this train of reasoning they will have the soul to pass into nothing: thus a return once more to the better state is impossible for it: and yet they make the soul return from a bush to the man: they therefore prove that the life in a bush is more precious than an incorporeal state.

6. It has been shown that the process of deterioration which takes place in the soul will probably be extended downwards; and lower than the insensible we find the inanimate, to which, by consequence, the principle of their doctrine brings the soul: but as they will not have this, they either exclude the soul from insensibility, or, if they are to bring it back to human life, they must, as has been said, declare the life of a tree to be preferable to the original state—if, that is, the fall towards vice took place from the one, and the return towards virtue takes place from the other.

7. Thus this doctrine of theirs, which maintains that souls have a life by themselves before their life in the flesh, and that they are by reason of wickedness bound to their bodies, is shown to have neither beginning nor conclusion: and as for those who assert that the soul is of later creation than the body, their absurdity was already demonstrated above.

8. The doctrine of both, then, is equally to be rejected; but I think that we ought to direct our own doctrine in the way of truth between these theories: and this doctrine is that we are not to suppose, according to the error of the heathen that the souls that revolve with the motion of the universe weighed down by some wickedness, fall to earth by inability to keep up with the swiftness of the motion of the spheres.

Chapter 29

1. Nor again are we in our doctrine to begin by making up a human being like a clay figure, and to say that the soul came into being for the sake of this; for surely in that case the intellectual nature would be shown to be less precious than the clay figure. But as the human being is one, the being consisting of soul and body, we are to suppose that the beginning of human existence is one, common to both parts, so that the individual should not be found to be antecedent and posterior to himself, if the bodily element were first in point of time, and the other were a later addition; but we are to say that in the power of God's foreknowledge (according to the doctrine laid

down a little earlier in our discourse), all the fullness of human nature had pre-existence (and to this the prophetic writing bears witness, which says that God "knoweth all things before they be" [Sus. 42]), and in the creation of individuals not to place the one element before the other, neither the soul before the body, nor the contrary, that the human being may not be at strife against himself, by being divided by the difference in point of time.

2. For as our nature is conceived as twofold, according to the apostolic teaching, made up of the visible human being and the hidden human being, if the one came first and the other supervened, the power of Him that made us will be shown to be in some way imperfect, as not being completely sufficient for the whole task at once, but dividing the work, and busying itself with each of the halves in turn.

3. But just as we say that in wheat, or in any other grain, the whole form of the plant is potentially included—the leaves, the stalk, the joints, the grain, the beard (and do not say in our account of its nature that any of these things has pre-existence, or comes into being before the others, but that the power abiding in the seed is manifested in a certain natural order, not by any means that another nature is infused into it)—in the same way we suppose the human germ to possess the potentiality of its nature, sown with it at the first start of its existence, and that it is unfolded and manifested by a natural sequence as it proceeds to its perfect state, not employing anything external to itself as a stepping-stone to perfection, but itself advancing its own self in due course to the perfect state; so that it is not true to say either that the soul exists before the body, or that the body exists without the soul, but that there is one beginning of both, which according to the heavenly view was laid as their foundation in the original will of God; according to the other, came into existence on the occasion of generation.

4. For as we cannot discern the articulation of the limbs in that which is implanted for the conception of the body before it begins to take form, so neither is it possible to perceive in the same the properties of the soul before they advance to operation; and just as no one would doubt that the thing so implanted is fashioned into the different varieties of limbs and interior organs, not by the importation of any other power from without, but by the power which resides in it transforming it to this manifestation of energy, so also we may by like reasoning equally suppose in the case of the soul that even if it is not visibly recognized by any manifestations of activity it nonetheless is there; for even the form of the future human being is there potentially, but is concealed because it is not possible that it should be made visible before the necessary sequence of events allows it; so also the soul is there, even though it is not visible, and will be manifested by means of its own proper and natural operation, as it advances concurrently with the bodily growth.

5. For since it is not from a dead body that the potentiality for conception is secreted, but from one which is animate and alive, we hence affirm

that it is reasonable that we should not suppose that what is sent forth from a living body to be the occasion of life is itself dead and inanimate; for in the flesh that which is inanimate is surely dead; and the condition of death arises by the withdrawal of the soul. Would not one therefore in this case be asserting that withdrawal is antecedent to possession—if, that is, he should maintain that the inanimate state which is the condition of death is antecedent to the soul? And if any one should seek for a still clearer evidence of the life of that particle which becomes the beginning of the living creature in its formation, it is possible to obtain an idea on this point from other signs also, by which what is animate is distinguished from what is dead. For in the case of human beings we consider it an evidence of life that one is warm and operative and in motion, but the chill and motionless state in the case of bodies is nothing else than deadness.

6. Since then we see that of which we are speaking to be warm and operative, we thereby draw the further inference that it is not inanimate; but as, in respect of its corporeal part, we do not say that it is flesh, and bones, and hair, and all that we observe in the human being, but that potentially it is each of these things, yet does not visibly appear to be so; so also of the part which belongs to the soul, the elements of rationality, and desire, and anger, and all the powers of the soul are not yet visible; yet we assert that they have their place in it, and that the energies of the soul also grow with the subject in a manner similar to the formation and perfection of the body.

7. For just as human beings when perfectly developed have a specially marked activity of the soul, so at the beginning of their existence they show in themselves that co-operation of the soul which is suitable and conformable to existing need, in its preparing for itself its proper dwelling-place by means of the implanted matter; for we do not suppose it possible that the soul is adapted to a strange building, just as it is not possible that the seal impressed on wax should be fitted to an engraving that does not agree with it.

8. For as the body proceeds from a very small original to the perfect state, so also the operation of the soul, growing in correspondence with the subject, gains and increases with it. For at its first formation there comes first of all its power of growth and nutriment alone, as though it were some root buried in the ground; for the limited nature of the recipient does not admit of more; then, as the plant comes forth to the light and shows its shoot to the sun, the gift of sensibility blossoms in addition, but when at last it is ripened and has grown up to its proper height, the power of reason begins to shine forth like a fruit, not appearing in its whole vigor all at once, but by care increasing with the perfection of the instrument, bearing always as much fruit as the powers of the subject allow.

9. If, however, you seek to trace the operation of the soul in the formation of the body, "take heed to thyself" [Deut. 4:23], as Moses says, and you

will read, as in a book, the history of the works of the soul; for nature itself expounds to you, more clearly than any discourse, the varied occupations of the soul in the body, alike in general and in particular acts of construction.

10. But I deem it superfluous to declare at length in words what is to be found in ourselves, as though we were expounding some wonder that lay beyond our boundaries. Who that looks on himself needs words to teach him his own nature? For it is possible for one who considers the mode of his own life, and learns how closely concerned the body is in every vital operation, to know in what the vegetative principle of the soul was occupied on the occasion of the first formation of that which was beginning its existence; so that hereby also it is clear to those who have given any attention to the matter, that the thing which was implanted by separation from the living body for the production of the living being was not a thing dead or inanimate.

11. Moreover we plant in the ground the kernels of fruits, and portions torn from roots, not deprived by death of the vital power which naturally resides in them, but preserving in themselves, hidden indeed, yet surely living, the property of their prototype; the earth that surrounds them does not implant such a power from without, infusing it from itself (for surely then even dead wood would proceed to growth), but it makes that manifest which resides in them, nourishing it by its own moisture, perfecting the plant into root, and bark, and pith, and shoots of branches, which could not happen were not a natural power implanted with it, which drawing to itself from its surroundings its kindred and proper nourishment, becomes a bush, or a tree, or an ear of grain, or some plant of the class of shrubs.

SELECTION **3**

John Chrysostom

Homilies Concerning the Statues

John Chrysostom (ca. 350–407) spent most of his life in Antioch, but his reputation for eloquence ("Chrysostom" means "golden mouthed" in Greek) led to his not altogether willing promotion to the office of Patriarch of Constantinople. There his criticism of the powerful made him many enemies, with the result that he was deposed and banished, eventually dying in exile. Yet his reputation for holiness and the brilliance of his sermons resulted in his being canonized and revered as a doctor of the church by Greek and Latin Christians alike.

The following extract is taken from the seventh and last of Chrysostom's *Homilies Concerning the Statues*, which date from 397, toward the end of his career in Antioch. They were given in response to local riots that had led to the destruction of statues of the Emperor Theodosius I and other members of the imperial family. Though the sermons were effective in their immediate aim of inducing sufficient repentance to avert the full force of imperial punishment of the city, they also served as an occasion for fairly wide-ranging theological reflection, including this interpretation of humanity's creation "in the image of God" in functional terms, as referring to human dominion over the rest of creation.

> From *Chrysostom: On the Priesthood, Ascetic Treatises, Select Homilies and Letters, Homilies on the Statues*, NPNF[1] 9:391–94.

3. What then is this introduction? "In the beginning God made the heaven and the earth, and the earth was invisible, and unformed, and darkness was upon the face of the abyss" [Gen. 1:2]. Do these words seem to some of you incapable of affording consolation under distress? Is it not an historical narrative, and an instruction about the creation?

Would you then that I show the consolation that is hidden in this saying? Arouse yourselves then, and attend with earnestness to the things which are about to be spoken. For when you hear that God made the heaven, the earth, the sea, the air, the waters, the multitude of stars, the two great lights, the plants, the quadrupeds, the swimming and the flying animals, and all things without exception which you see, for you, and for your safety and honor; do you not straightway take comfort and receive this as the strongest proof of the love of God, when you think that He produced such a world as this, so fair, so vast and wonderful, for such a puny being as yourself! When therefore you hear that, "In the beginning God made the heaven and the earth," run not hastily over the declaration; but traverse in thy mind the breadth of the earth; and reflect how He hath spread out so sumptuous and exquisite a table for us, and provided us with such abundant gladness. And this is, indeed, the most marvelous thing, that He gave us not such a world as this in payment for services done; or as a recompense for good works; but at the very time He formed us, He honored our race with this kingdom. For He said, "Let us make man after our image, and after our likeness" [Gen. 1:26]. What is the sense of this, "after our image, and after our likeness?" The image of government is that which is meant; and as there is no one in heaven superior to God, so let there be none upon earth superior to man. This then is one, and the first respect, in which He did him honor; by making him after His own image; and secondly, by providing us with this principality, not as a payment for services, but making it entirely the gift of His own love toward man; and thirdly, in that He conferred it upon us as a thing of nature. For of governments there are some natural, and others which are elective; natural as of the lion over the quadrupeds, or as that of the eagle over the birds; elective, as that of an Emperor over us; for he doth not reign over his fellow-servants by any natural authority. Therefore it is that he oftentimes loses his sovereignty. For such are things which are not naturally inherent; they readily admit of change and transposition. But not so with the lion; he rules by nature over the quadrupeds, as the eagle doth over birds. The character of sovereignty is, therefore, constantly allotted to his race; and no lion hath ever been seen deprived of it. Such a kind of sovereignty God bestowed upon us from the beginning, and set us over all things. And not only in this respect did He confer honor upon our nature, but also, by the very eminence of the spot in which we were placed, fixing upon Paradise as our choice dwelling, and bestowing the gift of reason, and an immortal soul.

4. But I would not speak of these things: for I say that such was the abundance of God's care, that we may know His goodness, and His love towards man, not only from the way in which He hath honored, but also from the way in which He hath punished us. And this, I especially exhort you to consider with attention, that God is alike good, not only whilst He is treating us with honor and beneficence, but also whilst He is punishing and chastising. And whether we should have to carry on our contest and combat against the heathen, or against the heretics, respecting the loving-kindness and goodness of God, we shall make His goodness evident, not only from the cases in which He bestows honor, but also from the cases in which He inflicts punishment. For if He is good only whilst honoring us, and not good whilst punishing us, He were but half good. But this is not the case. God forbid! Among men this may probably happen, when they inflict punishments in anger and passion; but God being free from passion, whether He exercise kindness, or whether He punish, He is alike good. Nor less does the threat of hell serve to show His goodness, than the promise of the kingdom. But how? I answer. If He had not threatened hell, if He had not prepared punishment, there are not many who would have attained the kingdom. For the promise of good things doth not so strongly induce the multitude to virtue; as doth the threat of evil things compel by fear, and arouse them to the care of the soul. So that, although hell be the opposite of the kingdom of heaven, yet each hath respect to the same end—the salvation of men; the one alluring to itself, the other driving them towards its opposite, and by the operation of fear correcting those who are carelessly disposed.

5. I do not enlarge upon this subject without reason; but because there are many who often, when famines, and droughts, and wars take place, or when the wrath of an Emperor overtakes them, or when any other unexpected events of this kind happen, deceive the simpler class by saying, that these things are unworthy of the Providence of God.

I am therefore compelled to dwell on this part of my discourse, that we may not be beguiled by words, but that we may plainly perceive, that whether He brings upon us a famine, or a war, or any calamity, whatsoever,

He doth it out of His exceeding great care and kindness. For even those fathers, who especially love their offspring, will forbid them the table, and inflict stripes, and punish them by disgrace, and in endless other ways of this kind correct their children when they are disorderly; yet are they nevertheless fathers, not only while doing them honor, but when acting thus; yea, they are preeminently fathers when they act thus. But if men, who are frequently carried away beyond what is meet by the force of angry feelings, are yet held to punish those whom they love, not from cruelty and inhumanity, but from a kind care and regard; much rather is it proper to be thus minded concerning God; who in the exceeding abundance of His goodness, far transcends every degree of paternal fondness. And that you may not suppose that what I say is a mere conjecture, let us, I pray you, direct our discourse to the Scripture itself. When man, then, had been deceived and beguiled by the wicked demon, let us observe how God treated him, after his committing so great a sin. Did He then altogether destroy him? Yet the reason of the thing in justice demanded this, that one who had displayed nothing that was good, but, after enjoying so much favor, had waxed wanton even from the very first, should be made away with, and utterly destroyed; yet God acted not so; neither did He regard with disgust and aversion him who had been so ungrateful towards his Benefactor, but He comes to him as a physician cometh to a sick man.

6. Do not, O beloved, pass over unthinkingly, what has just been said! but consider what an act it was, not to send an angel, or archangel, or any other of his fellow-servants, but that the Lord Himself should have descended to him who had fallen from the right way, and should have raised him when thus cast down; and should have approached him, One to one, as a friend comes to a friend when he is unfortunate, and is plunged in great distress! For that He acted thus out of His great kindness, the very words too which He spoke to him evidently show His ineffable affection. And why do I say, *all* the words? The first utterance signifies at once His tenderness. For He said not, what it was probable a person treated so contemptuously would say, "O wicked, yea most wicked man! When you had enjoyed so great favor from Me, and had been honored with such a sovereignty, being exalted above all the creatures upon the earth for no merit of your own; and having received in actual deeds the pledges of My care, and a true manifestation of My Providence, didst thou esteem a wicked and pestiferous demon, the enemy of thy salvation, to be worthy of more credit than thy Lord and Benefactor? What proof did he give of regard for thee, like that which I have done? Did I not make for thee the heaven, the earth, the sea, the sun, the moon, and all the stars? For truly none of the angels needed this work of creation; but for you, and for your recreation, I made so great and excellent a world; and did you esteem mere words alone, a false engagement, and a promise full of deceit, as more worthy to be believed than the kindness and providence that was manifested by deeds; that you gave yourself over

to him, and did trample My laws under foot!" These words, and more of this kind, one who had been treated contemptuously would probably say. But God acted not so; but quite in the contrary manner. For by His first word He at once raised him up from his dejection, and gave the fearful and trembling man confidence, by being the first Himself to call him, or rather, not by merely calling him first, but by addressing him by his own familiar appellation, and saying, "Adam, where art thou?" [Gen. 3:9]. Thus He showed His tenderness, and the great regard He had for him. For you must all know, that this is a mark of intimate friendship. And thus those who call upon the dead are wont to do, continually repeating their names. And so, on the other hand, those who entertain hatred and enmity against any, cannot bear to mention the very names of those who have aggrieved them. Saul, for instance, though he had sustained no injury from David, but had wronged him exceedingly, since he abhorred and hated him, could not endure to mention his proper name; but when all were seated together, not seeing David to be present, what said he? He said not, "Where is David?" but, "Where is the son of Jesse?" [1 Sam. 20:27] calling him by his father's name. And again, the Jews did the same with respect to Christ, for since they abhorred and hated Him, they did not say, "Where is Christ?" but, "Where is that man?" [John 7:35; 9:29].

7. But God, willing to show even by this that sin had not quenched His tenderness, nor disobedience taken away His favor toward him, and that He still exercised His Providence and care for the fallen one, said, "Adam, where art thou?" not being ignorant of the place where he was, but because the mouth of those who have sinned is closed up; sin turning the tongue backward, and conscience taking hold of it; so that such persons remain speechless, held fast in silence as by a kind of chain. And God wishing therefore to invite him to freedom of utterance, and to give him confidence, and to lead him to make an apology for his offences, in order that he might obtain some forgiveness, was Himself the first to call; cutting off much of Adam's distress by the familiar appellation, and dispelling his fear, and opening by this address the mouth that was shut. Hence also it was that he said, "Adam, where art thou?" "I left thee," says he, "in one situation, and I find thee in another. I left thee in confidence and glory; and I now find thee in disgrace and silence!" And observe the care of God in this instance. He called not Eve; He called not the serpent; but him who had sinned in the lightest degree of all, he brings first to the tribunal, in order that beginning from him who was able to find some degree of excuse, He might pass a more merciful sentence, even against her who had sinned the most. And judges, indeed, do not deign to make inquiry in their own person of their fellow-servants, and those who are partakers of a common nature with them, but putting forward some one of their attendants to intervene, they instruct him to convey their own questions to the criminal; and through him they say and hear whatever they wish, when they exam-

ine the offenders. But God had no need of a go-between in dealing with man; but Himself in His own person at once judges and consoles him. And not only this is wonderful, but also that he corrects the crimes that had been committed. For judges in general, when they find thieves and grave-robbers, do not consider how they may make them better, but how they may make them pay the penalty of the offences committed. But God, quite on the contrary, when He finds a sinner, considers not how He may make him pay the penalty, but how He may amend him, and make him better, and invincible for the future. So that God is at the same time a Judge, a Physician, and a Teacher; for as a Judge He examines, and as a Physician He amends, and as a Teacher He instructs those who have sinned, directing them unto all spiritual wisdom.

SELECTION 4

Maximus the Confessor

Difficulty 41

Although Maximus (580–662) remained a simple monk throughout his career, he was the leading theologian of his age, best known for his defense of the doctrine that Christ possessed a human will against the proponents of monothelitism, who argued that Christ had a divine will only. Though his position was ultimately vindicated at the Third Council of Constantinople in 680 as integral to the church's confession that Christ was fully human as well as fully divine, in his own lifetime Maximus was condemned by the imperial authorities to mutilation and exile, thereby earning the title "Confessor."

The following text predates Maximus's involvement in the monothelite controversy and is one of a series in which the Confessor seeks to explain difficult passages in the writings of earlier theologians. In this case a line from a sermon of Gregory of Nazianzus—"And natures are instituted afresh, and God became man"—serves as the occasion for an extended reflection on the structure of creation and humanity's place within it. Central to Maximus's thinking is the idea that each creature has been endowed by God with its own inner principle, or *logos*, that defines both its distinctiveness from and its relationship to all other creatures. Humanity is the linchpin by means of which the various orders of creation find their unity under God. In the fall humanity betrays this destiny, causing the natural differences among creatures to become the basis for division and mutual opposition. God therefore assumes human nature in Christ in order to renew that nature and thereby bring all creation to its destined unity under God, with the many created *logoi* finding their place within the one divine Logos.

From *Maximus the Confessor*, ed. Andrew Louth (New York: Routledge, 1996), 155–63.

"And natures are instituted afresh, and God becomes man."[1]

The saints have received the many divine mysteries from "those who became attendants and ministers of the word" (Luke 1:2), and were immediately initiated into knowledge of reality in accordance with the tradition passed down to them from those before them. They say that the substance of everything that has come into being is divided into five divisions.[2] The first of these divides from the uncreated nature the universal created nature, which receives its being from becoming. For they say that God in his goodness has made the radiant orderly arrangement of everything that is, and that it is not immediately plain what and how it is, and that therefore the division that divides creation from God is to be called ignorance. For what it is that naturally divides these one from another, so that they may not be united in a single essence, since they do not have one and the same *logos*, they grant to be ineffable. The second division is that in accordance with which the whole nature that receives being from creation is divided by God into that which is perceived by the mind and that perceived by the senses. The third is that in accordance with which the nature perceived by the senses is divided into heaven and earth. The fourth is that in accordance with which the earth is divided into paradise and the inhabited world [the *oikoumene*], and the fifth, that in accordance with which the human person, which is the laboratory in which everything is concentrated and in itself naturally mediates between the extremities of each division, having been drawn into everything in a good and fitting way through becoming, is divided into male and female.

For humanity clearly has the power of naturally uniting at the mean point of each division since it is related to the extremities of each division in its own parts. Through that capacity it can come to be the way of fulfillment of what is divided and be openly instituted in itself as the great mystery of the divine purpose. It proceeds harmoniously to each of the extremities in the things that are, from what is close at hand to what is remote, from what is worse to what is better, lifting up to God and fully accomplishing union. For this reason the human person was introduced last among beings,[3] as a kind of natural bond[4] mediating between the universal poles through their

---

1. From St. Gregory of Nazianzus, *Sermon* 39.13, on the Feast of Lights (i.e., the Theophany or Epiphany), in *PG* 36.384D.
2. For these divisions, cf. Gregory of Nyssa, *Against Eunomius* 1.270–72; 3.6.62–67 in Gregorii Nysemi, *Contra Eunomium Libri*, 2 vols., 2nd ed., ed. W. Jaeger (Leiden: E. J. Brill, 1960), 1:105–6; 2:66–67.
3. See Gregory of Nyssa, *On the Making of Humankind* 2, in *PG* 44.133A; ET, *NPNF*[2], 5:390.
4. *Syndesmos*: a key term in Maximus' theology, used by Nemesius of Emesa, *On Human Nature* 1, in Nemesii Emesini, *De natura hominis*, ed. M. Morani (Leipzig: Teubner Verlagsgesellschaft, 1987).

proper parts, and leading into unity in itself those things that are naturally set apart from one another by a great interval.[5]

In order to bring about the union of everything with God as its cause, the human person begins first of all with its own division, and then, ascending through the intermediate steps by order and rank, it reaches the end of its high ascent, which passes through all things in search of unity, to God, in whom there is no division. It accomplishes this by shaking off every natural property of sexual differentiation into male and female by the most dispassionate relationship to divine virtue. This sexual differentiation clearly depends in no way on the primordial reason behind the divine purpose concerning human generation.[6] Thus it is shown to be and becomes simply a human person in accordance with the divine purpose, no longer divided by being called male or female. It is no longer separated as it now is into parts, and it achieves this through the perfect knowledge, as I said, of its own *logos*, in accordance with which it is.[7] Then, by a way of life proper and fitting to Saints, the human person unites paradise and the inhabited world to make one earth, no longer is it experienced as divided according to the difference of its parts, but rather as gathered together, since no introduction at all of partition is allowed. Then, through a life identical in every way through virtue with that of the angels,[8] so far as is possible to human beings, the human person unites heaven and earth making the whole of creation perceived through the senses one with itself and undivided, not dividing it spatially by intervals in any way, since the human person has become as subtle as spirit and is no longer tied to earth by any bodily weight. Nor is it obstructed in its ascent to the heavens thanks to the perfect invisibility to these things of the mind that is genuinely hastening towards God, and wisely stretches out towards him step by step, as on an ordinary path, naturally overcoming any obstacles that stand in its way. And then the human person unites what is perceived by the mind and what is perceived by the senses with each other by achieving equality with the angels in its manner of knowing, and thus makes the whole creation one single creation, no longer divided by what it can know and what it cannot know, through its equality to the angels lacking nothing in their knowledge and understanding of the *logoi* in the things that exist, according to which the infinite pouring out of the gift of true wisdom inviolably and without intermediary furnishes, so far as is permitted to those who are worthy a concept of God

---

5. *Diastēma*: another key term of Maximus.
6. Cf. Gregory of Nyssa, *On the Making of Humankind* 16 in PG 44.181A-B; ET, NPNF[2], 5:404-6 [see pp. 105-9 above].
7. It sounds odd to refer to a human person as "it," but Maximus is talking about a human person transcending sexual differentiation, which would be obscured by the use of "he" or "she."
8. Cf. Gregory of Nyssa, *On the Making of Humankind* 17 in PG 44.189A and D, and frequently elsewhere; ET, NPNF[2], 5:406-7 [see pp. 109-11 above].

beyond understanding or explanation. And finally, beyond all these, the human person unites the created nature with the uncreated through love (O the wonder of God's love for us human beings!), showing them to be one and the same through the possession of grace, the whole [creation] wholly interpenetrated[9] by God, and become completely whatever God is, save at the level of being, and receiving to itself the whole of God himself, and acquiring as a kind of prize for its ascent to God the most unique God himself, as the end of the movement of everything that moves towards it, and the firm and unmoved rest of everything that is carried towards it, being the undetermined and infinite limit and definition of every definition and law and ordinance, of reason and mind and nature.

Since then the human person is not moved naturally, as it was fashioned to do, around the unmoved, that is its own beginning (I mean God), but contrary to nature is voluntarily moved in ignorance around those things that are beneath it, to which it has been divinely subjected, and since it has abused the natural power of uniting what is divided, that was given to it at its generation, so as to separate what is united, therefore "natures have been instituted afresh," and in a paradoxical way beyond nature that which is completely unmoved by nature is moved immovably around that which by nature is moved, and God becomes a human being, in order to save lost humanity. Through himself he has, in accordance with nature, united the fragments of the universal nature of the all, manifesting the universal *logoi* that have come forth for the particulars, by which the union of the divided naturally comes about, and thus he fulfils the great purpose of God the Father, "to recapitulate everything both in heaven and earth in himself" (Eph. 1:10), "in whom everything has been created" (Col. 1:16). Indeed being in himself the universal union of all, he has started with our division and become the perfect human being, having from us, on our account, and in accordance with our nature, everything that we are and lacking nothing, "apart from sin" (Heb. 4:15), and having no need of the natural intercourse of marriage. In this way he showed, I think, that there was perhaps another way, foreknown by God, for human beings to increase, if the first human being had kept the commandment and not cast himself down to an animal state by abusing his own proper powers. Thus God-made-man has done away with the difference and division of nature into male and female, which human nature in no way needed for generation, as some hold, and without which it would perhaps have been possible.[10] There was no necessity for these things to have lasted forever. "For in Christ Jesus, says the divine Apostle, there is neither male nor female" (Gal. 3:28). Then having sanctified the world we inhabit by his own humanly-fitting way of

---

9. *Perichōrēsas*: used also in the Greek tradition to express the interpenetration of the natures of Christ, and the persons of the Trinity (cf. Latin *circumincessio*).

10. Cf. Gregory of Nyssa, *On the Making of Humankind* 17, 22 in *PG* 44.189A–B, 205A; ET, *NPNF*², 5:406–7 [see pp. 109–11 above], 411–13.

life he opened a clear way into paradise after his death, as, without a lie, he promised the thief, "Today, you will be with me in paradise" (Luke 23:43). Then, since there was for him no longer any difference between paradise and the world we inhabit, he again made this clear to his disciples when he was with them after his resurrection from the dead, showing that the world is one and is not divided in itself, preserving the *logos* in accordance with which it exists free from any division caused by difference. Then by his ascension into heaven, he clearly united heaven and earth, and with his earthly body that is of the same nature and consubstantial with ours he entered into heaven and showed that the whole nature that can be perceived through the senses is, by the most universal *logos* of its being, one, thus obscuring the peculiar nature of the division which cuts it into two. Then, in addition to this, by passing with his soul and body, that is, with the whole of our nature, through all the divine and intelligible ranks of heaven, he united the sensible and the intelligible and showed the convergence of the whole of creation with the One according to its most original and universal *logos*, which is completely undivided and at rest in itself. And finally, considered in his humanity, he goes to God himself, having clearly "appeared," as it is written, "in the presence of God" the Father "on our behalf" (Heb. 9:24), as a human being. As Word, he cannot be separated in any way at all from the Father; as man, he has fulfilled, in word and truth, with unchangeable obedience, everything that, as God, he has predetermined is to take place, and has accomplished the whole will of God the Father on our behalf. For we had ruined by misuse the power that had been naturally given us from the beginning for this purpose. First he united us in himself by removing the difference between male and female, and instead of men and women, in whom above all this manner of division is beheld, he showed us as properly and truly to be simply human beings, thoroughly transfigured in accordance with him, and bearing his intact and completely unadulterated image, touched by no trace at all of corruption. With us and through us he encompasses the whole creation through its intermediaries and the extremities through their own parts. He binds about himself each with the other, tightly and indissolubly, paradise and the inhabited world, heaven and earth, things sensible and things intelligible, since he possesses like us sense and soul and mind, by which, as parts, he assimilates himself by each of the extremities to what is universally akin to each in the previously mentioned manner. Thus he divinely recapitulates the universe in himself, showing that the whole creation exists as one, like another human being, completed by the gathering together of its parts one with another in itself, and inclined towards itself by the whole of its existence, in accordance with the one, simple, undifferentiated and indifferent idea of production from nothing, in accordance with which the whole of creation admits of one and the same undiscriminated *logos*, as having not been before it is.

For in their true *logos* all beings have at least something in common one with another. Amongst the beings after God, which have their being from God through generation, there are no exceptions, neither the greatly honored and transcendent beings which have a universal relationship to the One absolutely beyond any relation, nor is the least honored among beings destitute and bereft since it has by nature a generic relationship to the most honored beings.[11] For all those things that are distinguished one from another by their particular differences are united by their universal and common identities, and forced together to the one and the same by a certain natural generic *logos*, so that the various kinds are united one with another according to their essence, and possess the one and the same and the undivided. For nothing of what is universal and containing [others] and generic can be divided into what is partial and contained and particular. For that is no longer generic which does not naturally unite what is separated, but which, participating in their separation, departs from its own singular unity. For everything generic, according to its own *logos*, is wholly present, indivisibly by the mode of unity, to those subordinate wholes, and the particular as a whole is considered as within the genus. The species, considered according to the genus, are released as it were from the variety caused by difference, and find identity one with another. The individuals, considered according to the species, finding agreement one with another, are in every way constituted as identical one with another, being indistinguishable from their same nature and free from any difference. Finally the accidents, brought together one with another by the substance in which they inhere, possess unity, not being scattered at all by their substance. And the unerring witness of all this is the true theologian, the great and holy Denys the Areopagite, in the chapter on the Perfect and the One in the *Divine Names*, where he speaks thus: "For multiplicity is not without participation in the One, but that which is many in its parts is one as a whole, and that which is many in its accidents is one in the subject, and that which is many in number or potentialities is one in species, and that which is many in species is one in genus, and that which is many in its processions is one in its source, and there is none of the beings that is without participation in the One."[12] And simply, to speak concisely, the *logoi* of everything that is divided and particular are contained, as they say, by the *logoi* of what is universal and generic, and the most universal and generic *logoi* are held together by wisdom, and the *logoi* of the particulars, held fast in various ways by the generic *logoi* are contained by sagacity, in accordance with which they are first simplified, and releasing the symbolic vari-

---

11. Reading *timiôtata*, not *atimiôtata*. See I. Hausherr, *Philautie. De la tendresse pour soi à la charité selon saint Maxime le Confesseur*. Orientalia Christiana Analecta, 137 (Rome: Pontificale Institutum Orientalium Studiorum, 1952).

12. Dionysius the Areopagite, *Divine Names* 13.2, in *PG* 3.980A; ET, *Pseudo-Dionysius: The Complete Works*, ed. Paul Rorem (New York: Paulist Press, 1987), 128.

ety in the actions of their subjects, they are unified by wisdom, receiving congruence making for identity from the more generic. For the wisdom and sagacity of God the Father is the Lord Jesus Christ, who holds together the universals of beings by the power of wisdom, and embraces their complementary parts by the sagacity of understanding, since by nature he is the fashioner and provider of all, and through himself draws into one what is divided, and abolishes war between beings, and binds everything into peaceful friendship and undivided harmony, "both what is in heaven and what is on earth" (Col. 1:20), as the divine Apostle says. . . .

SELECTION 5

Thomas Aquinas

Summa Theologiae 1.93

The following selection comes from Thomas's most famous and influential work, his *Summa Theologiae* (or *Summa Theologica*), composed between 1266 and 1273. Intended as a comprehensive introduction to Christian theology, the various topics are examined following the highly structured format of the disputed question (*quaestio disputata*), which demanded careful consideration of arguments on all sides of a question. Each particular issue (or article) is introduced as an open-ended question of the form "Whether it is the case that. . . ." Thomas then lists a series of objections that highlight theological problems raised by the question, before giving his own opinion in the sections labeled "On the Contrary" and "Answer." Finally, he offers a reply to each of the initial objections. The result is a balanced examination in which Thomas develops his own theology in dialogue with opposing points of view.

The following four articles from the first part of the *Summa* offer a carefully nuanced examination of the concept of the image of God. Thomas begins by arguing that the concept of image implies a capacity for activity corresponding to God's (specifically, the knowing and loving of God) that is limited to creatures with intellectual natures. This focus on activity leads to the further consideration that the divine image appears with different degrees of intensity in creation depending on the perfection of the intellectual nature in question. As a result, angels may be said to be more in God's image than people, while among human beings factors like gender and level of faith will also result in different individuals reflecting the divine image in different degrees. In this way, Thomas's anthropology is characterized by a certain tension between the basic equality of all human beings as created in God's image with an inequality caused by the ways in which differences between people allow them to be ranked as relatively more or less in God's image.

From *The Summa Theologica of St. Thomas Aquinas*, 2nd ed.
(London: Burns, Oates, & Washbourne, 1927), 4:284–89, 292–96.

Article 2: Whether the image of God is to be found in irrational creatures?

Objections:

1. It would seem that the image of God is to be found in irrational creatures. For Dionysius says: "Effects are contingent images of their causes."[1] But God is the cause not only of rational, but also of irrational creatures. Therefore the image of God is to be found in irrational creatures.

2. Further, the more distinct a likeness is, the nearer it approaches to the nature of an image. But Dionysius says that "the solar ray has a very great similitude to the Divine goodness."[2] Therefore it is made to the image of God.

3. Further, the more perfect anything is in goodness, the more it is like God. But the whole universe is more perfect in goodness than man; for though each individual thing is good, all things together are called "very good" [Gen. 1:31]. Therefore the whole universe is to the image of God, and not only man.

4. Further, Boethius says of God: "Holding the world in His mind, and forming it into His image."[3] Therefore the whole world is to the image of God, and not only the rational creature.

On the Contrary:

Augustine says: "Man's excellence consists in the fact that God made him to His own image by giving him an intellectual soul, which raises him above the beasts of the field."[4] Therefore things without intellect are not made to God's image.

Answer:

Not every likeness, not even what is copied from something else, is sufficient to make an image; for if the likeness be only generic, or existing by virtue of some common accident, this does not suffice for one thing to be the image of another. For instance, a worm, though from man it may originate, cannot be called man's image, merely because of the generic likeness. Nor, if anything is made white like something else, can we say that it is the image of that thing; for whiteness is an accident belonging to many species. But the nature of an image requires likeness in species; thus the image of the king exists in his son: or, at least, in some specific accident, and

---

1. Dionysius the Areopagite, *Divine Names* 2.8, in PG 3.645C; ET, *Pseudo-Dionysius: The Complete Works*, ed. Paul Rorem (New York: Paulist Press, 1987), 64.
2. Dionysius, *Divine Names* 4.4, in PG 4.697C; ET, *Pseudo-Dionysius*, 74.
3. Boethius, *The Consolation of Philosophy* 3.9, in PL 63.759; ET, Boethius, *The Consolation of Philosophy*, ed. P. G. Walsh (Oxford: Clarendon, 1999), 56.
4. Augustine, *Literal Interpretation of Genesis* 6.12, in PL 34.348.

chiefly in the shape; thus, we speak of a man's image in copper. Whence Hilary says pointedly that "an image is of the same species."

Now it is manifest that specific likeness follows the ultimate difference. But some things are like to God first and most commonly because they exist; secondly, because they live; and thirdly because they know or understand; and these last, as Augustine says "approach so near to God in likeness, that among all creatures nothing comes nearer to Him."[5] It is clear, therefore, that intellectual creatures alone, properly speaking, are made to God's image.

Replies to the Objections:

1. Everything imperfect is a participation of what is perfect. Therefore even what falls short of the nature of an image, so far as it possesses any sort of likeness to God, participates in some degree the nature of an image. So Dionysius says that effects are "contingent images of their causes"; that is, as much as they happen to be so, but not absolutely.

2. Dionysius compares the solar ray to Divine goodness, as regards its causality; not as regards its natural dignity which is involved in the idea of an image.

3. The universe is more perfect in goodness than the intellectual creature as regards extension and diffusion; but intensively and collectively the likeness to the Divine goodness is found rather in the intellectual creature, which has a capacity for the highest good. Or else we may say that a part is not rightly divided against the whole, but only against another part. Wherefore, when we say that the intellectual nature alone is to the image of God, we do not mean that the universe in any part is not to God's image, but that the other parts are excluded.

4. Boethius here uses the word "image" to express the likeness which the product of an art bears to the artistic species in the mind of the artist. Thus every creature is an image of the exemplar type thereof in the Divine mind. We are not, however, using the word "image" in this sense; but as it implies a likeness in nature, that is, inasmuch as all things, as being, are like to the First Being; as living, like to the First Life; and as intelligent, like to the Supreme Wisdom.

Article 3: Whether the Angels Are More to the Image of God Than Man Is?

Objections:

1. It would seem that the angels are not more to the image of God than man is. For Augustine says in a sermon *On the Image*, 43 that God granted to no other creature besides man to be to His image.[6] Therefore it is not true to say that the angels are more than man to the image of God.

---

5. Augustine, *Book of the 83 Questions*, 51, in *PL* 40.32.
6. Augustine, *Sermons*, 43.2, in *PL* 38.255.

2. Further, according to Augustine, "man is so much to God's image that God did not make any creature to be between Him and man: and therefore nothing is more akin to Him." But a creature is called God's image so far as it is akin to God. Therefore the angels are not more to the image of God than man.

3. Further, a creature is said to be to God's image so far as it is of an intellectual nature. But the intellectual nature does not admit of intensity or remissness; for it is not an accidental thing, since it is a substance. Therefore the angels are not more to the image of God than man.

On the Contrary:
Gregory says: "The angel is called a 'seal of resemblance' [Ezek. 28:12] because in him the resemblance of the Divine image is wrought with greater expression."[7]

Answer:
We may speak of God's image in two ways. First, we may consider in it that in which the image chiefly consists, that is, the intellectual nature. Thus the image of God is more perfect in the angels than in man, because their intellectual nature is more perfect, as is clear from what has been said [quest. 59.3; quest. 79.8]. Secondly, we may consider the image of God in man as regards its accidental qualities, so far as to observe in man a certain imitation of God, consisting in the fact that man proceeds from man, as God from God; and also in the fact that the whole human soul is in the whole body, as God from God; and also in the fact that the whole human soul is in the whole body, and again, in every part, as God is in regard to the whole world. In these and the like things the image of God is more perfect in man than it is in the angels. But these do not of themselves belong to the nature of the Divine image in man, unless we presuppose the first likeness, which is in the intellectual nature; otherwise even brute animals would be to God's image. Therefore, as in their intellectual nature, the angels are more to the image of God than man is, we must grant that, absolutely speaking, the angels are more to the image of God than man is, but that in some respects man is more like to God.

Replies to the Objections:
1. Augustine excludes the inferior creatures bereft of reason from the image of God; but not the angels.

2. As fire is said to be specifically the most subtle of bodies, while, nevertheless, one kind of fire is more subtle than another; so we say that nothing is more like to God than the human soul in its generic and intellectual nature, because as Augustine had said previously, "things which

---

7. Gregory the Great, *Homilies on the Gospels*, 2.34, in *PL* 76.1250.

have knowledge, are so near to Him in likeness that of all creatures none are nearer." Wherefore this does not mean that the angels are not more to God's image.

3. When we say that substance does not admit of more or less, we do not mean that one species of substance is not more perfect than another; but that one and the same individual does not participate in its specific nature at one time more than at another; nor do we mean that a species of substance is shared among different individuals in a greater or lesser degree.

Article 4: Whether the Image of God Is Found in Every Man?
Objections:
1. It would seem that the image of God is not found in every man. For the Apostle says that "man is the image of God, but woman is the image of man" [1 Cor. 11:7]. Therefore, as woman is an individual of the human species, it is clear that every individual is not an image of God.

2. Further, the Apostle says [Rom. 8:29]: "Whom God foreknew, He also predestined to be made conformable to the image of His Son." But all men are not predestined. Therefore all men have not the conformity of image.

3. Further, likeness belongs to the nature of the image, as above explained [art. 1]. But by sin man becomes unlike God. Therefore he loses the image of God.

On the Contrary:
It is written [Ps. 38:7]: "Surely man passeth as an image."

Answer:
Since man is said to be the image of God by reason of his intellectual nature, he is the most perfectly like God according to that in which he can best imitate God in his intellectual nature. Now the intellectual nature imitates God chiefly in this, that God understands and loves Himself. Wherefore we see that the image of God is in man in three ways. First, inasmuch as man possesses a natural aptitude for understanding and loving God; and this aptitude consists in the very nature of the mind, which is common to all men. Secondly, inasmuch as man actually and habitually knows and loves God, though imperfectly; and this image consists in the conformity of grace. Thirdly, inasmuch as man knows and loves God perfectly; and this image consists in the likeness of glory. Wherefore on the words, "The light of Thy countenance, O Lord, is signed upon us [Ps. 4:7], the gloss distinguishes a threefold image of "creation," of "re-creation," and of "likeness." The first is found in all men, the second only in the just, the third only in the blessed.

Replies to the Objections:
1. The image of God, in its principal signification, namely the intellectual nature, is found both in man and in woman. Hence after the words, "To

the image of God He created him," it is added, "Male and female He created them" [Gen. 1:27]. Moreover it is said "them" in the plural, as Augustine remarks,[8] lest it should be thought that both sexes were united in one individual. But in a secondary sense the image of God is found in man, and not in woman: for man is the beginning and end of woman; as God is the beginning and end of every creature. So when the Apostle had said that "man is the image and glory of God, but woman is the image of man," he adds his reason for saying this: "For man is not of woman, but woman of man; and man was not created for woman, but woman for man."

2 and 3. These reasons refer to the image consisting in the conformity of grace and glory. . . .

Article 6: Whether the Image of God Is in Man As Regards the Mind Only?

Objections:

1. It would seem that the image of God is not only in man's mind. For the Apostle says [1 Cor. 11:7] that "the man is the image . . . of God." But man is not only mind. Therefore the image of God is to be observed not only in his mind.

2. Further, it is written [Gen. 1:27]: "God created man to His own image; to the image of God He created him; male and female He created them." But the distinction of male and female is in the body. Therefore the image of God is also in the body, and not only in the mind.

3. Further, an image seems to apply principally to the shape of a thing. But shape belongs to the body. Therefore the image of God is to be seen in man's body also, and not in his mind.

4. Further, according to Augustine there is a threefold vision in us, "corporeal," "spiritual," or imaginary, and "intellectual."[9] Therefore, if in the intellectual vision that belongs to the mind there exists in us a trinity by reason of which we are made to the image of God, for the like reason there must be another trinity in the others.

On the Contrary:

The Apostle says [Eph. 4:23, 24]: "Be renewed in the spirit of your mind, and put on the new man." Whence we are given to understand that our renewal which consists in putting on the new man, belongs to the mind. Now, he says [Col. 3:10]: "Putting on the new" man; "him who is renewed unto knowledge" of God, "according to the image of Him that created him," where the renewal which consists in putting on the new man is ascribed to the image of God. Therefore to be to the image of God belongs to the mind only.

---

8. Augustine, *Literal Interpretation of Genesis*, 3.22, in PL 34.294.
9. Augustine, *Literal Interpretation of Genesis*, 12.7, 24, in PL 34.459-60, 474-75.

Answer:

While in all creatures there is some kind of likeness to God, in the rational creature alone we find a likeness of "image" as we have explained above [art. 1-2]; whereas in other creatures we find a likeness by way of a "trace." Now the intellect or mind is that whereby the rational creature excels other creatures; wherefore this image of God is not found even in the rational creature except in the mind; while in the other parts, which the rational creature may happen to possess, we find the likeness of a "trace," as in other creatures to which, in reference to such parts, the rational creature can be likened. We may easily understand the reason of this if we consider the way in which a "trace," and the way in which an "image," represents anything. An "image" represents something by likeness in species, as we have said; while a "trace" represents something by way of an effect, which represents the cause in such a way as not to attain to the likeness of species. For imprints which are left by the movements of animals are called "traces": so also ashes are a trace of fire, and desolation of the land a trace of a hostile army.

Therefore we may observe this difference between rational creatures and others, both as to the representation of the likeness of the Divine Nature in creatures, and as to the representation in them of the uncreated Trinity. For as to the likeness of the Divine Nature, rational creatures seem to attain, after a fashion, to the representation of the species, inasmuch as they imitate God, not only in being and life, but also in intelligence, as above explained [art. 2]; whereas other creatures do not understand, although we observe in them a certain trace of the Intellect that created them, if we consider their disposition. Likewise as the uncreated Trinity is distinguished by the procession of the Word from the Speaker, and of Love from both of these, as we have seen [quest. 28.3]; so we may say that in rational creatures wherein we find a procession of the word in the intellect, and a procession of the love in the will, there exists an image of the uncreated Trinity, by a certain representation of the species. In other creatures, however, we do not find the principle of the word, and the word and love; but we do see in them a certain trace of the existence of these in the Cause that produced them. For in the fact that a creature has a modified and finite nature, proves that it proceeds from a principle; while its species points to the [mental] word of the maker, just as the shape of a house points to the idea of the architect; and order points to the maker's love by reason of which he directs the effect to a good end; as also the use of the house points to the will of the architect. So we find in man a likeness to God by way of an "image" in his mind; but in the other parts of his being by way of a "trace."

Replies to the Objections:

1. Man is called to the image of God; not that he is essentially an image; but that the image of God is impressed on his mind; as a coin is an image

of the king, as having the image of the king. Wherefore there is no need to consider the image of God as existing in every part of man.

2. As Augustine says, some have thought that the image of God was not in man individually, but severally.[10] They held that "the man represents the Person of the Father; those born of man denote the person of the Son; and that the woman is a third person in likeness to the Holy Spirit, since she so proceeded from man as not to be his son or daughter." All of this is manifestly absurd; first, because it would follow that the Holy Ghost is the principle of the Son, as the woman is the principle of the man's offspring; secondly, because one man would be only the image of one Person; thirdly, because in that case Scripture should not have mentioned the image of God in man until after the birth of the offspring. Therefore we must understand that when Scripture had said, "to the image of God He created him," it added, "male and female He created them," not to imply that the image of God came through the distinction of sex, but that the image of God belongs to both sexes, since it is in the mind, wherein there is no sexual distinction. Wherefore the Apostle [Col. 3:10], after saying, "According to the image of Him that created him," added, "Where there is neither male nor female" [Gal. 3:28].

3. Although the image of God in man is not to be found in his bodily shape, yet because "the body of man alone among terrestrial animals is not inclined prone to the ground, but is adapted to look upward to heaven, for this reason we may rightly say that it is made to God's image and likeness, rather than the bodies of other animals," as Augustine remarks.[11] But this is not to be understood as though the image of God were in man's body; but in the sense that the very shape of the human body represents the image of God in the soul by way of a trace.

4. Both in the corporeal and in the imaginary vision we may find a trinity, as Augustine says.[12] For in corporeal vision there is first the species of the exterior body; secondly, the act of vision, which occurs by the impression on the sight of a certain likeness of the said species; thirdly, the intention of the will applying the sight to see, and to rest on what is seen.

Likewise, in the imaginary vision we find first the species kept in the memory; secondly, the vision itself, which is caused by the penetrative power of the soul, that is, the faculty of imagination, informed by the species; and thirdly, we find the intention of the will joining both together. But each of these trinities falls short of the Divine image. For the species of the external body is extrinsic to the essence of the soul; while the species in the memory, though not extrinsic to the soul, is adventitious to it; and thus in both cases the species falls short of representing the connaturality

---

10. Augustine, *The Trinity*, 12.5, in *PL* 42.1000; ET, *NPNF*², 3:156–57.
11. Augustine, *Book of the 83 Questions*, 51, in *PL* 40.33.
12. Augustine, *The Trinity*, 11.2, in *PL* 42.985; ET, *NPNF*², 3:145–47.

and co-eternity of the Divine Persons. The corporeal vision, too, does not proceed only from the species of the external body, but from this, and at the same time from the sense of the seer; in like manner imaginary vision is not from the species only which is preserved in the memory, but also from the imagination. For these reasons the procession of the Son from the Father alone is not suitably represented. Lastly the intention of the will joining the two together, does not proceed from them either in corporeal or spiritual vision. Wherefore the procession of the Holy Ghost from the Father and the Son is not thus properly represented.

SELECTION 6

Sojourner Truth

"Ar'n't I a Woman?"

Born a slave in upstate New York, Sojourner Truth (ca. 1797–1883) was owned by several masters, married, and gave birth to thirteen children before finally escaping bondage in 1826. Originally named Isabella Baumfree, she changed her name in obedience to a divine revelation that in 1843 summoned her to be a witness to truth. She then moved to Massachusetts, where she became a leading figure in the abolitionist movement, working closely with other prominent abolitionists, including William Lloyd Garrison (who later wrote the preface to her autobiography).

The speech below was given in 1851 at a convention for women's rights in Akron, Ohio. Truth herself was illiterate, and her extemporaneous response to several men who had spoken against women's demand for equal rights was recorded by the president of the Convention, Frances Gage. The accuracy of Gage's transcription (which was not published until 1863) is disputed, but it remains one of the most concise and theologically penetrating critiques of the overwhelming tendency in traditional Christian anthropology to privilege men over women; it also includes an equally devastating (if somewhat more implicit) critique of the racist doctrines used to justify chattel slavery.

From *Narrative of Sojourner Truth, A Bondswoman of Olden Time Emancipated by the New York Legislature in the Early Part of the Present Century, with a History of Her Labors and Correspondence Drawn from Her Book of Life* (Chicago: Johnson Publishing Co., 1970 [1875], 104–6.

"Well, chilern, whar dar is so much racket dar must be something out o'kilter. I tink dat 'twixt de niggers [*sic*] of de Souf and de women at de Norf, all a talkin' 'bout rights, de white men will be in a fix pretty soon. But what's all diss here talkin' 'bout? Dat man ober dar say dat woman needs to be helped into carriages, and lifted ober ditches, and to have de best place every whar. Nobody eber help me into carriages, or ober mud puddles, or gives me any best place . . . and ar'n't I a woman? Look at me! Look at my arm! . . . I have plowed, and planted, and gathered into barns, and no man could head me—and ar'n't I a woman? I could work as much and eat as much as a man (when I could get it) and bear the lash as well—and ar'n't I a woman? I have borne thirteen children, and seen 'em mos' all sold off to slavery, and when I cried out with my mother's grief, none but Jesus heard me—and ar'n't I a woman? Den dey talks 'bout dis ting in de head—what dis dey call it?"

"Intellect," whispered someone near.

"Dat's it, honey. What's dat got to do with women's rights or niggers' [sic] rights? If my cup won't hold but a pint, and yours holds a quart, would n't ye be mean not to let me have my little half measure full? . . .

"Den dat little man in black dar, he say women can't have as much rights as man, cause Christ wasn't a woman! Whar did your Christ come from? . . . Whar did your Christ come from? From God and a woman. Man had nothing to do with Him. . . .

"If de fust woman God ever made was strong enough to turn the world upside down, all 'lone, dese togedder . . . ought to be able to turn it back and get it right side up again, and now dey is asking to do it, de men better let 'em.

"Bleeged to ye for hearin' on me, and now ole Sojourner ha'n't got nothing more to say."

SELECTION 7

Karl Barth

"The Basic Form of Humanity"

The Reformed thinker Karl Barth (1886–1968) is widely regarded as the most influential Protestant theologian of the twentieth century. His *Epistle to the Romans* constituted a sharp challenge to the theological liberalism that had dominated European and American theology throughout the latter half of the nineteenth century. In it, Barth argued for the essential strangeness of God and God's word over against the liberal tendency to stress continuity between God and human experience. His *Church Dogmatics* (running to thirteen part-volumes and still incomplete at the time of Barth's death) is a comprehensive exposition of Christian doctrine, shaped throughout by the insistence that all theological discourse be rooted in and tested against God's word as revealed in Jesus Christ.

In the following selection, taken from the second of the four part-volumes of the *Dogmatics* that deal with the doctrine of creation, Barth outlines the implications of his radical christocentrism for Christian reflection on human being. Over against more traditional attempts to define the essence of humanity individualistically in terms of the personal possession of some attribute like rationality or freedom, Barth maintains that the defining feature of human existence is life-with-another (or fellow-humanity), on the grounds that Christ's human life is fundamentally a matter of encounter with others. In this way, Barth articulates a form of relational anthropology, according to which one's humanity is disclosed in the act of addressing—and of being addressed by—another as "Thou."

From Karl Barth, *Church Dogmatics*, III/2, ed. G. W. Bromiley and T. F. Torrance (Edinburgh: T. & T. Clark, 1960), 225-28, 243-49.

When we ask: What is humanity, human creatureliness? We must first ask: What is its basic form? In other words, to what extent does human essence correspond to the determination of man to be the covenant-partner of God? Our criterion in answering this question is the humanity of the man Jesus. If, for all the distance, there is between His humanity and ours a common factor, a similarity for all the dissimilarity, now that we turn to ourselves, to man generally, we must first make a great distinction and differentiation in respect of the human essence presupposed in our question. We cannot start with the assumption that there is a known and accepted picture of man and humanity before which we can pause and from the contours of which we can read off that which corresponds and is similar in man to the humanity of Jesus, and therefore supremely his participation in the image of God actualized in the humanity of Jesus. In theological anthropology there can be no question of giving a theological meaning to a given text (in this case a picture of man assumed to be generally known and accepted). This procedure would merely arouse the justifiable suspicion that the text itself (the known and accepted picture of man) is the constant and certain factor, whereas the theological interpretation is variable and uncertain like any other. No, in theological anthropology what man is, is decided by the primary text, i.e., by the humanity of the man Jesus. And the application of this criterion means that a whole sphere of supposed humanity is ruled out as non-human from the very first, and cannot be considered, because that which in it is regarded and alleged to be human stands in a contradiction to the humanity of Jesus which denies the essential similarity between Him and us and therefore excludes the possibility, of the human creature as a covenant-partner of God, thus destroying the unity of creation and covenant. It is against any line of anthropological investigation and exposition which results in this denial, exclusion and destruction that we are warned *a limine* by our Christological basis, even though we may seem to have very good reasons for accepting the picture of man proposed. We do not have to regard as human, as the essence of man which God created good, that which measured by this criterion is non-human, i.e., not yet or no longer human. On the contrary, in the application of this criterion we are free to excise from the proposed picture of man all those features which are incompatible with the similarity which we presuppose for all the dissimilarity between the man Jesus and us other men. That which is incompatible with this similarity is *ipso facto* non-human.

The excision with which we must begin will be as follows. It is not yet or no longer seen what humanity is when there is ascribed to man an existence which is abstract, i.e., abstracted from the co-existence of his fellows. No enriching, deepening or heightening of this concept of humanity in other directions, even religious, can excuse, make good or compensate this basic defect. If we see man in and for himself, and therefore without his fellows, we do not see him at all. If we see him in opposition or even neutrality towards his fellows, we do not see him at all. If we think that his humanity is only subsequently and secondarily determined, as an incidental enrichment, by the fact that he is not alone, we do not see him at all. If we do not realise and take into account from the very outset, from the first glance and word, the fact that he has a neighbour, we do not see him at all. At this point we have no option either to be tolerant or intolerant. We can only exclude. If a picture of man does not satisfy this demand, it has nothing whatever to do with the human essence in question, and it cannot be brought under discussion. We ask concerning the brightness of man in the light of the man Jesus, in the light of the fact that the man Jesus is for him, and therefore can be for him, because between the man Jesus and this other man there is similarity as well as dissimilarity. A man without his fellows, or radically neutral or opposed to his fellows, or under the impression that the co-existence of his fellows has only secondary significance, is a being which *ipso facto* is fundamentally alien to the man Jesus and cannot have him as Deliverer and Saviour. To be sure, He is the Deliverer and Saviour of sinful man, and therefore of the man who denies His fellow-humanity, acting as though he had no God and no neighbour, and therefore showing himself to be supremely non-human. But this does not mean that this sinner has ceased to be a man, or that we are allowed or even obliged to interpret His inhumanity as his humanity or the work of sin as the good creation of God. Even the sinful man who denies his humanity and in a blatant or more refined way turns his back on his fellows stands in the light of the humanity of Jesus. He acts contrary to his humanity, and he cannot be excused the guilt which he incurs by projecting a picture of man according to which his inhumanity—his isolation from his fellows, or neutrality or opposition in relation to them, or the casualness of their significance for him—belongs to his humanity as a possibility of the nature which he has been given by his Creator. No, even as he denies it, his creaturely nature stands in the light of the humanity of Jesus, and it is bright in this light, accusing him of sinning in his inhumanity not only against God and his neighbour but also primarily and finally against himself, and yet not ceasing to bind him to his Saviour and Deliverer. To sin is to wander from a path which does not cease to be the definite and exclusive path of man even though he leaves it. The fact that man sins does not mean that God ceases to be God and therefore man man. In this context, too, we must say that man does not accomplish a new creation by sinning. He cannot achieve any essential alteration of the human nature which he has been given. He can only shame this nature and himself. He can only bring himself into supreme peril. But the fact that he has in the man Jesus his Saviour and Deliverer is the pledge that he has not ceased to be a man, a being ordered in relation to this Jesus. The fact that the Good Shepherd has acted on behalf of His lost sheep shows that he does not give it up for the lost but still numbers it with His flock and deals with it as His own and not an alien possession. This is what makes the idea of a man without his fellows, in any form, quite intolerable. This is what rules it out from the very first. Theological anthropology cannot enter the sphere where this man without his fellows is considered as a serious possibility. It knows man well enough as the man of sin, but not as the man who actualizes his creaturely nature in his sin, whom God has created for this actualization. It cannot blame God for what man has made of himself. And it cannot exculpate man from the permanent reproach of the transgression with which he denies the truth, the truth of his Creator and his own truth. We take sin lightly if we spare sinful man this reproach, giving him the evasion that as a sinner he has forfeited and lost his humanity, or that God has created him in a humanity in which he can choose either to be man or not, and in which inhumanity is more probable than humanity. Every supposed humanity which is not radically and from the very first fellow-humanity is inhumanity. At this point a distinction must be made *a limine*, and humanity must be protected against its decisive and definitive destruction. If we take away fellow-man from the picture of man, and describe the latter as a being which is alien, opposed or casual in relation to him, we have not merely given an inadequate or partially false representation of man, but described a different being altogether. There is nothing else for it. In this respect theological anthropology must be quite pitiless in its opposition to every attempt to seek real man outside the history of his responsibility to God. The very reality of man in his responsibility before God necessarily gives us the negative rule for an understanding of the basic form of his humanity—that in no circumstances may it be sought in that abstraction, in a humanity without the fellow-man. . . .

Before we move on from this point, we must try to clarify three of the terms employed in this definition.

1. We describe humanity as a determination of human being. Man is, as he is created by God for God, as this creature of God for covenant-partnership with God. But this being is a wholly definite being. It corresponds in its own way to its particular creation and to the meaning and goal of the particularity of its creation. The manner of its being is a likeness of its purpose and therefore of the fact that it is created by God for God. This parabolic determination of human being, this correspondence and similarity of its nature in relation to its being as such, is humanity.

2. We describe humanity as a being of man with others. With this cautious expression we distinguish humanity generally from the humanity of Jesus. There is also a being for others in the relation of man to man. But only the humanity of Jesus can be absolutely exhaustively and exclusively described as a being for man. There can be no question of a total being for others as the determination of any other men but Jesus. And to the humanity of the other men there necessarily belongs reciprocity. Others are for them as they are for others. This reciprocity cannot arise in the humanity of Jesus with its irreversible "for." We are thus satisfied to describe the humanity generally with which we are now dealing as a being of the one with the other, and we shall have to show to what extent this includes a certain being of the one for the other.

3. We describe humanity as a being of the one man with the other. Fundamentally we speak on both sides in the singular and not in the plural. We are thinking here in terms of individualism. But the basic form of humanity, the determination of humanity, according to its creation, in the light of the humanity of Jesus—and it is of this that we speak—is a being of the one man with the other. And where one is with many, or many with one, or many with many, the humanity consists in the fact that in truth, in the basic form of this occurrence, one is always with another, and this basic form persists. Humanity is not in isolation, and it is in pluralities only when these are constituted by genuine duality, by the singular on both sides.

The singular, not alone but in this duality, is the presupposition without which there can never be humanity in the plural.

We may now move forward, and for the sake of clarity we shall begin with an analysis of the statement "I am," which we have so far understood only as the axiom of humanity without the fellow-man, but which will help us to a true understanding and exposition once we appreciate its true significance. The statement "I am" is ultimately a confession—and perhaps *the* confession—of the man Jesus; He therefore permits and requires of us an interpretation on which, as at least a corresponding and similar if not an equal confession in the mouth of others, it has a human and not an inhuman form; an interpretation which does not point us in the direction which we cannot take, but in the opposite and right direction, the being of one man with the other.

What is meant by "I"? I pronounce the word, and in so doing, even if I only do so mentally or to myself, I make a distinction, but also a connexion. In thinking and speaking this word, I do not remain in isolation. I distinguish myself from another who is not I and yet also not It, not an object, but one who can receive and estimate and understand my declaration "I" because he can make a similar declaration to me. In making this distinction, I presuppose, accept and make, as far as I am able, a connexion with him as one who is like me. Addressing this object as I, I distinguish him not only from myself but from all other objects, from every It, placing myself on the same level or in the same sphere with him, acknowledging that I am not without him in my sphere, that this sphere is not just mine but also his. The mere fact that I say "I" means that I describe and distinguish the object to which I say it as something like myself; in other words, that with my "I" I also address him as "Thou." But saying "I," I implicitly address and treat him as "Thou." Not, be it noted, as "He" or "She." So long and so far as he is only He or She, he is really It, an object like others, in a different sphere from mine, unlike myself; and my distinction from him and connexion with him are not yet human. But in this case I do not speak to him; I speak about him. And the word "I" is meaningful in relation to the one with whom I speak about him. It has no reference to himself. If I speak to him and not about him, he is neither It, He nor She, but Thou. I then make the distinction and connexion in relation to him in the specific form of a demarcation in virtue of which my sphere is no longer my own but his, and he is like me. But there is more to it than this. For when I say "I" in what I say is the declaration of my expectation that the other being to which I declare myself in this way will respond and treat and describe and distinguish me as something like himself. When he accepts my "I"—and in turning to him I count on it that he is able to do so—he cannot possibly regard me as an It or a mere He or She, but I am distinguished from all other objects for him as he is for me, and distinguished from and connected to me as I am from and to him. And it can only be a matter of fulfillment that he for his part should admit his recognition of this fact by pronouncing the word "Thou" and thus proclaim himself not merely as something like an I but actually as an I. Thus the word "Thou," although it is a very different word, is immanent to "I." It is not a word which is radically alien, but one which belongs to it. The word "I" with which I think and declare my humanity implies as such humanity with and not without the fellow-man. I cannot say "I," even to myself, without also saying "Thou," without making that distinction and connexion in relation to another. And only as I think and say "I" in this way, only as I make this specific distinction and connexion with this word, can I expect to be recognized and acknowledged by others as a "Thou," as something like an "I," and more than that as a real "I," and therefore to be confirmed in the human determination of my being, and regarded, treated and addressed as human being.

On this basis, what is meant by "I am?" It certainly means that I posit myself: myself as this being in the cosmos; myself in all the freedom and necessity of my being; myself in the totality of the movement of my distinctions and connexions in relation to what is for me the outside world; myself in my desire and ability to project myself into this world. There can be no objection to this formal description of "I am." But what does all this mean if I cannot say "I" without also saying "Thou," and being a Thou for this "Thou," and only in this way receiving confirmation that I am? What does "I am" mean on this presupposition? Who and what am I myself as I confirm my being in this way? What kind of being is it in the freedom and necessity of which I posit myself, distinguishing and connecting myself, projecting myself outwards? One thing at least is certain. A pure, absolute and self-sufficient I is an illusion, for, as an I, even as I think and express this I, I am not alone or self-sufficient, but am distinguished from and connected with a Thou in which I find a being like my own, so that there is no place for an interpretation of the "I am" which means isolation and necessarily consists in a description of the sovereign self-positing of an empty subject by eruptions of its pure, absolute and self-sufficient abyss. On the contrary, as I am—the genuine I—I am in distinction and connexion to the other which in the fact that I am is Thou, my Thou, and for which I am a Thou in return, thus receiving confirmation of my own being, of the "I am." "I am" is not an empty but a filled reality. As I am, the other is like me. I am as I am in relation. And this means that as I posit myself—I should not be myself if it were otherwise—I at once come up against the fact that there takes place a corresponding self-positing and being on the part of the one whom I must see and treat as Thou as I think and declare myself as I. With this self-positing and being of his he comes towards me, or rather the Thou comes (for that is what he is as I am I in relation to him), and comes in such a way that I cannot evade him, since he is like myself and therefore Thou as surely as I am I, and therefore my sphere is not mine alone but his as well. What I am and posit as myself, I am and posit in relation to his positing and being, in distinction from and connexion with this alien happening which is characterized by the fact that I can see and recognize and accept this alien being and positing as one which corresponds to my own. This alien being and positing does not belong, therefore, to the general mass of happenings in the external world. In face of it I cannot refer back to myself, asserting and developing myself from myself as from a neutral point quite apart from it. The being and positing of this Thou reaches and affects me, for it is not that of an It, but of the Thou without which I should not be I. In its decisive content as a work of the Thou it is not the outside world which I can leave to itself, avoid or control. The work of the Thou cannot be indifferent to me, nor can I evade or master it. I cannot do this because as I do my own work, as I am myself and posit myself, I am necessarily claimed by and occupied with the being and positing of the

Thou. My own being and positing takes place in and with the fact that I am claimed by that of the other and occupied with it. That of the other sets limits to my own. It indicates its problems. It poses questions which must be answered. And there are answers for which it asks. I am in encounter with the other who is in the same way as I am. I am under the conditions imposed by this encounter. I am as either well or badly I fulfill the conditions imposed by this encounter. Even if I fulfill them badly, I am as measured by these conditions. I have no being apart from them. I cannot posit myself without coming up against the self-positing other. I have no line of retreat to a place where he does not come up against me with his self-positing. If I had, it could only be that of a return to the inhumanity of a being without the being of the other, of the "I am" of an empty subject, of an I which cannot be more than an illusion. And here, too, we must consider the matter from the other side. As I myself am, and posit myself, I confront the other no less than he does me with his being and positing. He is my Thou, and therefore something like myself, in the sphere which is my own. My being and positing is for him more than the external world. Hence he cannot retreat before me into himself, and in this way exist without me. Since I am not an It, but an I and therefore a Thou, he is reached and affected by me no less than I am by him. He, too, is unable to leave aside or to evade or control my work. He, too, is claimed by and occupied with my being and positing. He, too, stands under the conditions which I create for him. I am his encounter as he is mine. In being myself, I cannot help being what I am for him. In this sense, too, there is no line of retreat to a place where I exist neutrally for him, where I do not affect him, where I do not owe him anything, where I with my being and positing do not have to take any account of his. The only line of retreat is again that of a retreat to inhumanity—to the inhumanity of a being without the Thou in relation to which I can be alone, to the "I am" of an empty subject which cannot find fulfillment or really be a human subject, but is always, or always becomes again, an illusion.

"I am"—the true and filled "I am"—may thus be paraphrased: "I am in encounter." Nor am I in encounter before or after, incidentally, secondarily or subsequently, while primarily and properly I am alone in an inner world in which I am not in this encounter, but alongside which there is an outer world in which amongst other things I certainly come up against being, against the being of the Thou, and have to reckon with it, but in such sort that this is not at all essential, since essentially I am always outside this encounter, and can always retreat into this world apart. No, at the very root of my being and from the very first I am in encounter with the being of the Thou, under his claim and with my own being constituting a claim upon him. And the humanity of human being is this total determination as being in encounter with the being of the Thou, as being with the fellow-man, as fellow-humanity. To this extent we must oppose humanity without the fellow-man. This is the reach of the likeness in unlikeness, of the correspondence and similarity between the man Jesus and us other men. The minimal definition of our humanity, of humanity generally, must be that it is the being of man in encounter, and in this the determination of man as a being with the other man. We cannot go back on this. We cannot be content with anything less or weaker. We cannot accept any compromise or admixture with the opposite conception which would have it that at bottom—in the far depths of that abyss of an empty subject—man can be a man without the fellow-man, an I without the Thou.

But we must be more precise. Being with means encounter. Hence being with the other man means encounter with him. Hence humanity is the determination of our being as a being in encounter with the other man. We shall now try to understand the content of this encounter.

The basic formula to describe it must be as follows: "I am as Thou art." Naturally the word "as" does not imply that the "Thou art" is the cause, even the instrumental cause, or the true substance of the "I am." In this respect an excess of zeal in conflict with the idealistic concept of humanity has sometimes led to the emptying out of the baby with the bath-water. Man has been constructed wholly in the light of the fellow-man, and the "I am" has formally disappeared in the "Thou art." The word "as" does not tell us where human being is created—for this we can turn only to God the Creator—but how. It tells us that every "I am" is qualified, marked and determined by the "Thou art." Owing it to God the creator that I am, I am only as Thou art; as created by the same God, Thou art with me. Neither the I am nor the Thou art loses its own meaning and force. I do not become Thou, nor Thou I, in this co-existence. On the contrary, as I and Thou are together, their being acquires the character, the human style, of always being I for the self and Thou for the other. As we are in this encounter we are thus distinguished. On both sides—we shall return to this—the being has its own validity, dignity and self-certainty. Nor is this human being static, but dynamic and active. It is not an *esse* but an *existere*. To say man is to say history. On a false understanding no less than a true we are forced to put the statement "I am" in the form of a little history, describing it as that self-positing. Similarly, the statement "Thou art" denotes a history. Therefore in our formula: "I am as Thou art," we do not describe a relationship between two static complexes of being, but between two which are dynamic, which move out from themselves, which exist, and which meet or encounter each other in their existence. The "I am" and the "Thou art" encounter each other as two histories. It is to be noted that they do not just do this subsequently, as though there were one history here and another there which at a certain point became a common history; as though there were an "I am" here and a "Thou art" there which in the continuation of their two-sided movement came together and became a partnership. But in and with their creation, and therefore in and with the two-sided beginning of their movement and history, they are in encounter: I am as Thou art, and Thou art as I am. To say man is to say history, and this is to speak of the encounter between I and Thou. Thus the formula: "I am as Thou art," tells us that the encounter between I and Thou is not arbitrary or accidental, that it is not incidentally but essentially proper to the concept of man. It tells us noologically that this concept would at once be empty if the view basic to it were that of a pure subject and not of the subject in this encounter. And it tells us ontologically that we have to do with real man only when his existence takes place in this encounter, only in the form of man with his fellow-man.

On this basis we shall now try to see what are the categories, the constant, decisive and necessary elements in this history or encounter, and to that extent what are the categories of the distinctively human. Great caution is needed at this point. Things which might be said about man without his fellow, qualities and characteristics of that empty subject, are out of place here, because they have no categorical significance in the description of humanity, i.e., they tell us nothing about being in encounter and therefore about that which is properly and essentially human. Thus the fact that I am born and die; that I eat and drink and sleep; that I develop and maintain myself; that beyond this I assert myself in face of others, and even physically propagate my species; that I enjoy and work and play and fashion and possess; that I acquire and have and exercise powers; that I take part in all the works of the race either accomplished or in process of accomplishment; that in all this I satisfy religious needs and can realize religious possibilities; and that in it all I fulfill my aptitudes as an understanding and thinking, willing and feeling being—all this as such is not my humanity. In it I can be either human or inhuman. In it I am only asked whether I am human or inhuman. In it all I must first answer the question whether I will affirm or deny my humanity. It is only the field on which human being either takes place or does not takes place as history, as the encounter of I and Thou; the field on which it is revealed or obscured that "I am as Thou art." That I exist on this field, and do so in a particular way, does not of itself mean that I am human. But as I exist on this field and in this way, in this restriction or development, poverty or wealth, impotence or intensity, it has to become true and actual that I am human and not inhuman in my existence. There is no reason why in the realization of my vital, natural and intellectual aptitudes and potentialities, in my life-act as such, and my participation in scholarship and art, politics and economics, civilization and culture, I should not actualize and reveal that "I am as Thou art." But it may well be that in and with all this I deny it. It may well be that in all this I am only man without my fellow-man, and therefore not really human at all. Nothing of all this is in itself and as such the glory of my humanity.

SELECTION 8

Hans Urs von Balthasar

"Woman as Answer"

Hans Urs von Balthasar (1905–1988) is widely regarded as one of the most influential Catholic theologians of the twentieth century. After taking his doctorate in German Romantic literature, Balthasar joined the Jesuits but left the order in 1950 to found a lay contemplative society (the Community of Saint John) in collaboration with the mystic Adrienne von Speyr. His reputation in official Catholic circles grew steadily through the later decades of his life, and at the time of his death he had just been elevated to the office of cardinal. His comprehensive theological vision was published in three parts (*The Glory of the Lord*, *Theo-Drama*, and *Theo-Logic*), comprising a total of fifteen volumes. In these texts Balthasar interprets the Christian faith as a Trinitarian drama in which creation functions as the theater of God's glory. For though the principal actor in this "theo-drama" is the Son (with the Father as author and the Holy Spirit as director), the fact that the second person performs this role by taking flesh as Jesus Christ implicates the whole of creation in the fulfillment of God's purposes and gives human beings a central role as the focus of God's work and as leading actors alongside Christ.

In the following excerpt from the third volume of *Theo-Drama*, Balthasar focuses on the significance of human sexual differentiation for the structure of the theo-drama, with particular attention to the role of woman. Balthasar attempts to walk a fine line here. On the one hand, he wants to argue that the difference between male and female is integral to theological anthropology—an attention to the importance of gender that unites him with many feminists against a tendency in the Christian tradition to treat sexual difference as incidental to reflection on human existence. On the other hand, he maintains that woman's distinctiveness lies in her status as response with respect to man, suggesting to some critics a subordination of female to male that stands in tension with Balthasar's claim that each is equally made the image of God.

From Hans Urs von Balthasar, *Dramatis Personae: Persons in Christ*, vol. 3 of *Theo-Drama: Theological Dramatic Theory* (San Francisco: Ignatius Press, 1978), 283–92.

All we have said so far concerning the nature of the Person of Christ, and the prospect of his being followed by a community or by individuals, has left aside a fundamental feature of human nature: the polarity of man and woman. . . . If God's Word has really become man, this fundamental modality cannot be bracketed out of the realm of theo-drama, nor can it remain neutral to it.... Now, therefore, we must go on to discuss the significance of the difference between the sexes. We saw it to be a cosmic, creaturely reality that, in man, together with his whole being, extends right up to the level of the *theion* [divine]. In pagan terms it was seen in the *hieros gamos*,[1] and in the Bible it was part of the context of God's image in man. Here too, therefore, if we are to get near its theodramatic meaning, we must start from an interpretation of the creaturely sphere. Not as if the meaning that descends upon it from above were nothing but the full unfolding of what is latent in, and deducible from, the "natural" datum; all the same, if a real incarnation of the divine Word has taken place, this final meaning will *at least* bring what is human to its perfection (and superabundantly so).

The Word of God appears in the world as a man, as the "Last Adam." This cannot be a matter of indifference. But it is astonishing on two counts. For if the Logos proceeds eternally from the eternal Father, is he not at least quasi-feminine vis-à-vis the latter?[2] And if he is the "Second Adam," surely he is incomplete until God has formed the woman from his side? We can give a provisional answer to these two questions as follows: However the One who comes forth from the Father is designated, as a human being he must be a man if his mission is to represent the Origin, the Father, in the world. And just as, according to the second account of creation, Eve is fashioned from Adam (that is, he carried her within him, potentially), so the feminine, designed to complement the man Christ, must come forth from within him, as his "fullness" (Eph. 1:23). This will take a long time to clarify before we advance to theo-drama proper. Our starting point will be woman's nature and task.

A. Answer, Face

The first Adam calls nature's animals by name, and as he names them, so they are called. But no adequate response comes to him from them. Only when God forms woman from his side does nature reply ("at last!") with an appropriate word. "This at last is bone of my bones and flesh of my flesh; she shall be called Woman, because she was taken out of Man" (Gen. 2:23). Thus woman is essentially an answer (*Ant-Wort*), in the most fundamental sense of *ant*, which is common to all Indo-European languages, meaning "over against," as in German *entgegen* (for example,

---

1. Ed. note: Greek for "holy wedding," referring to the sexual coupling of a god and a human being, generally associated with myths and/or rites of fertility.

2. Thus, in the Old Testament, the principle that comes forth from God, embodying him in creation and for creation, is predominantly female: *shekinah* (indwelling), *ruach* (spirit) and *memra* (word). In [August] Strindberg's *A Dream Play*, it is Indra's daughter who visits the world in order to learn of her torment, taking her "petition" up with her....

Greek *anti*, Sanskrit *anti*, and so on); or "toward" (Old Saxon, Old Norse, Gothic *and*); the word implies both "direction toward" and the counterpart to something. The German *Ende* [English *end*] is cognate insofar as, in Old High German (and so forth) it means "front," "forehead," "apex." If man is the word that calls out, woman is the answer that comes to him at last (in the *end*). The two are related and ordered to each other. Furthermore, the second account of creation shows that the word that calls out only attains fulfillment when it is understood, accepted and given back as a word. This clearly shows us the way in which man can be primary and woman secondary, where the primary remains unfulfilled without the secondary. The primary needs a partner of equal rank and dignity for its own fulfillment. Moreover, the man is incapable of providing this answering dimension; it is latent within him—for there can be no word without an answering word—but it has to be given to him as grace. It can only come about in freedom, and only God, fundamentally, can give such freedom.

What *Antwort* (answer) denotes in the realm of speech, *Antlitz* (face) signifies in the visual realm. The phoneme -*litz* is cognate with the Anglo-Saxon *wlitan*, Old Norse *lita*, "see, look," and the corresponding *wlite*, "appearance, form." Words for "seer, poet" (cf. *veleda*) come from the same Indo-European root. Thus the face is what "faces" us, "looks toward" us. Man and woman are face to face. Here their equal rank is given even more emphasis: man looks around him and meets with an answering gaze that turns the one-who-sees into the one-who-is-seen.

The paradise legend has no way of expressing the substantial unity and equality of *Wort* and *Antwort* (word and answer), *Litz* and *Antlitz* (the "look" and the "face" that returns it) but by speaking of Eve being taken from Adam's side (not from his reproductive organ!) and being fashioned by God. Had God not formed Eve from Adam but (like him) from the dust of the earth, their unity would have been an external one, and Adam could not have recognized her as "flesh of my flesh." And if the making of woman from man had not been an act of God but a natural process, the original meeting of these two free human beings would not have had the miraculous character it does have and must have: it would be merely an instance of sexual correlation at the natural level. Both sides—the "from within" and the "from without," "from above"—are equally essential. In other words, Eve is potentially in Adam, but he himself cannot produce her from within him. "It is not good for man to be alone" (Gen. 2:18): this state of affairs cannot be remedied by man on his own; the action of Adam's ("man's") Creator is required if man is to be complete: "Male and female he created them" (Gen. 1:27).

Thus the woman, who is both "answer" and "face," is not only man's delight: she is the help, the security, the home man needs; she is the vessel of fulfillment specially designed for him. Nor is she simply the vessel of *his* fruitfulness: she is equipped with her own explicit fruitfulness. Yet her fruitfulness is not a primary fruitfulness: it is an answering fruitfulness, designed to receive man's fruitfulness (which, in itself, is helpless) and bring it to its "fullness." In this way she is the "glory" of the man (1 Cor. 11:7). So we can speak of a kind of natural *vocation* on woman's part much more explicitly than in man's case; for the call to "be fruitful" and "subdue the earth" is addressed to both of them (Gen. 1:28). To that extent, the woman's *missio* vis-à-vis Adam can be described as the extrapolation and continuation of her *processio* from Adam. Of course this aspect must not obscure the other truth, namely, that both man and woman *individually* (and not only *together*) constitute an "image of God"; thus each has a guaranteed direct access to God.[3]

Something more remains to be said here. Since it is woman's essential vocation to receive man's fruitfulness into her own fruitfulness, thus uniting in herself the fruitfulness of both, it follows that she is actually the fruit-bearing principle in the creaturely realm. (But as we have said elsewhere, we must not be misled into equating man with the principle of "spirit" or "heaven" and woman with the principle of "nature" or "earth.")[4] In the most general terms, this means that the woman does not merely give back to man what she has received from him: she gives him something new, something that integrates the gift he gave her but that "faces" him in a totally new and unexpected form. In this way the woman gives him a twofold answer: a "personal" answer and one that goes beyond the I-thou relationship (and which, in the absence of a more precise word, one may call "generic" or "of the species"). She responds through reproduction. We deliberately leave this expression vague, because initially it takes no account of the manner of reproduction. In the wake of the Fall, reproduction is explicitly sexual, but we cannot say whether it was so, in the same form, when man was in the original (paradisal) state, for sexuality is intimately bound up with the death of individuals. Once again we must refer, therefore, to Karl Barth's insight that Genesis 2 speaks of man and wife in their relationship *as such*, that is, not of human father and motherhood, not of the founding of the family[5] on the basis of sexual relationship and the succession of generations. While what he is saying here does not address the question of sexual reproduction, it does assert

---

3. Cf. in Hans Urs von Balthasar, *Theo-Drama* II (San Francisco: Ignatius Press, 1990), 370, the quotation from E. Przywara: "On the one hand, we cannot regard sexuality as a closed circle, as if man cannot be human except within the sexual relationship between man and woman. . . ." *Mensch* 1 (1959): 134.

4. Balthasar, *Theo-Drama* II, 367-68.

5. Karl Barth, *Church Dogmatics* III/1, ed. Geoffrey W. Bromiley and T. F. Torrance (Edinburgh: T. & T. Clark, 1958), 312, quoted in Balthasar, *Theo-Drama* II, 381-82. Cf. also Barth, *Church Dogmatics* III/2, 300.

that, whereas the man represents a single principle (word, seed), the woman represents a double principle: she is the "answer" and the common "fruit" of both of them.

B. Feminine Creature

This yields an analogy for the relationship between God and the creature. We have already indicated that the creature can only be secondary, responsive; "feminine" vis-à-vis God. On the other hand, we may not in any way equate the Creator with Adam, for God does not need the creature for his fulfillment (as all pantheism assumes, be it of the static or the dynamic-evolutionist kind). In particular, according to Christian dogmatics, God the Father is under no necessity to separate himself from the product of his fruitfulness. He does not generate the Son in order to have a vessel into which to pour his richness but out of the superabundant fullness of his "selfless" love, which is not stimulated to self-communication by anything outside itself. Similarly, the answer in the form of the Son does not come, as it were, to the Father's "aid": he is a response of equal stature; and the Spirit, the fruit of their love, proceeds from their union—as their essence, their product, their testimony, their matrix—but he does not become an independent and separate instance, founding new generations himself. Thus the life of the Trinity is a circle, eternally fulfilled in itself; it does not need the world. As for the act of creation, it is founded on trinitarian freedom, "selflessly" granting to needy creatures a share in this life of blessed selflessness.

However, insofar as every creature—be it male or female in natural order—is originally the fruit of the primary, absolute, self-giving divine love, there is a clear analogy to the female principle in the world. Parthenogenesis can have no place here, by way of exception; yet the analogy goes farther: if the creature is to be God's "image", it must be equipped with its fruit-bearing principle, just like the woman (vis-à-vis the man). So we can say that every conscious creaturely being has a "mission" at a natural level (by remote analogy to what we have described as the christological mission): to be ready and open to receive the seed of the divine Word, to bear it and give it its fully developed form.

C. Wider Implications

Once the intramundane (man-woman) aspect and the supra-mundane (God-world) aspect come together in Jesus Christ, we can begin to see what woman's christological position might be. For the present we will just state the main principles, keeping to Scripture. Later these principles will have to be discussed in detail.

First, since the man Jesus Christ is an individual human being, his relationship to woman will be individual too; the woman to whom he relates is a particular person. On the other hand, insofar as he is the incarnate

Word of God, carrying out in his earthly existence the Father's commission to reconcile God's entire creation with God (2 Cor. 5:19), there will necessarily be a social aspect to his "helpmate," since she represents mankind (which, in relation to God, is female). These two aspects will be neither identical nor separable, reflecting the "unconfused" and "undivided" relationship of the human and divine sides in Jesus Christ, as set forth at Chalcedon (DS 302).

Furthermore we must distinguish between incarnation per se and incarnation "in the form of sinful flesh" (Rom. 8:3). Here we make a couple of observations on each of these two aspects.

If we consider the Incarnation per se of the Word insofar as he is *God*, we cannot say that he is incomplete without his female complement (like a Gnostic *syzygia* [dyad] or the first Adam). In fact, the Incarnate One possesses all "fullness" in himself (Col. 1:19; 2:9); out of his fullness he creates a vessel, then pours his fullness into it, fulfilling both it and—in a certain sense—himself through the realization of its possibilities (Eph. 1:23; cf. 4:13, 16).

But Christ, as a divine Person, is also truly *human* and a *man*. To that extent, as the Second and Last Adam, he bears a particular analogy to the First Adam. What the profound legend tells of the latter comes true in the case of the former, beyond all expectation: from the side of the sleeping Adam, the woman is drawn; now, from the (wounded) side of the sleeping Savior (on the Cross), the answering "face" of the woman is taken and "fashioned" (Eph. 5:27)—the woman who is essential to man's completeness. This is shown forth in the mystery of man and woman in the first creation, but the fullness of mystery is only attained in the mystery of Christ and his Church (Eph. 5:27, 33). The immediate reference here is to Genesis 2:24, that is, man and woman are "one flesh" because the woman comes from the man (who stands in need of her).

On the other hand, if we consider the specifically redemptive aspect of the Incarnation of the divine Word, the above remarks need to be complemented by the whole complex of issues arising from the sexual relationship in its post-paradisal form, where there is a correlation between begetting (and the birth resulting from it) and death. The difficulty is this: incarnation must take place *in* the sequence of generations if there is to be genuine humanity (otherwise we should be left with the Gnostic *illusion* of corporeality); yet the very purpose of this incarnation is to break the vicious circle of begetting and death (by the power of the Resurrection—anticipated by the Virgin Birth). Here, therefore, we have a unique soteriological situation that cannot be constructed a priori but must be read from the data of historical revelation. This again yields two propositions.

The Word of God can only genuinely enter into mankind's sequence of generations through conception, pregnancy and birth from a woman. As Paul observes, this reverses the situation as found in Adam: "As woman was made from man, so man is now born of woman" (1 Cor. 11:12). Here, for the first time, the relationship between mother and (male) child is explicitly highlighted. If the woman concerned is the Mother of a human Child who, in his person, is God, she will rightly be called Theotokos, God-bearer.

However, if this human Child is really God's Word, we are once again confronted by the two sides of the first aspect, and the question arises: What is the relationship between the woman as mother and woman as "helpmate" (or "bride" or "spouse": 2 Cor. 11:2; Eph. 5:26–27; Rev. 19:7; 21:2, 9), both in the personal and in the social dimension? This is a pressing question: the whole purpose of the redemption of the race of the First Adam by the Second Adam is to liberate mankind from all "futility" (Rom. 8:20) and to bring about that ultimate relationship between man and woman that is dimly anticipated in the paradise legend and set forth as a final destination in the "marriage of the Lamb" in the Book of Revelation.

The man-woman relationship is thus shown to be an ultimate one. All attempts to overcome it in the direction of an androgynous primal being or a sexless first nun must be dismissed. If woman is essentially an answer to man's call (she is created "for man," 1 Cor. 11:9), there are *two complexes of questions* with which a theodramatic theory must deal.

In the first, the individual woman, Mary, and the woman in-community, the Church, and the doctrine concerning them (Mariology, ecclesiology) are seen as functionally dependent on Christology. We shall develop this doctrine along these lines. But since Christology cannot be separated from soteriology, the problem of sexuality will become particularly acute for woman: she is bride and spouse to the man but mother to the child. To that extent she is not only "second" ("answer") but "dual" (*dyad*)—bearing in mind that we must not adopt the Greek subordination of the female dyad to the male monad.[6] We shall have to ask how this dyad can be brought from a form in which it is subject to sin to a form that is finally and definitively redeemed.

The second complex is intimately connected with the first. It concerns the specifically dramatic dimension of Mariology/ecclesiology. Here again we see very clearly that it is impossible to focus on the theodramatic roles unless, right from the start, we also bring out their inner dramatic potential. Thus from the very outset the person of Mary (and, accordingly, that of the Church, understood as *civitas Dei* [city of God]) goes through all the varied *status* of human nature. She must share in mankind's "original *status*," but also in its fallen *status*, since she must display solidarity with humanity in the concrete. Finally she must share in the "ultimate *status*," which her Son has initiated and, in his Resurrection, has himself assumed

---

6. As a sexual being, the man is explicitly monadic, whereas the woman is dyadic: the area of woman that interests the man sexually is not the same that the child desires for its sustenance.

once for all. We can already see that all the classical problems, particularly those associated with Mariology, arise from this twofold complex of questions.

It is clear from what we have said that Mariology and ecclesiology are closely intertwined. Which of these two roles comes first? Although the doctrine concerning the Church (of which, in a particular respect, Mary is a member) has the wider object, Mariology must claim priority insofar as it concerns the Mother of the Redeemer; for without him there would be neither a structured Church nor any divine grace whatsoever in world history before and after Christ. There is no question of a collective, not even the "faithful people," producing the Redeemer-Messiah out of itself, in virtue of its own faith. The fact that the Church can become the "Mother" of those who believe in Christ always presupposes that Mary conceived the Messiah and brought him to birth. That is why she can rightly be given the title "Mother of the Church."[7] But just as Christ came in order to serve, so Mary's motherhood vis-à-vis the Son and his Church is pure selflessness. No one has put this more beautifully than Ephrem the Syrian, who discerns the many-layered relationship between this Mother and this Son:

> My Son, I do not insist / that you will be with me
> and with all people. / Be God
> for him who confesses you, / and Lord
> for him who serves you, / and Brother
> to him who loves you; / in this way you will redeem them all.
>
> When you dwelt within me, / your majesty lived
> in me and outside of me. / And when I bore you
> visibly, / your invisible power
> did not part from me. / How you confuse your Mother;
> for you are in me / and outside of me!
>
> I see your image, / that external image
> which is before my eyes. / As for your invisible image,
> it is fashioned in my heart. / In your visible image
> I saw Adam, / and in that invisible image
> I saw your Father, / who is one with you.
>
> And did you / manifest your beauty
> two images only? / No; may your bread mold you,
> may the mind fashion you / Dwell in the bread
> and in those who eat it / Let your Church see you
> hidden and visible, / as your Mother does.[8]

---

7. Peter Damian was very clear in his teaching on this relationship. He calls Mary "the source of the living Source, the origin of the Beginning" (*Sermo* 45, in *PL* 144, 740ff.). He points out that Christ took flesh of Mary, whereas the Church was born from him, water and blood flowing from his side. "Thus we see that the Church also came forth from Mary" (*Sermo* 65, in *PL* 144, 861).

8. *De Nativitate* 16, 1–4 (Cod. Vat. syr. 113), quoted from E. Beck, "Die Mariologie der echten Schriften Ephraïms," in *Oriens Christianus* 40 (1956): 35.

SELECTION 9

Rosemary Radford Ruether

"Toward a Feminist Anthropology beyond Liberalism and Romanticism"

Rosemary Radford Ruether (1936–) is perhaps the most influential of the first generation of modern feminist theologians, having written the first comprehensive feminist systematic theology, *Sexism and God-Talk*, from which the following extract is taken. Ruether takes as her theological touchstone the conviction that every Christian doctrine should be judged according to whether or not it promotes the full humanity of women. In the face of the pervasive marginalization of women both from the practice and the content of theological reflection from biblical times onward, she insists on the need to invoke women's experience as both source and norm of theological reflection.

Trained as a historian of doctrine, Ruether builds her own constructive proposals in conversation with past trajectories in the history of the church, incorporating marginalized individuals and movements that are affirming of women's lives. In her anthropology she seeks to avoid both a liberal reduction of humanity to capacities privileged by a patriarchal social order (e.g., rationality, autonomy) and a one-sided affirmation of qualities (e.g., intuition, relationality) traditionally coded as female. Instead, she advocates a holistic affirmation of the full range of human psychological capacities while at the same time challenging the way in which these have been conventionally socialized. This leads to a certain relativization of the authority of traditional theological resources, including Scripture and even the person of Christ himself, who is affirmed as *a* but not *the* model of complete humanity.

From Rosemary Radford Ruether, *Sexism and God-Talk: Toward a Feminist Theology* (Boston: Beacon, 1983), 109–15.

Contemporary feminism inherits the traditions of both liberal and romantic feminism. It becomes divided and confused over the opposite values and directions espoused by each viewpoint. Both liberalism and romanticism are inadequate and yet both testify to important truths that I wish to affirm. A more adequate feminist anthropology would be one that finds a creative synthesis between the two. Liberal feminism too readily identifies normative human nature with those capacities for reason and rule identified with men and with the public sphere. It claims that women, while appearing to have lesser capacities for these attributes, actually possess them equally;

they have simply been denied the educational cultivation of them and the opportunity to exercise them. Opening up equal education and equal political rights to women will correct this and allow women's suppressed capacities for reason and rule to appear in their actual equivalence to men's.

There is important truth to this. Women, through the opening of equal education and political rights, have indeed demonstrated their ability to exercise the "same" capacities as men. But liberalism does not entirely recognize the more complex forms of women's psychological and economic marginalization that result in only token integration of women into "equal" roles in the public sphere. Liberalism assumes the traditional male sphere as normative and believes it is wrong to deny people access to it on the basis of gender. But once women are allowed to enter the public sphere, liberalism offers no critique of the modes of functioning within it.

Romanticism, in contrast, recognizes the moral ambiguity of the roles traditionally associated with masculinity. It idealizes the home, the private sphere of interpersonal relations, and places of "unspoiled nature" outside of urbanization and industrialization as havens of a more integrated humanity. It idealizes women precisely in their segregation from this ambiguous world. It tends to overlook the ambiguity and violence present in the sphere of private relationships, both the violation of women to keep them there and the way in which unexpressed angers and frustrations from the work world can be unleashed in the home. Altruism and service, while compensating women for acquiescence to relations of domination, also become a means of passive aggression masquerading as "helping others."

Romanticism is not entirely wrong in believing there are clues to a better humanity in the virtues relegated to women and the home in bourgeois society. But these virtues exist in deformed and deforming ways within the institutionalization of "woman's sphere." Moreover, the capacities traditionally associated with men and with public life also contain some important human virtues that women should not be forbidden to cultivate.

Thus neither masculinity traditionally defined nor femininity traditionally defined discloses an innately good human nature, and neither is simply an expression of evil. Both represent different types of alienation of humanity from its original potential. Socially, both home and work represent realms of corruption. If women will not be automatically redeemed by being incorporated into male political power and business in its present form, men will not automatically be redeemed by learning to nurture infants and keep house.

Androgyny has been used in recent feminist thought to express the human nature that all persons share. *Androgyny* refers to the possession by both males and females of both halves of the psychic capacities that have been traditionally separated as masculinity and femininity. The word *androgyny* is misleading, however, because it suggests that males and females possess both "masculine" and "feminine" sides to their psychic capacity. The term thus continues to perpetuate the ideas that certain psychic attributes are to be labeled masculine and others are to be labeled feminine and that humans, by integrating these "masculine" and "feminine" sides of themselves, become "androgynous."

There is no valid biological basis for labeling certain psychic capacities, such as reason, "masculine" and others, such as intuition, "feminine." To put it bluntly, there is no biological connection between male gonads and the capacity to reason. Likewise, there is no biological connection between female sexual organs and the capacity to be intuitive, caring, or nurturing. Thus the labeling of these capacities as masculine and feminine simply perpetuates gender role stereotypes and imports gender complementarity into each person's identity in a confusing way. Moreover, the idea of androgyny still preserves the idea of complementarity in complex form, since it suggests that males should integrate their androgynous identity around a "masculine" core of psychic capacities and females should integrate their androgyny around a "feminine" core.[1] We need to affirm not the confusing concept of all androgyny but rather that all humans possess a full and equivalent human nature and personhood, *as male and female*.

Maleness and femaleness exist as reproductive role specialization. There is no necessary (biological) connection between reproductive complementarity and either psychological or social role differentiation. These are the work of culture and socialization, not of "nature." Recent research on the bicameral brain has shown that the right brain specializes in intuitive, musical, relational, and spatial capacities and the left brain in linguistic and mathematical thinking. But this is, in no way, a basis for differentiating males and females as masculine and feminine, since obviously males and females possess both sides of the brain.

We referred [earlier in the book] to recent evidence that women mature earlier and create a more integrated relationship between right- and left-brain capacities. Males mature later and tend to have greater left- and right-brain specialization.[2] Added to this are cultural factors that identify

---

1. This way of defining androgyny is typical of Jungianism; it makes Jungianism seductive for women who fail to perceive its fundamentally androcentric and antifeminist bias. See C. J. Jung, *Aion: Research into the Phenomenology of the Self*, in *Collected Works*, vol. 9, pt. 2 (New York: Pantheon, 1959).

2. The experimental evidence for more lateralized brain development in males and more integrated brain development in females is controversial. See the article by Jeannette McGlone and the accompanying discussion in *The Behavioral and Brain Sciences* 3 (1980): 215–63. It is important to note that the evidence for gender difference in brain lateralization cannot be construed as invariable. At most, one can say there is evidence of a statistical tendency for women to integrate the functions of the brain across left and right hemispheres and males to separate brain functions between the hemispheres and to create left-brain dominance. But there is greater difference between females and between males on brain lateralization than between males and females. Moreover, there has been insufficient cross-cultural research to determine whether this tendency is more pronounced among white Western Europeans, while cultures that encourage males to develop intuitive and artistic capacities might differ. At most, we can say that the human brain has a capacity to develop either in more balanced and integrated modes of functioning between the two hemispheres or more lateralized modes and that, among white Westerners, there is some evidence that females tend more toward the first type of brain development and males more toward the second.

maleness, particularly in Western societies, with left-brain characteristics. Male culture forces on males further specialization in left-brain capacities, repressing the development and integration of right-brain characteristics. Females, in turn, have been prevented from developing their left-brain characteristics.

This research discloses *not* a biological basis for differentiation of males and females into different psychic profiles but rather the capacity of both sexes for psychic wholeness. It also suggests that women have a tendency toward greater integration and males toward a more dualistic perception of these characteristics. Thus brain research discloses a possible biological basis of men's cultural tendency to identify their ego with left-brain characteristics and to see right-brain characteristics as the "repressed" part of themselves, which they in turn project upon and identify with women. Androgyny, then, is basically a male and not a female problem. Females do not need to adopt this concept to express their quest for psychic wholeness.

Women should not identify themselves with those repressed parts of the male psyche that males have projected upon them as "feminine." Nor should they adopt the male, one-sided psychic profile that identifies the ego with linear, rational types of thinking. Rather they need to appropriate and deepen the integration of the whole self—relational with rational modes of thought—that is already theirs. This may mean that they need to extend the development of those capacities for rational thought that have been culturally denied them. They need to do this not in a dualistic way but in a way that integrates these rational capacities with relational modes of thought. In this sense women are right when they instinctively feel they have a specifically female way of developing their persons that is different from men's. But the understanding of this has been confused by its identification with the male-defined "feminine."

The extension and deepening of psychic integration lead women necessarily toward a critique not just of male psychic dualism but also of male sociological dualism. Psychic integration demands a social revolution. This means not just the integration of women into roles in the public sphere, defined by rational action, and the integration of males into domestic roles of caring and nurturing. These are indeed important beginnings, but the crossing of the psychic-social boundaries of the male dualistic world leads women on to a further vision, a transformation of the relationship between the spheres of psychic capacities and social roles.

Women, building upon psychic integration, seek a new sociological integration that overcomes the schizophrenia of mind and of society. Women want to integrate the public and the private, the political and the domestic spheres in a new relationship that allows the thinking-relational self to operate throughout human life as one integrated self, rather than fragmenting the psyche across a series of different social roles. Women want to tear down the walls that separate the self and society into "male" and "female" spheres. This demands not just a new integrated self but a new integrated social order.³

Thus the recovery of holistic psychic capacities and egalitarian access to social roles point us toward that lost full human potential that we may call "redeemed humanity." Redeemed humanity, reconnected with the *imago dei*, means not only recovering aspects of our full psychic potential that have been repressed by cultural gender stereotypes; it also means transforming the way these capacities have been made to function socially. We need to recover our capacity for relationality, for hearing, receiving, and being with and for others, but in a way that is no longer a tool of manipulation or of self-abnegation. We need to develop our capacities for rationality, but in a way that makes reason no longer a tool of competitive relations with others. Recovering our full psychic potential beyond gender stereotypes thus opens up an ongoing vision of transformed, redeemed, or converted persons and society, no longer alienated from self, from others, from the body, from the cosmos, from the Divine.

In traditional Christian theology, Christ is the model for this redeemed humanity that we have lost through sin and recover through redemption. But Christ as symbol is problematic for feminist theology. The Christological symbols have been used to enforce male dominance, and even if we go back behind masculinist Christology to the praxis of the historical Jesus of the synoptic Gospels, it is questionable whether there is a single model of redeemed humanity fully revealed in the past. This does not mean that feminist theology may not be able to affirm the person of Jesus of Nazareth as a positive model of redemptive humanity. But this model must be seen as partial and fragmentary, disclosing from the perspective of one person, circumscribed in time, culture, and gender, something of the fullness we seek. We need other clues and models as well, models drawn from women's experience, from many times and cultures.

The fullness of redeemed humanity, as image of God, is something only partially disclosed under the conditions of history. We seek it as a future self and world, still not fully achieved, still not fully revealed. But we also discover it as our true self and world, the foundation and ground of our being. When we experience glimpses of it, we recognize not an alien self but our own authentic self. We experience such glimpses through encounters with other persons whose own authenticity discloses the meaning of such personhood. By holding the memory of such persons in our hearts and minds, we are able to recognize authenticity in ourselves and others.

The life and death of Jesus of Nazareth is one such memory, one such paradigm.⁴ It is no less paradigmatic when we recognize that it is partial

---

3. See Lynda M. Glennon, *Women and Dualism: A Sociology of Knowledge Analysis* (New York: Longman & Green, 1979), 97–115.

4. Sallie McFague, *Metaphorical Theology: Models of God in Religious Language* (Philadelphia: Fortress Press, 1982). See chapter 4 on models in theology.

and needs to be joined by other models, other memories, particularly those that disclose the journey to redemptive personhood from women's experience. Thus the question of anthropology leads us, theologically, to the problem of Christology. Has Christology, in fact, been a model of redemptive personhood for women, or has it become a tool for enforcing female subjugation in patriarchal society? What are the possibilities, and limits, of discovering an alternative, usable Christology, a paradigm of redemptive personhood, for women in the praxis of the historical Jesus?

SELECTION 10

John Zizioulas

"From Biological to Ecclesial Existence: The Ecclesiological Significance of the Person"

John Zizioulas (1931–), Metropolitan Bishop of Pergamon, is one of the most widely read contemporary Orthodox theologians, having taught in Britain and published extensively in English. His theological writing is focused on the Trinitarian concept of the person or hypostasis, which for him is the key to understanding the destiny of human beings for life with God. Though he draws heavily on the Orthodox theological tradition as represented by figures like Gregory of Nyssa and Maximus the Confessor (especially in his relatively low appraisal of the ultimate significance of human sexual difference), he is also influenced by more contemporary currents in Western thought, including existentialist reflection on the defining role of freedom for genuinely human life.

The argument in the following extract from Zizioulas's book *Being as Communion* depends on a distinction between the concept of person (or hypostasis), on the one hand, and nature, on the other. For Zizioulas "nature" refers to those shared (especially biological) properties that shape (and thereby limit) the basic form of human existence, while "person" refers to the freedom through which one is able to transcend one's nature (e.g., the power of love whereby the ties of communion in the church prove stronger than purely biological relationships). Within this framework Zizioulas argues that although the human potential for personal existence is normally frustrated by the facts of their biology, in Christ human beings are offered the possibility of existence like God's own, in which the exercise of freedom is no longer constrained by nature but rather defines the terms in which the nature exists.

From John Zizioulas, *Being as Communion: Studies in Personhood and the Church*
(Crestwood, NY: St. Vladimir's Seminary Press, 1997), 49–65.

The eternal survival of the person as a unique, unrepeatable and free "hypostasis," as loving and being loved, constitutes the quintessence of salvation, the bringing of the Gospel to man. In the language of the Fathers this is called "divinization" (*theosis*), which means participation not in the nature or substance of God, but in His personal existence. The goal of salvation is that the personal life which is realized in God should also be realized on the level of human existence. Consequently salvation is identified with the realization of personhood in man. But is not "man" a person even without salvation? Is it not sufficient for him to be a "man" in order to be also a person?

Patristic theology considers the person to be an "image and likeness of God." It is not satisfied with a humanistic interpretation of the person. From this standpoint patristic theology sees man in the light of two "modes of existence." One may be called the *hypostasis of biological existence*, the other the *hypostasis of ecclesial existence*. A brief analysis and comparison of these two modes of human existence will explain why the concept of the person is inextricably bound up with theology.

1. *The hypostasis of biological existence* is "constituted" by a man's conception and birth. Every man who comes into the world bears his "hypostasis," which is not entirely unrelated to love: he is the product of a communion between two people. Erotic love, even when expressed coldly without emotional involvement, is an astounding mystery of existence, concealing in the deepest act of communion a tendency towards an ecstatic transcendence of individuality through creation. But this biological constitution of man's hypostasis suffers radically from two "passions" which destroy precisely that towards which the human hypostasis is thrusting, namely the person. The first "passion" is what we may call "ontological necessity." Constitutionally the hypostasis is inevitably tied to the natural instinct, to an impulse which is "necessary" and not subject to the control of freedom. Thus the person as a being "subsists" not as freedom but as necessity. As a result it does not have the power to affirm its hypostasis with absolute ontological freedom as I have described it above: if it attempts to raise freedom to the level of its ontological absoluteness, it will be confronted with the dilemma of nihilism.[1]

The second "passion" is a natural consequence of the first. At its earliest stage it may be called the "passion" of *individualism*, of the *separation* of the hypostases. Finally, however, it is identified with the last and greatest

---

[1]. The youth in adolescence, in the very period in which he becomes conscious of his freedom, asks: "and who consulted me when I was brought into the world?" Unconsciously he articulates the great theme of the ontological necessity which exists in the biological hypostasis.

passion of man, with the disintegration of the hypostasis, which is death. The biological constitution of the human hypostasis, fundamentally tied as it is to the necessity of its "nature," ends in the perpetuation of this "nature" through the creation of bodies, that is, of hypostatic unities which affirm their identity as *separation* from other unities or "hypostases." The body, which is born as a biological hypostasis, behaves like the fortress of an ego, like a new "mask" which hinders the hypostasis from becoming a person, that is, from affirming itself as love and freedom. The body tends towards the person but leads finally to the individual. The result of this situation is that for a man to take the affirmation of his hypostasis further he has no need of a relationship (an ontological relationship, not simply a psychological one) with his parents. On the contrary, the breaking of this relationship constitutes the *precondition* of his self-affirmation.

Death is the "natural" development of the biological hypostasis, the cession of "space" and "time" to other individual hypostases, the sealing of hypostasis as individuality. At the same time it is also the definitely tragic "self-negation" of its own hypostasis (dissolution and annihilation of the body and of individuality), which in its attempt to affirm itself as hypostasis discovers that finally its "nature" has led it along a false path towards death. This "failure" of nature, as it is expressed in the biological identity of man, reveals two things simultaneously. The first is that, contrary to the "assurance" of its biological drive, for the "hypostasis" to survive it must express itself as "ecstasy"—not sequentially but simultaneously, not first as being and then as person. The second is that this "failure" of the survival of the biological hypostasis is not the result of some acquired fault of a moral kind (a transgression), but of the very *constitutional make-up* of the hypostasis, that is, of the biological act of the perpetuation of the species.[2]

All this means that man as a biological hypostasis is intrinsically a tragic figure. He is born as a result of an *ecstatic* fact—erotic love—but this fact is interwoven with a natural necessity and therefore lacks ontological freedom. He is born as a *hypostatic* fact, as a body, but this fact is interwoven

---

2. St. Maximus the Confessor, following Gregory of Nyssa (*On the Making of Humankind* 16–18, *PG* 44.177 ff.; ET, *NPNF*[2], 5:404–9 [see pp. 105–13 above]), comes to the very root of the problem of human existence when he regards the biological mode of procreation as a result of the Fall (*Difficulties* 41–42, *PG* 81:1309A, 1340C ff.; [ET, *Difficulty* 41, in Andrew Louth, *Maximus the Confessor* (New York: Routledge, 1996), 156–62; (see pp. 123–29 above); ET, *Difficulty* 42 in St. Maximus the Confessor, *On the Cosmic Mystery of Jesus Christ: Selected Writings from St. Maximus the Confessor* (Crestwood, NY: St. Vladimir's Seminary Press, 2003), 79–95]; cf. *To Thalassius: On Various Questions* 61, *PG* 90:626 ff.; [ET, *On the Cosmic Mystery of Jesus Christ*, 131–43)]. Those who attribute this view of Maximus to a monastic or ascetic bias ignore the fact that he is not an ordinary thinker but perhaps one of the greatest and most creative geniuses in history, and that it is therefore impossible for him to say something without this being an organic and integral part of his whole thought. Maximus' position on this question is inspired by Matt. 22:30, that is, by the basic presupposition that the true "being" of man is found only in his eschatological state (see below). Victory over death, the survival of the person, is incomprehensible without a change in the constitutive mode of the human hypostasis, without a transcendence of the biological hypostasis. This does not imply Manichaeism: the biological and eschatological hypostases are not mutually exclusive (see below at note 16).

with individuality and with death. By the same erotic act with which he tries to attain ecstasy he is led to individualism. His body is the tragic instrument which leads to communion with others, stretching out a hand, creating language, speech, conversation, art, kissing. But at the same time it is the "mask" of hypocrisy, the fortress of individualism, the vehicle of the final separation, death. "Wretched man that I am! Who will deliver me from this body of death?" (Rom. 7:24). The tragedy of the biological constitution of man's hypostasis does not lie in his not being a person because of it; it lies in his tending towards becoming a person through it and failing. Sin is precisely this failure. And sin is the tragic prerogative of the person alone.

Consequently, for salvation to become possible, for the unsuccessful hypostasis to succeed, it is necessary that eros and the body, as expression of ecstasy and of the hypostasis of the person, should cease to be the bearers of death. Two things therefore appear to be indispensable: (a) that the two basic components of the biological hypostasis, eros and the body, should *not* be destroyed (a flight from these elements would entail for man a privation of those means by which he expresses himself equally as ecstasy and as hypostasis, that is, as person[3]); and (b) that the *constitutional make-up of the hypostasis* should be changed—not that a moral change or improvement should be found but a kind of new birth for man. This means that although neither eros nor the body are abandoned, they nevertheless change their activity, adapt themselves to the new "mode of existence" of the hypostasis, reject from this activity of theirs which is constitutive of the human hypostasis whatever creates the tragic element in man, and retain whatever makes the person to be love, freedom and life. This is precisely what constitutes that which I have called the "hypostasis of ecclesial existence."

2. The *hypostasis of ecclesial existence* is constituted by the new birth of man, by baptism. Baptism as new birth is precisely an act constitutive of hypostasis. As the conception and birth of a man constitute his biological hypostasis, so baptism leads to a new mode of existence, to a regeneration (1 Pet. 1:3, 23), and consequently to a new "hypostasis." What is the basis of this new hypostasis? How is man hypostasized by baptism and what does he become?

We have seen that the fundamental problem of the biological hypostasis of man lies in the fact that the ecstatic activity which leads to his birth is bound up with the "passion" of ontological necessity, in the fact that ontologically nature precedes the person and dictates its laws (by "instinct"), thus

---

3. Soteriologies which are not inspired by genuine patristic theology have created the following dilemma: either hypostasis without ecstasy (a kind of individual pietism), or ecstasy without hypostasis (a form of mystical escape from the body, an ecstasy of the type of the Hellenistic mysteries). The key to the soteriological problem lies in the safeguarding of both the ecstatic and the hypostatic dimensions of the person equally, without the "passions" of ontological necessity, individualism and death.

destroying freedom at its ontological base. This "passion" is closely connected with createdness, that is, with the fact that man as a person confronts, as we have already seen, the necessity of existence. Consequently it is impossible for created existence to escape ontological necessity in the constitution of the biological hypostasis: without "necessary" natural laws, that is, without ontological necessity, the biological hypostasis of man cannot exist.[4]

Consequently, if, in order to avoid the consequences of the tragic aspect of man which we have discussed, the person as absolute ontological freedom needs a hypostatic constitution without ontological necessity, his hypostasis must inevitably be rooted, or constituted, in an ontological reality which does not suffer from createdness. This is the meaning of the phrase in Scripture about being born "anew" or "from above" (John 3:3, 7). It is precisely this possibility that patristic Christology strives to proclaim, to announce to man as the good news.

Christology, in the definitive form which the Fathers gave it, looks towards a single goal of purely existential significance, the goal of giving man the assurance that the quest for the person, not as a "mask" or as a "tragic figure," but as the authentic person, is not mythical or nostalgic but is a *historical reality*. Jesus Christ does not justify the title of Savior because he brings the world a beautiful revelation, a sublime teaching about the person, but because He realizes in history *the very reality of the person* and makes it the basis and "hypostasis" of the person for every man. Patristic theology therefore regarded the following points as the indispensable elements of Christology:

a) The identification of the person of Christ with the hypostasis of the Son of the Holy Trinity. The long dispute with Nestorianism was not an exercise of academic theology but a hard struggle with the existential question: how is it possible for Christ to be the Savior of man if His hypostasis is what I have called here the "hypostasis of biological existence"? If Christ as a person "subsists" not in freedom but according to the necessity of nature, then He too finally, that is, definitively, fails to escape the tragic aspect of the human person.[5] The meaning of the virgin birth of Jesus is

---

4. The artificial conception of a human being, if it is ever achieved, will by no means imply freedom as regards the constitutive mode of the human hypostasis. Instead it will imply the henceforth unfree replacement of nature and its laws with the laws of human reason.

5. I stress the word "finally" because this is of vital importance in Christology. All things in Christology are judged in the light of the resurrection. The incarnation in itself does not constitute a guarantee of salvation. The fact that *finally* death is conquered gives us the right to believe that the conqueror of death was also *originally* God. This is the way in which Christology in the New Testament has developed—from the resurrection to the incarnation, not the other way round—and patristic theology has never lost this eschatological approach to Christology. Consequently, when we say that Christ escaped the necessity and the "passions" of nature, we do not imply that He remained a stranger to the conditions of biological existence (for example, He suffered the supreme passion of the biological hypostasis, the passion of death). But the fact that He rose from the dead rendered this passion "without hypostasis": the real hypostasis of Christ was proved to be not the biological one, but the eschatological or trinitarian hypostasis.

the negative expression of this existential concern of patristic theology. The positive expression of the same concern consists in the Chalcedonian doctrine that the person of Christ is *one* and is identified with the *hypostasis of the Son of the Trinity*.

b) The *hypostatic* union of the two natures—divine and human—in Christ. At this point it is important that a difference of emphasis should be stressed between the Greek and the Western Fathers which is parallel to that which was noted earlier in relation to the doctrine of the Holy Trinity. In the West, as is apparent in the *Tome* of Pope Leo I, the starting-point of Christology is found in the concept of the "natures" or "substances," whereas in the Greek Fathers, for example in Cyril of Alexandria, the starting-point of Christology is the hypostasis, the person. However much this might seem at first sight a mere detail, it is of the greatest significance. For it stresses not only, as we have seen, with regard to God but now also with regard to man that the basis of ontology is the person: just as God "is" what He is in His nature, "perfect God," only as person, so too man in Christ is "perfect man" only as hypostasis, as person, that is, as freedom and love. The perfect man is consequently only he who is authentically a person, that is, he who subsists, who possesses a "mode of existence" which is constituted as being, *in precisely the manner in which God also subsists as being*—in the language of human existence this is what a "hypostatic union" signifies.

Christology consequently is the proclamation to man that his nature can be "assumed" and hypostasized in a manner free from the ontological necessity of his biological hypostasis, which, as we have seen, leads to the tragedy of individualism and death. Thanks to Christ man can henceforth himself "subsist," can affirm his existence as personal not on the basis of the immutable laws of his nature, but on the basis of a relationship with God which is identified with what Christ in freedom and love possesses as Son of God with the Father. This adoption of man by God, the identification of his hypostasis with the hypostasis of the Son of God, is the essence of baptism.[6]

I have called this hypostasis which baptism gives to man "ecclesial" because, in fact, if one should ask, "How do we see this new biological hypostasis of man realized in history?" the reply would be, "In the Church." In early patristic literature the image of the Church as mother is often employed. The spirit of this image is precisely that in the Church a birth is brought about;

---

6. The structure of the sacrament of baptism was identified at the outset with the structure of the evangelical narrative of the baptism of Jesus. The words, "this is my beloved [or: only-begotten] Son in whom I am well pleased," uttered by the Father with reference to the Son of the Trinity in the presence of the Spirit, are pronounced at baptism with reference to the person being baptized. In this way the structure of the Trinity is made the structure of the hypostasis of the person being baptized, a fact which makes Paul summarize the sense of baptism with the phrase, "Spirit of adoption, in which we cry Abba, Father" (Rom. 8:15).

man is born as "hypostasis," as person. This new hypostasis of man has all the basic characteristics of what I have called authentic personhood, characteristics which distinguish the ecclesial hypostasis from the first hypostasis, the biological one. In what do these characteristics consist?

The first and most important characteristic of the Church is that she brings man into a kind of relationship with the world which is not determined by the laws of biology. The Christians of the early centuries, when their consciousness of what the Church is was lucid and clear, expressed this transcendence over the relationships created by the biological hypostasis by transferring *to the Church* the terminology which is used of the family.[7] Thus for the new ecclesial hypostasis "father" was not the physical progenitor but He "who is in heaven," and "brothers" were the members of the Church, not of the family. That this signified not a parallel co-existence of the ecclesial with the biological hypostasis but a transcendence of the latter by the former is apparent from the harshness of sayings like those which demand of Christians the abandonment—even the "hatred"—of their own relations.[8] These sayings do not signify a simple denial. They conceal an affirmation: the Christian through baptism stands over against the world, he exists as a relationship with the world, as a person, in a manner free from the relationship created by his biological identity. This means that henceforth he can love not because the laws of biology oblige him to do so—something which inevitably colors the love of one's own relations—but *unconstrained* by the natural laws. As an ecclesial hypostasis man thus proves that what is valid for God can also be valid for man: the nature does not determine the person; the person enables the nature to exist; freedom is identified with the being of man.

The result of this freedom of the person from the nature, of the hypostasis from biology, is that in the Church man transcends exclusivism. When man loves as a biological hypostasis, he inevitably excludes others: the family has priority in love over "strangers," the husband lays exclusive claim to the love of his wife—facts altogether understandable and "natural" for the biological hypostasis. For a man to love someone who is not a member of his family *more* than his own relations constitutes a transcendence of the exclusiveness which is present in the biological hypostasis. Thus a characteristic of the ecclesial hypostasis is the capacity of the person to love without exclusiveness, and to do this not out of conformity with a moral commandment ("Love thy neighbor," etc.), but out of his "hypostatic constitution," out of the fact that his new birth from the womb

---

7. "And I take it to mean Christ and the Church" (Eph. 5:32).

8. "You are all brethren; and call no man your father on earth, for you have one Father, who is in heaven" (Matt. 23:8–9). Cf. Matt. 4:21; 10:25, 27; 19:29 and parallel texts, especially Luke 14:26: "If anyone comes to me and does not hate his own father and mother and wife and children and brothers and sisters, yes, and even his own life . . ." that is, the whole network of relations that constitutes the biological hypostasis.

of the Church has made him part of a network of relationships which transcends every exclusiveness.[9] This means that only in the Church has man the power to express himself as a catholic person. Catholicity, as a characteristic of the Church, permits the person to become a hypostasis without falling into individuality, because in the Church two things are realized simultaneously: the world is presented to man not as mutually exclusive portions which he is called upon to unite *a posteriori*, but as a single whole, which is expressed in a catholic manner without division in every concrete being; simultaneously the same man, while relating to the world precisely through this catholic mode of existence that he has, comes to express and realize a catholic presence in the world, a hypostasis which is not an individual but an authentic person. Thus the Church becomes Christ Himself in human existence, but also every member of the Church becomes Christ[10] and Church.[11] The ecclesial hypostasis exists historically in this manner as a confirmation of man's capacity not to be reduced to his tendency to become a bearer of individuality, separation and death. The ecclesial hypostasis is the *faith* of man in his capacity to become a person and his *hope* that he will indeed become an authentic person. In other words it is faith and hope in the immortality of man as a person.

This last sentence leads us to a most important point, to which we must address ourselves at once. For all that I have said so far leaves a question unanswered: what happens to the biological hypostasis of man when that which I have called the ecclesial hypostasis is brought into being? Experience tells us that in spite of the existence of baptism and the ecclesial hypostasis, man does not cease at the same time to be born and to die in accordance with his biological hypostasis. What kind of experience of authentic personhood is it that the ecclesial hypostasis offers?

In order to reply to this question we really need a new ontological category—not to destroy the distinction which I have made between biological and ecclesial hypostases, but to express the relationship of these two to each other. In fact the encounter between the ecclesial and the biological hypostases creates a paradoxical relationship in human existence. Man appears to exist in his ecclesial identity not as that which he is but as that which he *will* be; the ecclesial identity is linked with eschatology, that is, with the final outcome of his existence.

This consideration of the human person from the point of view of a *telos* must not be interpreted with the help of an Aristotelian entelechy, that is,

---

9. Thus the Church proves (a) that salvation is not a matter of moral perfection, an improvement of nature, but a new hypostasis of nature, a new creation, and (b) that this new hypostasis is not something theoretical, but a historical *experience*, even though it is not permanent.

10. It is characteristic that according to the Fathers every baptized person becomes "Christ."

11. St. Maximus the Confessor in his *Mystagogy* 4 (*PG* 91.672B-C; ET, *Maximus Confessor: Selected Writings* [New York: Paulist Press, 1985], 189–90) applies the catholicity of the Church to the existential make-up of each believer.

with the help of a potentiality existing in man's nature which enables him to become something better and more perfect than that which he is now.[12] Through all that I have said in this study, I have excluded every possibility of regarding the person as an expression or emanation of the substance or nature of man (or even of God Himself as "nature"). Consequently there is no question of the ecclesial hypostasis, the authentic person, emerging as a result of an evolution of the human race, whether biological or historical.[13] The situation created by the expectation and hope of the ecclesial identity, by this paradoxical hypostasis which has its roots in the future and its branches in the present,"[14] could perhaps have been expressed by another ontological category, which I would call here a *sacramental* or *eucharistic hypostasis*.

3. All that I have said above to describe the ecclesial hypostasis as something different from the biological corresponds historically and experientially only to the holy eucharist. The transcendence of the ontological necessity and exclusiveness entailed by the biological hypostasis constitutes an experience which is offered by the eucharist. When it is understood in its correct and primitive sense—and not how it has come to be regarded even in Orthodoxy under the influence of Western scholasticism—the eucharist is first of all an assembly (*synaxis*),[15] a community, a network of relations, in which man "subsists" in a manner different from the biological as a member of a body which transcends every exclusiveness of a biological or social kind. The eucharist is the only historical context of human existence where the terms "father," "brother," etc., lose their biological exclusiveness and reveal, as we have seen, relationships of free and universal love.[16] Patristic theology saw in the eucharist the historical realization

---

12. Teilhard de Chardin's understanding of man bears no relation to patristic theology.

13. Herein also lies a fundamental distinction between Christianity and Marxism.

14. The Epistle to the Hebrews (11:1) uses the term "hypostasis" precisely with the meaning which I am endeavoring to describe here, that is, as an ontology which has its roots in the future, in eschatology.

15. The term *ekklēsia* is not unrelated in its original Christian usage to the fact of the eucharistic community. For the relevant sources see my work, *The Unity of the Church in the Holy Eucharist and the Bishop during the First Three Centuries* (in Greek—1965), 29–59.

16. If the Lord's prayer was indeed, as it appears, a eucharistic prayer from the beginning, there is special significance in the fact that the expression, "our Father, who are in heaven," appears there evidently in contradistinction to the relation of every believer with his earthly father. Also illuminating is the history of the use of the term "father" for the clergy. Originally it was used only of the bishop, precisely because only he was seated "in the place of God" (Ignatius) and offered the eucharist. Then it was transferred to the presbyter when he finally assumed a role of leadership in the eucharistic community with the creation of parishes. With regard to the catholicity of the eucharistic community, that is, the transcendence of natural and social divisions, let us note the strict ancient canonical requirement that only one eucharist should be celebrated in the same place on the same day. This prescription (which today among the Orthodox is circumvented "intelligently" by the erection of a new altar and the services of another priest in the same church on the same day) had as its aim precisely the practical safeguarding of the possibility for all the faithful of the same locality to participate in the same eucharistic community. I leave aside the other new custom of celebrating the eucharist only for certain groups of Christians, whether social (for students, scholars, etc.) or natural (for small children, etc.), or even specially for members of organizations. What we have here is the establishment of a heresy in the midst of Orthodoxy, the denial of the catholicity of the eucharistic community.

of the philosophical principle which governs the concept of the person, the principle that the hypostasis expresses the whole of its nature and not just a part. There Christ is "parted but not divided" and every communicant is the whole Christ and the whole Church. The ecclesial identity, consequently, in its historical realization is eucharistic. This explains why the Church has bound every one of her acts to the eucharist, which has as its object man's transcendence of his biological hypostasis and his becoming an authentic person, like those acts which we call "sacraments." The sacraments when not united with the eucharist are a blessing and confirmation which is given to nature as biological hypostasis. United, however, with the eucharist, they become not a blessing and confirmation of the biological hypostasis, but a rendering of it transcendent and eschatological.[17]

It is precisely this eschatological character of the eucharist that helps us to reply to the question, "What is the relationship of the ecclesial with the biological hypostasis?" The eucharist is not only an assembly in one place, that is, a historical realization and manifestation of the eschatological existence of man; it is at the same time also *movement*, a progress towards this realization. Assembly and movement are the two fundamental characteristics of the eucharist, which unfortunately have lost their vigor in the modern teaching of dogma, even in the Orthodox Church. However, they constitute the vital core of patristic eucharistic theology.[18] Besides this, they make the eucharist *liturgy*. This liturgical, progressive movement of the eucharist, its eschatological orientation, proves that in its eucharistic expression the ecclesial hypostasis is not of this world—it belongs to the eschatological transcendence of history and not simply to history. The ecclesial hypostasis reveals man as a person, which, however, has its roots in the future and is perpetually inspired, or rather maintained and nourished, by the future. *The truth and the ontology of the person belong to the future, are images of the future.*[19]

What exactly does this hypostasis mean for the existence of man, this hypostasis which is "the assurance (*hypostasis*) of things hoped for, the

---

17. On the fact that sacraments were all formerly linked with the eucharist see P. Trembelas, "I Theia Efcharietia kata tin synarthrosin aftis pros ta alla mystiria kai mystirioeideis teletas," *Efcharisitirion*, essays in honour of H. Alivisatos, 1958, 462–72. The theological significance of this liturgical fact is immense. For example, it would be a mistake to regard marriage as a simple confirmation and blessing of a biological fact. Linked with the eucharist it becomes a reminder that although the newly married couple have been blessed in order to created their own family, nevertheless the ultimate and essential network of relationships which constitutes their hypostasis is not the family but the Church as expressed in the eucharistic assembly. This eschatological transcendence of the biological hypostasis is also conveyed by the "crowning" of the bride and groom, but is lost essentially and existentially from the moment the rite of marriage is separate from the eucharist.

18. In St. Maximus' *Mystagogy* the holy eucharist is understood as movement, as progress towards the goal (*to peras*). This dimension of the eucharist is weakened in the interpretations of the eucharist towards the end of the Byzantine age, and is lost entirely in the modern dogmatic handbooks.

19. Maximus gives a philosophical summary of the authentic patristic (and one would also say "biblical") ontology when he identifies the true nature of beings with the future, with the last things: "For 'shadow' refers to the things of the Old Testament, 'image' to the things of the New Testament, and 'truth' to the future state" (Scholion on *The Ecclesiastical Hierarchy* 3.3.2, in PG 4:137D).

conviction of things not seen" (Heb. 11:1)? Does not this situation bring us back to the tragic aspect of the person?

This eschatological character of the ecclesial hypostasis contains, of course, a kind of dialectic, the dialectic of "already but not yet." This dialectic pervades the eucharist.[20] It makes man as a person always sense that his true home is not in this world, a perception which is expressed by his refusal to locate the confirmation of the hypostasis of the person in this world, in the goods and values of this world.[21] The ecclesial hypostasis, as a transcendence of the biological, draws its being from the being of God and from that which it will itself be at the end of the age. It is precisely this which makes the ecclesial hypostasis ascetic.[22]

The ascetic character of the ecclesial hypostasis does not come from a denial of the world or of the biological *nature* of existence itself.[23] It implies a denial of the biological *hypostasis*. It accepts the biological nature but wishes to hypostasize it in a non-biological way, to endow it with real being, to give it a true ontology, that is, eternal life. It is for this reason that I stated previously that neither eros nor the body must be abandoned but must be hypostasized according to the "mode of existence" of the ecclesial hypostasis. The ascetic character of the person, derived as it is from the eucharistic form of the ecclesial hypostasis, expresses the authentic person precisely when it does not deny eros and the body but hypostasizes them in an ecclesial manner. In accordance with what I have said so far, in practice this means basically that eros as ecstatic movement of the human person drawing its hypostasis from the future, as it is expressed in the eucharist (or

---

20. See, for example, the Revelation of St. John: although nothing is more certain there than the presence of Christ in the eucharist, and yet the cry, "Come, Lord," and the assurance, "I am coming soon" (22:8–17) change Him who is already present into Him who is expected, or rather, make Him present precisely as the expected one. Cf. *Didache* 9–10 (ET, *LCC* 1:175–76).

21. It is therefore better understood for example why "the root of all evils is avarice" (1 Tim. 6:10) and wealth excludes from the Kingdom of God (Luke 6:24, etc.). This has to do not with a moral fault but with the location of the hypostasis of being, of its security, in this world, in the substance and not in the person. (Is it simply a coincidence that the term *ousia* came also to mean "property" or "possessions" very early on? See Luke 15:12. Cf. Euripides, *Madness of Herakles* 337; Aristophanes, *Ekklesiazousai* 729.)

22. The meaning of asceticism consists in the fact that the less one makes one's hypostasis rely on nature, on the substance, the more one is hypostasized as a person. In this way asceticism does not deny "nature" but frees it from the ontological necessity of the biological hypostasis; it enables it to *be* in an authentic manner. It is superfluous to stress that this does not suffice to bring about the transcendence of the biological hypostasis if nature is not "hypostasized" simultaneously in the eucharistic community. Other, non-Christian soteriological systems also exhibit asceticism as a transcendence of the biological hypostasis. But only the Church offers the positive side of this transcendence in the way I have just described with reference to the eucharist. (From the point of view of the historical phenomenology of religions it must some day be understood that only the eucharist in its correct sense is the specific differentiating factor of Christianity.) Without the ascetic dimension, the person is inconceivable. But in the end the context of the manifestation of the person is not the monastery: it is the eucharist.

23. The *logos phuseōs* [structure of nature] has no need of transformation; the *tropos phuseōs* [mode in which the nature subsists] demands it. Maximus, *Difficulty* 42, in *PG* 91:1340B–C, 1341C; [ET, *Difficulty* 42, in *On the Cosmic Mystery of Jesus Christ: Selected Writings from St. Maximus the Confessor* (Crestwood, NY: St. Vladimir's Seminary Press, 2003), 79–95].

from God through the eucharist, as it is expressed in the Trinity), is freed from ontological necessity and does not lead any more to the exclusiveness which is dictated by nature. It becomes a movement of free love with a universal character, that is, of love which, while it can concentrate on one person as the expression of the whole of nature, sees in this person the hypostasis through which all men and all things are loved and in relation to which they are hypostasized.[24] The body, for its part, as the hypostatic expression of the human person, is liberated from individualism and egocentricity and becomes a supreme expression of *community*—the Body of Christ, the body of the Church, the body of the eucharist. Thus it is proved experientially that the body is not in itself a negative or exclusive concept, but the reverse: a concept of communion and love. In this hypostasis which it has, the body transcends together with its individualism and separation from other beings even its own dissolution, which is death. Since it has been shown as a body of communion to be free from the laws of its biological nature with regard to individualism and exclusiveness, why should it not also be shown finally to be free even from the very laws relating to death, which are only the other side of the same coin? The ecclesial existence of man, his hypostasization in a eucharistic manner, thus constitutes a pledge, an "earnest," of the final victory of man over death. This victory will be a victory not of nature but of the person, and consequently not a victory of man in his self-sufficiency but of man in his hypostatic union with God, that is, a victory of Christ as the man of patristic Christology.

It is precisely on this point that the eucharistic hypostasis differs from the tragic person of humanism, that is, on the fact that in spite of living the tragic aspect of the biological hypostasis intensely and absolutely—from which Christian asceticism also comes[25]—it does not draw its being from what it is now but is rooted ontologically in the future, the pledge and earnest of which is the resurrection of Christ. As often as he tastes and experiences this hypostasis in the eucharist, man is confirmed in his certitude that the person which is hypostasized by love freed from biological necessity and exclusiveness will not finally die. When the eucharistic community keeps alive the memory of our loved ones—living as well as dead—it does not just preserve a psychological recollection; it proceeds to an act of ontology, to the assurance that the person has the final word over nature, in the same way that God the Creator as person and not as nature had the very first word. Belief in creation *ex nihilo*—biblical faith—thus encounters

---

24. The great existential significance of patristic Christology consists in the fact that the capacity of the person to love in one person alone all things and all men is an attribute of God, who as *Father*, although He hypostasizes and loves one Son alone (the "only-begotten"), can, "through the Son" love and bestow hypostasis on all creation ("all things were created through Him and for Him." Col. 1:16).

25. The similarities which appear at first sight to exist between the understanding of man in the works of the ascetic Fathers and the insights of contemporary existentialism arise from this. But the ascetic Fathers do not exhaust the concept of the person in the reality of the biological hypostasis; they also recognize its eschatological transcendence.

belief in ontology—Greek faith—to give to human existence and thought its most dear and precious good, the concept of the person. This and nothing less than this is what the world owes to Greek patristic theology.

SELECTION 11

Mary McClintock Fulkerson

"Contesting the Gendered Subject: A Feminist Account of the *Imago Dei*"

Mary McClintock Fulkerson (1950–) teaches at the Divinity School of Duke University and is among the leading second-generation feminist theologians. Though building on the work of earlier feminists, Fulkerson is in the following essay critical of attempts like Ruether's to construct a theological anthropology that affirms the full humanity of women by simply adopting a more inclusive account of the image of God. Instead, Fulkerson uses poststructuralist insights into the way language generates meaning to argue that any account of the *imago Dei* will invariably exclude some human group. In the face of this situation, Fulkerson argues that the chief task of theological anthropology should be to identify and destabilize the implicit content of the divine image in traditional theological discourse in order to help bring to light those persons whose humanity has been ignored. Thus, over against nearly two millennia of theological attempts to define the positive content of the *imago Dei*, Fulkerson argues that the most urgent task of theological anthropology is to identify what the divine image is not, so as to avoid the selective privileging of some human beings over others.

From *Horizons in Feminist Theology: Identity, Tradition, and Norms*,
ed. Rebecca S. Chopp and Sheila Greeve Davaney (Minneapolis: Fortress, 1997), 99–115.

There is no better place to look for the intersection of feminist theological and secular thinking than at the problem of the gendered subject, one of the most important and contested issues in current feminist thinking. Referring to the ways a subject comes to be defined as woman, the gendered subject first arose as a challenge to the false universal mankind. Early criticisms from women of color, lesbian women, and class-based feminisms noted the false universal in feminist appeals to woman. The recent jargon of feminist theory calls these problems of essentialism and the politics of identity. Feminist theologians need to care about the gendered subject because secular feminist accounts of the subject are unavoidable and embedded in our thinking. Put simply, the dilemma is how a feminism defined by the desire to alleviate women's oppression can avoid being hopelessly hegemonic with its focus on a limited subject.

My point of departure for this topic is theological feminism and its liberating frame for the gendered subject, the *imago Dei* of women. When we assess feminist theories of the subject, some of the problems related to hegemonic difference appear in the classic feminist theological treatment of women as *imago Dei*. However, a poststructuralist intervention offers a different kind of "difference" worth consideration, which can helpfully chasten a reconfigured story of the *imago Dei*. Finally, my assumption that feminist theory and theology are social-change practices leads me out of the potential paralysis of poststructuralist destabilizations to argue for the distinctive contribution provided by new Christian feminist narrations of the creation of a loving, just God. I begin with a quick review of major feminist accounts of the gendered subject.

The Subject Changes

Contesting the notion of the subject is definitional to feminist explorations. This is best illustrated in the elegantly simple statement of Simone de Beauvoir—"One is not born a woman"—an insight which originated all modern feminist accounts of gender, says Donna Haraway.[1] Major types of feminism have explored the "constructed" character of the designation woman to varying degrees over these past decades. To see the emancipatory implications and problems of this development, we begin with nineteenth-century liberal feminism.

The now-familiar subject of liberal feminism emerged out of the "woman movement" in the United States. Defining women as potential citizens and rational creatures, this group thought education and legislative action would solve women's problems. This rationalistic notion of woman as person assumed masculinity and femininity to be secondary attributes of human being, a position that implied the existence of a common humanity. This generic concept has been judged suspect by later feminisms, and it is fair to say that many view this as an androcentric rather than a generic notion of human nature.[2]

A feminist alternative to the ostensibly genderless liberal subject emerged in the late 1960s when use of *gender* as a term for language forms was overtaken by its use to refer to constructions of maleness and femaleness.[3] Although its early expression in "gender identity" studies (focused

---

1. Donna Haraway, "'Gender' for a Marxist Dictionary: The Sexual Politics of a Word," in *Simians, Cyborgs, and Women: The Reinvention of Nature* (New York: Routledge, 1992), 31.
2. Alison Jaggar, *Feminist Politics and Human Nature* (Totowa, NJ: Rowman & Allanheld, 1983), 46–47.
3. Linda Nicholson, "Interpreting Gender," *Signs: Journal of Women in Culture and Society* 20 (Autumn 1994): 80.

on normal gender "roles") had a conservative effect, the possibilities for social criticism opened up with this change in definition. This work assumed that a biological difference grounded accounts of masculinity and femininity (a view that characterized feminist theorizing into the early 1970s).[4] However, even with its limits, an impulse toward more radical possibilities of criticism is evident in this move to constructionism in the treatment of gender.

Feminist thinkers developed these possibilities in the 1960s and 1970s, when the concept of gender could increasingly "contest the naturalization of sexual difference in multiple arenas of struggle," as Donna Haraway put it.[5] Marxist and socialist feminisms expanded feminist constructionism on the basis of Marxist, historicizing concepts of human nature. Human being as maker is *being made* in history in these systems.[6] Although such feminisms get stuck in the problem of expanding production to include "women's work," and continue to assume a biologically sexed subject, at their best they define human nature as *in process*. They thereby imply that historical change could (potentially) challenge even that binary subject, particularly if reproduction could be detached from women's bodies.

The expansion of the category *gender* takes a slightly different turn in lesbian and radical feminism.[7] These feminisms correct the Marxist failure to interrogate constructions of sexuality properly. From some radical feminisms we also get a revalorization of the female body. With that recovery radical feminism offers a notion of the subject that is sometimes judged to be essentialist. Such a view assumes that the authentic human is a woman, defined as a naturally gendered/sexed body. Despite this continuing naturalization, these feminisms expose the centrality of sexuality and heterosexuality, in particular, in the oppression of women.

I offer this hasty and unnuanced sketch of feminist accounts of the gendered subject to highlight the ways they employ the idea that a subject is *made a woman*, as de Beauvoir put it. Gender is a moving concept. It extends de Beauvoir's modest pronouncement by pressing the question, How are subjects constructed into something called woman? What it means to be a woman has increasingly been understood by feminists as a function of social definition rather than a natural essence or subjectivity. As such these accounts are exercises in social constructionism, asking how ideas about reality are products of their contexts and how they reflect the biases, limits, and possibilities of their contexts. They assume, then,

---

4. Haraway, "Gender," 132–34.
5. Ibid., 131.
6. Marxist feminists include Frederick Engels, Heidi Hartmann, Paddy Quick, and Julie Mitchell. See Jaggar, *Feminist Politics*, 51–82, 207–47. Socialist feminists are too numerous to name. See, in the same volume, 123–71, 302–50.
7. Also called or linked with "cultural feminism." Jaggar, Hester Eisenstein, Josephine Donovan, and Rosemarie Tong have typologies that treat this subject with more nuance.

the finite or partial nature of constructions such as gender. Although each feminism considered has a different frame for defining women's oppression and liberation, to some degree each assumes the emancipatory thrust of constructionism: that to recognize the *made* character of the female/male is to create an opening for things to be different.

This expanding application of the sociology of knowledge to the concept of the gendered subject does not, however, exempt these feminist interrogations from hegemonies, that is, from commitments to particular identities that deny the validity of the Other. According to a liberal feminist notion of the subject, one is a woman but aspires to be a neutral citizen; the stable, unacknowledged hegemonic subject is still white male. Marxist/socialist feminisms define the production of the subject through social and historical conditions, but remain generic on gender. Despite the expansion of feminist concern into the production of sexuality, for significant forms of radical feminism authenticity is ostensibly classless and colorless. The continual use of "woman" as a nonclassed or nonracial category to which class/race can be added is, according to Elizabeth Spelman, clear evidence of the serious ethnocentrism of feminism.[8]

Yet a commitment to women or to any group brings assumptions that cannot be avoided. Social constructionism, which is emancipatory for feminists, implies that it is impossible to produce liberatory discourse without particularity, which is necessarily a choosing of this and not that—a kind of exclusion. By virtue of being historical and contextual, the particular is partial and finite. There is, then, a risk entailed in any feminist commitment to particular accounts of women, at least the risk of partiality.

However, to further characterize and identify the nature of this risk we need to know feminists' visions of their emancipatory subjects. Only that knowledge would tell us what counts as the relevant form of hegemony. At least two possibilities seem likely for the reach of that vision. If the vision of feminism's emancipatory subject includes all women, then we would expect that its account explaining the basic oppression of women should be adequate for all women. Or at least we would expect that it had a frame for expanding the horizon of concern beyond its particular focus and analysis. However, the primary frames for feminism are specific accounts of the oppression of women. A liberatory discourse must analyze the constitutive parts of oppression and how to address it. It is clear from the continual criticisms that none has yet accounted for the oppression of all women. Only secondarily do these feminisms show how the category woman could expand beyond its limitations to recognize the subject who is different, particularly that woman not subject to the particular form of oppression under discussion. Implicit frames for humanism employed in

---

8. Elizabeth V. Spelman, *Inessential Woman: Problems of Exclusion in Feminist Thought* (Boston: Beacon, 1988).

feminist thinking and the potential to add categories (race, class, and so forth) via the logic of social constructionism strike me as the basic frames for expansion.

Although this assessment needs further argument, I find these treatments less than satisfactory for answering how feminism can expand its focus beyond a particular subject. While explaining the specific conditions that make woman an element in an oppressive set of social arrangements is the lifeblood of feminism, feminists should also enable the focus on the particular to resist rather than create new hegemonies. It is not clear to me how feminist commitments to the particular satisfactorily address the production of those capacities.

This is not the end of feminist theory's interrogation of the subject, however. An alternative to these approaches to the subject woman is poststructuralism, in which antihumanism effectively destabilizes the notion of subjects altogether. Feminist poststructuralist interventions will confirm my suspicion that constructionism is inadequate for a nonhegemonic account of the gendered subject and that a feminist theological project should be simply a project of inclusion. With it, feminist thinking about difference becomes more complex.

The Subject Disappears

First, I offer some background to poststructuralism. With the term poststructuralism I refer to a set of discussions about signification within but not identical with postmodernism. With roots in the linguistics of Ferdinand de Saussure and structuralism, poststructuralism developed from thinking about language as an organizing structure or process of differentiation rather than a set of labels that reflect or mirror reality. Out of his realization that the synchronic (present structural) relations of words are more important for understanding language than their diachronic (historical, temporal) relations, Saussure determined that language makes meaning through differential and arbitrary relations of sounds and concepts which are ordered by systems.[9]

Poststructuralist corrections of Saussure's structuralism include the view that these relations do not occur simply in structures that function as closed or self-contained producers of meaning. Rather they intersect with and unravel into endless processes of differentiation—a mark of deconstructionist poststructuralism. Departures from his work also include attention to practices of meaning production rather than formal systems of relations—a mark of liberationist appropriations of poststructuralism.[10]

---

9. C. Bally and A. Sechehaye, eds., in collaboration with A. Reidlinger, *Ferdinand de Saussure: A Course in General Linguistics* (New York: Philosophical Library, 1959).

10. Poststructuralist feminism includes much variety: French feminists, Catherine Belsey, Chris Weedon, and Rosalind Coward. For background to my argument, see Philip Lewis, "The Poststructuralist Condition," *Diacritics* 12 (Spring 1982): 2–22.

However, what continues to characterize poststructuralism of all sorts is the gap between signifier and signified.

So far I have made poststructuralism sound like simply another, more far-reaching version of constructionism in the nonnecessity of signification. In fact my argument is that poststructuralism exposes the inadequacy of the latter. To suggest the difference I will explore an insight of Saussure's that endures in these interventions and constitutes the move away from or beyond social constructionism. The force of this move is to open up the possibility of epistemological nonfoundationalism and an alternative account of difference. Saussure explored the mechanics of the claim that differential relations constitute meaning. It is the differential relation between sounds that produces meaning at the level of the sign, the relation between the signifier (sound image) and signified (concept). At the semantic level another differential operates, but a differential all the same: that between the meanings of the signs. *High* makes meaning by virtue of its difference from *low*, *woman* in differential relation to *man*.

In this view the *foundation* of meaning is neither the external referent of a sign nor the context. Insofar as there is a foundation to meaning, it is the unheard, the unsaid reality *between* sounds, between signs, and between whole patterns that buttress the said and the heard. Otherwise put, it is the differential relation that makes concrete meanings possible. One can distinguish and understand the signs pat and bat because of the difference between the /p/ and the /b/. That difference is not heard, for it is not sayable. As Jane Tompkins puts it, "Rather than the differences themselves, you hear *the words that the differences make available*."[11]

Similarly, one understands *woman* from the differential relation between it and its opposite, *man*. The distinction is the "unsaid." Thus knowing what the word is *not*, neither *man* nor those things that define maleness, is the closest we come to knowing what *woman* is. This semantic difference can be said, in the sense of unearthed, in contrast with the phonetic difference. Yet in both examples the unsaid is the basis for the possibility of meaning; it is the *outside* that accompanies the understanding of these or any signs.[12] Difference operates not simply in phonetics, but throughout an entire structure or language game to produce intelligibility. By offering the possibility for relations of contrast and similarity, Tompkins says, difference is "that which makes any such opposition come into being."[13] The instability of language becomes a metaphor for the instabilities of all discursive systems and practices in poststructuralism. Again, Tompkins puts

---

11. Jane Tompkins, "A Short Course in Poststructuralism," *College English* 50 (November 1988): 740.

12. Derrida is the best known for his elaboration of the *outside* and its inextricable link to meaning (indicated by his pseudoterm *différance*, which cannot be aurally distinguished from the real word, *différence*). However, the fundamental insight is found in Saussure.

13. Tompkins, "A Short Course," 743.

it well by saying that language "becomes a metaphor for understanding or intelligibility itself."[14]

In a sense this inescapable connection among meaning, difference, and exclusion appears banal: meaning simply depends on exclusions and "nots," somewhat like the notion of the particular implied by the constructionist view. However, the understanding of partiality and exclusion, and the implications for defining difference, are not the same. Let me explain.

The Other that is created by the exclusion of *woman* in the identification of *man* as human is not simply a word not chosen or a different perspective that can be added; it is a foundation of sorts on which the systems that define *man* as ideal human rest. That foundation is a source of destabilization, not of the "truth" in the sense of bare reality behind the signifying systems. We might say that the *excluded* or the outside in poststructuralism becomes a metaphor for the Other, as the constructions of reality that threaten the unity of the reigning arrangement.[15] The kind of foundation offered by such an outside is not that of particular knowledges acknowledged as finite or partial—for such are always pieces of a potential explanation that may become certain. Unlike the theories of feminism as social constructionism, there is no fixed knowledge base in poststructuralism, however transient, from which to explain or to dissect the causes of a phenomenon. There will be no explanation that is not subject to destabilization. For what we might take as particular discourse is part of a configuration, a system, that always dissembles, that always hides an Other.[16]

The contrast between the treatment of a particular discourse as finite or partial and as a system of exclusion is helpfully illustrated with the work of feminist Judith Butler. Butler investigates the power/knowledge arrangements and cultural specificity that constitute binary gender difference. Her criticism of the identity *woman* is exemplary feminist poststructuralist investigation yielding new terrain for liberation, specifically, the previously occluded "outside" that supports the binary man/woman. Her argument challenges the view we found persisting in feminist theories that, regardless of how expansive gender became as a critical category, never questioned the givenness of male and female sexed bodies.[17]

---

14. Ibid., 739.

15. Thus I disagree with some feminist categorization of this as only "negativism and nominalism." By doing so I am closer to Foucault's take on the outside as image of the Other. See Linda Nicholson, "Feminism and the Politics of Postmodernism," in *Feminism and Postmodernism*, ed. Margaret Ferguson and Jennifer Wicke (Durham, NC: Duke University Press, 1994), 77–84.

16. I am grateful to Ellen Armour for her application of this critique to race/gender in feminist theology and theory via Derrida and Irigaray. See her "Deconstruction and Feminist Theology: Toward Forging an Alliance with Derrida and Irigaray" (Ph.D. diss., Vanderbilt University, 1993).

17. In what follows I summarize Judith Butler, *Gender Trouble: Feminism and the Subversion of Identity* (New York and London: Routledge, 1990). Butler assesses the degree to which a figure like Monique Wittig asks the question.

Butler poses a poststructuralist inquiry: what is being excluded, unsaid, in the assumption of bodies divided into male and female? The outside that she uncovers has two elements. First, the conviction that there really are men and women rests on the hidden notion that being a man/woman is a deep truth about one's body and psyche, that it is, in fact, "the supreme secret (the 'mystery of sex') and the general substratum of our existence"— a complex of notions that are now recognized as modern Western ideas.[18] It does not rest on the access to the prediscursive bodied reality of real men and women that our language provides, but on the notions that sex *causes* desire and that desire is binary and naturally directed toward the opposite "sex." These are the hidden conditions of a discursive system of binary heterosexual definitions of human subjects.

This destabilization also exposes the outside or the excluded as "perverted" or "abnormal" subjects. Bodies with desires at odds with the oppositional arrangement fall outside the system of heterosexual binarism. The multiply sexed subject of Foucault's writing, Herculine Barbin, is used by Butler to display the outside of the heterosexual binary and the cracks and slippages in the heterosexual regime that s/he represents. These slippages give the regime away, just as authorities attempt unsuccessfully to unify features of Barbin's body and to match that unity with a gender and a deeply inscribed source of sexual identity. However, her/his body refuses to be unified satisfactorily under the binary options—male or female. Barbin is the outside to this regime, and s/he puts pressure on the inside, even as s/he is counted by that regime as the "abnormal," the pervert (or the lesbian/homosexual).

Butler's work rearranges "common sense" about binary, gendered subjects. The power of heterosexuality is not the power of the natural—the real apart from its being signified. It is the power of the dominant systems of discourse—the power of hegemony. From her analysis Butler argues that soliciting women to join the politics of identity through feminist theory or practice functions as an appeal to the real that is, in fact, an appeal to a discursive power regime. It is a regime of heterosexism that reinforces and reproduces the connections between binary, sexed identity, the collapse of sexual desire into gender, and the normative linking of desire with the opposite (binary) sex. To reiterate "woman" is to support and maintain heterosexual, binary arrangements.

The point here is that Butler's work is not a relativization or contextualization of oppressive views of men and women. Her poststructuralist intervention assumes an inextricable connection between specificity of meaning and exclusion in a way that constructionism does not. To make Butler's case in the terms of constructionism, the assumption that a view

---

18. Jeffrey Weeks, *Sex, Politics, and Society: The Regulation of Sexuality since 1800* (London and New York: Longman Group Ltd., 1981), 12.

is a perspective and that what is excluded might be added, is to suggest that the categorical system man/woman of the heterosexual regime can accommodate the bodies and desires that fall outside. However, the Other, in these terms of difference, would be defined *in the categories of the dominant regime*, and virtually obliterated.[19]

What we can learn from this account of poststructuralism is that an identity is a function of a position within a system of differences. Subject identity does not depend on substance or natural essence, just as it does not depend on the sameness of the body. Rather it depends on the outside on which it rests. That outside supports the specificity of meaning, man/woman, and provides pressure to move out of the established definitions, thereby offering the possibility of a reconfiguration of differential relations. In contrast to constructionist criticism, the poststructuralist intervention requires us to look at the relation of identities to dominant constructions of reality and to ask what they occlude. This is why it contradicts what is implicit to constructionism, namely, that we might combine relative perspectives. Not only will they be mutually exclusive, but the addition of another Other woman to the feminist account of the subject will likely be a process of *saming*—of *incorporating* the Other under the terms of the current discursive regime. My earlier question about the risk entailed by the commitment to finitude has a preliminary answer. What is risked by a feminism operating with tools of constructionism is a notion of identity, which, however much it confesses its partiality, deploys operations of equivalence and, therefore, hegemony.

Feminist Theology and the *Imago Dei*

In the hands of feminist theologians the Christian belief that all are created *imago Dei* becomes the application of the "feminist critical principle" to issues of the gendered subject. Articulated by Rosemary Radford Ruether, the feminist principle states that the "promotion of the full humanity of women" is normative for theology.[20] One of the most cited ideas associated with feminist theology, this formulation of the woman-centeredness of theological feminism is rendered distinct by the grammar of Christian theology. Central to theological thinking about the human is this *imago* doctrine, which operated classically to identify the features of human being which are most like, or in the image of, God. Thus it refers to the idea of an original authentic human nature which is fallen or damaged in

---

19. Thus, the lesbians will always be a lesser copy of a "real woman." See my "Gender: Being It or Doing It? The Church, Homosexuality, and the Politics of Identity," *Union Seminary Quarterly Review* 47 (1993): 29–46. See Romand Coles for a discussion of the contrast between the Western notion of "difference," displayed in social constructionism, and Foucault's (*Self/Power/Other: Political Theory and Dialogical Ethics* [Ithaca, NY: Cornell University Press, 1992], 76–82).

20. Rosemary Radford Ruether, *Sexism and God-Talk: Toward a Feminist Theology* (Boston: Beacon, 1983), 18–19.

"man" and authentically displayed in the person of Jesus Christ. The *imago Dei* indicates the attributes of human being that make it capable of a relationship to God. Most important, it conveys the theologically appropriate affirmation of the goodness of finitude—of creatures. There is, then, an incipient universal referent to the *imago*; by definition, to be creaturely is to be worthy of regard. The important question is how the notion of authentic is defined, and that depends in no small part on the way the Jesus figure is used to define ideal human attributes.

The feminist charge is that tradition's compliment to humanity with the *imago Dei* has never been fully paid to women. Instead, Jesus' maleness has long been used to characterize authentic human being and to limit the implicit universal reach of *imago Dei*. The beauty of its formal grammatical function, however, is that the *imago* can warrant the correction of centuries of misnaming the ideal human as male. Employing this doctrine to expose the "false generic" of mankind, Ruether (and others) have a theological warrant for liberation of women. As a naming of subjects of God's saving care, the *imago Dei* entails no essential definition of the subject, characterized only by finitude and God-dependence. This is how feminists can use it to create a woman-affirming anthropology that never existed. The doctrine's basic work is to say that being female is "like God," too, even as it is God-dependent, and in so doing produce new insights about creation.[21] As such, feminist theologians employ a traditional frame to focus on a particular subject, woman, and enhance the potential reach of that frame by inserting woman in the category of finitely good human subjects, exposing the problematic character of the male-identified constructions of *imago Dei*.

Feminist theological use of the *imago Dei* appears to work well. It would seem that the previously ignored "outsiders" to Western Christian hegemonies might easily be added via the *imago Dei*: the subjects whose race, sexuality, or class has been deemed less than human can be affirmed as good in their creatureliness, just as women are. However, feminist theologies are at risk along with feminist theories. Ruether, to continue my example, criticizes many of the contributions and inadequacies of the very feminist theories considered here. She enhances social constructionist critique of gender, which is crucial to her work, to uncover gender asymmetries. Refusal of idolatry strengthens the theological strategies and authorizes the addition of women to the class, "ideal humanity." Missing only a poststructuralist take on difference, she calls for consideration of racism and class. Her summary portrayal of the subject walks a careful line between recognizing psychic and biological tendencies of male/female and calling for a transformation of both.[22]

---

21. Since it is new, the implications of this affirmation extend to all theological doctrine.

22. One need only look at her definition of revelation to see how important the sociology of knowledge approach is (Ruether, *Sexism*, 12–18, 93–115).

However, with a poststructuralist intervention, occlusions appear. In Ruether's terms males cannot be absolutized as authentic human beings, created so the argument proceeds that we, *too*, are of value; we, *too*, are *imago Dei*. However, the converse is also true. She says, "Women cannot affirm themselves as *imago Dei* and subjects of full human potential in a way that diminishes male humanity."[23] The feminist appeal to *imago Dei* becomes, then, affirmation that the world is divided into two kinds of people, and what we want is respect for both kinds.[24] But this implies that gender criticism is a kind of "me, too" theory. Taking Butler's view, what is going on here is the deployment of the heterosexual binary. The continual affirming of man means that, minimally, what lurks behind the sign "woman" in Ruether's formulation are certain constructions of heterosexual, male-desiring subjects who know their deep identities to be sexually female. For that is all that can be accommodated by the system of discourse that Ruether leaves in place. We remember that poststructuralism assumes that occlusions support this binary, and we might fairly assume they are racial, too.

Producing Antihegemonic Positivity

With a destabilizing of the feminist theological option, we seem to be at an impasse. But the real question is how such destabilizing can be understood to converge with positive commitment to concrete women. Here my view is that feminisms are social practices for change; thus we are not guided by some frame of permanent deconstruction. The function of a liberatory poststructuralist intervention is to identify the outside or the Other that is being occluded. What it does not do is frame the inevitable commitment to a particular with a "why" and a "what for." For that some of the early investigations of the instabilities of signifying are again helpful.

We see how meaning can be claimed even in the face of the pressure to destabilize by looking at what happens in actual communication. Two processes are important. What Saussure called the associative or similarity-based linguistic operation, which refers to the paradigmatic axis of language; this is analogous to the process of identity/difference. For a speaker it is the capacity to make identity or similarity/contrast judgments. This means that one can *substitute*, which is a process requiring the relating of elements of meaning according to their degrees of similarity. The paradigmatic operation allows one to have categories, that is, to use and understand the sign "man" in a particular communication and to recognize the same sign in a different context. It is, in short, to know what "the same" is.

The speaker/hearer who cannot make similarity or identity associations is unable to carry out operations that require some distance from context,

---

23. Ibid., 20. Ruether insists this is not a matter of "sameness." My argument questions that.
24. I thank Meg Gandy for this observation.

such as beginning a conversation, or dealing with metalinguistic discourse. S/he is unable to make connections between the same word when it is used in different contexts and, thus, can only be reactive.[25]

The capacity to make identity judgments (or substitutions), however, is not enough for communication. To communicate, one needs the syntagmatic axis of language as well as the paradigmatic axis. The syntagmatic refers to the capacity for discerning relations of *contiguity*, that is, the constituents of a context, in Roman Jakobson's terms.[26] This is the capacity to combine the "next to's," whether successive or spatial/simultaneous, that is, to know how words are to be properly ordered in a particular language, to know what words should come next in a sentence, and to know what response comes next in a particular communication. One exercises the capacity for contiguity relations by knowing how to respond when greeted by "May I help you?" on entering a shop.

Without this capacity (contiguity aphasia), a person cannot make connections. S/he can only speak in terms of categories or identities. Since context is a multilevel phenomenon, from the context of words in a sentence to that of gender in a specific social code, contiguity judgments obviously differ according to the complexity of a situation. What is shared in the deficit is the inability to respond to context.

These capacities are suggestive for thinking about feminist theology as a social-change practice. Poststructuralist interventions, again, are for the identification of the refused outside; they are not to disable us.[27] To depend on these alone would be to create an analogous deficit in the ability to communicate. We need not be paralyzed by poststructuralism. Clearly both communicative capacities are necessary to and implicit in feminist theological and secular practice. Both have facilities for selection and combination. Knowing what counts as a proper substitution for the word *God* in a particular community, for example, must come with knowing how to use *God* in a sentence or with how an account of *God* is contextually useful in a situation of poverty.

Let me illustrate further. Knowing what could count as *imago Dei* is an exercise of the capacity for distinguishing similarity or identity/difference. What *is imago Dei* rests on differential relations that produce what is *not* as the necessary outside of the definition. (It is obvious that knowing a situation or a system of rules is necessary to the capacity to make specific intelligible identity judgments.) The feminist principle is based on an ability to read situations, to interpret contiguity relations as

---

25. See Roman Jakobson, "Two Aspects of Language and Two Types of Aphasic Disturbances," in *On Language*, ed. Linda R. Waugh and Monique Monville-Burston (Cambridge, MA: Harvard University Press, 1990 [1956]), 120–25.

26. Ibid.

27. The standard question of its effects on signifying God is not unimportant, but beyond the bounds of this article.

well. On the basis of that ability, the feminist judgment is that the claim of traditional theological rules, that any subject is a proper candidate for the *imago*, has been false. The system of differences of traditional theology has rested, we might say, on an outside—the domain of women (but also on pagans, and Jews). In Ruether's and others' work with the *imago Dei*, feminists have displayed their analogous facility to make "good sentences" by exercising capacities for paradigmatic and syntagmatic relations.

It may be that capacities for identity/contrast and contiguity judgments move us away from the suspicion that the enterprise is dissolved by destabilizing identities. (They also lessen the threat of the crime of essentialism; saying "woman" in a particular context may be the exercise of contiguity judgments.) However, the question of antihegemonic response to context requires consideration of what *connects* these episodic situations.

Now we take up the earlier question of the *why* or *for what* of a social-change practice, after a summary of the clues thus far. It has been the capacity to see the excluded, the outside, in what counted as ideal human being that has led feminism to become a powerful liberation movement. There is, in short, some operative notion of how to use *woman* in a "better" sentence going on in the practices of feminists. Their "better sentences" break through these exclusions, a facility I see in the theological vision of feminist theologians such as Ruether, Daly, and a host of fore-mothers. Minimally this is to say that facility with context or contiguity is necessary to the employment of poststructuralist interventions. But it is to say more. Neither a poststructuralist flair for destabilizing, contextual skills nor their combination can account for or extend feminists' gift for recognizing the excluded.

Feminists must be able to trace connections between episodes in the life of the church and society in order to work for change. The missing piece in a frame of communicative practice is *narrative*. With this category for connection we can answer the question of how feminist theology refuses hegemony.

Narrating *Imago Dei* in a Story of the Outsider

Again Saussure's founding destabilizing move is helpful. By bracketing the temporal, historical trajectories of signification, the focus on language as a system of differences sunders the relation of signification to fixed referents. Analysis of the synchronic brings into view a freeze-frame or a still life. To get the temporal and successive back into the picture requires the discursive form of connection. According to Fredric Jameson, this is the rhetorical form of story. Story brings the two dimensions of meaning together in a display of history.[28]

---

28. I show I am not finally a poststructuralist here. Fredric Jameson, "The Vanishing Mediator; or, Max Weber as Storyteller," in *The Ideologies of Theory: Essays, 1971–1986*, vol. 2, *Syntax of History* (Minneapolis: University of Minnesota Press, 1988), 3–34.

By "history" I mean something rather simple. We do history in order to look at two situations together. Relating the situation of white middle-class women in the nineteenth century to that of twentieth-century women is a historical project. However, we can only make the connections discursively, or rhetorically. Narrative is the rhetorical mode that relates the two situations synchronically: it is the rhetorical mode that makes meaning by finding the similarities/differences of various situations. It is in some sense where we answer "why it matters." Explanation is the rhetorical mode for history in its diachronic or successive sense; it relates episodes causally. While these are surely more complexly related, we might say that narrative offers us the theoretical mode for transformative connections.[29]

That feminist theology tells us about the different conditions of being woman is the discourse of doing history; it can be done as an explanatory science. *How* it relates those conditions is a story about the world and God's relation to it. It is displayed through a particular rhetorical mode, and it is necessary to an assessment of how feminisms invoke a trajectory beyond the particular system of differences. Feminist theology looks at different conditions of being woman and interrogates certain similarities/contrasts to display how women should count in the class of ideal humanity in those situations where they do not. The logic that has allowed them to "pick up" woman as the outside is not one of explanation, but a story that has an imperative to change, a commitment to value denigrated forms of creation.

Similarly, stories are working in secular feminist thinking, whether acknowledged or not, because episodes of defining woman are connected and ordered toward the evoking of change; they are not simply explained. It is these narratives that shape our notion of hegemony and suggest the expansiveness of the emancipatory subject. My earlier criticism of secular feminisms resulted from my judgment that they offer ambiguous narratives to this end. My point here is not to dwell on that case, but to suggest that narratives are endemic to social-change practice and that poststructuralist intervention has exposed the risk of overreliance on explanatory discourse. Without a story that universalizes the emancipatory subject for new discernments, feminisms are best at offering explanation. As important as these explanations are, they may "same" the outsider, even with expanding trajectories of humanism.

My point relates to Butler's work, as well, but raises another issue. Despite poststructuralism's aversion to grand narrative, her account invokes a logic of liberation, however modest. It must make the connections to which "history" aspires. The "story" that implicitly connects Butler's episodes is an impulse to better human social arrangements, or one

---

29. I thank Gil Greggs for conversations on this topic. See Fredric Jameson, *The Political Unconscious: Narrative as a Socially Symbolic Act* (Ithaca, NY: Cornell University Press, 1981).

she may count on readers to contribute. However, when one unearths the excluded, as she has done, one has not successfully applied poststructuralism and found the basis of oppression. One is able to see this outside, the heterosexual regime, because *one is already governed by another system of differences*, another outside, which, by definition, *cannot be seen*.[30] What narrative of liberation remains after the defeat of this first oppressive regime, heterosexism, given that one has, in fact, simply moved to another, possibly more pernicious one?

The implications of this investigation of the gendered subject are several. I will close with suggestions about what needs to be different about feminist theological use of the *imago Dei*, and what feminist theologies contribute. To review, I have suggested that the hegemonies recognized in feminist appeals to woman are best taken up through poststructuralist questions. These help expose the potential hegemony in social constructionist or explanatory grids, for the latter account for difference by accommodating the Other to their categories. Yet I have argued that destabilization is insufficient for communicative and social-change capacities. I conclude that stories are the way that we make connections between situations and invoke change. The final question, then, is what counts as a good story, and that will differ between secular and religious feminist communities.

I am not arguing for a false universalizing narrative, or that secular feminist theories should commit to humanity rather than to women. Any commitment to women is an exercise of one's sense of episodic contiguity. One resists particular hegemonies by saying what needs to be said in a particular setting and marks the refusal of hegemony in one's discourse when occlusions are exposed. My point is that commitment to woman may not be the adequate *connecting* story, even though the discoveries that emerge through this commitment should change the traditions of the stories. Insofar as secular feminists need to tell stories that compel a sense for the outside, I am suggesting that they need to examine the limits of humanism as a story for doing that. Minimally, this is what poststructuralism requires. Donna Haraway comments, "Gender is a category to explore what counts as a woman, what has previously been taken for granted, and to problematize what counts as a human."[31]

What I propose for feminist theological use of the *imago Dei* is development of its strength—stories, rather than explanations. Feminist theologians must develop stories of a God of justice in light of poststructuralist destabilization. A narrative of this God-creation relation cannot use *imago Dei* to add women to the class of human creatures. Poststructuralism

---

30. Tompkins, "A Short Course," 746–47.
31. Donna Haraway, "Ecce Homo, Ain't (Ar'n't) I a Woman, and Inappropriate/d Others: The Human in a Post-humanist Landscape," in *Feminists Theorize the Political*, ed. Judith Butler and Joan W. Scott (New York: Routledge, 1992), 96.

reminds us that there must be a purely negative function for the claim that woman is created *imago* and a story that tries to match it. The work of Ruether's principle should be that "men are not" *imago Dei* because the need to affirm *women* is constructed out of a pernicious system of significations which constitute *men*. This is not to say that woman is the real image of God; it is not even to say that both are. It is only to say that in this particular set of discursive arrangements, in this context of male dominance, what the reigning discursive system means by *man* is not the *imago Dei*. It is to make a contextual, contiguity-based judgment about the effects of the reigning hegemonic (white male) identities that control the current accompanying contrast/exclusion. If this is not recognized, then the exclusions operative in any definition of *woman* and its supporting discursive setting will continue to go unrecognized.

A good feminist theological story will be an incomplete story of a God-loved creation, a creation for which the only requisite features of imaging God are finitude and dependence. That story must allow the commitment to the particular situation to develop new sensibilities for the outside, defined as violations of the goodness of the finite, God-dependent creation. It must sponsor the capacity for total self-criticism, for commitment to the goodness of the partial, and for the possibility that all is redeemable. For the outside, as a place where the occlusions of a situation appear, is not a stable foundation. A theological story might name it as the lure of an eschatological future, but, by definition, it will require disruption of the present system. Therefore it will not look like God's eschatological future to many.

Such stories will not, of course, escape hegemonies. Those who tell them must mark the occlusions when they appear, but know that they are already determined by others. Thus, Ellen Armour suggests that we speak of "whitefeminism" to mark that system of discourse that is only able to see Other women as having race.[32] Because of the new knowledges from "whitefeminist," womanist, and other liberation critiques of the tradition, this is a story, a set of stories, that Christians must construct anew.

These stories have hegemonic ones to replace, of course, given that the formal constructive function of the *imago Dei* is shaped by the relation of authentic humanity to Jesus. The implicit universal referent in the story of the God-loved and dependent *imago Dei* can become a form of hegemony in a number of ways. However, it does not always. Even an outsider to Christianity hears the possibilities in a newly told Jesus story. Haraway tells a story of the suffering servant as trickster figure, as the "original mime" who "redeems" the hegemonies of humanism: Jesus the "original mime" is "the actor of a history that mocks especially the recurrent tales

---

32. Armour, "Deconstruction, Feminist Theology."

that insist that 'man makes himself' in the deathly onanistic nightdream of coherent wholeness and correct vision."[33]

If there is insight in telling Christian stories, it might be that they can invite us to move ceaselessly toward the discovery of new "outsides," new strangers and the conditions that support them. It is not a story for all feminists, but it raises questions for their stories as well as for Christian communities. We do not abandon particular commitments, or particular stories; we simply expect that they will always contribute to dissembling. The best we can do is tell stories that enable us to confess that and to hear from rather than explain the Other.

---

33. Donna Haraway, "Ecce Homo," 96. For work on this see Elisabeth Schussler Fiorenza, *Jesus: Miriam's Child, Sophia's Prophet: Critical Issues in Feminist Christology* (New York: Continuum, 1995).

CHAPTER 3
Evil and Sin

SELECTION **1**

Origen of Alexandria

On First Principles, Book 1

Origen's understanding of the origin of evil is closely related to his understanding of the eternity of creation, and the two together were an important factor in his condemnation in the sixth century. Though Origen himself was a virulent opponent of Gnosticism, aspects of his own cosmology as outlined in his book *On First Principles* have important parallels with the Gnostic tendency to correlate the emergence of evil with the creation of matter. Like the Gnostics, Origen believed that originally the world consisted exclusively of spiritual beings enjoying a perfect existence in endless contemplation of God. As the following selection describes, however, virtually all these beings fell away from this ideal state out of carelessness: neglecting their place in the cosmic order, they became distracted from their orientation to the highest good. This pretemporal "fall" is the source of evil (which simply describes the character of life apart from the divine presence) and is also the occasion for the differences between various levels of rational beings, with angels having experienced the smallest "fall" and demons the greatest, with human beings falling somewhere in between.

At this point, however, Origen's scheme differs significantly from the Gnostic cosmologies attacked by Irenaeus in his *Against Heresies*. For while the Gnostics saw the creation of the material world as a largely accidental side effect of this pretemporal fall (and thus as fundamentally a mistake), Origen insisted that God deliberately created matter as a kind of safety net designed to check the fall of human souls and serve as a proving ground to help them reascend to their primordial state. Thus, while Origen agreed with the Gnostics that human beings were not originally intended to inhabit material bodies, he denied that our bodies were for this reason to be regarded as evil or defective. On the contrary, because they had been deliberately created by God for a specific purpose, they were fundamentally good. Moreover, this understanding of the role of physical bodies in the divine economy provided Origen with a ready solution to the problem of evil, since he could explain the different material circumstances into which people found themselves (e.g., healthy or sickly) as reflecting the degree to which they had fallen away from God, in much the way that the different states of angels and demons reflect the degree to which they had declined from their initial perfection.

From *The Fathers of the Third Century: Tertullian, etc.*, ANF 4:256–60.

Chapter 4
1. To exhibit the nature of defection or falling away on the part of those [spiritual beings] who conduct themselves carelessly, it will not appear

out of place to employ a similitude by way of illustration. Suppose, then, the case of one who had become gradually acquainted with the art or science, say of geometry or medicine, until he had reached perfection, having trained himself for a lengthened time in its principles and practice, so as to attain a complete mastery over the art: to such a person it could never happen, that, when he lay down to sleep in the possession of his skill, he should awake in a state of ignorance. (It is not our purpose to adduce or to notice here those accidents which are occasioned by any injury or weakness, for they do not apply to our present illustration.) According to our point of view, then, so long as that geometer or physician continues to exercise himself in the study of his art and in the practice of its principles, the knowledge of his profession abides with him; but if he withdraw from its practice, and lay aside his habits of industry, then, by his neglect, at first a few things will gradually escape him, then by and by more and more, until in course of time everything will be forgotten, and be completely effaced from the memory. It is possible, indeed, that when he has first begun to fall away, and to yield to the corrupting influence of a negligence which is small as yet, he may, if he be aroused and return speedily to his senses, repair those losses which up to that time are only recent, and recover that knowledge which hitherto had been only slightly obliterated from his mind. Let us apply this now to the case of those who have devoted themselves to the knowledge and wisdom of God, whose learning and diligence incomparably surpass all other training; and let us contemplate, according to the form of the similitude employed, what is the acquisition of knowledge, or what is its disappearance, especially when we hear from the apostle what is said of those who are perfect, that they shall behold face to face the glory of the Lord in the revelation of His mysteries.

Chapter 5
2. Then, in the next place, we must know that every being which is endowed with reason, and transgresses its statutes and limitations, is undoubtedly involved in sin by swerving from rectitude and justice. Every rational creature, therefore, is capable of earning praise and censure: praise, if, in conformity to that reason which it possesses, it advances to better things; censure, if it falls away from the plan and course of rectitude, for which reason it is justly liable to pains and penalties. And this also is to be held as applying to the devil himself, and those who are with him, and are called his angels. Now the character of these beings have to be explained, that we may know what they are of whom we have to speak. The name, then, of Devil, and Satan, and Wicked One, who is also described as Enemy of God, is mentioned in many passages of Scripture. Moreover, certain angels of the devil are mentioned, and also a prince of this world, who, whether the devil himself or some one else, is not yet clearly manifest. There are also certain princes of this world spoken of as possessing a kind of wis-

dom which will come to nothing; but whether these are those princes who are also the principalities with whom we have to wrestle, or other beings, seems to me a point on which it is not easy for any one to pronounce. After the principalities, certain powers also are named with whom we have to wrestle, and carry on a struggle even against the princes of this world and the rulers of this darkness. Certain spiritual powers of wickedness also, in heavenly places, are spoken of by Paul himself. What, moreover, are we to say of those wicked and unclean spirits mentioned in the Gospel? Then we have certain heavenly beings called by a similar name, but which are said to bend the knee, or to be about to bend the knee, at the name of Jesus; nay, even things on earth and things under the earth, which Paul enumerates in order. And certainly, in a place where we have been discussing the subject of rational natures, it is not proper to be silent regarding ourselves, who are human beings, and are called rational animals; nay, even this point is not to be idly passed over, that even of us human beings certain different orders are mentioned in the words, "The portion of the Lord is His people Jacob; Israel is the cord of His inheritance." [Deut. 32:9]. Other nations, moreover, are called a part of the angels; since "when the Most High divided the nations, and dispersed the sons of Adam, He fixed the boundaries of the nations according to the number of the angels of God." [Deut. 32:8, LXX]. And therefore, with other rational natures, we must also thoroughly examine the reason of the human soul.

3. After the enumeration, then, of so many and so important names of orders and offices, underlying which it is certain that there are personal existences, let us inquire whether God, the creator and founder of all things, created certain of them holy and happy, so that they could admit no element at all of an opposite kind, and certain others so that they were made capable both of virtue and vice; or whether we are to suppose that He created some so as to be altogether incapable of virtue, and others again altogether incapable of wickedness, but with the power of abiding only in a state of happiness, and others again such as to be capable of either condition. In order, now, that our first inquiry may begin with the names themselves, let us consider whether the holy angels, from the period of their first existence, have always been holy, and are holy still, and will be holy, and have never either admitted or had the power to admit any occasion of sin. Then in the next place, let us consider whether those who are called holy principalities began from the moment of their creation by God to exercise power over some who were made subject to them, and whether these latter were created of such a nature, and formed for the very purpose of being subject and subordinate. In like manner, also, whether those which are called powers were created of such a nature and for the express purpose of exercising power, or whether their arriving at that power and dignity is a reward and desert of their virtue. Moreover, also, whether those which are called thrones or seats gained that stability of happiness at the same time

with their coming forth into being, so as to have that possession from the will of the Creator alone; or whether those which are called dominions had their dominion conferred on them, not as a reward for their proficiency, but as the peculiar privilege of their creation, so that it is something which is in a certain degree inseparable from them, and natural. Now, if we adopt the view that the holy angels, and the holy powers, and the blessed seats, and the glorious virtues, and the magnificent dominions, are to be regarded as possessing those powers and dignities and glories in virtue of their nature, it will doubtless appear to follow that those beings which have been mentioned as holding offices of an opposite kind must be regarded in the same manner; so that those principalities with whom we have to struggle are to be viewed, not as having received that spirit of opposition and resistance to all good at a later period, or as falling away from good through the freedom of the will, but as having had it in themselves as the essence of their being from the beginning of their existence. In like manner also will it be the case with the powers and virtues, in none of which was wickedness subsequent or posterior to their first existence. Those also whom the apostle termed rulers and princes of the darkness of this world, are said, with respect to their rule and occupation of darkness, to fall not from perversity of intention, but from the necessity of their creation. Logical reasoning will compel us to take the same view with regard to wicked and malignant spirits and unclean demons. But if to entertain this view regarding malignant and opposing powers seem to be absurd, as it is certainly absurd that the cause of their wickedness should be removed from the purpose of their own will, and ascribed of necessity to their Creator, why should we not also be obliged to make a similar confession regarding the good and holy powers, that, *viz.*, the good which is in them is not theirs by essential being, which we have manifestly shown to be the case with Christ and the Holy Spirit alone, as undoubtedly with the Father also? For it was proved that there was nothing compound in the nature of the Trinity, so that these qualities might seem to belong to it as accidental consequences. From which it follows, that in the case of every creature it is a result of his own works and movements, that those powers which appear either to hold sway over others or to exercise power or dominion, have been preferred to and placed over those whom they are said to govern or exercise power over, and not in consequence of a peculiar privilege inherent in their constitutions, but on account of merit.

4. But that we may not appear to build our assertions on subjects of such importance and difficulty on the ground of inference alone, or to require the assent of our hearers to what is only conjectural, let us see whether we can obtain any declarations from holy Scripture, by the authority of which these positions may be more credibly maintained. And, firstly, we shall adduce what holy Scripture contains regarding wicked powers; we shall next continue our investigation with regard to the others, as the Lord

shall be pleased to enlighten us, that in matters of such difficulty we may ascertain what is nearest to the truth, or what ought to be our opinions agreeably to the standard of religion. Now we find in the prophet Ezekiel two prophecies written to the prince of Tyre, the former of which might appear to any one, before he heard the second also, to be spoken of some man who was prince of the Tyrians. In the meantime, therefore, we shall take nothing from that first prophecy; but as the second is manifestly of such a kind as cannot be at all understood of a man, but of some superior power which had fallen away from a higher position, and had been reduced to a lower and worse condition, we shall from it take an illustration, by which it may be demonstrated with the utmost clearness, that those opposing and malignant powers were not formed or created so by nature, but fell from a better to a worse position, and were converted into wicked beings; that those blessed powers also were not of such a nature as to be unable to admit what was opposed to them if they were so inclined and became negligent, and did not guard most carefully the blessedness of their condition. For if it is related that he who is called the prince of Tyre was amongst the saints, and was without stain, and was placed in the paradise of God, and adorned also with a crown of comeliness and beauty, is it to be supposed that such an one could be in any degree inferior to any of the saints? For he is described as having been adorned with a crown of comeliness and beauty, and as having walked stainless in the paradise of God: and how can any one suppose that such a being was not one of those holy and blessed powers which, as being placed in a state of happiness, we must believe to be endowed with no other honor than this? But let us see what we are taught by the words of the prophecy themselves. "The word of the Lord," says the prophet, "came to me, saying, Son of man, take up a lamentation over the prince of Tyre, and say to him, Thus saith the Lord God, Thou hast been the seal of a similitude, and a crown of comeliness among the delights of paradise; thou wert adorned with every good stone or gem, and wert clothed with sardonyx, and topaz, and emerald, and carbuncle, and sapphire, and jasper, set in gold and silver, and with agate, amethyst, and chrysolite, and beryl, and onyx: with gold also didst thou fill thy treasures, and thy storehouses within thee. From the day when thou wert created along with the cherubim, I placed thee in the holy mount of God. Thou wert in the midst of the fiery stones: thou wert stainless in thy days, from the day when thou wert created, until iniquities were found in thee: from the greatness of thy trade, thou didst fill thy storehouses with iniquity, and didst sin, and wert wounded from the mount of God. And a cherub drove thee forth from the midst of the burning stones; and thy heart was elated because of thy comeliness, thy discipline was corrupted along with thy beauty: on account of the multitude of thy sins, I cast thee forth to the earth before kings; I gave thee for a show and a mockery on account of the multitude of thy sins, and of thine iniquities: because of thy trade thou hast polluted thy holy places. And I shall bring forth fire from the midst of thee, and it shall devour thee, and I shall give thee for ashes and cinders on the earth in the sight of all who see thee: and all who know thee among the nations shall mourn over thee. Thou hast been made destruction, and thou shalt exist no longer for ever" [Ezek. 28:11–19]. Seeing, then, that such are the words of the prophet, who is there that on hearing, "Thou wert a seal of a similitude, and a crown of comeliness among the delights of paradise," or that "From the day when thou wert created with the cherubim, I placed thee in the holy mount of God," can so enfeeble the meaning as to suppose that this language is used of some man or saint, not to say the prince of Tyre? Or what fiery stones can he imagine in the midst of which any man could live? Or who could be supposed to be stainless from the very day of his creation, and wickedness being afterwards discovered in him, it be said of him then that he was cast forth upon the earth? For the meaning of this is, that He who was not yet on the earth is said to be cast forth upon it: whose holy places also are said to be polluted. We have shown, then, that what we have quoted regarding the prince of Tyre from the prophet Ezekiel refers to an adverse power, and by it, it is most clearly proved that that power was formerly holy and happy; from which state of happiness it fell from the time that iniquity was found in it, and was hurled to the earth, and was not such by nature and creation. We are of the opinion, therefore, that these words are spoken of a certain angel who had received the office of governing the nation of the Tyrians, and to whom also their souls had been entrusted to be taken care of. But what Tyre, or what souls of Tyrians, we ought to understand, whether that Tyre which is situated within the boundaries of the province of Phoenicia, or some other of which, this one which we know on earth is the model; and the souls of the Tyrians, whether they are those of the former or those which belong to that Tyre which is spiritually understood, does not seem to be a matter requiring examination in this place; lest perhaps we should appear to investigate subjects of so much mystery and importance in a cursory manner, whereas they demand a labor and work of their own.

5. Again, we are taught as follows by the prophet Isaiah regarding another opposing power. The prophet says, "How is Lucifer, who used to arise in the morning, fallen from heaven! He who assailed all nations is broken and beaten to the ground. Thou indeed saidst in thy heart, I shall ascend into heaven; above the stars of heaven shall I place my throne; I shall sit upon a lofty mountain, above the lofty mountains which are towards the north; I shall ascend above the clouds; I shall be like the Most High. Now shalt thou be brought down to the lower world, and to the foundations of the earth. They who see thee shall be amazed at thee, and shall say, This is the man who harassed the whole earth, who moved kings, who made the whole world a desert, who destroyed cities, and did not unloose those who

were in chains. All the kings of the nations have slept in honor, every one in his own house; but thou shalt be cast forth on the mountains, accursed with the many dead who have been pierced through with swords, and have descended to the lower world. As a garment cloned with blood, and stained, will not be clean; neither shall thou be clean, because thou hast destroyed my land and slain my people: thou shall not remain for ever, most wicked seed. Prepare thy sons for death on account of the sins of thy father, lest they rise again and inherit the earth, and fill the earth with wars. And I shall rise against them, saith the Lord of hosts, and I shall cause their name to perish, and their remains, and their seed" [Isa. 14:12–22]. Most evidently by these words is he shown to have fallen from heaven, who formerly was Lucifer, and who used to arise in the morning. For if, as some think, he was a nature of darkness, how is Lucifer said to have existed before? Or how could he arise in the morning, who had in himself nothing of the light? Nay, even the Savior Himself teaches us, saying of the devil, "Behold, I see Satan fallen from heaven like lightning." [Luke 10:18]. For at one time he was light. Moreover our Lord, who is the truth, compared the power of His own glorious advent to lightning, in the words, "For as the lightning shineth from the height of heaven even to its height again, so will the coming of the Son of man be." [Matt. 24:17]. And notwithstanding He compares him to lightning, and says that he fell from heaven, that He might show by this that he had been at one time in heaven, and had had a place among the saints, and had enjoyed a share in that light in which all the saints participate, by which they are made angels of light, and by which the apostles are termed by the Lord the light of the world. In this manner, then, did that being once exist as light before he went astray, and fell to this place, and had his glory turned into dust, which is peculiarly the mark of the wicked, as the prophet also says; whence, too, he was called the prince of this world, i.e., of an earthly habitation: for he exercised power over those who were obedient to his wickedness, since "the whole of this world"—for I term this place of earth, world—"lieth in the wicked one" [1 John 5:19], and in this apostate. That he is an apostate, i.e., a fugitive, even the Lord in the book of Job says, "Thou wilt take with a hook the apostate dragon," i.e., a fugitive [Job 40:20, LXX]. Now it is certain that by the dragon is understood the devil himself. If then they are called opposing powers, and are said to have been once without stain, while spotless purity exists in the essential being of none save the Father, Son, and Holy Spirit, but is an accidental quality in every created thing; and since that which is accidental may also fall away, and since those opposite powers once were spotless, and were once among those which still remain unstained, it is evident from all this that no one is pure either by essence or nature, and that no one was by nature polluted. And the consequence of this is, that it lies within ourselves and in our own actions to possess either happiness or holiness; or by sloth and negligence to fall from happiness into wickedness and ruin, to such a degree that, through too great proficiency, so to speak, in wickedness (if a man be guilty of so great neglect), he may descend even to that state in which he will be changed into what is called an "opposing power."

SELECTION 2

Athanasius

Against the Heathen

Best known for his tenacious defense of the full divinity of the Son during the Arian controversy, Athanasius (ca. 295–373) spent most of his long tenure as bishop of Alexandria (an office he held from 328 until his death) struggling to vindicate the orthodoxy of his views amid the shifting sands of imperial church politics. His efforts to forge theological consensus among key church leaders in the midst of repeated periods of exile from his see helped to lay the conceptual and terminological ground for the formal definition of the doctrine of the Trinity at the First Council of Constantinople in 381.

In the following excerpt, taken from what is generally viewed as a comparatively early work, Athanasius outlines the basic shape of what had by this time become the orthodox understanding of evil. Like his fellow Alexandrian, Origen, Athanasius maintains that evil is the product of creaturely will. Unlike Origen, however, he affirms that its emergence follows the creation of the material order rather than serving as the occasion for matter's being created in the first place. Thus, he interprets the story of the fall in Genesis 3 as teaching that evil resulted when humanity became distracted from contemplating God by excessive preoccupation with material reality. Inasmuch as the only cause of evil is the creaturely rejection of what is good, it follows that evil has no proper existence of its own and is thus neither itself a creature (since whatever God creates is by definition good) nor a substance equiprimordial with God (since any such reality would undermine Christian confession of God's sole, sovereign lordship).

From *Athanasius: Select Works and Letters*, NPNF[2] 4:4–7.

§2. In the beginning wickedness did not exist. Nor indeed does it exist even now in those who are holy, nor does it in any way belong to their nature. But men later on began to contrive it and to elaborate it to their own hurt. Whence also they devised the invention of idols, treating what was not as though it were. For God Maker of all and King of all, that has His Being beyond all substance and human discovery, inasmuch as He is good and exceeding noble, made, through His own Word our Savior Jesus Christ, the human race after His own image, and constituted man able to see and know realities by means of this assimilation to Himself, giving him also a conception and knowledge even of His own eternity, in order that, preserving his nature intact, he might not ever either depart from his idea of God, nor recoil from the communion of the holy ones; but having the grace of Him that gave it, having also God's own power from the Word of the Father, he might rejoice and have fellowship with the Deity, living the life of immortality unharmed and truly blessed. For having nothing to hinder his knowledge of the Deity, he ever beholds, by his purity, the Image of the Father, God the Word, after Whose image he himself is made. He is awe-struck as he contemplates that Providence which through the Word extends to the universe, being raised above the things of sense and every bodily appearance, but cleaving to the divine and thought-perceived things in the heavens by the power of his mind.

For when the mind of men does not hold converse with bodies, nor has mingled with it from without aught of their lust, but is wholly above them, dwelling with itself as it was made to begin with, then, transcending the things of sense and all things human, it is raised up on high; and seeing the Word, it sees in Him also the Father of the Word, taking pleasure in contemplating Him, and gaining renewal by its desire toward Him; exactly as the first of men created, the one who was named Adam in Hebrew, is described in the Holy Scriptures as having at the beginning had his mind turned to God in a freedom unembarrassed by shame, and as associating with the holy ones in that contemplation of things perceived by the mind which he enjoyed in the place where he was—the place which the holy Moses called in figure a Garden. So purity of soul is sufficient of itself to reflect God, as the Lord also says, "Blessed are the pure in heart, for they shall see God" [Matt. 5:8].

§3. Thus then, as we have said, the Creator fashioned the race of men, and thus meant it to remain. But men, making light of better things, and holding back from apprehending them, began to seek in preference things nearer to themselves. But nearer to themselves were the body and its senses; so that while removing their mind from the things perceived by thought, they began to regard themselves; and so doing, and holding to the body and the other things of sense, and deceived as it were in their own surroundings, they fell into lust of themselves, preferring what was their own to the contemplation of what belonged to God. Having then made themselves at home in these things, and not being willing to leave what was so near to them, they entangled their soul with bodily pleasures, vexed and turbid with all kind of lusts, while they wholly forgot the power they originally had from God. But the truth of this one may see from the man who was first made, according to what the holy Scriptures tell us of him. For he also, as long as he kept his mind to God, and the contemplation of God, turned away from the contemplation of the body. But when, by counsel of the serpent, he departed from the consideration of God, and began to regard himself, then they not only fell to bodily lust, but knew that they were naked, and knowing, were ashamed. But they knew that they were naked, not so much of clothing as that they were become stripped of the contemplation of divine things, and had transferred their understanding to the contraries. For having departed from the consideration of the one and the true, namely, God, and from desire of Him, they had thenceforward embarked in diverse lusts and in those of the several bodily senses. Next, as is apt to happen, having formed a desire for each and sundry, they began to be habituated to these desires, so that they were even afraid to leave them: whence the soul became subject to cowardice and alarms, and pleasures and thoughts of mortality. For not being willing to leave her lusts, she fears death and her separation from the body. But again, from lusting, and not meeting with gratification, she learned to commit murder and wrong. We are then led naturally to show, as best we can, how she does this.

§4. Having departed from the contemplation of the things of thought, and using to the full the several activities of the body, and being pleased with the contemplation of the body, and seeing that pleasure is good for her, she was misled and abused the name of good, and thought that pleasure was the very essence of good: just as though a man out of his mind and asking for a sword to use against all he met, were to think that soundness of mind. But having fallen in love with pleasure, she began to work it out in various ways. For being by nature mobile, even though she had turned away from what is good, yet she does not lose her mobility. She moves then, no longer according to virtue or so as to see God, but imagining false things, she makes a novel use of her power, abusing it as a means to the pleasures she has devised, since she is after all made with power over herself. For she is able, as on the one hand to incline to what is good, so on the other to reject it; but in rejecting the good she of course entertains the thought of what is opposed to it, for she cannot at all cease from movement, being, as I said before, mobile by nature. And knowing her own power over herself, she sees that she is able to use the members of her body in either direction, both toward what is, or toward what is not. But good is, while evil is not; by what is, then, I mean what is good, inasmuch as it has its pattern in God Who is. But by what is not I mean what is evil, in so far as it consists in a false imagination in people's thoughts. For though the body has eyes so as to see Creation, and by its entirely harmonious construction to recognize the Creator; and ears to listen to the divine oracles and the laws of God, and hands both to perform works of necessity and to raise to God in prayer; yet the soul, departing from the contemplation of what is good and from moving in its sphere, wanders away and moves toward its contraries. When seeing, as I said before, and abusing her power, she has perceived that she can move the members of the body also in an opposite way: and so, instead of beholding the Creation, she turns the eye to lusts, showing that she has this power too; and thinking that by the mere fact of moving she is maintaining her own dignity, and is doing no sin in doing as she pleases; not knowing that she is made not merely to move, but to move in the right direction. For this is why an apostolic utterance assures us "All things are lawful, but not all things are expedient" [1 Cor. 10:23].

§5. But the audacity of men, having regard not to what is expedient and becoming, but to what is possible for it, began to do the contrary; whence, moving their hands to the contrary, it made them commit murder, and led away their hearing to disobedience, and their other members to adultery instead of to lawful procreation; and the tongue, instead of right speaking, to slander and insult and perjury; the hands again, to stealing and striking fellow-men; and the sense of smell to many sorts of lascivious odors; the feet, to be swift to shed blood, and the belly to drunkenness and insatiable gluttony [Rom. 3:10]. All of which things are a vice and sin of the soul: neither is there any cause of them at all, but only the rejection of better things. For just as if a charioteer, having mounted his chariot on the race-course, were to pay no attention to the goal, toward which he should be driving, but, ignoring this, simply were to drive the horse as he could, or in other words as he would, and often drive against those he met, and often down steep places, rushing wherever he impelled himself by the speed of the team, thinking that thus running he has not missed the goal (for he regards the running only, and does not see that he has passed wide of the goal), so the soul too, turning from the way toward God, and driving the members of the body beyond what is proper, or rather, driven herself along with them by her own doing, sins and makes mischief for herself, not seeing that she has strayed from the way, and has swerved from the goal of truth, to which the Christ-bearing man, the blessed Paul, was looking when he said, "I press on toward the goal unto the prize of the high calling of Christ Jesus" [Phil. 3:14], so that the holy man, making the good his mark, never did what was evil.

§6. Now certain of the Greeks, having erred from the right way, and not having known Christ, have ascribed to evil a substantive and independent existence. In this they make a double mistake: either in denying the Creator to be maker of all things, if evil had an independent subsistence and being of its own; or again, if they mean that He is maker of all things, they will of necessity admit Him to be maker of evil also. For evil, according to them, is included among existing things. But this must appear paradoxical and impossible. For evil does not come from good, nor is it in, or the result of, good, since in that case it would not be good, being mixed in its nature or a cause of evil. But the sectaries, who have fallen away from the teaching of the Church, and made shipwreck concerning the Faith [1 Tim. 1:19], they also wrongly think that evil has a substantive existence. But they arbitrarily imagine another god besides the true One, the Father of our Lord Jesus Christ, and that he is the unmade producer of evil and the head of wickedness, who is also artificer of Creation. But these men one can easily refute, not only from the divine Scriptures, but also from the human understanding itself, the very source of these their insane imaginations. To begin with, our Lord and Savior Jesus Christ says in His own gospels confirming the words of Moses: "The Lord God is one" [Mark 12:29] and "I thank thee, Father, Lord of heaven and earth" [Matt. 11:25]. But if God is one, and at the same time Lord of heaven and earth, how could there be another God beside Him? Or what room will there be for the God whom they suppose, if the one true God fills all things in the compass of heaven and earth? Or how could there be another creator of that, whereof, according to the Savior's utterance, the God and Father of Christ is Himself Lord? Unless indeed they would say that it were, so to speak, in an equipoise, and the evil god capable of getting the better of the good God. But if they say this, see to what a pitch of impiety they descend. For when powers are equal, the superior and better cannot be discovered. For if the one exist even if the other will it not, both are equally strong and equally weak: equally strong, because the very existence of either is a defeat of the other's will; equally weak, because what happens is counter to their wills, for while the good God exists in spite of the evil one, the evil god exists equally in spite of the good.

SELECTION 3

Augustine of Hippo

The City of God, Book 14

Although Augustine's influence on subsequent Western theology extends to virtually every area of Christian doctrine, there is no subject with which his name is more closely associated than the topic of original sin. While others (including Augustine's great African predecessor, Cyprian of Carthage) had made reference to the idea of guilt inherited from Adam, Augustine developed the idea of congenital sinfulness with a power and consistency that became normative for traditional Catholic and Protestant theology—even as it has caused unease among Orthodox theologians and others down to the present day. Whereas it was widely agreed that Adam's sin had weakened human nature in such a way as to give it a propensity to sin, Augustine's concern to emphasize the absolute necessity and sufficiency of God's grace for salvation led him to conclude that human nature had been so distorted by the fall that human beings are now born sinful and incapable of anything but sin.

In this excerpt from his monumental *The City of God*, Augustine summarizes his understanding of the relationship between sin and evil by way of a running commentary on Genesis 2–3. He affirms that evil is a product of sin and, as such, has no independent existence; it is instead a corruption of the good and is thus parasitic upon the good. The root of sin, in turn, is pride, understood as the desire to elevate oneself to the place of God and therefore to deny one's status as a creature under God. The effects of this primal transgression radiate outward to corrupt the whole of the natural order, but its center remains the (male) human being, whose utter helplessness and guilt after the fall is for Augustine symbolized by the twin facts of the physiological inability to control sexual arousal and the resulting shame that accompanies all sexual intercourse.

From *Saint Angustin: The City of God, Christian Doctrine*, NPNF[1] 2:271–77.

Chapter 11

But because God foresaw all things, and was therefore not ignorant that man also would fall, we ought to consider this holy city in connection with what God foresaw and ordained, and not according to our own ideas, which do not embrace God's ordination. For man, by his sin, could not disturb the divine counsel, nor compel God to change what He had decreed; for God's foreknowledge had anticipated both: that is to say, both how evil the man whom He had created good should become, and what good He Himself should even thus derive from him. For though God is said to change His determinations (so that in a figurative sense the Holy Scripture says even that God repented [see, e.g., Gen. 6:6]), this is said with reference to man's expectation, or the order of natural causes, and not with reference to that which the Almighty had foreknown that He would do. Accordingly God, as it is written, made man upright [Eccl. 7:29], and consequently with a good will. For if he had not had a good will, he could not have been upright. The good will, then, is the work of God; for God created him with it. But the first evil will, which preceded all man's evil acts, was rather a kind of falling away from the work of God to its own works than any positive work. And therefore the acts resulting were evil, not having God, but the will itself for their end; so that the will or the man himself, so far as his will is bad, was as it were the evil tree bringing forth evil fruit. Moreover, the bad will, though it be not in harmony with, but opposed to nature, inasmuch as it is a vice or blemish, yet it is true of it as of all vice, that it cannot exist except in a nature, and only in a nature created out of nothing, and not in that which the Creator has begotten of Himself, as He begot the Word, by whom all things were made. For though God formed man of the dust of the earth, yet the earth itself, and every earthly material, is absolutely created out of nothing; and man's soul, too, God created out of nothing, and joined to the body, when He made man. But evils are so thoroughly overcome by good, that though they are permitted to exist, for the sake of demonstrating how the most righteous foresight of God can make a good use even of them, yet good can exist without evil, as in the true and supreme God Himself, and as in every invisible and visible celestial creature that exists above this murky atmosphere; but evil cannot exist without good, because the natures in which evil exists, in so far as they are natures, are good. And evil is removed, not by removing any nature, or part of a nature, which had been introduced by the evil, but by healing and correcting that which had been vitiated and depraved. The will, therefore, is then truly free, when it is not the slave of vices and sins. Such was it given us by God; and this being lost by its own fault, can only be restored by Him who was able at first to give it. And therefore the truth says, "If the Son shall make you free, ye shall be free indeed" [John 8:36]; which is equivalent to saying, If the Son shall save you, ye shall be saved indeed. For He is our Liberator, inasmuch as He is our Savior.

Man then lived with God, for his rule in a paradise at once physical and spiritual. For neither was it a paradise only physical for the advantage of the body, and not also spiritual for the advantage of the mind; nor was it only spiritual to afford enjoyment to man by his internal sensations, and not also physical to afford him enjoyment through his external senses. But obviously it was both for both ends. But after that proud and therefore envious angel . . . preferring to rule with a kind of pomp of empire rather than to be another's subject, fell from the spiritual Paradise, and essaying to insinuate his persuasive guile into the mind of man, whose unfallen condition provoked him to envy now that himself was fallen, he chose the serpent as his mouthpiece in that bodily Paradise in which it and all the other earthly animals were living with those two human beings, the man and his wife, subject to them, and harmless; and he chose the serpent because, being slippery, and moving in tortuous windings, it was suitable for his purpose. And this animal being subdued to his wicked ends by the presence and superior force of his angelic nature, he abused as his instrument, and first tried his deceit upon the woman, making his assault upon the weaker part of that human alliance, that he might gradually gain the whole, and not supposing that the man would readily give ear to him, or be deceived, but that he might yield to the error of the woman. For as Aaron was not induced to agree with the people when they blindly wished him to make an idol, and yet yielded to constraint; and as it is not credible that Solomon was so blind as to suppose that idols should be worshipped, but was drawn over to such sacrilege by the blandishments of women; so we cannot believe that Adam was deceived, and supposed the devil's word to be truth, and therefore transgressed God's law, but that he by the drawings of kindred yielded to the woman, the husband to the wife, the one human being to the only other human being. For not without significance did the apostle say, "And Adam was not deceived, but the woman being deceived was in the transgression" [1 Tim. 2:14]; but he speaks thus, because the woman accepted as true what the serpent told her, but the man could not bear to be severed from his only companion, even though this involved a partnership in sin. He was not on this account less culpable, but sinned with his eyes open. And so the apostle does not say, "He did not sin," but "He was not deceived." For he shows that he sinned when he says, "By one man sin entered into the world" [Rom. 5:12], and immediately after more distinctly, "In the likeness of Adam's transgression" [Rom. 5:14]. But he meant that those are deceived who do not judge that which they do to be sin; but he knew. Otherwise how were it true that "Adam was not deceived?" But having as yet no experience of the divine severity, he was possibly deceived in so far as he thought his sin venial. And consequently he was not deceived as the woman was deceived, but he was deceived as to the judgment which would be passed on his apology: "The woman whom thou gavest to be with me, she gave me, and I did eat" [Gen. 3:12]. What need of saying more? Although they were not both deceived by credulity, yet both were entangled in the snares of the devil, and taken by sin.

Chapter 12

If any one finds a difficulty in understanding why other sins do not alter human nature as it was altered by the transgression of those first human beings, so that on account of it this nature is subject to the great corruption we feel and see, and to death, and is distracted and tossed with so many furious and contending emotions, and is certainly far different from what it was before sin, even though it were then lodged in an animal body; if, I say, any one is moved by this, he ought not to think that that sin was a small and light one because it was committed about food, and that not bad nor noxious, except because it was forbidden; for in that spot of singular felicity God could not have created and planted any evil thing. But by the precept He gave, God commended obedience, which is, in a sort, the mother and guardian of all the virtues in the reasonable creature, which was so created that submission is advantageous to it, while the fulfillment of its own will in preference to the Creator's is destruction. And as this commandment enjoining abstinence from one kind of food in the midst of great abundance of other kinds was so easy to keep, so light a burden to the memory, and, above all, found no resistance to its observance in lust (which only afterwards sprung up as the penal consequence of sin) the iniquity of violating it was all the greater in proportion to the ease with which it might have been kept.

Chapter 13

Our first parents fell into open disobedience because already they were secretly corrupted; for the evil act had never been done had not an evil will preceded it. And what is the origin of our evil will but pride? For "pride is the beginning of sin" [Sir. 10:13]. And what is pride but the craving for undue exaltation? And this is undue exaltation, when the soul abandons Him to whom it ought to cleave as its end, and becomes a kind of end to itself. This happens when it becomes its own satisfaction. And it does so when it falls away from that unchangeable good which ought to satisfy it more than itself. This falling away is spontaneous; for if the will had remained steadfast in the love of that higher and changeless good by which it was illumined to intelligence and kindled into love, it would not have turned away to find satisfaction in itself, and so become frigid and benighted; the woman would not have believed the serpent spoke the truth, nor would the man have preferred the request of his wife to the command of God, nor have supposed that it was a venial transgression to cleave to the partner of his life even in a partnership of sin. The wicked deed, then—that is to say, the transgression of eating the forbidden fruit—was committed by persons who were already wicked. That "evil fruit" [Matt. 7:18] could be brought forth only by "a corrupt tree." But that the tree was evil was not the result of nature; for certainly it could become so only by the vice of the will, and vice is contrary to nature. Now nature could not have been depraved by vice had it not been made out of nothing. Consequently, that it is a nature is because it is made by God; but that it falls away from Him is because it is made out of nothing. But man did not so fall away as to become absolutely nothing; but being turned towards himself, his being became more contracted than it was when he cleaved to Him who supremely is. Accordingly, to exist in himself, that is, to be his own satisfaction after abandoning God, is not quite to become a nonentity, but to approximate to that. And therefore the holy Scriptures designate the proud by another name, "self-pleasers." For it is good to have the heart lifted up, yet not to one's self, for this is proud, but to the Lord, for this is obedient, and can be the act only of the humble. There is, therefore, something in humility which, strangely enough, exalts the heart, and something in pride which debases it. This seems, indeed, to be contradictory, that loftiness should debase and lowliness exalt. But pious humility enables us to submit to what is above us; and nothing is more exalted above us than God; and therefore humility, by making us subject to God, exalts us. But pride, being a defect of nature, by the very act of refusing subjection and revolting from Him who is supreme, falls to a low condition; and then comes to pass what is written: "Thou castedst them down when they lifted up themselves" [Ps. 78:18]. For he does not say, "when they had been lifted up," as if first they were exalted, and then afterwards cast down; but "when they lifted up themselves" even then they were cast down—that is to say, the very lifting up was already a fall. And therefore it is that humility is specially recommended to the city of God as it sojourns in this world, and is specially exhibited in the city of God, and in the person of Christ its King; while the contrary vice of pride, according to the testimony of the sacred writings, specially rules his adversary the devil. And certainly this is the great difference which distinguishes the two cities of which we speak, the one being the society of the godly men, the other of the ungodly, each associated with the angels that adhere to their party, and the one guided and fashioned by love of self, the other by love of God.

The devil, then, would not have ensnared man in the open and manifest sin of doing what God had forbidden, had man not already begun to live for himself. It was this that made him listen with pleasure to the words, "Ye shall be as gods" [Gen. 3:5], which they would much more readily have accomplished by obediently adhering to their supreme and true end than by proudly living to themselves. For created gods are gods not by virtue of what is in themselves, but by a participation of the true God. By craving to be more, man becomes less; and by aspiring to be self-sufficing, he fell away from Him who truly suffices him. Accordingly, this wicked desire which prompts man to please himself as if he were himself light, and which thus turns him away from that light by which, had he followed it, he would himself have become light,—this wicked desire, I say, already secretly existed in him, and the open sin was but its consequence. For that is true which is written, "Pride goeth before destruction, and before honor is humility" [Prov. 18:12]; that is to say, secret ruin precedes open ruin, while the former is not counted ruin. For who counts exaltation ruin, though no sooner is the Highest forsaken than a fall is begun? But who does not recognize it as ruin, when there occurs an evident and indubitable transgression of the commandment? And consequently, God's prohibition had reference to such an act as, when committed, could not be defended on any pretense of doing what was righteous. And I make bold to say that it is useful for the proud to fall into an open and indisputable transgression, and so displease themselves, as already, by pleasing themselves, they had fallen. For Peter was in a healthier condition when he wept and was dissatisfied with himself, than when he boldly presumed and satisfied himself. And this is averred by the sacred Psalmist when he says, "Fill their faces with shame, that they may seek Thy name, O Lord" [Ps. 83:16]; that is, that they who have pleased themselves in seeking their own glory may be pleased and satisfied with Thee in seeking Thy glory.

Chapter 14
But it is a worse and more damnable pride which casts about for the shelter of an excuse even in manifest sins, as these our first parents did, of whom the woman said, "The serpent beguiled me, and I did eat;" and the man said, "The woman whom Thou gavest to be with me, she gave me of the tree, and I did eat" [Gen. 3:12-13]. Here there is no word of begging pardon, no word of entreaty for healing. For though they do not, like Cain, deny that they have perpetrated the deed, yet their pride seeks to refer its wickedness to another: the woman's pride to the serpent, the man's to the woman. But where there is a plain transgression of a divine commandment, this is rather to accuse than to excuse oneself. For the fact that the woman sinned on the serpent's persuasion, and the man at the woman's

offer, did not make the transgression less, as if there were any one whom we ought rather to believe or yield to than God.

Chapter 15
Therefore, because the sin was a despising of the authority of God—who had created man, who had made him in His own image, who had set him above the other animals, who had placed him in Paradise, who had enriched him with abundance of every kind and of safety, who had laid upon him neither many, nor great, nor difficult commandments, but, in order to make a wholesome obedience easy to him, had given him a single very brief and very light precept by which He reminded that creature whose service was to be free that He was Lord—it was just that condemnation followed, and condemnation such that man, who by keeping the commandments should have been spiritual even in his flesh, became fleshly even in his spirit; and as in his pride he had sought to be his own satisfaction, God in His justice abandoned him to himself, not to live in the absolute independence he affected, but instead of the liberty he desired, to live dissatisfied with himself in a hard and miserable bondage to him to whom by sinning he had yielded himself, doomed in spite of himself to die in body as he had willingly become dead in spirit, condemned even to eternal death (had not the grace of God delivered him) because he had forsaken eternal life. Whoever thinks such punishment either excessive or unjust shows his inability to measure the great iniquity of sinning where sin might so easily have been avoided. For as Abraham's obedience is with justice pronounced to be great, because the thing commanded, to kill his son, was very difficult, so in Paradise the disobedience was the greater, because the difficulty of that which was commanded was imperceptible. And as the obedience of the second Adam was the more laudable because He became obedient even "unto death" [Phil. 2:8], so the disobedience of the first Adam was the more detestable because he became disobedient even unto death. For where the penalty annexed to disobedience is great, and the thing commanded by the Creator is easy, who can sufficiently estimate how great a wickedness it is, in a matter so easy, not to obey the authority of so great a power, even when that power deters with so terrible a penalty?

In short, to say all in a word, what but disobedience was the punishment of disobedience in that sin? For what else is man's misery but his own disobedience to himself, so that in consequence of his not being willing to do what he could do, he now wills to do what he cannot? For though he could not do all things in Paradise before he sinned, yet he wished to do only what he could do, and therefore he could do all things he wished. But now, as we recognize in his offspring, and as divine Scripture testifies, "Man is like to vanity" [Ps. 144:4]. For who can count how many things he wishes which he cannot do, so long as he is disobedient to himself, that is, so long as his mind and his flesh do not obey his will? For in spite of himself his mind is both frequently disturbed, and his flesh suffers, and grows old, and dies; and in spite of ourselves we suffer whatever else we suffer, and which we would not suffer if our nature absolutely and in all its parts obeyed our will. But is it not the infirmities of the flesh which hamper it in its service? Yet what does it matter *how* its service is hampered, so long as the fact remains, that by the just retribution of the sovereign God whom we refused to be subject to and serve, our flesh, which was subjected to us, now torments us by insubordination, although our disobedience brought trouble on ourselves, not upon God? For He is not in need of our service as we of our body's; and therefore what we did was no punishment to Him, but what we receive is so to us. And the pains which are called bodily are pains of the soul in and from the body. For what pain or desire can the flesh feel by itself and without the soul? But when the flesh is said to desire or to suffer, it is meant, as we have explained, that the man does so, or some part of the soul which is affected by the sensation of the flesh, whether a harsh sensation causing pain, or gentle, causing pleasure. But pain in the flesh is only a discomfort of the soul arising from the flesh, and a kind of shrinking from its suffering, as the pain of the soul which is called sadness is a shrinking from those things which have happened to us in spite of ourselves. But sadness is frequently preceded by fear, which is itself in the soul, not in the flesh; while bodily pain is not preceded by any kind of fear of the flesh, which can be felt in the flesh before the pain. But pleasure is preceded by a certain appetite which is felt in the flesh like a craving, as hunger and thirst and that generative appetite which is most commonly identified with the name "lust," though this is the generic word for all desires. For anger itself was defined by the ancients as nothing else than the lust of revenge; although sometimes a man is angry even at inanimate objects which cannot feel his vengeance, as when one breaks a pen, or crushes a quill that writes badly. Yet even this, though less reasonable, is in its way a lust of revenge, and is, so to speak, a mysterious kind of shadow of [the great law of] retribution, that they who do evil should suffer evil. There is therefore a lust for revenge, which is called anger; there is a lust of money, which goes by the name of avarice; there is a lust of conquering, no matter by what means, which is called opinionativeness; there is a lust of applause, which is named boasting. There are many and various lusts, of which some have names of their own, while others have not. For who could readily give a name to the lust of ruling, which yet has a powerful influence in the soul of tyrants, as civil wars bear witness?

Chapter 16
Although, therefore, lust may have many objects, yet when no object is specified, the word lust usually suggests to the mind the lustful excitement of the organs of generation. And this lust not only takes possession of the whole body and outward members, but also makes itself felt within, and

moves the whole man with a passion in which mental emotion is mingled with bodily appetite, so that the pleasure which results is the greatest of all bodily pleasures. So possessing indeed is this pleasure, that at the moment of time in which it is consummated, all mental activity is suspended. What friend of wisdom and holy joys, who, being married, but knowing, as the apostle says, "how to possess his vessel in sanctification and honor, not in the disease of desire, as the Gentiles who know not God" [1 Thess. 4:4], would not prefer, if this were possible, to beget children without this lust, so that in this function of begetting offspring the members created for this purpose should not be stimulated by the heat of lust, but should be actuated by his volition, in the same way as his other members serve him for their respective ends? But even those who delight in this pleasure are not moved to it at their own will, whether they confine themselves to lawful or transgress to unlawful pleasures; but sometimes this lust importunes them in spite of themselves, and sometimes fails them when they desire to feel it, so that though lust rages in the mind, it stirs not in the body. Thus, strangely enough, this emotion not only fails to obey the legitimate desire to beget offspring, but also refuses to serve lascivious lust; and though it often opposes its whole combined energy to the soul that resists it, sometimes also it is divided against itself, and while it moves the soul, leaves the body unmoved.

Chapter 17

Justly is shame very specially connected with this lust; justly, too, these members themselves, being moved and restrained not at our will, but by a certain independent autocracy, so to speak, are called "shameful." Their condition was different before sin. For as it is written, "They were naked and were not ashamed" [Gen. 2:25], not that their nakedness was unknown to them, but because nakedness was not yet shameful, because not yet did lust move those members without the will's consent; not yet did the flesh by its disobedience testify against humanity's disobedience. For they were not created blind, as the unenlightened vulgar fancy; for Adam saw the animals to whom he gave names, and of Eve we read, "The woman saw that the tree was good for food, and that it was pleasant to the eyes" [Gen. 3:6]. Their eyes, therefore were open, but were not open to this, that is to say, were not observant so as to recognize what was conferred upon them by the garment of grace, for they had no consciousness of their members warring against their will. But when they were stripped of this grace, that their disobedience might be punished by fit retribution, there began in the movement of their bodily members a shameless novelty which made nakedness indecent: it at once made them observant and made them ashamed. And therefore, after they violated God's command by open transgression, it is written: "And the eyes of them both were opened, and they knew that they were naked; and they sewed fig leaves together, and made themselves aprons" [Gen. 3:7]. "The eyes of them both were opened," not to see, for already they saw, but to discern between the good they had lost and the evil into which they had fallen. And therefore also the tree itself which they were forbidden to touch was called the tree of the knowledge of good and evil from this circumstance, that if they ate of it, it would impart to them this knowledge. For the discomfort of sickness reveals the pleasure of health. "They knew," therefore, "that they were naked,"—naked of that grace which prevented them from being ashamed of bodily nakedness while the law of sin offered no resistance to their mind. And thus they obtained a knowledge which they would have lived in blissful ignorance of, had they, in trustful obedience to God, declined to commit that offence which involved them in the experience of the hurtful effects of unfaithfulness and disobedience. And therefore, being ashamed of the disobedience of their own flesh, which witnessed to their disobedience while it punished it, "they sewed fig leaves together, and made themselves aprons" [Gen. 3:7], that is, cinctures for their privy parts; for some interpreters have rendered the word by *succinctoria*. . . . Shame modestly covered that which lust disobediently moved in opposition to the will, which was thus punished for its own disobedience. Consequently all nations, being propagated from that one stock, have so strong an instinct to cover the shameful parts, that some barbarians do not uncover them even in the bath, but wash with their drawers on. In the dark solitudes of India also, though some philosophers go naked, and are therefore called gymnosophists, yet they make an exception in the case of these members and cover them.

Chapter 18
Lust requires for its consummation darkness and secrecy; and this not only when unlawful intercourse is desired, but even such fornication as the earthly city has legalized. Where there is no fear of punishment, these permitted pleasures still shrink from the public eye. Even where provision is made for this lust, secrecy also is provided; and while lust found it easy to remove the prohibitions of law, shamelessness found it impossible to lay aside the veil of retirement. For even shameless men call this shameful; and though they love the pleasure, dare not display it. What! does not even conjugal intercourse, sanctioned as it is by law for the propagation of children, legitimate and honorable though it be, does it not seek retirement from every eye? Before the bridegroom fondles his bride, does he not exclude the attendants, and even the paranymphs, and such friends as the closest ties have admitted to the bridal chamber? The greatest master of Roman eloquence says, that all right actions wish to be set in the light, i.e., desire to be known. This right action, however, has such a desire to

be known, that yet it blushes to be seen. Who does not know what passes between husband and wife that children may be born? Is it not for this purpose that wives are married with such ceremony? And yet, when this well-understood act is gone about for the procreation of children, not even the children themselves, who may already have been born to them, are suffered to be witnesses. This right action seeks the light, in so far as it seeks to be known, but yet dreads being seen. And why so, if not because that which is by nature fitting and decent is so done as to be accompanied with a shame-begetting penalty of sin?

Chapter 19
Hence it is that even the philosophers who have approximated to the truth have avowed that anger and lust are vicious mental emotions, because, even when exercised towards objects which wisdom does not prohibit, they are moved in an ungoverned and inordinate manner, and consequently need the regulation of mind and reason. And they assert that this third part of the mind is posted as it were in a kind of citadel, to give rule to these other parts, so that, while it rules and they serve, man's righteousness is preserved without a breach. These parts, then, which they acknowledge to be vicious even in a wise and temperate man, so that the mind, by its composing and restraining influence, must bridle and recall them from those objects towards which they are unlawfully moved, and give them access to those which the law of wisdom sanctions (so that anger, for example, may be allowed for the enforcement of a just authority, and lust for the duty of propagating offspring), these parts, I say, were not vicious in Paradise before sin, for they were never moved in opposition to a holy will towards any object from which it was necessary that they should be withheld by the restraining bridle of reason. For though now they are moved in this way, and are regulated by a bridling and restraining power, which those who live temperately, justly, and godly exercise, sometimes with ease, and sometimes with greater difficulty, this is not the sound health of nature, but the weakness which results from sin. And how is it that shame does not hide the acts and words dictated by anger or other emotions, as it covers the motions of lust, unless because the members of the body which we employ for accomplishing them are moved, not by the emotions themselves, but by the authority of the consenting will? For he who in his anger rails at or even strikes some one, could not do so were not his tongue and hand moved by the authority of the will, as also they are moved when there is no anger. But the organs of generation are so subjected to the rule of lust, that they have no motion but what it communicates. It is this we are ashamed of; it is this which blushingly hides from the eyes of onlookers. And rather will a man endure a crowd of witnesses when he is unjustly venting his anger on some one, than the eye of one man when he innocently copulates with his wife.

SELECTION 4

Thomas Aquinas

On Evil, Quest. 3

Thomas devoted an entire treatise to the problem of evil. While the material is presented using the same *quaestio disputata* format found in the *Summa Theologiae*,[1] the treatment of individual topics is much more detailed, with a dozen or more objections normally considered in each case as opposed to the handful typical of the *Summa*. This difference may well reflect the respective audiences for which the two works were composed, for while the *Summa* was designed as a general introduction to theology for beginners, the minute examination of questions in *On Evil* seems to reflect the more rarified atmosphere of private disputations held between a teacher and a small group of advanced students.

The three articles that follow deal with the cause of sin. Thomas is convinced that God, as Creator, is irresistibly sovereign over the whole of creation. How then is God to escape the charge of being the cause of sin? Thomas answers the question by denying that God can be said to cause sin, since a cause naturally draws the effects to itself, and anything drawn to God is invariably good, since God is the supreme good. At the same time, Thomas concedes that God can be said to cause acts of sin insofar as God is the cause of every creaturely happening. He reconciles these two apparently contradictory positions by arguing that God always communicates the divine goodness to creatures—and is as such the cause of every creaturely act—but that because the sinfulness of any act comes from some deficiency in the creature's reception of this goodness, the cause of the sin lies in the sinner and not in God (or in the devil, since the will, even when deficient in its operation, remains ineluctably self-moved and thus responsible for its own actions).

From Thomas Aquinas, *On Evil*, ed. Brian Davies
(Oxford: Oxford University Press, 2003), 141–54.

First Article: Does God Cause Sin?
Objections:
It seems that God does, for the following reasons:
1. The Apostle says in Rom. 1:28: "God delivered them up to a depraved way of thinking, so that they do unrighteous things." And a gloss of Augustine on this text says: "God is evidently active in the hearts of human beings by inclining their wills to whatever he willed, whether to good or to evil."[2] But the inclination of the will to evil is sin. Therefore, God causes sin.

---

1. For a discussion of this format, see p. 129 above.
2. The reference is actually to Peter Lombard, *Gloss*, on Rom. 1:24, in *PL* 191.1332A. But cf. Augustine, *On Grace and Free Choice* 21.3, *PL* 44.909; ET, *NPNF*[1], 5:462–63.

2. People have said that the will's inclination to evil is attributed to God insofar as such inclination is a punishment, and that is why Augustine in the cited text speaks of the judgment of God. But the same thing cannot in the same respect be a punishment and a moral wrong, since punishment is by its nature contrary to the will, and moral wrong is by its nature voluntary, as I have said before.[3] And the will's inclination belongs to the nature of voluntariness. Therefore, if God inclines the will to evil, it seems that he himself also causes moral wrong as such.

3. As moral wrong is contrary to the good of grace, so punishment is contrary to the good of nature. But God is not prevented from causing punishment because he causes nature. Therefore, neither is he prevented from causing moral wrong because he causes grace.

4. What causes a cause causes the effect of the caused cause. But free choice causes sin, and God causes free choice. Therefore, God causes sin.

5. God caused the objects toward which the powers he bestowed incline. But some powers bestowed by God incline to sin (e.g., the irascible power toward homicide and the concupiscible power toward adultery). Therefore, God causes sin.

6. Those who incline their own wills or the wills of others to evil cause sin. For example, such would be the case if persons giving alms should incline their wills to seek vainglory. But God inclines human wills to evil, as I have already said [in Objection 1 above]. Therefore, God causes sin.

7. Dionysius says in his work *Divine Names* that there are causes of evil in God.[4] But causes in God are not in vain. Therefore, God causes evils, among which we reckon sins.

8. Augustine says in his work *On Nature and Grace* that the soul has grace as the light whereby human beings do good, and without which they cannot do good.[5] Therefore, grace causes merit. Therefore, by contrast, the withdrawal of grace causes sin. But God is the one who withdraws grace. Therefore, God causes sin.

9. Augustine says in his *Confessions*: "I ascribe to your grace whatever evils I have not committed."[6] But he would not need to impute to grace that human beings did no evil if they, lacking grace, could not sin. Therefore, sin does not cause persons to be deprived of grace; rather, the privation of grace causes sin. And so, as before, God causes sinning.

10. We should especially attribute to God everything we praise in creatures. But Sir. 31:10 says in praise of a just human being that the person "could have transgressed and did not." Therefore, much more can we say this about God. Therefore, God can sin and so cause sin.

---

3. See *On Evil* 1.4–5.
4. Dionysius the Areopagite, *Divine Names* 4.30, in *PG* 3.729C; ET, *Pseudo-Dionysius: The Complete Works*, ed. Paul Rorem (New York: Paulist Press, 1987), 93.
5. Augustine, *On Nature and Grace* 26, in *PL* 44.261; ET, *NPNF*[1] 5:131.
6. Augustine, *Confessions* 2.7, in *PL* 32.681; ET, *LCC* 7:58.

11. The Philosopher [Aristotle] says in the *Topics*: "God and the zealous can do evil things."[7] But to do evil things is to sin. Therefore, God can sin.

12. It is a valid argument to say: "Socrates can run if he so wills. Therefore, absolutely speaking, he can run." But it is true to say that God can sin if he so wills, since the very willing to sin is sinning. Therefore, absolutely speaking, God can sin. And so we reach the same conclusion as before.

13. One who provides the occasion for injury seems to have inflicted the injury. But God by giving the law provided the occasion for human beings to sin, as Rom. 7:7–8 says. Therefore, God causes sin.

14. Since good causes evil, it seems that the greatest good causes the greatest evil. But the greatest evil is moral wrong, which makes a good human being or a good angel evil. Therefore, the greatest good, that is, God, causes moral wrong.

15. The same person has the authority to grant dominion and to take it away. But God has the authority to grant to the soul dominion over the body. Therefore, he also has the authority to take dominion over the body away from the soul. But only sin, which subjects the spirit to the flesh, takes away the soul's dominion over the body. Therefore, God causes sin.

16. The cause of a nature causes the characteristic and natural movement of that very nature. But God causes the nature of the will, and the characteristic and natural movement of the will is turning away from God, just as the characteristic and natural movement of a stone is downward, as Augustine says in his work *On Free Choice*.[8] Therefore, God causes the will's turning away from him. And so it seems that God causes moral wrong, since the nature of moral wrong consists of turning away from him.

17. One who commands a sin causes the sin. But God has commanded sin. For example, as 1 Kgs. 22:22 says, since the spirit of lies had said, "I shall go forth and be a lying spirit in the mouth of the prophets," the Lord said, "Go forth and do so." And Hos. 1:2 says that the Lord commanded Hosea to take a wanton woman for his wife and to beget children of wantonness from her. Therefore, God causes sin.

18. Action and the power to act belong to the same subject, since action belongs to one with the power to act, as the Philosopher says.[9] But God causes the power to sin. Therefore, God causes the action of sinning.

On the Contrary:

1. Augustine says in his work *Book of the 83 Questions* that human beings are not made worse by God, their author.[10] But sin makes human beings worse. Therefore, God is not the author of sin.

---

7. Aristotle, *Topics* 4.5; ET, *LCL* 2:463.
8. Augustine, *On Free Choice*, 3.1.2, in PL 32.1271.
9. Aristotle, *On Sleep and Wakefulness* 1.
10. Augustine, *Book of the 83 Questions* 3–4, in PL 40.11–12.

2. Fulgentius says that God is not the author of what he punishes.[11] But God punishes sin. Therefore, God is not the author of sin.

3. God causes only what he loves, since Wis. 11:25 says: God loves everything that exists, "and you [God] hated nothing that you have made." And he hates sin, as Wis. 14:9 says: "The wicked and their wickedness are alike hateful to God." Therefore, God is not the author of sin.

Answer:

One causes sin in two ways: in one way because the very one sins; in the second way because one causes someone else to sin. And neither of these ways can belong to God.

For it is evident, both from the general nature of sin and from the particular nature of moral sin that we call moral wrong, that God cannot sin. For sin in the general sense, as found in things of nature and artifacts, comes about because persons' actions do not attain the ends they intend. And this happens because of a deficiency in the causal source. For example, a grammarian's poor composition, if he intends to write well, comes about because of his deficient skill. And nature's sin in forming animals, as happens in the birth of monsters, comes about because of the deficient causal power of semen. And sin as we properly speak of it in moral matters, and as it has the nature of moral wrong, comes about because the will by tending toward an improper end fails to attain its proper end. And in the case of God, the causal source cannot be deficient, since his power is infinite, nor can his will fail to attain its proper end, since his very will, which is also his nature, is supreme goodness that is the final end and first rule of all wills. And so his will by nature adheres to, and cannot defect from, the supreme good, just as the natural appetites of things cannot fail to seek their natural good. Therefore, God cannot cause sin because he himself sins.

Likewise, he also cannot cause sin because he causes others to sin. For sin as we are now speaking of it consists of the created will's turning away from the final end. And God cannot cause anyone's will to be turned away from the final end, since he himself is the final end. For whatever created causes universally possess, they necessarily have by imitating the first cause, who gives all of them his likeness insofar as they can receive it, as Dionysius says in his work *Divine Names*.[12] And every created cause through its activity in some way draws other things to its very self by making the things like itself. A created cause does this either by likeness of form, as when heat makes something hot, or by directing other things to its own end, as when human beings by their commands move others to attain the ends those commanding intend. Therefore, it belongs to God to direct everything to his very self and so not to divert anything from his

---

11. Fulgentius, *To Monimus* 1.19, in *PL* 65.167C.
12. Dionysius, *Divine Names* 9.6, in *PG* 3.913C; ET, *Pseudo-Dionysius*, 117.

very self. But he himself is the supreme good. And so he cannot cause the will to turn away from the supreme good, and the nature of moral wrong, as we are now speaking about it, consists of turning away from that good.

Therefore, God cannot cause sin.

Replies to the Objections:
1. The Apostle says that God delivers some up to a depraved way of thinking or inclines their wills to evil by withdrawing his support or by not preventing evil, not indeed by his activity or movement. Just so, for example, we would say that a person who were to fail to extend a hand to someone falling would cause the latter's fall. But it is by just judgment that God does not bestow assistance on some to prevent their fall.

2. The foregoing also makes clear the reply to the second objection.

3. Punishment is contrary to a particular good. And taking away a particular good is not contrary to the nature of the supreme good, since the addition of other, sometimes better, goods takes away particular goods. For example, the addition of the form of fire takes away the form of water, and likewise the addition of a higher good, namely, that God has established an order of justice regarding things, takes away the good of a particular nature as a punishment. But the evil of moral wrong occurs by turning away from the supreme good, from which the supreme good cannot turn away. And so God can cause punishment but not moral wrong.

4. We trace to the prior cause the effect produced by the caused cause as such. But if something does not proceed from the caused cause as such, we do not need to trace the effect to the prior cause. For example, an animal's power to move its legs causes the animal's leg movement. But limping comes from the fact that a leg by reason of its deficiency lacks the capacity to receive the influence of the animal's locomotive power, not from the fact that the leg is moved by the animal's locomotive power. And so the animal's locomotive power does not cause the limping. Therefore, free choice, as it defects from God, causes sin. And so God, although he causes free choice, need not cause sin.

5. Sins do not come from the inclination of the irascible and concupiscible power, as instituted by God, but as the powers depart from the ordination that God himself instituted, for the powers were instituted in human beings to be subject to reason. And so it is not from God when they incline to sin contrary to the ordination of reason.

6. The argument of this objection is not valid, since God inclines the will by adding grace, not by activity or movement, as I have said [in the answer above].

7. The causes of evils are particular goods that can be deficient. But such particular goods are in God as effects in their cause insofar as they are goods. And we say that the causes of evils are in God to this extent, not that he himself causes the evils.

8. God as he is in himself communicates himself to all things in proportion to their receptivity. And so if something should deficiently share in his goodness, this is because the thing has an obstacle to participating in God. Therefore, God does not cause grace not to be supplied to someone; rather, those not supplied with grace offer an obstacle to grace insofar as they turn themselves away from the light that does not turn itself away, as Dionysius says.[13]

9. We should speak in one way about human beings in the state of nature as instituted, and in another way about human beings in the state of fallen nature, since human beings in the state of nature as instituted had nothing impelling them to evil, although natural good was insufficient to attain glory. And so human beings needed the help of grace in order to merit but not in order to avoid sins, since human beings by their natural powers could remain upright. But human beings in the state of fallen nature have an impulse to evil and so need the help of grace in order not to fall. And it was regarding the latter state that Augustine attributed to divine grace the evils he did not commit. And a previous moral wrong brought about such a state.

10. Things that do not belong to the praise of higher beings can be praiseworthy in lower beings. For example, ferociousness is praiseworthy in dogs but not in human beings, as Dionysius says.[14] And likewise, not transgressing when one could belongs to the praise of human beings but is absent from the praise of God.

11. We understand the words of the Philosopher about those called gods, whether by unfounded opinion as in the case of pagan gods or by participation as in the case of human beings virtuous beyond human measure, to whom the *Ethics* attributes heroic or divine virtue.[15] Or as some say, it is possible to hold that we can say that God can do evil things because he can if he wishes.

12. The protasis of the conditional proposition, "Socrates can run if he so wills," is possible, and so it follows that the apodasis is possible. But in the case of the conditional proposition, "God can sin if he so wills," the protasis is impossible, since God cannot will evil. And so there is no similarity between the two propositions.

13. There are two ways of being an occasion of sin, namely, one when an occasion is offered for sin, the second when an occasion is taken for sin. But the commandments are occasions for sin as taken by those to whom the commandments are imparted, not indeed as given by the one who gave the commandments. And so the Apostle in Rom. 7:8 significantly adds: "Taking the occasion, sin through the law worked in me all kinds of lust-

---

13. Dionysius, *Divine Names* 4.23, in PG 3.725C; ET, *Pseudo-Dionysius*, 91.
14. Dionysius, *Divine Names* 4.25, in PG 3.728B; ET, *Pseudo-Dionysius*, 92.
15. Aristotle, *Nicomachean Ethics* 7.1; ET, LCL 19:376–78.

ful desires." For we say that persons provide an occasion for sinning when they do something less virtuous that by their example leads others to sin. And if one should perform a virtuous deed, and another should thereby be led into sinning, there will be an occasion taken but not offered for sinning. For example, such was the case when the Pharisees were scandalized at the teaching of Christ [e.g., Matt. 15:12]. And the commandments were holy and just, as Rom. 7:12 says. And so God by the commandments does not offer an occasion to sin, but human beings take the commandments as the occasion to sin.

14. If good as such were to cause evil, it would follow that the greatest good causes the greatest evil. But good insofar as it is deficient causes evil. And so the greater the good, the lesser the cause of evil.

15. Taking away the dominion of the spirit over the flesh is contrary to the order of natural justice, and such cannot belong to God, who is justice itself.

16. We call the movement of turning away from God characteristic and natural for the will in the state of fallen nature, not in the state of nature as instituted.

17. We should not understand the statement "Go forth and do so" by way of command but by way of permission, just like the statement to Judas "What you do, do quickly" [John 13:27], in the manner of speaking whereby we call permission by God his will. And we should understand the statement to Hosea "Take to yourself a wanton woman as your wife," etc., by way of command. But God's command causes what would otherwise be a sin not to be a sin. For as Bernard says,[16] God can dispense in regard to the commandments of the second tablet, commandments whereby human beings are directly regulated regarding their neighbor, since the good of one's neighbor is a particular good. But God cannot dispense in regard to the commandments of the first tablet, commandments whereby human beings are regulated regarding God, who cannot turn others away from his very self, since he cannot deny his very self, as 2 Tim. 2:13 says. Nonetheless, some say that we should understand that the things described about Hosea happened in a prophetic vision.

18. We understand by the words of the Philosopher that it is one thing to be able to act and another thing to act, and not what causes a power also causes the power's act.

Second Article: Do Acts of Sin Come from God?

Objections:
It seems that they do not, for the following reasons:
1. We say that human beings cause sin only because they cause acts of sin, since we do not do anything aiming to do evil, as Dionysius says in his

---

16. Bernard of Clairvaux, *On Precept and Dispensation* 3, in PL 182.864B–C.

work *Divine Names*.¹⁷ But God does not cause sin, as I have said before [in the previous article].

2. Every cause of something causes what belongs to the thing by reason of its species. For example, if a person causes Socrates, then the person causes the human being that Socrates is. But some acts are indeed sins by reason of their species. Therefore, if acts of sin come from God, then sin comes from God.

3. Everything from God is a thing. But acts of sin are not things, as Augustine says in his work *On the Perfection of the Justice of Human Beings*.¹⁸ Therefore, acts of sin do not come from God.

4. Acts of sin are acts of free choice, which we call free because the will moves its very self to act. But everything whose acts are caused by another is moved by the other, and if the thing does not move itself, it is not free. Therefore, acts of sin do not come from God.

On the Contrary:

Augustine says in his work *On the Trinity* that the will of God causes every species and movement.¹⁹ But acts of sin are indeed movements of free choice. Therefore, the acts come from God.

Answer:

Ancient thinkers held two opinions regarding this matter. For some of old, stressing the very deformity of sin, which does not come from God, said that acts of sin do not come from God. And some, stressing the very entity of the acts, said that acts of sin come from God. And we need for two reasons to hold that the entity of the acts comes from God. The first reason is general. Since God is by his essence being, for his essence is his existing, everything existing in whatever way derives from himself. For there is nothing else that can be its own existing; rather, we call everything else a being by some participation. And everything we call such a thing by participation derives from what is such by essence. For example, everything on fire derives from what is fire by essence. But acts of sin are evidently beings and classified in the category of being. And so we need to say that the acts are from God.

And second, a particular reason evidences the same thing. For every movement of secondary causes needs to be caused by the first mover, just as all the movements of earthly material substances are caused by the movements of heavenly bodies. But God is the first mover regarding all movements, both spiritual and material, just as a heavenly body is the source of all the movements of earthly material substances. And so, since

---

17. Dionysius, *Divine Names* 4.19, in *PG* 3.716C; ET, *Pseudo-Dionysius*, 85.
18. Augustine, *On the Perfection of the Justice of Human Beings* 2, in *PL* 44.294.
19. Augustine, *On the Trinity* 3.4.9, in *PL* 42.873; ET, *NPNF*¹ 3:58–59.

acts of sin are movements of free choice, we need to say that such acts as acts come from God.

And yet we should note that the movement from the first mover is not received in all moveable things in only one way but received in each kind of moveable thing in its own way. For example, heavenly movements cause the movements of inanimate material substances, which do not move themselves, in one way, and the movements of animals, which move themselves, in another way. And further, heavenly bodies cause plants whose reproductive power is not wanting, and whose reproductive power produces perfect shoots, to sprout in one way, and plants whose reproductive power is weak and produces fruitless shoots to sprout in another way. For when something is properly disposed to receive the causal movement of the first cause, a perfect causal action in accord with the aim of the first mover results. But if something is not properly disposed or fit to receive the causal movement of the first mover, imperfect action results. And then we trace what belongs to the activity in it to the first mover as the cause. And we do not trace what is in it regarding deficiency to the first mover as the cause, since such deficiency in the activity results because the secondary cause defects from the ordination of the first mover, as I have said [in the first article]. For example, everything regarding the movement in limping is from an animal's locomotive power, but everything in limping regarding deficiency is from the leg insofar as the leg lacks the aptitude to be moved by the animal's locomotive power, not from the locomotive power.

Therefore, we need to say that God, since he is the first source of the movement of everything, moves certain things in such a way that they also move their very selves, as in the case of those with the power of free choice. And if those with free choice be properly disposed and rightly ordered to receive movement by God, good acts will result, and we completely trace these acts to him as their cause. But if those with free choice should defect from the requisite order, disordered acts that are acts of sin result. And so we trace what regards the activity of those with the power of free choice to God as the cause, while only free choice, not God, causes what regards the deordination or deformity of those with the power of free choice. And that is why we say that acts of sin come from God, but that sin does not.

Replies to the Objections:
1. Although sinners do not intrinsically will the deformity of sin, the deformity of sin nonetheless in some way falls within the compass of the sinner's will, namely, as the sinner prefers to incur the deformity of sin than to desist from the act. But the deformity of sin in no way falls within the compass of the divine will; rather, the deformity results because free choice withdraws from the ordination of the divine will.

2. The deformity of sin does not result from the species of acts as the acts belong to a type of nature, and God causes the acts as they belong to a

type of nature. Rather, the deformity of sin results from the species of acts as moral, as caused by free choice, as I have said in connection with other questions.[20]

3. We speak of being and thing absolutely in regard to substances but with qualifications regarding accidents. And it is in this regard that Augustine says that acts are not things.

4. When we say that something moves its very self, we posit that the same thing causes the movement and is moved. And when we say that one thing moves another, we posit that one thing causes the movement, and that the other is moved. But it is evident that when one thing moves another, we do not posit that the cause of movement, by that fact, is the first cause of movement. And so we do not preclude that the cause of movement is moved by another and has from the other the very power to cause movement. Likewise, when something moves its very self, we do not preclude that such a thing be moved by another from which it has the very power to move itself. And so it is not contrary to freedom that God cause acts of free choice.

Third Article: Does the Devil Cause Sin?
Objections:
It seems that he does, for the following reasons:

1. Wis. 2:24 says: "Death entered the world through the devil's envy." But death is the consequence of sin. Therefore, the devil causes sin.

2. Sin consists of desire. But Augustine says in his work *On the Trinity* that the devil inspires wicked desires in his companions.[21] And Bede says in his *Commentary on the Acts of the Apostles* that the devil entices the soul to wicked desires.[22] Therefore, the devil causes sin.

3. Nature constitutes lower things to be moved by higher things. But as nature ordains that the human intellect is inferior to the angelic intellect, so does nature ordain that the human will is inferior to the angelic will, since appetitive power is proportioned to cognitive power. Therefore, a bad angel by his evil will can move human wills to evil and so cause sin.

4. Isidore says in his work *On the Supreme Good* that the devil inflames human hearts with hidden inordinate desires.[23] But the root of all evils is inordinate desire, as 1 Tim. 6:10 says. Therefore, it seems that the devil can cause sin.

5. Everything equally related to each of two things needs something to determine it in order that it proceed to act. But the power of free choice of human beings is equally related to each of two things, namely, good and evil. Therefore, in order to proceed to an act of sin, the power of free choice

---

20. See article 1 above and quest. 2.2–3.
21. Augustine, *On the Trinity* 4.12.15, in *PL* 42.897; ET, *NPNF*² 3:77.
22. Bede, *Commentary of Acts*, on 5:3, in *PL* 92.954D.
23. Isidore of Seville, *On the Supreme Good* 3.5.33, in *PL* 83.666B.

needs to be determined to evil by something. And the devil, whose will is determined to evil, seems especially to do this. Therefore, it seems that the devil causes sin.

6. Augustine says in his *Enchiridion* that the cause of sin is the mutable will, first indeed that of the angels and then of human beings.[24] But the first in any genus causes the others. Therefore, it seems that the devil's evil will causes the evil will of human beings.

7. Sin consists of designs, and so Isa. 1:16 says: "Take away the evil of your designs from my eyes." But it seems that the devil can cause us to have designs, since the cogitative power is linked to bodily organs, and the devil can change material substances. Therefore, it seems that the devil can directly cause sin.

8. Augustine says [*The City of God*, 19.4.3] that we should not think that there is no vice when the flesh lusts against the spirit.[25] But it seems that the devil can cause such concupiscence, since the concupiscible power is the actuality of a bodily organ. Therefore, it seems that he can directly cause sin.

9. Augustine says in his *Literal Interpretation of Genesis* that when images of things are so presented to human beings as not to be distinguishable from the things, disorder in the flesh results.[26] And he says that the spiritual power of a good or bad angel can accomplish this. But there is no disorder in the flesh without sin. Therefore, it seems that the devil can directly cause sin.

10. The Commentator [Averroes] in his *Commentary on the Metaphysics* cites the words of Themistius, who said that a lower nature acts as if inspired by higher causes.[27] But higher causes properly and directly cause what lower causes do. Therefore, what can inspire things in lower causes seems to cause the acts of the lower causes. But the devil can inspire in human beings things whereby they are moved to sin. Therefore, it seems that the devil can directly cause sin.

11. The Philosopher in the *Eudemian Ethics* inquires about the source of the soul's activity and shows that the source needs to be something external, since everything that begins to exist has a cause.[28] For example, human beings begin to act because they will to do so, and they begin to will because they deliberate beforehand. And if they should deliberate beforehand by reason of an antecedent deliberation, either there is an infinite regress or we need to posit an external source that first moves human beings to deliberate. (Someone may suggest that deliberation happens by chance, but then it would follow that every human act happens by chance.)

---

24. Augustine, *Enchiridion* 23, in *PL* 40.244; ET, *LCC* 7:353–54.
25. Augustine, *The City of God* 19.4.3, in *PL* 41.629; ET, *NPNF*[1] 2:402.
26. Augustine, *Literal Interpretation of Genesis* 12.12.25, in *PL* 34.463.
27. Averroes, *On Aristotle's Metaphysics* 11.18.
28. Aristotle, *Eudemian Ethics* 8.2; ET, *LCL* 20:465–67.

And the Philosopher says that the external source in the case of good acts is indeed God, who does not cause sin, as I have demonstrated before [in article 1 above]. Therefore, since human beings begin to act, to will, and to deliberate regarding sin, it seems that this process needs to have an external cause, which can only be the devil. Therefore, the devil himself causes sin.

12. To the power of whatever a cause of movement is subject, the movement caused is subject. But the cause of the will's movement is something apprehended by the senses or the intellect, both of which are subject to the power of the devil. For Augustine says in his work *Book of the 83 Questions*: "This evil," namely, the one from the devil, "creeps in through all the accesses of the senses, gives itself shapes, adapts itself to colors, adheres to sounds, is hidden in anger and false speech, underlies odors, infuses with flavors, and clouds all avenues of understanding."[29] Therefore, the devil has the power to move the will and so directly causes sin.

13. The devil buys human beings for their sins, as Isa. 50:1 says: "Behold, you were sold for your sins." But buyers offer money to sellers. Therefore, the devil causes sin in human beings.

14. Jerome says that just as God perfects good, so the devil perfects evil, although human beings have certain inclinations that incite them to vices.[30] But God intrinsically causes our good acts. Therefore, it seems that the devil likewise directly causes our sins.

15. Bad angels are related to evil as good angels are related to good. But good angels lead human beings to good, since it is the divine law to lead to ultimate things through intermediaries, as Dionysius says.[31] Therefore, it seems that a bad angel can lead human beings to evil, and so that the devil causes sin.

On the Contrary:

1. Augustine says in his work *Book of the 83 Questions* [4] that "the cause of the depravity of human beings is traceable to their will, whether they have been perverted at the persuasion of someone or no one."[32] But sin perverts human beings. Therefore, the human will, not the devil, causes the sin of human beings.

2. Augustine says in his work *On Free Choice* [1.1.1] that each human being causes his or her own wickedness, and no one else causes human sin.[33]

3. The sin of human beings comes about by free choice. But the devil cannot cause movement by free choice. Therefore, the devil does not cause sin.

---

29. Augustine, *Book of the 83 Questions* 12, in *PL* 40.14.
30. Jerome, *Against Jovinian* 2.3, in *PL* 23.286–87.
31. Dionysius, *On Ecclesiastical Hierarchy*, 5.1.4, in *PG* 3.504C; ET, *Pseudo-Dionysius*, 236.
32. Augustine, *Book of the 83 Questions* 4, in *PL* 40.12.
33. Augustine, *On Free Choice* 1.1.1, in *PL* 32.1223.

Answer:

We speak in many ways about causes inducing something. For example, we sometimes call what disposes or commends or commands, a cause. And we sometimes call what brings about an effect a cause. And we properly and truly call the latter a cause, since causes result in effects. But effects result directly from the activity of what brings them about, and not from the activity of what disposes or commends or commands, "since persuasion does not compel one who is unwilling," as Augustine says in his *Book of the 83 Questions*.[34] Therefore, we need to say that the devil can cause sin as one who disposes or persuades internally or externally, or even as one who commands, as is apparent in the case of those who have openly surrendered themselves to the devil. But he cannot cause sin as an efficient cause. For as the efficient causes in producing forms are the causes by whose activity the forms result, so the efficient causes in eliciting acts are the causes by whose activity human agents are induced to act. But sin is an act, not a form. Therefore, only what can directly move the will to an act of sin can intrinsically cause sin.

And we should consider that we speak in two ways about the will being induced to something: in one way by something external; in the second way by something internal. The will is indeed moved by something external, for example, an apprehended object. For we say that the apprehended object moves the will, and we say that one who commends or persuades moves the will in this way, namely, inasmuch as such a one makes something seem good. And the will is moved by something internal, for example, what produces the very act of the will. And the object proposed to the will does not necessarily move the will, although the intellect sometimes necessarily assents to a proposed truth. And the reason for this difference is that both the intellect and the will necessarily tend toward what nature has ordained as their object, for it is characteristic of nature to be determined to one thing. And so the intellect necessarily assents to the first principles known naturally, nor can it assent to their contraries, and the will likewise naturally and necessarily wills happiness, nor can anyone will unhappiness. And so regarding the intellect, things necessarily linked to naturally known first principles necessarily move the intellect. For example, such is the case of demonstrated conclusions, where it is evident that denial of the conclusions necessitates denial of the first principles from which the conclusions necessarily result. But the intellect is not compelled to assent to conclusions if they be not necessarily linked to naturally known first principles, as is the case with contingent and probable things. Likewise, neither does the intellect necessarily assent to necessary things necessarily linked to first principles before it knows there is such a necessary connection. Therefore, regarding the will, the will will not be necessarily moved

---

34. Augustine, *Book of the 83 Questions* 4, in *PL* 40.12.

to anything that does not even seem to have a necessary connection with happiness, which is naturally willed. And it is obvious that such particular goods have no necessary connection with happiness, since human beings can be happy without any one of them. And so however much one of them is presented to human beings as good, the will does not necessarily incline to it. And the perfect good, that is, God, indeed has a necessary connection with the happiness of human beings, since human beings cannot be happy without that good, but the necessity of this connection is not fully evident to human beings in this life, since they do not in this life behold the essence of God. And so the human will in this life also does not necessarily adhere to God, but the will of those who, beholding the essence of God, evidently know that he himself is the essence of goodness and the happiness of human beings cannot not adhere to God, just as our will in this life cannot not will happiness. Therefore, it is evident that the will's object does not necessarily move the will, and so no persuasion necessarily moves the will to act.

Therefore, we conclude that the efficient and proper cause of a voluntary act is only what acts internally, and this can only be the will itself as secondary cause and God as first cause. And the reason for this is that the will's act is simply an inclination of the will to the thing willed, just as a natural appetite is simply a natural inclination to something. But a natural inclination comes from a natural form and from what gave the form. And so we say that the upward movement of fire comes from its lightness and from the cause that created such a form. Therefore, the will's movement directly comes from the will and God, who causes the will, who alone acts within the will and can incline the will to whatever he should will. But God cannot cause sin, as I have shown before [in article 1 above]. Therefore, we conclude that only the will directly causes human sin. Therefore, it is clear that the devil does not, properly speaking, directly cause sin but causes sin only as a persuader.

Replies to the Objections:

1. Death entered the world through the devil's envy insofar as he persuaded the first human being to sin.

2. We say that the devil as a persuader inspires wicked desires in human beings or even draws souls to wicked desires.

3. Nature constitutes something lower, as passive, to be moved by something higher, as active, through an external change, as, for example, air is moved by fire. But external change does not impose necessity on the will, as I have shown [in the answer]. And so the devil, although he belongs to a rank of nature superior to the human soul, cannot affect a human will necessarily. And so he does not, properly speaking, cause sin, since we properly speak of a cause as something from which something else necessarily results.

4. We say that the devil inflames the hearts of human beings by persuading them with inordinate desires.

5. The will, although it is equally related to each of two alternatives, is determined to one of them by something, namely, the deliberation of reason. And this determination does not need to be by an external cause.

6. The sin of the angels and the sin of human beings do not have a natural relationship to one another but only a temporal relationship. For it happens that the devil sinned before human beings did, but it could have happened conversely. And so the sin of the devil does not necessarily cause the sin of human beings.

7. There is sin in thoughts only insofar as they incline someone to evil or withdraw someone from good. And this remains subject to the will's power of free choice, no matter what thoughts arise. And so it is not necessary that something which causes thought thereby causes sin.

8. The lusting of the flesh against the spirit is an act of sensuality, which can involve sin insofar as reason can prevent or restrain its movement. And so there is no sin in the act if the movement of sensuality arises from a bodily change, and reason resists the movement. And resistance is within the will's power of choice. And so it is clear that every sin rests in the will's power of choice.

9. The fact that we do not distinguish the images and likenesses of things from the things themselves results from the fact that the higher power capable of distinguishing and judging is fettered. For example, one thing touched by two fingers seems to the sense of touch to be two things unless another power (e.g., sight) contradicts the perception. Therefore, the power of imagination, when likenesses are presented to it, is bound to them as if they were the things themselves, unless another power, namely, an external sense or reason, contradicts the perception. But if reason is fettered, and the external senses are inactive, the power of imagination is bound to the likenesses as if they were the things themselves, as happens in sleepers' dreams and the demented. Therefore, devils can cause human beings not to distinguish images from things insofar as devils, God permitting, disturb internal sense powers, and the disturbed powers fetter the operation of human reason, which needs such powers for its activity. For example, such is evidently the case with those possessed by the devil. But we impute nothing to human beings as sin when their use of reason is fettered, just as we impute nothing to irrational animals as sin. And so the devil will not cause sin even if he should cause acts that would otherwise be sins.

10. Lower natures are moved necessarily by higher causes, and so the higher causes that we speak of as inspiring lower natures cause natural effects properly and directly. But the devil's inspiration does not necessarily move the will, and so there is no comparison.

11. God is the universal source of every deliberation and willing and human act, as I have said before [in the answer]. But every misstep and sin

and deformity in deliberation, willing, and human action comes from the deficiency of human beings. Nor do we need to attribute these to another, extrinsic cause.

12. The apprehended thing does not move the will necessarily, as I have shown [in the answer]. And so the thing apprehended by the senses or the intellect, however much it be subject to the power of the devil, cannot be sufficient to move the will to sin.

13. The devil offers sin to human beings as a persuader.

14. We do not note the cited similarity in every respect. For God is the author of our good acts both as external persuader and internal mover, while the devil causes sin only as external persuader, as I have shown [in the answer].

15. Good angels as persuaders, not indeed by directly moving the will, lead human beings to God. And so also does the devil induce human beings to sin.

SELECTION 5

John Calvin

Institutes of the Christian Religion, Book 2, Chapter 1

John Calvin (1509–1564) was one of the pivotal figures of the Reformation and the most well-known among those theologians grouped with the Reformed (as opposed to Lutheran) Protestant tradition. His *Institutes of the Christian Religion*, perhaps the most influential text of the Reformation, went through several revisions between its initial appearance in 1536 and the final edition published by Calvin in 1559. In every case, however, Calvin's aim was to provide a summary theological framework for the education of ministers. As such, he sought to be comprehensive but also to be pastoral, subsuming all theological topics to the proclamation of the gospel of grace. It is therefore significant that Calvin's treatment of the difficult topic of original sin in the following excerpt opens the section of the *Institutes* titled "The Knowledge of God the Redeemer."

Calvin defends a strongly Augustinian version of the doctrine of original sin, stressing its hold on all humankind and insisting (in terms that later Reformed theologians would name "total depravity") that no part of the human person is free from its effects. At the same time, he denies that it is in any way "natural" in the sense of having been created by God. The origin of sin is attributed entirely to human perversity, though Calvin maintains that it is by divine decree rather than by genetic transmission that all human beings share the consequences of Adam's initial disobedience. That

God should so decree may seem arbitrary, but for Calvin it actually serves to reinforce the graciousness of the gospel, since it is the good news that we are counted righteous in Christ apart from our own actions that demands the admission that we are equally counted sinful (and thus in need of Christ's righteousness) apart from our own actions.

From John Calvin, *Institutes of the Christian Religion*, LCC 20:244–55.

4. The History of the Fall Shows Us What Sin Is [Gen., ch. 3]: Unfaithfulness

Because what God so severely punished must have been no light sin but a detestable crime, we must consider what kind of sin there was in Adam's desertion that enkindled God's fearful vengeance against the whole of mankind. To regard Adam's sin as gluttonous intemperance (a common notion) is childish. As if the sum and head of all virtues lay in abstaining solely from one fruit, when all sorts of desirable delights abounded everywhere; and not only abundance but also magnificent variety was at hand in that blessed fruitfulness of earth!

We ought therefore to look more deeply. Adam was denied the tree of the knowledge of good and evil to test his obedience and prove that he was willingly under God's command. The very name of the tree shows the sole purpose of the precept was to keep him content with his lot and to prevent him from becoming puffed up with wicked lust. But the promise by which he was bidden to hope for eternal life so long as he ate from the tree of life, and, conversely, the terrible threat of death once he tasted of the tree of the knowledge of good and evil, served to prove and exercise his faith. Hence it is not hard to deduce by what means Adam provoked God's wrath upon himself. Indeed, Augustine speaks rightly when he declares that pride was the beginning of all evils.[1] For if ambition had not raised man higher than was meet and right, he could have remained in his original state. But we must take a fuller definition from the nature of the temptation which Moses describes. Since the woman through unfaithfulness was led away from God's Word by the serpent's deceit, it is already clear that disobedience was the beginning of the Fall. This Paul also confirms, teaching that all were lost through the disobedience of one man [Rom. 5:19]. Yet it is at the same time to be noted that the first man revolted from God's authority, not only because he was seized by Satan's blandishments, but also because, contemptuous of truth, he turned aside to falsehood. And surely, once we hold God's Word in contempt, we shake off all reverence for him. For, unless we listen attentively to him, his majesty will not dwell among us, nor his worship remain perfect. Unfaithfulness, then, was the root of the Fall. But thereafter ambition and pride, together with ungratefulness,

---

1. Augustine, *Psalms*, Ps. 18.2.15, in *PL* 36.163; ET, *NPNF*[1], 8:56.

arose, because Adam by seeking more than was granted him shamefully spurned God's great bounty, which had been lavished upon him. To have been made in the likeness of God seemed a small matter to a son of earth unless he also attained equality with God—a monstrous wickedness! If apostasy, by which man withdraws from the authority of his Maker— indeed insolently shakes off his yoke—is a foul and detestable offense, it is vain to extenuate Adam's sin. Yet it was not simple apostasy, but was joined with vile reproaches against God. These assented to Satan's slanders, which accused God of falsehood and envy and ill will. Lastly, faithlessness opened the door to ambition, and ambition was indeed the mother of obstinate disobedience; as a result, men, having cast off the fear of God, threw themselves wherever lust carried them. Hence Bernard rightly teaches that the door of salvation is opened to us when we receive the gospel today with our ears, even as death was then admitted by those same windows when they were opened to Satan [cf. Jer. 9:21].[2] For Adam would never have dared oppose God's authority unless he had disbelieved in God's Word. Here, indeed, was the best bridle to control all passions: the thought that nothing is better than to practice righteousness by obeying God's commandments; then, that the ultimate goal of the happy life is to be loved by him. Therefore Adam, carried away by the devil's blasphemies, as far as he was able extinguished the whole glory of God.

5. The First Sin as Original Sin

As it was the spiritual life of Adam to remain united and bound to his Maker, so estrangement from him was the death of his soul. Nor is it any wonder that he consigned his race to ruin by his rebellion when he perverted the whole order of nature in heaven and on earth. "All creatures," says Paul, "are groaning" [Rom. 8:22], "subject to corruption, not of their own will" [Rom. 8:20]. If the cause is sought, there is no doubt that they are bearing part of the punishment deserved by man, for whose use they were created. Since, therefore, the curse, which goes about through all the regions of the world, flowed hither and yon from Adam's guilt, it is not unreasonable if it is spread to all his offspring. Therefore, after the heavenly image was obliterated in him, he was not the only one to suffer this punishment—that, in place of wisdom, virtue, holiness, truth, and justice, with which adornments he had been clad, there came forth the most filthy plagues, blindness, impotence, impurity, vanity, and injustice—but he also entangled and immersed his offspring in the same miseries.

This is the inherited corruption, which the church fathers termed "original sin," meaning by the word "sin" the depravation of a nature previously good and pure. There was much contention over this matter, inasmuch as

---

2. Bernard, *Sermons on the Song of Songs* 28, in PL 183.923; ET, S. J. Eales, *Life and Works of St. Bernard*, 4:179.

nothing is farther from the usual view than for all to be made guilty by the guilt of one, and thus for sin to be made common. This seems to be the reason why the most ancient doctors of the church touched upon this subject so obscurely. At least they explained it less clearly than was fitting. Yet this timidity could not prevent Pelagius from rising up with the profane fiction that Adam sinned only to his own loss without harming his posterity.[3] Through this subtlety Satan attempted to cover up the disease and thus to render it incurable. But when it was shown by the clear testimony of Scripture that sin was transmitted from the first man to all his posterity [Rom. 5:12], Pelagius quibbled that it was transmitted through imitation, not propagation. Therefore, good men (and Augustine above the rest) labored to show us that we are corrupted not by derived wickedness, but that we bear inborn defect from our mother's womb.[4] To deny this was the height of shamelessness. But no man will wonder at the temerity of the Pelagians and Coelestians when he perceived from that holy man's warnings what shameless beasts they were in all other respects. Surely there is no doubt that David confesses himself to have been "begotten in iniquities, and conceived by his mother in sin" [Ps. 51:5]. There he does not reprove his father and mother for their sins; but, that he may better commend God's goodness toward himself, from his very conception he carries the confession of his own perversity. Since it is clear that this was not peculiar to David, it follows that the common lot of mankind is exemplified in him.

Therefore all of us, who have descended from impure seed, are born infected with the contagion of sin. In fact, before we saw the light of this life we were soiled and spotted in God's sight. "For who can bring a clean thing from an unclean? There is not one"—as The Book of Job says [Job 14:4, cf. Vulg.].

6. Original Sin Does Not Rest upon Imitation

We hear that the uncleanness of the parents is so transmitted to the children that all without any exception are defiled at their begetting. But

---

3. Pelagius (ca. 354–420), a British monk who combated Augustine's doctrine of man's innate depravity resulting from Adam's sin, thus calling forth a body of treatises and letters by Augustine in exposition and defense of this doctrine. With his more aggressive associate, Coelestius . . . Pelagius emerged from Rome, visited North Africa, Palestine, and Asia Minor, and won numerous adherents. Pelagianism was condemned in Councils of Carthage (in 412 and 418) and in an imperial edict (418), after which Pope Zosimus withdrew the favor in which he had held Coelestius and joined in his condemnation. But elements of this heresy were perpetuated. It is essentially an assertion of the natural moral ability of man. For a useful brief selection of documents on the controversy, see H. Bettenson, *Documents of the Christian Church* (Oxford: Oxford University Press, 1944), 74–87.

4. Cf. Augustine, *The City of God* 16.27: "Infants . . . according to the common origin of the human race, have all broken God's covenant in that one in whom all have sinned. . . . Infants are . . . born in sin not actual but original," in *PL* 41.506; ET, *NPNF*[1], 2:326. The first opposition of Pelagius to Augustine had been called forth against the implications of man's helplessness in the well-known sentence in the *Confessions* (10.29.40; 10.31.45): *Da quod iubes et iube quod vis* ("Give what you command and command what you will"); in *PL* 32.796, 798; ET, *LCC* 7:225, 228.

we will not find the beginning of this pollution unless we go back to the first parent of all, as its source. We must surely hold that Adam was not only the progenitor but, as it were, the root of human nature; and that therefore in his corruption mankind deserved to be vitiated. This the apostle makes clear from a comparison of Adam with Christ. "As through one man sin came into the world and through sin death, which spread among all men when all sinned" [Rom. 5:12], thus through Christ's grace righteousness and life are restored to us [Rom. 5:17]. What nonsense will the Pelagians chatter here? That Adam's sin was propagated by imitation? Then does Christ's righteousness benefit us only as an example set before us to imitate? Who can bear such sacrilege! But if it is beyond controversy that Christ's righteousness, and thereby life, are ours by communication, it immediately follows that both were lost in Adam, only to be recovered in Christ; and that sin and death crept in through Adam, only to be abolished through Christ. These are no obscure words: "Many are made righteous by Christ's obedience as by Adam's disobedience they had been made sinners" [Rom. 5:19]. Here, then, is the relationship between the two: Adam, implicating us in his ruin, destroyed us with himself; but Christ restores us to salvation by his grace.

In such clear light of truth, I think that there is no need for longer or more laborious proof. In the first letter to the Corinthians, Paul wishes to strengthen the faith of the godly in the resurrection. Here he accordingly shows that the life lost in Adam is recovered in Christ [1 Cor. 15:22]. Declaring that all of us died in Adam, Paul at the same time plainly testifies that we are infected with the disease of sin. For condemnation could not reach those untouched by the guilt of iniquity. The clearest explanation of his meaning lies in the other part of the statement, in which he declares that the hope of life is restored in Christ. But it is well known that this occurs in no other way than that wonderful communication whereby Christ transfuses into us the power of his righteousness. As it is written elsewhere, "The Spirit is life to us because of righteousness" [Rom. 8:10]. There is consequently but one way for us to interpret the statement, "We have died in Adam": Adam, by sinning, not only took upon himself misfortune and ruin but also plunged our nature into like destruction. This was not due to the guilt of himself alone, which would not pertain to us at all, but was because he infected all his posterity with that corruption into which he had fallen.

Paul's statement that "by nature all are children of wrath" [Eph. 2:3] could not stand, unless they had already been cursed in the womb itself. Obviously, Paul does not mean "nature" as it was established by God, but as it was vitiated in Adam. For it would be most unfitting for God to be made the author of death. Therefore, Adam so corrupted himself that infection spread from him to all his descendants. Christ himself, our heavenly judge, clearly enough proclaims that all men are born wicked and depraved when he says that "whatever is born of flesh is flesh" [John 3:6], and therefore the door of life is closed to all until they have been reborn [John 3:5].

7. The Transmission of Sin from One Generation to Another

No anxious discussion is needed to understand this question, which troubled the fathers not a little—whether the son's soul proceeds by derivation[5] from the father's soul—because the contagion chiefly lies in it. With this we ought to be content: that the Lord entrusted to Adam those gifts which he willed to be conferred upon human nature. Hence Adam, when he lost the gifts received, lost them not only for himself but for us all. Who should worry about the derivation of the soul when he hears that Adam had received for us no less than for himself those gifts which he lost, and that they had not been given to one man but had been assigned to the whole human race? There is nothing absurd, then, in supposing that, when Adam was despoiled, human nature was left naked and destitute, or that when he was infected with sin, contagion crept into human nature. Hence, rotten branches came forth from a rotten root, which transmitted their rottenness to the other twigs sprouting from them. For thus were the children corrupted in the parent, so that they brought disease upon their children's children. That is, the beginning of corruption in Adam was such that it was conveyed in a perpetual stream from the ancestors into their descendants. For the contagion does not take its origin from the substance of the flesh or soul, but because it had been so ordained by God that the first man should at one and the same time have and lose, both for himself and for his descendants, the gifts that God had bestowed upon him.

But it is easy to refute the quibble of the Pelagians, who hold it unlikely that children should derive corruption from godly parents, inasmuch as the offspring ought rather to be sanctified by their parents' purity [cf. 1 Cor. 7:14]. For they descend not from their parents' spiritual regeneration but from their carnal generation. Hence, as Augustine says, whether a man is a guilty unbeliever or an innocent believer, he begets not innocent but guilty children, for he begets them from a corrupted nature.[6] Now, it is a special blessing of God's people that they partake in some degree of their

---

5. Calvin here uses the debated word *tradux* and has in mind the arguments among the fathers on the origin of the individual soul. Though both Augustine and Calvin hold strongly the unity of mankind in creation, neither commits himself to traducianism, by which Adam's soul is regarded as bearing an element transmitted from the divine essence and as the source of all human souls. Calvin, indeed, completely rejects this teaching. But Augustine opposed the alternate view of creationism as it was somewhat crudely presented by Vincentius Victor. See Augustine, *On the Soul and Its Origin* 1.4; 2.14, in *PL* 44.477; 507–8; ET, in *NPNF*[1], 5:316; 340–41. For the prevailing medieval view, cf. E. R. Fairweather's note on a passage from Anselm of Laon in *LCC* 10:261, note 2. On the whole controversy, see C. Hodge, *Systematic Theology* (New York: Scribner, Armstrong and Co., 1873), II. iii, and J. F. Bethune-Baker, *An Introduction to the Early History of Christian Doctrine* (London: Methuen, 1903), 302 ff. Calvinist theology has favored creationism, the doctrine that each soul is a new creation of God.

6. Cf. Augustine, *On the Grace of Christ and on Original Sin* 2.40.45, in *PL* 44.407; ET, *NPNF*[1], 5:253.

parents' holiness. This does not gainsay the fact that the universal curse of the human race preceded. For guilt is of nature, but sanctification, of supernatural grace.

8. The Nature of Original Sin

So that these remarks may not be made concerning an uncertain and unknown matter, let us define original sin.[7] It is not my intention to investigate the several definitions proposed by various writers, but simply to bring forward the one that appears to me most in accordance with truth. Original sin, therefore, seems to be a hereditary depravity and corruption of our nature, diffused into all parts of the soul, which first makes us liable to God's wrath, then also brings forth in us those works which Scripture calls "works of the flesh" [Gal. 5:19]. And that is properly what Paul often calls sin. The works that come forth from it—such as adulteries, fornications, thefts, hatreds, murders, carousings—he accordingly calls "fruits of sin" [Gal. 5:19–21], although they are also commonly called "sins" in Scripture, and even by Paul himself.

We must, therefore, distinctly note these two things. First, we are so vitiated and perverted in every part of our nature that by this great corruption we stand justly condemned and convicted before God, to whom nothing is acceptable but righteousness, innocence, and purity. And this is not liability for another's transgression. For, since it is said that we became subject to God's judgment through Adam's sin, we are to understand it not as if we, guiltless and undeserving, bore the guilt of his offense but in the sense that, since we through his transgression have become entangled in the curse, he is said to have made us guilty. Yet not only has punishment fallen upon us from Adam, but a contagion imparted by him resides in us, which justly deserves punishment. For this reason, Augustine, though he often calls sin "another's" to show more clearly that it is distributed among us through propagation, nevertheless declares at the same time that it is peculiar to each.[8] And the apostle himself most eloquently testifies that "death has spread to all because all have sinned" [Rom. 5:12]. That is, they have been enveloped in original sin and defiled by its stains. For that reason, even infants themselves, while they carry their condemnation along with them from the mother's womb, are guilty not of another's fault but of their own. For, even though the fruits of their iniquity have not yet come forth, they have the seed enclosed within them. Indeed, their whole nature is a seed of sin; hence it can be only hateful and abhorrent to God. From this it follows that it is rightly considered sin in God's sight, for without guilt there would be no accusation.

---

7. *Acts of the Synod of Trent with the Antidote* I, session 5, decree 1, in CR 7:425–26; ET, Calvin, *Tracts and Treatises* (Grand Rapids: Wm. B. Eerdmans Publishing Co., 1958), 3:86 ff.

8. Augustine, *On the Grace of Christ and on Original Sin*, 2.40.45 in PL 44.407; ET, NPNF[1], 5:253.

Then comes the second consideration: that this perversity never ceases in us, but continually bears new fruits—the works of the flesh that we have already described—just as a burning furnace gives forth flame and sparks, or water ceaselessly bubbles up from a spring. Thus those who have defined original sin as "the lack of the original righteousness, which ought to reside in us," although they comprehend in this definition the whole meaning of the term, have still not expressed effectively enough its power and energy. For our nature is not only destitute and empty of good, but so fertile and fruitful of every evil that it cannot be idle. Those who have said that original sin is "concupiscence"[9] have used an appropriate word, if only it be added—something that most will by no means concede—that whatever is in man, from the understanding to the will, from the soul even to the flesh, has been denied and crammed with this concupiscence. Or, to put it more briefly, the whole man is of himself nothing but concupiscence.

9. Sin Overturns the Whole Man

For this reason, I have said that all parts of the soul were possessed by sin after Adam deserted the fountain of righteousness. For not only did a lower appetite seduce him, but unspeakable impiety occupied the very citadel of his mind, and pride penetrated to the depths of his heart. Thus it is pointless and foolish to restrict the corruption that arises thence only to what are called the impulses of the senses; or to call it the "kindling wood" that attracts, arouses, and drags into sin only that part which they term "sensuality." In this matter Peter Lombard has betrayed his complete ignorance. For, in seeking and searching out its seat, he says that it lies in the flesh, as Paul testifies; yet not intrinsically, but because it appears more in the flesh.[10] As if Paul were indicating that only a part of the soul, and not its entire nature, is opposed to supernatural grace! Paul removes all doubt when he teaches that corruption subsists not in one part only, but that none of the soul remains pure or untouched by that mortal disease. For in his discussion of a corrupt nature Paul not only condemns the inordinate impulses of the appetites that are seen, but especially contends the mind is given over to blindness and the heart to depravity.

The whole third chapter of Romans is nothing but a description of original sin [vss. 1–20]. From the "renewal" that fact appears more clearly. For the Spirit, who is opposed to the old man and to the flesh, not only marks the grace whereby the lower or sensual part of the soul is corrected, but

---

9. The term "concupiscence" is much used by Augustine, e.g., in his treatise *On Marriage and Concupiscence*, where in its broadest sense the word means "the law of sin in our sinful flesh" (1.24); see *PL* 44.435; ET, *NPNF*[1], 5:277). Peter Lombard, in discussing the transmission of Adam's sin to his posterity, describes original sin as *fomes peccati, id est, concupiscentia* [the tinder of sin, that is, concupiscence], and also calls it "a vice of nature vitiating all men, who through Adam are born in concupiscence." *Sentences*, 2.30.7–8, in *PL* 192.722. Cf. the interesting and typically Scholastic argument of Stephen Langton on original sin in *LCC* 10:352 ff.

10. Lombard, *Sentences*, 2.30.7–8 and 2.31.2–4, in *PL* 192.722, 724.

embraces the full reformation of all the parts. Consequently, Paul not only enjoins that brute appetites be brought to nought but bids us "be renewed in the spirit of our mind" [Eph. 4:23]; in another passage he similarly urges us to "be transformed in newness of mind" [Rom. 12:2]. From this it follows that that part in which the excellence and nobility of the soul especially shine has not only been wounded, but so corrupted that it needs to be healed and to put on a new nature as well. We shall soon see to what extent sin occupies both mind and heart. Here I only want to suggest briefly that the whole man is overwhelmed—as by a deluge—from head to foot, so that no part is immune from sin and all that proceeds from him is to be imputed to sin. As Paul says, all turnings of the thoughts to the flesh are enmities against God [Rom. 8:7], and are therefore death [Rom. 8:6].

10. Sin Is Not Our Nature, But Its Derangement

Now away with those persons who dare write God's name upon their faults, because we declare that men are vicious by nature![11] They perversely search out God's handiwork in their own pollution, when they ought rather to have sought it in that unimpaired and uncorrupted nature of Adam. Our destruction, therefore, comes from the guilt of our flesh, not from God, inasmuch as we have perished solely because we have degenerated from our original condition.

Let no one grumble here that God could have provided better for our salvation if he had forestalled Adam's fall.[12] Pious minds ought to loathe this objection, because it manifests inordinate curiosity. Furthermore, the matter has to do with the secret of predestination, which will be discussed later in its proper place. Let us accordingly remember to impute our ruin to depravity of nature, in order that we may not accuse God himself, the Author of nature. True, this deadly wound clings to nature, but it is a very important question whether the wound has been inflicted from outside or has been present from the beginning. Yet it is evident that the wound was inflicted through sin. We have, therefore, no reason to complain except against ourselves. Scripture has diligently noted this fact. For Ecclesiastes says: "This I know, that God made man upright, but they have sought out many devices" [Eccl. 7:29]. Obviously, man's ruin is to be ascribed to man alone; for he, having acquired righteousness by God's kindness, has by his own folly sunk into vanity.

11. "Natural" Corruption of the "Nature" Created by God

Therefore we declare that man is corrupted through natural vitiation, but a vitiation that did not flow from nature. We deny that it has

---

11. This is one of the charges brought against the Libertines in Calvin's *Contre la secte phantastique des Libertins* (1545), in CR 7:184–85; and in his *Epistre contre un certain Cordelier* (1547), in CR 7:347, 350 ff.

12. Cf. Augustine, *Literal Interpretation of Genesis* 11.4, 6, 10, 13, in *PL* 34.431–34.

flowed from nature in order to indicate that it is an adventitious quality which comes upon man rather than a substantial property which has been implanted from the beginning. Yet we call it "natural" in order that no man may think that anyone obtains it through bad conduct, since it holds all men fast by hereditary right. Our usage of the term is not without authority. The apostle states: "We are all by nature children of wrath." [Eph. 2:3.] How could God, who is pleased by the least of his works, have been hostile to the noblest of all his creatures? But he is hostile toward the corruption of his work rather than toward the work itself. Therefore if it is right to declare that man, because of his vitiated nature, is naturally abominable to God, it is also proper to say that man is naturally depraved and faulty. Hence Augustine, in view of man's corrupted nature, is not afraid to call "natural" those sins which necessarily reign in our flesh wherever God's grace is absent.[13] Thus vanishes the foolish trifling of the Manichees, who, when they imagined wickedness of substance in man, dared fashion another creator for him in order that they might not seem to assign the cause and beginning of evil to the righteous God.

SELECTION 6

Teresa of Avila

The Interior Castle, 1

Teresa of Avila (1515–1582) is for Catholics both a saint and a doctor of the church (one of only three women to have been accorded the latter designation). Born to a family of Jewish descent, she entered Avila's Carmelite convent in 1534. Her life in the cloister was marked by profound spiritual experiences, but the extreme hostility toward deviant forms of Christianity in sixteenth-century Spain meant that her experiences were viewed as suspect by many, and it was not until 1559 that a sympathetic confessor helped Teresa overcome her own doubts. The last twenty years of her life were devoted to the founding and promotion of a reformed religious order (the Discalced Carmelites), in which Teresa's vision of spiritual community for women could be realized.

The Interior Castle, composed in 1577, is generally considered Teresa's masterpiece. Addressed to her sisters in community, it is a guide to spiritual growth based on the image of the soul as a crystalline "castle" containing many chambers (or "dwelling places"). Through prayer and reflection the contemplative gradually penetrates to the castle's inner chambers,

---

13. Augustine, *Literal Interpretation of Genesis* 1.1.3, in *PL* 34.221; *Contra Julianum, opus imperfectum* 5.40, in *PL* 45.1477.

culminating in the light of the Trinity at the center. The following selection describes the situation in the soul's outermost chambers, where the contemplative is so distracted by wordly concerns as hardly to be able to discern the light at the center. Yet though battling these distractions is the responsibility of the individual, success is inseparable from the relations maintained with others in the community. Teresa stresses in particular the importance of mutual support and trust in overcoming the feelings of fear, false humility, and suspicion sown by the devil to prevent the growth in self-knowledge that is crucial to spiritual advancement. In this way she depicts sin as profoundly individuating and suggests that proper relation to God is inseparable from relations with one's neighbors.

From Teresa of Avila, *The Interior Castle* (New York: Paulist Press, 1979), 39–47.

1. Before going on I want to say that you should consider what it would mean to this so brilliantly shining and beautiful castle, this pearl from the Orient, this tree of life planted in the very living waters of life[1]—that is, in God—to fall into mortal sin; there's no darker darkness nor anything more obscure and black. You shouldn't want to know anything else than the fact that, although the very sun that gave the soul so much brilliance and beauty is still in the center, the soul is as though it were not there to share in these things. Yet, it is as capable of enjoying His Majesty as is crystal capable of reflecting the sun's brilliance. Nothing helps such a soul, and as a result all the good works it might do while in mortal sin are fruitless for the attainment of glory. Since these works do not proceed from that principle, which is God, who is the cause of our virtue's being really virtue, and are separated from Him, they cannot be pleasing in His sight. Since, after all, the intention of anyone who commits a mortal sin is to please the devil, not God, the poor soul becomes darkness itself because the devil is darkness itself.

2. I know a person to whom our Lord wanted to show what a soul in mortal sin was like.[2] That person says that in her opinion if this were understood it would be impossible to sin, even though a soul would have to undergo the greatest trials imaginable in order to flee the occasions. So the Lord gave her a strong desire that all might understand this. May He give you, daughters, the desire to beseech Him earnestly for those who are in this state, who have become total darkness, and whose works have become darkness also. For just as all the streams that flow from a crystal-clear fount are also clear, the works of a soul in grace, because they proceed from this fount of life in which the soul is planted like a tree, are most

---

1. Ps. 1:3.
2. The person is Teresa herself. See her *Spiritual Testimonies*, in vol. 1 of *The Collected Works of St. Teresa of Avila* (Washington, DC: Institute of Carmelite Studies, 1976).

pleasing in the eyes of both God and man. There would be no freshness, no fruit, if it were not for this fount sustaining the tree, preventing it from drying up, and causing it to produce good fruit. Thus in the case of a soul that through its own fault withdraws from this fount and plants itself in a place where the water is black and foul smelling, everything that flows from it is equally wretched and filthy.

3. It should be kept in mind here that the fount, the shining sun that is in the center of the soul, does not lose its beauty and splendor; it is always present in the soul, and nothing can take away its loveliness. But if a black cloth is placed over a crystal that is in the sun, obviously the sun's brilliance will have no effect on the crystal even though the sun is shining on it.[3]

4. O souls redeemed by the blood of Jesus Christ! Understand and take pity on yourselves. How is it possible that in realizing these things you don't strive to remove the pitch from this crystal? See that if your life comes to an end you will never again enjoy this light. O Jesus, how sad a thing it is to see a soul separated from this light! How miserable is the state of those poor rooms within the castle! How disturbed the senses are, that is, the people who live in these rooms! And in the faculties, that is, among the custodians, the stewards, and the chief waiters, what blindness, what bad management! In sum, since the tree is planted where the devil is, what fruit can it bear?

5. I once heard of a spiritual man who was not surprised at things done by a person in mortal sin, but at what was not done. May God in His mercy deliver us from so great an evil. There is nothing, while we are living, that deserves this name "evil" except mortal sin, for such sin carries in its wake everlasting evils. This, daughters, is what we must go about in fear of and what we must ask God in our prayers to protect us against. For if He doesn't guard the city, our labor will be in vain,[4] since we are vanity itself.

That person I mentioned[5] said she received two blessings from the favor God granted her: the first, an intense fear of offending Him, and so in seeing such terrible dangers she always went about begging Him not to let her fall; the second, a mirror for humility, in which she saw how none of our good deeds has its principle in ourselves but in this fount in which the tree, symbolizing our souls, is planted and in this sun that gives warmth to our works. She says that this truth was represented to her so clearly that in doing something good, or seeing it done, she gave heed to the source and understood how without this help we could do nothing. As a result she would begin immediately to praise God and usually not think of herself in any good thing that she did.

---

3. For similar comparisons see Teresa of Avila, *The Book of Her Life*, ch. 40 (in vol. 1 of *The Collected Works*) and *Spiritual Testimonies*, 52.
4. Ps. 127:1.
5. See §2 above.

6. The time you spend in reading this, or I in writing it, Sisters, would not be lost if we were left with these two blessings. Learned and wise men know about these things very well, but everything is necessary for our womanly dullness of mind; and so perhaps the Lord wills that we get to know comparisons like these. May it please His goodness to give us grace to profit by them.

7. These interior matters are so obscure for our minds that anyone who knows as little as I will be forced to say many superfluous and even foolish things in order to say something that's right. Whoever reads this must have patience, for I have to have it in order to write about what I don't know. Indeed, sometimes I take up the paper like a simpleton, for I don't know what to say or how to begin. I understand well that it's important for you that I explain some things about the interior life as best I can. We always hear about what a good thing prayer is, and our constitutions oblige us to spend so many hours in prayer. Yet only what we ourselves can do in prayer is explained to us; little is explained about what the Lord does in a soul, I mean about the supernatural.[6] By speaking about this heavenly interior building and explaining and considering it in many ways we shall find great comfort. It is so little understood by mortals, even though many walk through it. And although in other things I've written the Lord has given me some understanding,[7] I know there were certain things I had not understood as I have come to understand them now, especially certain more difficult things. The trouble is that before discussing them, as I have said, I will have to repeat matters that are well known; on account of my stupidity things can't be otherwise.

8. Well now let's get back to our castle with its many dwelling places. You mustn't think of these dwelling places in such a way that each one would follow in file after the other; but turn your eyes toward the center, which is the room or royal chamber where the King stays, and think of how a palmetto[8] has many leaves surrounding and covering the tasty part that can be eaten. So here, surrounding this center room are many other rooms; and the same holds true for those above. The things of the soul must always be considered as plentiful, spacious, and large; to do so is not an exaggeration. The soul is capable of much more than we can imagine, and the sun that is in this royal chamber shines in all parts. It is very important for any soul that practices prayer, whether little or much, not to

---

6. Teresa laments the fact there are few books that explain mystical (supernatural) prayer in depth. In the next chapter she asserts that there are many books dealing with ascetical matters. Thus her orientation in this book is toward the mystical.

7. She is referring to her *Life* and *The Way of Perfection* (the latter in vol. 2 of *The Collected Works of St. Teresa of Avila* [Washington, DC: Institute of Carmelite Studies, 1980]), and alludes to a divine influence in the composition of her mystical writings. See *Life*, ch. 39, §8: "Many of the things I write about here do not come from my own head, but my heavenly Master told them to me."

8. A plant about elbow-length, which grows in Andalusia and Valencia, resembling the palm tree. Only the center or heart, the tender part, is eaten.

hold itself back and stay in one corner. Let it walk through these dwelling places which are up above, down below, and to the sides, since God has given it such great dignity. Don't force it to stay a long time in one room alone. Oh, but if it is in the room of self-knowledge! How necessary this room is—see that you understand me—even for those whom the Lord has brought into the very dwelling place where He abides. For never, however exalted the soul may be, is anything else more fitting than self-knowledge; nor could it be even were the soul to so desire. For humility, like the bee making honey in the beehive, is always at work. Without it, everything goes wrong. But let's remember that the bee doesn't fail to leave the beehive and fly about gathering nectar from the flowers. So it is with the soul in the room of self-knowledge; let it believe me and fly sometimes to ponder the grandeur and majesty of its God. Here it will discover its lowliness better than by thinking of itself, and be freer from the vermin that enter the first rooms, those of self-knowledge. For even though, as I say, it is by the mercy of God that a person practices self-knowledge, that which applies to what is less applies so much more to what is greater, as they say. And believe me, we shall practice much better virtue through God's help than by being tied down to our own misery.

9. I don't know if this has been explained well. Knowing ourselves is something so important that I wouldn't want any relaxation ever in this regard, however high you may have climbed into the heavens. While we are on this earth nothing is more important to us than humility. So I repeat that it is good, indeed very good, to try to enter first into the room where self-knowledge is dealt with rather than fly off to other rooms. This is the right road, and if we can journey along a safe and level path, why should we want wings to fly? Rather, let's strive to make more progress in self-knowledge, for in my opinion we shall never completely know ourselves if we don't strive to know God. By gazing at His grandeur, we get in touch with our own lowliness; by looking at His purity, we shall see our own filth; by pondering His humility, we shall see how far we are from being humble.

10. Two advantages come from such activity. First, it's clear that something white seems much whiter when next to something black, and vice versa with the black next to the white. The second is that our intellects and wills, dealing in turn now with self, now with God, become nobler and better prepared for every good. And it would be disadvantageous for us never to get out of the mire of our miseries. As we said of those who are in mortal sin, that their streams are black and foul smelling, so it is here; although not entirely—God deliver us—for we are just making a comparison. If we are always fixed on our earthly misery, the stream will never flow free from the mud of fears, faintheartedness, and cowardice. I would be looking to see if I'm being watched or not; if by taking this path things will turn out badly for me; whether it might be pride to dare begin a certain work; whether it would be good for a person so miserable to engage in

something so lofty as prayer; whether I might be judged better than others if I don't follow the path they all do. I'd be thinking that extremes are not good, even in the practice of virtue; that, since I am such a sinner, I might have a greater fall; that perhaps I would not advance and would do harm to good people; that someone like myself has no need of special things.

11. Oh, God help me, daughters, how many souls must have been made to suffer great loss in this way by the devil! These souls think that all such fears stem from humility. And there are other things I could mention. The fears come from not understanding ourselves completely. They distort self-knowledge; and I'm not surprised if we never get free from ourselves, for this lack of freedom from ourselves, and even more, is what can be feared. So I say, daughters, that we should set our eyes on Christ, our Good, and on His saints. There we shall learn true humility, the intellect will be enhanced, as I have said,[9] and self-knowledge will not make one base and cowardly. Even though this is the first dwelling place, it is very rich and so precious that if the soul slips away from the vermin within it, nothing will be left to do but advance. Terrible are the wiles and deceits used by the devil so that souls may not know themselves or understand their own paths.

12. I could give some very good proofs from experience of the wiles the devil uses in these first dwelling places. Thus I say that you should think not in terms of just a few rooms but in terms of a million;[10] for souls, all with good intentions, enter here in many ways. But since the devil always has such a bad intention, he must have in each room many legions of devils to fight souls off when they try to go from one room to the other. Since the poor soul doesn't know this, the devil plays tricks on it in a thousand ways. He's not so successful with those who have advanced closer to where the King dwells. But since in the first rooms souls are still absorbed in the world and engulfed in their pleasures and vanities, with their honors and pretenses, their vassals (which are these senses and faculties) don't have the strength God gave human nature in the beginning. And these souls are easily conquered, even though they may go about with desires not to offend God and though they do perform good works. Those who see themselves in this state must approach His Majesty as often as possible. They must take His Blessed Mother and His saints as intercessors so that these intercessors may fight for them, for the soul's vassals have little strength to defend themselves. Truly, in all states it's necessary that strength come to us from God. May His Majesty through His mercy give it to us, amen.

13. How miserable the life in which we live! Because elsewhere I have said a great deal about the harm done to us by our failure to understand

---

9. See §10 above.
10. See §8 above. Teresa avoids any arrangement of these dwelling places into neatly structured rows with set numbers. She thereby in her allegory makes it easy for us to imagine a marvelous depth and abundance of inner riches.

well this humility and self-knowledge,[11] I'll tell you no more about it here, even though this self-knowledge is the most important thing for us. Please God, I may have now said something beneficial for you.

14. You must note that hardly any of the light coming from the King's royal chamber reaches these first dwelling places. Even though they are not dark and black, as when the soul is in sin, they nevertheless are in some way darkened so that the soul cannot see the light. The darkness is not caused by a flaw in the room—for I don't know how to explain myself—but by so many bad things like snakes and vipers and poisonous creatures that enter with the soul and don't allow it to be aware of the light. It's as if a person were to enter a place where the sun is shining but be hardly able to open his eyes because of the mud in them. The room is bright but he doesn't enjoy it because of the impediment of things like these wild animals or beasts that make him close his eyes to everything but them. So, I think, must be the condition of the soul. Even though it may not be in a bad state, it is so involved in worldly things and so absorbed with its possessions, honor, or business affairs, as I have said,[12] that even though as a matter of fact it would want to see and enjoy its beauty these things do not allow it to; nor does it seem that it can slip free from so many impediments. If a person is to enter the second dwelling places, it is important that he strive to give up unnecessary things and business affairs. Each one should do this in conformity with his state in life. It is something so appropriate in order for him to reach the main dwelling place that if he doesn't begin doing this I hold that it will be impossible for him to get there. And it will even be impossible for him to stay where he is without danger even though he has entered the castle, for in the midst of such poisonous creatures one cannot help but be bitten at one time or another.

15. Now then, what would happen, daughters, if we who are already free from these snares, as we are, and have entered much further into the castle to other secret dwelling places should turn back through our own fault and go out to this tumult? There are, because of our sins, many persons to whom God has granted favors who through their own fault have fallen back into this misery. In the monastery we are free with respect to exterior matters; in interior matters may it please the Lord that we also be free, and may He free us. Guard yourselves, my daughters, from extraneous cares. Remember that there are few dwelling places in this castle in which the devils do not wage battle. True, in some rooms the guards (which I believe I have said are the faculties)[13] have the strength to fight; but it is very necessary that we don't grow careless in recognizing the wiles of the devil, and that we not be deceived by his changing himself into an angel of light.[14]

---

11. See *Way of Perfection*, ch. 38, §5. See also *Life*, ch. 13, §15.
12. See *Interior Castle*, ch. 1, §8.
13. See §§4 and 12 above.
14. Cf. 2 Cor. 11:14.

There's a host of things he can do to cause us harm; he enters little by little, and until he's done the harm we don't recognize him.

16. I've already told you elsewhere[15] that he's like a noiseless file, that we need to recognize him at the outset. Let me say something that will explain this better for you.

He gives a Sister various impulses toward penance, for it seems to her she has no rest except when she is tormenting herself. This may be a good beginning; but if the prioress has ordered that no penance be done without permission, and the devil makes the Sister think that in a practice that's so good one can be rightly daring, and she secretly gives herself up to such a penitential life that she loses her health and doesn't even observe what the rule commands, you can see clearly where all this good will end up.

He imbues another with a very great zeal for perfection. Such zeal is in itself good. But it could follow that every little fault the Sisters commit will seem to her a serious breach; and she is careful to observe whether they commit them, and then informs the prioress. It could even happen at times that she doesn't see her own faults because of her intense zeal for the religious observance. Since the other Sisters don't understand what's going on within her and see all this concern, they might not accept her zeal so well.

17. What the devil is hereby aiming after is no small thing: the cooling of the charity and love the Sisters have for one another. This would cause serious harm. Let us understand, my daughters, that true perfection consists in love of God and neighbor; the more perfectly we keep these two commandments, the more perfect we will be. All that is in our rule and constitutions serves for nothing else than to be a means toward keeping these commandments with greater perfection. Let's forget about indiscreet zeal; it can do us a lot of harm. Let each one look to herself. Because I have said enough about this elsewhere,[16] I'll not enlarge on the matter.

18. This mutual love is so important that I would never want it to be forgotten. The soul could lose its peace and even disturb the peace of others by going about looking at trifling things in people that at times are not even imperfections, but since we know little we see these things in the worst light; look how costly this kind of perfection would be. Likewise, the devil could tempt the prioress in this way; and such a thing would be more dangerous. As a result much discretion is necessary. If things are done against the rule and constitutions, the matter need not always be seen in a good light. The prioress should be cautioned, and if she doesn't amend, the superior informed. This is charity. And the same with the Sisters if there is something serious. And to fail to do these things for fear of a temptation would itself be a temptation. But it should be carefully noted—so that the

---

15. See *Way of Perfection*, ch. 38, §2, ch. 39, passim.
16. See *Life*, ch. 13, §§8, 10; *Way of Perfection*, ch. 4.

devil doesn't deceive us—that we must not talk about these things to one another. The devil could thereby gain greatly and manage to get the custom of gossiping started. The matter should be discussed with the one who will benefit, as I have said. In this house, glory to God, there's not much occasion for gossip since such continual silence is kept; but it is good that we be on guard.

SELECTION 7

Friedrich Schleiermacher

**Christian Faith,
§§69, 71–72.2**

There are few areas where Schleiermacher's program of reinterpreting Christian doctrine as reflective descriptions of Christian self-consciousness has been more influential than the topic of sin. While he did not here reject the historicity of the biblical story of Adam and Eve, he found traditional theological accounts of the fall and its effects untenable. Instead, he derived the doctrine of original sin from what he took to be the Christian experience that every act of sin has its source outside of as well as within the individual, arguing that this experience is, in turn, based in the fact that our cultural and historical environment ineluctably shapes our attitudes and proclivities. In this way, Schleiermacher introduced the idea of a socio-cultural (versus genetic or hereditary) model of the transmission of original sin. Importantly, this approach does not commit him to a Pelagian understanding of human sinfulness as the imitation of sinful behavior in the environment, since Schleiermacher maintains that the dependence of the individual upon the collective precedes any sort of deliberate action on her part. At the same time, his insistence that this "inward ground of sinful actions" only become realized as sin through the voluntary action of the individual leads him to reject the Augustinian view that original sin merits punishment.

From Friedrich Schleiermacher, *Christian Faith*, trans. Terrence N. Tice, Catherine L. Kelsey, and Edwina Lawler (Louisville, KY: Westminster John Knox Press, forthcoming).

§69. We are conscious of sin in part as grounded in ourselves, in part as having its ground somewhere beyond our own individual existence.

1. In a particular manner, unevenly operative within each individual, the way various tendencies and functionings of one's sensory orientation stand in relation to the higher activity of one's mind[1] is grounded in an

---

1. *Richtungen und Verrichtungen der Sinnlichkeit zu der höheren Geistesthätigkeit.*

"innate difference"[2]—as we want to say provisionally—among these tendencies, which innate difference helps to constitute a personal existence distinctive to each one. However, in part, we see such differences as they are propagated within the same lineage and so also as they coalesce in the forming of new families out of different lineages; in part we find these differences in large masses of human beings, established as the distinctive character of tribes and peoples. Thus, by virtue of this dependence of a particular formation of individual life on some large type held in common, as well as by virtue of the dependence of later generations on earlier ones, the sin of each individual has its source in an earlier existence above and beyond one's own existence. Hence, even if someone, denying innate differences, simply ascribes these differences to education,[3] the matter remains the same, in that any given mode of education is grounded in leanings and experiences that have preceded the existence of the one who is to be educated. On the other hand, inasmuch as the urgent movement of some sensory stirring toward its goal, without placement in more elevated self-consciousness, is still undeniably the deed of any given individual, every particular sin of that individual has to be grounded in oneself.

By means of the first mode of observation we distinguish our good-naturedness[4]—in that many an inclination of our senses also makes no effort to strive beyond what is demanded of them by the mind itself—from our ill-naturedness, and we are conscious of both kinds of attitude as both received and obtained in company with other human beings. By virtue of the other mode of observation, however, we recognize our sin even in our ill-naturedness. That is, we do so because instead of having already surmounted that attitude by some deed of ours, we rather propagate it from one moment to another by our own self-initiated action.

2. To take two examples, one person may incline more to reflection, wherewith the person's external efficacy may then be either weak overall or even if it is strong may still be raw and uncultivated. In contrast, another person may apply oneself entirely to external efficacy, whereas, generally speaking, thinking either may rarely enter into the process or may at least remain obtuse and confused. Both of these cases we also reckon to innate differences. Now, even the first person is indeed drawn into the domain of efficacious action by life shared with others; and results of reflection that have currency within the domain one shares with others will somehow come into the imagination even of the second person. Yet, those original differences in disposition continue to have an effect nonetheless, and in the first person awakening piety will more readily unite with thought but

---

2. *Angeboren Differenz.* Ed. note: Or "inborn."

3. *Erziehung.* Ed. note: In German this term stands for both child rearing and any type of education outside the home, hence the general issue here is the familiar one of "nature vs. nurture."

4. *Gutartigkeit.* Ed. note: The concept points to an attitude of kindliness, good will. In contrast, *Bösartigkeit* points to an attitude of unkindliness, ill-will.

modes of action will remain of a fleshly nature, whereas in the second person awakening into piety will be more readily resistant to understanding. As a result, sin will take a different shape in each of these persons.

Now, to the extent that this differentiation coheres with the predisposition that is natural to each person and precedes every deed, to that extent the sin of any given person is, as to the shape it takes, also grounded beyond the person's own life. In contrast, to some extent every moment, be it filled with some notion or action in the narrower sense, nonetheless always comes to pass only by one's self-initiated activity. To that extent, even in a moment that does not bear God-consciousness within it, whether or not God-consciousness has already been aroused, in the same fashion the sin of each person is, in accordance with its reality, also grounded in oneself.

3. The same thing is true of the development of sensory life, which in all human beings enters in before mental development, namely that it is not dependent on the individual person oneself. That is to say, the entrance of "I"[5] into this world through conception and birth can in no way be recognized by our immediate self-consciousness as our own deed, even though occasionally speculation has tried to present precisely this entrance of "I" as the most primordial falling away of which the self can be guilty. Rather, just as this entrance of the "I" is for every later generation everywhere conditioned by the deed of the previous generation, in the same way the sin-ridden self-reliance[6] of orientation to the senses, itself being conditioned by its earlier development, is also grounded beyond the separate existence of any individual. However, once God-consciousness is in place as a distinct, active factor and as one capable of growth, then every moment in which it does not come to light as that factor and with a surplus, even if infinitesimal in comparison with previous similar instances, is a restraint upon higher activity, a restraint that is founded in one's own agency and is truly sin.

Postscript. This twofold relation, which on all sides we simply find once more, in varying degrees, within every consciousness of sin, is the most authentic and innermost ground on account of which explication of the Christian consciousness of sin in our ecclesial doctrine is split into two points of doctrine, regarding original sin[7] and actual sin.[8] The true sense of this division also clearly emerges from the explication given here thus far. That is, in the doctrine of original sin the state of sin is viewed as something received and brought along prior to any deed; yet, at the same time one's own guilt also lies hidden within it already. In the doctrine of actual

---

5. *Ich.* Ed. note: In his structural theory of the self, Freud later used *Es* (it), *Ich* (I), and *Überich* (above I); the Latin terms *Id*, *Ego*, and *Superego* were contributed by his English translators. "Ego" was not much used for "I" before that.

6. *Selbständigkeit.* Ed. note: Or strict autonomy, independence.

7. *Peccatum originis.* Ed. note: *Erbsünde.*

8. *Peccatum actuale.* Ed. note: *wirklichen Sünde.*

sin, that state is depicted as appearing in one's own sinful deeds, which themselves have their foundation in each individual; yet, that sin which is received and brought along is also disclosed within them.

In either case, only the conventional terms used for these sins are troublesome. The reasons are as follows. In the second formulation, "actual sin," the word "sin" is indeed posited of a person's own actual deed,[9] entirely in accordance with ordinary usage. However, the addition of "actual" to it easily occasions the confusing subordinate thought to the effect that original sin would not be anything actual, or at least that, in the same sense, next to actual sin there would be a kind of sin that is a mere semblance or that lies apart from one's deed. On the other hand, in the first formulation, "original sin," to be sure, the word "original"[10] does rightly express the connection of later generations with earlier ones and with the way the entire species is preserved. However, it is erroneous to add the word "sin," as if it would be taken in the same sense as that in the other formulation. In that case, moreover, only some actual sins would have had to be founded in some earlier occurrence but others would not. This cannot at all be what is meant, however, since the term "original sin" points to the inherited constitution of the acting subject that co-conditions the actual sins of every individual and prior to any deed.[11] Hence, an alteration of these inexact terms, which are not at all to be found in scripture, is greatly to be desired. Such an effort, however, must be introduced with considerable caution, to which the treatment to follow will provide some contribution. Moreover, the task ought to be carried out only by gradual adjustments if one does not want entirely to sever the doctrine from its historical connection and simply call forth new misconstruals and misunderstandings. . . .[12]

---

9. Ed. note: Here *eigentlichen Tat*, referring as it does to a person's own (*eigen*) deed, further explains the interpretation of *actuale* (*wirklich*) given here. In contrast, the term *actuale* could mean simply that the sin is actually happening, at present, not just being passed down as a consequence of another's (in this case, Adam's) original act.

10. Ed. note: *Erb* (or *Erbe*), without any further qualification, strictly means "heir," hence "inherited" sin, a property that could be gained only genetically in this case.

11. *Epitome, Formula of Concord*, I.10: "Original sin is not a sin that a person commits (*aliquod delictum quod actu perpetratur*); rather, it is embedded in the human being's nature, substance and essence." Ed. note: ET, *BC*, 490.

12. Ed. note: Indeed, the discussion of every proposition that follows concerning the operation and consequences of sin in human life (§§70–85) consists of a succession of adjustments to this doctrine. Thus, this treatment presents a continuous, highly refined argument, impossible to grasp without closely following Schleiermacher's "cautious" (*vorsichtig*), careful analysis. Still, it can be helpful to get an overall picture of what he comes to in the process.

Accordingly, §70 begins by using several sample statements in confessions and dogmatics in order meaningfully to assert that the individual's "complete incapacity for good," which can be removed only by redemption, precedes any deed performed and in part comes from a source, to be called "the collective life of sin" (cf. §71), that is beyond (*jenseits*) one's own existence. Yet, this incapacity does not obviate the capacity inherent in the original perfection of humanity to appropriate grace. Both capacities are still in us to some degree. Thus, we all have some ability to do good, and the regenerate can do ill, both within the reign of God and outside it. In both places, inseparably, the question is: How are we to do "spiritual" good?

§71. At the same time, however, original sin is so much the personal fault of every individual who takes part in it that it is best represented as the collective act and collective fault of the human race and that recognition of it is at the same time recognition of the general human need for redemption.

1. In not a few ... symbolic passages and among many teachers of faith-doctrine the thesis does indeed obtain the appearance as if the sinfulness that shows up in all human beings from birth,[13] precisely inasmuch as it is something received from elsewhere, is nonetheless to be regarded as the fault of each one, in fact a fault that implies unlimited deserving of punishment. As a result, even the greatest abundance of actual sins could not add anything to the culpability for sin to which everyone is thought to be subject already on account of this so-called "disease." Moreover, one must find it to be a natural consequence that in this form the proposition is denied by many who would rather declare original sin to be an "evil" so as not to recognize as a fault something that is entirely beyond one's own doing.

The proposition also acquires this twist into something unbelievable, this repellent and hostile tone, moreover, only when one tears original sin from its connection with actual sin. This move runs contrary to what would be natural and would inveigh against the quite generally recognized, correct rule.[14] Furthermore, all this does not intend to be understood in the sense that original sin would not be a fault until it breaks out into actual sins. This is the case in that indeed the sheer circumstance in which there is no opportunity for sin or any external enticement to it cannot be regarded as enhancing the spiritual worth of a human being. Rather, it is to be understood in the sense that original sin is the sufficient reason for all actual sins in any individual. In consequence, the individual needs only something outside oneself, and nothing new added within oneself, for actual sins to unfold. Original sin is something purely received only in the measure that the self-initiated activity[15] of the individual has not yet arisen. Original sin ceases to be something received strictly in the measure that the individual's self-initiated activity is developing. Until then, and only to that degree, original sin is rightly called "originated"[16] because it has its cause outside the individual. However, just as every aptitude in a human being gains proficiency through exercise and grows in this way, so

---

13. *Mitgeborene.* Ed. note: This word indicates a condition that can be observed, whereas the concept oft used, *angeborene* (innate), indicates a condition that must be implied or presupposed.

14. Philipp Melanchthon, *Loci praecipui theologici* (1543 to 1559) in the section on actual sin, states: "Accordingly, actual sins are always accompanied at the same time with the evil of original sin."

15. *Selbsttätigkeit.* Ed. note: In Schleiermacher's psychology, self-initiated activity (or spontaneous action) is always wrapped in a continually oscillating engagement with receptivity, though in a given moment one of the two elements may be predominant.

16. *Verursachte Ursünde: Peccatum originis originatum.* Ed. note: Or "caused."

too an individual's sinfulness from birth grows through exercise proceeding from one's self-initiated activity.

Now, although in this way this sinfulness is the effect of actual sin, this growing added component of self-initiated activity, of the same nature as that originally brought along from birth—that is, this persevering inner ground of sinful actions—is thus, nonetheless, consequently also still original sin. It is so in this same relation but viewed as strengthened sinfulness repeatedly preceding the actual sin that will emerge from it. Yet, in this relation it is no longer purely "originated" but is self-effected and "originating original sin,"[17] exactly the same expression as is customarily applied to the first sin of the first human beings. That is, it is applicable in both instances because this self-effected original sin pushes up and increases actual sin in each individual self and thereby in others as well.

Now, suppose if that this subsequent sinfulness, having grown out of an individual's own self-initiated activity, would be one and the same thing as the original sinfulness that appears from birth, then two things also follow. First, the added sinfulness would have emerged in the individual by one's free acts of life that are affixed to original sinfulness. Second, as this occurs, it holds just as well that original sinfulness, which in any case would recede more and more in comparison to that added sinfulness but with which one would always have started off, would not advance in oneself without one's will and would therefore also have emerged by one's own agency. Consequently, this advance of original sin in actual sin is rightly called the fault of each individual. To be sure, from this point on one could say that this fault could be assigned only to human beings to the extent that they themselves have already acted but not in the same way to children and not at all to the unborn; and here a distinction is indeed not to be denied.

However, if the matter has always rested in the claim that actual sin inevitably proceeds from original sin, then everywhere that human life is present actual sin is grounded internally and the connection on account of which original sin is one's fault likewise exists in children and the unborn as well, even if it has not exactly emerged in them as yet. As a result, one can say of them that they will be sinners by means of that tendency which already exists in them at a given time. It has probably never been seriously doubted that they are not yet sinners in that same sense and degree as are those in whom actual sin has already become constant, especially since here the issue is only one of fault.[18] However, this distinction does not apply to sinfulness at birth, and to the degree that the symbolic passages in which reference is made to children are intended especially to shed light on the degree of fault, we can also fully adopt them.

---

17. *Verursachende Ursünde: Peccatum originis originans.* Ed. note: Or "causing."
18. *Schuld.* Ed. note: Here this is the term regularly translated "fault." In German, the same word is also used for "guilt" or "blame."

2. Now, if, on the one hand, the sinfulness that precedes every deed is effected in each individual by the sin and sinfulness of others, but if, at the same time, it is also both propagated in others and secured in them by each individual through one's own free actions, then sinfulness is of a thoroughly collective nature.[19] Indeed, whether one were to consider sinfulness more as a fault and as a work or more as a motivating principle of life and as a condition, in both respects it is of a thoroughly collective nature, not present separately in each individual and not related to each individual alone; rather, in each individual sinfulness is the work of all and in all individuals it is the work of each. Indeed, sinfulness is to be understood rightly and fully only in this commonality.

Hence, the doctrinal propositions that treat of original sin and sinfulness are in no way to be conceived as expressions of personal self-consciousness, with which, in contrast, the doctrine of actual sin has to do; rather, these propositions are expressions of collective consciousness. This collectivity of sin and sinfulness comprises an inclusive solidarity[20] of all times and places in relation to what is set forth in these propositions. With respect to its shape, the distinctive formation of original sin in each individual is simply an integrating component of the formation of it in the sphere of life to which the individual belongs most closely. In consequence, that distinctive individual formation of original sin, not intelligible of itself alone, points to the remaining components as its complement. This whole complementary process, moreover, goes through all the gradations of shared feeling[21] that run through families, relatives, genealogy, peoples and racial identities of human beings. In consequence, the formation of sinfulness in each of these gradations of shared feeling points to that present in the others, viewed as its complement. Moreover, the collective power of the flesh in its resistance against the spirit, inasmuch as this power is the basis of all that is incompatible with God-consciousness in human actions can also be conceived only in terms of the collective existence of all who are living in association with one another[22] but never wholly in one part of that collective power of the flesh. Moreover, even that of the collective power of the flesh which appears in a single individual entity, be this a personal or a composite individual entity, is not to be described in relation to this individual entity alone nor to be explained from this individual entity alone.

The same, however, is also true of times. What appears from birth as the sinfulness of a generation is conditioned by the sinfulness of earlier

---

19. *Ein durchaus Gemeinschaftliches.* Ed. note: Schleiermacher's much-used concept of the "collective life (*Gesamtleben*) of sin" and that of its "commonality" (*Gemeinsamheit*) both also refer to the same shared processes over against "the collective life of grace" in the reign of God, and they are likewise brought to consciousness by participation in the latter.
20. *Zusammengehörigkeit.* Ed. note: Here, a broad solidarity, as in "we're all in this together" versus an exclusive, self-contained solidarity.
21. *Gemeingefühl.*
22. *Gesamtsein aller Zusammenlebenden.*

generations and itself conditions the sinfulness of generations yet to come. Moreover, only in the whole series of these formations, as that series interconnects with the advancing development of humanity, is the entire relationship expressed in the concept "original sin" given.

Likewise, the inclusive solidarity of times and of places also both mutually condition each other and refer back to each other. Probably anyone would readily testify, moreover, that only in relation to that collective existence does either the notion of the sinfulness of individuals or one's feeling of also having that sinfulness in common[23] reach the level of surety and satisfaction. Precisely by virtue of this interconnectedness, however, each individual is, in relation to that collective existence, a representative of the entire human race. This is so, because the sinfulness of each individual refers back to the collective sinfulness of all, spatially as well as temporally considered, and also helps to condition that collective sinfulness both around and after oneself.

Now, the various ways original sin is customarily designated, all of which have a relative truth in them, are most easily united in this view of it. First, it is called a *fault*[24] with complete correctness only if it is absolutely considered to be the collective deed of the entire human race, in that it cannot likewise be a fault of an individual, at least to the extent that it is engendered in that individual. It is called *natural corruption*[25] in contrast to original perfection insofar as the state of original perfection is in part overcome by original sin in the real unfolding of that state. It is also called *original defect*[26] insofar as it is the irremediable basis for malformations of the relationship between the spirit and the particular functions of sensory life, and *original disease*[27] insofar as a feature of death is posited to occur through it in all acts of spiritual life. Further, it is called *original evil*[28] insofar as it is within the individual a persistently effective basis of

---

23. *Mitgefühl*. Ed. note: Eventually in this work, this concept not only conveys the satisfaction of knowing that one is not anywhere near being solitary in one's sinfulness, in one's being out of touch with God and in need of redemption, but also takes on compassion for others who lack the joy and solace of redemptive blessedness.

24. *Schuld*. Ed. note: Schleiermacher supplies the word *reatus* here, one that bears the same range of meanings as *Schuld*. . . . In classical Latin it literally referred to the condition, offense or appearance (e.g. dress) of a person who stands accused.

25. *Verderben: Corruptio naturae*. A different meaning of this expression from that assumed here will be considered below.

26. *Urgebrechen: vitium originis*. Ed. note: In some prayers it is called "shortcoming," as with the familiar phrase "forgive us our shortcomings and offenses."

27. *Urkrankheit: morbus originis*. On *morbus* and *vitium* compare Cicero (106–43 B.C.E.), *Tusculan Disputations* 4.13. Ed. note: There Cicero states, "Disease (*morbus*) is the term applied to a breakdown of the whole body, sickness (*aegrotionem*) to disease attended by weakness, defect (*vitium*) when the parts of the body are not symmetrical with one another and there ensue crookedness of the limbs, distortion, ugliness." ET in Loeb Library (1960), 356–57. Accordingly, in medical lingo "morbidity" refers to an incidence of death and dying, becoming moribund, in a person or population.

28. *Urübel*. Ed. note: In Schleiermacher's view, this concept would include the natural consequences of human evil (*Böse*), even if these are either not immediately intended or within the non-human areas of nature.

obstacles to life that are independent of the individual's own doing. How difficult it is, however, to depict original sin as *punishment*[29]—I do not want to say exclusively but even if only at the same time—is doubtless self-evident. This is so for two reasons. In the first place, punishment is always something inflicted, but sin can never be something inflicted; thus punishment must always be something that is not sin in the person who undergoes it. In the second place, in every sin for which original sin is supposed to be punishment, original sin must itself always be presupposed to exist already, so that in the final analysis the punishment would have to exist before the sin.

3. Suppose that the self-consciousness the expression of which is the concept of original sinfulness developed up to now were no collective feeling but were rather a personal feeling in each individual. Then a consciousness of a general need of redemption would doubtless not be necessarily bound to it, in that each individual would have believed it to be necessary to rely above all on the collective body to which one belongs for strengthening of one's spiritual power. This is why denying that original sin is collective in nature and underrating the value of redemption through Christ usually go together. This connection of the two attitudes would also not be any firmer, moreover, if original sinfulness could be present within us without our having any consciousness of it. That is, in that case either consciousness of sin would be quite feeble if it emerged at all or it would emerge only each time an actual sin were committed and would be referred only to this actual sin. That is to say, each individual would have to rely on one's own resources, in weaker moments drawing from supposedly stronger resources available in the past.

Such a lack of consciousness regarding one's sinfulness, however, is possible only where God-consciousness has still not developed at all or where a tendency to have God-consciousness has not been awakened by communication. Thus, this is not possible within the domain of Christianity and of Christian proclamation. Only where God-consciousness has once been taken up will pre-eminence also be afforded it among the various features of self-consciousness and will its dominion be sought. Where this happens, moreover, the resistance of the flesh must also come into consciousness as something constant and as something that conditions the reality of particular sins.

Now, suppose that we first become quite clear about the resistance when we observe it to belong to our self-consciousness expanded to consciousness of the human species. Then either all hope of gaining pre-eminence for God-consciousness must be given up or the need must arise to obtain succor that comes from outside the domain of that expanded

---

29. *Apology Augsburg* (1531) II: "The deficiency and concupiscence are both penalty and sin." Ed. note: *BL,* 157; ET, *BC,* 119.

self-consciousness. Consequently, there must also arise either a surrender to the insurmountable futility of that striving or a presentiment of that succor. These alternatives display the appropriateness of that presentation which would also link an initial presentiment of redemption with the initial consciousness of sin that appears as God-consciousness arises.

... from the very beginning on, these two features of consciousness have been bound together in the Evangelical church too. Likewise, ... these two features of consciousness actually interconnect: first, the conviction that powers that surpass the human consciousness of sin already held in common from time immemorial could not be set in motion for us and among us and, second, the resolve to make do with this shared consciousness of sin and without any boost for the purpose from actual redemption overcome the resistance of the flesh, if only to a certain degree.

4. However, this natural interconnectedness between consciousness of general, original sinfulness and consciousness of a necessity of redemption[30] from it would be disrupted and misdirected, not without considerable detriment to genuine Christian piety, if consciousness of deserving punishment[31] for original sin were thrust into the mix. This is so, for suppose that by "punishment" one understands not the mounting intensity of sin itself but an evil that has been unfolding from sin or is ordered with reference to sin. In a teleological mode of faith the mounting intensity of sin can be comprehended only as fault and as still more sin. As a result, in this instance the relation between the consciousness of sin and consciousness of a need for redemption that we have discussed would not be a natural one here. If all this is true, then a feeling regarding the necessity of redemption that would first be mediated by consciousness of deserving punishment would no longer be so strictly unalloyed as what has been described up to now. That is, this is plainly the case when "to be deserving of punishment" is set forth only to draw attention to punishment itself and when the opinion is that the need for redemption from sin is to be awakened, or even simply enhanced, by fear of punishment. Furthermore, for at that point, removing the condition of sinfulness could not be desired for the purpose of doing away with restraint to God-consciousness and making room for God-consciousness. Rather, the purpose would be to secure distinct states of sensory self-consciousness and to guard against opposing states. Not wanting resistance of the flesh would be simply for the sake of fleshly consequences, and redemption would likewise be willed simply for the sake of fleshly consequences, whereby actual piety would thus entirely recede from the scene.

---

30. *Erlösung.* Ed. note: This concept literally refers to a process of being loosed or liberated from, hence there is no *prima facie*, built-in sense of substitutionary payment made in punishment sustained or sacrifice offered on behalf of sinners, as in customary atonement theories, even though the same concept is often used for those theories.

31. *Strafwürdigkeit.* Ed. note: Or, as some say, "penal desert."

Now, one could indeed also imagine that what is to be considered is not so much punishment itself as being deserving of it, and one could imagine that what is to be aroused is not so much fear of punishment as dread of deserving it. Even then, however, the relation to what is of a sensory nature would always be set forth as the criterion for what is spiritual. This would be so in that it would be presupposed that if a person were not in and of oneself disposed to have God-consciousness in control of one's life, then one could at least be led to this point by reflecting on the fact that otherwise one would appear to be someone who is unworthy of sensory well-being. By this route, moreover, Christian piety would be no less endangered than by the other route. For this reason, we have not adopted even this notion here, not at all. In contrast, one can see, based on the . . . creedal symbols, in comparison with what has just been explicated, how essential it is for these symbols to derive the need for redemption from the consciousness of sinfulness. One can also see, however, how easily the one can skip over the inserted notion of being deserving of punishment for original sin without doing damage to the interconnection we have discussed. Treatment of this notion, however, is reserved for another place.[32]

§72. Even though we cannot apply the notion of original sin explicated thus far to the first human beings in the same sense, nonetheless there is no reason to explain the general sinfulness of humanity based on some alteration that has taken place within human nature in the very person of the first human beings by the first sin.

1. This proposition is meant solely to fend off error and promises no intention of establishing anything concerning the way sin emerged in the first human beings. It presupposes, in keeping with our initial explanation,[33] that we are not able to set forth any proper doctrine of faith concerning this subject. The reason is as follows. Suppose that we expand our self-consciousness to that of the entire human race as well and are able in that way to bring self-consciousness into a combination with God-consciousness. Then we could not include the first human beings in this community of self-consciousness. We would not do so even directly in relation to that within them which would definitely and exactly connect with this community, namely that they were created but not born, because to that extent their self-consciousness would be quite different from our own. Now, if we were talking about sin in the further course of their lives, then this difference would disappear, the more so the longer they lived. The situation would be different, however, in regard to sinfulness, which is supposed to precede all deeds whatsoever. Suppose that we would then

---

32. Ed. note: See §76.
33. Cf. §15. Ed. note: Thus, here for the most part Schleiermacher critically examines a long string of positions that *might* be held. This examination leads to several general, more formal affirmations in §72.3–6.

be unable to have any shared feeling[34] with the first human beings in relation to sinfulness and that we would thus have no self-consciousness to expound on this subject. Then there would be no statement of faith to set forth on the matter either.

Suppose, however, that we had some information from some other quarter as to how sinfulness in them related to their having been created, be this information then speculative in nature or more historical. Then we would indeed have to look into how this information would stand in relation to our propositions regarding our faith. Moreover, inasmuch as this information would not be purely historical in nature but would be interlaced with presuppositions and combinations of its own, at that point safeguards could be set forth, as is done here, so that a Christian would not produce unawares doctrinal opinions that do not comport with the Christian's faith.

Now, in direct terms our consciousness of sin and its conjunction with the longing for some redemption from it will always remain the same whatever the situation might have been with the first human beings—unless, of course, it is claimed that they had not yet sinned at all during the period in which their work was to reproduce and raise offspring. Given this proviso, after that period anything they did further would be excluded from the domain of our expanded self-consciousness, in that the separate features of original sinfulness could have met only gradually. Suppose, however, that they had already sinned in that earlier period. Then their next of kin too could already have had some sinfulness in their own lives, just as we do, even before they had done any deed, a sinfulness that would have had its basis outside their own existence. This latter scenario, moreover, is sufficient to support our proposition, even if we could not also bring up any graphic image of how the sinfulness of the first human beings would have been transmitted to their offspring or would have continued to be transmitted.

Our creedal symbols also lay no particular value on any such graphic image. Even though they derive the loss of a state of sinlessness for all subsequent generations from the emergence of sin in the first ones,[35] nevertheless in part they do not get into further elucidations on the way this influence happened at all and in part they dismiss the question outright.[36]

---

34. *Mitgetfühl.* Ed. note: Depending on context, this word is also translated "feeling held in common," "common feeling" and "compassion" in this work; in each instance it is a feeling that connects individuals or groups with each other.

35. (1) *Augsburg Confession* (1530) II; (2) *Apology Augsburg* (1531) II; (3) *Second Helvetic Confession* (1566) VIII; (4) *Belgic Confession* (1561) XV; (5) *Schmalcald Articles* (1537) Pt. III.1. Ed. note: (1, 2, 5) BL, 53, 146, 433; ET, BC, 37, 111, 300; (3) Philip Schaff, *The Creeds of Christendom* (New York: Harper, 1919), 3:247–48; (4) Latin: A. H. Niemeyer, *Collectio cofessionum in ecclesiis reformatis publicatarum* (Lipsiae: Sumptibus Iulii Klinkhardti, 1840), 332; ET, Schaff, *Creeds*, 3:400–401.

36. *Gallican Confession* (1559) X: "... it is not necessary to inquire how sin was conveyed (*propagari*) from one man to another." Ed. note: Niemeyer, *Collectio*, 332; ET, Schaff, *Creeds*, 3:365.

2. On the other hand, the question as to how sin would have emerged in the first human beings after God-consciousness had developed is an eminently natural one nonetheless, even though it does not directly arise out of the interest of Christian piety. Obviously, however, we cannot answer it in regard to their situation with the same surety as we can with regard to our own situation in the propositions expounded here. This is so, in the first place, for we cannot form any graphic image of how sensory functions would have had a grip[37] on them earlier than higher spiritual[38] functions, since from the beginning their status would have had to be at the same level as that of newborns, in whom "spirit" also has some power already.

Now, suppose that we think of God-consciousness developing in them from within or even by means of some imaginable communion with God, though we simply do not know exactly how to picture it. In either case, there is no basis for imagining why God-consciousness should have formed more strongly and quickly as a consciousness at rest but more sluggishly and weakly as an impulse. This is true especially since in any such supposed development from within we can find no reason at all to assume, in general terms, an unequal progress of intellect and will as could accrue where there would be an unequal support of intellect through communicated notions and of will through pre-established customs. Moreover, we cannot picture to ourselves any innate one-sidedness in the first human beings—with the exception of those associated with gender—either in this respect or in any other. This is the case, in that the plenitude of contrasting formations that experience offers us today could not have developed out of them otherwise than as a quintessence of human nature.

Suppose, now, that by the very nature of the matter analogy fails us here. Then it all comes down to an attempt to explain the onset of sin in the first human beings without their having any sinfulness in them beforehand. This attempt too seems doomed to failure, however, whether the biblical narrative regarding the first sin is taken literally or whether some significant general characteristic is assigned to it. The prevailing explanations are that humankind first sinned by Satan's enticement[39] or by misuse of its free will.[40] In this instance, the two explanations hardly permit of being entirely separated, because sin is always a misuse of free will. However, the more

---

37. *Macht.* Ed. note: Or "some power in them," as in the reference to newborns just below.

38. Ed. note: The contrast is between lower, *sinnlichen* functions and higher, *geistigen* functions. In Schleiermacher's psychology the latter functions include various levels of self-consciousness contained in the immediacy of feeling and perception and the mediate qualities of cognition and action, both sets rising above mere sensation and sense perception. *Geistige* refers to all mental functions that gain control over merely sense-originated functions, hence they cannot always be "spiritual," strictly speaking. The same word has to do service for both spiritual functions and their expression in intellect and intelligent action.

39. *Belgic Confession* (1561) XIV: ". . . giving ear to the words and impostures of the devil." Cf. Gerhard, *Loci* (1610–1622) 4:294–95.

40. Augustine, *Enchiridion* (421) 9.30: "A human being misusing one's free will destroys both oneself and it." Ed. note: *PL* 40.246; ET, *FC* 2:395.

that sin is ascribed to Satan's activity, the closer Satan's enticement comes to being either magic or sheer force and the less there is of any human deed, consequently of any sin as well. In contrast, the less there is of Satan's enticement, the less likelihood there is of there being an act of sin apart from sinfulness already present. The latter is the case, in that misuse of free will in and of itself nevertheless offers no ground for explanation; rather, something must be assumed that has impelled one to that misuse. Suppose that at this point someone wants to go right back to the whispering innuendos of Satan. These promptings still could not have worked unless something were already present in the soul that contained a readiness to succumb to merely sensory desires. Moreover, such an inclination toward sin would therefore have to have existed in the first human beings already before the first sin, because otherwise no susceptibility to temptation could have taken place. It also does not help if one splits the first sin into several elements so as to arrive at the tiniest possible element to be viewed as its very outset,[41] for if one is talking about one specific deed, then one must also inquire as to what could serve to explain the deed as a whole. The answer could never be found, moreover, if one were to presuppose a state in which there was no self-initiated activity of the flesh but God-consciousness was alone in force. This is so, because then no sinful desire could itself have arisen in a person, nor could Satan have made it credible that God could have forbidden something out of bearing a grudge; rather, trust in God would have had to be destroyed beforehand. However, if this trust had already been destroyed, then existing in the likeness of God would also have been lost already,[42] consequently sinfulness would also have been present already, whether it would then be thought of as in the form of pride[43] or in some other form. Thus, the last recourse would be to explain the first sin as based on a misuse of free will such that it would have had no ground in a human's inner being—that is, that this human being would have chosen to do wrong[44] without any bases for deciding to do so. Here we are faced with two alternatives. The first of these alternatives is that the first sin would have to have occurred prior to all practice of what is good, because even through the briefest such exercise a skill for it would already have been produced that, given the absence of any countering grounds for deciding, would have to have proved to be fully active. In consequence, sin would thereupon have

---

41. Luther, *On Genesis* (1535) 3:3, finds the onset of sin in Eve's falsifying God's word and attaching the little word "perhaps" to God's command, as if this act would have been sinful if the preceding outbreak of lustful desire had not been its basis. Others like [Nicholas of] Lyra focus more on sensory lust itself and view looking at the tree as the onset of sin, which amounts to the very same thing. Ed. note: *WA*, 42:116–17; ET, *LW* 1:155.

42. Ambrose (ca 339–397), *Hexameron* (ca. 389) VI.8: "Is not that, therefore, in which God is ever-present made to the likeness of God?" Ed. note: *PL* 14.260; ET, *FC* 32:258.

43. Augustine, *Two Books on Genesis against the Manichees* (388) 2.15.22: "We see from these words that they were persuaded to sin through pride." Ed. note: *PL* 34.207; ET, *FC* 84:118.

44. *Böse*. Ed. note: Human evil (*Übel*) in contrast to other kinds.

to have been the first free deed, which cannot in the least be acceded to. The second alternative is that throughout the lives of the first human beings there must not have arisen any ability to do good through repeated action. In that case, however, any consolidation in their doing good or any increase in God-consciousness having a grip on them would have been impossible.[45] This outcome, in turn, is in contradiction to every notion of an original perfection[46] in humankind.

This difficulty of bringing to mind the emergence of the first sin without any underlying sinfulness is increased to the utmost degree by the circumstances in which we catch sight of the first human beings according to the Mosaic narrative.[47] That is to say, on the one hand one can least envisage an enticement or a misuse of free will given a great simplicity of life and a considerable ease in satisfying natural needs, because in such a state no stimulus coming from one particular object can be of any outstanding effect. On the other hand, one can certainly not in any way imagine keeping any direct company with God without one's having developed an intensified love toward God and without one's having formed an increased knowledge of God. By both means, human beings would have to have been secured against influences of nonsensical misrepresentations.[48] This situation has also been recognized already from long, long ago.[49] On account of that great "ability not to sin," moreover, the more one holds to that narrative in literal terms, the more one also has to assume a correspondingly greater inclination toward sin to be present already. In an indirect fashion, this point also seems to be assumed by those who express themselves in such a way that God did not will human beings to be "confirmed in what is good prior to any voluntary obedience."[50] That is to say, suppose that confirmation in what is good would have to have been a special work of God and not a work of practice by virtue of powers invested in human nature. Then, to be sure, this work of God would presuppose the incapacity, already mentioned above, to acquire such abilities as to practice what is good. At the same time, however, this work of God would also presuppose nevertheless that without that special divine succor the spiritual power of a human being could, in any given instance, just as well have been too slight to withstand a given sensory impulse.

---

45. Origen, *Commentary on Matthew* (246–48) 10.11: "Again, if he had been of a good and unchangeable nature, he would not have turned away from the good after being called righteous so as to commit unrighteousness." Ed. note: *PG* 13.861; ET, *ANF* 4:693.

46. Ed. note: This "perfection" lies specifically in the relation of human beings to God.

47. Ed. note: In the "First Book of Moses" of the Pentateuch, Genesis 3.

48. Ed. note: E.g. from Satan or some other delusive source. In Schleiermacher's view, the very figure of the devil stands for such a delusive source. Cf. §44.

49. Augustine, *Admonition and Grace* (427) 12.35: "Adam, with the use of his free will, affrighted by nothing, and actually in the face of God's fear-inspiring command, did not stand firm in his great happiness, in his ability not to sin." *PL* 44.937; ET, *FC* 2:287.

50. See Gerhard, *Loci* (1610–1622) 4:303.

SELECTION 8

Walter Rauschenbusch

"The Kingdom of Evil"

The leading theologian of the social gospel movement, Walter Rauschenbusch (1861–1918) turned to Protestant liberalism while a student at Rochester Theological Seminary, though retaining throughout his life the strong emphasis on personal piety of his Baptist upbringing. Convinced that the point of Jesus' ministry had been to instruct humanity in the building of the kingdom of God, he believed that the primary calling of the church was the practical one of creating social conditions of justice and equality in which the kingdom could grow. He correspondingly dedicated his own ministry to the alleviation of the poverty and alienation produced by unrestrained capitalism, focusing especially on urban poverty, child labor, and workers' rights.

Rauschenbusch labeled the collective forces that impeded the growth of the kingdom of God "the kingdom of evil," the scope and character of which are outlined in the following selection from his book, *A Theology for the Social Gospel*. Rauschenbusch followed Schleiermacher in viewing the transmission of sin as a fundamentally social rather than a biological phenomenon, though he went beyond Schleiermacher in attributing the persistence of sin to particular social structures, including especially the economic and political interests of the powerful, on the one hand, and the depredation and misery of the poor, on the other. By arguing that the cumulative effects of these structures implicated the whole of society, Rauschenbusch sought to affirm the sense of universal human solidarity in sin characteristic of traditional Christian teaching on the pervasiveness of evil while correcting what he saw as its mythological and fatalistic elements.

From Walter Rauschenbusch, *A Theology of the Social Gospel*
(New York: MacMillan, 1917), 78–92.

In some of our swampy forests the growth of ages has produced impenetrable thickets of trees and undergrowth, woven together by creepers, and inhabited things that creep or fly. Every season sends forth new growth under the urge of life, but always developing from the old growth and its seeds, and still perpetuating the same rank mass of life.

The life of humanity is infinitely interwoven, always renewing itself, yet always perpetuating what has been. The evils of one generation are caused by the wrongs of the generations that preceded, and will in turn condition the sufferings and temptations of those who come after. Our Italian immigrants are what they are because Church and the land system of Italy have made them so. The Mexican peon is ridden by the Spanish past. Capitalistic Europe has fastened its yoke on the neck of Africa. When negroes are hunted from a northern city like beasts, or when a Southern city degrades the whole nation by turning the savage inhumanity of a mob into a public festivity, we are continuing because our fathers created the conditions of sin by the African slave trade and by the unearned wealth gathered from slave labour for generations.

Stupid dynasties go on reigning by right of the long time they have reigned. The laws of the ancient Roman despotism were foisted by ambitious lawyers on mediaeval communities, to which they were in no wise fitted, and once more strangled liberty, and dragged free farmers into serfdom. When once the common land of a nation, and its mines and waters, have become private property of a privileged band, nothing short of a social earthquake can pry them from their right collecting private taxes. Superstitions which originated in the third century are still faithfully cultivated by great churches, compressing the minds of the young with fear and cherished by the old as their most precious faith. Ideas struck out by a wrestling mind in the heat of an argument are erected by later times into proof-texts more decisive than masses of living facts. One nation arms because it fears another; the other arms more because this armament alarms it; each subsidizes a third and a fourth to aid it. Two fight; all fight; none knows how to stop; a planet is stained red in a solidarity of hate and horror.

The entomologist Fabre investigated the army caterpillar, which marches in dense thousands, apparently under some leadership which all obey. But Fabre found there is no leadership. Each simply keeps in touch with the caterpillar just ahead of it and follows, follows on. The one article of faith is to follow the leaders, though none of the leaders knows whither they are going. The experimenter led the column to march in a circle by getting the front rank in touch with the rear, and now they milled around helplessly like lost souls in Dante's hell.

If this were the condition of humanity, we should be in a state of relative innocency and bliss. The front-rank caterpillars are at least not trying to make something out of the rest, and are not leading them to the destruction by assuring them that they are doing it for their good and for the highest spiritual possessions of the caterpillar race. Human society has leaders who know what they want, but many of them have manipulated the fate of thousands for their selfish ends. The sheep-tick hides in the wool of the sheep and taps the blood where it flows warm and rich. But the tick has no power to alter the arterial system of the sheep and to bring the aorta close to the skin where it can get at it. Human ticks have been able to do this. They have gained control of legislation, courts, police, military, royalty, church, property, religion, and have altered the constitution of nations in order to make things easy for tick class. The laws, institutions, doctrines, literature, art, and manners which these ruling classes have secreted have been social means of infection which have new evils for generations.

Any reader who doubts these sad statements can find the facts in the books, though mostly in foot-notes in fine print. It is also going on in real life. We can watch it if we look at any nation except our own.

This is what the modern social gospel would call the Kingdom of Evil. Our theological conception of sin is but fragmentary unless we see all men in their natural groups bound together in a solidarity of all times and all places, bearing the yoke of evil and suffering. This is the explanation of the amazing regularity of social statistics. A nation registers so and so many suicides, criminal assaults, bankruptcies, and divorces per 100,000 of the population. If the proportion changes seriously, we search for the disturbing social causes, just as we search for the physical causes if the rhythm of our pulse-beat runs away from the normal. The statistics of social morality are the pulse-beat of the social organism. The apparently free and unrelated acts of individuals are also the acts of the social group. When the group is evil, evil is over all.

The conception of a Kingdom of Evil is not a new idea. It is as old as the Christian Church and older. But while our modern conception is naturally historical and social, the ancient and mediaeval Church believed in a Kingdom of evil spirits, with Satan at their head, which is the governing power in the present world and the source of all temptation.

The belief in evil spirits is so common in ethnic religions that the relative absence of that belief in the Old Testament is proper cause for wonder. There are only a few passages referring to evil spirits, and a few referring to a spiritual being called Satan. It is altogether likely that the belief in dangerous and malicious spirits held a much larger place in the popular religious life of the Jewish people than we would gather from their literature. If the higher religious minds, who wrote the biblical books, purposely kept the popular beliefs down and out of sight, that gives remarkable support to those who regard the belief in personal evil spirits as a seamy and dangerous element of religion.

After the Exile the religion of the Jews was filled with angels and devils, each side built up in a great hierarchy, rank above rank. Evidently this systematized and theological belief in a satanic kingdom was absorbed from the Eastern religions with which the Jews came into close contact during the Exile. The monotheism of the Hebrew faith held its own against the dualism of the East, but the belief in Satan is a modified dualism compatible with the reign of Jehovah. The apocalyptic system is a theology built up on this semi-dualistic conception, describing the conflict of the Kingdom of Satan against God and his angels and his holy nation, and the final triumph of God.

The belief in the Satanic Kingdom and the apocalyptic theology were transferred from Judaism to Christianity as part of the initial inheritance of the new religion from the old, and any one familiar with patristic literature and with popular mediaeval religion needs no reminder that this was one of the most active and effective parts of the religious consciousness. The original belief was reinforced by the fact that all the gods and the daimonia of the Graeco-Roman world were dyed black and classified as devils and evil spirits by the aggressive hostility of the Church. This process was repeated when the mediaeval Church was exorcising the pagan gods from the minds and customs of the Teutonic nations. All these gods remained realities, but black realities.

Popular superstition, systematized and reinforced by theology, and inculcated by all the teaching authority of the mediaeval Church, built up an overwhelming impression of the power of evil. The Christian spirit was thrown into an attitude of defense only. The best that could be done was to hold the powers of darkness at bay by the sign of the cross, by holy water, by sacred amulets, by prayer, by naming holy names. The church buildings and church yards were places of refuge from which the evil spirits were banned. The gargoyles of Gothic architecture are the evil spirits escaping from the church buildings because the spiritual power within is unbearable to them. I recently witnessed a cornerstone laying at a new Catholic church. The bishop and the clergy thrice moved in procession around the foundation walls, chanting; an acolyte carried a pailful of holy water, and the bishop liberally applied it to the walls. So the rectangle of masonry became an exempt and disinfected area of safety. Under the sunshine of an American afternoon, and with a crowd of modern folks around, it was an interesting survival.

The belief in a demonic Kingdom was in no wise attacked in the Reformation. Luther's sturdy belief in devils is well known. Indeed, the belief which had been built up for centuries by the Church came to its terrible climax during the age of the Reformation in the witch trials. From A.D. 1400 to 1700, hundreds of thousands of women and girls were imprisoned, tortured, and burned. These witch trials were grounded on the belief in the satanic kingdom. Thomas Aquinas furnished the theological basis; the Inquisition reduced it to practice; Innocent VIII in 1484 in the bull *Summis desiderantes* lent it the highest authority of the Church; the *Malleus Maleficarum* (1487 or 1488) codified it; lawyers, judges, informers, and executioners exploited it for gain; information given by malice, fear, or the shrieks of the tortured made the contagion self-perpetuating and ever spreading. It prevailed in Protestant countries equally with Catholic. To believe in the machinations of evil spirits and their compact with witches was part of orthodoxy, part of profounder piety. If the devil and his spirits are not real but a figment of social imagination, yet at that time the devil was real, just as real as any flesh and blood being and far more efficient. Theology had made him real. The Reformation theology did not end this craze of horror. Aside from the humane religious spirit of a few who wrote against it, it was the blessed skepticism of the age of Enlightenment and the dawn of modern science which saved humanity from the furies of a theology which had gone wrong.

The passive and defensive attitude toward the satanic Kingdom of Evil still continues wherever the belief in evil spirits and in the apocalyptic theology is active. Bunyan's "Pilgrim's Progress" presents a dramatic record of the Calvinistic religious consciousness in its prime. In all the wonderful adventures and redoubtable combats of Christian and his companions and heavenly aids, they are on the defensive. The only exception that I can remember occurs in the second part, when Christian's wife and children, personally conducted by Great-Heart, pass by Doubting Castle where Christian and Hopeful were imprisoned by Giant Despair.

> So they sat down and consulted what was best to be done: to wit, now they were so strong, and had got such a man as Mr. Great-Heart for their conductor, whether they had not best to make an attempt upon the giant, demolish his castle, and if there were any pilgrims in it, to set them at liberty, before they went any further. So one said one thing, and another said the contrary. One questioned if it was lawful to go upon unconsecrated ground; another said they might, provided their end was good; but Mr. Great-Heart said, "Though that assertion offered last cannot be universally true, yet I have a commandment to resist sin, to overcome evil, to fight the good fight of faith; and pray, with whom should I fight this good fight, if not with Giant Despair? I will therefore attempt the taking away of his life and the demolishing of Doubting Castle.

So they passed from the defensive to the offensive attitude and demolished the castle. The serious deliberations of the party show that Bunyan realized that this was a new departure. He was, in fact, at that moment parting company with the traditional attitude of theology and religion, and putting one foot hestitatingly into the social gospel and the preventive methods of modern science. Note that it was Mr. Great-Heart who made the move.

To-day the belief in a satanic kingdom exists only where religious and theological tradition keeps it alive. It is not spontaneous, and it would not originate anew. Its lack of vitality is proved by the fact that even those who accept the existence of a personal Satan without question are not influenced in their daily life by the practical belief in evil spirits. The demons have faded away into poetical unreality. Satan alone remains, but he has become a literary and theological devil, and most often a figure of speech. He is a theological necessity rather than a religious reality. He is needed to explain the fall and the temptation, and he re-appears in eschatology. But our most orthodox theology on this point would have seemed cold and skeptical to any of the great theologians of the past.

No positive proof can be furnished that our universe contains no such spiritual beings as Satan and his angels. Impressive arguments have been made for their existence. The problem of evil is simplified if all is reduced to this source. But the fact confronts us,—and I think it can not be denied,— that Satan and his angels are a fading religious entity, and that a vital belief in demon powers is not forthcoming in modern life.

In that case we can no longer realize the Kingdom of Evil as a demonic kingdom. The live realization of this belief will be confined to narrow circles, mostly of premillennialists; the Church would have to use up its precious moral authority in persuading its members to hold fast a belief which all modern life bids them drop. Yet we ought to get a solidaristic and organic conception of the power and reality of evil in the world. If we miss that, we shall see only disjointed facts. The social gospel is the only influence which can renew the idea of the Kingdom of Evil in modern minds, because it alone has an adequate sense of solidarity and a sufficient grasp of the historical and social realities of sin. In this modern form the conception would offer religious values similar to those of the old idea, but would not make such drafts on our credulity, and would not invite such unchristian superstitions and phantasms of fear.

The ancient demonic conception and the modern social conviction may seem at first sight to be quite alien to each other. In fact, however, they are blood-kin.

The belief in a Satanic kingdom, in so far as it was not merely theology but vital religious faith, has always drawn its vitality from political and social realities. The conception of an empire of evil fastened on Jewish thought after the Jews had an opportunity during the Exile to observe imperialism at close range and to be helpless under its power. The splendor of an Oriental court and its court language deeply influenced the Jewish conception of God. He was surrounded with a heavenly retinue, and despotic ideas and phraseology were applied. The same social experiences also enlarged the conception of the reign of evil. The little evil spirits had been enough to explain the evil of local Jewish communities. But a great malign power was needed as the religious backing of the oppressive international forces in whose talons the Jewish race was writhing. Satan first got his vitality as an international political concept.

The political significance of the belief in the Satanic kingdom becomes quite clear in the relation of the early Church to the Roman Empire. The Apocalypse of John is most enlightening on this fact. The Empire is plainly described as the creature and agent of the Satanic powers. The Beast with the seven heads had received its dominion from the great Dragon. The great city, which is described as the commercial and financial centre of the world, falls with a crash when Satan and his host are overthrown by the Messiah. Evidently the political system of Rome and the demonic powers are seen as the physical and spiritual side of the same evil power.

Early Christianity is usually described as opposed to paganism, and we think of the pagan religion as a rival religious system. But it was also a great social force penetrating all community life, the symbol of social coherence and loyalty. Its social usages let no one alone. It became coercive and threatening where religious actions had political significance, especially in the worship of the emperor. Christians believed the pagan gods to be in reality demon powers, who had blinded and enticed men to worship them. Whoever did worship them came under their defiling power. Idolatry was an unforgivable sin. All the life of the Church aimed to nerve Christians to suffer anything rather than come under the control of the dark powers again from which baptism had saved them. When the choice confronted them they were pinned to the wall, the hand that gripped them was the hand of the Roman Empire, but the face that leered at them was the face of the adversary of God. So the belief in a Satanic kingdom of evil drew its concrete meaning and vitality from social and political realities. It was their religious interpretation.

In the Middle Ages, when the Roman Empire had become a great memory, the Papacy was the great international power, rich, haughty, luxurious, domineering, commanding the police powers of States for its coercive purposes, and claiming the heritage of the emperors. The democratic movements which sprang up during the eleventh and twelfth centuries and headed toward a freer religion and a more fraternal social life, found the papacy against them. Then the Apocalypse took on new life. The city on the seven hills, drunk with the blood of the saints, and clad in scarlet, was still there. The followers of Jesus who suffered in the grip of the international hierarchy did not see this power as a Christian Church using oppressive measures, but as an anti-Christian power, the tool of Satan and adversary of God. This belief was inherited by Protestantism and was one of its fighting weapons. Once more it was a political and social reality which put heat and vitality into the belief in the reign of Satan.

To-day there is no such world-wide power of oppression as the Roman Empire or the mediaeval papacy. The popular, superstitious beliefs in demonic agencies have largely been drained off by education. The conception of Satan has paled. He has become a logical devil, and that is an attenuated and precarious mode of existence. At the same time belief in original sin is also waning. These two doctrines combined,—the hereditary racial unity of sin, and the supernatural power of evil behind all sinful human action,—created a solidaristic consciousness of sin and evil, which I think is necessary for the religious mind. Take away these two doctrines, and both our sense of sin and our sense of the need of redemption will become much more superficial and will be mainly concerned with the transient acts and vices of individuals.

A social conception of the Kingdom of Evil, such I have tried to sketch, makes a powerful appeal to our growing sense of racial unity. It is modern and grows spontaneously out of our livest interests and ideas. Instead of appealing to conservatives, who are fond of sitting on antique furniture, it would appeal to the radicals. It would contain the political and social protest against oppression and illusion for which the belief in a Satanic kingdom stood in the times of its greatest vitality. The practical insight into the solidarity of nations in their sin would emphasize the obligation to share with them all every element of salvation we possess and thus strengthen the appeal for missionary and educational efforts.

The doctrine of original sin was meant to bring us under the sense of guilt. Theology in the past has labored to show that we are in some sense partakers of Adam's guilt. But the conscience of mankind has never been convinced. Partakers in his wretchedness we might well be by our family coherence, but guilt belongs only to personality, and requires will and freedom. On the other hand an enlightened conscience can not help feeling a growing sense of responsibility and guilt for common sins under which humanity is bound and to which we all contribute. Who of us can say that he has never by word or look contributed to the atmospheric pressure of lubricious sex stimulation which hems in young and old, and the effect of which bears down the war no man can predict without sickening? Whose hand has never been stained with income for which no equivalent had been given in service? How many business men have promoted the advance of democracy in their own industrial kingdom when autocracy seemed safer and more efficient? What nation has never been drunk with a sense of its glory and importance, and which has never seized colonial possessions or developed its little imperialism when the temptation came its way? The sin of all is in each of us, and every one of us has scattered seeds of evil, the final multiplied harvest of which no man knows.

At the close of his great invective against the religious leaders of his nation (Matthew 23), Jesus has a solidaristic vision of the spiritual unity of the generations. He warns his contemporaries that by doing over again the acts of their forefathers, they will bring upon them not only the blood they shed themselves, but the righteous blood shed long before. By solidarity of action and spirit we enter into solidarity of guilt. This applies to our spiritual unity with our contemporaries. If in the most restricted sphere of life we act on the same sinful principles of greed and tyranny on which the great exploiters and despots act, we share their guilt. If we consent to the working principles of the Kingdom of Evil, and do not counteract it with all our strength, but perhaps even fail to see its ruinous evil, then we are part of it and the salvation of Christ has not set us free.

SELECTION 9

Karl Barth

"The Reality of Nothingness"

Among Barth's many contributions to theological discussion, few have proved more contentious than his interpretation of evil as "nothingness" (*das Nichtige*) developed in the third volume of *Church Dogmatics*. At one level, Barth's proposal can be seen as simply a version of the traditional Augustinian interpretation of evil as the privation of the good, inasmuch as he defines nothingness as that which God does not will and which, therefore, has no proper being of its own. Even his insistence that "nothingness is not nothing" (i.e., that it cannot be dismissed as not existing) can be seen as a conventional refusal to regard evil as simply an illusion. Nevertheless, many have charged that Barth's insistence that nothingness "is"—albeit in a manner qualitatively different from either God or creation—represents a theologically unwarranted piece of speculative metaphysics that brings him dangerously close to a form of ontological dualism. Barth rejects this charge, arguing that the fact that nothingness "is" only in the face of God's electing (viz., as that which God rejects)—and thus as from the beginning subject to the divine lordship—rules out the possibility of its being interpreted as either equiprimordial with or autonomous with respect to God. Yet the criticism retains an edge insofar as it is unclear how the evil which "is" inevitably as the reflex of God's election of the good can also be contingent enough to be destroyed in the way Barth insists it has been in Christ.

From Karl Barth, *Church Dogmatics*, III/3, ed. G. W. Bromiley and T. F. Torrance (Edinburgh: T. & T. Clark, 1960), 349–62.

What Is Real Nothingness?

1. In this question objection may well be taken to the word "is." Only God and His creature really and properly are. But nothingness is neither God nor His creatures. But it would be foolhardy to rush to the conclusion that it is therefore nothing, i.e., that it does not exist. God takes it into account. He is concerned with it. He strives against it, resists and overcomes it. If God's reality and revelation are known in His presence and action in Jesus Christ, He is also known as the God who is confronted by nothingness, for whom it constitutes a problem, who takes it seriously, who does not deal with it incidentally but in the fullness of the glory of His deity, who is not engaged indirectly or mediately but with his whole being, involving Himself to the utmost. If we accept this, we cannot argue that because it has nothing in common with God and His creature nothingness is nothing, i.e., it does not exist. That which confronts God in this way, and is seriously treated by Him, is surely not nothing or non-existent. In the light of God's relationship to it we must accept the fact that in a third way of its own nothingness "is." All conceptions or doctrine which would deny or diminish or minimize this "is" are untenable from the Christian standpoint. Nothingness is not nothing. Quite apart from the inadmissibility of its content, this position would be self-contradictory. But it "is" nothingness. Its nature and being are those which can be assigned to it within this definition. But because it stands before God as such they must be assigned to it. They cannot be controverted without misapprehending God himself.

2. Again, nothingness is not simply to be equated with what is *not*, i.e., not God and not the creature. God is God and not the creature, but this does not mean that there is nothingness in God. On the contrary, this "not" belongs to His perfection. Again, the creature is creature and not God, yet this does not mean that as such it is null or nothingness. If in the relationship between God and creature a "not" is involved, the "not" belongs to His perfection. Again, the creature is creature and not God, yet this does not mean that as such it is null or nothingness. If in the relationship between God and creature a "not" is involved, the "not" belongs to the perfection of the relationship, and even the second "not" which characterizes the creature belongs to its perfection. Hence it would be blasphemy against God and His work if nothingness were to be sought in this "not," in the non-divinity of the creature. The diversities and frontiers of the creaturely world contain many "nots." No single creature is all-inclusive. None is or resembles another. To each belongs its own place and time, and in these its own manner, nature and existence. What we have called the "shadow side" of creation is constituted by the "not" which in this twofold respect, as its distinction from God and its individual distinctiveness, pertains to creaturely nature.[1] On this shadow side the creature is contiguous to nothingness, for this "not" is at once the expression and frontier of the positive will, election and activity of God. When the creature crosses the frontier from the one side, and it is invaded from the other, nothingness achieves actuality in the creaturely world. But in itself and as such this frontier is not nothingness, nor has the shadow side of creation any connexion with it. Therefore all conceptions and doctrines which view nothingness as an essential and necessary determination of being and existence and therefore of the creature, or as an essential determination of the original and creative being of God Himself, are untenable from the Christian standpoint. They are untenable on two grounds, first, because they misrepresent the creature and even the Creator Himself, and second, because they confound the legitimate "not" with nothingness, and are thus guilty of a drastic minimisation of the latter.

3. Since real nothingness is real in this third fashion peculiar to itself, not resembling either God or the creature but taken seriously by God Himself, and since it is not identical either with the distinction and frontier between God and creation or with those within the creaturely world, its revelation and knowledge cannot be a matter of the insight which is accessible to the creature itself and is therefore set under its own choice and control. Standing before God in its own characteristic way which is very different from that of the creature, the object of His concern and action,

---

1. Ed. note: Barth characterizes those aspects of the created order that stand in contrast to the plenitude of creaturely existence (e.g., darkness over against light, weakness over against power) and yet remain absolutely part of God's will for creation as creation's "shadow side" (Schattenseite).

His problem and adversary and the negative goal of His victory, nothingness does not possess a nature which can be assessed nor an existence which can be discovered by the creature. There is no accessible relationship between the creature and nothingness. Hence nothingness cannot be an object of the creature's natural knowledge. It is certainly an objective reality for the creature. The latter exists objectively in encounter with it. But it is disclosed to the creature only as God is revealed to the latter in His critical relationship. The creature knows it only as it knows God in His being and attitude against it. It is an element in the history of the relationship between God and the creature in which God precedes the creature in His acts, thus revealing His will to the creature and informing it about Himself. As this occurs and the creature attains to the truth—the truth about God's purpose and attitude and therefore about itself—through the Word of God, the encounter of the creature with true nothingness is also realized and recognized. Of itself, the creature cannot recognize this encounter and what it encounters. It experiences and endures it. But it also misinterprets it, as has always happened. Calumniating God and His work, it misrepresents it as a necessity of being or nature, as a given factor, as a peculiarity of existence which is perhaps deplorable, perhaps also justifiable, perhaps to be explained in terms of perfection or simply to be dismissed as non-existent, as something which can be regarded as supremely positive in relation to God, or even as a determination of God Himself. All these conceptions and doctrines, whatever their content, are untenable from a Christian standpoint if only because they are contingent upon an arbitrary and impotent appraisal of what can only make itself known in the judgment of God, and is thus knowable only as God pronounces His sentence, while its malignity and corruption find supreme expression in the assumption of the creature that of itself and at its own discretion it is able to discover its nature and existence.

4. The ontic context in which nothingness is real is that of God's activity as grounded in His election, of His activity as the Creator, as the Lord of His creatures, as the King of the covenant between Himself and man which is the goal and purpose of His creation. Grounded always in election, the activity of God is invariably one of jealousy, wrath and judgment. God is also holy, and this means that His being and activity take place in a definite opposition, in a real negation, both defensive and aggressive. Nothingness is that from which God separates Himself and in face of which He asserts Himself and exerts His positive will. If the biblical conception of the God whose activity is grounded in election and is therefore holy fades or disappears, there will also fade and disappear the knowledge of nothingness, for it will necessarily become pointless. Nothingness has no existence and cannot be known except as the object of God's activity as always a holy activity. The biblical conception, as we now recall it, is as follows. God elects, and therefore rejects what he does not elect. God wills, and therefore opposes what He does not will. He says Yes, and therefore says No to that to which

He has not said Yes. He works according to His purpose, and in so doing rejects and dismisses all that gainsays it. Both of these activities, grounded in His election and decision, are necessary elements in His sovereign action. He is Lord both on the right hand and on the left. It is only on this basis that nothingness "is," but on this basis it really "is." As God is Lord on the left hand as well, He is the basis and Lord of nothingness too. Consequently it is not adventitious. It is not a second God, nor self-created. It has no power save that which it is allowed by God. It, too, belongs to God. It "is" problematically because it is only on the left hand of God, under his No, the object of His jealousy, wrath and judgment. It "is," not as God and His creation are, but only in its own improper way, as inherent contradiction, as impossible possibility. Yet because it is on the left hand of God, it really "is" in this paradoxical manner. Even on His left hand the activity of God is not in vain. He does not act for nothing. His rejection, opposition, negation and dismissal are powerful and effective like all his works because they, too, are grounded in Himself, in the freedom and wisdom of his election. That which God renounces and abandons in virtue of His decision is not merely nothing. It is nothingness, and has as such its own being, albeit malignant and perverse. A real dimension is disclosed, and existence and form are given to a reality *sui generis*, in the fact that God is wholly and utterly not the Creator in this respect. Nothingness is that which God does not will. It lives only by the fact that it is that which God does not will. But it does live by this fact. For not only what God wills, but what he does not will, is potent, and must have a real correspondence. What really corresponds to that which God does not will is nothingness. . . .

Nothingness "is," therefore, in its connexion with the activity of God. It "is" because and as and so long as God is against it. It "is" only in virtue of the fact that God is against it in jealousy, wrath and judgment. It is "only within the limits thus ordained. But within these limits it is." From the Christian standpoint, therefore, any conception must be regarded as untenable if it ascribes to nothingness any other existence than in confrontation with God's non-willing. It would be untenable from a Christian point of view to ascribe autonomous existence independent of God or willed by Him like that of His creature. Only the divine non-willing can be accepted as the ground of its existence. Equally untenable from a Christian standpoint, however, is any conception in which its existence in opposition to the divine non-willing is denied and it is declared to be a mere semblance. Within this limit nothingness is no semblance but a reality, just as God's non-willing in relation to it, and the whole *opus alienum* [alien work] of the divine jealousy, wrath and judgment, is no semblance but a reality.

5. The character of nothingness derives from its ontic peculiarity. It is evil. What God positively wills and performs in the *opus proprium* [proper work] of His election, of His creation, of His preservation and overruling rule of the creature revealed in the history of His covenant with man, is His grace—the free goodness of His condescension in which He wills,

identifying Himself with the creature, to accept solidarity and to be present with it, to be Himself its Guarantor, Helper and King, and therefore to do the best possible for it. What God does not will and therefore negates and rejects, what can thus be only the object of His *opus alienum*, of His jealousy, wrath and judgment, is a being that refuses and resists and therefore lacks His grace. This being which is alien and adverse to grace and therefore without it, is that of nothingness. This negation of His grace is chaos, the world which He did not choose or will, which He could not and did not create, but which, as He created the actual world, He passed over and set aside, marking and excluding it as the eternal past, the eternal yesterday. And this is evil in the Christian sense, namely, what is alien and adverse to grace, and therefore without it. In this sense nothingness is really privation, the attempt to defraud God of His honor and right and at the same time to rob the creature of its salvation and right. For it is God's honor and right to be gracious, and this is what nothingness contests. It is also the salvation and right of the creature to receive and live by the grace of God, and this is what it disturbs and obstructs. Where this privation occurs, nothingness is present; and where nothingness is present this privation occurs, i.e., evil, that which is utterly inimical first to God and then to His creature. The grace of God is the basis and norm of all being, the source and criterion of all good. Measured by this standard, as the negation of God's grace, nothingness is intrinsically evil. It is both perverting and perverted. In this capacity it does not confront either God or the creature neutrally. It is not merely a third factor. It opposes both as an enemy, offending God and threatening His creature. From above as from below, it is the impossible and intolerable. By reason of this character, whether in the form of sin, evil or death, it is inexplicable as a natural process or condition. It is altogether inexplicable. The explicable is subject to a norm and occurs within a standard. But nothingness is absolutely without norm or standard. The explicable conforms to a law, nothingness to none. It is simply aberration, transgression, evil. For this reason it is inexplicable, and can be affirmed only as that which is inherently inimical. For this reason it can be apprehended in its aspect of sin only as guilt, and in its aspect of evil and death only as retribution and misery, but never as a natural process or condition, never as a subject of systematic formulation, even though the system be dialectical. Being hostile before and against God, and also before and against His creature, it is outside the sphere of systematisation. It cannot even be viewed dialectically, let alone resolved. Its defeat can be envisaged only as the purpose and end of the history of God's dealings with His creature, and in no other way. As it is real only by reason of the *opus Dei alienum*, the divine negation and rejection, so it can be seen and understood only in the light of the *opus Dei proprium*, only in relation to the sovereign counter-offensive of God's free grace. It "is" only as the disorder at which this counter-offensive is aimed, only as the non-essence which it judges, only as the enemy of God and His creation. We thus affirm that it is necessary to dismiss as non-Christian all those conceptions in which its character as evil is openly or secretly, directly or indirectly, conjured away, and its reality is in some way regarded or grouped with that of God and His creature. Where God and His creature are known, and His free grace as the basic order of their relationship, nothingness can only be understood as opposition and resistance to this basic order and cannot therefore be regarded or grouped with God and His creature.

6. The controversy with nothingness, its conquest, removal and abolition, are primarily and properly God's own affair. It is true, of course, that it constitutes a threat to the salvation and right of the creature, but primarily and supremely it contests the honor and right of God the Creator. It is also true that in the form of sin nothingness is the work and guilt, and in the form of evil and death the affliction and misery, of the creature. Yet in all these forms it is first and foremost the problem of God Himself. Even the man who submits to nothingness and becomes its victim is still His creature. His care for His creature takes substance as its work and guilt and affliction and misery engender such rebellion and ruin, such disturbance and destruction. It is true, again, that God does not contend with nothingness without allowing His creature a share in the contention, without summoning His creature to His side as His co-belligerent. Yet the contention remains His own. His is the cause at stake, His all the power, His all the wisdom, His every weapon profitable and effectual in the strife. His free grace alone is victorious even where it is given to His creature to be victorious in this conflict. Everything depends upon the performance of His *opus proprium*. Only with the operation of His election and grace, and only as its converse, is His *opus alienum* also performed, and the sovereign No pronounced by which nothingness is granted its distinctive form and existence. Only within the limit of His No does nothingness have its reality, and in its reality its character as that which is evil, alien and adverse to grace, and therefore without it. And the limit of His No, and therefore of nothingness, is His Yes, the work of His free grace. As God performs this work, espousing the cause of the creature, He engages in controversy with nothingness, and deals with it, as is fitting, as that which [is] separated, passed over and abandoned, as the eternal yesterday. He exercises the non-willing by which it can have existence, and His jealousy, wrath and judgment achieve their purpose and therefore their end, which is also the end and destruction of nothingness. It is God's *opus proprium*, the work of His right hand, which alone renders pointless and superfluous His *opus alienum*, the work of His left. This penetration and victory of His free grace as the achievement of the separation already recognizable in creation, and therefore as the destruction of chaos, is the meaning of the history of the relationship between God and His creature. He alone, His activity grounded in His election, can master nothingness and guide the course of

history towards this victory. God alone can defend His honor, ensure His creature's salvation, and maintain His own and His creature's right in such a way that every assault is warded off and the assailant himself is removed. God alone can summon, empower and arm the creature to resist and even to conquer this adversary. This is what has taken place in Jesus Christ. But it has taken place in Him as the work of the creature only in the strength of the work of the Creator. The creature as such would be no match for nothingness and certainly unable to overcome it. . . .

The incredible and real mystery of the free grace of God is that He makes His own the cause of the creature which is not even the equal of nothingness, let alone its master, but its victim. There is a grain of truth in the erroneous view that in virtue of His Godhead God Himself has absolutely done away with nothingness, so that for Him it is not only nothingness but nothing. In Him there is room only for its negation. And as the Creator He has effected this negation once and for all. In creation He separated, negated, rejected and abandoned nothingness. How, then, can it still assail, oppose, resist and offend Him? How can it concern Him? But we must not pursue this thought to its logical end. We have not to forget the covenant, mercy and faithfulness of God, nor should we overlook the fact that God did not will to be God for His own sake alone, but that as the Creator He also became the covenant Partner of His creature, entering into a relationship with it in which He wills to be directly and primary involved in all that concerns it. His grace as the basis of His relationship with His creature means that whatever concerns and affects the creature concerns and affects Himself, not indirectly but directly, not subsequently and incidentally but primarily and supremely. Why is this so? Because, having created the creature, He has pledged His faithfulness to it. The threat of nothingness to the creature's salvation is primarily and supremely an assault upon His own majesty. That is to say, He whom nothingness has no power to offend is prepared on behalf of His creature to be primarily and properly offended and humiliated, attacked and injured by nothingness. For the sake of the creature which of itself can be no match for it, He Himself is willing not to be an easy match for it. He thus casts Himself into this conflict which is not necessarily His own. Where His creature stands or succumbs, He comes and exposes Himself to the threat of assault, to the confrontation with nothingness which the creature cannot escape and in which it falls an easy prey. God is not too great, nor is He ashamed, to enter this situation which is not only threatened but already corrupted, to confess Himself the Friend and Fellow of the sinful creature which is not only subject to the assault but broken by it, to acknowledge Himself the Neighbor of the sinful creature stricken and smitten by its own fault, and to act accordingly He Himself inaugurates the history of His covenant with this impotent and faithless partner. His grace does not stop short because it sees that, in spite of the nature which He has given it and the freedom for which He has determined it, the creature is alien and adverse to grace and therefore without it. Though Adam is fallen and disgraced, he is not too low for God to make Himself his Brother, and to be for him a God who must strangely contend for his status, honor and right. For the sake of this Adam God becomes poor. He identifies His own honor and right, which nothingness is obviously unable to contest, with the salvation and right of His creature, which is not only exposed but has already succumbed to its threat. He lets a catastrophe which might be quite remote from Him approach Him and affect His very heart. He makes this alien conflict His very own. He does this of His free grace. For He is under no compulsion. He might act as the erroneous view postulates. He might remain aloof and detached from nothingness. He need not involve Himself. Having given free course to His jealousy, wrath and judgment once and for all in creation, He might have refrained from any further exercise of them. He might have been a majestic, passive and beatific God on high. But He descends to the depths, and concerns Himself with nothingness, because in His goodness He does not will to cease to be concerned for His creature. He thus continues to act in relation to nothingness with the same holiness with which He acted as the Creator when He separated light from darkness. He continues to be the Adversary of this adversary because His love for the creature has no limit nor end. He does not will to be faithful to Himself except as He is faithful to His creature, adopting its cause and therefore constantly making the alien problem of nothingness His own.

Thus it follows that the controversy with nothingness, its conquest, removal and abolition, is primarily and properly the cause of God Himself. At first sight we might regard the converse as true. Nothingness is the danger, assault and menace under which the creature as such must exist. Therefore the creature as such is surely the hero who must suffer and fight and finally conquer this adversary, and the conflict with it is the problem of his destiny and decision, his tragedy and courage, his impotence and comparative successes. But there can be no greater delusion nor catastrophe than to take this view. For it would not be real nothingness, but only an ultimately innocuous counterfeit, if the attack were primarily and properly directed against the creature, and its repulse could and should be primarily and properly the creature's concern. And while the creature is preoccupied with the assault and repulse of these counterfeits, it is already subject to the attack of real nothingness and its defense against it is already futile. In face of real nothingness the creature is already defeated and lost. For, as Gen. 3 shows, it regards the conflict with it as its own cause, and tries to champion it as such. It tries to be itself the hero who suffers and fights and conquers, and therefore like God. And because this decision is a decision against the grace of God, it is a choice of evil. For good—the one and only good of the creature—is the free grace of God, the action of His mercy, in which He who has no need to do so has made the controversy with nothingness His own, exposing Himself to its attack and undertaking to repel it. He knows nothingness. He knows that which He did not elect or will as the Creator. He knows chaos and its terror. He knows its advantage over His creature. He knows how inevitably it imperils His creature. Yet He is Lord over that which imperils His creature. Against Him, nothingness has no power of its own. And He has sworn fidelity to His threatened creature. In creating it He has covenanted and identified Himself with it. He Himself has assumed the burden and trouble of confrontation with nothingness. He would rather be unblest with His creature than be the blessed God of an unblest creature. He would rather let Himself be injured and humiliated in making the assault and repulse of nothingness His own concern than leave His creature alone in this affliction. He deploys all His majesty in the work of His deepest condescension. He intervenes in the struggle between nothingness and the creature as if He were not God but Himself a weak and threatened and vulnerable creature. "As if"—but is that all? No, for in the decisive action in the history of His covenant with the creature, in Jesus Christ, He actually becomes a creature, and thus makes the cause of the creature His own in the most concrete reality and not just in appearance, really taking its place. This is how God Himself comes on the scene.

But it is really God who does so in His free grace. And therefore it is He as the first and true and indeed the only man, as the Helper who really takes the creature's place, lifting from it all its need and labor and problem and placing them upon Himself, as the Warrior who assumes the full responsibility of a substitute and suffers and does everything on its behalf. In the light of this merciful action of God, the arrogant delusion of the creature that it is called and qualified to help and save and maintain itself in its infinite peril is well shown to be evil as foolish and unnecessary. So, too, is the arrogant illusion that it is the principal party affected, that its own strength or weakness, despair or elation, folly or wisdom, modicum of "existential" insight and freedom, is the problem in solution of which there takes place the decisive encounter with nothingness, the repelling of its assault, and perhaps its defeat. In the light of the merciful action of God, only God Himself, and trust in Him, and perseverance in His covenant, can be called good, even for the creature too. Hence the creature has only one good to choose, namely, that it has God for it, and that it is thus opposed by nothingness as God Himself is opposed, the God who can so easily master it.

In this way, in this trust and perseverance, in this choice of God's help as its only good, the creature can and will have a real part in the conflict with nothingness. It is certainly no mere spectator. But only in this way does it cease to be such. Only in this way is it rescued from illusory struggles and strivings with what are only counterfeits of nothingness, and from inaction in the event in which the onslaught of nothingness is real but its repulse is effective and its conquest in sight. In this way alone is the situation of the creature, its fall and rehabilitation, its suffering, action and inaction, full of meaning and promise. As the action of God is primary, the creature can and will also play its part. For it is the salvation of the creature which God makes a matter of His own honor. It is for the right of the creature that He establishes and defends His own right. The *opus alienum* of divine jealousy, wrath and judgment is no less for the creature than the *opus proprium* of divine grace. For it is the sin and guilt, the suffering and misery of the creature that God makes His own problem. The creature is not its own. It is the creature and possession of God. It is thus the object of His concern. And therefore conflict with nothingness is its own problem as it is the cause of God. The full intervention of God is needed, and this action of His mercy is the only compelling force, to make the creature willing and able to act on its own behalf in the conflict with nothingness. As God takes action on its behalf, the creature itself is summoned and empowered. It has no arrogant illusion as to its own authority or competence. It really trusts in God, perseveres in His covenant and chooses His help as the only effective good. But if it does this it can and will take action in the conflict with nothingness. It is not under the wings of divine mercy but in the vacuum of creaturely self-sufficiency that the laziness thrives which induces man to yield and succumb to nothingness. And it is not in the vacuum of creaturely self-sufficiency but under the wings of divine mercy that the fortitude thrives in which man is summoned and equipped to range himself with God, so that in his own place he opposes nothingness and thus has a part in the work and warfare of God.

The concluding delimitation which must be made is self-evident. We must reject as non-Christian all conceptions of nothingness which obscure or deny the fact that God Himself is primarily affected by its contradiction and opposition and primarily confronts it with His own contradiction and opposition. There are few heresies so pernicious as that of a God who faces nothingness more or less unaffected and unconcerned, and the parallel doctrine of man as one who must engage in independent conflict against it. We know well enough what it means to be alien and adverse to grace and therefore without it. A graceless God would be a null and evil God, and a self-sufficient, self-reliant creaturely subject a null and evil creature. If a doctrine of nothingness is not unyielding on this point, nothingness itself will triumph. But from another angle, too, we are here at the heart of the whole question. If God Himself were not the primary victim and foe of nothingness, there would be no reason for the unyielding recognition (1) that nothingness is not nothing but exists in its own curious fashion, (2) that it is in no way to be understood as an essential attribute of divine or creaturely being but only as their frontier, (3) that we are capable of knowing nothingness only as we know God in His self-revelation, (4) that nothingness has its being on the left hand of God and is grounded in His non-willing, and (5) that it is evil by nature and therefore we cannot regard or group it in any sense with God and His creature. All these insights, and therefore the whole theological concept of nothingness, depend upon the fact that the primal antithesis or encounter in which it has its being is its confrontation with God Himself, which God freely allows because His freedom is that of His grace and love and faithfulness, and His glory is that of His condescension, to His creature. Everything ultimately depends on this one point, and we remember that it is not a theory or notion but the concrete event at the core of all Christian reality and truth—the self-giving of the Son of God, His humiliation, incarnation and obedience unto death, even the death of the cross. It is here that the true conflict with nothingness takes place. And it is here that it is unmistakeably clear that it is God's own affair. All the statements and delimitations which we have made rest on this point and can be made only on this noetic and ontic basis.

7. On this one point, again, rests our final and decisive insight that nothingness has no perpetuity. God not only has perpetuity, but is Himself the basis, essence and sum of all being. And for all its finiteness and mutability even His creature has perpetuity—the perpetuity which He wills to grant it in fellowship with Himself, and which cannot be lacking in this fellowship but is given it to all eternity. Nothingness, however, is not created by God, nor is there any covenant with it. Hence it has no perpetuity. It is from the very first that which is past. It was abandoned at once by God in creation. He did not even give it time, let alone any other essence than that of non-essence. As we have already pointed out, in all the power of its peculiar being it is nothing but a receding frontier and fleeting shadow. It has no substance. How can it have when God did not will to give it substance or to create it? It has only its own emptiness. How can it be anything but empty when it is only by God's non-willing that it is what it is? It is thus insubstantial and empty. Only in this way does it have being, form and space on the left hand of God as the object of His *opus alienum*.

But this *opus alienum Dei* is jealousy, wrath and judgment. It does not confer substance and fullness on nothingness but prevents it from assuming them. It gives it only the truth of falsehood, the power of impotence, the sense of non-sense. It establishes it only as that which has no basis. It admits it, but only as that which can have no perpetuity. Nor is this *opus alienum Dei* an interminable process. It moves towards a definite goal and end. It is not effected for its own sake. Unlike the *opus proprium Dei*, the work of His grace, it does not take place by an inner and autonomous necessity. On the contrary, it is subsidiary and complementary to the divine *opus proprium*. The *opus alienum Dei* can have only the significance, weight and scope proper to it as the inevitable divine negation and rejection. If it is inevitable, i.e., as the obverse of the divine election and affirmation, it is nevertheless as such a basically contingent and transient activity. As God fulfils His true and positive work, His negative work becomes pointless and redundant and can be terminated and ended. It is of major importance at this point that we should not become involved in the logical dialectic that if God loves, elects and affirms eternally He must also hate and therefore reject and negate eternally. There is nothing to make God's activity on the left hand as necessary and perpetual as His activity on the right. It takes place only with the necessity with which it can take place according to its nature and meaning—not with the higher, true and primary necessity with which God is gracious to His creature, but only with the subordinate and transient necessity with which, in virtue of His grace, and to establish its rule, He wills to keep it from evil and save it from its power, and has thus to reckon with evil and take it seriously. This negative activity of God has as such, in accordance with its meaning and nature, a definite frontier, and this is to be found at the point where it attains its goal and accomplishes its purpose. With the attainment of the goal the *opus alienum* of God also reaches its end. God is indeed eternally holy, pure, distinct and separated from the evil which is nothingness. But this does not mean that He must always strive with this adversary, enduring its opposition and resistance, and Himself exercising His jealousy, wrath and judgment upon it. Surely He will be holy, and all the more so, when judgment is executed, when the triumph of His love is unchallenged and boundless, and therefore when He is the God who no longer has to do with an enemy but only with His creature. If He now has to do with nothingness, it is only that He may have to do with it no more, but only with His creature in eternally triumphant love. No eternal enemy is needed for this. And because nothingness is His enemy, because it is He who allows it to be this, because He has made the controversy with it His affair, it cannot be an eternal enemy or have perpetuity.

SELECTION 10

Reinhold Niebuhr

"Sin and Man's Responsibility"

Reinhold Niebuhr (1892–1971) was the most influential Christian thinker of mid-twentieth-century America. His "Christian realism" was honed in direct response to what he viewed as the naivete of the social gospel movement, with its comparatively optimistic assessment of the capacity of human beings to overcome the power of sin through programs of social reform. As the following selection from one of his most important works, *The Nature and Destiny of Man*, makes clear, Niebuhr saw sin as a much more intractable feature of human existence than did Rauschenbusch, though he shares the latter's appreciation of sin's social dimensions. Eschewing traditional appeals to revelation, Niebuhr's understanding of sin is grounded primarily in a phenomenological analysis of the human situation.

While Rauschenbusch analyzed sin primarily from the perspective of social structures, Niebuhr focused on the structures of the human psyche. Drawing on the work of the nineteenth-century Danish philosopher Søren Kierkegaard, he interpreted sin as the result of the tension between the self-transcending possibilities of human freedom on the one hand and the constraints of human finitude on the other. According to this analysis, the anxiety caused by the experience of finitude invariably leads people to use their freedom to try to secure their existence in disregard of God, who made human existence good in its finitude. In this way, Niebuhr retrieves an Augustinian emphasis on sin as an inevitable consequence of finite freedom for which human beings nevertheless remain responsible (insofar as it is a product of that freedom).

From Reinhold Niebuhr, *Human Nature*, Vol. 1 of *The Nature and Destiny of Man: A Christian Interpretation* (Louisville, KY: Westminster John Knox Press, 1996), 251–60.

Temptation and the Inevitability of Sin

The full complexity of the psychological facts which validate the doctrine of original sin must be analyzed, first in terms of the relation of temptation to the inevitability of sin. Such an analysis may make it plain why man sins inevitably, yet without escaping responsibility for his sin. The temptation to sin lies, as previously observed, in the human situation itself. This situation is that man as spirit transcends the temporal and natural process in which he is involved and also transcends himself. Thus his freedom is the basis of his creativity but it is also his temptation. Since he is involved in the contingencies and necessities of the natural process on the one hand and since, on the other, he stands outside of them and foresees their caprices and perils, he is anxious. In his anxiety he seeks to transmute his finiteness into infinity, his weakness into strength, his dependence into independence. He seeks in other words to escape finiteness and weakness by a quantitative rather than qualitative development of his life. The quantitative antithesis of finiteness is infinity. The qualitative possibility of human life is its obedient subjection to the will of God. This possibility is expressed in the words of Jesus: "He that loseth his life for my sake shall find it" (Matt. 10:39).

It will be noted that the Christian statement of the ideal possibility does not involve self-negation but self-realization. The self is, in other words, not evil by reason of being a particular self and its salvation does not consist in absorption into the eternal. Neither is the self divided, as in Hegelianism, into a particular or empirical and a universal self; and salvation does not consist in sloughing off its particularity and achieving universality. The Christian view of the self is only possible from the standpoint of Christian theism in which God is not merely the *x* of the unconditioned or the undifferentiated eternal. God is revealed as loving will; and His will is active in creation, judgment and redemption. The highest self-realization for the self is therefore not the destruction of its particularity but the subjection of its particular will to the universal will.

But the self lacks the faith and trust to subject itself to God. It seeks to establish itself independently. It seeks to find its life and thereby loses it. For the self which it asserts is less than the true self. It is the self in all the contingent and arbitrary factors of its immediate situation. By asserting these contingent and arbitrary factors of an immediate situation, the self loses its true self. It increases its insecurity because it gives its immediate necessities a consideration which they do not deserve and which they cannot have without disturbing the harmony of creation. By giving life a false centre, the self then destroys the real possibilities for itself and others. Hence the relation of injustice to pride, and the vicious circle of injustice, increasing as it does the insecurity which pride was intended to overcome.

The sin of the inordinate self-love thus points to the prior sin of lack of trust in God. The anxiety of unbelief is not merely the fear which comes from ignorance of God. "Anxiety," declares Kierkegaard, "is the dizziness of freedom,"[1] but it is significant that the same freedom which tempts to anxiety also contains the ideal possibility of knowing God. Here the Pauline psychology is penetrating and significant. St. Paul declares that man is without excuse because "the invisible things of him from the creation of the world are clearly seen, being understood by the things that are made, even his eternal power and Godhead" (Romans 1:20). The anxiety of freedom leads to sin only if the prior sin of unbelief is assumed. This is the meaning of Kierkegaard's assertion that sin posits itself.[2]

The sin of man's excessive and inordinate love of self is thus neither merely the drag of man's animal nature upon his more universal loyalties, nor yet the necessary consequence of human freedom and self-transcendence. It is more plausibly the consequence of the latter than of the former because the survival impulse of animal nature lacks precisely those boundless and limitless tendencies of human desires. Inordinate self-love is occasioned by the introduction of the perspective of the eternal into natural and human finiteness. But it is a false eternal. It consists in the transmutation of "mutable good" into infinity. This boundless character of human desires is an unnatural rather than natural fruit of man's relation to the temporal process on the one hand and to eternity on the other. If man knew, loved and obeyed God as the author and end of his existence,

---

1. Søren Kierkegaard, *Begriff der Angst*, 57; ET, *The Concept of Anxiety: A Simply Psychologically Orienting Deliberation on the Dogmatic Issue of Hereditary Sin*, ed. Reidar Thomte (Princeton, NJ: Princeton University Press, 1980), 61.
2. Ibid., *Begriff*, 27; ET, *Anxiety*, 32.

a proper limit would be set for his desires including the natural impulse of survival.³

The fact that the lie is so deeply involved in the sin of self-glorification and that man cannot love himself inordinately without pretending that it is not his, but a universal, interest which he is supporting, is a further proof that sin presupposes itself and that it is neither ignorance nor yet the ignorance of ignorance which forces the self to sin. Rather it "holds the truth in unrighteousness" [Rom. 1:18].

The idea that the inevitability of sin is not due merely to the strength of the temptation in which man stands by reason of his relation to both the temporal process and eternity, is most perfectly expressed in the scriptural words: "Let no man say when he is tempted, I am tempted of God: for God cannot be tempted with evil, neither tempteth he any man: But every man is tempted, when he is drawn away of his own lust, and enticed. Then when lust hath conceived, it bringeth forth sin: and sin, when it is finished, bringeth forth death."⁴ But on the other hand the idea that the situation of finiteness and freedom is a temptation once evil has entered it and that evil does enter it prior to any human action is expressed in Biblical thought by the conception of the devil. The devil is a fallen angel, who fell because he sought to lift himself above his measure and who in turn insinuates temptation into human life. The sin of each individual is preceded by Adam's sin: but even this first sin of history is not the first sin. One may, in other words, go farther back than human history and still not escape the paradoxical conclusion that the situation of finiteness and freedom would not lead to sin if sin were not already introduced into the situation. This is, in the words of Kierkegaard, the "qualitative leap" of sin and reveals the paradoxical relation of inevitability and responsibility. Sin can never be traced merely to the temptation arising from a particular situation or condition in which man as man finds himself or in which particular men find themselves. Nor can the temptation which is compounded of a situation of

---

3. Failure to understand the difference between a natural and an unnatural though inevitable characteristic of human behaviour confuses otherwise clear analyses such as that of Bertrand Russell's. He declares: "Between man and other animals there are various differences some intellectual and some emotional. One chief emotional difference is that human desires, unlike those of animals, are essentially boundless and incapable of complete satisfaction." Bertrand Russell, *Power: A New Social Analysis* (New York: W. W. Norton, 1938), 9.

Thus Mr. Russell is forced to regard the boundless will-to-power as natural in his analysis of human nature and as the very principle of evil in his analysis of society.

4. James 1:13-15. This word succinctly expresses the general attitude of the Bible which places it in opposition to all philosophical explanations which attribute the inevitability of sin to the power of temptation. One of the most ingenious of these is the theory of Schelling, who, borrowing from the mystic system of Jakob Boehme, declares that God has a "foundation that He may be"; only this is not outside himself but within him and he has within him a nature which though it belongs to himself is nevertheless different from him. In God this foundation, this "dark ground," is not in conflict with His love, but in man it "operates incessantly and arouses egotism and a particularized will, just in order that the will to love may arise in contrast to it." F. W. J. von Schelling, *Philosophical Inquiries into the Nature of Human Freedom* (LaSalle, IL: Open Court, 1936), 51-53. Thus in this view sin is not only a prerequisite of virtue but a consequence of the divine nature.

finiteness and freedom, plus the fact of sin, be regarded as leading necessarily to sin in the life of each individual, if again sin is not first presupposed in that life. For this reason even the knowledge of inevitability does not extinguish the sense of responsibility.

Responsibility Despite Inevitability

The fact of responsibility is attested by the feeling of remorse or repentance which follows the sinful action. From an exterior view not only sin in general but any particular sin may seem to be the necessary consequence of previous temptations. A simple determinism is thus a natural characteristic of all social interpretations of human actions. But the interior view does not allow this interpretation. The self, which is privy to the rationalizations and processes of self-deception which accompanied and must accompany the sinful act, cannot accept and does not accept the simple determinism of the exterior view. Its contemplation of its act involves both the discovery and the reassertion of its freedom. It discovers that some degree of conscious dishonesty accompanied the act, which means that the self was not deterministically and blindly involved in it. Its discovery of that fact in contemplation is a further degree of the assertion of freedom than is possible in the moment of action.

The remorse and repentance which are consequent upon such contemplation are similar in their acknowledgment of freedom and responsibility and their implied assertion of it. They differ in the fact that repentance is the expression of freedom and faith while remorse is the expression of freedom without faith. The one is the "Godly sorrow" of which St. Paul speaks, and the other is "the sorrow of this world which worketh death" [2 Cor. 7:10]. It is, in other words, the despair into which sin transmutes the anxiety which precedes sin.

There are of course many cases in which the self seems so deeply involved in its own deceptions and so habituated to standards of action which may have once been regarded as sinful that it seems capable of neither repentance nor remorse. This complacency is possible on many levels of life from that of a natural paganism in which the freedom of spirit is not fully developed, to refined forms of Pharisaism in which pride as self-righteousness obscures the sin of pride itself. It is not true, however, that habitual sin can ever destroy the uneasy conscience so completely as to remove the individual from the realm of moral responsibility to the realm of unmoral nature.[5]

---

5. James Martineau erroneously regards the state of habitual sin as a reversion to natural necessity. He writes: "The forfeiture of freedom, the relapse into automatic necessity, is doubtless a most fearful penalty for persistent unfaithfulness; but once incurred it alters the complexion of all subsequent acts. They no longer form fresh constituents in the aggregate of guilt but stand outside in a separate record after its account is closed.... The first impulse of the prophets of righteousness when they see him thus is, 'he cannot cease from sin' and perhaps to predict for him eternal retribution; but looking a little deeper, they will rather say, 'he has lost the privilege of sin and sunk away from the rank of persons into the destiny of things.'" James Martineau, *A Study of Religion, Its Sources and Contents*, 2 vols. (Oxford: Clarendon, 1888), 2:108.

The religious sacrifices of nature religions, in which primitive peoples express an uneasy conscience and assume that natural catastrophe is the expression of their god's anger against their sins, is a proof of the reality of some degree of freedom even in primitive life.[6] The brutality with which a Pharisee of every age resists those who puncture his pretensions proves the uneasiness of his conscience. The insecurity of sin is always a double insecurity. It must seek to hide not only the original finiteness of perspective and relativity of value which it is the purpose of sin to hide, but also the dishonesty by which it has sought to obscure these. The fury with which oligarchs, dictators, priest-kings, ancient and modern, and ideological pretenders turn upon their critics and foes is clearly the fury of an uneasy conscience, though it must not be assumed that such a conscience is always fully conscious of itself.

An uneasy conscience which is not fully conscious of itself is the root of further sin, because the self strives desperately to ward off the *denouement* of either remorse or repentance by accusing others, seeking either to make them responsible for the sins of the self, or attributing worse sins to them. There is a certain plausibility in this self-defense, because social sources of particular sins may always be found and even the worst criminal can gain a certain temporary self-respect by finding some one who seems more deeply involved in disaster than he is. On the other hand such social comparisons always increase the force of sin, for they are efforts to hide a transaction between the self and God, even though God is not explicitly known to the sinner. While all particular sins have both social sources and social consequences, the real essence of sin can be understood only in the vertical dimension of the soul's relation to God because the freedom of the self stands outside all relations, and therefore has no other judge but God.[7] It is for this reason that a profound insight into the character of sin must lead to the confession, "Against thee, thee only, have I sinned, and done this evil in thy sight" (Ps. 51). All experiences of an uneasy conscience, of remorse and of repentance, are therefore religious experiences, though they are not always explicitly or consciously religious. Experiences of repentance, in distinction to remorse, presuppose some knowledge of God. They may not be consciously related to Biblical revelation but yet they do presuppose some, at least dim, awareness of God as redeemer as well as God as judge. For without the knowledge of divine love remorse cannot be transmuted into repentance. If man recognizes only judgment and knows only that his sin is discovered, he cannot rise above the despair of remorse to the hope of repentance.

---

6. Cf. W. E. Hocking, *The Meaning of God in Human Experience: A Philosophic Study of Religion* (New Haven, CT: Yale University Press, 1912), 235.

7. Cf. 1 Cor. 4:3–4: "But with me it is a very small thing that I should be judged of you, or of man's judgement: yea, I judge not mine own self. For I know nothing against myself; yet I am not hereby justified: but he that judgeth me is the Lord."

The vertical dimension of the experience of remorse and repentance explains why there is no level of moral goodness upon which the sense of guilt can be eliminated. In fact the sense of guilt rises with moral sensitivity: "There are only two kinds of men," declares Pascal, "the righteous who believe themselves sinners; the rest, sinners, who believe themselves righteous." Pascal does not fully appreciate, at least as far as this statement is concerned, how infinite may be the shades of awareness of guilt from the complacency of those who are spiritually blind to the sensitivity of the saint who knows that he is not a saint. Yet it is obviously true that awareness of guilt arises with spiritual sensitivity and that such an awareness will be regarded as morbid only by moralists who have no true knowledge of the soul and God. The saint's awareness of guilt is no illusion. The fact is that sin expresses itself most terribly in its most subtle forms. The sinful identification of the contingent self with God is less crass on the higher levels of the spiritual life but it may be the more dangerous for being the more plausible. An example from the realm of political life may explain why this is true. The inevitable partiality of even the most impartial court is more dangerous to justice than the obvious partiality of contending political factions in society, which the impartiality of the court is intended to resolve. The partiality of the contending forces is so obvious that it can be discounted. The partiality of the court, on the other hand, is obscured by its prestige of impartiality. Relative degrees of impartiality in judicial tribunals are important achievements in political life. But without a judgment upon even the best judicial process from a higher level of judgment, the best becomes the worst.[8]

The fact that the sense of guilt rises vertically with all moral achievement and is, therefore, not assuaged by it nor subject to diminution or addition by favorable and unfavorable social opinion, throws a significant light on the relation of freedom to sin. The ultimate proof of the freedom of the human spirit is its own recognition that its will is not free to choose between good and evil. For in the highest reaches of the freedom of the spirit, the self discovers in contemplation and retrospect that previous actions have invariably confused the ultimate reality and value, which the self as spirit senses, with the immediate necessities of the self. If the self assumes that because it realizes this fact in past actions it will be able to avoid the corruption in future actions, it will merely fall prey to the Pharisaic fallacy.

This difference between the self in contemplation and the self in action must not be regarded as synonymous with the distinction between the self

---

8. Surely this is the significance of the words of Isaiah: "He maketh the judges of the earth as vanity" (Isa. 40:23). In one of the great documents of social protest in Egypt, "The Eloquent Peasant," the accused peasant standing in the court of the Grand Visier declares: "Thou hast been set as a dam to save the poor man from drowning, but behold thou art thyself the flood." Cf. J. H. Breasted, *The Dawn of Conscience* (New York: Charles Scribner's Sons, 1934), 190.

as spirit and the self as natural vitality. To regard the two distinctions as identical is a plausible error, and one which lies at the root of all idealistic interpretations of man. But we have already discovered that the sins of the self in action are possible only because the freedom of spirit opens up the deterministic causal chains of the self in nature and tempts the self to assume dignities, to grasp after securities and to claim sanctities which do not belong to it. The contemplating self which becomes conscious of its sins does not therefore view some other empirical self which is not, properly speaking, its true self. There is only one self. Sometimes the self acts and sometimes it contemplates its actions. When it acts it falsely claims ultimate value for its relative necessities and falsely identifies its life with the claims of life *per se*. In contemplation it has a clearer view of the total human situation and becomes conscious, in some degree, of the confusion and dishonesty involved in its action. It must not be assumed, however, that the contemplating self is the universal self, judging the finite and empirical self. At its best the contemplating self is the finite self which has become conscious of its finiteness and its relation to God as the limit and the fulfillment of its finiteness. When the self in contemplation becomes contritely aware of its guilt in action it may transmute this realization into a higher degree of honesty in subsequent actions. Repentance may lead to "fruits meet for repentance" [Matt. 3:8]; and differences between the moral quality in the lives of complacent and of contrite individuals are bound to be discovered by observers. But the self cannot make too much of them; for its real standard is not what others do or fail to do. Its real standard is its own essential self and this in turn has only God's will as norm. It must know that judged by that standard, the experience of contrition does not prevent the self from new dishonesties in subsequent actions. The self, even in contemplation, remains the finite self. In one moment it may measure its situation and discover its sin. In the next moment it will be betrayed by anxiety into sin. Even the distinction between contemplation and action must, therefore, not be taken too literally. For any contemplation which is concerned with the interests, hopes, fears and ambitions of this anxious finite self belongs properly in the field of action; for it is a preparation for a false identification of the immediate and the ultimate of which no action is free.

We cannot, therefore, escape the ultimate paradox that the final exercise of freedom in the transcendent human spirit is its recognition of the false use of that freedom in action. Man is most free in the discovery that he is not free. This paradox has been obscured by most Pelagians and by many Augustinians. The Pelagians have been too intent to assert the integrity of man's freedom to realize that the discovery of this freedom also involves the discovery of man's guilt. The Augustinians on the other hand have been so concerned to prove that the freedom of man is corrupted by sin that they have not fully understood that the discovery of this sinful taint is an achievement of freedom.

SELECTION 11

Valerie Saiving

"The Human Situation: A Feminine View"

Few theological essays have proved more influential than Valerie Saiving's (1921–1992) analysis of the Christian doctrine of sin. Her argument is essentially a critique of the Augustinian tradition, as defended in the twentieth century by Niebuhr and others, on the grounds that its identification of pride as the primal sin and selflessness as the primal virtue is one-sidedly focused on the experience of men, whose socialization renders them vulnerable to excessive self-assertion. By contrast, she contends that women's orientation to the nurturing of children tends to promote the cultivation of selfless behavior and render women correspondingly liable to the corresponding sins of "triviality, distractibility, and diffuseness . . . in short, underdevelopment or negation of self." Saiving's work is recognized as a groundbreaking contribution to feminist theology for its pioneering use of women's experience to expose the gender bias of established doctrinal forms; but it is no less significant for the broader claim that if sin is a deformation of an individual's relationship with God, then its precise form in any particular instance cannot be identified without attention to persons' social location.

From *Journal of Religion* 40 (April 1960): 100–112.

I am a student of theology; I am also a woman. Perhaps it strikes you as curious that I put these two assertions beside each other, as if to imply that one's sexual identity has some bearing on his theological views. I myself would have rejected such an idea when I first began my theological studies. But now, thirteen years later, I am no longer as certain as I once was that, when theologians speak of "man," they are using the word in its generic sense. It is, after all, a well-known fact that theology has been written almost exclusively by men. This alone should put us on guard, especially since contemporary theologians constantly remind us that one of man's strongest temptations is to identify his own limited perspective with universal truth.

I purpose to criticize, from the viewpoint of feminine experience, the estimate of the human situation made by certain contemporary theologians. Although the views I shall outline receive their most uncompromising expression in the writings of Anders Nygren and Reinhold Niebuhr, I believe that they represent a widespread tendency in contemporary theology to describe man's predicament as rising from his separateness and the anxiety occasioned by it and to identify sin with self-assertion and love with selflessness.

The human condition, according to many contemporary theologians, is universally characterized by anxiety, for, while man is a creature, subject to the limitations of all finite existence, he is different from other creatures because he is free. Although his freedom is qualified by his participation in the natural order, he is not simply bound by inherited instinct to a repetitious living-out of the life-pattern common to all members of the species. Instead, he can stand apart from the world and survey it, envision multiple possibilities and make choices, elaborate his own private ends and imagine larger harmonies, destroy given natural structures and create new ones in their place. This freedom of man, which is the source of his historical and cultural creativity, is also the source of his temptation to sin. For man's freedom, which from another point of view can be called his individuality and his essential loneliness, brings with it a pervasive fear for the survival of the self and its values. Sin is the self's attempt to overcome that anxiety by magnifying its own power, righteousness, or knowledge. Man knows that he is merely a part of the whole, but he tries to convince himself and others that he is the whole. He tries, in fact, to become the whole. Sin is the unjustified concern of the self for its own power and prestige; it is the imperialistic drive to close the gap between the individual, separate self and others by reducing those others to the status of mere objects which can then be treated as appendages of the self and manipulated accordingly. Sin is not an occasional, isolated act but pervades everything man does, even those acts which he performs for the most pure and "unselfish" motives. For the human creature has a marvelous capacity for blinding himself to the fact that, no matter how altruistic his goals may be, he always inserts his own limited individual goals into his attempts to achieve them.

Love is the precise opposite of sin. It is the true norm of human existence and the one real solution to the fundamental predicament in which man stands. Love, according to these theologians, is completely self-giving, taking no thought for its own interests but seeking only the good of the other. Love makes no value judgments concerning the other's worth; it demands neither merit in the other nor recompense for itself but gives itself freely, fully, and without calculation. Love is unconditional forgiveness; concerning the one to whom it is given, it beareth all things, believeth all things, hopeth all things, endureth all things. Love is personal; it is the concrete relatedness of an *I* to a *Thou*, in which the *I* casts aside all its particularities, all its self-affirmations, everything which separates it from the *Thou*, and becomes wholly receptive to the other.

It is important, I think, to emphasize that the foregoing analysis of the human situation and the definitions of love and sin which accompany it are mutually dependent concepts. The kind of love described is normative and redemptive precisely insofar as it answers to man's deepest need. If human nature and the human situation are not as described by the theologians in question, then the assertion that self-giving love is the law of man's being is irrelevant and may even be untrue. To the extent that contemporary theology has, in whole or in part, described the human condition inaccurately, to that same extent is its doctrine of love in question.

It is my contention that there are significant differences between masculine and feminine experience and that feminine experience reveals in a more emphatic fashion certain aspects of the human situation which are present but less obvious in the experience of men. Contemporary theological doctrines of love have, I believe, been constructed primarily upon the basis of masculine experience and thus view the human condition from the male standpoint. Consequently, these doctrines do not provide an adequate interpretation of the situation of women—nor, for that matter, of men, especially in view of certain fundamental changes now taking place in our own society.

But can we speak meaningfully about feminine experience as something fundamentally different from masculine experience? Is there such a thing as an underlying feminine character structure which always and everywhere differs from the basic character structure of the male? Are not all distinctions between the sexes, except the purely biological ones, relative to a given culture? Are we not all, men and women alike, members of a single species?

Of course it would be ridiculous to deny that there is a structure of experience common to both men and women, so that we may legitimately speak of the "human situation" without reference to sexual identity. The only question is whether we have described the human situation correctly by taking account of the experiences of both sexes. We know, too, that we can no longer make any hard-and-fast distinctions between the *potentialities* of men and women as such. The twentieth century has witnessed the shattering of too many of our traditional conceptions of sexual differences for us any longer to ignore the tremendous plasticity of human nature. But perhaps the most telling evidence of all that every distinction between the sexes above the physiological level is purely arbitrary comes from the descriptions given by cultural anthropologists of many primitive societies whose ideas about the behavior appropriate to each sex are widely different from, and in many instances contradictory to, those held in our own tradition.

And yet, curiously enough, it is the anthropologists themselves who have begun in recent years to question the assumption that the characters of men and women are essentially alike in all respects. It is even more startling to note that among them are two women of unquestioned professional competence.

It was Ruth Benedict—who in *Patterns of Culture* stressed the relativity of the character ideals held by various societies and the inability of science to account for their diversity on a biological basis—who also wrote these words: "To me it seems a very terrible thing to be a woman." And again: "Nature lays a compelling and very distressing hand upon woman, and she struggles in vain who tries to deny it or escape it—life loves the little irony of proving it upon the very woman who has denied it; she can only hope for success by working according to Nature's conception of her make-up—not against them."[1]

Margaret Mead's concern with the problem of sex differentiation has been expressed in much of her research and writing. In 1935 she published *Sex and Temperament in Three Primitive Societies*,[2] in which she came to the conclusion that there are no natural—that is to say, innate—differences between the character traits of men and women. Rather, the way any particular society defines masculinity and femininity is by a purely arbitrary assignment to one or the other sex of qualities to which members of either sex could be trained with equal ease.

Fourteen years later Margaret Mead published *Male and Female*, in which she returned to the problem, but this time from a slightly different perspective:

> In every known society, mankind elaborated the biological division of labor forms often very remotely related to the original biological differences that provided the original clues. . . . Sometimes one quality has been assigned to one sex, sometimes to the other. . . . Whether we deal with small matters or with large, with the frivolities of ornament and cosmetics or the sanctities of man's place in the universe, we find this great variety of ways, often flatly contradictory one to the other in which the roles of the two sexes have been patterned.
> But we always find the patterning. We know of no culture that has said, articulately, that there is no difference between men and women except in the way they contribute to the creation of the next generation; that otherwise in all respects they are simply human with varying gifts, no one of which can be assigned to either sex. . . .
> So . . . we are faced with a most bewildering and confusing array of apparently contradictory evidence about sex differences. We may well ask: Are they important? Do real differences exist, in addition to the obvious and physical ones—but just as biologically based—that may be masked by the learnings appropriate to any given society, but which will nevertheless be there? Will such differences run through all of men's and all of women's behavior?[3]

Miss Mead answers this question in the affirmative, not because she has found new evidence which contradicts the evidence presented in her earlier book, but because she has put the question in a different way. Instead

---

1. Quoted by Clyde Kluckhohn in a review of Margaret Mead, *An Anthropologist at Work: Writings of Ruth Benedict* (Boston: Houghton Mifflin Co., 1959), *New York Times Book Review*, May 31, 1959.

2. Margaret Mead, *Sex and Temperament in Three Primitive Societies* (New York: William Morrow & Co., 1935).

3. Margaret Mead, *Male and Female* (New York: New American Library, 1959 [1949]), 16–17.

of asking the question most of us ask: "Are character differences between the sexes the result of heredity or environment, of biology or culture?" she asks, rather, whether there may not be certain basic similarities in the ways in which men and women in every culture have experienced what it means to be a man or to be a woman. Cultures may and do superimpose upon the fundamental meanings of sex membership other ideas which are irrelevant or contradictory to the basic structure of sexuality. Nevertheless, if such regularities do exist, then we may find that, underneath the specific additions which each culture has imposed, there remains a substratum or core of masculine and feminine orientations which, if too drastically contradicted by the superstructure, may threaten the very existence of the society and its members.

In my description of a few of these biocultural differences between masculine and feminine experience, I shall draw heavily upon Margaret Mead's analysis because I personally find it most illuminating. Nevertheless, I wish to make it clear that I am not attempting to summarize her thought, which is far too complex to present fully here, nor (since even anthropologists are not in agreement in these matters) do I present her as an authority. Primarily, what I shall say is based upon my own experience and observation as it has been clarified and substantiated by Miss Mead and by a number of other writers, including Helene Deutsch,[4] Erich Fromm,[5] and Theodor Reik[6] (psychoanalysts), Talcott Parsons[7] (sociologist), and Ashley Montagu[8] (anthropologist).

What, then, are the distinctions between the experiences of men and the experiences of women as they occur in any human society, and in what way do these contribute to the formation of differences between the masculine and the feminine character and orientation?

We must begin with the central fact about sexual differences: that in every society it is women—and only women—who bear children. Further, in every society the person closest to the infant and young child is a woman. This fact, based on the physiology of lactation, remain true even in our own culture, in which the formula has so largely replaced the mother's breast.

The close relationship between mother and infant plays the first and perhaps the most important role in the formation of masculine and feminine character, for it means that the person with whom the child originally identifies himself is a woman. Both male and female children must learn to overcome this initial identification by differentiating themselves from the

---

4. Helene Deutsch, *Psychology of Women* (New York: Grune & Stratton, 1944), vols. 1 and 2.
5. Erich Fromm, "Sex and Character," in *The Family: Its Function and Destiny*, ed. Ruth Nanda Anshen (New York: Harper & Bros., 1949), chap. xix.
6. Theodor Reik, *Of Love and Lust* (New York: Grove Press, 1957 [1949]).
7. Talcott Parsons, "The Social Structure of the Family," in *The Family*, 186–88.
8. Ashley Montagu, *The Natural Superiority of Women* (New York: Macmillan Co., 1953).

mother. But the kind and degree of differentiation required of the boy are strikingly different from what is required of the girl. The little girl learns that, although she must grow up (become a separate person), she will grow up to be a woman, like her mother, and have babies of her own: she will, in a broad sense, merely take her mother's place. She learns, too, that she will attain womanhood quite naturally—merely by the maturation of her body. In fact she already is a woman, if in miniature, and must therefore be protected against the premature exploitation of her femininity. And so the emphasis for the girl is upon the fact that she *is* a female and that all she needs to do to realize her full femininity is to wait.

The boy's process of differentiation from his mother is much more complex and difficult. He learns not only that he must grow up but that he must grow up to be a man; that men are different from women, since they do not have babies; and that he must therefore become quite a different sort of creature from his mother. Instead of imitating her, he must relinquish completely his original identification with her. He also finds that, while he is not and never will be a woman, neither is he yet a man. It will be many years before he can perform sexually as a man, and therefore he does not need to be guarded, like his sister, against sexual activity before he is ready for it. He is thus permitted far greater freedom than the girl. But this freedom has its drawbacks for him, since along with it goes a certain set of standards which he must meet before he will be judged to have achieved manhood. He must learn this or that skill, acquire this or that trait or ability, and pass this or that test of endurance, courage, strength, or accomplishment. He must *prove* himself to be a man. True, he has certain advantages over the girl, particularly in the fact that he has visible organs which demonstrate his sex. But, on the whole, the process of self-differentiation plays a stronger and more anxiety-provoking role in the boy's maturation than is normally the case for the girl. Growing up is not merely a natural process of bodily maturation; it is, instead, a challenge which he must meet, a proof he must furnish by means of performance, achievement, and activity directed toward the external world. And even so his reward for achieving manhood is not easily grasped in imagination. It is quite obvious to a child what motherhood is; it is not nearly so obvious what it means to be a father.

This early divergence between masculine and feminine sexual development is repeated, reinforced, and elaborated in later stages of the individual's life. For instance, the girl's history as a female is punctuated and authenticated by a series of definite, natural, and irreversible bodily occurrences: first menstruation, defloration, childbirth, menopause. Each of these events to be sure, occasions anxiety for the girl and thus might seem to be the female equivalent of the constant anxiety regarding his maleness which besets the boy. Yet these physiological events which mark the woman's life have a reassuring aspect, too, for each of them is concrete.

unmistakable proof of her femaleness. The boy's history will provide no such dramatic, once-for-all physical signals of his masculinity.

Even more significant are the differences between male and female roles in the various aspects of adult sexuality. The processes of impregnation, pregnancy, childbirth, and lactation have a certain passivity about them; they are things which *happen* to a woman more than things that she *does*. The sexual act itself, for example, has for her this basically passive quality. The woman, of course, *may* take an active role, but it is not necessary for her to do so, either to satisfy the man or to fulfill her reproductive function. In fact, she may be quite without desire or may even have strong feelings of revulsion, and yet she may, for any number of reasons, submit to the man—sometimes with sufficient grace so that he is completely unaware of her feelings. In the extreme case—rape—the passive structure of female sexuality unquestionably appears. The case is quite otherwise for the male, whose *active* desire and *active* performance in the sexual act is absolutely required for its completion. And here again the demand for performance is coupled with an inevitable anxiety; in order to prove his maleness, he *must* succeed in what he has undertaken—and it is possible for him to fail.

Considered in terms of its reproductive consequences, the sexual act has greatly different meanings for men and women. The male's part in the creation of a child seems indirect and is completed very quickly, while a woman's participation is direct, immediate, and prolonged. It is true that we now know as scientific fact what some primitive peoples have only suspected and others denied: that the man's role in reproduction is essential and that his genetic contribution is equal to the woman's. Yet the birth of a child is never an absolute guaranty to a man of his maleness, as it is to a woman of her femaleness. For, while there can be no doubt as to who is the mother of the child, "paternity remains, with all our modern biological knowledge, as inferential as it ever was, and considerably less ascertainable than it has seemed to be in some periods of history."[9] There is a sense, too, in which woman's biological creativity appears to present a challenge to a man; he perhaps feels his inability to bear children as a deficiency for which he must compensate by other kinds of creativity.

The man's sense of his own masculinity, then, is throughout characterized by uncertainty, challenge, and the feeling that he must again and again prove himself a man. It also calls for a kind of objective achievement and a greater degree of self-differentiation and self-development than are required of the woman as woman. In a sense, masculinity is an endless process of *becoming*, while in femininity the emphasis is on *being*. Another way of putting the distinction is that woman is more closely bound to nature than is man. This has advantages and disadvantages for her as a human being. The advantages lie in her greater degree of natural security and the

9. Mead, *Male and Female*, 125.

lesser degree of anxiety to which she is subject, both of which make it easier, all other things being equal, for her to enter into loving relationships in which self-concern is at a minimum. Yet if it is true, as Niebuhr says, that man stands at the juncture of nature and spirit, then woman's closeness to nature is a measure of the distance she must travel to reach spirit. That she, too, is a free human being is proved by the fact that she can reject the feminine role: but, having chosen it, she has chosen a kind of bondage which is not involved in a man's acceptance of his sexual identity.

For masculinity can with good reason be defined as the distance between spirit and nature. Because of his less direct and immediate role in the reproductive process, including nurture during the long period of human infancy, man is, in his greater freedom, necessarily subject to a kind of anxiety—and, consequently, to a kind of creative drive—which is experienced more rarely and less intensely by most women.

I have drawn the distinctions between masculine and feminine experience in the sharpest possible terms in order to clarify the divergence between them. But it is important to remind ourselves of the countless changes which have been rung on these basic themes in human societies. Every culture, we have said, superimposes upon the necessities of sexual roles a whole structure of masculine and feminine character traits. Many of these addenda are only tenuously related to the foundation on which they rest, and they may even be completely contradictory to that foundation. When this phenomenon is carried to its extreme, so that women, for example, are educated by their society to despise the functions of childbearing and nurture, then the society is in grave danger of bringing about its own destruction. Similarly, where procreation is valued so highly that men attempt to participate directly in the processes of pregnancy, birth, and the rearing of children to the exclusion of other kinds of creative activity, the social fabric again becomes dangerously weak. Both types of society have been discovered among preliterate peoples,[10] and, as we shall see, our own society has not escaped the tendency to overvalue the traits characteristic to one or the other sex.

The truth is, of course, that there is no impassable gulf between the ways in which men and women may look at themselves and at their world. Just as sexuality is not the whole of human existence, so the individual's sense of his own identity is not derived solely from his sexual role. Human beings of both sexes have certain basic experiences in common from earliest infancy—hunger and satiety, constriction and freedom, defenselessness and power, resentment and love. Men and women can and do learn from each other, too; women can be aggressive and ambitious, and men can be fatherly. Neither sex is exempt from anxiety, and both experience the temptations of passivity. Yet the individual's sense of being male or female, which

---

10. See, among others, Mead, *Male and Female*, passim.

plays such an important part in the young child's struggle for self-definition, can never be finally separated from his total orientation to life; in those cases—which are the majority—in which adult men and women accept and are able to actualize their respective sexual roles, the characterological tendencies based on sex membership are reinforced and strengthened. This is surely the reason why, although there have been women philosophers, musicians, and murderers, there have been no female Platos, Bachs, or Hitlers. It is also the reason why even those men who enjoy being fathers most fully can scarcely be imagined as finding complete self-fulfillment in fatherhood. "A woman, as Madame de Staël remarked, either has children or writes books."[11] As for men, Margaret Mead has observed:

> In every known human society the male's need for achievement can be recognized. Men may cook, or weave or dress dolls or hunt hummingbirds, but if such activities are appropriate occupations of men, then the whole society, men and women alike votes them as important. When the same occupations are performed by women, they are regarded as less important. In a great number of human societies men's sureness of their sex role is tied up with their right, or ability, to practice some activity that women are not allowed to practice. Their maleness, in fact, has to be underwritten by preventing women from entering some field or performing some feat. Here may be found the relationship between maleness and pride; that is, a need for prestige that will outstrip the prestige which is accorded to any woman. There seems no evidence that it is necessary for men to surpass women in any specific way, but rather that men do need to find reassurance in achievement, and because of this connection, cultures frequently phrase achievement as something that women do not or cannot do, rather than directly as something which men do well.
>
> The recurrent problem of civilization is to define the male role satisfactorily enough—whether it be to build gardens or raise cattle, kill game or kill enemies, build bridges or handle bank-shares—so that the male may in the course of his life reach a solid sense of irreversible achievement, of which his childhood knowledge of the satisfactions of childbearing have given him a glimpse. In the case of women, it is only necessary that they be permitted by the given social arrangements to fulfill their biological role, to attain this sense of irreversible achievement. If women are to be restless and questing, even in the face of childbearing, they must be made so through education. If men are ever to be at peace, ever certain that their lives have been lived as they were meant to be, they must have, in addition to paternity, culturally elaborated forms of expression that are lasting and sure. Each culture—in its own way—has developed forms that will make men satisfied in their constructive activities without distorting their sure sense of their masculinity. Fewer cultures have yet found ways in which to give women a divine discontent that will demand other satisfactions than those of childbearing.[12]

It seems to me that a more realistic appraisal of contemporary theological doctrines of sin and love is possible against this general background,

---

11. Robert Briffault, *The Mothers* (New York: Macmillan Co., 1927), 2:443.
12. Mead, *Male and Female*, 125–26.

for the prevalent theologies today were created by men who lived amid the tensions of a hypermasculine culture. What is usually called the "modern era" in Western civilization, stretching roughly from the Renaissance and Reformation up to very recent times and reaching the peak of its expression in the rise of capitalism, the industrial revolution, imperialism, the triumphs of science and technology, and other well-known phenomena of the eighteenth, nineteenth, and twentieth centuries—this modern era can be called the "masculine age par excellence," in the sense that it emphasized, encouraged, and set free precisely those aspects of human nature which are peculiarly significant to men. It placed the highest value on external achievement, on the creation of structures of matter and meaning, on self-differentiation and the separation of man from nature. By its emphasis on laissez faire competition and economic uncertainty, on scientific and geographic explorations, on the widening of the gulf between family relationships, on the one hand, and the public life of business and politics, on the other—by these and many more innovations, the modern era presented a heightened challenge to men; and, by the same token, it increased their natural sense of insecurity and anxiety. It was a masculine era, too, in the degree to which it devalued the functions of women and children and the whole reproductive process. It thereby provoked a new restlessness in women, too.[13]

It is clear that many of the characteristic emphases of contemporary theology—its definition of the human situation in terms of anxiety, estrangement, and the conflict between necessity and freedom; its identification of sin with pride, will-to-power, exploitation, self-assertiveness, and the treatment of others as objects rather than persons; its conception of redemption as restoring to man what he fundamentally lacks (namely, sacrificial love, the I-Thou relationship, the primacy of the personal, and, ultimately, peace)—it is clear that such an analysis of man's dilemma was profoundly responsive and relevant to the concrete facts of modern man's existence. Insofar as modern woman, too, increasingly accepted the prevailing values of the age and took on the challenges and opportunities, risks and insecurities of participation in the masculine world, this theology spoke directly to her condition also. And, since the most striking features of modern culture were but heightened expressions of one aspect of the universal human situation, the adequacy of this theology as a description of man's fundamental predicament seemed assured.

As a matter of fact, however, this theology is not adequate to the universal human situation; its inadequacy is clearer to no one than to certain contemporary women. These women have been enabled, through personal

---

13. This point is discussed at some length by Ferdinand Lundberg and Marynia F. Farnham, M.D., *Modern Women, the Lost Sex* (New York: Grosset & Dunlap, 1959 [1947]).

experience and education, to transcend the boundaries of a purely feminine identity. They now stand closer to the juncture of nature and spirit than was possible for most women in the past. They believe in the values of self-differentiation, challenge, and adventure and are not strangers to that "divine discontent" which has always driven men. Yet these same women value their femininity also; they do not wish to discard their sexual identity but rather to gather it up into a higher unity. They want, in other words, to be both women *and* full human beings.

Many of these women, who were brought up to believe in the fundamental equality of the sexes and who were given the same kind of education and the same encouragement to self-realization as their male contemporaries, do not really discover until they marry and bear children—or, perhaps, have been forced to admit to themselves that they never will marry—that there are real differences between the masculine and feminine situations which cannot be blamed upon a cultural lag in the definitions of femininity or upon the "selfishness" and "stupidity" of men. It is only at this point, when the ultimate actualization of their specific sexuality must be either accepted or given up for good, that they become aware of the deep need of almost every woman, regardless of her personal history and achievements or her belief in her own individual value, to surrender her self-identity and be included in another's "power of being." And, if she is fortunate enough to bear a child, she very soon discovers that the one essential, indispensable relationship of a mother to her child is the I-Thou relationship. In infancy the very existence of the child depends upon the mother's ability to transcend her own patterns of thought, feeling, and physical need. As Margaret Mead puts it, "The mother who must learn that the infant who was but an hour ago a part of her own body is now a different individual, with its own hungers and its own needs, and that if she listens to her own body to interpret the child, the child will die, is schooled in an irreplaceable school."[14] At a later stage in the child's life, too, the essential relationship continues to be one of love. To take just one example—the least sentimental one, perhaps the child, when he has learned to talk, is almost constantly absorbed in trying to understand the world around him. It is so full of strange and wonderful and lovely and terrifying things. He is full of questions, and upon his learning the true and adequate answers to them depends the whole process of acculturation upon which the uniqueness of human societies rests. But, in order to answer a child's eager questions, the mother must be able to transcend her own habitual patterns of thought; she must meet the child where *he* is at that moment. It is absolutely impossible to communicate with a young child without in some way abandoning one's own perspective and looking at the world through *his* eyes.

14. Mead, *Male and Female*, 284.

A mother who rejoices in her maternal role—and most mothers do most of the time—knows the profound experience of self-transcending love. But she knows, too, that it is not the whole meaning of life. For she learns not only that it is impossible to sustain a perpetual I-Thou relationship but that the attempt to do so can be deadly. The moments, hours, and days of self-giving must be balanced by moments, hours, and days of withdrawal into, and enrichment of, her individual selfhood if she is to remain a whole person. She learns, too, that a woman can give too much of herself, so that nothing remains of her own uniqueness: she can become merely an emptiness, almost a zero, without value to herself, to her fellow men, or, perhaps, even to God.

For the temptations of woman *as woman* are not the same as the temptations of man *as man*, and the specifically feminine forms of sin—"feminine" not because they are confined to women or because women are incapable of sinning in other ways but because they are outgrowths of the basic feminine character structure—have a quality which can never be encompassed by such terms as "pride" and "will-to-power." They are better suggested by such items as triviality, distractibility, and diffuseness; lack of an organizing center or focus; dependence on others for one's own self-definition; tolerance at the expense of standards of excellence; inability to respect the boundaries of privacy; sentimentality, gossipy sociability, and mistrust of reason—in short, underdevelopment or negation of the self.

This list of specifically feminine sins could be extended. All of them, however, are to be understood as merely one side of the feminine coin. For just as man's distance from nature is the precondition of his creativity, on the one hand, and his self-concern, on the other, so does woman's closeness to nature have dipolar potentialities. Her sureness of her own femininity and thus of her secure place in the scheme of things may, if she accepts the feminine role with joy, enable her to be a source of strength and refreshment to her husband, her children, and the wider community. If she has been brought up to devalue her femininity, on the other hand, this same sense that for her "anatomy is destiny" may create an attitude of stolid and sterile resignation, a feeling that there is no use in trying. Again, the fact that her whole growth toward womanhood has the character of an inevitable process of bodily maturation rather than that of a challenge and a task may lead her to dissipate herself in activities which are merely trivial. Yet it is the same lack of creative drive which may make it possible for her to perform cheerfully the thousand-and-one routine tasks—the woman's work which is never done—which someone must do if life is to go on. Her capacity for surrendering her individual concerns in order to serve the immediate needs of others—a quality which is so essential to the maternal role—can, on the other hand, induce a kind of diffuseness of purpose, a tendency toward being easily distracted, a failure to discriminate between the more and the less important, and an inability to focus in a sustained manner on the pursuit of any single goal.[15] Her receptivity to the mood and feelings of others and her tendency to merge her selfhood in the joys, sorrows, hopes, and problems of those around her are the positive expressions of an aspect of the feminine character which may also take the negative forms of gossipy sociability, dependence on others (such as husband or children) for the definition of her values, or a refusal to respect another's right to privacy. And her capacity for forgiving love, for cherishing all her children equally without regard to beauty, merit, or intelligence, can also express itself in a kind of indiscriminate tolerance which suspects or rejects all objective criteria of excellence.

All this is not meant to constitute an indictment of the feminine character as such. I have no wish, certainly, to add to the burden of guilt which has been heaped upon women—by themselves as well as by men—for centuries. My purpose, indeed, as far as it concerns women in particular, is quite the opposite. It is to awaken theologians to the fact that the situation of woman, however similar it may appear on the surface of our contemporary world to the situation of man and however much it may be echoed in the life of individual men, is, at bottom, quite different—that the specifically feminine dilemma is, in fact precisely the opposite of the masculine. Today, when for the first time in human history it really seems possible that those endless housewifely tasks—which, along with the bearing and rearing of children, have always been enough to fill the whole of each day for the average woman—may virtually be eliminated; today, when at last women might seem to be in a position to begin to be both feminine and fully developed, creative human beings; today, these same women are being subjected to pressures from many sides to return to the traditional feminine niche and to devote themselves wholly to the tasks of nurture, support, and service of their families. One might expect of theologians that they at least not add to these pressures. One might even expect them to support and encourage the woman who desires to be both a woman and an individual in her own right, a separate person some part of whose mind and feelings are inviolable, some part of whose time belongs strictly to herself, in whose house there is, to use Virginia Woolf's marvelous image, "a room of one's own." Yet theology, to the extent that it has defined the human condition on the basis of masculine experience, continues to speak of such desires as sin or temptation to sin. If such a woman believes the theologians, she will try to strangle those impulses

---

15. "The tendency to identification sometimes assumes very valuable forms. Thus, many women put their qualities, which may be excellent, at the disposal of their object of identification.... They prefer to love and enjoy their own qualities in others.... There are women endowed with rich natural gifts that cannot, however, develop beyond certain limits. Such women are exposed to outside influences and changing identifications to such an extent that they never succeed in consolidating their achievements. Instead of making a reasonable choice among numerous opportunities at their disposal, they constantly get involved in confusion that exerts a destructive influence on their own lives and the lives of those around them." Deutsch, *Psychology of Women*, 132–33.

in herself. She will believe that, having chosen marriage and children and thus being face to face with the needs of her family for love, refreshment, and forgiveness, she has no right to ask anything for herself but must submit without qualification to the strictly feminine role.

Perhaps, after all, the contemporary woman who wants to participate in the creative tasks of the world outside her home—those tasks upon which mankind has built all that is distinctively human, that is, history and culture—and yet remain a woman is attempting an impossible task. Perhaps the goal we should set ourselves is to rear our daughters in the older way, without too much formal education and without encouraging them to be independent, differentiated, free human beings of whom some contribution is expected other than the production of the next generation. If we could do this, our daughters might be able to find secure fulfillment in a simple femininity. After all, the division of labor between the sexes worked fairly well for thousands of years, and we may be only asking for trouble by trying to modify that structure.

And yet I do not think we can turn back this particular clock. Nor do I think that the feminine dilemma is of concern only to women. To understand it is important for men, too, not only because it is a loss to every man when a woman fails to realize her full self-identity, but because there is, it seems to me, a growing trend in contemporary life toward the feminizing of society itself, including men as well as women.

To document and explore this trend would require a lengthy exposition beyond the scope of the present paper. I can only refer here briefly to two recent analyses of contemporary Western culture which have impressed me greatly in this connection. Neither of these books—David Riesman's *The Lonely Crowd*[16] and Hannah Arendt's *The Human Condition*[17]—deals with the masculine-feminine theme as such. Yet both of them see a quite recent shift in the fundamental orientation of our present society, one which presages an era as different from what we call the "modern age" as the modern age differs from the medieval. And the analysis of each presents, in its own way, the picture of a society in which the character traits inherent in femininity are being increasingly emphasized, encouraged, and absolutized, just as the modern era raised the essentially masculine character traits to their highest possible power. Lionel Trilling has noted the same trend in our contemporary life and has characterized both its virtues and its dangers with great clarity:

> Our culture is in process of revision, and of revision in a very good and right direction, in the direction of greater openness, greater socialization, greater cooperativeness, greater reasonableness. There are, to be sure, tendencies to be observed which go counter to this one, but they are not, I believe, so momentous

---

16. David Riesman, *The Lonely Crowd* (New York: Doubleday & Co., 1950).
17. Hannah Arendt, *The Human Condition* (Chicago: University of Chicago Press, 1958).

as the development of the tendency toward social peace. It must always seem ill-natured to raise any question at all about this tendency. It goes against the grain to do so.... The American educated middle class is firm in its admiration of nonconformity and dissent. The right to be nonconformist, the right to dissent, is part of our conception of community. Everybody says so: in the weekly, monthly, quarterly magazines and in *The New York Times*, at the cocktail party, at the conference of psychiatrists, at the conference of teachers. How good this is, and how right! And yet, when we examine the content of our idea of nonconformity, we must be dismayed at the smallness of the concrete actuality this very large idea contains. The rhetoric is as sincere as it is capacious, yet we must sometimes wonder whether what is being praised and defended is anything more than the right to have had some sympathetic connection with Communism ten or twenty years ago.... We cannot really imagine non-conformity at all, not in art, not in moral or social theory, certainly not in the personal life—it is probably true that there never was a culture which required so entire an eradication of personal differentiation, so bland a uniformity of manner. Admiring non-conformity and loving community, we have decided that we are all non-conformists together. We assert the right of our egos to court adventure without danger and of our superegos to be conscientious without undue strain. We make, I think, what is in many ways a very attractive culture, but we really cannot imagine what it means to take an intellectual chance, or to make an intellectual mistake, or to have a real intellectual difference. You have but to read our novels to understand that we have a growing sense of the cooperative virtues and a diminishing sense of the self that cooperates.[18]

It is true that the kind of "selflessness" and "community" described here is hardly what the theologians who identify love with selflessness and community mean when they speak of the redemptive power of love. Yet there is no mistaking the fact that there is a strong similarity between theology's view that salvation lies in selfless love and contemporary man's growing tendency to avoid any strong assertion of the self as over against others and to merge his individual identity in the identities of others. In truth, the only element that is lacking in the latter picture is the theological presupposition of man's inherent Sinfulness, the stubborn refusal of the individual human being to give up his individuality and separateness and to unite in harmonious love. But, if this refusal to become selfless is wholly sinful, then it would seem that we are obliged to try to overcome it; and, when it is overcome, to whatever extent this may be possible, we are left with a chameleon-like creature who responds to others but has no personal identity of his own.

If it is true that our society is moving from a masculine to a feminine orientation, then theology ought to reconsider its estimate of the human condition and redefine its categories of sin and redemption. For a feminine society will have its own special potentialities for good and evil, to which a theology based solely on masculine experience may well be irrelevant.

---

18. Lionel Trilling, *Freud and the Critics of Our Culture* (Boston: Beacon Press, 1955), 50–53.

SELECTION **12**

James H. Cone

"God and Black Suffering"

James H. Cone (1938–) is one of the founders of academic black theology and a leading figure in the broader field of liberation theology. In much the same way that Saiving's analysis of the theological tradition highlights its implicit male bias, Cone's theology has from its inception indicted the failure of white American theologians to see the systematic oppression of blacks in the United States as relevant to theological reflection. Yet while Saiving's analysis is more focused on women as individuals, Cone and other black theologians do their theological work in conversation with the accumulated experience of African Americans as a self-identified community shaped by a common history. Thus, while Cone is fully conversant with the leading figures of the Western theological tradition, his primary sources are taken from the life of the black church.

In the following extract from his book *The Spirituals and the Blues*, Cone explores the way in which black Christians have faced the experience of evil, drawing especially on the evidence of the slave spirituals. He notes first that the concrete situation of African Americans in a racist society has precluded the dispassionate analysis of theodicy as a theoretical question: because suffering has been the basic form of black existence rather than a more or less exceptional "problem" intruding on it, the community's ability to respond to evil is inseparable from its survival. Correspondingly, Cone observes that the primary challenge identified by black folk in the face of their collective suffering has not been belief in God's justice as such, but the community's ability to wait on the vindication of that justice instead of giving in to despair. In this way, theodicy comes to be a function of worship, as the work of reminding the community of God's continuing presence rather than a form of argument designed to justify God's ways.

From James H. Cone, *The Spirituals and the Blues: An Interpretation* (Maryknoll, NY: Orbis Books, 1991), 53–77.

> Oh, Lord, Oh, My Lord!
> Oh, My Good Lord!
> Keep me fo'm sinkin' down.

Although black slaves believed that the God of Jesus Christ was involved in the historical liberation of oppressed people from bondage, the continued existence of American slavery seemed to contradict that belief. If God is omnipotent and is in control of human history, how can God's goodness be reconciled with human servitude? If God has the power to deliver black people from the evil of slavery as God delivered Moses from Pharaoh's army, Daniel from the lion's den, and the Hebrew children from the fiery furnace, why then are black slaves still subject to the rule of white masters? Why are we still living in wretched conditions when God could end this evil thing with one righteous stroke?

These are hard questions, and they are still relevant today. In the history of theology and philosophy, these questions are the core of the "problem of evil"; and college and seminary professors have spent many hours debating them. But black slaves did not have the opportunity to investigate the problem of suffering in the luxury of a seminar room with all the comforts of modern living. They encountered suffering in the cotton fields of Georgia, Arkansas, and Mississippi. They had to deal with the absurdities of human existence under whip and pistol. Every time they opened their eyes and visualized the contradictions of their environment, they realized that they were "rolling through an unfriendly world." How could a good and powerful God be reconciled with white masters and overseers? What explanation could the Holy One of Israel give for allowing the existence of an ungodly slave institution?

Faith and Suffering in the Bible
In order to understand the black slaves' reaction to their enslavement, it is necessary to point out that their reflections on the problem of suffering were not "rational" in the classical Greek sense, with its emphasis on abstract and universal distinctions between good and evil, justice and injustice. The black slaves had little time for reading books or sitting in the cool of the day, thinking about neat philosophical answers to the problem of evil. It was not only illegal to teach slaves to read, but most were forced to work from daybreak to nightfall, leaving no spare time for the art of theological and philosophical discourse. The black slaves' investigation of the absurdities of human existence was concrete, and it was done within the context of the community of faith. No attempt was made to transcend the faith of the community by assuming a universal stance common to "all" people. In this sense, black reflections on human suffering were not unlike the biblical view of God's activity in human history. It was grounded in the historical realities of communal experience.

The classic examples in biblical literature are found in the books of Habakkuk the prophet and of Job. In both, questions are raised about the justice of God, but they were clearly questions for the faithful, not for philosophers. They had significance only for members of the community of faith. Habakkuk was concerned about the cruelty of Assyrian oppression against Judah and also about the internal corruption of Judah under the inept rule of Jehoiakim. Why was God silent and inactive as the wicked oppressed the righteous?

> Oh Lord, how long shall I cry for help,
>   and thou wilt not hear?
> Or cry to the "Violence!"
>   and thou wilt not save?
> Why dost thou make me see wrongs
>   and look upon trouble?
>
> Destruction and violence are before me;
>   strife and contention arise.
> So the law is slacked
>   and justice never goes forth.
> For the wicked surround the righteous,
>   so justice goes forth perverted.
>   (1:2–4)

And God's contention that God is "rousing the Chaldeans" (1:6) to put down the wicked Assyrians does not really satisfy the prophet, even though he recognizes that the Lord "hast ordained them as a judgment; and thou, O Rock, hast established them for chastisement" (1:12). The issue is *justice*! How can the Holy One of Israel justify the use of wicked and faithless men as the instrument of divine righteousness?

> Thou who art of purer eyes than to behold evil
>   and canst not look on wrong,
> Why dost thou look on faithless men,
>   and art silent when the wicked swallows up
>   the man more righteous than he?
>   (1:13)

If God is righteous and is in control of history, why is God not setting things right?

The author of the book of Job had a similar concern about the justice of God. Writing probably during the Exile (sixth century B.C.E.), he protested against the deuteronomic doctrine of retribution, according to which God rewards people according to their obedience and punishes them in proportion to their disobedience. The author contended that not all suffering is on account of disobedience; for although Job was "blameless and upright, one who feared God, and turned away from evil" (1:1), he suffered severe mental and physical anguish. If the deuteronomic success formula is true, then God is a demon and does not know righteousness.

Both Habakkuk and Job are concerned about the faithfulness of the people who are condemned to live in the midst of injustice and suffering. How can the people depend upon God, when so much historical evidence seems to point toward God's being either an evildoer or uninterested in the fate of the people? Is faith in God possible when the righteousness of God seems to be absent in everyday affairs? Neither Job nor Habakkuk questioned the ultimate sovereignty of God. What was requested was a divine explanation of God's righteousness in history so that the faithful could understand the ways of the Almighty.

The "answer" came, not in thought but in *encounter*. There was no philosophical resolution to the problem of evil. Both Job and Habakkuk recognized that suffering was a reality of life. But they wanted to know: "How can the believer live in pain without losing faith in God?" Habakkuk and Job received God's answer in the form of divine self-disclosure.

> And the Lord answered me:
> "Write the vision;
>   make it plain upon tablets,
>   so he may run who reads it.
> For still the vision awaits its time;
>   it hastens to the end—it will not lie.
> If it seem slow, wait for it;
>   it will surely come, it will not delay.
> Behold, he whose soul is not upright in him shall fail,
>   but the righteous shall live by his faith."
> (Habakkuk 2:2–4)

And Job says, after the disclosure of God's mighty presence: "I had heard of thee by the hearing of the ear, but now my eye sees thee" (42:5).

Because the faithful can experience the reality of divine presence, they can endure suffering and transform it into an event of redemption. An encounter with God is the ultimate answer to the question of faith, and it comes only in and through the struggle for righteousness—not in passivity.

Black Faith and Suffering
The black slaves' response to the experience of suffering corresponded closely to the biblical message and its emphasis that God is the ultimate answer to the question of faith. In the spirituals, the black slaves' experience of suffering and despair defined for them the major issue in their view of the world. They do not really question the justice and goodness of God. It was taken for granted that God is righteous and will vindicate the poor and the weak. Indeed it was the point of departure for faith. The singers of spirituals had another concern, centered on the faithfulness of the community of believers in a world full of trouble. They wondered not whether God is just and right but whether the sadness and pain of the world would cause them to lose faith in the gospel of God. They were concerned about the solidarity of the community of sufferers. Will the wretched of the earth be able to experience the harsh realities of despair and loneliness and take this pain upon themselves and not lose faith in the faithfulness of God? There was no attempt to evade the reality of suffering. Black slaves faced the reality of the world "ladened wid trouble, an' burden'd wid grief," but they believed that they could go to Jesus in secret and get relief. They

appealed to Jesus not so much to remove the trouble (though that was included), but to keep them from "sinkin' down."

> Oh, Lord, Oh, My Lord!
> Oh, My Good Lord! Keep me fom sinkin' down.
> Oh, Lord, Oh, My Lord!
> Oh, My Good Lord! Keep me fom sinkin' down.

Significantly, the note of despair was usually intertwined with confidence and joy that "trouble don't last always." To be sure, the slaves sang "Sometimes I feel like a motherless child, A long way from home"; but because they were confident that Jesus was with them and had not left them completely alone, they could still add (in the same song!), "Glory Hallelujah!" The same conjunction also occurred in:

> Nobody knows the trouble I've seen
> Nobody knows my sorrow.
> Nobody knows the trouble I've seen,
> Glory, Hallelujah!

The "Glory, Hallelujah!" was not a denial of trouble; it was an affirmation of faith: God is the companion of sufferers, and *trouble* is not the last word on human existence. This was why they could sing with assurance:

> Soon-a-will be done with the trouble of the world;
> Soon-a-will be done with the trouble of the world;
> Going home to live with God.

Or again, they sang:

> All-a-my troubles will soon be over with,
> All-a-my troubles will soon be over with,
> All over this world.

It appears that slaves were not troubled by the problem of evil in its academic guise; they knew intuitively that nothing would be solved through a debate on that problem. They dealt with the world as it was, not as it might have been if God had acted "justly." They attended to the present realities of despair and loneliness that disrupted the community of faith. The faithful seemed to have lost faith, and the brother or sister experienced the agony of being alone in a world of hardship and pain.

> I couldn't hear nobody pray,
> Oh, I couldn't hear nobody pray.
> Oh, way down yonder by myself,
> And I couldn't hear nobody pray.

Thus it is the loss of community that constitutes the major burden. Suffering is not too much to bear, if there are brothers and sisters to go down in the valley to pray with you.

> O brothers let's go down, let's go down, let's go down,
> O brothers let's go down, down in the valley to pray.
>
> O sisters let's go down, let's go down, let's go down,
> O sisters let's go down, down in the valley to pray.
>
> O children let's go down, let's go down, let's go down,
> O children let's go down, down in the valley to pray.
>
> By-an'-by we'll all go down, all go down, all go down,
> By-an'-by we'll all go down, down in the valley to pray.

The actual physical brutalities of slavery were minor in comparison to the loss of the community. That was why most of the slave songs focused on "going home." Home was an affirmation of the need for community. It was the place where mother, father, sister, and brother had gone. To be sure, the slaves wanted to make it to heaven so they could put on their "golden slippers and walk all over God's heaven"; they wanted to see the "pearly gates" and the "golden streets"; and they wanted to "chatter with the Father, argue with the Son" and "tell um 'bout the world [he] just come from." But most of all, they wanted to be reunited with their families which had been broken and scattered in the slave marts.

> I'm just a-goin' 'way over Jordan
> I'm just a-goin' over there,
> I'm goin' home to see my brother,
> I'm just a-goin' over there.
>
> I'm just a-goin' 'way over Jordan
> I'm just a-goin' over there,
> I'm goin' home to see my mother,
> I'm just a-goin' over there.

In the midst of a broken community, slaves might wonder whether existence had any meaning at all without mother, father, brother, or sister.

> If I had-a my way,
> If I had-a my way, little children,
> If I had-a my way,
> I'd tear this building down.
> Great God, then, if I had-a my way,
> If I had-a my way, little children,
> If I had-a my way,
> I'd tear this building down.

Nevertheless, despite the brokenness of community and family inflicted by slavery, slaves continued to hold on doggedly to what life and existence they had. The affirmation of life, as expressed in their strivings for being, was possible because they believed that they were sheltered in the care of the Lord. They "remembered" the Exodus, the Covenant, the prophets;

and, most of all, Jesus' life, death, and resurrection. Through the remembrance of these events, they encountered God, and they realized that they were not (as an old prayer says) "put here for any ship-shape form nor fashion, nor for any outside show to this unfriendly world." God the Creator and Jesus Christ the Savior have included them in the plan of salvation, and it does not matter ultimately what wicked men do with mama and papa, sister and brother. The authentic community of saints is bound up with the encounter of God in the midst of a broken existence, struggling to be free. God is the Community! And all earthly communities must be evaluated in the light of the divine presence. To those who know God in their strivings for being, God is a mother to the motherless, a father to the fatherless. "He is a very present help in trouble"—and much more. God is the Liberator of black people and gives them a victory that is not made with human hands.

However, slaves realized that the victory which God gives is not cheap. The journey of salvation is like a lonesome valley with hard trials, and the believer has to travel the valley for herself.

> I must walk my lonesome valley
> I got to walk it for myself,
> Nobody else can walk it for me,
> I got to walk it for myself.
>
> I must go and stand my trial,
> I got to stand it for myself,
> Nobody else can stand it for me,
> I got to stand it for myself.
>
> Jesus walked his lonesome valley,
> He had to walk it for himself,
> Nobody else could walk it for him,
> He had to walk it for himself.

It is commonplace among many interpreters of black religion to account for the emphasis on the "I" in the spirituals and other black church expressions by pointing to the influence of white pietism and revivalism in the nineteenth century.[1] But that assumption, while having some merit, is too simplistic; it does not take seriously enough the uniqueness of black religion. Black people did not unquestioningly adopt the white interpretation of scriptural language. Rather, they invested scriptural language with the meaning that was consistent with their struggle to affirm themselves as people, their identity and their freedom. The existential "I" in black religion, then, did not have as its content the religious individualism and guilt of white religion or refer to personal conversion in those terms. Neither

---

1. See Joseph Washington, *Black Religion* (Boston: Beacon, 1964); E. Franklin Frazier, *The Negro Church in America* (New York: Shocken, 1964).

was it simply a black duplication of the Protestant idea of the priesthood of all believers. The "I" of black slave religion was born in the context of the brokenness of black existence. It was an affirmation of self in a situation where the decision to be was thrust upon the slaves. But the slaves did not determine the historical setting in which they had to make this affirmation; it had been determined by others against them. And so to affirm their being meant that their existence had to be managed in that inimical setting. That was the situation of blacks who found themselves slaves in "the land of the free." The "I," then, who cries out in the spirituals is a particular black self affirming both his or her being and being-in-community, for the two are inseparable. Thus the struggle to be both a person and a member of community was the major focus of black religion. The slaves knew that an essential part of this struggle was to maintain this affirmation even and especially when alone and separated from the community and its support. They knew that they alone were accountable to God, because somewhere in the depth of the soul's search for meaning, they met the divine. The revelation from that encounter made it plain to them that the divine and human are bound inseparably together. When black slaves suffered, God suffered. Evil was not just their problem; it was God's problem too. That was why they could not believe that God willed his slavery. In the agony of this contradiction, the slaves cried for deliverance:

> O wretched man that I am
> O wretched man that I am
> O wretched man that I am,
> O who will deliver po' me.
>
> I'm bowed down with a burden of woe
> I'm bowed down with a burden of woe
> I'm bowed down with a burden of woe,
> O who will deliver po' me.

In this context one may wonder why there were no direct attacks upon God in the spirituals, like those found in Habakkuk and Job? If slaves really believed that God was in control of history, why were they silent about the apparent divine neglect to end slavery? There are at least two responses. In the first place, not all slaves were silent. There is evidence of open rebellion against God; some of it is found in another style of black music that is almost as old as the spirituals. These songs are commonly called slave "seculars," and today they are known as the *blues*. More will be said in Chapter 6 about the significance of the "seculars." Here we simply note the evidence that not all slaves accepted an unquestioning faith in God. Sterling Brown reports that blacks sang: "I don't want to ride no golden chariot; I don't want no golden crown; I want to stay down here and be, just as I am without one plea." "'Live a humble to the Lord' was changed to 'Live a humbug.'" And they also sang:

> Our father, who is in heaven,
> White man owe me eleven and pay me seven,
> Thy kingdom come, thy will be done,
> And if I hadn't took that, I wouldn't had none.[2]

Daniel Payne (elected Bishop of the African Methodist Episcopal Church in 1852) reported that many slaves denied the existence of God because they could not reconcile divine revelation with human servitude.

> The slaves are sensible of the oppression exercised by their masters; and they see these masters on the Lord's day worshipping in his holy Sanctuary. They hear their masters professing Christianity; they see their masters preaching the gospel; they hear these masters praying in their families, and they know that oppression and slavery are inconsistent with the Christian religion; therefore they scoff at religion itself—mock their masters, and distrust both the goodness and justice of God. Yes, I have known them even to question his existence. I speak not of what others have told me, but of what *I have both seen and heard from the slaves themselves*. I have heard the mistress ring the bell for family prayer, and I have seen the servants immediately begin to sneer and laugh; and have heard them declare they would not go in to prayers; adding if I go in she will not only just read, "Servants obey your master;" but she will not read "break every yoke, and let the oppressed go free." I have seen colored men at the church door, scoffing *at the ministers*, while they were preaching, and saying, you had better go home, and set your slaves free. A few nights ago ... a runaway slave came to the house where I live for safety, and succor. I asked him if he were a Christian; "no sir," said he, "white men treat us so bad in Mississippi that we can't be Christians."[3]

Payne also reported his own personal difficulties in reconciling the justice of God with human slavery.

> I began to question the existence of the Almighty, and to say, if indeed there is a God, does he deal justly? Is he a just God? Is he a holy Being? If so, why does he permit a handful of dying men thus to oppress us? ... Thus I began to question the Divine government, and to murmur at the administration of his providence. And could I do otherwise, while slavery's cruelties were pressing and grinding my soul in the dust, and robbing me and my people of these privileges which it was hugging to its breast, and giving thousands to perpetuate the blessing which it was tearing away from us?[4]

Other black preachers had similar difficulties, and they protested not just to whites or to blacks, but to God. They demanded, in words similar to Habakkuk and Job, that God give an account of God's sovereignty. Nathaniel Paul made it plain:

---

2. Sterling Brown, "Negro Folk Expression: Spirituals, Seculars, Ballads and Work Songs," in *The Making of Black America*, ed. A. Meier and E. Rudwick (New York: Atheneum, 1969), 2:215–16.

3. Daniel Payne, "Bishop Daniel Alexander Payne's Protestation of American Slavery," *Journal of Negro History* 52 (1967): 63. Emphasis in original.

4. Payne, "Protestation," 63–64.

> Tell me, ye mighty waters, why did ye sustain the ponderous load of misery? Or speak, ye winds, and say why it was that ye executed your office to waft them onward to the still more dismal state; and ye proud waves, why did you refuse to lend your aid and to have overwhelmed them with your billows? . . . And, oh thou immaculate God, be not angry with us, while we come into this thy sanctuary, and make the bold inquiry in this thy holy temple, why it was that thou didst look on with the calm indifference of an unconcerned spectator when thy holy law was violated, thy divine authority despised and a portion of thine own creatures reduced to a state of mere vassalage and misery?[5]

These are difficult theological questions, and they belong to the biblical tradition that took seriously the righteousness and goodness of God. Like Job and Habakkuk, Nathaniel Paul did not receive a philosophical answer. He did not ask a philosophical question! It was a question of faith, and the answer which came focused on revelation as the only clue to historical absurdities.

> Hark! while he answers from on high: hear Him proclaiming from the skies— Be still, and know that I am God! Clouds and darkness are round about me; yet righteousness and judgment are the habitation of my throne. I do my will and pleasure in the heavens above, and in the earth beneath; it is my sovereign prerogative to bring good out of evil, and cause the wrath of man to praise me, and the remainder of that wrath I will restrain.[6]

In the second place, there was a good reason for the measure of restraint shown in the spirituals. They do not make direct attacks upon God, because questions about God's justice did not represent a major religious problem for black slaves. The spirituals are not songs of protest against God because black slaves did not perceive the source of their oppressed condition as being ordained by God or Jesus Christ.

Sociology of knowledge and its emphasis on the relation between ideas and the social condition of the people expounding them is worth remembering here. The social and cultural environment of the people determine the kinds of religious questions they ask. This is not to deny that revelation provides its own questions or has its own integrity (a concern that dominated Karl Barth's theological works). But the integrity of revelation must be encountered to the human situation. The situation of being an American slave created certain kinds of theological problems, but they were not the same theological problems of white slave masters or others who did not live out their lives as slaves. Therefore, to use European or Western theological and philosophical methodologies as a means of evaluating the significance of black reflections on the slave condition is not only theoretically inappropriate but very naive. To evaluate correctly

---

5. Nathaniel Paul, "An Address Delivered on the Celebration of the Abolition of Slavery in the State of New York, July 5, 1827," in *Negro Orators and Their Orations*, ed. Carter G. Woodson (New York: Russell and Russell, 1969), 69.

6. Ibid.

the slaves' theological reflection on their servitude in relation to divine justice, it is necessary to suspend the methodology of the enslavers and to enter the cultural and religious milieu of the victims. What were the theological questions of the slave community? What were the assumptions that defined the movement of that community?

The theological assumption of black slave religion as expressed in the spirituals was that *slavery contradicts God, and God will therefore liberate black people.* All else was secondary and complemented that basic perspective. But how did black slaves know that God was liberating them? Black slaves did not ask that epistemological question. As with all faith assumptions, the truth of a theological assertion is found in the givenness of existence itself and not in theory. Black slaves did not devise philosophical and theological methodologies in order to test the truth of God's revelation as liberation. From their viewpoint it did not need testing. They had already encountered its truth and had been liberated by it. Instead of testing God, they *ritualized* God in song and sermon. That was what the spirituals were all about—a ritualization of God in song. They are not documents for philosophy; they are material for worship and praise to the One who had continued to be present with black humanity despite European insanity.

According to Ernst Bloch, "need is the mother of thought." In other words, reflective thought directly relates to perceived wants. Bloch's observation can be very helpful to us at this point in understanding the prominence of certain themes in the spirituals and, conversely, the absence of others. The spirituals nowhere raise questions about God's existence or matters of theodicy, and it is safe to assume that the slave community did not perceive a theoretical solution of the problem of evil as a felt need. Rather, their needs were defined by the existential realities which they encountered. As slaves, they felt sharply their oppression and complete lack of freedom. In the Bible, the black slaves found the God who liberated the Israelites from bondage and whose will was the liberation of the oppressed. This same God also came to humanity in Jesus Christ the Oppressed One, who disclosed that God's will from all eternity was not to be reconciled with human slavery. Moreover, the death and resurrection of Jesus made clear God's will to deliver the oppressed. This biblical disclosure the slaves appropriated as speaking directly to their own condition. Whether they reasoned correctly about the Bible's message is irrelevant, a question for speculative discussion by those not entrapped in their situation.

That this theme of God's involvement in history and the liberation of the oppressed from bondage should be central in black slave religion and the spirituals is not surprising, for it corresponded with the black people's need to know that their slavery was not the divine Creator's intention for them. In fastening on this knowledge, they experienced the awareness of divine liberation. Their experience of it and their faith in its complete fulfillment became factual reality and self-evident truth for the slave community. Only those outside the community and the experience could dare question it or remain unconvinced. To be sure, they did not deny:

> Sometimes I'm up, sometimes I'm down,
> Oh, yes, Lord!
> Sometimes I'm almost to the ground,
> Oh, yes, Lord!

But the certain fact is always that God is present with them and trouble will not have the last word. Penultimately, white masters may torture and kill slaves capriciously, and the world seem only chaos and absurdity. But ultimately God is in control and black slaves believed that they had encountered the infinite significance of God's liberation. And so they lifted up their voices and sang:

> Do, Lord, remember me.
> Do, Lord, remember me.
> When I'm in trouble,
> Do, Lord, remember me.
>
> When I'm low down,
> Do, Lord, remember me.
> Oh, when I'm low down,
> Do, Lord, remember me.

SELECTION 13

David Ray Griffin

"The Furies and the Goodness of God"

Along with his teacher John B. Cobb Jr., David Ray Griffin (1939–) is widely regarded as one of the leading contemporary proponents of process theology. The following selection from his *God, Power, and Evil: A Process Theodicy* gives a concise summary of the process approach to the problem of evil. As noted in the introduction to this volume, process theodicy is characterized by a willingness to compromise divine power: because in Whiteheadian metaphysics creatures have a power of self-determination that is beyond God's control, it is impossible to lay the full burden of responsibility for evil at God's door. Yet Ray notes that this move does not absolve God from all responsibility for evil, since God is responsible for having lured creation from a primordial condition of "trivial chaos" into those more complexly ordered states where evil is possible. In this way, the question of God's goodness remains open.

The heart of Griffin's response is that insofar as the primordial state of "trivial chaos" is itself properly regarded as an evil, God would have been more culpable for not creating a more complex world (in which case the continuing presence of evil would be guaranteed) than for having done so (which allows the possibility for the emergence of greater good). While this argument bares a superficial similarity to more conventional solutions to the problem of evil (viz., that the possibility of evil is a necessary consequence of God's desire to maximize the good), the process insistence that evil would have been present even apart from God's creative activity gives Griffin's argument a moral cohesion more traditional theodicies lack.

From David Ray Griffin, *God, Power, and Evil: A Process Theodicy* (Philadelphia: Westminster Press, 1976), 300–310.

God is clearly responsible in one sense for all of the evil of discord in the world, even though God is not ever fully responsible for the details of the events that occur. In order that the perfect forms of experience might be achieved, God's persuasive activity has led the finite realm out of a state of trivial chaos, and discord has appeared as "the half-way house between perfection and triviality."[1] And [Alfred North] Whitehead does not underestimate the extent and depth of this evil. In discussing Plato's treatment in the *Symposium* of the urge toward ideal perfection, Whitehead comments: "It is obvious that he should have written a companion dialogue which might have been named *The Furies*, dwelling on the horrors lurking within imperfect realization."[2]

God is not totally responsible for any of the horrors, of course, since all creatures have the power of self-determination and other-determination. But God is responsible in the sense of having urged the creation forward to those states in which discordant feelings could be felt with great intensity. The question is whether God is indictable. In other words, is the God of process theology morally perfect? There are three dimensions of this more general question that have been raised as objections against the moral goodness of God as conceived by Whiteheadian process thought: Is this God not morally deficient (1) since aesthetic considerations are primary in the goodness God seeks, (2) since evil is overcome by good in God's own experience, and (3) since this God, while lacking the power to prevent discord, has nevertheless led the creation to a stage where horrendous evils of this type can occur? I will deal with these three questions in order.

1. As the previous discussion has made clear, the criteria of intrinsic goodness are aesthetic criteria—harmony and intensity of experience. Does this fact make God's aim morally unapprovable? Some critics have

1. Alfred North Whitehead, *Adventures of Ideas* (New York: Macmillan, 1933), 355.
2. Ibid., 189.

claimed that it does. Stephen Ely concludes his critical interpretation with this judgment as to the meaning of Whitehead's view:

> All values are then fundamentally aesthetic.... God ... is not concerned with our finite sufferings, difficulties, and triumphs—except as material for aesthetic delight. God, we must say definitely, is not primarily good. He does not will the good. He wills the beautiful.[3]

Similarly, Edward Madden and Peter Hare claim that Whitehead's God "sacrifices human feelings to aesthetic ends,"[4] and say that "a God who is willing to pay any amount in moral and physical evil to gain aesthetic value is unlovable."[5] Their conclusion is that, since this deity is concerned only for aesthetic value, it is "not all good as a theistic God should be."[6]

Common to these two criticisms is the assumption that aesthetic goodness is to be distinguished from both physical and moral goodness, i.e., that neither physical suffering nor moral evil detracts from aesthetic enjoyment. Both aspects of this assumption represent misinterpretations of what Whitehead means by "beauty" and "aesthetic" enjoyment.

The fact that "physical" goodness cannot be played off against aesthetic goodness is obvious from the above discussion. Aesthetic goodness requires harmony as well as intensity, and physical pain is a primary example of dis-harmony or discord. In discussing the Whiteheadian criteria of aesthetic value, Madden and Hare do not mention "harmony" but only "massiveness" and "intensity" of experience. This oversight probably lies behind their assumption that pain is not only compatible with but contributes to God's aesthetic enjoyment.

It is also the case that moral goodness is not excluded from the type of beauty or aesthetic enjoyment which is the chief end of creation. When Whitehead makes this kind of statement, he is referring to "beauty" or "aesthetic experience" in a deeper sense than the simple sense in which these terms are often understood. By the "simple" sense I mean aesthetic experience as one dimension of human experience among others. That Whitehead does not mean that aesthetic experience in this simple sense is the aim of God is made clear in his discussion of "important" experience. After listing aesthetic enjoyment as one form of importance along with others—logical, moral, religious, and practical being the other forms—he says:

> Not one of these specializations exhausts the final unity of purpose in the world. The generic aim of process is the attainment of importance, in that species and to that extent which in that instance is possible.[7]

---

3. Stephen Lee Ely, *The Religious Accessibility of Whitehead's God: A Critical Analysis* (Madison: University of Wisconsin Press, 1942), 52.
4. Edward H. Madden and Peter H. Hare, *Evil and the Concept of God* (Springfield, IL: Charles C. Thomas, 1968), 124.
5. Ibid., 239–40.
6. Ibid., 242.
7. Alfred North Whitehead, *Modes of Thought* (New York: Macmillan, 1938), 12.

He says that this generic aim is "at greatness of experience in the various dimensions belonging to it."⁸ However, he then uses aesthetic categories to explain what he means by "greatness of experience." It is that union of harmony, intensity, and vividness which involves the perfection of importance for that occasion.⁹ This is aesthetic experience in the deeper sense. Likewise, Whitehead can use "beauty" in the simple sense, distinguishing it from truth and moral goodness, and accordingly concluding: "All three types of character partake in the highest ideal of satisfaction possible for actual realization."¹⁰ But then he shifts to the use of "beauty" in the deeper sense, saying that the three together "can be termed that beauty which provides the final contentment for the Eros of the Universe."¹¹ Elsewhere he says that rightness of conduct is one of the forms of beauty.¹² So the beauty which God seeks is not one which is indifferent to moral goodness, but one which includes it.¹³

2. The second charge that has been leveled against the moral approvability of Whitehead's God is based on some statements which say that worldly evil is transmuted into good when it is taken into God's experience. Two implications have been drawn. First, it is claimed that Whitehead's God selfishly overcomes evil with good only in the privacy of the divine experience and not in the world. Second, it is claimed that this means that the reality of genuine evil is ultimately denied, since the divine experience is the ultimate standard of truth and reality. The second implication is reflected in the comment by Madden and Hare that "what appears as gratuitous evil [their term for 'genuine evil'] is really just the makings of aesthetic value in the Consequent Nature of God."¹⁴ Both implications are reflected in Ely's criticism:

> We can hardly suppose that many will take pleasure in the reflection that God enjoys himself by making mental additions to one's pain and grief and frustra-

---

8. Ibid., 14.
9. Ibid.
10. Whitehead, *Adventures*, 12–13.
11. Ibid., 13.
12. Ibid., 190.

13. Incidentally, this deeper beauty or aesthetic enjoyment which Whitehead's God seeks is also distinct from aesthetic enjoyment in the "superficial" sense, by which I mean a limitation to those forms of pleasure which we share with other animals, which the term "hedonism" usually suggests. For example, Whitehead refers to humans as "a race of beings sensitive to values beyond those of mere animal enjoyment" (*Adventures*, 204). He says that "it is not true that the finer quality [of life] is the direct associate of obvious happiness or obvious pleasure" (Alfred North Whitehead, *Religion in the Making* [New York: Macmillan, 1926], 77). He speaks of our lives as expressing "perfections proper to our finite natures," and thereby including "a mode of satisfaction deeper than joy or sorrow" (*Adventures*, 221). And he indicates that this deeper mode of satisfaction is the aim of deity: "God in the world is the perpetual vision of the road which leads to the deeper realities" (*Religion*, 151). Hence, when the deeper sense is distinguished from the simple and superficial senses of aesthetic enjoyment, it is clear that it would be misleading to think of Whitehead's God as either a Divine Aesthete (in the usual sense of that term) or a Cosmic Hedonist.

14. Madden and Hare, *Evil*, 123.

tion. It is no help for present ills to know that God sees them in such a way that they are valuable for him.... The affirmation that what is evil for us is not evil for God does not help. For such an affirmation is merely a denial that we experience real evil.[15]

This interpretation results in part from the misunderstanding of the meaning of "aesthetic value" discussed above. But it also follows in part from taking some of Whitehead's statements about the "transformation" or "transmutation" of worldly occasions in God's experience (God's "consequent nature") out of the context of Whitehead's total position on this subject.

Whitehead does say that worldly events which are intrinsically evil are transformed or transmuted as they are received into the divine experience, and he even sees this as a generalization of "the aesthetic value of discords in art."[16] But he does not mean this in such a way that the evil loses its character of evil so that the divine experience would be, as traditional theism said, "pure bliss." For example, he says that it is a profanation to ascribe mere happiness to God—the divine happiness is always conjoined with sympathy and tragedy.[17] The beauty of the divine experience is always "tragic beauty."[18] Furthermore, Whitehead says:

> God has in his nature the knowledge of evil, of pain, and of degradation, but it is there as overcome with what is good. Every fact is what it is, a fact of pleasure, of joy, of pain, or of suffering.[19]

This statement shows that for a fact of suffering to be "overcome with what is good" in God does not keep that fact from being "what it is, a fact . . . of suffering." By looking closely at Whitehead's meaning, one can see that no self-contradiction is involved.

Whitehead's meaning is that the evil is "overcome by good" in the sense that God, in responding to the evil facts in the world, provides ideal aims for the next state of the world designed to overcome the evil in the world. In *Religion in the Making*, in which the ideal aim is termed the "ideal consequent," Whitehead says:

> Each actual occasion gives to the creativity which flows from it a definite character in two ways. In one way, as a fact . . . it contributes a ground. . . . In another way, as transmuted in the nature of God, the ideal consequent as it stands in his vision is also added.[20]

---

15. Ely, *Religious Accessibility*, 40–41.
16. Alfred North Whitehead, *Process and Reality: An Essay in Cosmology* (New York: Macmillan, 1929), 531.
17. Alfred North Whitehead, "Immortality," in *The Philosophy of Alfred North Whitehead*, ed. Paul A. Schilpp (New York: Tudor, 1951), 698.
18. Whitehead, *Adventures*, 381.
19. Ibid., 149.
20. Ibid., 151.

This passage shows that "transmuting" an occasion means providing an ideal aim for the next stage of the creative advance. Hence, for an evil fact to be overcome by good in God means for it to be transformed into an ideal aim which can serve to overcome evil in the world.

> Its very evil becomes a stepping stone in the all-embracing ideals of God. Every event on its finer side introduces God into the world. Through it his ideal vision is given a base in actual fact to which He provides the ideal consequent, as a factor saving the world from the self-destruction of evil.[21]

Accordingly, it is a misinterpretation to say that evil is overcome only in and for the benefit of the consequent nature of God, and that evil is overcome in such a manner as to negate its genuineness. The falsity of this interpretation is shown most clearly by the following passage, in which Whitehead uses the term "kingdom of heaven" for God's consequent nature:

> The kingdom of heaven is not the isolation of good from evil. It is the overcoming of evil by good. This transmutation of evil into good enters into the actual world by reason of the inclusion of the nature of God, which includes the ideal vision of each actual evil so met with a novel consequent as to issue in the restoration of goodness.[22]

Part of the source of confusion in interpreting Whitehead on this issue arises from his doctrine that it is God's own experience which is finally most important, being "the final end of creation"[23] and "the final Beauty with which the Universe achieves its justification."[24] This could lead one to suppose that God's experience in itself is thought to be the only important experience, which would imply that it is only important that evil be overcome by God in the privacy of the divine experience.

However, there is no experience which is purely private; what is first experienced privately then becomes a public fact, conditioning the future world.[25] Whitehead gives terminological application of this doctrine to God by speaking of God's "superjective nature."[26] And he points out that the transformation of a worldly fact into a "perfected actuality" in the consequent nature does condition the future world.

> For the perfected actuality passes back into the temporal world, and qualifies this world so that each temporal actuality includes it as an immediate fact of relevant experience. For the kingdom of heaven is with us today. What is done in the world is transformed into a reality in heaven, and the reality in heaven passes back into the world.[27]

---

21. Ibid., 149.
22. Ibid., 148–49.
23. Whitehead, *Process*, 530.
24. Whitehead, *Adventures*, 381.
25. Whitehead, *Process*, 443–44.
26. Ibid., 135.
27. Ibid., 532.

Hence, there is no basis for a dichotomy between the overcoming of evil in God and in the world. In fact, since it is "overcome" in God's consequent nature in the sense that it is responded to with an ideal aim which aims at restoring goodness in the world, this "overcoming" in God is precisely for the sake of overcoming evil in the world.

The manner in which God seeks to overcome a chief source of evil in the world connects the present point with the previous one about the place of moral goodness in the highest forms of aesthetic experience. As stated earlier, a chief source of evil in the present state of the world is that those beings—ourselves—with the greatest destructive power also have the power deliberately to intend to be destructive of the potential intrinsic good of others. This capacity for moral evil is the chief source of the threat we pose for each other and the planet as a whole. Hence, one of the most relevant things God could be doing toward overcoming evil with good in the world would be to be seeking to overcome our proclivity for moral evil. Whitehead contends that God is doing just that.

For Whitehead, "the effect of the present on the future is the business of morals."[28] More specifically, in a passage in which "importance" is used for beauty in the deeper sense, he says:

> Morality consists in the control of process so as to maximize importance.... Our action is moral if we have ... safeguarded the importance of experience so far as it depends on that concrete instance in the world's history.[29]

In the words that we have been using, this means that morality involves actualizing oneself in the present so that one's potential instrumental value will be such as to maximize the opportunities for the intrinsic good of future experiences.

Further, Whitehead understands our prehension of God to be the source of our feeling that we should be moral.

> God, as conditioning the creativity with his harmony of apprehension, issues into the mental creature as moral judgment according to a perfection of ideals.[30]

> There are experiences of ideals—of ideals entertained, of ideals aimed at, of ideals achieved, of ideals defaced. This is the experience of the deity of the universe.[31]

> God is that function in the world by reason of which our purposes are directed to ends which in our own consciousness are impartial as to our own interests.... He is that element in virtue of which our purposes extend beyond values for ourselves to values for others.[32]

---

28. Whitehead, *Adventures*, 346.
29. Whitehead, *Modes*, 13–15.
30. Whitehead, *Religion*, 114.
31. Whitehead, *Modes*, 103.
32. Whitehead, *Religion*, 152.

Finally, Whitehead suggests that this functioning of God is not disconnected from God's functioning to lure us to achieve the greatest intrinsic good open to us; in fact, it is part of that functioning. This coalescence of the two divine aims for us—to actualize both aesthetic and moral goodness—is based upon the fact that the twofold aim of an occasion of experience—to achieve value in the immediate present and in the relevant future—is not as divided as it might appear at first.[33] The "relevant future" consists of those elements which are effectively "anticipated" by the decision of the present occasion, in the sense that the occasion considers the real potentiality for those elements to be derived from itself.[34] This anticipation of its own effects in the future is not divided from the aim to achieve intrinsic value, since this anticipation enters into the quality of the occasion's present value experience.[35] This means that the anticipation that our present decision will contribute to the good of others in the future contributes to our present enjoyment.

Of course, we all know that there can be a strong tension between these two aspects of our essential aim, the tension we normally describe as that between desire and duty. But there is the possibility that this tension can be overcome, Whitehead suggests:

> The antithesis between the general good and the individual interest can be abolished only when the individual is such that its interest is the general good, thus exemplifying the loss of the minor intensities in order to find them again with finer composition in a wider sweep of interest.[36]

When this occurs, even though we have given up some of the "minor intensities," we will enjoy the "extreme ecstasy of Peace,"[37] which is the highest good. In other words, the highest aesthetic enjoyment open to human beings requires the incorporation of moral goodness.

> God is luring us to realize this highest form of enjoyment.
> He is that element in virtue of which the attainment of such a value for others transforms itself into value for ourselves.[38]

Hence, while moral good is not of the essence of intrinsic goodness (since there can be intrinsic goodness in those beings who are incapable of moral goodness or evil), or even of the intrinsic goodness of human life, it is of the essence of that type of intrinsic good which God seeks to promote in us; and this promotion involves God's enlistment of our deliberate support in the drive to overcome evil in the world by maximizing good. In Whitehead's words:

---

33. Whitehead, *Process*, 41.
34. Ibid.
35. Whitehead, *Adventures*, 346.
36. Whitehead, *Process*, 23.
37. Whitehead, *Adventures*, 372.
38. Whitehead, *Religion*, 152.

The function of being a means is not disjoined from the function of being an end. The sense of worth beyond itself is immediately enjoyed as an overpowering element in the individual self-attainment.[39]

This statement, which is more or less true of finite actualities, is ideally true for God. It is precisely because of this ideal harmony, between immediate enjoyment and aims for future welfare, that there is no tension between God's overcoming of evil in the divine consequent nature and in the world. The self-determining response by God (in distinction from God's purely receptive response to the values achieved in the previous moments of creation) which brings the greatest immediate enjoyment to God is the provision of ideal aims which will influence the future state of the world toward the greatest good open to it. This is why the provision of ideal aims for the future can be referred to as the overcoming of evil by good in God's own experience.

Incidentally, Whitehead points out that "in a purified religion . . . you study his [God's] goodness in order to be like him."[40] To the extent that the tension between our interest and the general good is overcome, we imitate the goodness of God. God is perfectly good, not, as traditional theism said, because the divine activity in relation to the world is free from any self-interest, but because God's self-interest is not selfish interest but is an interest in the welfare of the world. There is no tension in God between desire and duty, since God, being completely receptive of all the joys and sufferings in creation, desires nothing other than the greatest possible joy for the entire creation. To the extent that the scope of our sympathy is enlarged, to that extent the scope of the interest behind our aims will be enlarged, and to that extent we will experience a resolution of the tension between desire and duty.

3. A third objection that could be raised against the moral goodness of Whitehead's God is this: Since God does not have controlling power, and therefore cannot prevent the occurrence of genuine evil, should not God have abstained from creating a world, at least one in which the more intense forms of evil are possible?[41] This question raises directly the issue as to whether God can be seen as responsible in an important sense for the suffering in the world without being morally indictable for it.

Although not totally responsible for any evil event, of course, God is responsible for all the suffering in the world in an important sense. If God had ceased stimulating novelty prior to the advent of life, there would be no pain in the world. If God had rested content with the state of creation prior to the emergence of animals with central nervous systems, the intensity

---

39. Whitehead, *Process*, 531.
40. Whitehead, *Religion*, 40.
41. Madden and Hare raise this question in relation to the position of E. S. Brightman (Madden and Hare, *Evil*, 111). But the question is also relevant to Whitehead's position.

of pain in the creation would have been low. Or if God had even ceased stimulating the development of mentality before the rise of rational creatures, the planet would have been spared its most intense horrors. Human beings have been the causes and the victims of the most horrible forms of evil experienced on our planet; and it is our species which threatens to bring all the life of the planet to a premature end.

Should God have avoided bringing order out of chaos, or at least avoided the higher forms of order, so that the higher forms of evil would not have been possible? An unambiguously positive answer would seem to assume that discord is the only type of evil to take into consideration. From that assumption it would follow that a being who is morally perfect (defined as one who wants to prevent all genuine evil) but lacks controlling power would refrain from creating a world. But if it is recognized that unnecessary triviality is also genuinely evil, then genuine evil cannot be avoided by leaving the world in chaos, or by calling off at some stage the quest for the higher perfections. In fact, to do so would be to guarantee the existence of genuine evil (since all experience which is more trivial than it need be is evil by comparison with what it could be). To stimulate more complex and thereby more intense forms of experience is to risk the possibility of more intense discord; but it is also to make possible the enjoyment of the more intense harmonies.

In this context, the question as to whether God is indictable is to be answered in terms of the question as to whether the positive values that are possible in our world are valuable enough to be worth the risk of the negative experiences which have occurred, and the even greater horrors which stand before us as real possibilities for the near future. Should God, for the sake of avoiding the possibility of persons such as Hitler, and horrors such as Auschwitz, have precluded the possibility of Jesus, Gautama, Socrates, Confucius, Moses Mendelssohn, El Greco, Michelangelo, Leonardo da Vinci, Florence Nightingale, Abraham Lincoln, Mahatma Gandhi, Chief Joseph, Chief Seattle, Alfred North Whitehead, John F. Kennedy, Oliver Wendell Holmes, Sojourner Truth, Helen Keller, Louis Armstrong, Albert Einstein, Dag Hammarskjold, Reinhold Niebuhr, Carol Channing, Margaret Mead, and millions of other marvelous human beings, well known and not well known alike, who have lived on the face of this earth? In other words, should God, for the sake of avoiding "man's inhumanity to man," have avoided humanity (or some comparably complex species) altogether? Only those who could sincerely answer this question affirmatively could indict the God of process theology on the basis of the evil in the world.

Another point that is relevant to this third question is the fact that God responds to the world sympathetically. If God were an impassive absolute, then all the previous talk about the necessity of risk-taking in order to achieve higher values would mean that it is the creatures alone which suffer the consequences of God's decision to take risks. But in process thought, the quality of God's experience depends in part upon that of the creatures. As clarified above, worldly events of pain and sorrow are received into God just as they are. God suffers with our sufferings, as well as enjoying our enjoyments. Since the world always contains a mixture of good and evil, beauty and ugliness, the divine beauty is always tragic beauty. Accordingly, the risks which God asks the creation to take are also risks for God. Stimulating the world toward greater intensity means the risk that God too will experience more intense suffering.

Awareness of this aspect of God as envisioned by process thought not only removes the basis for that sense of moral outrage which would be directed toward an impassive spectator deity who took great risks with the creation. It also provides an additional basis, beyond that of our own immediate experience, for affirming that the risk was worth taking. That being who is the universal agent, goading the creation to overcome triviality in favor of the more intense harmonies, is also the universal recipient of the totality of good and evil that is actualized. In other words, the one being who is in position to know experientially the bitter as well as the sweet fruits of the risk of creation is the same being who has encouraged and continues to encourage this process of creative risk-taking.

Why, then, can we say that God is good in spite of all the evil within the divine creation? Because all individuals within the creation necessarily have power partially to determine themselves and others; because both intensity and harmony are necessary for intrinsic goodness, so seeking to increase intrinsic goodness means seeking to overcome triviality as well as avoiding discord; because the conditions for the possibilities of greater good are necessarily the conditions for the possibilities of greater suffering; because God does not promote any new level of intensity without being willing to suffer the possible consequences; because God constantly works to overcome the evil in the creation with good, and in human experience does this by simultaneously seeking to increase our enjoyment of life and to enlist our support in the effort to overcome evil by maximizing good.

SELECTION **14**

Stephen G. Ray Jr.

"Redeeming Sin-Talk"

Stephen Ray (1960–) is a Reformed theologian who shares Valerie Saiving's insistence on the importance of reference to social location in the construction of an adequate Christian doctrine of sin. He is particularly attentive to the way in which the images theologians use to characterize sin tend to stigmatize members of marginalized groups in ways that eclipse their particularity and thereby exacerbate the social dynamics which led to their being marginalized in the first place. Yet his final position is less a rejection of the Augustinian tradition than a plea for its intensification, on the grounds that it is precisely theologians' insensitivity to their own complicity in the dynamics of sin—and thus a failure to take with full seriousness Augustine's insistence on sin's universality—that leads them to deploy the language of sin in such damaging ways. In this selection from the concluding chapter of his book *Do No Harm: Social Sin and Christian Responsibility*, Ray proposes four rules to help Christians chasten their sin-talk in ways that render it capable of identifying and correcting rather than furthering the harm caused by sin in people's lives.

From Stephen G. Ray Jr., *Do No Harm: Social Sin and Christian Responsibility* (Minneapolis: Fortress Press, 2003), 121–35.

I have sought to highlight the unfortunate practice by many contemporary theologians of deploying sin-talk (theoretical and functional doctrines of sin) that trades in images and language that are destructive of marginalized persons and communities in these theologians' contexts. We have seen how inattention to the discursive economies at work in these sociocultural contexts reflects these economies in harmful ways in their sin-talk. This seeming unawareness significantly compromises these theologians' engagements with sin in its social dimension.

The rhetorical participation of these theologians in oppressive systems and marginalizing discourses is not born of a particular malice harbored by these writers toward those marginalized within their societies. In fact, in two cases they apparently believed that they were being sympathetic to the marginalized persons about whom they were writing ([Reinhold] Niebuhr and African Americans, and [Dietrich] Bonhoeffer and Jews). Nonetheless, for the theologians discussed, the effect of their sin-talk is to legitimate cultural "common sense" that primarily functions to buttress systems of social, religious, and political oppression.

In my analysis of [Cornelius] Plantinga and Niebuhr, I illustrated results arising from two discrete instances of a theologian's unexamined use of cultural and rhetorical figures to exemplify his sin-talk. The primary consequences that I identified were that the sin-talk of these theologians participates in (1) the discursive legitimization of oppressive social, economic, and political systems, and (2) the abstraction of marginalized persons and communities into exotic, pathological monoliths. To use the language deployed earlier, the sin-talk of Plantinga and Niebuhr rhetorically constructs social and cultural margins and then essentializes oppressed persons and communities into those margins. Neither of these practices is a fitting aim or method for a Christian theologian concerned about engaging sin in its social dimension.

In identifying these problematic tendencies in the works of Plantinga and Niebuhr, I sought to make the further point that to the extent that both theologians use and thereby legitimate stereotypic figures, they are denying the full humanity of the persons to whom these figures putatively refer. This denial is always the consequence of objectifying persons and their communities because it does not allow for the type of "thick" account of existence that is necessary for a true rendering of human experience. This denial has serious implications for other aspects of the discourse of these theologians. An area that is immediately affected is, of course, theological anthropology. The first implication is made evident in the recognition that stereotyping persons and rendering their communities as monolithic denies those persons the elements of identity and subjectivity that have been identified in modernity—both philosophically and theologically—as hallmarks of human uniqueness within creation.[1]

The denial of personal identity and subjectivity has the second implication of discursively distorting the theological description of human agency as a venue for responsive relatedness to God. A failure to recognize the individuality of persons precludes the further recognition of their response in freedom to God. This is an important consequence because much of the Protestant tradition holds that it is precisely in our response to God as *free individuals* that we are responsibly claiming our creaturehood.[2] Indeed, the capacity to do more than simply respond to our environment by instinct or conditioning is the facet of our being that much of the tradition describes as the *imago Dei* in humanity.[3] This capacity which is most often identified in the tradition as free will is the font of both positive response to God (love and the pursuit of justice) and negative (sin).[4] Because it is an integral part of the Christian account of humanity, any circumscription of the capacity for free will diminishes the humanity of those persons so set apart. Thus, to the extent that persons are rhetorically constructed, as they are by Niebuhr, without a full and robust capacity for free will and agency, they are depicted as less than fully human. Correlatively, to posit some sort of unique propensity to sin, or a distinct condition of sin apart from the general human condition of sin, as Plantinga does, is to participate in the denial of full humanity to persons thus circumscribed. Obviously, this is not what Plantinga or Niebuhr intended; but these are unavoidable consequences of the weaknesses in their work.

---

1. Georg Friedrich Hegel, *Philosophy of the Right* (Oxford: Oxford University Press, 1967), 20–30; Reinhold Niebuhr, *The Nature and Destiny of Man* (New York: Scribner's, 1941), 54–65.
2. Niebuhr, *Nature*, 57–58.
3. Christoph Schwöbel, "*Imago Libertatis*: Human and Divine Freedom," in *God and Freedom: Essays in Historical and Systematic Theology*, ed. Colin E. Gunton (Edinburgh: T. & T. Clark, 1995), 57–81.
4. Colin E. Gunton, "God, Grace and Freedom," in *God and Freedom*, 119–33.

In my analysis of the work of Dietrich Bonhoeffer, my concern was to demonstrate how accepting a discursive economy surrounding a type of difference can blind theologians to the potentially dangerous mediation of that difference in their particular contexts. Specifically, I demonstrated how Bonhoeffer's acceptance of the idea of Jewish difference impeded him from seeing that the category itself was being rendered as defilement in the midst of a ritual purification by his society, and, thus, treated as a presence that must be eradicated. I argued that a keener awareness of the character of this cultural enactment, which was exemplified in the [anti-Semitic] Aryan clauses, might have helped Bonhoeffer to see the potentially lethal material consequences of this cultural designation for Jewish persons and communities. This was a case of a cultural response to sin expressed as defilement going unrecognized by a theologian who was ostensibly writing on behalf of those stigmatized in this cultural enactment.

Bonhoeffer's oversight was closely related to his unquestioned acceptance of the notion of essential Jewish difference. While he rejected biological explanations of this difference, he was entirely caught up in Christian anti-Semitism, which did not allow him to see that the theological significance that he attributed to the distinctiveness of "Israel before God" was every bit as essentializing as claims rooted in genealogy. In order to accomplish the type of intervention he desired, he would have had to (1) recognize the absolutely defiling way in which Jewish difference was being mediated in his context, and (2) challenge the notion of Jewish difference in any form in which it could be essentialized. Because he did not do this, he trapped himself in the same anti-Semitic language loop that the Nazi regime was using as currency for its project, and legitimated the notion of essential Jewish difference.

The difficulties that I identified in the works of Plantinga, Niebuhr, and Bonhoeffer raised the question of whether sin-talk that emerges from a Protestant trajectory necessarily privileges discursive economies produced by the centers of social, economic, and political power and is thus unable to address social sin adequately. While there may exist a propensity within the tradition to privilege these discursive economies, it is not inevitable, which becomes apparent in my interpretation of Augustine, Martin Luther, and John Calvin. As a way to confirm this assessment, I identified two specific resources in the Augustinian tradition on sin that counter the co-option of Christian sin-talk by destructive discursive economies.

The first resource was the concept of participation. Here I interpreted Augustine, Luther, and Calvin, whose assertion of our participation in Adam as analogous to our being saved in Christ does not allow the problematic practices in the works of Plantinga, Niebuhr, and Bonhoeffer. The first of these practices is any mediation of sin that discursively creates unique conditions of sin beyond the general human condition of sin. A discourse of participation precludes the establishment of a hierarchy of sinners by emphasizing our "equality in sinfulness" in the eyes of God. The second practice is any interpretation of sin that validates an essentialized difference related to or emanating from sin, whether this difference is mediated in biological or cultural terms. Maintaining awareness of this concept of participation subverts the functioning of the discursive economies that reiterate social marginalization through, or explain it by appeals to, essentialized difference.

The principle of participation serves also to remind us of the essential unity of all humanity—first in Adam and now in Christ. This reminder subverts what is perhaps the most destructive outcome of social sin and problematic sin-talk: denying the humanity of marginalized persons. Also, this principle effectively challenges, and, one hopes, overthrows, the long-standing practice of rationalizing oppression, exclusion, and eradication by appeals to the aberrant humanity we assign to our enemies.

The second resource that I found in the Protestant tradition was its insistence on recognizing the overesteem that humanity has for its own moral capacities. This reminder cuts against the propensity of theologians to believe blithely that there is a point of objectivity from which they can assess the full contours of social sin at work. It makes plain the reality that our sin-talk is corrupted by the sin that is at work in our social context—whatever its character may be. Cognizance of this reality may persuade theologians that responsible reflection requires more than a perusal of the headlines. Responsible reflection requires that we interrogate the cultural common senses, ideas, and beliefs at work in our contexts, and assess the material relations of power that underlie them.

Before naming the discrete practices that can help to redeem Christian sin-talk to be prophetic proclamation in the public square, let me reiterate the importance of this project. I have spent the previous chapters describing the conceptual difficulties present in much contemporary social sin-talk. Let me again call attention to the conviction that underlies this entire work: wrongheaded sin-talk deployed in the public square has destructive effects on the lives of flesh-and-blood human beings.

Recall my presentation [earlier in the book] about how sin-talk was used in the recent welfare debates. For a moment, let us ask what is really at stake in this social debate and the consequences of sin-talk gone askew. First, let us be clear: Christian moralizing played a significant role in the unfolding of that debate. Sin-talk was, and is, implicated in these discussions—more often than not, in an unhelpful way. Notwithstanding the fact that commentators like [Lawrence] Mead focus almost all of their attention on the behavior of adults, the primary beneficiaries of welfare (or Aid to Families with Dependent Children, as it was once known) are the most vulnerable people in our society—poor children. These are the ones who suffer most when draconian measures are taken to teach "moral turpitude" and the "work ethic" to poor adults. From my experience in working with the socially and economically vulnerable (I directed an inner-city crisis intervention program for three years), I know that many families are never more than a hairsbreadth away from hunger and a day or two from homelessness. I also know that each worry-fraught mother has a name, and each hungry child a face. These human dimensions are erased by discursive representation: the *welfare queen* and her scion. That erasure makes it possible for nonsense like Mead's suggestion that the poor accept the system that maintains their poverty as something "fine as gold" to seem something more altruistic than the callous, classist condescension that it is. One wonders whether a hungry child or a homeless family would qualify as "the least of these" for moralists like Mead.

While this example is focused on a recent debate, the issues I raise with it are perennial ones facing human society. The distribution of resources, the claim that persons have on the wealth of their society, and the extent to which segments of the population can be cast aside are quandaries as old as human society itself. So also are the questions that face Christians within these societies: Where do we look for sin in our social setting? How do we name it? What kind of difference should our sin-talk make?

What I hope to do with this example, and the others used throughout the book, is to show how knee-jerk agreement by Christians with the cultural assignment of others to a liminal space of marginalization is finally nothing more than baptizing oppression in their contexts. Further, I am trying to illustrate the way that this unreflective agreement leads to a callousness of spirit that deadens the sense of empathy and compassion for the weak. I define callousness of spirit as the rationalization of human suffering in a way that either ignores or furthers the suffering of others. This callousness often evidences itself in the relegation of those who suffer to the inescapable identity of sinner. So, whether it is the person whose body and life are wasting away because of HIV/AIDS, or the child who is doomed to a life of poor education and want, or the "urban tough" whose life expectancy is twenty-five years, the response is always the same: "Repent sinner! Repent!" And when the reply to this call to repentance is: "And still we are not saved!" The return reply? "Repent sinner! Repent!"

Could *the Jew* have repented in Nazi Germany and been saved from the camps? Could *the Negro* have repented and been saved from Jim Crow? Can the malnourished child of the *welfare queen* repent and be saved from hunger tonight? The answer to these questions should be clear: No. Because there is no repentance possible for those who are essentialized into a social margin not of their own making. These margins are by definition inescapable cultural representations that doom their supposed flesh-and-blood referents to the margins of society.

There is a type of repentance, however, that is possible in these situations. The opportunity for repentance is available to all Christian theologians, pastors, and laypeople who have allowed their sincere concern about social sin to be co-opted and corrupted by systems of oppression and marginalization. Substantially, this repentance takes the form of receiving those who are despised and marginalized by the type of cultural depictions we have seen and challenging the systems that have so stigmatized them. This repentance does not mean remaining silent about sin in its social dimension. Rather, it means taking a new type of care in the way we talk about and exemplify sin in our particular context. This type of repentance will go far to address the sins of sin-talk. What follows is a way to begin that journey of repentance.

Rules of Engagement: Constructive Approaches to Sin-Talk
Beyond identifying problematic practices in the sin-talk of some important theologians, I wish to make some positive intervention into the practices of Protestant theologians who write about social sin. Thus far I have only sounded cautionary notes about the dangers that await theologians who attempt to write about social sin without adequately appreciating the discursive economies at work in their contexts. At this point I want to offer constructive comments about appropriate discourse about social sin using the resources that I have identified in the Protestant tradition. Since I have been most concerned about the relationship between discursive economies and the unexamined rhetoric of sin-talk, I will offer my interventions as grammatical and analytic rules of engagement.

Rule 1: Do Not Seek Only Your Own Privilege
The substance of much of my critique of contemporary Protestant sin-talk is that it has not taken seriously enough its tendency to participate in social marginalization. A significant piece of this critique is that theologians in their sin-talk rarely marginalize themselves or their own communities. It is more often the case that they marginalize "others." What goes unspoken is usually this: In their discursive acts that marginalize others, theologians are simultaneously privileging themselves and their communities. It is important to notice this dual character of marginalizing discourse, because it highlights the self-interest that may be involved in our discussions of social sin. This recognition also highlights the validity of the second resource that I drew from the Protestant tradition: Our reflections are never wholly untainted by the sin of our own self-interest.

This rule of engagement points to the reality that the theological formulations of sin-talk that we are most comfortable with are those that render our ecclesial, economic, social positions and perspectives normative. As we saw in Plantinga's work, the more egregious "sinners" we identify in our sin-talk are usually persons and communities whom we had little affinity for in the first place. More often than not, these "sinners" have also been tagged as aberrant by the general customs of society. So, our sin-talk not only reinforces our privilege, but the very structure of society that allows us to hold that privilege. If, as a result of our sin-talk, we and our communities are rendered normative and privileged in relation to others, it is a clear indication that we are perpetuating social sin. We know that we are in trouble when our sin-talk violates the principle of participation by fundamentally denying our mutuality with others in sin and redemption.

Let me make a point about privilege—it is relative! There is no community, no matter what its particular social or economic position, that is safe from the danger of reflecting on sin in a way that profoundly marginalizes others. As has been observed by a number of theologians such as Jacquelyn Grant and [Elizabeth] Johnson, even the oppressed can oppress.[5] A noteworthy example of this is the continuing homophobia of the Evangelical African American churches (the Black Church). Here we have a case of members of a community using the very types of biblical interpretation and theological reflection on sin as a tool of oppression that were used against them not many years ago.[6] No one is immune, as Augustine and the reformers reminded us earlier, from talking about the sin of others in a way that minimizes the reality of one's own sin.

Rule 2: Follow the Money: Who Gets Paid?

This second rule is also concerned with the material relationships that are affected by particular theological formulations of sin. By seeking to identify how some enactments of sin-talk direct privilege in certain ways, we are explicitly recognizing that our sin-talk is somehow corrupted by our own implication in sinful systems. Every theologian who writes about sin is prone to some aspect of the sins of sin-talk. What I am contending is not that we can never get it quite right, but that, with care, we might not get it so wrong. It was this lack of care that I critiqued in Plantinga, Niebuhr, and Bonhoeffer.

If the first rule compels us to ask how our sin-talk serves our own self-interest, then this rule admonishes us to ask how others' sin-talk works to their advantage in their context. These two rules invite us to a dialectical posture of humility and suspicion that will not allow us blindly to accept or promulgate enactments of sin-talk that harm other persons and communities. This posture can encourage enough contextual attentiveness to engender more careful language, helping theologians minimize any harmful elements in their sin-talk.

---

5. Jacquelyn Grant, *White Woman's Christ and Black Woman's Jesus: Feminist Christology and Womanist Response* (Atlanta: Scholars, 1989), chap. 7; Elizabeth A. Johnson, *She Who Is: The Mystery of God in Feminist Theological Discourse* (New York: Crossroad, 1992), 28.

6. Gary David Comstock has collected a number of essays by preachers and theologians about the issue of the Black Church and gays and lesbians in a helpful volume titled *A Whosoever Church: Welcoming Lesbians and Gay Men into African American Congregations* (Louisville, KY: Westminster John Knox Press, 2001).

Rule 3: Physician, Heal Yourself!

This rule deals with how the answers to the questions raised by the first two rules might be made meaningful in particular contexts by addressing the actual cultural significations attached to the images, figures, and metaphors we use in our sin-talk. It counsels that we need to ascertain the specific discursive economies at work in our sin-talk. Because the categories that we use to talk about social sin are deeply implicated in the material relations of power in our contexts, we must gain as much clarity as possible about the sensibilities, common sense, and beliefs that are most immediate to us.

Starting from the posture suggested by the first two rules, it is incumbent upon us to ask very definite questions about our contexts. So, using myself as an example, it is important to recognize that I inhabit, minimally, four positions of privilege—I am a male in a largely patriarchal society; I am a first-world resident in a world that has drastic inequities of wealth; I am middle-class in a society that esteems wealth as a sign of God's grace; and I am "straight" in a heterosexist society. The consequence of recognizing these positions of privilege is that I should be keenly aware of the discursive economies that are at work in each of these situations but that may be largely invisible to me given my particular privilege. Thus, if I, as a heterosexual man, were writing about the supposed sinfulness of the "gay lifestyle," I should first ask: Is there any way to be gay and not be a "sinner" in the social or religious context that I inhabit? In other words, is the social identity labeled "gay" rendered in a totally negative way in my context? Based on the terms of "normative" sexuality is it possible, according to common sense, to be at once gay and a faithful Christian? If it is not, why? These types of questions will lead to the sort of material and cultural analysis that may enable me to write about sin in a way that does not immediately reproduce marginalization in my context.

Rule 4: Listen to the "Sinner"

The preceding rules leave out one element of careful sin-talk. What is missing, of course, is the type of engagement that will give us sensitivity to the features of our contexts that reflection in solitude can never do. It is imperative that we incorporate the perspectives of marginalized persons in our sin-talk. With this rule I make explicit use of a methodological move I first suggested [earlier in the book]—integrating the testimony of those deemed "sinners" by popular renderings of sin-talk.

This rule also admonishes us to take context and privilege seriously. By recognizing that I cannot engage in sin-talk concerning persons who do not hold a similar privilege to mine without importing discursive economies that undergird that power differential, I should demonstrate an enhanced appreciation of the testimony given by persons who are marginalized in my work. Privilege should be given to the testimony of those persons who bear the brunt of social sin in a given context. That is to say, we must explicitly recognize that materially excluded or culturally disdained persons and communities are in a far better position to describe how social sin is working in that context than persons who are culturally empowered. By methodologically giving this privilege to the testimony of oppressed persons and communities, we significantly enhance the value of our sin-talk. We accomplish an expansion of our vision—the workings of social sin that may be invisible to us are exposed in a way that simple reflection could not attain. Also, this exposure increases the chance that our work will be in solidarity with "the least of these" in any given circumstance.

The Final Statement: Do No Harm!

The interventions that I have outlined above reflect a consequentialist approach to sin-talk. . . . [I]t is the absence of this concern about consequences that lies behind many of the failures of sin-talk discussed in this book. *Do No Harm* provides the beginning of a method that can help theologians be attentive not only to the ways our sin-talk rearticulates and legitimizes structures of social sin, but also to the consequences of those works. This is a necessary task because our sin-talk should intervene in situations that deny the full humanity of any class or group of persons. Our sin-talk should take seriously its capacity to be a restorative discourse—restoring the humanity of those on the margins of society in public and theological discourse. So, far from being the venue through which marginalization is reiterated, the purpose of our sin-talk should be to challenge and dismantle the discursive economies that participate in and enable marginalization to occur in the first place. Active concern for the way that our sin-talk intervenes in particular cultural contexts can go a long way toward avoiding having our work co-opted by systems of marginalization and exclusion. In the end, a consequentialist approach to sin-talk affirms our conviction that the way we talk about sin in its social dimension matters. It matters because persons hurt by social sin matter.

SELECTION **15**

Rowan Williams

"Against Symbols"

Rowan Williams (1950–), Archbishop of Canterbury and leader of the worldwide Anglican communion, is widely respected as one of the leading theologians of the English-speaking world. He also happened to be at Trinity Church, Wall Street, on the morning of September 11, 2001, and was thus an eyewitness to what for many has come to be the defining symbol of evil for the twenty-first century: the terrorist attacks on the twin towers of the World Trade Center. Williams's reflections on that experience in the following essay are a caution against the ways the language we use to talk about evil all too easily become iconic. He argues that our natural proclivity to invest events with symbolic significance tempts us to give suffering meaning (whether positive or negative) in a way that encourages its use in service of ideology. He concludes that we do well to resist this temptation, on the grounds that the refusal of consoling interpretations both honors the ultimate inexplicability of evil and also opens us to the possibility of a grief that moves beyond the interests of our own group to include the pain of others as well.

>From Rowan Williams, *Writing in the Dust: After September 11*
(Grand Rapids: Wm. B. Eerdmans Publishing Co., 2002), 61–74.

Recognizing common experience is the exact opposite of using someone else to fit with your agenda, using them to play out roles you have worked out and assigned. We have been very resourceful in this over the centuries. Christians have conscripted Jews into their version of reality and forced them into a role that has nothing to do with how Jews understand their own past or current experience—what one scholar called "using Jews to think with." In the Middle Ages, Muslims too were made to play a part in the drama written by Christians, as a kind of diabolical mirror image of Christian identity, worshipping a trinity of ridiculous idols. This was a distortion nurtured by popular religion, of course; responsible theologians studied the Qur'an and knew better. But those very writers who were so careful not to parody Islam were also capable of calmly and authoritatively writing nonsense about women; it would not have occurred to them that there was a Christian principle involved in listening to what women had to say about themselves.

And yes, of course, Jews and Muslims cherished equally bizarre beliefs about Christianity at times. They, like us, needed to assert some kind of control over the stranger, the other, by "writing them in" in terms that could be managed and manipulated. What happens is that the stranger is assigned a meaning, a value, in the dominant system. When, as with Christians and Jews in Europe, this is allied to a hugely disproportionate distribution of power, the effects are dreadful.

"Using other people to think with"; that is, using them as symbols for points on your map, values in your scheme of things. When you get used to imposing meanings in this way, you silence the stranger's account of who they are; and that can mean both metaphorical and literal death. Death as the undermining of a culture, language, or faith, and, at the extreme, the death of tyranny and genocide. I have been using religious examples, but it isn't essentially a failing of religion itself. The collective imagination needs the outsider to give itself definition—which commonly means that it needs somewhere to project its own fears and tensions. The history of modern Europe's attitudes to the non-Western world, the history of what has come to be called "Orientalism," the imagining of the East as a mysterious opposite to the West, both devilish and subtly attractive, spells this out clearly.

Living realities are turned into symbols, and the symbolic values are used to imprison the reality. At its extreme pitch, people simply relate to the symbols. It is too hard to look past them, to look into the complex humanity of a real other. The World Trade Center and the Pentagon were massively obvious symbols of American dominance, economic and military. To target them was clearly a blow against that entire system of dominance. The trouble is that, while burning the Stars and Stripes in a demonstration is one thing, the Twin Towers and the Pentagon were inhabited buildings; they may have been "natural" symbols, but the people in them were not (people never are). It is a point that was missed even by some commentators who wrote as if the Trade Center were entirely full of prosperous bond traders and the Pentagon full of military strategists. It's easy to forget cleaners and maintenance staff, the anonymous and necessary background for large enterprises like these, many of them people of uncertain civic status (how many illegal immigrants died on September 11th? We are not going to know because they had no official existence)—the Third World on the doorstep of Manhattan and Washington.

But even if the buildings had been full of professionals working for American domination, not even then could we say that these people could be reduced to symbols: they had families, hobbies, a "hinterland" of human life not consumed in professional identities. It is always people who suffer and are killed, not symbols. When we strike out at a symbol such as a flag, we hurt nothing except perhaps the self-esteem of those who use the language of which it's a part. When we decide to treat people as symbols, the story is different.

But the effect of this symbolic outrage against the tokens of dominance has been to populate our own world with more symbols. The Muslim world is now experiencing—as it has for some time, but now with so much more intensity—that "conscription" into someone else's story which once characterized the Church's attitude to Jews. And individual "strangers" in the UK and USA (including people born and raised in these countries) who are recognizable by speech, pigmentation, dress, or whatever are discovering what it is like to be loaded with meanings by the majority around them, to be forced into the role of "potential terrorist." Muslim mothers with small children are attacked or insulted in the streets; Sikhs are abused as Muslims (i.e., enemies) because anyone in a turban is a terrorist. Some have already been killed. And on the other side of the world, it is not only flags that are being burned; presumably the Christians massacred in Pakistan in October [2001] were seen as "signs" of Western (i.e., American) presence and power.

So the drama continues, both sides engaging in the same terrible simplifications, striking against symbols that have closed around the flesh and history of human beings. And the whole process of turning people into symbols in this murderous way has its roots in our shared inability to face the fact, already mentioned, of division, failure, and ambiguity within our systems. There is, I've said, a certain relief in being able to point to a clear outside agency responsible for terror (we should not forget the assumption instantly made after the Oklahoma bombing that it was the work of Muslim extremists). But there are a good many Muslims who will also admit that the USA is equally a convenient scapegoat for the political dysfunctionalism of much of the Islamic world today, an excuse for not addressing the internal problems of some despotic and corrupt regimes.

Once the concreteness of another's suffering has registered, you cannot simply use them to think with. You have to be patient with the meanings that the other is struggling to find or form for themselves. Acknowledging the experience you share is the only thing that opens up the possibility of finding a meaning that can be shared, a language to speak together.

I'm not sure, but perhaps this is something of what some of our familiar Christian texts and stories point us towards. In the ninth chapter of the Gospel of John, Jesus encounters a man blind from birth, and his disciples encourage him to speculate on why he should suffer in this way: who is being punished, this man or his parents? They are inviting Jesus to impose a meaning on someone's suffering within a calculus that assumes a neat relation between suffering and guilt.

Jesus declines; guilt is irrelevant, and all that can be said is that this blindness is an opportunity for God's glory to become manifest. The meaning is not in the system being operated by the disciples, but in the unknown future where healing will occur. As the story proceeds, we see how the fact of healing becomes a problem in turn, because it does not fit into the available categories; it has been performed by an outsider, a suspected heretic. The blind man is again faced with people, this time the religious authorities, who want him to accept a meaning imposed by others, and he resists. It is this resistance, which proves costly for him, that brings him finally to faith. What should strike us is Jesus' initial refusal to make the blind man's condition a proof of anything—divine justice or injustice, human sin or innocence. We who call ourselves Christian have every reason to say no to any system at all that uses suffering to prove things: to prove the sufferer's guilt as a sinner being punished, or—perhaps more frequently in our world—to prove the sufferer's innocence as a martyr whose heroism must never be forgotten or betrayed. If this man's condition is to have a symbolic value—and in some sense it clearly does in the text—it is as the place where a communication from God occurs—the opening up of something that is not part of the competing systems operated by human beings.

I want to say that it is only here, with the renunciation of all our various ways of making suffering a weapon or a tool of ideology, that we are going to learn how to grieve properly. Of course, we just grieve anyway, "properly" or not; but where does our grief take us? And what do we mourn for? If, as St Augustine says in his *Confessions*, we can fail to "love humanly," then surely we can also fail to grieve humanly, to grieve without the consolation of drama, martyrdom, resentment, and projection. Are there words for grief that can make us more human, so that we mourn, not just for ourselves but for those whose experience we have come to share, even for those whose moral poverty is responsible for murder and terror?

What use is faith to us if it is only a transcription into mythological jargon of the mechanisms of that inhuman grief that grasps its own suffering to itself as a ground of justification and encloses the suffering of others in interpretations that hold it at a safe distance?

And Christian faith? Can we think about our focal symbol, the cross of Jesus, and try to rescue it from its frequent fate as the banner of our own wounded righteousness? If Jesus is indeed what God communicates to us, God's language for us, his cross is always both ours and not ours; not a magnified sign of our own suffering, but the mark of God's work in and through the deepest vulnerability; not a martyr's triumphant achievement, but something that is there for all human sufferers because it belongs to no human cause. Breathing spaces again: if the cross is what we say it is, it requires that kind of hesitation, that kind of silence.

CHAPTER 4
Providence

SELECTION **1**

Irenaeus of Lyons

Against Heresies, Book 3

Irenaeus's idea of providence is strongly bound up with his concern to preserve the unity both of the Old and New Testaments and of the God to which they bear witness over against a Gnostic hermeneutic that would drive a wedge between the God of Israel and the God of Jesus Christ. Correspondingly, his discussion of God's direction of history in the following excerpt from book 3 of *Against Heresies* is strongly shaped by typological interpretation of Scripture, according to which the stories of Old Testament figures like Jonah are understood to foreshadow the destiny of humankind as a whole and thereby illustrate the fundamental unity and cohesion of God's saving work across both testaments.

In addition to making this hermeneutical point, however, Irenaeus is also interested in the purposes behind God's way of bringing humankind to salvation. As noted earlier, Irenaeus believes that human beings benefit from having been made to grow toward perfection through time, and this same pedagogical perspective shapes his discussion of providence. The fact that salvation comes by way of the long path of biblical history has the effect of awakening in human beings a vivid awareness of their incapacity to secure their well-being on their own and a correspondingly profound appreciation for God's graciousness in taking flesh. In this way, Irenaeus's doctrine of providence takes the form of a meditation on the beauty and fittingness of God's ways with humankind rather than more abstract reflection on the extent of God's power over creation.

From *The Apostolic Fathers with Justin Martyr and Irenaeus*, ANF 1:449–51.

Chapter 20

1. Long-suffering therefore was God, when man became a defaulter, as foreseeing that victory which should be granted to him through the Word. For, when strength was made perfect in weakness [2 Cor. 12:9], it showed the kindness and transcendent power of God. For as He patiently suffered Jonah to be swallowed by the whale, not that he should be swallowed up and perish altogether, but that, having been cast out again, he might be the more subject to God, and might glorify Him the more who had conferred upon him such an unhoped-for deliverance, and might bring the Ninevites to a lasting repentance, so that they should be convened to the Lord who would deliver them from death, having been struck with awe by that portent which had been wrought in Jonah's case, as the Scripture says of them, "And they returned each from his evil way, and the unrighteousness

which was in their hands, saying, Who knoweth if God will repent, and turn away His anger from us, and we shall not perish?" [Jon. 3:8–9]—so also, from the beginning, did God permit man to be swallowed up by the great whale, who was the author of transgression, not that he should perish altogether when so engulfed; but, arranging and preparing the plan of salvation, which was accomplished by the Word, through the sign of Jonah, for those who held the same opinion as Jonah regarding the Lord, and who confessed and said, "I am a servant of the Lord, and I worship the Lord God of heaven, who hath made the sea and the dry land" [Jon. 1:9]. [This was done] that man, receiving an unhoped-for salvation from God, might rise from the dead, and glorify God, and repeat that word which was uttered in prophecy by Jonah: "I cried by reason of mine affliction to the Lord my God, and He heard me out of the belly of hell" [Jon. 2:2]; and that he might always continue glorifying God, and giving thanks without ceasing for that salvation which he has derived from Him, "that no flesh should glory in the Lord's presence" [1 Cor. 1:29]; and that man should never adopt an opposite opinion with regard to God, supposing that the incorruptibility which belongs to him is his own naturally, and by thus not holding the truth, should boast with empty superciliousness, as if he were naturally like to God. For he [Satan] thus rendered him [man] more ungrateful towards his Creator, obscured the love which God had towards man, and blinded his mind not to perceive what is worthy of God, comparing himself with, and judging himself equal to, God.

2. This, therefore, was the [object of the] long-suffering of God, that man, passing through all things, and acquiring the knowledge of moral discipline, then attaining to the resurrection from the dead, and learning by experience what is the source of his deliverance, may always live in a state of gratitude to the Lord, having obtained from Him the gift of incorruptibility, that he might love Him the more; for "he to whom more is forgiven, loveth more" [Luke 7:43]: and that he may know himself, how mortal and weak he is; while he also understands respecting God, that He is immortal and powerful to such a degree as to confer immortality upon what is mortal, and eternity upon what is temporal; and may understand also the other attributes of God displayed towards himself, by means of which being instructed he may think of God in accordance with the divine greatness. For the glory of man [is] God, but [His] works [are the glory] of God; and the receptacle of all His wisdom and power [is] man. Just as the physician is proved by his patients, so is God also revealed through men. And therefore Paul declares, "For God hath concluded all in unbelief, that He may have mercy upon all" [Rom. 11:32]; not saying this in reference to spiritual Aeons, but to man, who had been disobedient to God, and being cast off from immortality, then obtained mercy, receiving through the Son of God that adoption which is [accomplished] by Himself. For he who holds, without pride and boasting, the true opinion regarding cre-

ated things and the Creator, who is the Almighty God of all, and who has granted existence to all; [such a one,] continuing in His love [John 15:9] and subjection and thanksgiving, shall also receive from Him the greater glory of promotion, looking forward to the time when he shall become like Him who died for him, for He, too, "was made in the likeness of sinful flesh" [Rom. 8:3], to condemn sin, and to cast it, as now a condemned thing, away beyond the flesh, but that He might call man forth into His own likeness, assigning him as [His own] imitator to God, and imposing on him His Father's law, in order that he may see God, and granting him power to receive the Father; [being] the Word of God who dwelt in man, and became the Son of man, that He might accustom man to receive God, and God to dwell in man, according to the good pleasure of the Father.

3. On this account, therefore, the Lord Himself, who is Emmanuel from the Virgin, is the sign of our salvation, since it was the Lord Himself who saved them, because they could not be saved by their own instrumentality; and, therefore, when Paul sets forth human infirmity, he says: "For I know that there dwelleth in my flesh no good thing" [Rom. 7:18], showing that the "good thing" of our salvation is not from us, but from God. And again: "Wretched man that I am, who shall deliver me from the body of this death?" [Rom. 7:24]. Then he introduces the Deliverer, [saying,] "The grace of Jesus Christ our Lord." And Isaiah declares this also, [when he says:] "Be ye strengthened, ye hands that hang down, and ye feeble knees; be ye encouraged, ye feeble-minded; be comforted, fear not: behold, our God has given judgment with retribution, and shall recompense: He will come Himself, and will save us" [Isa. 25:3]. Here we see, that not by ourselves, but by the help of God, we must be saved.

4. Again, that it should not be a mere man who should save us, nor [one] without flesh—for the angels are without flesh—[the same prophet] announced, saying: "Neither an elder, nor angel, but the Lord Himself will save them because He loves them, and will spare them. He will Himself set them free" [Isa. 63:9]. And that He should Himself become very man, visible, when He should be the Word giving salvation, Isaiah again says: "Behold, city of Zion: thine eyes shall see our salvation" [Isa. 33:20]. And that it was not a mere man who died for us, Isaiah says: "And the holy Lord remembered His dead Israel, who had slept in the land of sepulture; and He came down to preach His salvation to them, that He might save them" [see Justin Martyr, *Dialogue with Trypho*, ch. 72]. And Amos [Micah] the prophet declares the same: "He will turn again, and will have compassion upon us: He will destroy our iniquities, and will cast our sins into the depths of the sea [Mic. 7:9]. And again, specifying the place of His advent, he says: "The Lord hath spoken from Zion, and He has uttered His voice from Jerusalem" [Joel 3:16]. And that it is from that region which is towards the south of the inheritance of Judah that the Son of God shall come, who is God, and who was from Bethlehem, where the Lord was

born [and] will send out His praise through all the earth, thus says the prophet Habakkuk: "God shall come from the south, and the Holy One from Mount Ephraim. His power covered the heavens over, and the earth is full of His praise. Before His face shall go forth the Word, and His feet shall advance in the plains" [Hab. 3:3, 5]. Thus he indicates in clear terms that He is God, and that His advent was [to take place] in Bethlehem and from Mount Ephraim, which is towards the south of the inheritance, and that [He is] human. For he says, "His feet shall advance in the plains," and this is an indication proper to a human being.

SELECTION 2

Augustine of Hippo

On the Holy Trinity, Book 3

In the following selection from his treatise *On the Holy Trinity*, Augustine argues for the importance of decoupling God's providential government of the world from our own parochial views of what is or is not part of the natural order. Noting that things like eclipses, which appear extraordinary to the uneducated, are in fact governed by definite laws, he maintains that the Christian should view all happenings, however unusual they may seem, as the product of God's good creative will and thus, in their own sphere, as no less natural and well ordered than the changing of the seasons. Augustine thereby argues that all apparent novelty in creation is in fact subordinate to the overruling sovereignty of God, even where God arranges for more proximate causes to effect particular results in any given instance. Thus, in a series of reflections that are particularly arresting in light of modern theories of biological evolution, Augustine contends that God at the beginning planted "seeds" of novelty in the creation: though these would only be manifest at a later time under particular conditions, they were nonetheless part of God's intention for creation from the beginning.

From *Saint Augustin: On the Holy Trinity, Doctrinal Treatises, Moral Treatises*, NPNF[1] 3:57–63.

7. But there is one kind of natural order in the conversion and changeableness of bodies, which, although itself also serves the bidding of God, yet by reason of its unbroken continuity has ceased to cause wonder; as is the case, for instance, with those things which are changed either in very short, or at any rate not long, intervals of time, in heaven, or earth, or sea; whether it be in rising, or in setting, or in change of appearance from time to time; while there are other things, which, although arising from that same order, yet are less familiar on account of longer intervals of time. And

these things, although the many stupidly wonder at them, yet are understood by those who inquire into this present world, and in the progress of generations become so much the less wonderful, as they are the more often repeated and known by more people. Such are the eclipses of the sun and moon, and some kinds of stars, appearing seldom, and earthquakes, and unnatural births of living creatures, and other similar things; of which not one takes place without the will of God; yet, that it is so, is to most people not apparent. And so the vanity of philosophers has found license to assign these things also to other causes, true causes perhaps, but proximate ones, while they are not able to see at all the cause that is higher than all others, that is, the will of God; or again to false causes, and to such as are not even put forward out of any diligent investigation of corporeal things and motions, but from their own guess and error.

8. I will bring forward an example, if I can, that this may be plainer. There is, we know, in the human body, a certain bulk of flesh and an outward form, and an arrangement and distraction of limbs, and a temperament of health; and a soul breathed into it governs this body, and that soul a rational one; which, therefore, although changeable, yet can be partaker of that unchangeable wisdom, so that "it may partake of that which is in and of itself"; as it is written in the Psalm concerning all saints, of whom as of living stones is built that Jerusalem which is the mother of us all, eternal in the heavens. For so it is sung, "Jerusalem is builded as a city, that is partaker of that which is in and of itself" [Ps. 122:3, Vulg.]. For "in and of itself," in that place, is understood of that chiefest and unchangeable good, which is God, and of His own wisdom and will. To whom is sung in another place, "Thou shalt change them, and they shall be changed; but Thou art the same" [Ps. 102:26–27].

Let us take, then, the case of a wise man, such that his rational soul is already partaker of the unchangeable and eternal truth, so that he consults it about all his actions, nor does anything at all, which he does not by it know ought to be done, in order that by being subject to it and obeying it he may do rightly. Suppose now that this man, upon counsel with the highest reason of the divine righteousness, which he hears with the ear of his heart in secret, and by its bidding, should weary his body by toil in some office of mercy, and should contract an illness; and upon consulting the physicians, were to be told by one that the cause of the disease was overmuch dryness of the body, but by another that it was overmuch moisture; one of the two no doubt would allege the true cause and the other would err, but both would pronounce concerning proximate causes only, that is, corporeal ones. But if the cause of that dryness were to be inquired into, and found to be the self-imposed toil, then we should have come to a yet higher cause, which proceeds from the soul so as to affect the body which the soul governs. Yet neither would this be the first cause, for that doubtless was a higher cause still, and lay in the unchangeable wisdom itself, by serving which in love, and by obeying its ineffable commands, the soul of the wise man had undertaken that self-imposed toil; and so nothing else but the will of God would be found most truly to be the first cause of that illness. But suppose now in that office of pious toil this wise man had employed the help of others to cooperate in the good work, who did not serve God with the same will as himself, but either desired to attain the reward of their own carnal desires, or shunned merely carnal unpleasantnesses. Suppose, too, he had employed beasts of burden, if the completion of the work required such a provision, which beasts of burden would be certainly irrational animals, and would not therefore move their limbs under their burdens because they at all thought of that good work, but from the natural appetite of their own liking, and for the avoiding of annoyance. Suppose, lastly, he had employed bodily things themselves that lack all sense, but were necessary for that work, as, for example, corn, and wine, and oils, clothes, or money, or a book, or anything of the kind. Certainly, in all these bodily things thus employed in this work, whether animate or inanimate, whatever took place of movement, of wear and tear, of reparation, of destruction, of renewal or of change in one way or another, as places and times affected them. Now I ask, could there be any other cause of all these visible and changeable facts, except the invisible and unchangeable will of God, using all these, both bad and irrational souls, and lastly bodies, whether such as were inspired and animated by those souls, or such as lacked all sense, by means of that upright soul as the seat of His wisdom, since primarily that good and holy soul itself employed them, which His wisdom had subjected to itself in a pious and religious obedience?

9. What, then, we have alleged by way of example of a single wise man, although of one still bearing a mortal body and still seeing only in part, may be allowably extended also to a family, where there is a society of such men, or to a city, or even to the whole world, if the chief rule and government of human affairs were in the hands of the wise, and of those who were piously and perfectly subject to God; but because this is not the case as yet (for it behooves us first to be exercised in this our pilgrimage after mortal fashion, and to be taught with stripes by force of gentleness and patience), let us turn our thoughts to that country itself that is above and heavenly, from which we here are pilgrims. For there the will of God, "who maketh His angels spirits, and His ministers a flaming fire" [Ps. 104:4], presiding among spirits which are joined in perfect peace and friendship, and combined in one will by a kind of spiritual fire of charity, as it were in an elevated and holy and secret seat, as in its own house and in its own temple, thence diffuses itself through all things by certain most perfectly ordered movements of the creature first spiritual, then corporeal; and uses all according to the unchangeable pleasure of its own purpose, whether incorporeal things or things corporeal, whether rational or irrational spirits, whether good by His grace or evil through their own will. But as the

most gross and inferior bodies are governed in due order by the more subtle and powerful ones, so all bodies are governed by the living spirit; and the living spirit devoid of reason, by the reasonable living spirit; and the reasonable living spirit that makes default and sins, by the living and reasonable spirit that is pious and just; and that by God Himself, and so the universal creature by its Creator, from whom and through whom and in whom it is also created and established [Col. 1:16]. And so it comes to pass that the will of God is the first and the highest cause of all corporeal appearances and motions. For nothing is done visibly or sensibly, unless either by command or permission from the interior palace, invisible and intelligible, of the supreme Governor, according to the unspeakable justice of rewards and punishments, of favor and retribution, in that far-reaching and boundless commonwealth of the whole creature.

10. If, therefore, the Apostle Paul, although he still bare the burden of the body, which is subject to corruption and presseth down the soul [Wis. 9:15], and although he still saw only in part and in an enigma [1 Cor. 13:12], wishing to depart and be with Christ [Phil. 1:23], and groaning within himself, waiting for the adoption, to wit, the redemption of his body [Rom. 8:23], yet was able to preach the Lord Jesus Christ significantly, in one way by his tongue, in another by epistle, in another by the sacrament of His body and blood (since, certainly, we do not call either the tongue of the apostle, or the parchments, or the ink, or the significant sounds which his tongue uttered, or the alphabetical signs written on skins, the body and blood of Christ; but that only which we take of the fruits of the earth and consecrate by mystic prayer, and then receive duly to our spiritual health in memory of the passion of our Lord for us: and this, although it is brought by the hands of men to that visible form, yet is not sanctified to become so great a sacrament, except by the spirit of God working invisibly; since God works everything that is done in that work through corporeal movements, by setting in motion primarily the invisible things of His servants, whether the souls of men, or the services of hidden spirits subject to Himself): what wonder if also in the creature of heaven and earth, of sea and air, God works the sensible and visible things which He wills, in order to signify and manifest Himself in them, as He Himself knows it to be fitting, without any appearing of His very substance itself, whereby He is, which is altogether unchangeable, and more inwardly and secretly exalted than all spirits whom He has created?

11. For since the divine power administers the whole spiritual and corporeal creature, the waters of the sea are summoned and poured out upon the face of the earth on certain days of every year. But when this was done at the prayer of the holy Elijah; because so continued and long a course of fair weather had gone before, that men were famished; and because at that very hour, in which the servant of God prayed, the air itself had not, by any moist aspect, put forth signs of the coming rain; the divine power was

apparent in the great and rapid showers that followed, and by which that miracle was granted and dispensed [1 Kgs. 18:45]. In like manner, God works ordinarily through thunders and lightnings: but because these were wrought in an unusual manner on Mount Sinai, and those sounds were not uttered with a confused noise, but so that it appeared by most sure proofs that certain intimations were given by them, they were miracles [Exod. 19:6]. Who draws up the sap through the root of the vine to the bunch of grapes, and makes the wine, except God; who, while man plants and waters, Himself giveth the increase [1 Cor. 3:7]? But when, at the command of the Lord, the water was turned into wine with an extraordinary quickness, the divine power was made manifest, by the confession even of the foolish [John 2:9]. Who ordinarily clothes the trees with leaves and flowers except God? Yet, when the rod of Aaron the priest blossomed, the Godhead in some way conversed with doubting humanity [Num. 17:8]. Again, the earthy matter certainly serves in common to the production and formation both of all kinds of wood and of the flesh of all animals: and who makes these things, but He who said, "Let the earth bring them forth" [Gen. 1:24]; and who governs and guides by the same word of His, those things which He has created? Yet, when He changed the same matter out of the rod of Moses into the flesh of a serpent, immediately and quickly, that change, which was unusual, although of a thing which was changeable, was a miracle [Exod. 4:3]. But who is it that gives life to every living thing at its birth, unless He who gave life to that serpent also for the moment, as there was need?

And who is it that restored to the corpses their proper souls when the dead rose again [Ezek. 37:1–10], unless He who gives life to the flesh in the mother's womb, in order that they may come into being who yet are to die? But when such things happen in a continuous kind of river of ever-flowing succession, passing from the hidden to the visible, and from the visible to the hidden, by a regular and beaten track, then they are called natural; when, for the admonition of men, they are thrust in by an unusual changeableness, then they are called miracles.

12. I see here what may occur to a weak judgment, namely, why such miracles are wrought also by magic arts; for the wise men of Pharaoh likewise made serpents, and did other like things. Yet it is still more a matter of wonder, how it was that the power of those magicians, which was able to make serpents, when it came to very small flies, failed altogether. For the lice, by which third plague the proud people of Egypt were smitten, are very short-lived little flies; yet there certainly the magicians failed, saying, "This is the finger of God" [Exod. 7:12; 8:7, 18–19]. And hence it is given us to understand that not even those angels and powers of the air that transgressed, who have been thrust down into that lowest darkness, as into a peculiar prison, from their habitation in that lofty ethereal purity, through whom magic arts have whatever power they have, can do any-

thing except by power given from above. Now that power is given either to deceive the deceitful, as it was given against the Egyptians, and against the magicians also themselves, in order that in the seducing of those spirits they might seem admirable by whom they were wrought, but to be condemned by the truth of God; or for the admonishing of the faithful, lest they should desire to do anything of the kind as though it were a great thing, for which reason they have been handed down to us also by the authority of Scripture; or lastly, for the exercising, proving, and manifesting of the patience of the righteous. For it was not by any small power of visible miracles that Job lost all that he had, and both his children and his bodily health itself [Job 1–2].

13. Yet it is not on this account to be thought that the matter of visible things is subservient to the bidding of those wicked angels; but rather to that of God, by whom this power is given, just so far as He, who is unchangeable, determines in His lofty and spiritual abode to give it. For water and fire and earth are subservient even to wicked men, who are condemned to the mines, in order that they may do therewith what they will, but only so far as is permitted. Nor, in truth, are those evil angels to be called creators, because by their means the magicians, withstanding the servant of God, made frogs and serpents; for it was not they who created them. But, in truth, some hidden seeds of all things that are born corporeally and visibly, are concealed in the corporeal elements of this world. For those seeds that are visible now to our eyes from fruits and living things, are quite distinct from the hidden seeds of those former seeds; from which, at the bidding of the Creator, the water produced the first swimming creatures and fowl, and the earth the first buds after their kind, and the first living creatures after their kind [Gen. 1:20–25]. For neither at that time were those seeds so drawn forth into products of their several kinds, as that the power of production was exhausted in those products; but oftentimes, suitable combinations of circumstances are wanting, whereby they may be enabled to burst forth and complete their species. For, consider, the very least shoot is a seed; for, if fitly consigned to the earth, it produces a tree. But of this shoot there is a yet more subtle seed in some grain of the same species, and this is visible even to us. But of this grain also there is further still a seed, which, although we are unable to see it with our eyes, yet we can conjecture its existence from our reason; because, except there were some such power in those elements, there would not so frequently be produced from the earth things which had not been sown there; nor yet so many animals, without any previous commixture of male and female; whether on the land, or in the water, which yet grow, and by commingling bring forth others, while themselves sprang up without any union of parents. And certainly bees do not conceive the seeds of their young by commixture, but gather them as they lie scattered over the earth with their mouth. For the Creator of these invisible seeds is the Creator of all things Himself; since whatever comes

forth to our sight by being born, receives the first beginnings of its course from hidden seeds, and takes the successive increments of its proper size and its distinctive forms from these as it were original rules. As therefore we do not call parents the creators of men, nor farmers the creators of corn, although it is by the outward application of their actions that the power of God operates within for the creating these things, so it is not right to think not only the bad but even the good angels to be creators, if, through the subtlety of their perception and body, they know the seeds of things which to us are more hidden, and scatter them secretly through fit temperings of the elements, and so furnish opportunities of producing things, and of accelerating their increase. But neither do the good angels do these things, except as far as God commands, nor do the evil ones do them wrongfully, except as far as He righteously permits. For the malignity of the wicked one makes his own will wrongful; but the power to do so, he receives rightfully, whether for his own punishment, or, in the case of others, for the punishment of the wicked, or for the praise of the good.

14. Accordingly, the Apostle Paul, distinguishing God's creating and forming within, from the operations of the creature which are applied from without, and drawing a similitude from agriculture, says, "I planted, Apollos watered; but God gave the increase" [1 Cor. 3:6]. As, therefore, in the case of spiritual life itself, no one except God can work righteousness in our minds, yet men also are able to preach the gospel as an outward means, not only the good in sincerity, but also the evil in pretence [Phil. 1:18]; so in the creation of visible things it is God that works from within; but the exterior operations, whether of good or bad, of angels or men, or even of any kind of animal, according to His own absolute power, and to the distribution of faculties, and the several appetites for things pleasant, which He Himself has imparted, are applied by Him to that nature of things wherein He creates all things, in like manner as agriculture is to the soil. Wherefore I can no more call the bad angels, evoked by magic arts, the creators of the frogs and serpents, than I can say that bad men were creators of the corn crop, which I see to have sprung up through their labor.

15. Just as Jacob, again, was not the creator of the colors in the flocks, because he placed the various colored rods for the several mothers, as they drank, to look at in conceiving [Gen. 30:41]. Yet neither were the cattle themselves creators of the variety of their own offspring, because the variegated image, impressed through their eyes by the sight of the varied rods, cleaved to their soul, but could affect the body that was animated by the spirit thus affected only through sympathy with this commingling, so far as to stain with color the tender beginnings of their offspring. For that they are so affected from themselves, whether the soul from the body, or the body from the soul, arises in truth from suitable reasons, which immutably exist in that highest wisdom of God Himself, which no extent of place contains; and which, while it is itself unchangeable, yet quits not one even

of those things which are changeable, because there is not one of them that is not created by itself. For it was the unchangeable and invisible reason of the wisdom of God, by which all things are created, which caused not rods, but cattle, to be born from cattle; but that the color of the cattle conceived should be in any degree influenced by the variety of the rods, came to pass through the soul of the pregnant cattle being affected through their eyes from without, and so according to its own measure drawing inwardly within itself the rule of formation, which it received from the innermost power of its own Creator. How great, however, may be the power of the soul in affecting and changing corporeal substance (although certainly it cannot be called the creator of the body, because every cause of changeable and sensible substance, and all its measure and number and weight, by which are brought to pass both its being at all and its being of such and such a nature, arise from the intelligible and unchangeable life, which is above all things, and which reaches even to the most distant and earthly things), is a very copious subject, and one not now necessary. But I thought the act of Jacob about the cattle should be noticed, for this reason, *viz.* in order that it might be perceived that, if the man who thus placed those rods cannot be called the creator of the colors in the lambs and kids; nor yet even the souls themselves of the mothers, which colored the seeds conceived in the flesh by the image of variegated color, conceived through the eyes of the body, so far as nature permitted it; much less can it be said that the creators of the frogs and serpents were the bad angel, through whom the magicians of Pharaoh then made them.

16. For it is one thing to make and administer the creature from the innermost and highest turning-point of causation, which He alone does who is God the Creator; but quite another thing to apply some operation from without in proportion to the strength and faculties assigned to each by Him, so that what is created may come forth into being at this time or at that, and in this or that way. For all these things in the way of original and beginning have already been created in a kind of texture of the elements, but they come forth when they get the opportunity. For as mothers are pregnant with young, so the world itself is pregnant with the causes of things that are born; which are not created in it, except from that highest essence, where nothing either springs up or dies, either begins to be or ceases. But the applying from without of adventitious causes, which, although they are not natural, yet are to be applied according to nature, in order that those things which are contained and hidden in the secret bosom of nature may break forth and be outwardly created in some way by the unfolding of the proper measures and numbers and weights which they have received in secret from Him "who has ordered all things in measure and number and weight" [Wis. 11:20]: this is not only in the power of bad angels, but also of bad men, as I have shown above by the example of agriculture.

17. But lest the somewhat different condition of animals should trouble any one, in that they have the breath of life with the sense of desiring those things that are according to nature, and of avoiding those things that are contrary to it; we must consider also, how many men there are who know from what herbs or flesh, or from what juices or liquids you please, of whatever sort, whether so placed or so buried, or so bruised or so mixed, this or that animal is commonly born; yet who can be so foolish as to dare to call himself the creator of these animals? Is it, therefore, to be wondered at, if just as any, the most worthless of men, can know whence such or such worms and flies are produced; so the evil angels in proportion to the subtlety of their perceptions discern in the more hidden seeds of the elements whence frogs and serpents are produced, and so through certain and known opportune combinations applying these seeds by secret movements, cause them to be created, but do not create them? Only men do not marvel at those things that are usually done by men. But if any one chance to wonder at the quickness of those growths, in that those living beings were so quickly made, let him consider how even this may be brought about by men in proportion to the measure of human capability. For whence is it that the same bodies generate worms more quickly in summer than in winter, or in hotter than in colder places? Only these things are applied by men with so much the more difficulty, in proportion as their earthly and sluggish members are wanting in subtlety of perception, and in rapidity of bodily motion. And hence it arises that in the case of any kind of angels, in proportion as it is easier for them to draw out the proximate causes from the elements, so much the more marvelous is their rapidity in works of this kind.

18. But He only is the creator who is the chief former of these things. Neither can any one be this, unless He with whom primarily rests the measure, number, and weight of all things existing; and He is God the one Creator, by whose unspeakable power it comes to pass, also, that what these angels were able to do if they were permitted, they are therefore not able to do because they are not permitted. For there is no other reason why they who made frogs and serpents were not able to make the most minute flies, unless because the greater power of God was present prohibiting them, through the Holy Spirit; which even the magicians themselves confessed, saying, "This is the finger of God" [Exod. 7:12; 8:7, 18–19]. But what they are able to do by nature, yet cannot do, because they are prohibited; and what the very condition of their nature itself does not suffer them to do; it is difficult, nay, impossible, for man to search out, unless through that gift of God which the apostle mentions when he says, "To another the discerning of spirits" [1 Cor. 12:10]. For we know that a man can walk, yet that he cannot do so if he is not permitted; but that he cannot fly, even if he be permitted. So those angels, also, are able to do certain things if they are permitted by more powerful angels, according to the supreme commandment

of God; but cannot do certain other things, not even if they are permitted by them; because He does not permit from whom they have received such and such a measure of natural powers: who, even by His angels, does not usually permit what He has given them power to be able to do.

SELECTION 3

Thomas Aquinas

Summa Theologiae, 1.22, 103

At a fundamental level Thomas's doctrine of providence governs the overall structure of the *Summa Theologiae*, which begins with God as the source of an outward movement of being in creation and ends with the divinely enabled return of the creature to God. Thomas's more explicitly dogmatic reflections on providence come in the first of the *Summa*'s three parts, where he describes the general character of God's ordering of creation toward an end, as well as the means by which God executes this plan. The following two excerpts from questions 22 ("The Providence of God") and 103 ("Of the Government of Things in General") illustrate Thomas's fundamental convictions regarding these two dimensions of Christian belief in providence.

Central to Thomas's thinking is the conviction that God's providence is all-encompassing: because God is the sole source of everything that is, God's providence extends to every part of creation, from the general to the individual. At the same time, Thomas insists that it is completely illegitimate to equate the comprehensiveness and irresistibility of divine government with a fatalism that undermines genuine contingency and freedom in creation. On the contrary, because God is the source of all things, God (the "primary cause") is free to achieve God's ends by means of creaturely intermediaries ("secondary causes"). Such intermediaries act according to their own natures as these have been created by God, such that God is able to achieve some particular effects by the operation of causes that operate necessarily (e.g., physical laws) and others by causes that act contingently (e.g., free human agents). In short, Thomas argues that while the *fact* that God's ends for creation will be achieved is certain, this implies nothing about the *mode* by which they are achieved at the level of creaturely causation, because God is equally the source of (and thus equally sovereign over) all creaturely causes in their various forms. (Ed. note: The format of the following selection has been modified to highlight the different sections of Thomas's argument in each article.)

From *The Summa Theologica of St. Thomas Aquinas*, 2nd ed.
(London: Burns, Oates, & Washbourne, 1927), 1:309–17; 5:15–18.

Article 2 (Question 22): Whether Everything Is Subject to the Providence of God?

Objections:
1. It seems that everything is not subject to divine providence. For nothing foreseen can happen by chance. If then everything was foreseen by God, nothing would happen by chance. And thus hazard and luck would disappear; which is against common opinion.

2. Further, a wise provider excludes any defect or evil, as far as he can, from those over whom he has a care. But we see many evils existing. Either, then, God cannot hinder these, and thus is not omnipotent; or else He does not have care for everything.

3. Further, whatever happens of necessity does not require providence or prudence. Hence, according to the Philosopher [Aristotle]: "Prudence is the right reason of things contingent concerning which there is counsel and choice."[1] Since, then, many things happen from necessity, everything cannot be subject to providence.

4. Further, whatsoever is left to itself cannot be subject to the providence of a governor. But men are left to themselves by God in accordance with the words: "God made man from the beginning, and left him in the hand of his own counsel" [Sir. 15:14]. And particularly in reference to the wicked: "I let them go according to the desires of their heart" [Ps. 80:13]. Everything, therefore, cannot be subject to divine providence.

5. Further, the Apostle says [1 Cor. 9:9]: "God doth not care for oxen;"[2] and we may say the same of other irrational creatures. Thus everything cannot be under the care of divine providence.

On the Contrary:
It is said of Divine Wisdom: "She reacheth from end to end mightily, and ordereth all things sweetly" [Wis. 8:1].

Answer:
Certain persons totally denied the existence of providence, as Democritus and the Epicureans, maintaining that the world was made by chance. Others taught that incorruptible things only were subject to providence and corruptible things not in their individual selves, but only according to their species; for in this respect they are incorruptible. They are represented as saying [Job 22:14]: "The clouds are His covert; and He doth not consider our things; and He walketh about the poles of heaven." Rabbi

---

1. Aristotle, *Nicomachean Ethics* 6.5; ET, *LCL* 19:337.
2. Vulgate: "Doth God take care for oxen?"

Moses, however, excluded men from the generality of things corruptible, on account of the excellence of the intellect which they possess, but in reference to all else that suffers corruption he adhered to the opinion of the others.

We must say, however, that all things are subject to divine providence, not only in general, but even in their own individual selves. This is made evident thus. For since every agent acts for an end, the ordering of effects towards that end extends as far as the causality of the first agent extends. Whence it happens that in the effects of an agent something takes place which has no reference towards the end, because the effect comes from a cause other than, and outside the intention of the agent. But the causality of God, Who is the first agent, extends to all being, not only as to constituent principles of species, but also as to the individualizing principles; not only of things incorruptible, but also of things corruptible. Hence all things that exist in whatsoever manner are necessarily directed by God towards some end; as the Apostle says: "Those things that are of God are well ordered"[3] [Rom. 13:1]. Since, therefore, as the providence of God is nothing less than the type of the order of things towards an end, as we have said; it necessarily follows that all things, inasmuch as they participate in existence, must likewise be subject to divine providence. It has also been shown [quest. 14.6, 11] that God knows all things, both universal and particular. And since His knowledge may be compared to the things themselves, as the knowledge of art to the objects of art, all things must of necessity come under His ordering; as all things wrought by art are subject to the ordering of that art.

Replies to the Objections:
1. There is a difference between universal and particular causes. A thing can escape the order of a particular cause, but not the order of a universal cause. For nothing escapes the order of a particular cause, except through the intervention and hindrance of some other particular cause; as, for instance, wood may be prevented from burning, by the action of water. Since then, all particular causes are included under the universal cause, it could not be that any effect should take place outside the range of that universal cause. So far then as an effect escapes the order of a particular cause, it is said to be casual or fortuitous in respect to that cause; but if we regard the universal cause, outside whose range no effect can happen, it is said to be foreseen. Thus, for instance, the meeting of two servants, although to them it appears a chance circumstance, has been fully foreseen by their master, who has purposely sent to meet at the one place, in such a way that the one knows not about the other.

---

3. Vulgate: "Those powers that are, are ordained of God" (*Quae autem sunt, a Deo ordinate sunt*). St. Thomas often quotes this passage, and invariably reads, *Quae a Deo sunt, ordinate sunt.*

2. It is otherwise with one who has care of a particular thing, and one whose providence is universal, because a particular provider excludes all defects from what is subject to his care as far as he can; whereas, one who provides universally allows some little defect to remain, lest the good of the whole should be hindered. Hence, corruption and defects in natural things are said to be contrary to some particular nature; yet they are in keeping with the plan of universal nature; inasmuch as the defect in one thing yields to the good of another, or even to the universal good: for the corruption of one is the generation of another, and through this it is that a species is kept in existence. Since God, then, provides universally for all being, it belongs to His providence to permit certain defects in particular effects, that the perfect good of the universe may not be hindered, for if all evil were prevented, much good would be absent from the universe. A lion would cease to live, if there were no slaying of animals; and there would be no patience of martyrs if there were no tyrannical persecution. Thus Augustine says: "Almighty God would in no wise permit evil to exist in His works, unless He were so almighty and so good as to produce good even from evil."[4] It would appear that it was on account of these two arguments to which we have just replied, that some were persuaded to consider corruptible things—e.g. casual and evil things—as removed from the care of divine providence.

3. Man is not the author of nature; but he uses natural things in applying art and virtue to his own use. Hence human providence does not reach to that which takes place in nature from necessity; but divine providence extends thus far, since God is the author of nature. Apparently it was this argument that moved those who withdrew the course of nature from the care of divine providence, attributing it rather to the necessity of matter, as Democritus, and others of the ancients.

4. When it is said that God left man to himself, this does not mean that man is exempt from divine providence; but merely that he has not a prefixed operating force determined to only the one effect, as in the case of natural things, which are only acted upon as though directed by another towards an end, and do not act of themselves, as if they directed themselves towards an end, like rational creatures, through the possession of free will, by which these are able to take counsel and make a choice. Hence it is significantly said: "In the hand of his own counsel." But since the very act of free will is traced to God as to a cause, it necessarily follows that everything happening from the exercise of free will must be subject to divine providence. For human providence is included under the providence of God, as a particular under a universal cause. God, however, extends His providence over the just in a certain more excellent way than over the wicked; inasmuch as He prevents anything happening which would impede their

---

4. Augustine, *Enchiridion* 11, in *PL* 40.; ET, *LCC* 7:342.

final salvation. For "to them that love God, all things work together unto good" [Rom. 8:28]. But from the fact that He does not restrain the wicked from the evil of sin, He is said to abandon them: not that He altogether withdraws His providence from them, since they would return to nothing, if they were not preserved in existence by His providence. This was the reason that had weight with Tully [Cicero], who withdrew from the care of divine providence human affairs concerning which we take counsel.

5. Since a rational creature has, through its free will, control over its actions, as was said above [quest. 19.10], it is subject to divine providence in a special manner, so that something is imputed to it as a fault, or as a merit; and there is given it accordingly something by way of punishment or reward. In this way, the Apostle withdraws oxen from the care of God: not, however, that individual irrational creatures escape the care of divine providence, as was the opinion of the Rabbi Moses.

Article 3: Whether God Has Immediate Providence over Everything?
Objections:

1. It seems that God does not have immediate providence over all things. For whatever is contained in the notion of dignity, must be attributed to God. But it belongs to the dignity of a king, that he should have ministers; through whose mediation he provides for his subjects. Therefore much less has God Himself immediate providence over all things.

2. Further, it belongs to providence to order all things to an end. Now the end of everything is its perfection and its good. But it appertains to every cause to direct its effect to good; wherefore every active cause is a cause of the effect of providence. If therefore God were to have immediate providence over all things, all secondary causes would be withdrawn.

3. Further, Augustine says that, "It is better to be ignorant of some things than to know them (for example, vile things),"[5] and the Philosopher says the same.[6] But whatever is better must be assigned to God. Therefore He has not immediate providence over bad and vile things.

On the Contrary:

It is said [Job 34:13]: "What other hath He appointed over the earth? or whom hath He set over the world which He made?" On which passage Gregory says: "Himself He ruleth the world which He Himself hath made."[7]

Answer:

Two things belong to providence: namely, the type of the order of things foreordained towards an end; and the execution of this order,

---

5. Augustine, *Enchiridion* 17, in *PL* 40.239; ET, *LCC* 7:347.
6. *Metaphysics*, 12.9; ET, *LCL* 18:165.
7. Gregory the Great, *Moralia* 24.20, in *PL* 76.344.

which is called government. As regards the first of these, God has immediate providence over everything, because He has in His intellect the types of everything, even the smallest; and whatsoever causes He assigns to certain effects, He gives them the power to produce those effects. Whence it must be that He has beforehand the type of those effects in His mind. As to the second, there are certain intermediaries of God's providence; for He governs things inferior by superior, not on account of any defect in His power, but by reason of the abundance of His goodness; so that the dignity of causality is imparted even to creatures. Thus Plato's opinion, as narrated by Gregory of Nyssa,[8] is exploded. He taught a threefold providence. First, one which belongs to the supreme Deity, Who first and foremost has provision over spiritual things, and thus over the whole world as regards genus, species, and universal causes. The second providence, which is over the individuals of all that can be generated and corrupted, he attributed to the divinities who circulate in the heavens; that is, certain separate substances, which move corporeal things in a circular direction. The third providence, over human affairs, he assigned to demons, whom the Platonic philosophers placed between us and the gods, as Augustine tells us.[9]

Replies to the Objections:
1. It pertains to a king's dignity to have ministers who execute his providence. But the fact that he has not the plan of those things which are done by them arises from a deficiency in himself. For every operative science is the more perfect, the more it considers the particular things with which its action is concerned.

2. God's immediate provision over everything does not exclude the action of secondary causes; which are the executors of His order, as was said above [quest. 19.5].

3. It is better for us not to know low and vile things, because by them we are impeded in our knowledge of what is better and higher; for we cannot understand many things simultaneously; because the thought of evil sometimes perverts the will towards evil. This does not hold with God, Who sees everything simultaneously at one glance, and whose will cannot turn in the direction of evil.

Article 4: Whether Providence Imposes
Any Necessity on Things Foreseen?
Objections:
1. It seems that divine providence imposes necessity upon things foreseen. For every effect that has a *per se* cause, either present or past, which

---

8. The citation is actually from Nemesius of Emesa, *On Human Nature* 44, in *PG* 40.794.
9. Augustine, *The City of God*, 8.14, in *PL* 41.238; ET, *NPNF*[2], 2:153–54.

it necessarily follows, happens from necessity, as the Philosopher proves.[10] But the providence of God, since it is eternal, pre-exists; and the effect flows from it of necessity, for divine providence cannot be frustrated. Therefore divine providence imposes a necessity upon things foreseen.

2. Further, every provider makes his work as stable as he can, lest it should fail. But God is most powerful. Therefore He assigns the stability of necessity to things provided.

3. Further, Boethius says: "Fate from the immutable source of providence binds together human acts and fortunes by the indissoluble connection of causes."[11] It seems therefore that providence imposes necessity upon things foreseen.

On the contrary:
Dionysius says that "to corrupt nature is not the work of providence."[12] But it is in the nature of some things to be contingent. Divine providence does not therefore impose any necessity upon things so as to destroy their contingency.

Answer:
Divine providence imposes necessity upon some things; not upon all, as some formerly believed. For to providence it belongs to order things towards an end. Now after the divine goodness, which is an extrinsic end to all things, the principal good in things themselves is the perfection of the universe; which would not be, were not all grades of being found in things. Whence it pertains to divine providence to produce every grade of being. And thus it has prepared for some things necessary causes, so that they happen of necessity; for others contingent causes, that they may happen by contingency, according to the nature of their proximate causes.

Replies to the Objections:
1. The effect of divine providence is not only that things should happen somehow; but that they should happen either by necessity or by contingency. Therefore whatsoever divine providence ordains to happen infallibly and of necessity happens infallibly and of necessity; and that happens from contingency, which the plan of divine providence conceives to happen from contingency.

2. The order of divine providence is unchangeable and certain, so far as all things foreseen happen as they have been foreseen, whether from necessity or from contingency.

---

10. Aristotle, *Metaphysics* 6.3; ET, *LCL* 17:305.
11. Boethius, *The Consolation of Philosophy* 4.6, in *PL* 63.817; ET, Boethius, *The Consolation of Philosophy*, ed. P. G. Walsh (Oxford: Clarendon, 1999), 89.
12. Dionysius the Areopagite, *Divine Names* 4.23, in *PG* 3.725A; ET, *Pseudo-Dionysius: The Complete Works*, ed. Paul Rorem (New York: Paulist Press, 1987), 90.

3. That indissolubility and unchangeableness of which Boethius speaks, pertain to the certainty of providence, which fails not to produce its effect, and that in the way foreseen; but they do not pertain to the necessity of the effects. We must remember that properly speaking "necessary" and "contingent" are consequent upon being as such. Hence the mode both of necessity and of contingency falls under the foresight of God, who provides universally for all being; not under the foresight of causes that provide only for some particular order of things.

Article 7 (Question 103): Whether Anything Can Happen outside the Order of the Divine Government?

Objections:

1. It would seem possible that something may occur outside the order of the Divine government. For Boethius says that "God disposes all for good."[13] Therefore, if nothing happens outside the order of the Divine government, it would follow that no evil exists.

2. Further, nothing that is in accordance with the pre-ordination of a ruler occurs by chance. Therefore, if nothing occurs outside the order of the Divine government, it follows that there is nothing fortuitous and casual.

3. Further, the order of Divine Providence is certain and unchangeable; because it is in accordance with the eternal design. Therefore, if nothing happens outside the order of the Divine government, it follows that all things happen by necessity, and nothing is contingent; which is false. Therefore it is possible for something to occur outside the order of the Divine government.

On the contrary:

It is written [Esth. 13:9]: "O Lord, Lord, almighty King, all things are in Thy power, and there is none that can resist Thy will."

Answer:

It is possible for an effect to result outside the order of some particular cause; but not outside the order of the universal cause. The reason of this is that no effect results outside the order of a particular cause, except through some other impeding cause; which other cause must itself be reduced to the first universal cause; as indigestion may occur outside the order of the nutritive power by some such impediment as the coarseness of the food, which again is to be ascribed to some other cause, and so on till we come to the first universal cause. Therefore as God is the first universal cause, not of one genus only, but of all being in general, it is impossible for anything to occur outside the order of the Divine government; but from the very fact that from one point of view something seems to evade the order

---

13. Boethius, *The Consolation of Philosophy* 3.12, in *PL* 63.779; ET, *Consolation*, 6.

of Divine providence considered in regard to one particular cause, it must necessarily come back to that order as regards some other cause.

Replies to the Objections:
1. There is nothing wholly evil in the world, for evil is ever founded on good, as shown above [quest. 48.3]. Therefore something is said to be evil through its escaping from the order of some particular good. If it wholly escaped from the order of the Divine government, it would wholly cease to exist.

2. Things are said to be fortuitous as regards some particular cause from the order of which they escape. But as to the order of Divine providence, "nothing in the world happens by chance," as Augustine declares.[14]

3. Certain effects are said to be contingent as compared to their proximate causes, which may fail in their effects; and not as though anything could happen entirely outside the order of Divine government. The very fact that something occurs outside the order of some proximate cause, is owing to some other cause, itself subject to the Divine government.

Article 8: Whether Anything Can Resist the Order of the Divine Government?

Objections:
1. It would seem possible that some resistance can be made to the order of the Divine government. For it is written [Isa. 3:8]: "Their tongue and their devices are against the Lord."

2. Further, a king does not justly punish those who do not rebel against his commands. Therefore if no one rebelled against God's commands, no one would be justly punished by God.

3. Further, everything is subject to the order of the Divine government. But some things oppose others. Therefore some things rebel against the order of the Divine government.

On the Contrary:
Boethius says: "There is nothing that can desire or is able to resist this sovereign good. It is this sovereign good therefore that ruleth all mightily and ordereth all sweetly,"[15] as is said [Wis. 8:1] of Divine wisdom.

Answer:
We may consider the order of Divine providence in two ways: in general, inasmuch as it proceeds from the governing cause of all; and in particular, inasmuch as it proceeds from some particular cause which executes the order of the Divine government.

---

14. Augustine, *Book of the 83 Questions* 24, in *PL* 40.17.
15. Boethius, *The Consolation of Philosophy* 3.12, in *PL* 63.779; ET, *Consolation*, 67.

Considered in the first way, nothing can resist the order of the Divine government. This can be proved in two ways: firstly from the fact that the order of the Divine government is wholly directed to good, and everything by its own operation and effort tends to good only, "for no one acts intending evil," as Dionysius says:[16] secondly from the fact that, as we have said above [art. 1, 5], every inclination of anything, whether natural or voluntary, is nothing but a kind of impression from the first mover; as the inclination of the arrow towards a fixed point is nothing but an impulse received from the archer. Wherefore every agent, whether natural or free, attains to its divinely appointed end, as though of its own accord. For this reason God is said "to order all things sweetly" [Wis. 8:1].

Replies to the Objections:
1. Some are said to think or speak or act against God: not that they entirely resist the order of the Divine government (for even the sinner intends the attainment of a certain good), but because they resist some particular good, which belongs to their nature or state. Therefore they are justly punished by God.
2. The reply is clear from the above.
3. From the fact that one thing opposes another, it follows that some one thing can resist the order of a particular cause; but not that order which depends on the universal cause of all things.

SELECTION **4**

Julian of Norwich

Showings (Long Text)

Little is known of the life of Julian of Norwich (1342–ca. 1420) beyond the fact that she spent much of her adult life as an anchorite enclosed in a cell attached to the cathedral in Norwich. Her familiarity with Scripture and the fact that she was literate suggest that she may have entered a religious order in her youth. Her book *Showings* (also known as *Revelations of Divine Love*) is based on a series of visions of the crucified Christ she experienced during a near-fatal illness in 1373. The text survives in two recensions, the longer, from which this selection is taken, composed some fifteen to twenty years after the visions. The short text appears to have been written earlier, though exactly when is unclear.

The whole sequence of Julian's reflections can be read as an attempt to reconcile the official church's teachings about the power of sin, death, and

---

16. Dionysius, *Divine Names* 4.19, in *PG* 3:716C; ET, *Pseudo-Dionysius*, 85.

damnation with the equally orthodox principle—at the heart of Julian's own vision—of God's sovereign love for the whole creation. The three chapters excerpted below illustrate stages in Julian's attempt to vindicate the victory of God's love over every conceivable obstacle. In chapter 5 she has a vivid experience of God's love as the sole power preserving every creature in existence. Chapter 11 focuses more specifically on divine sovereignty as the sole cause behind every event, such that the inherent goodness (or, in Julian's language, "rightfulness") of God's will eclipses –without denying—the experience of sin. Finally, in chapter 32 God resolves Julian's doubts with the assurance that in a way not to be known prior to Christ's coming God "will make well all which is not well" so that "every kind of thing will be well."

From Julian of Norwich, *Showings* (New York: Paulist Press, 1978), 183–84, 197–99, 231–33.

The Fifth Chapter

At the same time as I saw this sight of the head bleeding, our good Lord showed a spiritual sight of his familiar love. I saw that he is to us everything which is good and comforting for our help. He is our clothing, who wraps and enfolds us for love, embraces us and shelters us, surrounds us for his love, which is so tender that he may never desert us. And so in this sight I saw that he is everything which is good, as I understand.

And in this he showed me something small, no bigger than a hazelnut, lying in the palm of my hand, as it seemed to me, and it was as round as a ball. I looked at it with the eye of my understanding and thought: What can this be? I was amazed that it could last, for I thought that because of its littleness it would suddenly have fallen into nothing. And I was answered in my understanding: It lasts and always will, because God loves it; and thus everything has being through the love of God.

In this little thing I saw three properties. The first is that God made it, the second is that God loves it, the third is that God preserves it. But what did I see in it? It is that God is the Creator and the protector and the lover. For until I am substantially united to him, I can never have perfect rest or true happiness, until, that is, I am so attached to him that there can be no created thing between my God and me.

This little thing which is created seemed to me as if it could have fallen into nothing because of its littleness. We need to have knowledge of this, so that we may delight in despising as nothing everything created, so as to love and have uncreated God. For this is the reason why our hearts and souls are not in perfect ease, because here we seek rest in this thing which is so little, in which there is no rest, and we do not know our God who is almighty, all wise and all good, for he is true rest. God wishes to be known, and it pleases him that we should rest in him; for everything which is beneath him is not sufficient for us. And this is the reason why no soul is at rest until it has despised as nothing all things which are created. When it by its will has become nothing for love, to have him who is everything, then is it able to receive spiritual rest.

And also our good Lord revealed that it is very greatly pleasing to him that a simple soul should come naked, openly and familiarly. For this is the loving yearning of the soul through the touch of the Holy Spirit, from the understanding which I have in this revelation: God, of your goodness give me yourself, for you are enough for me, and I can ask for nothing which is less which can pay you full worship. And if I ask anything which is less, always I am in want; but only in you do I have everything.

And these words of the goodness of God are very dear to the soul, and very close to touching our Lord's will, for his goodness fills all his creatures and all his blessed works full, and endlessly overflows in them. For he is everlastingness, and he made us only for himself, and restored us by his precious Passion and always preserves us in his blessed love; and all this is of his goodness. . . .

The Eleventh Chapter
And after this I saw God in an instant of time, that is to say in my understanding, by which vision I saw that he is present in all things. I contemplated it carefully, seeing and recognizing through it that he does everything which is done. I marveled at that vision with a gentle fear, and I thought: What is sin? For I saw truly that God does everything, however small it may be, and that nothing is done by chance, but all by God's prescient wisdom. If it seem chance in man's sight, our blindness and lack of prescience is the reason. For those things which are in God's Prescient wisdom since before time, which duly and to his glory he always guides to their best conclusion, as things come about, come suddenly upon us when we are ignorant; and so through our blindness and our lack of prescience we say that these things are by chance.

So I understood in this revelation of love, for I know well that in our Lord's sight there is no chance; and therefore I was compelled to admit that everything which is done is well done, for our Lord God does everything. For at this time the work of creatures was not revealed, but the work of our Lord God in creatures; for he is at the centre of everything, and he does everything. And I was certain that he does no sin; and here I was certain that sin is no deed, for in all this sin was not shown to me. And I did not wish to go on wondering about this, but I contemplated our Lord and waited for what he would show. And thus the rightfulness of God's dealing was shown to the soul, as well as could be in that time. Rightfulness has two fine qualities: It is right and it is full. And so are all the works of our Lord, and they lack no operation of mercy or of grace, for they are all rightful and nothing whatever is lacking in them. And on another occasion he did show sin, undisguised, for my contemplation, as I shall tell afterwards, when he performs works of mercy and of grace.

This vision was revealed to my understanding, for our Lord wants to have the soul truly converted to contemplation of him and of all his works in general. For they are most good, and all his judgments are easy and sweet, bringing to great rest the soul which is converted from contemplating men's blind judgments to the judgments, lovely and sweet, of our Lord God. For a man regards some deeds as well done and some as evil, and our Lord does not regard them so, for everything which exists in nature is of God's creation, so that everything which is done has the property of being of God's doing. For it is easy to understand that the best of deeds is well done; and the smallest of deeds which is done is as well done as the best and the greatest, and they all have the property and the order ordained for them as our Lord had ordained, without beginning, for no one does but he.

I saw most truly that he never changed his purpose in any kind of thing, nor ever will eternally. For there was nothing unknown to him in his just ordinance before time began, and therefore all things were set in order, before anything was made, as it would endure eternally. And no kind of thing will fail in that respect, for he has made everything totally good.

And therefore the blessed Trinity is always wholly pleased with all its works; and God revealed all this most blessedly, as though to say: See, I am God. See, I am in all things. See, I do all things. See, I never remove my hands from my works, nor ever shall without end. See, I guide all things to the end that I ordain them for, before time began, with the same power and wisdom and love with which I made them; how should anything be amiss? So was the soul examined, powerfully, wisely and lovingly, in this vision. Then I saw truly that I must agree, with great reverence and joy in God....

The Thirty-Second Chapter

On one occasion our good Lord said: Every kind of thing will be well; and on another occasion he said: You will see yourself that every kind of thing will be well. And from these two the soul gained different kinds of understanding. One was this: that he wants us to know that he takes heed not only of things which are noble and great, but also of those which are little and small, of humble men and simple, of this man and that man. And this is what he means when he says: Every kind of thing will be well. For he wants us to know that the smallest thing will not be forgotten. Another understanding is this: that there are many deeds which in our eyes are so evilly done and lead to such great harms that it seems to us impossible that any good result could ever come of them. And we contemplate this and sorrow and mourn for it so that we cannot rest in the blessed contemplation of God as we ought to do. And the cause is this: that the reason which we use is now so blind, so abject and so stupid that we cannot recognize God's exalted, wonderful wisdom, or the power and the goodness of the blessed Trinity.

And this is his intention when he says: You will see yourself that every kind of thing will be well, as if he said: Accept it now in faith and trust, and in the very end you will see truly, in fullness of joy.

And so in the same five words said before: I may make all things well, I understand a powerful comfort from all the works of our Lord God which are still to come.

There is a deed which the blessed Trinity will perform on the last day, as I see it, and what the deed will be and how it will be performed is unknown to every creature who is inferior to Christ, and it will be until the deed is done. The goodness and the love of our Lord God want us to know that this will be, and his power and his wisdom, through the same love, want to conceal it and hide it from us, what it will be and how it will be done. And the cause why he wants us to know it like this is because he wants us to be at ease in our souls and at peace in love, disregarding every disturbance which could hinder our true rejoicing in him.

This is the great deed ordained by our Lord God from without beginning, treasured and hidden in his blessed breast, known only to himself, through which deed he will make all things well. For just as the blessed Trinity created all things from nothing, just so will the same blessed Trinity make everything well which is not well. And I marveled greatly at this sight, and contemplated our faith, with this in my mind: Our faith is founded on God's word, and it belongs to our faith that we believe that God's word will be preserved in all things. And one article of our faith is that many creatures will be damned, such as the angels who fell out of heaven because of pride, who now are devils, and many men upon earth who die out of the faith of Holy Church, that is to say those who are pagans and many who have received baptism and who live unchristian lives and so die out of God's love. All these will be eternally condemned to hell, as Holy Church teaches me to believe.

And all this being so, it seemed to me that it was impossible that every kind of thing should be well, as our Lord revealed at this time. And to this I had no other answer as a revelation from our Lord except this: What is impossible to you is not impossible to me. I shall preserve my word in everything, and I shall make everything well. And in this I was taught by the grace of God that I ought to keep myself steadfastly in the faith, as I had understood before, and that at the same time I should stand firm and believe firmly that every kind of thing will be well, as our Lord revealed at that same time. For this is the great deed which our Lord will do, and in this deed he will preserve his Word in everything. And he will make well all which is not well. But what the deed will be and how it will be done, there is no creature who is inferior to Christ who knows it, or will know it until it has been done, according to the understanding which I received of our Lord's meaning at this time.

SELECTION 5

John Calvin

Institutes of the Christian Religion, Book 1, Chapter 16

Few doctrines are so closely associated with Calvin and the Reformed tradition than that of providence, usually closely associated with the doctrine of predestination. Interestingly, although providence and predestination are treated together in the early editions of the *Institutes*, in the final edition of 1559 they are separated, with the topic of providence (from which the following excerpt is taken) located under the topic of creation in book 1 and predestination treated much later in connection with redemption in book 3. Whether discussed together or separately, however, Calvin views both doctrines as among the most comforting truths of the faith, on the grounds that confidence in God's direction of events gives the believer courage and hope in the face of adversity.

In the selection that follows, Calvin works from the assumption that while people are generally happy to acknowledge God as creator of the world and even as sustainer of the basic forces of nature, they are reluctant to ascribe God direct control over every event. Against this perspective Calvin argues that both Scripture and the logic of divine omnipotence demand confidence that God so governs every creature that "nothing takes place by chance." He is willing to grant that a distinction may be drawn between God's watching over the order of nature as a whole (general providence) and God's determination of individual events (special providence), but his pastoral concern that the Christian look to God in all things leads him to focus on the particular.

From John Calvin, *Institutes of the Christian Religion*, LCC 20:197–205.

1. Creation and Providence Inseparably Joined

Moreover, to make God a momentary Creator, who once for all finished his work, would be cold and barren, and we must differ from profane men especially in that we see the presence of divine power shining as much in the continuing state of the universe as in its inception. For even though the minds of the impious too are compelled by merely looking upon earth and heaven to rise up to the Creator, yet faith has its own peculiar way of assigning the whole credit for Creation to God. To this pertains that saying of the apostle's to which we have referred before,[1] that only "by faith we understand that the universe was created by the word of God" [Heb. 11:3].

---

1. In *Institutes* 1.5.14.

For unless we pass on to his providence—however we may seem both to comprehend with the mind and to confess with the tongue—we do not yet properly grasp what it means to say: "God is Creator." Carnal sense, once confronted with the power of God in the very Creation, stops there, and at most weighs and contemplates only the wisdom, power, and goodness of the author in accomplishing such handiwork. (These matters are self-evident, and even force themselves upon the unwilling.) It contemplates, moreover, some general preserving and governing activity, from which the force of motion derives. In short, carnal sense thinks there is an energy divinely bestowed from the beginning, sufficient to sustain all things.

But faith ought to penetrate more deeply, namely, having found him Creator of all, forthwith to conclude he is also everlasting Governor and Preserver—not only in that he drives the celestial frame[2] as well as its several parts by a universal motion, but also in that he sustains, nourishes, and cares for, everything he has made, even to the least sparrow [cf. Matt. 10:29]. Thus David, having briefly stated that the universe was created by God, immediately descends to the uninterrupted course of His providence, "By the word of Jehovah the heavens were made, and all their host by the breath of his mouth" [Ps. 33:6; cf. Ps. 32:6, Vulg.]. Soon thereafter he adds, "Jehovah has looked down upon the sons of men" [Ps. 33:13; cf. Ps. 32:13-14, Vulg.], and what follows is in the same vein. For although all men do not reason so clearly, yet, because it would not be believable that human affairs are cared for by God unless he were the Maker of the universe, and nobody seriously believes the universe was made by God without being persuaded that he takes care of his works, David not inappropriately leads us in the best order from the one to the other. In general, philosophers teach and human minds conceive that all parts of the universe are quickened by God's secret inspiration. Yet they do not reach as far as David is carried, bearing with him all the godly, when he says: "These all look to thee, to give them their food in due season; when thou givest to them, they gather it up; when thou openest thy hand, they are filled with good things; when thou hidest thy face, they are dismayed; when thou takest away their breath, they die and return to the earth. If thou sendest forth thy spirit again, they are created, and thou renewest the face of the earth" [Ps. 104:27-30]. Indeed, although they subscribe to Paul's statement that we have our being and move and live in God [Acts 17:28], yet they are far from that earnest feeling of grace which he commends, because they do not at all taste God's special care, by which alone his fatherly favor is known.

2. There Is No Such Thing As Fortune or Chance

That this difference may better appear, we must know that God's providence, as it is taught in Scripture, is opposed to fortune and fortuitous hap-

---

2. *Orbis machinam*.

penings.³ Now it has been commonly accepted in all ages, and almost all mortals hold the same opinion today, that all things come about through chance. What we ought to believe concerning providence is by this depraved opinion most certainly not only beclouded, but almost buried. Suppose a man falls among thieves, or wild beasts; is shipwrecked at sea by a sudden gale; is killed by a falling house or tree. Suppose another man wandering through the desert finds help in his straits; having been tossed by the waves, reaches harbor; miraculously escapes death by a finger's breadth. Carnal reason ascribes all such happenings, whether prosperous or adverse, to fortune. But anyone who has been taught by Christ's lips that all the hairs of his head are numbered [Matt. 10:30] will look farther afield for a cause, and will consider that all events are governed by God's secret plan. And concerning inanimate objects we ought to hold that, although each one has by nature been endowed with its own property, yet it does not exercise its own power except in so far as it is directed by God's ever-present hand. These are, thus, nothing but instruments to which God continually imparts as much effectiveness as he wills, and according to his own purpose bends and turns them to either one action or another.

No creature has a force more wondrous or glorious than that of the sun. For besides lighting the whole earth with its brightness, how great a thing is it that by its heat it nourishes and quickens all living things! That with its rays it breathes fruitfulness into the earth! That it warms the seeds in the bosom of the earth, draws them forth with budding greenness, increases and strengthens them, nourishes them anew, until they rise up into stalks! That it feeds the plant with continual warmth, until it grows into flower, and from flower into fruit! That then, also, with baking heat it brings the fruit to maturity! That in like manner trees and vines warmed by the sun first put forth buds and leaves, then put forth a flower, and from the flower produce fruit! Yet the Lord, to claim the whole credit for all these things, willed that, before he created the sun, light should come to be and earth be filled with all manner of herbs and fruits [Gen. 1:3, 11, 14]. Therefore a godly man will not make the sun either the principal or the necessary cause of these things which existed before the creation of the sun, but merely the instrument that God uses because he so wills; for with no more difficulty he might abandon it, and act through himself. Then when we read that at Joshua's prayers the sun stood still in one degree for two days [Josh. 10:13], and that its shadow went back ten degrees for the sake of King Hezekiah

---

3. *Fortunae et casibus fortuitis*. Personified and deified in the ancient world, Fortuna retained a fascination for the Western mind and was a common term of discourse in the Renaissance, when ideas of chance and fate versus the divine ordering of events had a wide vogue. Here and in the other passages cited Calvin is probably thinking of the rejection of this notion by Lactantius in the *Divine Institutes* 3.28.45 (*L. Caeili Firmiani Lactanti Opera omnia*, vol. 19 of *Corpus Scriptorum Ecclesiasticorum Latinorum*, ed. Samuel Brandt and Georgius Laubmann [Leipsig: G. Freytag, 1890], 264; ET, ANF 7:97); and by Augustine, e.g., in *The City of God* 5.9–11 (*PL* 41.447–50; ET, NPNF¹, 2:90–93); *Retractations* 1.1.2 (*PL* 32.585).

[2 Kgs. 20:11 or Isa. 38:8], God has witnessed by those few miracles that the sun does not daily rise and set by a blind instinct of nature but that he himself, to renew our remembrance of his fatherly favor toward us, governs its course. Nothing is more natural than for spring to follow winter; summer, spring; and fall, summer—each in turn. Yet in this series one sees such great and uneven diversity that it readily appears each year, month, and day is governed by a new, a special, providence of God.

3. God's Providence Governs All

And truly God claims, and would have us grant him, omnipotence—not the empty, idle, and almost unconscious sort that the Sophists[4] imagine, but a watchful, effective, active sort, engaged in ceaseless activity. Not, indeed, an omnipotence that is only a general principle of confused motion, as if he were to command a river to flow through its once-appointed channels, but one that is directed toward individual and particular motions. For he is deemed omnipotent, not because he can indeed act, yet sometimes ceases and sits in idleness, or continues by a general impulse that order of nature which he previously appointed; but because, governing heaven and earth by his providence, he so regulates all things that nothing takes place without his deliberation. For when, in the Psalms, it is said that "he does whatever he wills" [Ps. 115:3; cf. Ps. 113(b):3, Vulg.], a certain and deliberate will is meant. For it would be senseless to interpret the words of the prophet after the manner of the philosophers, that God is the first agent because he is the beginning and cause of all motion; for in times of adversity believers comfort themselves with the solace that they suffer nothing except by God's ordinance and command, for they are under his hand.

But if God's governance is so extended to all his works, it is a childish cavil to enclose it within the stream of nature. Indeed, those as much defraud God of his glory as themselves of a most profitable doctrine who confine God's providence to such narrow limits as though he allowed all things by a free course to be borne along according to a universal law of nature. For nothing would be more miserable than man if he were exposed to every movement of the sky, air, earth, and waters. Besides, in this way God's particular goodness toward each one would be too unworthily reduced. David exclaims that infants still nursing at their mothers' breasts are eloquent enough to celebrate God's glory [Ps. 8:2], for immediately on coming forth from the womb, they find food prepared for them by his heavenly care. Indeed, this is in general true, provided what experience plainly demonstrates does not escape our eyes and senses, that some mothers have full and abundant breasts, but others' are almost dry, as God wills to feed one more liberally, but another more meagerly.

---

4. *Sophistae*. The word is used by Calvin, in common with the other Reformers and with many Humanists, to designate the Scholastic writers when these are treated adversely.

Those who ascribe just praise to God's omnipotence doubly benefit thereby. First, power ample enough to do good there is in him in whose possession are heaven and earth, and to whose beck all creatures are so attentive as to put themselves in obedience to him. Secondly, they may safely rest in the protection of him to whose will are subject all the harmful things which, whatever their source, we may fear; whose authority curbs Satan with all his furies and his whole equipage; and upon whose nod depends whatever opposes our welfare. And we cannot otherwise correct or allay these uncontrolled and superstitious fears, which we repeatedly conceive at the onset of dangers. We are superstitiously timid, I say, if whenever creatures threaten us or forcibly terrorize us we become as fearful as if they had some intrinsic power to harm us, or might wound us inadvertently and accidentally, or there were not enough help in God against their harmful acts.

For example, the prophet forbids God's children "to fear the stars and signs of heaven, as disbelievers commonly do" [Jer. 10:2]. Surely he does not condemn every sort of fear. But when unbelievers transfer the government of the universe from God to the stars, they fancy that their bliss or their misery depends upon the decrees and indications of the stars, not upon God's will; so it comes about that their fear is transferred from him, toward whom alone they ought to direct it, to stars and comets. Let him, therefore, who would beware of this infidelity ever remember that there is no erratic power, or action, or motion in creatures, but that they are governed by God's secret plan in such a way that nothing happens except what is knowingly and willingly decreed by him.

4. The Nature of Providence

At the outset, then, let my readers grasp that providence means not that by which God idly observes from heaven what takes place on earth, but that by which, as keeper of the keys, he governs all events. Thus it pertains no less to his hands than to his eyes. And indeed, when Abraham said to his son, "God will provide" [Gen. 22:8], he meant not only to assert God's foreknowledge of a future event, but to cast the care of a matter unknown to him upon the will of Him who is wont to give a way out of things perplexed and confused. Whence it follows that providence is lodged in the act; for many babble too ignorantly of bare foreknowledge. Not so crass is the error of those who attribute a governance to God, but of a confused and mixed sort, as I have said, namely, one that by a general motion revolves and drives the system of the universe, with its several parts, but which does not specifically direct the action of individual creatures. Yet this error, also, is not tolerable; for by this providence which they call universal, they teach that nothing hinders all creatures from being contingently moved, or man from turning himself hither and thither by the free choice of his will. And they so apportion things between God and man that God by His power inspires in man a movement by which he can act in accordance with the nature implanted in him, but He regulates His own actions by the plan of His will. Briefly, they mean that the universe, men's affairs, and men themselves are governed by God's might but not by His determination. I say nothing of the Epicureans (a pestilence that has always filled the world) who imagine that God is idle and indolent; and others just as foolish, who of old fancied that God so ruled above the middle region of the air that he left the lower regions to fortune. As if the dumb creatures themselves do not sufficiently cry out against such patent madness!

"General" and "Special" Providence

For now I propose to refute the opinion (which almost universally obtains) that concedes to God some kind of blind and ambiguous motion, while taking from him the chief thing: that he directs everything by his incomprehensible wisdom and disposes it to his own end. And so in name only, not in fact, it makes God the Ruler of the universe because it deprives him of his control. What, I pray you, is it to have control but so to be in authority that you rule in a determined order those things over which you are placed? Yet I do not wholly repudiate what is said concerning universal providence, provided they in turn grant me that the universe is ruled by God, not only because he watches over the order of nature set by himself, but because he exercises especial care over each of his works. It is, indeed, true that the several kinds of things are moved by a secret impulse of nature, as if they obeyed God's eternal command, and what God has once determined flows on by itself.

At this point we may refer to Christ's statement that from the very beginning he and the Father were always at work [John 5:17]; and to Paul's teaching that "in him we live, move, and have our being" [Acts 17:28]; also, what the author of the Letter to the Hebrews says, meaning to prove the divinity of Christ, that all things are sustained by his mighty command [Heb. 1:3]. But they wrongly conceal and obscure by this excuse that special providence which is so declared by sure and clear testimonies of Scripture that it is a wonder anyone can have doubts about it. And surely they who cast over it the veil of which I spoke are themselves compelled to add, by way of correction, that many things take place under God's especial care. But they wrongly restrict this to particular acts alone. Therefore we must prove God so attends to the regulation of individual events, and they all so proceed from his set plan, that nothing takes place by chance.

5. God's Providence Also Directs the Individual

Suppose we grant that the beginning of motion is with God, but that all things, either of themselves or by chance, are borne whither inclination of nature impels. Then the alternation of days and nights, of winter and summer, will be God's work, inasmuch as he, assigning to each one his part, has set before them a certain law; that is, if with even tenor they uninterruptedly maintain the same way, days following after nights, months after months, and years after years. But that sometimes immoderate heat joined with dryness burns whatever crops there are, that at other times unseasonable rains damage the grain, that sudden calamity strikes from hail and storms—this will not be God's work, unless, perhaps because clouds or fair weather, cold or heat, take their origin from the conjunction of the stars and other natural causes. Yet in this way no place is left for God's fatherly favor, nor for his judgments. If they say that God is beneficent enough to mankind because he sheds upon heaven and earth an ordinary power, by which they are supplied with food, this is too weak and profane a fiction. As if the fruitfulness of one year were not a singular blessing of God, and scarcity and famine were not his curse and vengeance! But because it would take too long to collect all the reasons, let the authority of God himself suffice. In the Law and in the Prophets he often declares that as often as he waters the earth with dews and rain [Lev. 26:3-4; Deut. 11:13-14; 28:12] he testifies to his favor; but when the heaven is hardened like iron at his command [Lev. 26:19], the grainfields consumed by a blight and other harmful things [Deut. 28:22], as often as the fields are struck with hail and storms [cf. Isa. 28:2; Hag. 2:18, Vulg.], these are a sign of his certain and special vengeance. If we accept these things, it is certain that not one drop of rain falls without God's sure command.

Indeed, David praises God's general providence, that he gives food to the young of the ravens which call upon him [Ps. 147:9; cf. Ps. 146:9, Vulg.]; but when God himself threatens the animals with famine, does he not sufficiently declare that he feeds all living things sometimes with a meager, at other times with a fuller, portion as seems best? It is childish, as I have already said, to restrict this to particular acts, since Christ says, without exception, that not even a tiny and insignificant sparrow falls to the ground without the Father's will [Matt. 10:29]. Surely if the flight of birds is governed by God's definite plan, we must confess with the prophet that he so dwells on high as to humble himself to behold whatever happens in heaven and on earth [Ps. 113:5-6].

6. God's Providence Especially Relates to Men

But because we know that the universe was established especially for the sake of mankind, we ought to look for this purpose in his governance also. The prophet Jeremiah exclaims, "I know, O Lord, that the way of man is not his own, nor is it given to man to direct his own steps" [Jer. 10:23; cf. Vulg.]. Moreover, Solomon says, "Man's steps are from the Lord [Prov. 20:24] and how may man dispose his way?" [Prov. 16:9, cf. Vulg.]. Let them now say that man is moved by God according to the inclination of his nature, but that he himself turns that motion whither he pleases. Nay, if that were truly said, the free choice of his ways would be in man's control. Perhaps they will deny this because he can do nothing without God's power. Yet they cannot really get by with that, since it is clear that the prophet and Solomon ascribe to God not only might but also choice and determination. Elsewhere Solomon elegantly rebukes this rashness of men, who set up for themselves a goal without regard to God, as if they were not led by his hand. "The disposition of the heart is man's, but the preparation of the tongue is the Lord's" [Prov. 16:1, 9, conflated]. It is an absurd folly that miserable men take it upon themselves to act without God, when they cannot even speak except as he wills!

Indeed, Scripture, to express more plainly that nothing at all in the world is undertaken without his determination, shows that things seemingly most fortuitous are subject to him. For what can you attribute more to chance than when a branch breaking off from a tree kills a passing traveler? But the Lord speaks far differently, acknowledging that he has delivered him to the hand of the slayer [Exod. 21:13]. Likewise, who does not attribute lots to the blindness of fortune? But the Lord does not allow this, claiming for himself the determining of them. He teaches that it is not by their own power that pebbles are cast into the lap and drawn out, but the one thing that could have been attributed to chance he testifies to come from himself [Prov. 16:33]. In the same vein is that saying of Solomon, "The poor man and the usurer meet together; God illumines the eyes of both" [Prov. 29:13; cf. 22:2]. He points out that, even though the rich are mingled with the poor in the world, while to each his condition is divinely assigned, God, who lights all men, is not at all blind. And so he urges the poor to patience; because those who are not content with their own lot try to shake off the burden laid upon them by God. Thus, also, another prophet rebukes the impious who ascribe to men's toil, or to fortune, the fact that some lie in squalor and others rise up to honors. "For not from the east, nor from the west, nor from the wilderness comes lifting up; because God is judge, he humbles one and lifts up another" [Ps. 75:6–7]. Because God cannot put off the office of judge, hence he reasons that it is by His secret plan that some distinguish themselves, while others remain contemptible.

SELECTION **6**

Friedrich Schleiermacher

Christian Faith, §§46–47

If Calvin is inclined to stress God's guidance at individual events, Schleiermacher focuses on God's direction of creation as a whole. He does this by arguing that belief in providence—that the whole of phenomenal reality is absolutely dependent on God for its continued existence—is simply a specifically religious interpretation of the experience of every event as the product of natural forces. From this perspective the idea of a special divine determination of individual events alongside God's general work of preservation becomes superfluous, since the feeling of absolute dependence already posits God as the fundamental cause behind every event. Indeed, for Schleiermacher it is precisely when we perceive all events as united with ourselves in a single causal nexus that we experience the feeling of absolute dependence most intensely—a perspective which leads him to view science and faith as standing in a relationship of mutual reinforcement rather than of conflict.

One important corollary of this interpretation of providence is a rejection of the idea of miracle, understood as special divine intervention in the world outside the nexus of natural causes. Aside from the fact that miracles have proved notoriously difficult to identify, Schleiermacher argues that the idea of divine supervention on the natural order is ruled out by the fact that the Christian experience of God's providential activity is experienced precisely in and through—and not in spite of or apart from—that order. Thus, a miracle is not to be understood objectively as a supernatural event, but rather subjectively as a natural event (albeit one whose exact cause may not be known) that stimulates and enhances individual piety.

From Friedrich Schleiermacher, *Christian Faith*, trans. Terrence N. Tice, Catherine L. Kelsey, and Edwina Lawler (Louisville, KY: Westminster John Knox Press, forthcoming).

§46. Religious self-consciousness, by virtue of which we locate all that bestirs us and influences us in our absolute dependence on God, wholly coincides with our discernment that precisely all of this is conditioned and determined by the interconnected process of nature.

1. In no way is it to be asserted that with every stirring of sensory self-consciousness that "religious self-consciousness" just referred to also actually arises. This is no more the case than that every sense perception also actually brings "the interconnected process of nature" to mind. In contrast, whenever some objective consciousness arrives at the degree of clarity indicated in our proposition we also posit[1] the interconnectedness of nature, in turn, as something entirely general and no less determinative even of all that wherewith the "discernment"[2] of this interconnected process of nature mentioned has not reached consciousness in us. By the same token, in those instances in which religious self-consciousness does occur we recognize those instances in which it has not occurred to be incomplete

---

1. Ed. note: "posit" (*setzen*) stands for what Christians are thought to "presuppose" (*voraussetzen*) in their religious self-consciousness, or affective states. In §32 Schleiermacher affirms that this is "the only way that in general terms, our own being and the infinite being of God can exist as one (*eines sein kann*) in self-consciousness."
2. *Einsicht*.

states. Moreover, we posit the feeling of dependence, because we also refer that feeling of dependence to our own being already inasmuch as we are parts of the world, just as we regard it to be true of all other such being, without exception.

It is also no more the case, however, that our proposition should also fall short of the concept of preservation, though in accordance with the nature of self-consciousness it is limited to what affects us and, to be sure, in a direct sense only to those movements and changes of things which stir us, not the things themselves and their internal being. That is to say, every stimulus that is directed to sense perception and knowledge, which do have the properties and being and nature of things as an object, also starts off with some stirring of self-consciousness, which stirring then also accompanies the operation of cognition from that point on; in this sense, then, the being and nature of things do also indirectly belong to that which affects us.

Now, within these bounds our proposition admits of no distinction. Rather, with respect to each and every thing we are to feel their absolute dependence on God, and to share that feeling, to the same extent that we conceive each and every thing to be completely conditioned by the interconnected process of nature. Entirely in opposition to this view, however, we do find the notion that these two states do not coincide but are rather mutually exclusive to be very widespread.

That is, it is asserted that the more clearly we conceive something in its complete conditionality[3] to exist through the interconnected process of nature, the less are we able to arrive at a feeling of its absolute dependence on God; and, conversely, the more lively this feeling is, the more we would have to leave the role of that interconnected process of nature in it undecided. It is plain to see, however, that from our standpoint and in agreement with all that has been established thus far, such a contrast between the two states cannot be validated. This is so, for in that case if we were to reach consummate knowledge of the world, the development of religious consciousness in ordinary life would have to cease entirely, because at that point everything would constantly present itself in terms of the interconnected process of nature, which would be entirely contrary to our presupposition that piety is an essential component of human nature. On the other hand, moreover, conversely our love of piety would have to strive against all zeal for research and all advancement of our knowledge of nature, which would be wholly opposed to the proposition that sense perception regarding the creation leads to consciousness of God. Furthermore, already even before the consummation of both tendencies every person most knowledgeable about nature would always have to be reli-

---

3. *Bedingtheit*. Ed. note: That is, in the unexceptionable restriction that it places on our existence, by virtue of which we are dependent on it.

gious least of all, and *vice versa*. Now, in the human psyche the tendency toward having knowledge of the world, however, is just as essential as is the tendency toward having God-consciousness. Thus, it can only be a pseudo-wisdom that would want to cancel out piety and a misconceived piety for love of which the advancement of knowledge would be taken to be obstructed.

The sole pretext that can be given for the assertion we are now examining is simply the circumstance that, to be sure, as a rule the more strongly objective consciousness comes to the fore in a given instance, the more will self-consciousness be suppressed in that same instance, and *vice versa*. This happens because, in the second case, in being more occupied with ourselves we tend to lose touch with any object affecting us, just as, in the first case, we tend toward being totally absorbed in the object. Emphasizing one activity over the other one, however, does not prevent either of these activities' stimulating and passing over to the other activity once it has been satisfied. Patently, moreover, one would wrongly rely on the claim that as a general experience what is not comprehended as such would always dispose us more than what is understood to be a stirring of religious feeling. As an example for this claim, people most love to cite the prodigious natural phenomena produced by elemental forces; yet, even the greatest confidence with which we accept any sort of hypothetical explanation of these impressive phenomena still does not put a stop to that religious feeling. The reason why those phenomena so prominently and readily stimulate religious feeling lies rather in the inscrutable complexity of their effects, both beneficial and destructive, on human existence and on the works of human art, thus in the aroused consciousness of our own efficacious action being conditioned by powers[4] of a general nature. Precisely this consciousness, however, is indeed the fullest recognition of the all-encompassing scope of the interconnected process of nature, and so this observation too could be used in just the opposite way, to support our proposition.

In another way, it is indeed a sign of human laziness to favor referring what is not understood directly to the supernatural. At that point, however, this referral to the supernatural does not belong to the tendency toward piety at all. Rather, in that the Supreme Being is then thought to substitute in place of the interconnected process of nature, one finds oneself in the tendency toward knowledge, just as in this sense too not everything but only what is incomprehensible is then placed in such an immediate dependence on God. Hence, based on this attitude people have just as easily invented morally evil and destructive powers holding sway over them as they have traced certain events back to powers of the highest good. This

---

4. *Potenzen*. Ed. note: This terms appears to be one borrowed from mathematics, a field in which Schleiermacher was quite adept; otherwise *Kräfte* would have been used. The term suggests higher and higher exponents of power, beyond ordinary comprehension, perhaps beyond any at present.

fact directly suggests that this sort of linkage to the "supernatural" has not proceeded from the interest of piety, in that by such a juxtaposition the unity and wholeness belonging to the relationship of dependence is unavoidably destroyed.

Still further, in that we posit everything that bestirs us as an object of this religious consciousness, even what is in itself miniscule and least significant is not to have been excluded from the relationship of absolute dependence. On this point, however, the following comments are to be made. On the one hand, not infrequently an improper value is placed on an explicit referral even of the tiniest particular to this relationship. On the other hand, often we resist such a reference with no greater justification. The first mistaken maneuver occurs in the opinion that even the smallest item must be expressly ordained by God, particularly because very often the most prominent item arises from the smallest. This opinion is mistaken, for the saying, so frequently heard, that great events issue from small causes, seems to be but an empty play of fantasy, though by no means an unquestionable one. This is so, in that thereby attention is simply distracted from the general interconnected process of nature, in which the true cases do actually lie. A pure calculation can be drawn up only on the basis of equivalence between cause and effect, whether this be in the historical domain or in that of nature, and in each instance only in well-defined relations may particular changes, along with their own causes, be extracted from the general interconnected process of nature and put on their own hook. As soon as religious feeling is combined with such an observation, however, it must revert to the general interconnected process of nature, this, as it were, so as not to impute to God an activity that is segregated off and partitioned,[5] the way human activity can be.

The second mistaken maneuver, which lies in a sense of resistance to referring the relationship of absolute dependence to the tiniest particular, is grounded in one's worrying that piety could become sacrilegious if reduced to arbitrariness in insignificant matters—for example, over which foot one should put down first—and to mere happenstance in matters that have no serious import—such as winning or losing in games and competitions—by considering that they too must be ordained by God.

Yet, what is disproportionate in both kinds of instance lies not in the given object but simply in the way it is observed—that is, in the isolating of particular cases, since in cases of the first kind seeming arbitrariness is always simply a particular expression, in part for an overall situation from which many things of the same kind follow and in part for a more general law by which a manifold set of similar things is regulated; and in cases of

---

5. *Vereinzelte und geteilte*. Ed. note: That is, split off from the exquisite interconnectedness of the whole and split up into arbitrary divisions. In the next paragraph "isolated" (*Isolieren*) seems roughly to stand for both descriptions, a word now chiefly used in the nominative for operations like "insulating," "screening" and "quarantining."

the second kind the outcome is always subsumed under a single will that they are taken to share. Neither of these kinds of cases can be regarded as insignificant. Thus, there will be nothing against their also being considered to be included within the concept "absolute dependence on God."

2. Now, if we consider our proposition purely in and of itself, in its entire compass, it must also be directly evident to anyone who grants in general terms, as a settled rule of experience, that the feeling of absolute dependence can be aroused by influences on our sensory self-consciousness. This is so, for that feeling rises to its fullest extent when we identify ourselves with the entire world in our self-consciousness and feel ourselves also to be no less dependent, so to speak, than this world is as a whole. This identification, however, can prosper in us only to the degree that we combine in thought all that is divided and segregated off in appearance and by means of this conjoining posit everything as one. Within this all-oneness of finite being the most complete and most all-encompassing interconnected process of nature is posited at this point. Thus, if we feel ourselves to be absolutely dependent, as this whole complex is, then these two things, the fullest conviction that everything is completely conditioned by and grounded in the totality of the interconnected process of nature and the inner surety regarding the absolute dependence of all that is finite on God wholly coincide.

Now, from this overall condition follow, at the same time, the possibility of religious self-consciousness for every element of objective consciousness and the possibility of a consummate world-consciousness for every element of a religious self-consciousness. That is to say, as concerns the second possibility, wherever a religious feeling has truly arisen there an interconnected process of nature is also always posited already. Accordingly, without detriment to that feeling, the effort to pursue this posited interconnected process of nature further and to bring it to the point of having a notion of the whole world can be effective to the degree that generally the tendency toward piety[6] is dominant. Likewise, as concerns the first possibility, wherever an objective notion is present, there an aroused self-consciousness is always present as well, and on this basis, without detriment to that notion, religious self-consciousness can develop, along with the notion of the whole world that is more or less clearly co-posited within it, to the degree that generally the tendency toward cognition is dominant in each person.

Now, if we imagine both tendencies to be fully formed in one human being, then each tendency would also call forth the other with complete ease. As a result, each thought, viewed as part of the concept "world," would lead that person toward the most unalloyed religious feeling possible, and

---

6. Ed. note: In this sentence all the texts have *Erkennen* (cognition) here; but at this exact spot in the first edition of 1821 the word is quite appropriately *Frömmigkeit* (piety) in counterpoint to *Erkennen* in the contrast being offered here. In turn, development of each of the two tendencies is dependent on that of the other tendency, even when the other tendency is dominant.

each religious feeling, viewed as called forth by some part of the world, would lead that person toward the fullest notion of the world possible. Conversely, if either tendency would not call forth the other but either tendency would curtail the other in some fashion, then the more completely developed one tendency would be, the more it would have to cancel out the other tendency.

Now, it has constantly been recognized by the most rigorous dogmaticians[7] precisely that divine preservation, viewed as the absolute dependence of all occurrences and changes on God, and natural causation, viewed as the complete conditionality of all that happens through the general interconnected process of nature, are neither sundered from nor curtailed by each other; rather, they recognize that the two are the same thing, only regarded from different viewpoints.

Anyone who nonetheless wants to find a semblance of pantheism in this position might simply consider that as long as wisdom concerning the world[8] sets forth no formula generally recognized to be valid for expressing the relationship between God and the world, so in the domain of dogmatics too, as soon as its talk is no longer about the origination of the world but is about its co-existence with God and its being related to God, a wavering cannot be avoided between formulas that approximate more toward a blended identity of the two and formulas that approximate more toward a contrasting severance between them. Further, so as not to confuse oneself in this manner, one ought simply to pay better attention to the difference between general and particular causes. This is so, for within the totality of finite being only a particular and partial causality is accorded each individual item, in that each is dependent not on *one* other item but on *all other* items; general causality exists only in that whereupon the totality of this divided causality is itself dependent.

Postscript. The method of division[9] in forming faith-doctrine, originally employed among the medieval scholastics, has broken up our simple proposition, in a most multiply categorized fashion, into a mass of distinct parts

---

7. Johann Andrea Quenstedt, *Theologia didactico-polemica, sive systema theologicum*, Tom I, 761: "Thus, that the same effect is produced not by God alone nor by creation alone but by one and the same efficient power from God and creation at the same time.... I say that this (concurrent) act is not prior to the action of a secondary cause nor subsequent to it ... but the act is such that it is included most profoundly in that very action of creation rather than that same action's being of creation alone." Cf. p. 762: "One action is not on its own the influence of God and other the work of creation, but there is one indivisible action regarding both and depending both on God as the general cause and on creation as the particular cause."

8. *Weltweisheit.* Ed. note: This word is a familiar substitute or synonym for "philosophy" (which is itself literally "the love of wisdom").

9. *Spaltende.* Ed. note: This important, generally authentic method of dividing up (*spaltende Methoda*) subject-matter for closer examination was an analytic tool first laid out and demonstrated by Socrates. By the period of the "Scholastics" it had sometimes reached an extreme, artificial form, later widely associated pejoratively with their name, called "hairsplitting" (*Haarespaltende*). Here Schleiermacher seems to leave the extent of its value itself open to examination, though ironically giving examples of the more extreme kind.

and specified sections. Moreover, there are so many of these that it becomes rather a matter of indifference which we choose so as to try to show in what sort of relationship they stand to our own presentation. Now, some scholars have divided the concept "preservation," which our proposition expresses as one undivided whole, into three parts: *general* preservation, which refers to the entire world, viewed as a unity, *special* preservation, which refers to the species, and *most special* preservation, which refers to particular things. For the purpose, this classification already seems not to be formed in the interest of piety, from which everything is nonetheless to proceed here, because it leads to the question, which entirely belongs to natural science, as to whether there might be something in the world that is not to be brought under the concept of species. However, suppose that this question has to be answered in the affirmative, so that the classification would also have to be expanded. Then, for all that, "general" preservation would still encompass everything else, and, since our basic feeling would rest only on the finitude of being in the world overall, any strict division[10] of categories would be superfluous for us.

Another aim to be served by this sort of classification can be anticipated, however, if one takes note of the addition that is usually made to the third member indicated here, namely that God preserves particular things in their mode of existence and their powers as long as God wills to do so. The reasons given are threefold: First, species, viewed in terms of the reproduction of particular things, are intransitory in a way. Thus, people have wanted to establish a distinction between what is relatively permanent and what is transitory. Meanwhile, for those who assume a beginning and end of the world, there is no reason at all to make a sharp distinction between the world and particular things. In any case, however, our proposition has just as well to hold true of the world's beginning and of its end. Second, we pretty much know regarding our world that species have existed that are no longer present and that present species have not always existed. Thus, our proposition must extend to all of these species as well. It thus expresses nothing other than that finite things' being temporal or enduring is also to be thought of only in their being absolutely dependent on God. Third, the endurance of particular things as well as of things that are of a general nature is nothing other than the expression of the sum total of their power in the co-existence of each with all the rest. Thus, nothing is contained in that addition we referred to, observed in and of itself, that our proposition would not also say. As it is formulated, however, it could very easily provoke an opinion that God's will to preserve would at some point or other begin or cease to operate. Thus, against that opinion the prefatory answer must be given that in preservation as much as in creation God would have to remain apart from all the means and occasions that belong to time.

10. *Zerteilung.*

Another allied classification lies in people's distinguishing between God's *preservation* and God's *cooperation*. This distinction, however, is not made in the same way by all teachers of faith-doctrine who use it, in that some refer the term "preservation" only to matter and form, reserving "cooperation" to refer to powers and actions, while others relate "preservation" to the mode of existence and powers of things and relate "cooperation" only to activities. Yet, it is not to be overlooked that a suggestion lies hidden in the term "cooperation" that within what is finite there might be an efficacious action that exists in and of itself, therefore independent of God's preserving activity. This suggestion must be entirely avoided and not perchance simply retained under the cover of its indefiniteness.[11] Thus, let us suppose that such a distinction is not made and that the powers of things are something no more apart from the divine activity of preservation than is their being, which latter could still be split up, by means of an abstraction that does not belong here, into matter and form. Then the distinction between preservation and cooperation would also be rooted only in an abstraction. This is the case, for any being that is to be posited in and of itself actually exists only where there is power, just as power unexceptionably exists only in activity of some being. Thus, a preservation that does not at the same time include in itself the fact that all activities of any finite being of any sort are positioned under the concept "absolute dependence on God" would, by the same token, be just as empty as a creation lacking in any preservation.

Likewise, if one should imagine a cooperation without the being of things over their entire duration being dependent on God, this being of things could also have been independent at its very first instant, and this status would indeed amount to a preservation such that it would not include creation within it but without positing creation either.

Now, the following observation also belongs here, that even teachers of faith-doctrine who have as a whole very correctly framed the subject have nonetheless been led to depict cooperation as something more direct than preservation.[12] They do this in such a way that they still separate activities of finite beings from preservation of powers that is engendered from some divine efficacious action. Thereby, strictly speaking, they in turn trace preservation of powers back to nothing, since in the domain of the interconnected process of nature this preservation is still repeatedly dependent on the activities that issue from the rest of things. Thus, in the domain that

---

11. As does Friedrich Nathanael Morus, *Commentarius exegetico-historicus in suam theologiae christianae epitomen*, ed. K.A. Hempel (Leipzig, 1797–1798), Tom I, 306: "For limits are not set by the extent to which the sun has an effect, or the farmer, or where God may begin.... God effects by aiding and by setting bounds, so that his plan may be carried out."

12. Quenstedt, *Theologia didactico-polemica*, Tom Ic, 760: "It should be observed that God not only gives the power of acting to secondary causes and also preserves it but that he directly influences the action and effect of creation."

pertains to absolute dependence on God one can only say that everything is directly mediated and directly unmediated, the first in the one relation and the second in the other relation.

Some then directly combine the concept "divine *government*" with these two concepts. To a certain extent, however, the intended meaning is a fulfillment of divine decrees[13] or a guidance of all things toward meeting divine ends, and by these assertions is to be understood something different from the view that by means of all powers that are distributed and preserved in the world everything happens or can happen as God originally and continually willed it—for the latter view is also already contained in our proposition. To that extent, then, we cannot treat of the concept of divine government at this point.[14] This is so in that here, where we have to do only with an overall description of the feeling of absolute dependence, a reflection that the contrast between purpose and means underlies, must be completely excluded, this quite apart from the issue of whether such a contrast can apply to God. That is to say, on the one hand, for our Christian religious self-consciousness it could in any case be only the reign of God that is to be grounded by redemption, thus something that lies beyond our present reflection, whereto everything else is related as to its purpose. On the other hand, however, if our self-consciousness is nonetheless to represent finite being overall at present, herewith purpose and means would be related as that which is posited for its own sake versus that which does not exist for its own sake, thus actually as that which is willed by God versus that which is not willed by God[15]— herewith a contrast that would have to be taken up into our religious self-consciousness but of which our present reflection knows nothing.

Thus, the only thing that this concept of divine governance could offer us here would be the following. To the extent that divine preservation, viewed as cooperation, is referred only to the powers and activities of every being that is to be posited as operating of itself, we require a counterpart to stand for the passive conditions of finite things. Now, these passive states are components just as essential for the attaining of divine purposes, and thus the absolute dependence of these passive states are also included within the concept of government. Yet, at this point even this consideration is superfluous. Such is the case, for, in the first place, passive states are already also assumed under the concept "absolute dependence" and, in the second place, they are also included in our general proposition.

---

13. Morus, *Commentarius*, Tom I, 319: "Governance is the work of God, effective in such a way that his plan may be carried out."
14. Ed. note: Thus, a discussion of the divine government of the world is postponed to a point in the presentation of doctrine by which it has been fully prepared for, under the rubric of "the divine wisdom" (§168–§169). *Regiergung* may be translated either as "government" or as "governance," as may *Regiment* for administrative activities in the church (*Kirchenregiment* vs. *Kirchenleitung*, "church leadership").
15. *Wie das um Sein-selbst-willen-Gesetzte und das Nicht-um-sein-selbst-willen, eigentlich also wie das von Gott Gewollte und Nichtgewollte.*

The first reason is applicable, since preservation has the being of things as its object, but in this being of things is contained the contrast between self-initiated activity and receptivity—this insofar as these things are a locus for exercise of powers and the passive states are also already assumed under the concept "absolute dependence."

The second reason is especially applicable, since these states belong to what affects our self-consciousness, both under the form of sense perception and under that of compassion,[16] thus they are also included in our general proposition. In addition, however, on the one hand, the passive states of one thing are simply what has proceeded from the active states of other things; and, on the other hand, the way in which the active states of things successively arise from each other and in what strength they appear depend on two things. They depend not alone on the distinctive mode in which a given thing exists but also on the actual engagement of each thing with others, consequently on the influences of other things and on the given thing's passive states.

Hence, one could imagine that one would perhaps form a still better differentiation if one were to say that if placed under the concept "absolute dependence on God" it would be a matter of indifference what arises from the being posited of each thing as existing of itself in accordance with its distinctive nature and what arises from its co-existence with everything else. Even this claim, however, would simply be an abstraction without any significance for our religious self-consciousness, for there the two processes, each viewed as a source of stimulation, are not distinguished from each other at all. Moreover, we would therefore do better to garner everything that bestirs our consciousness into the notion of finite being that is only relatively posited as existing of itself and that is itself conditioned through the general co-existence of things even in its being segregated from the rest. This notion is simply the very same thing as what our proposition designates by the expression "interconnected process of nature."

§47. Based on the interest of piety, it is never possible for a need to arise to conceive a fact in such a way that the fact's being conditioned by the interconnected process of nature[17] would be absolutely annulled by its dependence on God.

---

16. Ed. note: That is, both sense perception (*Wahrnehmung*) and compassion (*Mitgefühl*—literally, a feeling with or for another or shared with another). The first is a precondition for all other types and levels of perception (*Anschauung*). The second becomes a critically important component in Christ's redemptive work and in the life and work of the church; *Mitgefühl* can also be translated "sympathy," but in Schleiermacher's theological usage it is more than what is usually meant by that. It reaches out, empathically and actively, to the other.

17. *Naturzusammenhang*. Ed. note: In this context (§§46–47) especially, this characteristic of the natural order is indicated as a "process" by the translator, simply as a reminder that for Schleiermacher this order is far from static; it is a process in which the creative-preserving activity of God is taken to be very much engaged. In earlier, introductory discussions, the two points of special importance for Christian piety were that this intricately interrelated process is, in principle, ultimately to be grasped as natural and as accessible to human reason, including whatever may be affected by human,

1. This proposition is so much a direct consequence of the preceding one that achieving a natural progression would not at all have required expressly setting it forth. However, notions that are to a certain degree still widely held in the Christian church have to be carefully examined at the appropriate place in every systematic account of faith-doctrine.

Now, regarding "miracles," a notion of miracles that are implicated in the origination of Christianity or that are at least somehow reported in scripture is still quite familiar, and it is the notion that they are precisely events of the sort that our proposition describes. Moreover, since it is true that if the notion is itself untenable, it also cannot be assigned to this or that particular fact, teachers of faith-doctrine have long treated the issue in a general way. Here we do not have to adjudge the possibility of miracles in and of itself, however, but have only to consider the relationship of this assumption to the feeling of absolute dependence. That is to say, if the matter stands as our proposition states, then in our domain we will seek to apprehend every fact, as long as may be possible, with reference to the interconnected process of nature and without detriment to it.

Now, some have presented miracle defined in this way to be necessary for providing a complete exposition of divine omnipotence. However, on the one hand, it is difficult to grasp how omnipotence was ever to be more fully demonstrated in relation to interruptions within the interconnected process of nature than in the original yet indeed also, in accordance with divine order, unchanging course of it. This is difficult to grasp, since indeed the capacity to change things within what is ordered is but a prerogative of one who effects order if for the orderer there is a necessity to change that, in turn, can be grounded only in an incompleteness in the orderer as in the orderer's works. So, suppose that someone wanted to postulate such an intervention as a prerogative of the Supreme Being. In that case, one would first have to assume that something not ordered by the Supreme Being would exist that could be placed in opposition to the Supreme Being and thus could intervene in the very being and work of the Supreme Being. If we assumed this, our basic feeling would then be entirely contravened. On the other hand, yet to be considered is the fact that our basic feeling appears to be most weak and ineffective precisely when such a notion of miracles is most often employed—that is, in circumstances where there is as yet little acquaintance with nature. In contrast, the more widespread authentic information about nature is, thus the more sparingly that concept of miracle is employed, the more does that honoring of God which is an expression of our basic feeling arise. It then follows from this consideration that the most comprehensive exposition regarding divine omnipotence

---

relatively free choice. Whatever "chance" may be defined as including, this is not taken to abrogate the divine ordering in view of which the feeling regarding the absolute dependence of everything on God is seen to arise.

would occur in terms of a conception of the world that would make no use of this notion of miracle at all.

Along this line, others[18] have more shrewdly but hardly more tenably defended the matter in such a way that, in part, God would have needed miracle in order thereby to countermand the influences of free causes in the course of nature and, in part, God could generally have had reasons to remain in "direct" contact with the world. Now, the latter position in part presupposes an entirely lifeless view of divine preservation; in part it presupposes an overall contrast between indirect and direct activity in God, which contrast cannot be conceived without lowering the Supreme Being into the sphere of limited intelligence. The first position almost sounds as if free causes were not also objects of divine preservation—and indeed, just as the concept of preservation also implies the concept of creation, in such a way that they are both included and sustained within what is absolutely dependent on God. That is to say, if free causes thus came to be and are sustained, then for God there can no more arise a necessity to countermand their influences than to countermand the influences that one willless power of nature exercises on the area of another one. Neither, however, does anyone understand by the world that is the object of divine preservation the mechanism of nature alone; rather, this world includes the intertwining of this mechanism and freely acting beings, with the result that each of the two is inclusive of the other. Furthermore, the biblical miracles, for the sake of which this whole theory has been set forth, are much too isolated and encompass too little in their content to have a usable theory in relation to them that has posed for these miracles the task of restoring what free beings would have altered in the mechanism of nature. Rather, only one miracle, the sending of Christ,[19] definitely bears the purpose of restoring what free causes have changed, but in their own area, not in that of the mechanism of nature and also not against the course of nature originally ordered by God. Nor does it serve the interest of piety to insist that restorative free cause in the area of phenomenon must relate to the interconnected process of nature differently than other free causes do.

---

18. See Gottlob Christian Storr, *Lehrbuch der christlichen Dogmatik* (1803), §25.

19. Even in Christ, who is the greatest so-called "miracle," revelation, therefore, is always about "the supernatural becoming natural," not about breaking through the natural order. With respect to Christ, however, viewed as the completion of God's creation of human nature (§§89, 91, 93, 98)—in this sense as the prototypical "second Adam"—we may discern two roughly distinguishable but not strictly successive phases of God's activity in human history: a phase of "preparatory and introductory" activity before Christ appeared and a phase of spiritual "development and fulfillment" by God's grace in Christ (§164.2). By the Conclusion, then, we can have seen that the God on whom Christians are enabled to feel absolutely dependent is the triune God, manifested only from our temporal and finite perspective in a relatively successive way as Father, Christ and Holy Spirit—expressed in three circumscribed roles, as it were, as one God (*monos*). Thus, the entire systematic presentation of faith-doctrine has been organized so as to make as clear as possible what this one divine reality is. Cf. §46, notes 1 and 18.

Still, it is possible to advance two other reasons for the sake of which there can be an interest of piety in an absolute abrogation of the interconnected process of nature by miracle. Moreover, it cannot be denied that it is precisely for these reasons—even though they have never actually been set forth as ecclesial doctrine—that this notion of miracles has nonetheless kept at least a practical hold on many Christians. The first reason is "prayer being heard,"[20] because this very act would really seem to mean something only if on account of the prayer an outcome ensues that is different from what would have arisen otherwise, thus an outcome wherein there appears to lie an annulling of an event that would have resulted in accordance with the interconnected process of nature. The other reason is "regeneration,"[21] which tends to be presented as a "new creation" and thus in part may require an annulling of the same sort and in part may import into the interconnected process of nature a principle[22] that does not comport with preserving activity.

These two subjects cannot be fully discussed at this point. However, it will suffice to remark with respect to the first subject, which has more to do with piety in general terms, that our proposition also places prayer itself under divine preservation. As a result, prayer and its fulfillment or non-fulfillment are only aspects of the same original divine ordering, consequently that a "being would otherwise have been different" is simply an empty thought. As concerns the other subject, here we need only to rebuff something already mentioned above. That is to say, if God's revelation in Christ must not be considered to be something absolutely supernatural, then Christian piety too cannot be defined in advance to hold that anything that is associated with that revelation or that emerges from it is absolutely supernatural.

2. The closer determinations by which the assumption of such miracles is to be brought into connection with statements and concepts that designate the total dependence of the interconnected process of nature on God very clearly gives rise to the recognition of how little that notion of miracle is required by our religious stirrings. This is so, for the more definitely these stirrings intend to establish the existence of an absolute miracle, the farther away it is from being an expression of any religious stirring and the more something of a very different stamp enters in the place of genuine dogmatic content.[23]

---

20. *Gebetserhörung.* Implicit in the interpretation being discussed is the belief that what is asked for (petitioned) will presumably be answered in some fashion.
21. *Wiedergeburt.* Ed. note: Or "rebirth."
22. *Prinzip.* Ed. note: That is, a moving or motivating factor. On the sins and good works of the regenerate see §74.4 and §112. The contrast referred to is between the start-off factors of creation and regeneration and the otherwise not very strictly differentiated factors of preservation and sanctification.
23. (1) Johannes Laurentius Mosheim, in his *Elementa theologiae dogmaticae in academicis quondam praelectionibus proposita et demonstrata* I, §8, 462, calls the divine activity by which miracles are performed *gubernatio immediata* or *inordinata* (immediate or non-arranged government), whereby

In general, this topic can be most readily surveyed if one proceeds from two observations. The first observation is the following. Since anything in relation to which a miracle would come about would be bound together with all finite causes, every absolute miracle would severely disturb the entire interconnected process of nature. The second observation is that one can look at such a miracle from two points of view: a positive one, which extends into the whole future, and a negative one, which in a certain sense affects the entire past. That is, the latter would be the case in that what would have resulted from the totality of finite causes in accordance with the interconnected process of nature would not actually occur. Thus, an effect that would have happened would be blocked, and indeed this blocking would occur not by the influx of other finite causes countering it in a natural fashion, and thus present within the interconnected process of nature, but in spite of all effectual causes working in accord to bring about this effect. Therefore, everything that ever contributed to this end would to a certain degree be annihilated, and instead of installing at that spot within the entire interconnected process of nature only a single supernatural event, as one would actually want to have it, one would have to cancel out the concept of "nature" entirely.

Now, the positive point of view is that something would have to result that cannot be comprehended based on the totality of finite causes. However, in that this result of an absolute miracle would enter into the interconnected process of nature as an active component, in all future time everything would become different than it would have been if this particular miracle had not occurred. Moreover, not only would this absolute miracle annul the entire interconnected process of nature that belongs to the original ordering for all future time, but every subsequent miracle would also annul all earlier ones insofar as they had already entered into the series of effectual causes. Then, however, in order to describe the origination of what would follow, one would have to introduce the possibility of a divine influence apart from any natural

---

a contrast is made between miracles and God's preserving activity, to the advantage of the latter in the second formulation but to its disadvantage in the first formulation. However, pious feeling will likewise shy away from putting something in the middle between that which is and the divine activity by which it is, just as it shies away from ascribing something to the divine activity while at the same time wanting to call it subordinate to that activity. Moreover, the expression conflicts with the general definition that Mosheim gives of *gubernatio*, that it is to be a *directio virium alienarum* (a directing of power over alien forces), if a miracle is not to permit of being construed as based on pertinent natural forces.

(2) Franz Volkmar Reinhard, in his *Dogmatik*, 236 calls this same divine activity "extraordinary providence" and explains it in terms of "divine care in which God accomplishes some alteration or other that is quite inconsistent with the ordinary course of nature." If one may seek opposing elements in divine care, as here, preservation would then be a lack of care, or if it is to be sought in the normal course of nature, the latter would appear as something not dependent on divine care, and pious feeling would necessarily pronounce against both.

causes.[24] Yet, at whatever point one would also want to introduce this divine efficacious action as toward something particular, which action would always have to appear to be something magical, at which point one would conjure up a number of possible ways in which the same result could have been effected by natural causes if they had been arrayed to that end at the opportune time. The outcome would be that either one would be led to a purely epideictic[25] tendency of miracles for the sake of which God would intentionally not have arranged the interconnected process of nature in such a way that the entirety of what God wills would proceed from it—against which the above discussion concerning the relationship of omnipotence to this concept of miracle was directed; or, if the totality of finite causes could not be arranged in this way, then even what is not to be conceived as coming from the interconnected process of nature could never rightly arouse in us a feeling of the absolute dependence of all that is finite.

Now, others believe that they can more readily establish this notion of absolute miracles if from the very outset they classify divine cooperation into an ordinary type and an extraordinary type—which is only seemingly different from a subordinate type—and then they would assign the ordinary type to natural operations and the extraordinary type to supernatural operations. As a result, the negative aspect of miracle would consist in the withdrawal of ordinary cooperation.[26] In contrast, the positive aspect would consist in the entry of extraordinary cooperation. On the one hand, then, ordinary cooperation would nevertheless no longer be ordinary if it could be withdrawn and would no longer be at all distinctly different from extraordinary cooperation. Rather, we would then call more frequent occurrences "ordinary" and rare occurrences "extraordinary," a relationship that could just as well be reversed. Suppose, on the other hand, that miracle is still chiefly accomplished by finite causes, though by means of some divine cooperation even if it be an extraordinary one. Even so, in that something would come to pass by finite causes that could not have come to pass in accordance with their natural constitution, alternative consequences would then follow. First, they would not be causes in this case, and then the expression "cooperation" would be incorrect. For, second, they would have

---

24. The formulation that God is active in this case without being linked with any intermediate causes is on this account already in contradiction to our basic feeling, because therein God is presented as linked with the normal course of nature. In a hidden way, however, this very terminology, which describes natural causes as intermediate causes, is infected with the fundamental error of thinking that the dependence on God of that which happens as of the same sort as dependence on particular finite causes, only lying further back. Accordingly, then, where Storr intends to show how God can influence the world directly and alter the course of nature without abrogating natural laws (*Dogmatik*, 336), he in fact seems to represent God after the manner of a finite free cause.

25. Ed. note: In rhetoric, discourse for show or mere persuasion, not strictly a result of reasoning.

26. Quenstedt, *Theologia didactico-polemica*, Tom Ic, 760: "If God removes his concurrent action, the action of creation stops."

become something different from what they once were, and then every such extraordinary cooperation would truly be a "creation"; after this creation the restoration of a given active thing to its original status would be a reiterated creation that would, in turn, annul the previous one.

It is not to be denied, moreover, that of these two explanations the one is more suited to one class of biblical miracles, and the other is more suited to the other class,[27] and thus the different make-up of these purported events have borne significant influence on the construction of these different formulas. So, if someone should not find it easy to profess belief even in this notion of absolute miracle, one must still concede to the following. That is, first one notes that earlier theologians did hold fast to this notion of miracle, in its totality;[28] more recent theologians,[29] however, do not want to afford exclusive currency to this hypothesis but also find it reliable to hypothesize that, in a way inconceivable to us, God would have prepared for miracles in nature itself. Thus, in the interest of piety we also have to regard this position as a real step forward.

3. Accordingly, it appears also in relation to what is wondrous[30] overall to have the general interest of science,[31] particularly investigations into nature, and the interest of piety meet at the same point. That is, that point is where we let go of the notion of what is absolutely supernatural, because in no instance would we really know anything to be such, nor is such an acknowledgment ever required of us. Before long, in part it will be generally agreed that because our acquaintance with created nature is only in the process of growing, we have very little grounds for holding anything to be impossible. In part, it will also be admitted, in particular, that since by far the most New Testament miracles do lie within this broader area, we can indeed also neither exactly define what the boundaries are in the fluctuation of relationship between body and mind nor even simply assert that they are overall and always completely the same, not being able to undergo expansions or to be exposed to unsettled variations. In this way, everything

---

27. Friedrich Nathanael Morus puts the distinction this way: "For indeed, mention is made of natural support, or such mention is indeed made but the thing was done with the word having preceded it." See Morus, *Commentarius*, Tom I, 98–99.

28. Johann Franz Buddeus, *Theses theologicae de atheismo et superstione* (Leipzig, 1717), 291: "Operations that, in truth, are the laws of nature, by which the order and preservation of all this world are supported, are suspended." According to Thomas Aquinas, *Summa Theologiae*, 1.10.4: "It is for this reason that a miracle is defined as an event that happens outside the ordinary processes of the *whole* of created nature." Ed. Note: Latin text and ET in M. J. Charlesworth, ed. (London: Blackfriars, 1970), 17.

29. See Reinhard, *Dogmatik*, 238, to see how the expression "ordinary course of nature" adduced above was already prudently chosen in this respect as well. Morus treats of the matter in the same sense, albeit superficially, in his *Commentarius*, part 1, 97–98.

30. *Das Wunderbare*. Ed. note: In German usage, this is usually a broader concept than that of the absolutely miraculous, referring rather to what is wondrous, wonderful, marvelous, amazing or astounding.

31. *Wissenschaft*, then *Naturforschung*. Ed. note: Cf. §17, which articulates the twofold interest in dogmatics as "scientific" and "ecclesial," the latter interest focusing on piety.

remains a task for scientific investigation to tackle, even the most wondrous thing that occurs or has occurred. At the same time, however, wherever that wondrous event stimulates religious feeling, whether on account of what it aims at or for some other reason, the value of that event will not find itself to be detracted from in any way by pointing out that some future knowledge concerning it is possible. In addition, we are entirely released from the difficult and highly dubious task on which dogmatics has so long labored in vain,[32] namely that of discovering secure marks for distinguishing false and diabolical miracles from miracles that are divine and true.

SELECTION 7

Karl Barth

"The Christian Belief in Providence"

Barth's mature doctrine of providence reflects both his early "dialectical" insistence on the radical otherness of God and the profound christocentrism of *Church Dogmatics*. He begins by insisting that providence be understood exclusively as a matter of faith and not as any sort of inference from or explanation of worldly experience. Correspondingly, he cautions against the temptation to confuse providence with any empirically derived theory of history, whether conceived on a cosmic or purely personal scale, arguing that any attempt to read divine providence off the course of worldly events constitutes an idolatrous confusion of the world with God. In the same way, he eschews any equation of providence with a general confidence in the course of history that might be shared across different religious traditions, maintaining that the Christian belief in providence is constituted and justified exclusively by reference to Jesus Christ. It is in light of the relationship of the Father to the Son revealed in Christ, Barth contends, that the Christian conceives of God's lordship over the whole world as one of "fatherly" care.

From Karl Barth, *Church Dogmatics*, III/3, ed. G. W. Bromiley and T. F. Torrance (Edinburgh: T. & T. Clark, 1960), 14–30.

Belief in God's providence is the practical recognition that things are as we have said. It is the joy of the confidence and the willingness of the

---

[32]. Johann Gerhard, *Loci communes theologici* XXIII, §271. Ed. note: Apparently, Schleiermacher has derived some of the positions examined under this proposition from this source, or he has found them to be conveniently catalogued there.

obedience grounded in this reality and its perception. In the belief in providence the creature understands the Creator as the One who has associated Himself with it in faithfulness and constancy as this sovereign and living Lord, to precede, accompany and follow it, preserving, co-operating and overruling, in all that it does and all that happens to it. And in the belief in providence the creature understands itself as what it is in relation to its Creator, namely, as upheld, determined and governed in its whole existence in the world by the fact that the Creator precedes it every step of the way in living sovereignty, so that it has only to follow. And in the belief in providence this does not have the character of idle speculation, just as God's providence is not the idle onlooking of a divine spectator, but takes practical shape in the fact that the creature which enjoys this recognition may always and in every respect place itself under the guidance of its Creator, recognize its higher right, and give it its gratitude and praise....

In the light of this statement several sharp delimitations are indispensable.

1. The Christian belief in providence is faith in the strict sense of the term, and this means first that it is a hearing and receiving of the Word of God. The truth that God rules, and that the history of existent creation in its given time is also a history of His glory, is no less inaccessible and inconceivable, no less hard for man to grasp, than the truth of the origin of creation in the will and power of the Creator. In regard to the former there is as little to discover, comprehend and maintain, as little to conceive and postulate, as little room for pious or impious, practical or theoretical ventures, as there is in the latter. In both we find ourselves in the sphere of the confession which is possible only as the confession of faith or not at all. It is quickly said, and apparently easy to understand, that the history of created being takes place in every respect and in its whole range under the lordship of God. But we have only to consider one little portion of this history of created being even in outline, let alone in its concrete differentiations and details, and honesty forces us to ask whether these are not empty words. We start back from what we say, for it obviously goes far beyond what we know from our own experience and conviction, and what we can see and know and say responsibly falls far short of what is said with this confession. Indeed, it is better not to say it if in and in spite of this hesitation we do not have to say it as we confess our faith. Sincerely? Yes, if this sincerity consists in the fact that we are directed to say it by the Word of God, but not if it rests only on our own experiences and convictions. And we have only to ask how far, i.e., how little what we say with this confession squares with a corresponding heartfelt trust and obedience, to be honestly arrested afresh by the question whether it is not a cheap and unimpressive saying because we have never really answered it with our lives, and never will. If in spite of this more serious hesitation we do not have to say it as we confess our faith; if we do not know that we

can say it only to our own shame, it is better not to say it. In this matter, too, Christian faith begins where the sincerity of our own experiences and convictions reaches its limit with faith, where the measure of our corresponding trust and obedience obviously does not suffice, where we must completely abandon any self-confidence. It begins where we can cling only to the Word of God, where we may cling to this Word, but may do so with the indisputable certainty which is legitimate and obligatory and even self-evident when a man looks away from himself to God, when he has to do with His gift, when he makes use of the possibility which is created by the free work of the Holy Spirit within him, within his despondent heart, his foolish and fickle thoughts, his sinful life. In this faith man must say what a Christian has to say concerning the providence of God. If it is a confession of this faith, it is *eo ipso* a solid confession, because *eo ipso* one which has reference to this objective content and derives from the revelation of this objective content.

The notion against which we have to delimit ourselves at this point is that which regards the Christian belief in providence as an opinion, postulate or hypothesis concerning God, the world, man and other things, an attempt at interpretation, exposition and explanation based upon all kinds of impressions and needs, carried through in the form of a systematic construction, and ventured as if it were a pious outlook which has a good deal in its favor and may be adopted if we ourselves are pious. We can formulate and adopt opinions, postulates and hypotheses of this type, and sometimes abandon them again. But it is important to remember that even in the form of belief in providence Christian faith is grounded on the Word of God, and can draw its life from this alone. On this basis alone can we be sure, and on this basis we must, that it is not a non-obligatory and ultimately insecure view, and that the lordship of God over the history of created being is not therefore a problem, but an objective fact which is far more certain than anything else we think we know about this history or even ourselves. We can and must understand that the knowledge of this lordship of God can be compared only to the category of axiomatic knowledge, and that even in relation to this category it forms a class apart. If the Christian belief in this lordship were a view which ultimately had behind it only the thinking, feeling, choosing and judging human subject, both it and its confession would always be unstable. But it is not such a view. It consists in a realization of the possibility which God gives to man. It is the freedom which God Himself has given to man for God. And as such it cannot vacillate. The matter itself, God's lordship over the history of creaturely being, has spoken in the Word of God as in His revelation to man, and it no longer permits him even hypothetically to think as though it were not present and this history took place under no lordship at all, or that of another. Man has not elected himself, but is elected, to believe in the lordship of God. He has thus no option but to believe in it, and to confess this faith. In this sense the statement concerning providence is a statement of faith. We shall have to take pains to understand and assert it as such in all its details. We shall have to avoid the temptation of slipping back from the level of faith to the level where there can be only interpretations, opinions, postulates and hypotheses which it would be difficult to establish dogmatically....

2. The Christian belief in providence is also faith in the strict sense to the extent that, with reference to its object, it is simply and directly faith in God Himself, in God as the Lord of His creation watching, willing and working above and in world-occurrence. The consolation and impulse of this faith is that it points man to God in respect of the whole history of created being including his own. The man who lives by his faith may know that in everything which may happen to him he has to do with God. And beyond his own personal situation and history, as a near or distant witness and participant in all world-occurrence in all its dimensions, he may realize and count on it that God Himself not only has a hand in it all, but is in the seat of sovereign rule, so that no other will can be done than His. Whatever the distance, the heights or depths, they are all bounded by the horizon that God exists as and where His creatures exist, and that His existence as such controls theirs. God's disposing is the kernel by which faith in His providence is nourished, to which it always strives and must continually return. Much may vary in the sphere of the divine disposing. In it there is a place for prosperity and adversity, victory and defeat, peril and protection, life and death, angels and demons, even human sin and human liberation. God is Lord in all these things. He is so in very different ways. But properly and in the last resort exclusively it is He who is always Lord. And this reference to Him is the meaning and power of the belief in providence. In face of all the variations of world occurrence the trust and obedience of this belief always have Him in view as Helper, Commander, Judge and King. They look always to His mercy, holiness, faithfulness and omnipotence. Belief in providence depends on God and God alone: on God as the One who works all in all; but only on Him and on the fact that He is Lord of all.

It does not depend, therefore, on creatures and the different determinations proper to them in the world of His control, whether in detail, so that this or that good and fine and beautiful or in some way illuminating creaturely being is its true object, or as a whole, so that even though we say God we really mean creation and its life and their goodness or beauty or some other distinction. God is not creation. Neither in detail nor as a whole is He a determination of creation. To be sure, in its various determinations creation is, in the fine phrase of Luther, the mask of God, namely, to the extent that its history is also the history of the glory of its Creator. But it is only His mask and never His face, so that in it and its determinations in detail or as a whole we never have to do with God Himself. For as the history of God's glory takes place in, with and under that of creation, it is a hidden history, which is neither felt, seen, known, nor dialectically perceived by man, but can only be believed on the basis of this Word of God. We do not now speak of the divine manifestations, particularly that which fulfilled all others as the incarnation of the Word, the becoming creature of the Creator. In divine manifestation it is a matter of the establishment of faith in which the glory of God breaks through its concealment and man finds himself in direct confrontation with God. Even here the acting subject and therefore the basis of faith is God Himself and not His creaturely appearance in itself and as such. Even as the person of Jesus Christ it is the eternal Son of the Father, and only in unity with Him the man in whom this glory is revealed. Our present reference is to faith in God's more general presence and lordship in world-occurrence. Of this it falls to be said that it is real, and takes place in the world, but is concealed in world-occurrence as such, and therefore cannot be perceived or read off from this. Its revelation is not world-occurrence itself, but the Word of God, Jesus Christ. On the basis of this Word, in the freedom created by it, it may be believed, but prior to the consummation of the time of the world it can never be seen. Hence the object of the belief in providence can only be God Himself, as God Himself in His revelation in Jesus Christ is its only basis. The object of this belief cannot, then, be a creature, or any of its variable and varied determinations, instead of God. How could this belief stand if God were to it only what this or that glorious or apparently glorious creature is, or if He were only the Lord of the good and beautiful, of light and love and life, in the cosmic process, in a process which obviously stands so largely and we might often think totally under opposite determinations? If He is not the Lord in the latter, He is not in the former, and this is not the Christian belief. The Christian belief is not directed to any creature, or any modification or aspect of the creature, but to the Creator who is the Lord of His creature in all its modifications and aspects.

But this means—and here we come to the decisive point in this delimitation—that no human conception of the cosmic process can replace God as the object of the belief in providence. Man makes such conceptions. It is inevitable that he should do so, for otherwise he would not be capable of any practical orientation and decision. It is difficult to see how to forbid this. It belongs to his very life as man to do it. Every man has some conception at least of his own life and that of his nearest fellow; a picture of his own or someone else's life-work as it has so far developed and will do so, or should or should not do so, according to his insight, understanding and judgment. His particular notion of those different determinations of creaturely being, of good and evil, right and wrong, weal and woe, etc., will naturally play an important part in this. Such pictures may have a wider reference. They may be pictures of the life-process of a society, e.g., the Church, or a particular form of the Church, or a nation, or group of nations, or the whole of human history. Some standards, moral or amoral, technical, cultural, political or economic, will dominate the one who forms them, leading him to assert progress or decline, formation, reformation or deformation, and determining both his assessment of the past and his expectations, yearnings and fears for the future. And such pictures, always on the same assumptions on the part of the one who forms them, may have an even wider reference. They may embrace the whole of being known to man, perhaps as a kind of history of evolution, perhaps more modestly as an analysis and description of the eternal movement of all being and its laws and contingencies, possibly including or defiantly or gaily excluding the good God, who at bottom, subject to what the one who forms them thinks concerning Him, might well be able to call some place his own within this total picture. There is no objection to man making these small and great conceptions of the course of things. Indeed, there is much to be said for it. It is itself quite definitely part of the world-process, and therefore of the history of creaturely or at any rate human being, that there should always be such conceptions, which whether small or great can never be conceived as mere pictures of history, but raise the claim, and can always make it good in some depth and breadth, to shape and actually make history. Our present point is that no such conception can replace God as the object of the belief in providence. No such picture can come in question as a picture of God. The belief in providence does not rule out such conceptions. It can allow them their specific place and right as necessary expressions and media of human life. In certain circumstances it can take them very seriously. It can sometimes, transitorily and with a particular application, see its object in the similitude of such pictures. But it will realise that even in them, in the strict sense of the concept, it has to do only with the masks of God, or more accurately with the masks through which man—not without the divine appointment, will and permission—can see these masks of God, and behind which he usually hides himself from God and his fellows (under the name and pretext of an "ism"). The belief in providence embraces these conceptions, but it also limits them. It reckons with the truth which they contain. It also reckons with the distinctive dynamic with which they do not merely reflect but shape history. But it remains free in face of them. It does not rest on any of them. It cannot do this. For it is faith in God and His dominion and judgment to which all history, even that of the spirit, even that of human conceptions of human history, is wholly subject. It cannot, then, become belief in a human system of history invented by man, even when this system is the one to which the believer himself would give the preference and his heartiest approval. When a man believes, he will understand and apply even his own system, his own more or less distinct picture of history, only as a working hypothesis, and thus maintain the humility, the humor and the freedom to modify or abandon it as occasion may demand. He will treat it as an instrument which he has fashioned or taken over from others, which he uses so long as it can be used, but which he may see himself compelled and authorized to alter or to set aside and replace by another. He may give it much *fides humana* [faith in the human sphere], but he will not give it any *fides divina* [faith in the divine sphere]. He will be seriously convinced of its relative truth and goodness, but he will not believe in them. He will believe in God's providence, and not in his own as documented in his system. In all that follows we must beware of any aberration in this respect....

3. We now come to the third and most important delimitation. In its substance the Christian belief in providence is Christian faith, i.e., faith in Christ. The Word of God which it believes, in which it believes and which sets it in the light in which it may see the lordship of God in the history of creaturely being, is the one Word of God beside which there is no other—the Word which became flesh and is called Jesus Christ. And the history of creaturely being is—secretly but really—the history of the glory of God in the fact that it does not merely run alongside the history of Jesus Christ and therefore the history of the covenant of grace between God and man, but has its meaning in this, is conditioned and determined by it, serves it, and in its reflected light (and shadow) is the place, the sphere, the atmosphere and medium of its occurrence and revelation.

Hence the belief in providence is not a kind of forecourt, or common foundation, on which the belief of the Christian Church may meet with other conceptions of the relationship of what is called "God" with what is called "world." The lordship of God over world occurrence which is its theme is not a general form which might have a very different content. It is not a genus comprehending not only the lordship of the Father of Jesus Christ, the God of the election and covenant of grace, but also the sway of any other deities freely selected by religion or philosophy. In virtue of its relation to what God has done once for all in Jesus Christ, it is a happening *sui generis*....

The Christian belief in providence is given its content and form, and therefore its distinction from other views apparently similar, by the fact that the lordship of God over the world which is its object is not just any lordship, but the fatherly lordship of God. And this "fatherly" does not mean only "kind" and "friendly " and "loving." It means all this, yet not abstractly, but on a specific basis. Similar attributes of the supreme ruler or principle of the world are to be found elsewhere, but only in a way which is nonobligatory, contingent and problematical. In the language of the Christian belief in providence, "fatherly" means first of all, quite apart from any such predicates and as their solid foundation, that the God who sits in government is "the eternal Father of our Lord Jesus Christ." The Christian belief does not gaze into the void, into obscurity, into a far distance, height or depth, when it knows and confesses God as the Lord of the history of created being. It really knows this God, and therefore His rule. Under our second point we have established that it knows Him as it receives His Word. But His Word is not empty. It is not the reference to a supreme being which is supposed to have certain qualities. It is He Himself. But it is He Himself in a way in which He can be accepted by man. It is His person as a human person, His Word in the flesh, His eternal Son born in time as the Son of Mary, and crucified and raised for us. This "God with us" and "God for us" is God in eternity, the Son. And no other, but this God, is also "God over us," the eternal Father of this eternal Son. In the belief in providence it is a matter of "God over us," of God the Creator in His majesty, transcendence and lordship over His creature. But God the Creator is one God. The One who is for us as the Son is over us as the Father. As God has elected to be for us in His Son, He has elected Himself our Father and us His children. We are not in strange hands, nor are we strangers, when He is over us as our Creator and we are under Him as His children. We are His children for the sake of His Son and with Him (in whom He is so really for us that He becomes one with us). And it is as such that we are creatures in His fatherly hand. This fatherly hand is the divine power which rules the world. We can know no divine power over us, nor is there any such power, which is not this fatherly hand. As and because it is this fatherly hand, it is kind and friendly and loving. It has these qualities as the grace with which the same God who elected Himself our Father in His Son is also over us as our Creator. He is over us in a way which corresponds to this election of grace, to this eternal "for us" in His Son. Even as our Creator He is not alien or ungracious, but gracious. He is gracious as a Father to His children. And in this connection we have to remember that the truth of this relationship is not to be found in what might take place between a human father and his children, but in what has taken place from all eternity, and then in time, between God the Father and the Son. He is our heavenly Father, in a way which surpasses all that we can see or think. We are thus warned in advance that we cannot make what we think we know as fatherly or any other kindness, friendliness and love the measure and criterion of His. It is a matter of the eternal fatherly fidelity which we can only try to see and grasp where it is revealed to us. "He that hath seen me hath seen the Father" (John 14:9). It is here that the Christian belief in providence sees the Father, and therefore God over us, and therefore the Lord of the world-process. It is here that the will which rules the history of created being is not concealed. It looks to the history of the covenant which is fulfilled in the mission, in the person and work of the incarnate Son, of the "God for us." And through and beyond this it looks to the divine election of grace. And it thus sees the Father, the "God over us," as it sees the Son. As it sees Him it hears the Word of God, and as it hears the Word of God it receives the light on God's rule in the world beside which there is no other. The light which it receives and by which it lives will thus consist always in the fact that it may there perceive not only the will of an unknown Lord, not only the lines of an order and consistence, not only the stages of a process, but the demonstration of the Lord who is our Father for the sake of His Son, of the Lord of the covenant of grace, of the God of the eternal election of grace. In very general terms this is the specific and incomparable element in the Christian belief in providence.

SELECTION 8

Pierre Teilhard de Chardin

The Future of Man

          Pierre Teilhard de Chardin (1881–1955) is one of the most original and controversial among twentieth-century theologians. Trained both as a paleontologist and as a Catholic priest, he was one of the first to attempt a systematic reinterpretation of theology in light of evolutionary theory. It was his contention that evolution proceeded toward ever-greater complexity (a process he termed "orthogenesis") converging toward a transcendent spiritual presence that he called the "Omega point." Though his teachings were denounced by the Vatican after his death, his ideas still exercise considerable influence among both Catholic and non-Catholic theologians interested in the relationship between theology and science.

The following essay was originally delivered as a lecture in China (where Teilhard spent much of his career) in 1945. In it Teilhard argues that humanity stands at a turning point in the process of cosmic evolution, characterized by a shift from persons' functioning as more or less autonomous individual organisms to their coalescence into a superorganism. He takes pains to note that this process (which he terms "planetisation") does not mean the obliteration of individual identity found in totalitarian societies, but rather refers to a radical interdependence characteized by a common vision of and enthusiasm for the future, ultimately allowing human beings to transcend the limitations of biological existence. While Teilhard's views remain highly speculative and his equation of evolution with progress is open to criticism on scientific grounds, his theories represent a serious effort to reconcile the Christian belief in providence with scientific understandings of natural history, and his description of humanity as superorganism has found a favorable reception among some evolutionary biologists.

      From Pierre Teilhard de Chardin, *The Future of Man*
      (New York: Harper & Bros., 1964), 113–20.

The Present State of Mankind: The Phase of Planetization
To open any book treating scientifically, philosophically or sociologically of the future of the Earth (whether by a Bergson or a Jeans) is to be struck

at once by a presumption common to most of their authors, certain biologists excepted. Explicitly or by inference they talk as though Man today had reached a final and supreme state of humanity beyond which he cannot advance; or, in the language of this lecture, that, Matter having attained in *Homo sapiens* its maximum of centro-complexity on Earth, the process of super-molecularisation on the planet has for good and all come to a stop.

Nothing could be more depressing, but also, fortunately, more arbitrary and even scientifically false, than this doctrine of immobility. No proof exists that Man has come to the end of his potentialities, that he has reached his highest point. On the contrary, everything suggests that at the present time we are entering a peculiarly critical phase of super-humanisation. This is what I hope to persuade you of by drawing your attention to an altogether extraordinary and highly suggestive condition of the world around us, one which we all see and are subject to, but without paying any attention to it, or at least without understanding it: I mean the increasingly rapid growth in the human world of the forces of collectivization.

The phenomenon calls for no detailed description. It takes the form of the all-encompassing ascent of the masses; the constant tightening of economic bonds; the spread of financial and intellectual associations; the totalisation of political regimes; the closer physical contact of individuals as well as of nations; the increasing impossibility of being or acting or thinking alone—in short, the rise, in every form, of the Other around us. We are all constantly aware of these tentacles of a social condition that is rapidly evolving to the point of becoming monstrous. You feel them as I do, and probably you also resent them. If I were to ask your views you would doubtless reply that, menaced by this unleashing of blind forces, there is nothing we can do but evade them to the best of our ability, or else submit, since we are the victims of a sort of natural catastrophe against which we are powerless and in which there is no meaning to be discerned.

But is it true that there is nothing to understand? Let us look more closely, once again by the light of our principle of complexity.

The first thing to give us pause, as we survey the progress of human collectivization, is what I would call the inexorable nature of a phenomenon which arises directly and automatically out of the conjunction of two factors, both of a structural kind: first, the confined surface of the globe, and secondly, the incessant multiplication, within this restricted space, of human units endowed by ever-improving means of communication with a rapidly increasing scope for action; to which may be added the fact that their advanced psychic development makes them preeminently capable of influencing and inter-penetrating one another. Under the combined effect of these two natural pressures a sort of mass-hold of Mankind upon itself comes of necessity into operation.

But, the second noteworthy point, this phenomenon of holding, or cementing, turns out to be no sudden or unpredictable event. Looking at the picture as a whole we see that Life, from its lowest level, has never been able to effect its syntheses except through the progressively closer association of its elements, whether in the oceans or on land. Upon an imaginary earth of constantly increasing extent, living organisms, being only loosely associated, might well remain at the monocellular stage (if indeed they got so far); and certainly Man, if free to live in a scattered state, would never have reached even the neolithic stage of social development. The totalisation in progress in the modern world is in fact nothing but the natural climax and paroxysm of a process of grouping which is fundamental to the elaboration of organized matter. Matter does not vitalize or super-vitalize itself except by compression.

I do not think it is possible to reflect upon this twofold in-rooting, both structural and evolutionary, which characterizes the social events affecting us, without being at first led to the surmise, and finally overwhelmed by the evidence, that the collectivization of the human race, at present accelerated, is nothing other than a higher form adopted by the process of molecularization on the surface of our planet. The first phase was the formation of proteins up to the stage of the cell. In the second phase individual cellular complexes were formed, up to and including Man. We are now at the beginning of a third phase, the formation of an organico-social super-complex, which, as may easily be demonstrated, can only occur in the case of reflective, personalized elements. First the vitalization of matter, associated with the grouping of molecules; then the hominization of Life, associated with a super-grouping of cells; and finally the planetization of Mankind, associated with a closed grouping of people: Mankind, born on this planet and spread over its entire surface, coming gradually to form around its earthly matrix a single, major organic unity, enclosed upon itself; a single, hyper-complex, hyper-centrated, hyperconscious archmolecule, co-extensive with the heavenly body on which it was born. Is not this what is happening at the present time—the closing of this spherical, thinking circuit?

This idea of the planetary totalization of human consciousness (with its unavoidable corollary, that wherever there are life-bearing planets in the Universe, they too will become encompassed, like the Earth, with some form of planetized spirit) may at first sight seem fantastic: but does it not exactly correspond to the facts, and does it not logically extend the cosmic curve of molecularization? It may seem absurd, but in its very fantasy does it not heighten our vision of Life to the level of other and universally accepted fantasies, those of atomic physics and astronomy? However mad it may seem, the fact remains that great modern biologists, such as Julian Huxley and J. B. S. Haldane, are beginning to talk of Mankind, and to predict its future, as though they were dealing (all things being equal) with a brain of brains.

So why not?

Clearly this is a matter in which I cannot compel your assent. But I can assure you, of my own experience, that the acceptance of this organic and realistic view of the social phenomenon is both eminently satisfying to our reason and fortifying to our will.

Satisfying to the intelligence above all. For if it be true that at this moment Mankind is embarking upon what I have called its "phase of planetisation," then everything is clarified, everything in our field of vision acquires a new sharpness of outline.

The tightening network of economic and psychic bonds in which we live and from which we suffer, the growing compulsion to act, to produce, to think collectively which so disquiets us—what do they become, seen in this way, except the first portents of the super-organism which, woven of the threads of individual men, is preparing (theory and fact are at one on this point) not to mechanize and submerge us, but to raise us, by way of increasing complexity, to a higher awareness of our own personality?

The increasing degree, intangible, and too little noted, in which present-day thought and activity are influenced by the passion for discovery; the progressive replacement of the workshop by the laboratory, of production by research, of the desire for well-being by the desire for more-being—what do these things betoken if not the growth in our souls of a great impulse towards super-evolution?

The profound cleavage in every kind of social group (families, countries, professions, creeds) which during the past century has become manifest in the form of two increasingly distinct and irreconcilable human types, those who believe in progress and those who do not—what does this portend except the separation and birth of a new stratum in the biosphere?

Finally, the present war; a war which for the first time in history is as widespread as the earth itself; a conflict in which human masses as great as continents clash together; a catastrophe in which we seem to be swept off our feet as individuals—what aspect can it wear to our awakened eyes except that of a crisis of birth, almost disproportionately small in relation to the vastness of what it is destined to bring forth?

Enlightenment, therefore, for our intelligence. And, let it be added, *sustenance and necessary reassurance for our power of will*. Through the centuries life has become an increasingly heavy burden for Man the Species, just as it does for Man the Individual as the years pass. The modern world, with its prodigious growth of complexity, weighs incomparably more heavily upon the shoulders of our generation than did the ancient world upon the shoulders of our forebears. Have you never felt that this added load needs to be compensated for by an added passion, a new sense of purpose? To my mind, this is what is "providentially" arising to sustain our courage—the hope, the belief that some immense fulfillment lies ahead of us.

If Mankind were destined to achieve its apotheosis, if Evolution were to reach its highest point, in our small, separate lives, then indeed the enormous travail of terrestrial organization into which we are born would be no more than a tragic irrelevance. We should all be dupes. We should do better in that case to stop, to call a halt, destroy the machines, close the laboratories, and seek whatever way of escape we can find in pure pleasure or pure nirvana.

But if on the contrary Man sees a new door opening above him, a new stage for his development; if each of us can believe that he is working so that the Universe may be raised, in him and through him, to a higher level—then a new spring of energy will well forth in the heart of Earth's workers. The whole great human organism, overcoming a momentary hesitation, will draw its breath and press on with strength renewed.

Indeed, the idea, the hope of the planetisation of life is very much more than a mere matter of biological speculation. It is more of a necessity for our age than the discovery, which we so ardently pursue, of new sources of energy. It is this idea which can and must bring us the spiritual fire without which all material fires, so laboriously lighted, will presently die down on the surface of the thinking earth: the fire inspiring us with the joy of action and the love of life.

All this, you may say to me, sounds splendid: but is there not another side to the picture? You tell us that this new phase of human evolution will bring about an extension and deepening of terrestrial consciousness. But do not the facts contradict your argument? What is actually happening in the world today? Can we really detect any heightening of human consciousness even in the most highly collectivized nations? Does it not appear, on the contrary, that social totalisation leads directly to spiritual retrogression and greater materialism?

My answer is that I do not think we are yet in a position to judge recent totalitarian experiments fairly: that is to say, to decide whether, all things considered, they have produced a greater degree of enslavement or a higher level of spiritual energy. It is too early to say. But I believe this can be said, that in so far as these first attempts may seem to be tending dangerously towards the sub-human state of the ant-hill or the termitary, it is not the principle of totalisation that is at fault but the clumsy and incomplete way in which it has been applied.

We have to take into account what is required by the law of complexity if Mankind is to achieve spiritual growth through collectivization. The first essential is that the human units involved in the process shall draw closer together, not merely under the pressure of external forces, or solely by the performance of material acts, but directly, centre to centre, through internal attraction. Not through coercion, or enslavement to a common task, but through unanimity in a common spirit. The construction of molecules ensues through atomic affinity. Similarly, on a higher level, it is through sympathy, and this alone, that the human elements in a personalized universe may hope to rise to the level of a higher synthesis.

It is a matter of common experience that within restricted groups (the pair, the team) unity, far from diminishing the individual, enhances, enriches and liberates him in terms of himself. True union, the union of heart and spirit, does not enslave, nor does it neutralize the individuals which it brings together. It super-personalizes them. Let us try to picture the phenomenon on a terrestrial scale. Imagine men awakening at last, under the influence of the ever-tightening planetary embrace, to a sense of universal solidarity based on their profound community, evolutionary in its nature and purpose. The nightmares of brutalization and mechanization which are conjured up to terrify us and prevent our advance are at once dispelled. It is not harshness or hatred but a new kind of love, not yet experienced by man, which we must learn to look for as it is borne to us on the rising tide of planetisation.

Reflecting, even briefly, on the state of affairs which might evoke this universal love in the human heart, a love so often vainly dreamed of, but which now leaves the fields of Utopia to reveal itself as both possible and necessary, we are brought to the following conclusion: that for men upon earth, all the earth, to learn to love one another, it is not enough that they should know themselves to be members of one and the same thing; in "planetising" themselves they must acquire the consciousness, without losing themselves, of becoming one and the same person. For (and this is writ large in the Gospel) there is no total love that does not proceed from, and exist within, that which is personal.

And what does this mean except, finally, that the planetisation of Mankind, if it is to come properly into effect, presupposes, in addition to the enclosing Earth, and to the organization and condensation of human thought, yet another factor? I mean the rise on our inward horizon of a cosmic spiritual centre, a supreme pole of consciousness, upon which all the separate consciousnesses of the world may converge and within which they may love one another: the rise of a God.

It is here that reason may discern, conforming to and in harmony with the law of complexity, an acceptable way of envisaging "the end of the world."

The End of Planetary Life: Maturity and Withdrawal
The end of the world—for us, that is to say, the end of Earth.... Have you ever thought seriously, in human terms, about that somber and certain eventuality?

Life at the beginning seemed modest in its requirements. A few hours in the sun were all it seemed to ask. But this was only a semblance, belied at the earliest stages of vitalization by the tenacity with which the most humble cells reproduce themselves and multiply. This tenacity continues through all the enormous effusion of the animal kingdom, and bursts into the light of day with the appearance, in thinking Man, of the formidable power of pre-vision. It cannot but grow still more imperious with every forward stride of human consciousness. I have spoken of the impulse to act, without which there can be no action. But in practice it is not enough, if the impulse is to be sustained in face of the ever-growing onslaughts of the *taedium vitae*, for it to be offered nothing more than an immediate objective, even though this be as great as the planetisation of Mankind. We must strive for ever more greatness; but we cannot do so if we are faced by the prospect of an eventual decline, a disaster at the end. With the germ of consciousness hatched upon its surface, the Earth, our perishable earth that contemplates the final, absolute zero, has brought into the Universe a demand, henceforth irrepressible, not only that all things shall not die, but that what is best in the world, that which has become most complex, most highly centrated, shall be saved. It is through human consciousness, genetically linked to a heavenly body whose days are ultimately numbered, that Evolution proclaims its challenge: either it must be irreversible, or it need not go on at all! Man the individual consoles himself for his passing with the thought of the offspring or the works which he leaves behind. But what will presently be left of Mankind?

Thus every attempt to situate Man and the Earth in the framework of the Universe comes inevitably upon the heavy problem of death, not of the individual but on the planetary scale—a death which, if we seriously contemplate it, must paralyze all the vital forces of the Earth.

In an attempt to dispel this shadow, Jeans calculated that the Earth has many millions of years of habitability ahead of it, so that Man is still only on the threshold of his existence. He bade us warm our hearts, in this fresh dawn, with the almost limitless prospects of the glorious day that is only beginning. But a few pages previously he had talked of Mankind sadly growing old and disillusioned on a chilling globe, faced by inevitable extinction. Does not that first thought destroy the second?

Others seek to reassure us with the notion of an escape through space. We may perhaps move to Venus—perhaps even further afield. But apart from the fact that Venus is probably not habitable (is there water?) and that, if journeying between celestial bodies were practicable, it is hard to see why we ourselves have not already been invaded, this does no more than postpone the end.

We cannot resolve this contradiction, between the congenital mortality of the planets and the demand for irreversibility developed by planetised life on their surface, by covering it up or deferring it: we have finally to banish the specter of Death from our horizon.

And this we are enabled to do by the idea (a corollary, as we have seen, of the mechanism of planetisation) that ahead of, or rather in the heart of, a universe prolonged along its axis of complexity, there exists a divine centre of convergence. That nothing may be prejudged, and in order to stress its synthesizing and personalizing function, let us call it the point Omega. Let us suppose that from this universal centre, this Omega point, there constantly emanate radiations hitherto only perceptible to those persons whom we call "mystics." Let us further imagine that, as the sensibility or response to mysticism of the human race increases with planetisation, the awareness of Omega becomes so widespread as to warm the earth psychically while physically it is growing cold. Is it not conceivable that Mankind, at the end of its totalisation, its folding-in upon itself, may reach a critical level of maturity where, leaving Earth and stars to lapse slowly back into the dwindling mass of primordial energy, it will detach itself from this planet and join the one true, irreversible essence of things, the Omega point? A phenomenon perhaps outwardly akin to death: but in reality a simple metamorphosis and arrival at the supreme synthesis. An escape from the planet, not in space or outwardly, but spiritually and inwardly, such as the hyper-centration of cosmic matter upon itself allows.

This hypothesis of a final maturing and ecstasy of Mankind, the logical conclusion of the theory of complexity, may seem even more far-fetched than the idea (of which it is the extension) of the planetisation of Life. Yet it holds its ground and grows stronger upon reflection. It is in harmony with the growing importance which leading thinkers of all denominations are beginning to attach to the phenomenon of mysticism. In any event, of all the theories which we may evolve concerning the end of the Earth, it is the only one which affords a coherent prospect wherein, in the remote future, the deepest and most powerful currents of human consciousness may converge and culminate: intelligence and action, learning and religion.

SELECTION 9

John B. Cobb Jr. and David Ray Griffin

"Why an Evolutionary Process?"

John B. Cobb Jr. (1925–) and David Ray Griffin (1939–) are together recognized as leading exponents of process theology, both having taught for many years at the Claremont School of Theology and having jointly founded the Center for Process Studies at Claremont. The following selection from their text *Process Theology: An Introductory Exposition* illustrates how they defend a process doctrine of providence as both more internally coherent and more in accord with general experience than traditional alternatives. The authors argue that the idea of an omnipotent, fully self-sufficient deity suffers from two serious shortcomings: it can explain neither why God should create a world in the first place (since all perfections are already realized in God), nor why creation should take the form of a long evolutionary process (since God could have realized God's intentions immediately). By contrast, the process understanding of God as creating from chaos (versus from nothing) by means of persuasion (versus direct control) fits better with the modern evolutionary view. In process theism a long, slow process of development is to be expected, since God works in cooperation with creatures' own freedom, luring the cosmos to the greater levels of complexity needed if God's will that creatures experience the highest possible intensity of enjoyment is to be realized.

> From John B. Cobb Jr. and David Ray Griffin, *Process Theology: An Introductory Exposition* (Philadelphia: Westminster Press, 1976), 63–68.

Traditional theism had trouble explaining why there should be a world. The description of deity as *actus purus* meant that God had already (i.e., eternally) actualized all possible values. This was one way of stressing deity's total independence of the world. Process theology does not have this problem. Although the possible values all subsist in God, they subsist as merely possible values, not as actualized values. They are possible values for finite realization. They are in God only conceptually, or in the mode of appetition, not physically, or in the mode of enjoyment. Hence, there must be a world of finite actualities, or no values will be enjoyed.

However, since all actualities have value, the question still remains as to why these actualities should be involved in an evolutionary process. The basic element of the answer to this question is that there are gradations of value, and some actualities are capable of greater enjoyment than others. Roughly speaking, more complex actualities enjoy more value than simpler ones. The direction of the evolutionary process on the whole is toward more complex actualities, resulting from God's basic creative purpose, which is the evocation of actualities with greater and greater enjoyment.

If traditional theists gave up the idea of God as *actus purus*, but held to the notion of God as Controlling Power, they would still have difficulty explaining why there has been an evolutionary process. The difficulty is increased when it is anthropocentrically assumed, as it usually is, that the last (or at least latest) act of the drama of creation, the human species, is the only one with any real value, and that the rest was mere prologue. But it is still difficult on the more modest assumption, which we all in practice hold, that the more complex developments have more value than the earlier, simpler ones, since nothing has any inherent power to resist the divine Controlling Power. Whatever God wills can be brought about immediately. Why, then, take over four billion years to get to the more valuable creatures, if they could have been created at once?

This problem also does not exist for process theology, since it rejects the idea of God as Controlling Power. In [Alfred North] Whitehead's approving description of Plato's thought, God's influence "is always persuasive, and can only produce such order as is possible."[1] Another crucial assumption is that the more complex forms of order presuppose the simpler forms, and hence can only come after them. In the remainder of this section we will provide a sketch, based upon Whitehead's suggestions, of the major steps in this evolution of more complex forms of order.

But first the reason for the positive correlation between complexity and enjoyment must be made explicit. The two variables involved in the degree of enjoyment are harmony and intensity. Obviously, for experience to be enjoyable, it must be basically harmonious; the elements must not clash so strongly that discord outweighs harmony. Also, for great enjoyment there must be adequate intensity of experience. Without intensity there might be harmony, but the value enjoyed will be trivial. Intensity depends upon complexity, since intensity requires that a variety of elements be brought together into a unity of experience. To bring a variety of elements into a moment of experience means to *feel* these elements, to prehend them *positively*. Now, the more complex an actuality is, the more elements from its environment it can feel, and thereby take into itself. The simpler occasions of experience must exclude from feeling more of the potential values in the environment. This is why intensity depends upon complexity, and hence why the higher grades of enjoyment finally depend upon complexity. Furthermore, a complex actuality is possible only on the basis of an ordered environment. This is why order is promoted for the sake of increased enjoyment.

These criteria of harmony and intensity (based on variety held in contrast) are taken from aesthetics. Whitehead accordingly uses the word "beauty" to describe the achievement of an occasion of experience that fulfills these criteria. To maximize beauty is to maximize enjoyment. God's purpose, then, can be described as the aim toward maximizing either beauty or enjoyment. It is on the basis of these criteria of intrinsic value that the evolutionary process can be viewed as in part a product of divine providence.

Process theology rejects the notion of *creatio ex nihilo*, if that means creation out of *absolute* nothingness. That doctrine is part and parcel of the doctrine of God as absolute controller. Process theology affirms instead a doctrine of creation out of chaos (which was suggested not only by Plato but also by more Old Testament passages than those supporting the doctrine of creation out of nothing). A state of absolute chaos would be one in which there is nothing but very low-grade actual occasions happening at random, i.e., without being ordered into enduring individuals. An enduring individual is a series of occasions, each of which inherits more significantly from the preceding occasion in that series than it does from the other actualities in its environment. Electrons and protons are examples. By transmitting identical characteristics from occasion to occasion they

---

1. Alfred North Whitehead, *Adventures of Ideas* (New York: Macmillan, 1933), 189.

maintain individual identity through long periods of time. In a chaotic situation, on the contrary, each occasion would inherit equally from all the previous contiguous actualities. Whitehead suggests that what we refer to as the "empty space" between astronomical bodies is really full of chaotic occasions; it is only "empty" of any enduring individuals.[2]

There is value even when the situation is chaotic, since there are still actual occasions and all occasions have some intrinsic value. But the value enjoyed must be extremely trivial. With no order among the occasions, their respective contributions cannot be combined; the data provided for the enjoyment of a burgeoning subject are the outcome of mutually thwarting decisions.[3] This provides one sense in which the present world can be said to be the result of creation out of nothing. The chaos from which it emerged was a "nothingness of confusion."[4] We normally have an enduring individual in mind when we speak of a "thing"; in this sense the primordial chaos contained no-*thing*.

The first stage of creation of order out of this chaos, then, was the development of things, or enduring individuals. In Whitehead's words: "There must have been some epoch in which the dominant trend was the formation of protons, electrons, molecules. . . ."[5] Now, these simple enduring individuals involve the repetition of some particular form. This repetition in itself adds intensity to the actualization of the value in question.[6] This is the most primitive example of the fact that order is a condition for intensity of experience.[7] This development of primitive enduring individuals is the first stage in the escape from triviality.

However, besides increasing the enjoyment in the world, this degree of order provides the necessary basis for a higher degree of order to appear, which would allow for even greater enjoyment. This illustrates the connection between novelty and order. There is evidently an order among the possibilities themselves. They cannot be actualized in the world in simply any order; rather, some become real possibilities only after others have been actualized. Hence, at one stage certain novel possibilities are actualized for the first time. If they are then repeated, they become part of the order of the world. As such they provide the conditions for other novel possibilities to become actualized. And so on.

The development of enduring individuals at the level of electrons, protons, neutrons, etc., provided the necessary condition for the emergence of

---

2. See Alfred North Whitehead, *Process and Reality: An Essay in Cosmology* (New York: Macmillan, 1929), 141–42; *Science and the Modern World* (New York: Macmillan, 1925), 122, 220–21.
3. Whitehead, *Process*, 142.
4. Alfred North Whitehead, "Immortality," in *The Philosophy of Alfred North Whitehead*, ed. Paul A. Schilpp (New York: Tudor, 1951), 691.
5. Alfred North Whitehead, *The Function of Reason* (Princeton: Princeton University Press, 1929), 24.
6. Whitehead, *Science*, 137, 152–53; "Immortality," 688–90.
7. Alfred North Whitehead, *Modes of Thought* (New York: Macmillan, 1938), 87; *Process*, 373–74.

atoms. The atoms in turn provided the necessary condition for the appearance of molecules. These in turn were necessary ingredients in the emergence of the living cell.

Each stage of the evolutionary process represents an increase in the divinely given possibilities for value that are actualized. The present builds upon the past but advances beyond the past to the degree to which it responds to the divine impulses. This advance is experienced as intrinsically good, and it also provides the condition for an even richer enjoyment of existence in the future.

The increase of intrinsic value in the advance from chaos to events at the electronic-protonic level, and on to the atomic and molecular levels, is real but trivial. The increase is primarily in instrumental value. Atoms and molecules fit Whitehead's description of actualities "which, trivial in their own proper character of immediate 'ends,' are proper 'means' for the emergence of a world . . . intrinsically of immediate worth."[8]

The living cell is evidently another story. It is not ontologically different from the actualities that came before it. (The discovery of levels of actuality in between cells and "ordinary" molecules has further supported this Whiteheadian view.) However, it is significantly different. In Whitehead's words:

> In a sense, the difference between a living organism and the inorganic environment is only a question of degree; but it is a difference of degree which makes all the difference—in effect, it is a difference of quality.[9]

The word "living" points to the difference. All occasions of experience have at least the germ of mentality, for "mentality" is simply the capacity for self-determination: "The mental pole introduces the subject as a determinant of its own concrescence."[10] But in nonliving occasions, the mentality is "merely the appetition towards, or from, whatever in fact already is."[11] Although it is the element of final causation in the actualities, "it is degraded to being merely one of the actors in the efficient causation."[12] In other words, it brings nothing new into the world, but simply repeats the past, or lets it decay.

A "living" actuality is one in which the mental pole introduces a novel element into itself, one which was not derived from the past world.[13] This increases the value that can be enjoyed. The fact that a novel element is introduced by itself increases the variety and hence the intensity of the experience. And the novel response to the environment is a way of converting otherwise incompatible elements into compatible contrasts

---

8. Whitehead, *Process*, 517.
9. Ibid., 271.
10. Ibid., 380.
11. Whitehead, *Function*, 33.
12. Ibid., 34.
13. Whitehead, *Process*, 156, 159.

that can be internally appropriated. This further increases the intensity of enjoyment.

Accordingly, God's success as the goad toward novelty increases the present enjoyment in the world by stimulating the emergence of life. However, as before, this advance in intrinsic value has its instrumental value for the future. Cells can be so organized that a yet higher series of experiences can emerge from them. The reference here, of course, is to animals, especially those with a central nervous system. The higher stream of experience is the animal soul....

Each stage of this process of complexification (to use Teilhard's term), which increases the capacity for enjoyment, presupposes the previous stage. Each novel advance was possible only after the previous novel advance had become stabilized into a pervasive order. Also, only a limited advance is possible at each stage—it is not possible to jump directly from stage one to stage four; stages two and three have to come in between. Cells could not emerge directly out of electrons and protons, for the experiences they enjoy, and hence the data they have to contribute to others, are too trivial. Likewise, a soul as complex as that of a squirrel could not emerge directly out of molecules.

On the basis of this correlation between novelty and increasingly complex order, on the one hand, and increased capacity for enjoyment, on the other, the evolutionary development of our world propounded by modern science can be interpreted in harmony with the character and purpose of God. This creatively and responsively loving God is incarnately active in the present, bringing about immediate good on the basis of activity in the past, and with the purpose to bring about greater good in the future—a greater good that will involve a fuller incarnation of the divine reality itself.

SELECTION 10

Grace Jantzen

"Action and Embodiment"

Grace Jantzen (1948–2006) was a Quaker who taught at the University of Manchester. The following excerpt from her book *God's World, God's Body* explores one of the most challenging topics in contemporary doctrines of providence: how God's ongoing interaction with the world is to be understood. The problem is that the natural sciences' success in explaining natural phenomena in terms of the operation of quantifiable physical laws makes it difficult to find room within the causal network for special divine action. One can, of course, simply affirm God's capacity to override these laws, but then it becomes hard to understand why

God would have created such laws in the first place if they were not adequate to ensure the accomplishment of God's purposes in creation.

Jantzen addresses this problem by proposing that the world be understood as God's body, drawing on the idea that bodily actions are performed directly (e.g., while I need to move my arms before I can write, there is nothing I need to do before I can move my arms) to argue that this kind of unmediated "basic action" corresponds closely with traditional Christian understanding of how God influences the world. Indeed, she argues that insofar as God is for Christians far more immediately in control of the universe than we are of our bodies, God should be understood as more completely embodied than we are. She also maintains that under this model divine action is not in tension with the regularity of physical laws. They are understood as the way God normally acts, without prejudice to the possibility of acting differently when God so desires—in much the same way that we are free to override our own more routinized bodily actions in order to achieve particular ends.

From Grace Jantzen, God's World, God's Body
(Philadelphia: Westminster Press, 1984), 85–93.

A[n] ... argument ... can be constructed, which shows that the idea of God's action on the world ... makes more sense on the model that the world is God's body than on the traditional model. In order for us to act on the world, it is normally necessary for us to use an indirect method, originating in a movement of our own bodies. For example, if I wish to move a pen, I do so by moving my hand first. However, there are certain actions which I can do *without* doing anything else first; these are the direct actions of my own body. I do not have to do anything first, before I can move my hand. This latter sort of action, requiring no antecedent, has been called a "basic action."[1] Unless we can perform basic actions, we cannot do anything else either; all our action on the world begins with a movement of our bodies.

Now, a disembodied person would not have a body to move, and therefore could perform no basic actions. But then how can he get any action on the world started? Perhaps an appeal might be made to telekinesis—direct movement of a physical object at a distance, with no perceptible intervening mechanism. But as Anthony Kenny has pointed out, this is not really an analogue to the case of the disembodied agent, because the agent who claims paranormal ability is still an otherwise normal embodied person performing basic actions in other contexts. Indeed, if this were not the case, if we suspected that not even the movements of his own body were basic actions, then we would not be willing to say that he was the real agent of the paranormal activity.[2]

---

1. Arthur Danto, "Basic Actions," in *American Philosophical Quarterly* 2 (1965).
2. Anthony Kenny, *The God of the Philosophers* (Oxford: Clarendon, 1977), 126.

Now, just as theists wish to affirm that God's knowledge of the world is direct and immediate, they similarly wish to say that God can act directly, without any intervening action or mechanism: God did not wiggle his fingers to cause a mechanism to operate which sent fire from heaven to consume Elijah's sacrifice on Mount Carmel; he "spake and it was done." But in terms of the present discussion, this means that any action of God on the world is a basic action: he does not have to do anything else first. Terence Penelhum, discussing the action of disembodied spirits, says that if they can act at all, they do so, not by means of mechanisms, but directly: if a spirit raises a table, then the raising of the table is a basic action for the spirit. But then we might as well say that, at least for purposes of that action, the table has become the body of the spirit.[3] In the case of God, the conclusion to be drawn is spelled out by Kenny:

> If God can act in the world directly and without intermediary, as traditionally he has been held to, then on Danto's definition the world would be God's body. Most traditional theologians would have rejected this idea with horror.[4]

But would they? This seems to me to be too strong. It is true, of course, that most traditional theologians would not have expressed themselves in this way, because for various reasons, some of which we have already seen, they considered it more important to stress the disanalogies between God and material bodies. Throughout the Middle Ages, matter was conceived of as utterly inert; after the Enlightenment bodies were thought of as analogous to the interrelation of mechanistic clockwork: with such views of matter (which we will look at more closely later) it was of course important to insist that God was not material. But as Swinburne points out, when we think of God's interaction with the physical world:

> It is important ... not to overemphasize the extent of God's nonembodiment in the view of traditional theism.... The view of traditional theism is that in many ways God is not related to a material object as a person is to his body, but in other ways he is so related.[5]

In terms of his action on the world in particular, Swinburne argues that God is related to physical reality as a person is related to his body, in just the way that Kenny implies would have been repudiated by traditional theologians.

There are, however, also disanalogies, parallel to those we encountered in our discussion of divine knowledge. In the first place, a human person can perform only a limited range of basic actions, and a great many of the things he does are not basic, even if they must be initiated by basic

---

3. Terence Penelhum, *Survival and Disembodied Existence* (London: Routledge, 1970), 42.
4. Kenny, *God*, 126.
5. Richard Swinburne, *The Coherence of Theism* (Oxford: Clarendon, 1977), 107.

actions. Whenever human action involves the movement of some things other than the person's own body, non-basic, indirect action is initiated by direct, basic action. But a theist wants to say that *all* God's actions on the world are direct and basic; he never has to do anything first to accomplish his purposes, but does everything directly, without intervening apparatus. This would, indeed, be incompatible with the hypothesis that God has a finite body like our own, and lives on some planet of a distant galaxy from which he keeps his fingers on the control panel of the universe—if that were what was meant by having a body, then obviously God does not have one. But our considerations have already pushed us well away from such a view. What is important is that the direction of the push is not towards more restricted embodiment, as Swinburne suggests, but rather towards a concept of more complete embodiment. There are difficulties with the notion that an incorporeal spirit could perform any basic actions whatsoever which would result in physical movement; on the other hand, God can perform *any* physical action, and any such action on God's part is direct, basic. Just as in the discussion of divine perception, therefore, so here too we are led to the conclusion that the logical alternative to saying that God does not have a finite body is not to say that he is utterly incorporeal, but rather to say that the whole world is God's body. There is more than one alternative to the hypothesis that God has a finite body like a superman; thus to show the absurdity of such a concept of God does not rule out the attractiveness of divine embodiment.

Furthermore, just as we saw in the case of divine perception, God's control of the universe, like his awareness of it, is far more extensive than our awareness or our control of our own bodies. Much of the movement of our bodies is movement of which we are not even aware, let alone movement which we can voluntarily control. Most of us, for example, have very little idea of how our livers function, and although we can to a certain extent influence that function by what we eat and drink, we cannot bring it under deliberate control in any direct way. But just as an omniscient God must be aware of all parts of the universe, so an omnipotent God must be in direct control of all parts of it. Although this is disanalogous to our control over our bodies, however, this is once again not a disanalogy which would push us back towards saying that God is incorporeal, but rather forward to an idea of more complete embodiment.

It is worth pausing to be clear about the term "complete embodiment." Obviously I do not mean that more of God is embodied (that there is less spirit "left over") than is the case with humans: we have already seen how inadequate dualism is for a theological understanding of human persons, and our aim is to see to what extent a holistic model of human personhood is helpful for understanding the relationship between God and the world. Rather, I am contrasting the *degree* of deliberate knowledge and control that God has over the universe with the degree of knowledge and control that we have over our own bodies. Our bodies and their movements are to a very large extent independent of our desires and choices: the heart beats, the blood circulates without attention or will, nor is it through any choice of our own that we have hearts in the first place. There is a givenness about our bodies and their movements; consequently it is inappropriate to refer to their involuntary movements as basic actions, because strictly speaking, they are not actions at all.

But according to theological tradition, God is in immediate direct control of the whole universe; all of its movements are, in this sense, his basic actions. If we were to draw a scale showing the relative number of actions and movements of different sorts of entities which could be labelled "basic," an incorporeal spirit would have fewest, an embodied person would have more, and God would have most—this is what I mean by saying that God is more completely embodied than human persons. The differences between his actions and the involuntariness of many of our bodily movements is not a difference which pushes us in the direction of incorporeality but just the opposite: we acknowledge much more complete voluntary control on God's part than on our own. The moves here are parallel to those in the argument about divine knowledge in the previous section.

The idea that the universe is God's body and that all his actions are basic actions raises two large problems: the problem of evil, and a problem about natural law. Starting with the latter, how can we say that God is in continuous voluntary control of the whole of his body, the universe, if the universe displays the uniformity and causal regularity which makes it discoverable by the physical sciences? It would seem that either the natural laws which scientists have painstakingly discovered are unreliable, or else God does not have the voluntary control of the universe after all.

This dilemma, however, need not detain for long a theologian who believes that the world is God's body. It is easiest to see this by remembering what we would say about natural law if we hold that God is *not* corporeal. If God were a spirit, separate from the material world, we would account for natural law and the causal chain by saying that this is the way in which God deliberately organized the world and sustains it in being. If God is omnipotent, then he is perfectly free to change the natural laws if he chooses: he could, for example, change the rate of rotation of the earth if he wished to do so. Of course, that would have devastating consequences for us, and we trust God not to do it, but that has nothing to do with whether God is *powerful* enough to intervene in existing natural law. A theist after all maintains that in some sense God brought these causal regularities into being in the first place. If he wished to, he could change any or all of them in ways we cannot even conceive of (though of course we might not survive to discover the new causal regularities or lack of them). Thus on the traditional view of cosmic dualism, the uniformity of nature is not a logical necessity but a product of God's free choice, in both origin and duration: in traditional language, God freely creates and sustains the world and its regularities, though he is under no compulsion to do so.

I suggest that we can say just the same things of the world as God's body. If we assume, as I have argued, that God has complete control over all parts of his body all the time, then we can say that God has deliberately arranged it in the way it now is. Of course there is nothing (logically) to prevent him from changing its present organization except his own steadfast purposes; but that is true of the traditional view as well. Neither view makes God subject to natural law; both attribute the continuing uniformity of nature to his sustaining will. On either view, the laws of nature hold and are reliable because God has set them up in the first place and continually preserves them rather than interferes with their regularity; but by the same token, an omnipotent God is not bound by the regularities of nature if he should choose not to be: God *could* cause "the sun to be darkened and the moon be turned to blood" [Joel 2:31]. We can have confidence in scientific method, discovery and prediction, not because, like Deists, we believe that God has nothing to do with the ongoing course of the world, but because we believe that he is not arbitrary: he will continue to sustain the universe. But he does not have to: he chooses to. The danger of the cosmic dualism model in this connection is that it allows us to slip too easily into thinking of the universe and its laws as somehow independent of the ongoing sustenance of God: the model of the universe as the embodiment of God underscores the continuous dependence of the universe on his voluntary sustaining power.

Such a model also has the advantage of illuminating the notions of providence and miracle. If the world is God's body, and every part of it is sustained by his will, then he can arrange the natural order to suit his purposes (providence) and alter it in individual "miraculous" instances if he so chooses. Whether he ever would so choose to interrupt the causal sequence which he has ordained is of course an open question on this view as on any other, but at least we would not be tempted to think of some kind of monarch in the sky reaching down to intervene in the causal sequence: nor does this view encourage a "god-of-the-gaps" theology. The idea of the universe as the embodiment of God provides in these respects a religiously and philosophically satisfying picture of God's actions in the world in a way that is compatible with continuing scientific endeavour. The whole unfolding of nature, including at least to some degree humankind's part in it, will be the manifestation of divine activity. This does not mean that there can be no particularity in God's action: some events and processes, notably those surrounding the life and death of Jesus of Nazareth, can properly be seen as more revelatory of God than other events, just as some actions of a person are more significant than others for an estimate of his or her character. But this view does render unnecessary any concept of miracles which sees them as interventions from "out there" by some monarchical deity after the order of Zeus—a concept which many theologians would in any case abandon with relief.

But what can we say about the problem of evil? If every event in the universe is to be understood as willed by God—indeed, if the laws of nature are best understood as the regular activity of his body in his conscious control—then it follows that God not only permits hurricanes and earthquakes, he actually performs them and is responsible for all their destructive consequences. It was bad enough, on the traditional model, to have to say that God allows evil; but if God actually brings it about, is any theodicy possible?

But that is a misleading way of putting the problem. On any view of the relationship between God and the operation of nature, God organizes the universe into natural laws—consistent patterns of behavior, we might say—which, because of their consistency, can be said to have a quasi-autonomous status. In the course of this semi-independent nature, earthquakes and other physical disasters are bound to occur, but these are then seen as the natural consequences of a causal system which is on the whole good, rather than as direct performances of God. Thus to the extent that the "evilness" of these occurrences is mitigated by the fact that they are natural outworkings of the causal sequence, this response is open to the theologian who pursues the model of divine embodiment. As we have seen, a theist who takes this approach can be just as committed to the findings of science and the regularities of nature as a cosmic dualist is. If these regularities are in general good, even though they sometimes result in human and animal suffering, then one who believes that the universe is the embodiment of God can appeal to the inappropriateness of frequent divine intervention as readily as can a traditional theist. I am not suggesting that the problem of evil is not really a problem, nor even that an appeal to the regularities of nature can help to solve it. I am only saying that it is not a greater or even a different problem for this view than for a cosmic dualist; there is recourse to just the same sort of appeals in attempting to construct a theodicy. All the moves open to a traditional theist in constructing a theodicy are equally open to one who says that the world is God's body: he can appeal to the overriding goodness of regularities in natural law, to the free will of persons, and to the idea of the world as a vale of soul-making. And in addition he can say that, if the world is God's body, then although God is ultimately responsible for all our suffering, in another sense he shares it, he feels it with us in a more literal sense than would be possible for a cosmic dualist to affirm.

But if the world is God's body, then must we not say that there is evil in God himself—God containing evil? It is one thing to say that God permits evil and that he is ultimately responsible for it, but that is different from saying that God himself is evil. Yet if we say that the world is God's body, then the evil in the world appears to be evil in God—and how, then, can God be perfectly good?

From what I have already said, however, it is clear that this objection rests on taking the distinction between God and the world even in traditional theism too strongly. As we shall see in more detail in a later chapter, there is a sense in which any theist must affirm that all reality is from God: belief in creation *ex nihilo* is not the belief that the universe somehow owes its existence to something other than God, namely nothing, out of which God created it. Unless one is willing to adopt a Manichaean view, in which the material universe is irreducibly other than God, one must affirm that in some sense "God is All," all things have their origin in God and hence evil itself is in God. One simple way of pointing to what sense this has is just to recall that, if God were somehow to cease to exist, so would everything else, including evil. In that sense the universe and everything in it, evil not excepted, has no independent existence apart from God.

One of the most profound struggles with the problem of evil in Christian thought can be found in the writings of the Protestant mystic Jakob Boehme—profound because he takes just this point very seriously. Boehme's ideas are sometimes dismissed as an aberration; he is thought of as an obscure and heterodox curiosity. But though he is obscure and possibly heterodox, he should not be lightly dismissed, especially since his thought has been an influence on major twentieth-century theologians.[6] Boehme says:

> God is all. He is darkness and light, love and wrath, fire and light. For all things have their first beginning from the outflow of the divine will, be it evil or good, love or sorrow.[7]

The conflict between darkness and light, good and evil, which Boehme finds in the natural world and poignantly in human persons cannot have any origin except God himself, and must therefore somehow be a reflection of him. Hell itself cannot ultimately be outside of an omnipresent God.

But although I think that we must take Boehme's point seriously that ultimately nothing, not even evil itself, could exist without God, and hence that in that sense God is the origin of evil and evil is in God, we can make a distinction between saying that evil is in God and that God himself is evil. God is evil only if, to use a Kantian notion, he has an evil will: that is, if there is nothing to justify the evil for which he is ultimately responsible and which could not exist but for him. If a theodicy can be provided, whether in terms of a free-will defence or some other explanation of how evil is a necessary condition for bringing about God's good purposes, then we cannot say that God is evil. No special problem is raised by saying that the world is God's body. Although the "in" in "evil is in God" can then

---

6. For instance, Paul Tillich, who wrote the preface to John Joseph Stoudt's book on Boehme, *Sunrise to Eternity*.

7. Jakob Boehme, *The Way to Christ* (New York: Paulist/London: SPCK, 1978), 4.2.9; 7.1.23.

be taken literally (that is, spatially), this does not collapse the distinction between the statement, which all Christians must accept, that evil is finally ontologically dependent upon God, and the statement that God himself is evil, which means that he deliberately produces or allows evil without justification. Only if this distinction were collapsed would this be an objection to saying that the world is God's body.

I wish to emphasize that I do not think this to be any answer to the problems of evil in general. I do not even know whether such an answer is possible. But my point is that, if it is possible for cosmic dualism, then it is equally possible, on exactly the same lines, for one who sees the world as God's body. No special problems are raised; the new model leaves the problem of evil just where it was before. . . .

SELECTION 11

Wolfhart Pannenberg

"The Doctrine of Creation in an Age of Scientific Cosmology"

Like his compatriot Jürgen Moltmann, Wolfhart Pannenberg (1928–) has written extensively on the full range of theological topics and is respected as one of the most important German theologians of the latter part of the twentieth century. His theology has a distinctively apologetic cast, because Pannenberg is convinced that Christian faith is only credible if it is capable of contributing to the sum total of human knowledge on the same terms as any other discipline. He is thus sensitive to the charge that modern scientific explanations of the world render reference to God superfluous, and in the following excerpt from his short *Introduction to Systematic Theology* he argues that the necessarily limited character of scientific descriptions of reality find a necessary supplement in the Christian doctrine of a creator God.

Although Pannenberg denies that scientific explanations of reality are exhaustive, he is equally insistent that theological claims must be consistent with science, so that his own account of God's relationship to the world combines Trinitarian theology with modern physics. Specifically, he argues that while creation has its basis in the Son's eternal self-differentiation from the Father (which establishes a "generative principle of otherness" within God), the Bible portrays the Spirit as the force that both animates the creation and serves as the medium of God's continuing interaction with it. This leads to the provocative idea that God's presence to creation across space and time is best understood on analogy with the shaping of space-time by physical fields of force, which Pannenberg is inclined to see as mathematical approximations of the more fundamental reality of God's all-pervasive and continually creative Spirit providentially guiding history.

> From Wolfhart Pannenberg, *An Introduction to Systematic Theology* (Grand Rapids: Wm. B. Eerdmans Publishing Co., 1991), 37–52.

One of the greatest and continuing problems of Christian belief in God is presented by the difficulty of relating the concept of God to the world of nature and history or more precisely: to conceive of this world as dependent upon God. The idea of God becomes superfluous if all things and events in the world of nature and in the course of its history, including human history, do not depend on God's action. The worldview of modern science, however, untied the bonds of dependence that related the world of nature to the continuous activity of a creator God. In the rise of modern science, this effect was not intended. To the contrary, Isaac Newton reacted against Descartes's mechanical model of the universe, because he suspected it would dissolve the dependence of the physical world on its creator. Newton's own physics was designed as a means of restoring the dependence of all natural processes on material powers, and ultimately on God. But the historical effect of his mechanical description of nature was, contrary to his intentions, to render the physical world autonomous. Since the end of the 18th century this has become the dominant view of the world of nature, a view that profoundly influenced the presentation of human history, too. To many observers, the rise of Darwinism completed this view of the natural world and definitely excluded all reference to a creator from the description of the reality of nature. Though after the first shock theologians increasingly found it possible to combine the outlook of evolution with a Christian concept of salvation history, on the part of modern science the situation remained unchanged: Theological interpretations of the natural world appear at best as subjective additions to a self-sufficient and overwhelmingly successful scientific description of nature.

It is difficult to imagine even the possibility of a basic change in this situation. Since modern theories of nature are mathematical, such a change would require one of two conditions: Either God himself has to become an object of mathematical description, or all mathematical description has to be regarded as mere approximation to the true nature of physical reality, contrary to the widespread assumption that the very nature of things is mathematical.

I venture to opt for the second of these alternatives. Human intuition as well as physical reality always seem to exceed the formalism of mathematical description. One must not underestimate the subtlety and flexibility of mathematical description. It has proved adaptable to most intricate and puzzling data of experience. Yet its very precision entails its limitation: There is something in life which is not precise and systematically escapes that form of presentation. Considerations like this are required as legitimation for using ordinary language as an alternative way of describing reality; although such language notoriously lacks precision as compared to mathematics. The assertion that there are inherent limitations in mathematical language is on safe linguistic ground, since all formal languages continue to be in need of interpretation in terms of ordinary language from which they were derived. On that assumption, we need not think that philosophical or theological assertions on the nature of things or on the universe of nature are necessarily inferior to their mathematical description.

A theology of creation is related to the universe as well as to the nature of things in particular. In fact, both these aspects always belong together. It is only in the framework of some general assumptions about reality (e.g., theories of measurement in time and space) that more specific phenomena can be described. It does not necessarily indicate unwarranted speculation, then, that theology in its doctrine of creation focuses on sweeping statements about the world at large. This is due to the fact that in theology the idea of God provides the point of view for looking at the world. The idea of God necessarily implies the comprehension of anything else. If there is one God—and only one God—then everything else is to be regarded as finite and as comprised within his presence. The doctrine of creation explicates this relationship. Therefore, it produces primarily general assertions about the world of finite reality. These general assertions, of course, have to be specified in due course, and only in such a way can they be substantiated.

Because of its close connection to the very idea of God, the doctrine of creation in all its parts serves as a consolidation and corroboration of belief in God. This function, however, is not limited to the question of the origin of the world. It comprises the continuing existence and emergence of finite reality as well as the prospect of its ultimate completion. In traditional theological terminology, the doctrine of creation does not relate only to creation but also to conservation, redemption, and eschatology; in other words, to the entire economy of God's action.

This raises an issue that has been much debated recently: Is the word "creation" to be understood as referring to the first origin of finite existence, or does it relate to the continuing process in the course of which ever new creatures emerge and take shape? Often this question has been asked in the form of an alternative between two ideas of creation, *creatio ex nihilo* (meaning the creation of finite reality from nothing) and *continuing creation*, which is not restricted to the beginnings but covers the whole process of the world and of each creature's life. But to treat these issues as alternative conceptions of creation is unfortunate. Both come from the classical dogmatic tradition. There, the idea of continuous creation was related to the act of conservation, which is to say that the preservation of what has been created once is in fact the continuation of the creative act itself. While the idea of creation in the first place denotes the origin of the creature, it also extends to its continuing existence, because the creature cannot exist of itself. It would be reduced to nothing as soon as the creative act would discontinue. Therefore, the conception of creation as creation out of nothing also applies to continuous creation. The use of these terms as if they would indicate alternative models of creation is due to an inadequate understanding of the classical terminology.

Nevertheless, there is a problem with the classical doctrine at this point. The idea of creation was indeed primarily related to the beginning of created existence, even to the beginning of the whole world as reported in the first chapter of Genesis. Continuous creation was not understood as a continuous production of new forms of existence but as preservation of the created world in its original order. Although in the case of plants and animals new individual creatures continue to appear, their species were thought to be fixed in the original order of creation. At this point, the classical doctrine as well as the biblical reports on the creation of the world remained dependent on the mythical form of explaining the world: Everything was imagined as having been established in the origin of time. It is at this point that the modern conception of natural evolution differs profoundly from the classical doctrine of creation. Therefore, the expression "continuous correlation" itself acquired a new meaning in modern discussions, because now it actually refers to the continuous creation of new forms of being—a view which paradoxically is closer to the biblical way of looking at reality in terms of a history of God's action. The element of contingency in the ongoing process of nature has become the mark of the creative activity of God in the history of the universe. The emergence of enduring forms and even of patterns of events now appears itself as a contingent fact in the course of that history.

How is God the creator related to this process? On the one hand, the act of creation, though it now spans the entire temporal process, has to be conceived as an act in God's eternity, that is, as eternal in itself. How, then, is such an eternal act consistent with the contingency of events in their temporal sequence? On the other hand, the act of creation itself has to be perceived as contingent if there was not a world from eternity. How, then, is the origin of any creature at all possible on the basis of eternity? And if it is possible to imagine that the eternal God resolves upon a contingent act of creation, how can that act be conceived as contingent without becoming capricious?

In facing these issues, the Christian doctrine of creation need not take refuge in psychological considerations, as the classical Western tradition did, as if we disposed of a psychology of God's freedom of will in relation to the ideas contained in his intellect. I have suggested that this type of reasoning was very anthropomorphic. The trinitarian doctrine offers an alternative approach, which builds upon the biblical idea that the eternal

Son was cooperating in the creation of the world. The Son, then, in distinguishing himself from the Father in order to subordinate himself to his kingdom—as we perceive it in Jesus' relation to his heavenly Father in his earthly ministry—may be considered the origin of all that is different from God. The eternal act of the Son's self-differentiation from the Father would then contain the possibility of the separate existence of creatures. As the self-distinction of the Son from the Father is to be regarded as an act of freedom, so the contingency in the production of creatures would be in continuity with such freedom. In this way one could think of the Son as a generative principle of otherness, from which ever new creatures would come forth. The old Logos doctrine could be revised along those lines: While in the traditional doctrine the Logos was understood to comprise within himself all the ideas of God's intellect and therefore the plan and design of the world of creation, this function could now be reconceived in a more dynamic form, because from a generative principle of otherness, in generating ever new creatures, there would also issue a web of relationships between them.

Thus, a trinitarian concept of God disposes of resources to answer the questions that pertain to the contingency of creaturely existence and to the possibility of its origin from God. It helps to explain the related phenomenon of the multitude and variety of finite forms. It also provides a perspective within which the autonomous existence and life of creatures can be understood in relation to their dependence upon the creator. Here, the biblical tradition of the involvement of the divine Spirit in the act of creation is important.

I mentioned before, in connection with the concept of God, that the biblical idea of Spirit, especially as it occurs in the Old Testament, is not primarily related to the concept of mind but is of a more general nature. It evokes the images of wind and breath. Thus "spirit" is more appropriately conceived as a dynamic force, especially in terms of the creative wind that breathes the breath of life into animals and plants to the effect that, according to Ps. 104:30, they come alive: "When thou sendest forth thy Spirit, they are created; and thou renewest the face of the ground." The same idea underlies the account of the creation of Adam in Gen. 2:7: God "breathed into his nostrils the breath [spirit] of life; and man became a living being." Literally, it is the human soul that is here reported to be a creation of the spirit, but the modern translations are correct to interpret that phrase as "living being" and not in terms of a separate soul beside the body. Nor does the creator spirit consist of the power of intelligence that would produce the intelligent soul, which according to Greek philosophical tradition distinguishes the human being from the other animals. In the biblical story the spirit is simply the dynamic principle of life, and the soul is the creature which is alive and yet remains dependent on the spirit as the transcendent origin of its life.

The notions of spirit as well as of soul have been intellectualized in Christian theology under the influence of Platonic philosophy. The decisive figure in this process was Origen, who argued effectively against the Stoic idea of *pneuma*, which he charged to be materialistic. Origen's criticism was successful because of the apparent absurdities such a materialistic conception of spirit would cause in the concept of God who according to John 4:24 is spirit: God would be a body, could be divided and composed of parts, etc. In fact, however the Stoic conception of *pneuma* as a most subtle element like air was much closer to the biblical language than Origen's identification of *pneuma* with intelligence. The fateful effect of this identification was that the relation of the divine Spirit to the material world and to the process of its creation was obscured. In addition, the divine Spirit was also separated from the created spirit, the human soul. Consequently, the divine Spirit could be reduced almost to a principle of supernatural experience and insight. In the history of Christian thought, on the basis of the reading of the scriptures, there certainly occurred reactions against such a restrictive interpretation of the function of the Spirit. Thus in Orthodox as well as in Calvinist theology the involvement of the Spirit in the act of creation has been emphasized. But in order to recover the broad biblical vision of the Spirit as the creative origin of all life, not just of the new life of faith, it is necessary to overcome the intellectualization of the concept of spirit. In order to achieve this, it may be important to be reminded of the fact that the modern concept of fields of force, so influential in the history of modern physics, is historically rooted in the Stoic doctrine of *pneuma*. The biblical idea of spirit as dynamic movement of air in the forms of wind, storm, or breath is closer to the modern scientific concept of a field of force than to the notion of intellect. It is only by derivation from the phenomenon of life that the act of intelligence is related to the spirit. The human mind, then, is a phenomenon of heightened life. In this sense, all intellectual life is in need of inspiration, an inspiration that in a certain sense lifts up the creature beyond the limitations of its finite existence.

All spiritual experience has such an ecstatic tinge. But the same is true of life in general. There is no living being that could live without an ecological context. Each plant or animal in a certain way exists outside itself in seeking its food and nourishing itself from its surroundings. When modern biochemists describe the phenomenon of life as autocatalytic exploitation of an energy gradient, such a description yields the same idea of life as an ecstatic phenomenon, a phenomenon which is surprisingly close to the Christian idea of faith as described in the theology of the Reformation: an existence outside oneself, realized in the act of trust in God. Could it be that, basically, faith is the uncrippled and untainted enactment of the movement and rhythm of all life as it was intended by the creator? Could it be, conversely, that all life in its self-transcendence is related to God? The psalmist says of the young lions that when they "roar for their prey" they are "seeking their food from God" (Ps. 104:21). Can we take this as a clue to the understanding of all life, to the effect that its ecstatic self-transcendence is primarily related to God and that in this way the range of its finite object (including the prey of the lions) is opened up to a living being? Anyway, the ecstatic self-transcendence of life is not something that is in the power of the organism itself, but arises as its response to a power that seizes it and, by lifting it up beyond itself, inspires life into it.

This is, I think, what the biblical tradition intends by talking about the creative function of the Spirit of God. We may add that in arousing the ecstatic response of life, the Spirit cooperates with the Word of creation, because it is the Word that gives each creature its particular form of existence. In doing so, the Word itself is empowered by the Spirit and the Spirit animates the creatures in raising them beyond themselves to participate in some measure in the life of the eternal God, who is Spirit. Such a statement does not carry pantheistic or panentheistic connotations, because the Spirit is always transcendent, and only by transcending themselves do the creatures participate in the spiritual dynamics. But the biblical language requires us to admit that the Spirit of God himself is operative in such a way in all creatures. This is different from being imparted as a gift as it happens in connection with faith in the risen Christ. Since the life of the risen Christ is thoroughly united to the Spirit, the giver of life, the believer in the risen Christ receives in himself or herself the source of all life and therewith the hope of his or her own immortal life. In this way, the Spirit is not *given* to all creatures, but *operates* in all of them by arousing their self-transcendent response which is the movement of life itself.

What has been said so far with special reference to living creatures can now be generalized to comprise all of creation. The Spirit of God can be understood as the supreme field of power that pervades all of creation. Each finite event or being is to be considered as a special manifestation of that field, and their movements are responsive to its forces. The concept of field lends itself to such a theological application, because it does not conceive of force as a function of bodies, but rather of bodies as dependent on forces. In the early modern period, the mechanistic conception of physics tried to reduce all forces to bodies or masses. This contributed to the expulsion of the idea of God from the world of nature, because God cannot be conceived of as a body. If all forces are functions of bodies, then God can no longer be imagined to be operative in the world of nature, because he is not a body. The introduction of the field concept by Michael Faraday turned the issue around in rendering the concept of force independent from body, though in the actuality of natural processes masses may have a decisive role in structuring the dynamics of the field (e.g., as happens in the gravitational field). It is the independence in principle of the field concept of force from the notion of body that makes its theological application possible so as to describe all actions of God in nature and history as field effects. This does not mean to physicalize the theological conception of the creative, sustaining, and redeeming action of God. But it does relate the description of nature in modern physics to a theological perspective. We need only remind ourselves that the field language of science is rooted historically in the *pneuma* theories of classical antiquity. This demonstrates the legitimacy of using field concepts in a more general way than in the formalized mathematical fashion of physics. The field theories of science, then, can be considered as approximations to the metaphysical reality of the all-pervading spiritual field of God's creative presence in the universe. It may belong to the limitations of the approximative descriptions of science that the scientific descriptions usually treat field effects as correlative to masses rather than perceiving the occurrence of such a dependency as an inversion of the more profound nature of field effects.

The theological use of the field concept in describing God's creative presence and activity in the world of creation does require, however, a theological interpretation of space and time. There is a particularly intimate dependence of the field concept on space, because it is hardly possible to imagine a field without any form of space. In the perspective of modern thought, space in its turn is dependent on time, since space can be defined as simultaneousness: Everything that coexists simultaneously is somehow organized in spatial relations. The relativity of simultaneity therefore accounts for the relativity of distances in space.

In the history of modern thought, a theological interpretation of the concept of space was a hotly debated issue in the late 17th and 18th centuries. Isaac Newton and Samuel Clarke regarded space as the form of God's omnipresence to his creatures. The German philosopher Leibniz took these ideas of Newton's as evidencing a kind of pantheism not unlike that of Spinoza. He argued that as a consequence of associating God with space Newton had to conceive of God as a body and as having parts. But Clarke retorted that infinite space as such is undivided and without parts. It is coincident with God's immensity. It is only with the occurrence of finite entities within space (i.e., within the presence of God) that space gets parted, and the geometric construction of space is based on that form of space by way of abstraction from all differences of content, as if space were composed of equal parts, the units of measurement. However, it is not possible to imagine any parts without presupposing already infinite space as an undivided whole. This argument was also used by Immanuel Kant and in his view demonstrated the intuitive nature of our awareness of space, while the theological implications were passed over in silence, since they did not fit in Kant's phenomenalist scheme.

There is good reason, however, to insist that the intuition of infinite space can be appropriately accounted for only in theological terms, as expressing the immensity and omnipresence of God. The case of time is similar. Plotinus already argued that the transition from one temporal moment to another presupposes the intuition of time as a whole or rather of eternity, since eternity means the whole of time in the form of one undivided presence. Nevertheless, the separateness of temporal moments in the course of their sequence may be considered as connected with the situation of finite beings in the flow of time. Only from the point of view of a finite being is the past lost and the future not yet arrived, while God in his eternity is his own future as well as the world's, and whatever is past is kept in his presence. Thus, God's immensity and eternity can be regarded as constitutive of time and space, and consequently it makes sense to speak of a field of God's spiritual presence in his creation.

If the notion of energy can also be related to this concept of spirit as field, the presence of God's Spirit in his creation can be described as a field of creative presence, a comprehensive field of force that releases event after event into finite existence. Perhaps such a view of energy can be justified in terms of an interpretation of quantum indeterminacy. It would have to regard the indeterminacy of quantum events as not only epistemic but real in the sense that in the microstructure of natural processes individual future events are not derivable from any given situation. They occur contingently from a field of possibility which is another word for future. Such an interpretation of quantum indeterminacy substantiates a thesis which I tentatively proposed two decades ago in explicating the potential significance of the imminence of the kingdom of God for a Christian doctrine of creation: Every single event as well as the sequence of such events springs contingently from the future of God. This way of looking at the occurrence of events converges, furthermore, with the interrelatedness of time and eternity, because it is through the future that eternity enters into time.

It belongs to the essence of the act of creation that it aims at the autonomous existence of the creature. Such autonomous existence is possible only on condition of some permanence through time, and the first basic requirement for the emergence of permanent forms of finite existence—like atoms, molecules, and their aggregates—is regularities of natural processes. A second basic requirement is the expansion of the universe, as we know it from modern scientific cosmology, because cosmic expansion allows for temperatures to drop to a sufficiently low level so as to admit the formation of enduring creatures. Autonomous existence does not find its highest expression in sheer duration, however, but rather in some form of active self-preservation and self-organization. That is the level of independent existence that is obtained with the emergence of living creatures. Though other natural forms last longer than organisms do, living creatures represent an incomparably more intensified form of independent existence. Such intensified independence is bound up with the ecstatic form of existence that characterizes organic life. It is a peculiar combination of dependence and independence: The organism depends on its environment for its precarious existence and survival, but precisely thereby actively organizes itself.

Organisms obtain stability for their own life to the degree that they manage to control their environment. No other animal, however, has achieved this goal to such an extent as the human race. Since ancient times, notably so in the biblical story of creation, this has been noted as characteristic of human nature: It has the capacity of dominating all other creatures on earth. This human capacity, again, rests on a rather paradoxical basis. It is rooted in the peculiarly human ability to discern—to discern between objects, but above all to discern the objects themselves as self-centered entities, not simply as correlates to our own drives; that is to say: to discern them from ourselves and ourselves from everything else. Paradoxically, this ability of discernment empowers human beings to make themselves masters of their world. That is paradoxical because self-conscious discernment involves restraint, even self-effacement, which allows the particular nature of other beings to be perceived, but precisely thereby it puts the rest of creation to the service of humanity.

Since ancient times the peculiar capacity in human beings of self-conscious discernment has been regarded as evidence of their participation in the Logos. It has been considered so characteristic of human beings that the human being was called the logos-endowed animal or, in more familiar form, the rational animal. In the perspective of Christian patristic theology this also meant that the human being is the creature in which potentially the Son of God becomes manifest. And in a profound sense this is true. The Son of God, as he becomes apparent in Jesus' relationship with the Father, is characterized by distinguishing himself from the Father and thereby subordinating himself to the Father in acknowledging in the Father the one God and his kingdom. But what does that have in common with the human capability for self-conscious discernment?

Human discernment or self-discernment is primarily related to the finite things surrounding us. But it also includes the discernment of their finitude, and therefore it includes an awareness of what is other than finite. Thus, because the human being is the self-consciously discerning animal, it is also the religious animal. While all creatures are in fact related to God the creator, and the young lions seek their prey from God, they do not do so self-consciously. It is only in human beings that the relationship of the creature to God becomes an explicit issue. This, however, is intimately connected with the human capacity for self-conscious discernment.

Two characteristic features of human nature, then—religious awareness and the ability to dominate the earth—are both related to the discerning nature of the human mind. To keep them together in such a way as to subordinate the capacity for domination to the religious awareness of God is part of the destiny to which human beings are called. It is how the human being is described in the Genesis story as created in the image of God. To be created in the image of God is to exercise control over the earth, but to do so under God, so that self-discerning subordination to

God is at the basis of all other discernment. To the degree that this calling is realized, the Son in his relationship to the Father becomes manifest in the lives of human beings, and since only in this way can human creatures obtain communion with the eternal God, it is also the full accomplishment of independent existence of the creature. Creaturely independence is not achieved by emancipating oneself from subordination under God, nor by putting oneself in the place of God as ruler of the universe. Such experiments are doomed, as we know, to disaster and death. But independent existence is intended for the creature by the creator himself. It is the freedom the Son enjoys in his responsive relationship to the Father. To embody this freedom in the form of the creaturely existence has been the aim of the creator in creating the whole universe, and the human creature is the particular place where this aim is to be accomplished.

SELECTION 12

Arthur Peacocke

"God's Interaction with the World"

A respected biochemist as well as Christian theologian, Arthur Peacocke (1924–2006) was best known for his attempts to reconcile faith with contemporary science. Like Grace Jantzen, he was particularly concerned to come up with a coherent account of God's interaction with the universe, with particular attention to the identification of a plausible interface between God and the world that honors both God's sovereign freedom and the integrity of the phenomenal universe and its physical laws. This latter concern causes him to reject proposals that understand God as determining events through the undetectable manipulation events at the quantum level or in macroscopic chaotic systems. Instead of these "bottom-up" theories of divine action, Peacocke advocates a "top-down" or "whole-part" model.

This model examines how complex, multileveled systems, the structure of the system as a whole has an effect on the features of its constituent parts (e.g., changing climatic conditions within an ecosystem affect the behavior of individual organisms). This phenomenon, which counters the reductionist temptation to view the state of any systemic whole as entirely the product of its constituent parts, leads Peacocke to suggest that God acts on the universe as a whole, as the ultimate "boundary condition" affecting the state of the world's myriad constituent parts. Peacocke's proposal has certain disadvantages: it makes God's action highly indirect (since God can influence particular events only by way of the universe as a whole) and (because of the insistence that God never overrides physical laws) seems to limit God's ability to guarantee particular outcomes. It remains, however, one of the most engaging proposals in the contemporary discussion of the relationship between theology and science.

> From Arthur Peacocke, *Paths from Science towards God: The End of All Our Exploring* (Oxford: Oneworld, 2001), 108–15.

Whole-Part Influence and God's Interaction with the World

We have seen ... that causality in complex systems made up of units at various levels of interlocking organisation can best be understood as a two-way process. There is clearly a bottom-up effect of the constituent parts on the properties and behaviour of the whole complex. However, real features of the total system-as-a-whole are frequently an influence upon what happens to the units (which may themselves be complex) at lower levels. The units behave as they do because they are part of these particular systems. What happens to the component units is the joint effect of their own properties, explicable in terms of the lower-level science appropriate to them, and also the properties of the system-as-a-whole which result from its particular organisation. When that higher level can also be understood only in terms not reducible to lower-level ones, then new realities having causal efficacy can be said to have emerged at the higher levels.

We have also seen ... that the world-as-a-whole may be regarded as a kind of overall System-of-systems, for its very different (e.g., quantum, biological, cosmological) components systems are interconnected and interdependent across space and time, with wide variations in the degree of coupling. There will therefore be an influence on the component unit systems, at all levels, of the states and patterns of this overall world-System and of its succession of states and patterns. Moreover, God, by God's own very nature as omniscient, is the only being that could have an unsurpassed awareness of such states and patterns of the world-System in all its interconnectedness and interdependence. These would be totally and luminously clear to an omniscient God in all their ramifications and degrees of coupling across space and time. For God is present to and constitutes the circumambient Reality of all-that-is—that is what is meant by my emphasis on the immanence of God and what panentheism is all about.

I want now to explore the possibility that these theological insights informed by new scientific perspectives might provide a resource for exploring how we are to conceive of God interacting with the world. Let me make it clear from the outset that I am not postulating that the world is "God's body," for, although the world may best be regarded as "in" God (panentheism), God's Being is distinct from all created beings in a way that we are not distinct from our bodies. Yet, although the world is not organized like a human body, it is nevertheless a system, for all-that-is displays real interconnectedness and interdependence. So we shall continue to speak of the "world-System" without relying, at this stage, upon any analogy with the mind-brain-body relation or with personal agency.

If God interacts with the world-system as a totality, then God, by affecting its overall state, could be envisaged as being able to exercise influence upon events in the myriad sublevels of existence of which it is made without abrogating the laws and regularities that specifically apply to them. Moreover, God would be doing this without intervening within the supposed gaps provided by the in-principle, inherent unpredictabilities.... Particular events could occur in the world and be what they are because God intends them to be so, without any contravention of the laws of physics, biology, psychology or whatever is the pertinent science for the level in question—as in the exercise of whole-part influence within the many constituent systems of the world.

This model is based on the recognition that an omniscient God uniquely knows, over all frameworks of reference of time and space, everything that it is possible to know about the state(s) of the world-System, including the interconnectednesss and interdependence of the world's entities, structures and processes. By analogy with the operation of whole-part influence in real systems, the suggestion is that, because the ontological gap between the world and God is located simply everywhere in space and time, *God could affect holistically the state of the world-System.* Thence, *mediated by the whole-part influences of the world-System on its constituents, God could cause particular patterns of events to occur which would express God's intentions.* These latter would not otherwise have happened had God not so specifically intended.

Any such interaction of God with the world-System would be initially with it as a whole. One would expect this initial interaction to be followed by a kind of "trickle-down" effect as each level affected by the particular divine intention then has an influence on lower levels and so on down the hierarchies of complexity to the level at which God intends to effect a particular purpose. We have already seen ... how in "chaotic" systems, especially dissipative ones, states can differ in pattern and organization (and so in information content) yet be very close in energy. This provides a flexible route for the transmission of divinely influenced information from the world-System as a whole down to particular systems within that whole. These could well be those of individual human-brains-in-human-bodies-in-society ... and so this could be the means whereby God is experienced in acts of meditation and worship—as well as recognized as "special providence" in events judged to be responses to such human acts. If such divine responses were so transmitted then they would be indirect and elusive and could well take a long time by human reckoning—which corresponds to actual religious experience. This action of God on the world is to be distinguished from God's universal creative action in that particular intentions of God for particular patterns of events to occur are effected thereby.

The ontological interface at which God must be deemed to be influencing the world is, on this model, located in that which occurs between God and the totality of the world-System and this, from a panentheistic viewpoint, is within God's own self. What passes across this interface may perhaps be appropriately conceived of as a "flow of information" without energy transfer (as would necessarily accompany it in such flows within the world-System). But one has to recognize that there will always be a distinction, and so gulf, between the nature of God and that of all created entities, structures and processes (the notorious "ontological gap at the causal joint" of Austin Farrer[1]). Hence this model can attempt to postulate intelligibly only the "location" and tentative character of the initial effect of God on the world-System seen, as it were, from our side of the boundary. Whether or not this analogical use of the notion of information flow proves helpful in this context, we do need some way of indicating that the effect of God at this level, and so at all levels, is that of pattern shaping in its most general sense. I am encouraged in this kind of exploration by the recognition that the concept of the Logos, the Word, of God is usually taken to refer to God's self-expression in the world and so to indicate God's creative patterning of the world. . . .

The model is propounded to be consistent with the monist concept that all concrete particulars in the world-System are composed only of basic physical entities, and with the conviction that the world-System is causally closed. There are no dualistic, no vitalistic, no supernatural levels through which God might be supposed to be exercising special divine activity. In this model, the proposed kind of interactions of God with the world-System would not, according to panentheism, be from "outside" but from "inside" it. The world-System is regarded as being "in God." This seems to be a fruitful way of combining God's ultimate otherness with God's ability to interface holistically with the world-System.

These panentheistic interrelations of God with the world-System, including humanity, I have attempted to represent in figure 1. This is a kind of Venn diagram and represents ontological relationships; the infinity sign represents not infinite space or time but the infinitely "more" of God's Being in comparison with everything else. The diagram has the limitation of being in two planes so that the "God" label appears dualistically to be (ontologically) outside the world and although this conveys the truth that God is "more and other" than the world, it cannot represent God's omnipresence in and to the world. A vertical arrow has been placed at the centre of this circle to signal God's immanent influence and activity within

---

1. A. Farrer, *Faith and Speculation* (London: A & C Black, 1967), 66.

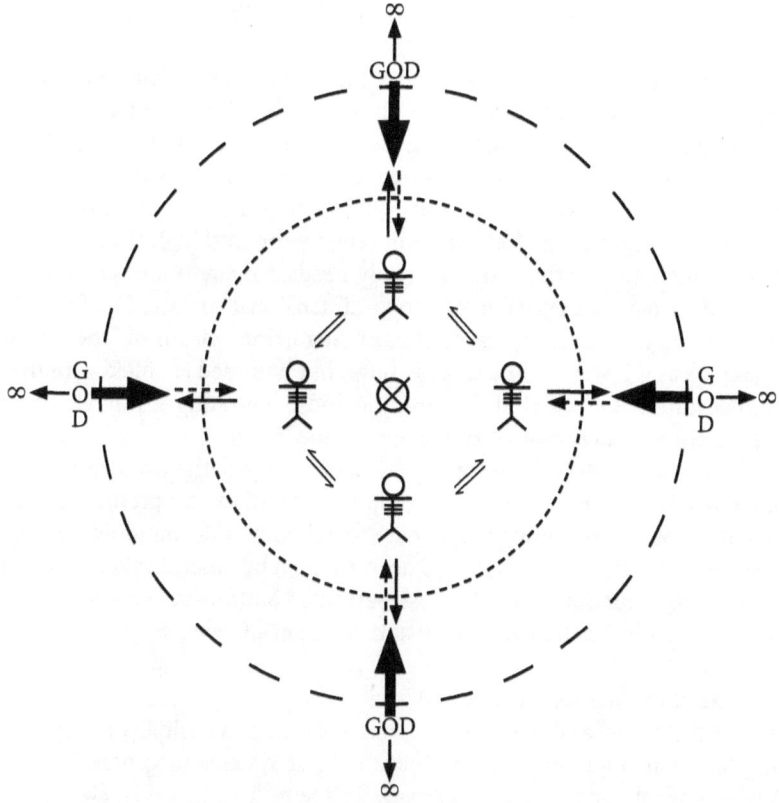

Figure 1.
Diagram representing spatially the ontological relation of, and the interactions between, God and the world (including humanity).

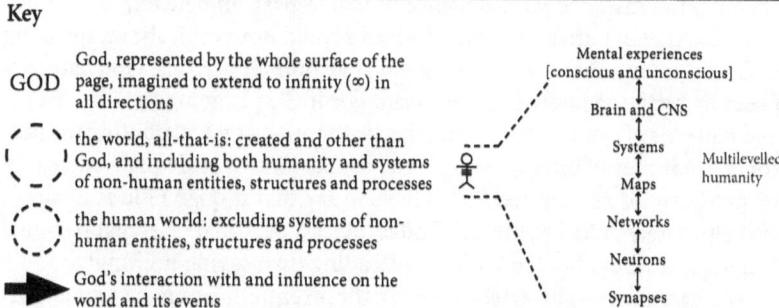

the world. It may also be noted that "God" is denoted by the (imagined) infinite planar surface of the page on which the circle representing the world is printed. For, it is assumed, God is "more than" the world, which is nevertheless "in" God. The page underlies and supports the circle and its contents, just as God sustains everything in existence and is present to all. So the larger dashed circle, representing the ontological location of God's interaction with all-that-is, really needs a many-dimensional convoluted surface not available on a two-dimensional surface. The figure is but a more mundane representation of Augustine's vision of "the whole creation" as if it were "some sponge, huge, but bounded . . . filled with that immeasurable sea" of God, "environing and penetrating it though every way infinite . . . everywhere and on every side."[2]

In conclusion, this model of God's interaction with the world as including a whole-part influence has proved, in my view, to be a promising path to take in our exploration from science towards an understanding of God's special providence and has indeed been adopted by other thinkers, though often in combination with other, less warranted bottom-up proposals, such as those involving chaotic systems and/or quantum events.

God As "Personal Agent" in the World

I hope the model as described so far has a degree of plausibility in depending on an analogy only with complex natural systems in general and on the way whole-part influence operates in them. It is, however, clearly too impersonal to do justice to the personal character of many (but not all) of the profoundest human experiences of God. So there is little doubt that it needs to be rendered more cogent by the recognition that, among natural systems, the instance *par excellence* of whole-part influence in a complex system is that of personal agency. Indeed I could not avoid, above, speaking of God's "intentions" and implying that, like human persons, God had purposes to be implemented in the world. For if God is going to affect events and patterns of event in the world, then we cannot avoid attributing the personal predicates of intentions and purposes to God—inadequate and easily misunderstood as they are. So we have to say that though God is ineffable and ultimately unknowable, yet God is "at least personal" and that personal language attributed to God is less misleading than saying nothing!

We can now legitimately turn to the exemplification of whole-part influence in the mind-brain-body relation . . . as a resource for modelling God's interaction with the world. When we do so the ascendancy of the "personal" as a category for explicating the wholeness of human agency comes to the fore and the traditional, indeed biblical, model of God as in some sense a personal agent in the world is rehabilitated. It is re-established here in a quite different metaphysical, non-dualist framework from that of

---

2. Augustine, *Confessions*, 7.5; ET, *LCC* 7:139.

much traditional theology but now consistently with the understanding of the world which the sciences provide. Accounts of religious experience are, of course, deeply suffused with the language of personal interaction with God and at this point our philosophical and theological explorations towards God begin to make contact with the common experiences of believers in God.

When we were using non-human systems in their whole-part relationships as a model for God's relation to the world in special providence, we resorted to the idea of a flow of information as a helpful pointer to what might be conceived as crossing the ontological gap between God and the world-as-a-whole. But now as we turn to more personal categories to explicate this relation and interchange, it is natural to interpret the flow of information between God and the world, including humanity, in terms of the communication that occurs between persons—rather in the way that a flow of information in the technical engineering sense transmutes, say in a telephone call, in the human brain into "information" in the ordinary sense of the word, so that communication occurs between persons. Thus, whatever else may be involved in God's personal interaction with the world, communication must be involved and this raises the question of to whom God might be communicating. There would not have been such intense investigations into scientific perspectives on divine action if it had not been the case that humanity distinctively and, it appears, uniquely has regarded itself as the recipient of communication from God. But in what ways has the reception of communication from God been understood and experienced?

SELECTION 13

Kathryn Tanner

"Is God in Charge?"

Kathryn Tanner (1957–) teaches systematic theology at the Divinity School of the University of Chicago. Her understanding of providence is closely bound up with her doctrine of creation and rests on a radical doctrine of divine transcendence. For Tanner divine transcendence means that God is "beyond kinds" and thus not describable in terms of any of the categories of phenomenal reality. This perspective allows her to stress that God is no closer to (or farther from) any one creature than any other, and, therefore, that God is not limited in the range of God's work in the world by the characteristics of particular creatures (as though God could only work effectively with spiritual or rational beings, for example).

Because God is equally the source of all beings, God's creative work is not limited to the beginning, but extends with equal intensity to every moment of creation's existence. This idea implies, in turn, a radically noncompetitive vision of the relation between divine and creaturely activity that is crucial to Tanner's understanding of providence. She maintains that it is impossible for God's activity in directing the course of history to compete with that of creatures, because God is the immediate cause of every creature's particular form of existence at every moment of its existence. Some charge that Tanner's insistence on God as the immediate source of the whole created causal nexus leaves no room for meaningful creaturely activity, but she counters that this objection falsely conceives of God as acting on the same level as creatures rather than as the Creator who is both the ground and enabler of all creaturely activity.

From Kathryn Tanner, *Essentials of Christian Theology*, ed. William C. Placher (Louisville, KY: Westminster John Knox Press, 2003), 116–30.

If Christians know anything about the Old Testament, they know the first few lines in which God is said to have created heaven and earth. Following the early ecumenical creeds in which God's creation of the world is cited first among the acts of salvation history, Christians often express such a belief in the routine course of worship—for example, in the thanksgiving portions of eucharistic services or when renewing baptismal vows.

Providence is another matter. The psalms are a mainstay of Christian worship, and the idea of God's providence does figure centrally in many of them. God's work is alive in nature: God visits the earth with showers and blesses the springs and crowns the year with goodness so that the pastures are full of flocks and the valleys covered in corn (Ps. 65). God is never far from the individual but will find and direct him or her wherever he or she may be—from the womb to the grave, whether in the heights of heaven or the depths of hell (Ps. 139). God is active throughout the history of the particular people Israel, leading them out of Egypt, parting the sea for them to escape their pursuers, providing them with food in the wilderness, giving the laws that define them as a nation, bringing them into the promised land, and so forth (e.g., Ps. 135–136). But direct Christian expression of belief in God's providence is probably more a fixture of popular piety than of formal worship.

In the events of daily life, Christians have occasion to express belief in God's providence where others might appeal to luck. It is providential that, held up by traffic, I missed my flight on a plane that crashed on takeoff. Or Christians may affirm belief in providence as a way of justifying refusal of human responsibility: Whether babies are born with birth defects is a matter of God's will and not a matter for technological intervention. Or Christians may make such an affirmation as an expression of resignation before the inevitable, seeking comfort and struggling to regain calm with the thought that God must know what we do not—how the death of a loved one, for example, is something more than simply a tragic loss. When Christians formally confess their belief in God, providence is likely to be simply the unexpressed subtext for the beliefs that really matter. God must have a hand in the world, directing its course according to a plan of God's own devising—that is the least one can say—if what Christians believe about Christ is true: Here, against all the forces of sin and death in the world, God fulfills and completes the covenant that God set up with Israel for all the nations.

If beliefs in creation and providence are clearly important components of the Christian faith, their meaning is not equally clear. The two-thousand-year history of Christian theology can be read as an effort to gain that clarity. Without such clarity, one cannot properly assess the seriousness of contemporary challenges to the faith. Do scientific descriptions of the universe's beginnings compete with the idea that God created it? Do those scientific descriptions tell us how God created the world, as a supplement or alternative to the description the Bible offers? If we can explain how things work in the world in the world's own terms, is appeal to God's providence superfluous? Are some accounts of how the world works incompatible with the idea of God's providence? Isn't, for example, the idea that outcomes in the world are determined by statistical probabilities, by some blind mechanism or chance, incompatible with the idea that God directs the world according to purposes, for ends, of God's own devising? In a world wracked, as ours is, by the havoc caused by the ignorant and sinful acts of men and women, mustn't one lose confidence in God's providence?

Without considerable clarity about the meaning of creation and providence, one cannot assess, either, the uses to which these ideas are put. Do Christian beliefs about creation and providence provide models of perfectly coercive power for our, unfortunate, imitation? Are these beliefs all about control and about who is in control, God or us? Is it proper for belief in God's providence to promote submission before the world's injustices and the world's tragedies as if they were an inexorable fate? Or is such a belief properly used in promoting childish hopes: We need not worry, we need not exert ourselves to improve the lot of the world, since God will intervene to save us, at the end, out of the blue? Does the idea of providence support a narrowly self-concerned smugness on the part of those whom the world favors, the sufferings of some serving the well-being of others by God's design? Does my good fortune—my good fortune not to be on that ill-fated plane, for example—suggest that I have an elevated place in God's plan not shared by those who perish?

These are complicated questions, and the present essay can give only hints about how to answer them. What this essay will do is sketch a meaning for creation and providence, culled from the two-thousand-year history of theological discussion of those topics, by means of which the questions may be answered. I hope that, this sketch in hand, the reader will return to these questions and begin to answer them all—in the negative.

My method here of generating a more precise meaning for these beliefs by focusing on the history of theological discussion of them is more controversial and complex in its implications than might appear at first glance. Such a focus in the first place might be thought overly restrictive, since beliefs about creation and providence are not on their face distinctively Christian. Beliefs like these are not limited to Christianity. One can find affirmations at least verbally indistinguishable from the ones Christians make about creation and providence in other world religions and in worldviews of primarily scientific or philosophical derivation (such as Neoplatonism and Stoicism).

Even in Christian use, these beliefs would seem explicable in their meaning apart from beliefs that are distinctively Christian in that they do not make mention of Christ, or seem to depend very directly on what Christians say about him. All this might suggest that there is no distinctively Christian meaning to such beliefs, and that one could therefore fill out their meaning in a freewheeling and eclectic way, providing content for them out of the common creation story or whatever philosophical resources might be currently available for discussing the origins and arrangement of the world. Beliefs about creation and providence would be then a kind of ground floor for explicitly Christian beliefs, specified independently of them and merely subsequently colored by them.

That assumption, and the procedures for determining the meaning of Christian beliefs about creation and providence that go with it, are in my view mistaken. It is true that ideas about creation and providence circulate everywhere, and Christian theologians do indeed work with such ideas—Christian theology is never a self-contained, insular enterprise. If, however, one wants to fill out the meaning that Christians give to those ideas, the trick is to see what Christians do with them, what Christians do with what other people mean by them, and to see what happens to such ideas in Christian use, especially at the time when Christian beliefs in creation and providence developed in the Greco-Roman milieu of the early church. The distinctiveness of that use is apparent, moreover—at the time it developed and, once established (at least in some Christian theological circles), ever after—in the way ideas about creation and providence are systematically shaped in relation to the rest of what Christians believe.

Thus, I do not believe that the meaning of creation in Christian circles is ascertainable apart from Christian beliefs about God, particularly about the transcendence of God as that comes to be developed in Trinitarian terms. This understanding of creation is, in turn, the lynchpin for understanding God's providence; certain ideas about providence follow from it by implication. Furthermore, the Christian interest in both claims—what is at stake for Christians in these affirmations—is only apparent in light of what Christians say about Jesus. Christian beliefs about creation and providence developed, then, at the time Christianity was wracked by controversies over the significance of Christ. The character of God's activity as either creator or providential guide of the world's arrangement and historical course is also concretely specified in much the same way—by what God's dealings with the world in Christ suggest about it. The meaning of both beliefs becomes clear, in short, only when they are set within the whole story of God's dealings with the world, as the nature of those dealings—their gracious beneficence—becomes clear in Christ.

Without this careful specification of the way creation and providence hang together with the whole Christian story, Christian beliefs about creation and providence can mean almost anything, they can be pushed this way and that with impunity, they become a blank screen for the projection of human worries and fantasies—worries, for example, about threatened privilege and fantasies about absolute power. As the often sordid history of Christianity exhibits, even with such efforts of careful specification, such temptations are ineradicable and failure likely.

God Beyond Kinds and Creation

Let us start, then, with connections between the doctrine of God and creation. The theologians of the early church who were responsible for developing a Christian account of creation tended to favor one of the ideas about God's transcendence circulating in the Hellenistic philosophical milieu of the day. In Greco-Roman religion and philosophy, divinity is most commonly identified with a general quality or set of qualities—eternity, rationality, order, simplicity, unity—in which a number of things can participate in differing degrees. These qualities might form a particular subset of those constituting the world as we know it, or they might be set off from the world as a whole as just what this disordered world of change, diversity, and division is not. In either case, such ideas about divinity are not easily reconcilable with the monotheism that Christianity shares with Judaism. Contrary to monotheism, in this Greco-Roman view, many things—whether within this world of time and change (e.g., numbers and eternal truths) or outside it (hierarchies of superior and subordinate deities)—are divine to differing degrees. Indeed, certain sorts of things within the world are simply identified with divinity in a fashion that smacks of idolatry.

Christians favor, instead, another understanding of divinity, which has its origins in the surrounding Greco-Roman milieu in what Plato says in the *Republic* about the mysterious "idea of the Good," an idea that seems beyond all forms or kinds of things as some sort of ineffable principle or source of their unity. Divinity is not a kind of thing at all, which might either be like some features of the world or simply opposed to them all, considered as a whole. Christians push this idea of a God beyond kinds in a distinctly monotheist direction. Since divinity is not a generic category in which distinct beings might share to varying degrees, the various deities of Greco-Roman religion and philosophy that lie outside the world of time and change must really only be names for what exists all together and at once in the one and only God. If they are anything at all, these divinities exist in that one and only God, and as such they are all equally God and bear no relations of superiority or subordination with respect to one another.

Christians also put this idea of God beyond distinctions of kind to novel use by arguing that there is one God who is directly responsible for the world as a whole—what Christians mean by God's creation of the world. If God is not a kind of thing but beyond identification by kind, it makes sense to say, first of all, that God is responsible, not just for those aspects of the world that are supposedly like God—for example, the world's rational arrangement, mind, and those aspects of the world suitable for rational comprehension according to timeless truths—but for the whole of the world, from the bottom up, so to speak, both the stuff or materials out of which the world takes shape and their organization, both the aspects that change and decay and those that have permanence, both materiality and mind.

If God is a kind of thing, then God's responsibility for the world is limited to just those aspects of the world that are most like itself; for example, if God is reason, then God is responsible for only the world's rational arrangement and intelligibility. If God is not a kind of thing, this limitation is removed and God can be responsible for every aspect of the world. And if God is responsible for every aspect of the world, God is not simply giving shape to its parts or arranging them, but producing the world, giving rise to it, as a whole. God is a comprehensive productive principle, in short—the creator of the whole world, both heaven and earth.

If God is beyond kinds, it makes sense to say, in the second place, that the one and only God produces the world directly or immediately. God is not a kind of thing whose nature needs to be protected from compromise and corruption when coming into close contact with things of an opposed nature—the way, say, fire needs to be kept from corruption, the loss of its own nature, through contact by water. Nor, conversely, is divinity a kind of thing that compromises the natures of others when brought into intimate relation with them the way fire compromises the nature of water—dissipating it into the air—by heating it. Kinds of things are essentially defined by not being like other kinds of things, and therefore their borders have to be guarded against those things that they are defined over and against.

A principle of this sort seems to be behind the penchant in religious philosophies of the Hellenistic world (the Greek-speaking world around the eastern Mediterranean in the centuries around the time of Jesus) for multiplying divinities to produce a buffer zone between the highest God and the world. In Hellenistic philosophy, inferior deities are the only ones directly responsible for the properties of the world that most contrast with divinity—matter, for example. Indeed, inferior deities must be the only ones directly responsible for even those properties that most resemble divinity just to the extent they differ from it, by being, say, found in material bodies subject to decay and change. If God is not a kind of thing, then the one God can be directly and intimately involved with the production of the world in all its aspects, without threatening to compromise or dilute either God's divinity or the natures of any of the things in the world.

Interest in both these points—that God produces the whole of the world and that God does so in an immediate way—was fueled by controversies in the early church over the significance of Christ. Take the matter of immediacy. The upshot of these controversies is that Christians want to maintain the closest possible relation between the man Jesus and God: God is identified with Jesus; Jesus is God. And Christians want to say that this God is no inferior or subordinate deity but very God, the one and only highest God. They claim, moreover, that in being so identified, neither the divinity of God nor the humanity of Jesus is compromised. When we are in touch with the man Jesus with the greatest possible physical intimacy (at the time of his existence on earth, grabbing the hem of his garments, receiving his spit on our faces, feeling his touch; or after his death, when drinking and eating of his flesh and blood in a eucharistic meal) we are in touch with God in the highest and with neither a demigod nor a superman.

Although not predictable from the fact of God's creation of the world—the identity between a human being and God is a surprising new level of intimacy between God and the world—the incarnation is therefore the paradigm in a remarkably extreme form of what the Christian doctrine of creation is saying about the immediacy of God's relation to the world, as that follows, we have seen, from the fact that God is beyond kinds. The doctrine of creation when explicated in relation to the doctrine of God helps makes sense of the central Christian affirmations about Christ. If what Christians say about creation makes sense in virtue of God's divinity beyond kinds, then so do the outrageous claims that they make about Christ: Here is God in the flesh! The intimacy of God's relation to a world of suffering, loss, and conflict may not be very apparent. But the most intimate identity of God with the one, Jesus, who saves us out of the world of suffering, violence, and conflict by taking it all on himself, proves God's capacity to be in intimate relations with that sort of world. Christ is the source of our confidence about what we say about God generally: From the very beginning God wishes to be near us, in intimate relation with us. Creation involves an intimate relationship with God on the way to the fulfillment of such relationship in Christ.

The comprehensive character of Christian claims about God's creation of the world is also promoted by Christian interest in making maximal claims for Jesus' significance. Jesus does not come to save a subset of humanity but, in intention if not in fact, to save the whole world—all the nations and the natural world too as it groans, as Paul says, under the powers of affliction and division. And Jesus comes to save the whole world in all its aspects; he brings total liberation, not just spiritual but physical healing, not just the liberation of individuals but of society, starting with the church, not just reconciliation among people but between them and the natural world. There are no irredeemable aspects of the world, which Christians must either flee in order to be saved or simply resign themselves to. God's comprehensive concerns as savior are matched, in short, by God's comprehensive concerns as creator.

The latter, indeed, makes sense of the former: Jesus' range of concern is unlimited because God's range of concern has always been such. As the first few lines of John's Gospel suggest, Jesus does not amount to a *deus ex machina* intervening in a world that is a stranger in most respects to God's designs. God's comprehensive creation of the world—indeed, God the Father's creation of the world through the very Word made flesh in Christ—means that the whole of it has been the object of God's concern from the very beginning. The incarnation simply brings that concern to its culmination and completion in overcoming the forces of sin and death. The sort of divine concern for the world completed in Christ was there from the very beginning when God created a whole world valuable in God's sight, when God looked with love upon all that had been made and declared it very good.

From Creation to Providence
Keeping in mind the comprehensive and immediate character of God's creation of the world and the idea that God is beyond kinds, one can unpack the meaning of God's creation of the world a bit more. Doing so will allow us to draw out the implications of creation for an understanding of God's providence. In fact, explicating the meaning of God's creation of the world is more like excising from that understanding all one's usual presuppositions about productive activity. If God is not a kind of thing, it is not permissible to identify God's creating with any particular kind of agency, operation, or principle of activity to be found in the world. None of those kinds of productive activity, moreover, gives rise to something totally new. The closest that ordinary processes come to this is where a new kind of thing begins to be, in the form of either a new species of thing or a new individual of an existing one. But this kind of production of things as we know it always works on something that already exists, or uses some preexisting stuff in the process, or depends on the cooperation of other productive powers not derived from its own activities.

A productive process employing only the preexisting stuff of its own substance might seem closest to the comprehensive creativeness of God.

But what is drawn out of the substance of its cause is similar to it in nature, and the world's relation to a God beyond kinds cannot be like that. Where already existing stuff and cooperative causal agencies have to be presumed, production of something is, moreover, not absolutely immediate, as God's agency is supposed to be; intervening media or processes of production come between a cause and its effect. If the whole of something is brought into existence by God, it is also not appropriate to talk of creation as any sort of change, movement, or process, within what is created. There is nothing to be moved or changed, nothing in which a process could occur, prior to creation, if creation is perfectly comprehensive. Nothing is happening to you in any ordinary sense of the term when you are being created by God. Furthermore, since God's creating is neither instigated by intervening motions (like birth throes or picking up a hammer), nor found within the world of time and change, the temporal progression, the lapse of time, that goes with movement or change is absent from God's creating of the world.

Finally, one should not even think of the creation of the world as a movement or change from a time when nothing existed to a time when everything does (or, for individuals, as a movement from one's nonexistence to existence—for example, at the moment of one's birth). One should think of the world being created by God as it exists, and not in the movement from nothing to something. If the world in its entirety is the creation of God, it is created not simply at its start (assuming it has one) but across the whole time of its existence. Because of the creative activity of God, there never is a time in the world's history when the world does not exist. The movement of the world away from its beginnings does not signal distance from the creative activity of God; it does not mean that the world exists on its own as time goes on, independently of God's action for it as creator.

When thinking properly of God's creating the world, one has to exclude, then, all ideas of cooperative agency (in which God would be one among other principles of production), all ideas of intermediate motion or process (God does not do anything to establish a kind of mediating causal bridge between God and the world), all ideas of time and change (nothing is happening in any ordinary sense of the term, as when something is generated or its qualities altered), and all ideas of beginnings in any simple contrast to what comes later. What is left, when all ideas of time, change, and finite process are excised, is the bare idea of a relation of utter dependence on God that holds for the whole world, in every respect, across the whole time of its existence.

What is left, in short, is a very abstract idea, one that might prompt praise and thankfulness—this is certainly a God majestic in giving beyond all comprehension—but one that might seem hardly intelligible. Theologians give the idea of God's creation a more concrete sense through a variety of images—more specifically, by merging in odd ways familiar images of causes of radically different sorts. That odd blending is a way of indicating that God's identity does not abide by the usual contrasts among kinds.

Personal Agency or Naturalistic Emanation
The two images with the widest currency in Christian theology are those of personal agency and naturalistic emanation: God creates the world by intelligence and will as a person would a house, or God creates the world like an overflowing source of water produces a stream or a source of light illumines the air. These images were the most common ones for talking about God's production of the world at the time the Christian doctrine of creation was formulated. Indeed, they were the images favored, respectively, by the two viewpoints Christianity came to oppose: God creates from something—for example, preexisting matter, like a human artificer would create a house from bricks—and the world arises out of the substance of God like heat from a flame or water from a spring; that is, what issues from God becomes progressively less divine the farther it gets from its source. For all their Hellenistic derivations, these are vivid images and rather commonsensical as an exhaustive division of types of causality—intentional agents on the one hand, and natural causes (whether physical or biological) on the other.

Christian theologians tend to highlight one of these images, using the other as a corrective. Thus, one can talk about God as a personal agent creating the world by thinking about what to create and then deciding to do so. This is one model for thinking of the creative action of the Trinity: God the Father creates the world through the Word out of the love that is the Holy Spirit. If one is trying to give concrete expression to the idea of a God beyond kinds who gives rise to the world as a whole, there are several reasons for the appeal of such imagery. First of all, compared with those of natural causes, images of personal agency seem to conform more easily with comprehensiveness. Natural causes seem to have the capacity to give rise to only one sort of thing like themselves (e.g., mares give birth only to horses), while personal agents act according to an intention whose complexity is potentially unlimited: I can choose to build a house, then go to the store, then cook dinner, and so forth.

Second, talking about God's creation of the world in terms of personal agency allows one to display the way in which God is beyond kinds. Unlike talk about natural causes, talk about someone thinking and willing has a peculiar grammatical structure: These verbs have (at least implicitly) clauses for their grammatical objects. Compare "The mare gives birth to a foal" with "I think that John is a rat." "Foal" is the grammatical object in the one case; the clause "that John is a rat" is the other. This grammatical fact brings with it several other odd ones. First, the nouns in the object clause refer to what is being talked about there only under a particular description; and therefore when nouns that describe the same thing differently are substituted, the new sentence may no longer be saying the same thing. So, substituting "the occupant of apartment 2C" for "John," the fact that I think John is a rat does not necessarily mean I think the occupant of apartment 2C is a rat, even if John and that occupant are the same person, since I might not know where John lives. This curiosity brings with it a second. The properties that characterize the thinking and willing need not also characterize what is being talked about in the object clause. So if it is true that I think John is a rat, that does not say anything about whether John is or isn't one—I might be mistaken. Similarly, my thinking him a rat might be necessary because I am such an ill-tempered person, but that suggests nothing about the necessity, or not, of John's being a rat. My thinking so might be petty, but that says nothing about the pettiness of John's being a rat. My act of thinking may be simple and single, without what I am thinking about—the whole complex lot of John's ratlike qualities—being so. And so on.

As the last examples make clear, these grammatical features do not depend on the ignorance of the one doing the thinking (or on the impotence of the one willing, in examples I have not provided) and therefore are not essentially unsuitable for use when talking about God. When so applied to God's creating the world, they display the idea of a God beyond kinds. Following these grammatical features in this new theological use, one sees that the world need not be like or unlike the God who intentionally brings it into existence. The character of God's thinking and willing by which the world is brought to be implies nothing either way about the character of the world, about the character of what God intends to bring into existence.

Other aspects, however, of talk about God's creating the world by acts of thinking and willing have to be severely modified in order to bring that way of speaking into conformity with the comprehensiveness and immediacy of God's creative activity. In doing so, such imagery is brought very close to imagery of natural causes such as fire and light. Thus, contrary to the comprehensiveness of God's creative activity, personal agents always work with materials they do not produce. To build a house, I need bricks and tools. I might make the bricks and tools too, but in order to do so, I require mud for the bricks, and metal and fire to forge the tools, and so on. The agency of fire or light is more serviceable here since fire and light seem (at least to the untutored eye) to be self-sufficient in their activity of heating or illuminating, apparently working even without substantial media to be heated or illumined, or without the need for outside implements.

Moreover, contrary to the immediacy of God's working, personal agents need to take additional steps to bring into existence what they think about and decide to do. If I think about the sort of house I want and decide to build it, the building of it still remains to be done. In order to avoid the suggestion of intervening action, one would have to say that acts of thinking and willing, which have no external effects in the case of humans, have such effects when God is the agent. The closest analogue again would be the way natural processes such as fire and sunlight produce their effects immediately, without needing to do anything and without any intervening process, just by being themselves.

In order to avoid suggesting that God creates through processes involving time and change—by beginning and ending, stopping and starting, in successive acts—one could extend this idea that God does not have to do anything in creating the world to God's even having to make a decision. God creates simply by being what God always is—the God who wants to create the world. If that is God's intention, it always was God's intention; God never came to so decide after a period of indecision. Again, the sun illuminating the air and fire heating things up would seem close analogues: Fire does not come to be what it needs to be in order to heat things up; it is always already in act, throwing off heat.

Something of the language of deliberation would still have to be retained here, however. Unlike what the cases of fire and light suggest, one should not say that God's intention to create the world is part of God's very nature; God may always intend to create the world, but this is by no necessity of nature. What needs to be retained of the idea of deliberation is the simple idea of a non-necessary relation between God's being and nature, on the one hand, and God's intention to create the world, on the other. From God's existence and nature one cannot infer with any logical necessity that God intends to create the world. Even if God never doesn't intend to create the world, God didn't have to so intend. Without this free character of intention, the necessity of God bleeds over onto the character of the world, in violation of the idea that God is beyond kinds, neither like nor unlike anything in the world or the world as a whole. If God's nature meant that God had to intend to create the world, then a similar "had to be" must also characterize the existence of the world (assuming that God's intentions cannot be frustrated!).

Finally, personalistic imagery for God's creating might suggest that the world is not equally the creation of God over its whole course, in much the way a house gains independence from its builder once built. Here again a better analogue might be found among natural causes, specifically in the relationship between a natural cause and those of its effects that lack the capacity to retain the properties communicated to them. Air, for example, does not have the ability to remain illuminated apart from the constant shining of a light source.

Other theologians prefer naturalistic imagery. We have already seen some of the positive reasons for its appeal: the way it helps avoid the ideas of creation out of preexisting stuff, of mediating process, temporal change, and narrow associations with the first moment of something's existence.

These theologians think the deficits of such language are not very serious and can be remedied through the use, for example, of personal imagery. Thus, images of fire and light need not imply that God's substance is parceled out to created things, or somehow thinned out to make them, like a thin stream from an overflowing basin of water or like a wave of heat from a much hotter stove. It can instead be thought of as a materially discontinuous imitation of the whole in an entirely different medium—less like the rays from the sun and more like a painted picture or photographic image of the sun itself. The world is not, then, quasi-divine; it is the distinctly non-divine reflection of God's own being and beauty. One could argue, moreover, that natural causes are no more limited in the range of their effects than intentional agents are. Fire, for example, can melt bronze or harden mud or make water evaporate.

Finally, natural causes are such because of their superabundance, and this suggests a kind of freedom to their working despite the fact that they must do what they do: Fire must give off heat, and the sun must shine. They do not act out of need; they have in a more perfect form anything that they might achieve by giving rise to light or heat outside themselves. So the triune God has in the divine superabundant life the perfect form of communicated good in the way the three persons of the Trinity give of their own good to one another in perfect equality. God must communicate the goodness of God's own nature outside God in creating a world that is not God; to do so is God's very nature in the way it is fire's nature to give off heat into its surroundings. But this is a free act, since God already has in God's own intra-Trinitarian life the perfect form of self-diffusing good, the perfect form of anything that God might hope to achieve in creating a good but non-divine world. One can talk then of this natural act of creating in personal terms; it is an act of generosity, an unforced demonstration of regard for the other, a gracious exhibition of concern for the good of others.

God, Providence, and the World
With this understanding of creation in hand, one can see how providence is implied by it. Talk of God's providence is just a way of singling out certain features of the world that God creates. If the world is created by God in all its respects, the world is being created by God as things within it act and form arrangements and move toward new ones, by way of natural and human causes. The activity, organization, and historical directionality of the world are all aspects of the world God creates; God gives rise to those aspects of the world as to every other. Since creation is not identified with the beginning of the world (should it have one) but means that the world is being held up into being at all times, the world's processes, and the arrangements of things they produce, are all included in what God creates. The world is the creation of God from start to finish, throughout the whole

of natural and human history, and throughout each created cause's course, from its beginning to act through its achievement of effects.

Providence refers to God's plan for the world but also to the way it is executed in a world that has its own powers of activity. By bringing into being a world with such powers, God gives the world a hand in the execution of God's plan; the world is made the partner of that plan, in stronger and weaker senses across the world's history—whether the world's creatures do so by natural instinct or by choice, and whether we do so as Christ does by a will aligned with God or as sinners and those ignorant of God's plans. The doctrines of God and creation reveal certain general features about how the plan is being executed—as that plan comes to fruition in Christ and elsewhere.

For example, because God is the creator of the world in all its respects, God does not need to replace the activities of creatures with God's own in order to achieve God's ends. God can instead give rise to the very powers and acts of creatures that further those ends. Nor do those actions of creatures replace the need for God's activity as creator; without God's holding of them into existence, such acts would not exist. As everywhere, so in a special way in Christ: God does not save us by replacing the human capacities of Jesus with God's own; God saves in and through the very human acts by which Jesus lives and dies. God works everywhere in and through creatures, while their activities remain their own (for better or worse)—fully finite and fully fallible.

Because God is beyond kinds, God does not carry out God's plans by entering into the world, as one kind of force among others, whether regularly or by spasmodic intervention. God is not the name of one kind of force or principle—say, creativity or a principle of novelty—operating within the world. God is not working alongside us, doing one part of the work that needs to be done while the world does another. Instead, God, as creator, is responsible for the working of the whole. Nor does God enter into the world after the fact, after the workings of the world are done, to coerce or redirect it. Because God brings them to be and holds them up into existence, God doesn't work on or from the outside of causes operating independently of God, in imitation of the way limited creatures have to coerce or redirect matters that preexist their activity.

Nor does God need creatures of any particular sort to achieve God's ends within the world. Remembering the complexities of language of intentional agency helps us to see how the characteristics of God's own planning imply nothing, one way or another, about the world God brings about to execute it. God's plans, for example, are by definition purposeful, but that need not mean that the contents of God's plans for the world include the creation of purposeful agents any more than my plan to hit a bull's-eye requires execution by an arrow with the same end in mind. God may be working in the world for our good out of the goodness of God's heart, but that does not mean that the world is.

The same loose relation with created causes of any particular sort follows from the immediacy of God's agency. Because God's creative powers extend to everything that happens in an equally direct fashion, what God wants to happen is not mediated by the activities of the creatures that carry it out in the strong way that, say, my wanting a submarine to be raised from the ocean bottom is mediated by the workings of heavy lifting equipment. (If that equipment is faulty or its operator has other plans, I'm in trouble!) Unlike the case of creatures bringing about effects through the workings of others, God's creative activity extends directly to everything and not indirectly to some things by way only of their causes. Created causes are not the means by which God brings into existence the effects of those causes, since the whole of those causes, their workings, and effects are the result of God's creative activity. Picture the whole world, in all its complexity of causal process, as a horizontal plane, suspended into existence, at each and every point, by the vertical threads (invisible and infinitesimal) of God's own working, and you will begin to see the sense this all makes.

God's creative activity extends directly to everything that happens, whether or not, therefore, sufficient created causes exist for those happenings or whatever the character of the causes that exist—whether they work purposely or blindly, accidentally or necessarily, and so forth. God can bring about what creatures, of their own powers, cannot, just as, beyond all human capacity, Christ's human powers for living and dying save us from sin and death. God does not have to make creatures the partners of God's plans; God might do without their powers altogether. God does not have to save us, for example, by becoming incarnate—God could, one supposes, simply destroy sin and death by fiat—but freely chooses to make human nature in Christ the partner of the process. God can make do with partners in only the weakest sense of that term—with creatures who work not at all, or blindly and without foresight, or with malice of intention. But as shown in Christ, God can also work with the full gamut of created causes, such as with the natural process of dying, willingly entered into by a man whose acts were in knowing conformity with God's, violently achieved through the ignorance and sin of everyone around him—Romans, his own people, and his chosen apostles.

Understanding God's providence in these ways—in light of Christian teachings about God and creation—protects against the idea of a God whose concerns are limited, a God who demands that creatures bend in submission to a tyrannical, inescapable will, a God who must fear frustration by the failure of creatures to match the characteristics of God's own will. But only in Christ is any of this known for sure. In Christ it becomes clear: The plan is one of steadfast, unbreakable love for the whole of what

God has created, a plan executed in and through the throes of a life like any other in its humanity, a life that sees the death to which all creatures come, hastened by violent sufferings wrought by the misguided, short-sighted acts of even those closest to him—the self-chosen disciples of his own mission of love. It is by that death, worked in that way, that Jesus saves. If, then, this same God holds up into existence a whole world with these flaws of both finitude and deliberate failing, it must be as an act of beneficent mercy, in which we may trust.

Permissions

These pages constitute a continuation of the copyright page. Grateful acknowledgment is made to the following for permission to quote from copyrighted material:

Thomas Aquinas, "Quest III: *On the Causes of Sin*," in *On Evil*, ed. Brian Davies (Oxford: Oxford University Press, 2003). Reprinted by permission of Oxford University Press, Inc. All rights reserved.

Hans Urs von Balthasar, "Woman as Answer," in *Dramatis Personae: Persons in Christ*, vol. 3 of *Theo-Drama: Theological Dramatic Theory* (San Francisco: Ignatius Press, 1978). Reprinted by permission of Ignatius Press. All rights reserved.

Karl Barth, "The Basic Form of Humanity," "The Reality of Nothingness," and "The Christian Belief in Providence," in *Church Dogmatics*, ed. G. W. Bromiley and T. F. Torrance (Edinburgh: T. & T. Clark, 1960). Reprinted by kind permission of Continuum International Publishing Group. All rights reserved.

Bonaventure, "Breviloquium," in *The Works of Bonaventure* (Paterson, NJ: St. Anthony Guild Press, 1963). Reprinted by permission of St. Anthony Guild Press. All rights reserved.

James H. Cone, "God and Black Suffering," in *The Spirituals and the Blues: An Interpretation* (Maryknoll, NY: Orbis Books, 1991). Reprinted by permission of Orbis Books. All rights reserved.

Julian of Norwich, *Showings*, from The Classics of Western Spirituality, translated from the critical text with an introduction by Edmund Colledge, OSA, and James Walsh, SJ. Copyright © 1978 by Paulist Press, Inc., New York/Mahwah, NJ. Used with permission. www.paulistpress.com.

Catherine Keller, "The Pluri-Singularity of Creation," in *Face of the Deep: A Theology of Becoming* (London: Routledge, 2003). Reprinted by permission of Taylor & Francis Books UK. All rights reserved.

David Kelsey, "The Doctrine of Creation from Nothing," in *Evolution and Creation*, ed. Ernan McMullin (Notre Dame, IN: University of Notre Dame Press, 1985). Reprinted by permission of University of Notre Dame Press. All rights reserved.

Andrew Louth, ed., *Maximus the Confessor* (New York: Routledge, 1996).Reprinted by permission of Taylor & Francis Books UK. All rights reserved.

Mary McClintock Fulkerson, "Contesting the Gendered Subject: A Feminist Account of the *Imago Dei*" in *Horizons in Feminist Theology*, ed. Rebecca S. Chopp and Sheila Greeve Davaney (Minneapolis: Fortress, 1997). Reprinted by permission of Augsburg Fortress. All rights reserved.

Jürgen Moltmann, "Creation Out of Nothing," in *God in Creation: A New Theology of Creation and the Spirit of God* (New York: Harper & Row, 1991; London: SCM Press, Ltd., 1985). Reprinted by permission of HarperCollins Publishers and SCM Press. All rights reserved.

Origen of Alexandria, *On First Principles* (London: SPCK, 1936). Reprinted by permission of SPCK. All rights reserved.

Wolfhart Pannenberg, "The Doctrine of Creation in an Age of Scientific Cosmology," in *An Introduction to Systematic Theology* (Grand Rapids: Wm. B. Eerdmans Publishing Co., 1991). Reproduced by permission of Wm. B. Eerdmans Publishing Company. Used by permission. All rights reserved.

Arthur Peacocke, "God's Interaction with the World, in *Paths from Science towards God: The End of All Our Exploring* (Oxford: Oneworld, 2001). Reprinted by permission of Oneworld Publications. All rights reserved.

Regin Prenter, "The Biblical Witness Concerning Creation" in *Creation and Redemption* (Philadelphia: Fortress Press, 1967). Reprinted by permission of Augsburg Fortress. All rights reserved.

Stephen G. Ray Jr., *Do No Harm: Social Sin and Christian Responsibility* (Minneapolis: Fortress Press, 2003). Reprinted by permission of Augsburg Fortress. All rights reserved.

Rosemary Radford Ruether, *Sexism and God-Talk* by Rosemary Radford Ruether, copyright © 1983, 1993 by Rosemary Radford Ruether. Reprinted by permission of Beacon Press, Boston. All rights reserved.

Valerie Saiving, "The Human Situation: A Feminine View," in *Journal of Religion* 40, no. 2 (April 1960). Copyright 1960 University of Chicago Press. Reprinted by permission of University of Chicago Press. All rights reserved.

Dumitru Staniloae, "Creation 'Ex Nihilio' in Time," in *The World: Creation and Deification*, vol. 2 of *The Experience of God: Orthodox Dogmatic Theology* (Brookline, MA: Holy Cross Orthodox Press, 2005). Reprinted by permission of Holy Cross Orthodox Press. All rights reserved.

Pierre Teilhard de Chardin, "The Present State of Mankind," in *The Future of Man* by Pierre Teilhard de Chardin. Copyright © 1959 by Editions du Seuil. English translation copyright © 1964 by William Collins Sons & Co., Ltd., London and Harper & Row, Inc., New York. Originally published in French as *L'Avenir de L'Homme*. Reprinted by permission of Georges Borchardt, Inc., for Editions de Seuil. All rights reserved.

Teresa of Avila, *The Interior Castle*, from the Classics of Western Spirituality, translated by Kieran Kavanaugh, OCD, and Otillo Rodriguez, OCD. Copyright 1979 by the Washington Province of Discalced Carmelites, Inc., Paulist Press, Inc., New York/Mahwah, NJ. Used with permission. www.paulistpress.com.

Rowan Williams, "Against Symbols," in *Writing in the Dust: After September 11* (Grand Rapids: Wm. B. Eerdmans Publishing Co., 2002; London: Hodder and Stoughton, 2002). Copyright 2002 Rowan Williams. Reproduced by permission of Wm. B. Eerdmans Publishing Company and Hodder and Stoughton Limited. Used by permission. All rights reserved.

John Zizioulas, "From Biological to Ecclesial Existence," in *Being as Communion: Studies in Personhood and the Church* (Crestwood, NY: St. Vladimir's Seminary Press, 1997). Reprinted by permission of St. Vladimir's Seminary Press. www.svspress.com. All rights reserved.

Suggestions for Further Reading

The following list includes significant books (including many of those from which the selections in this volume have been taken) published over the last century on some aspect of the doctrine of creation. It is in no way exhaustive, but it does include a broad range of perspectives on the character of God's relationship to that which is not God.

Books on the Doctrine of Creation in General

Barth, Karl. *Church Dogmatics*, vol. 3 (in four parts). Ed. Geoffrey W. Bromiley and T. F. Torrance. Trans. G. W. Bromiley, H. Knight, et al. Edinburgh: T. & T. Clark, 1958–1961.

Brunner, Emil. *The Christian Doctrine of Creation and Redemption*, vol. 2 of *Dogmatics*. Trans. Olive Wyon. Philadelphia: Westminster Press, 1952.

Fergusson, David. *The Cosmos and the Creator: An Introduction to the Theology of Creation*. London: SPCK, 1998.

Gilkey, Langdon. *Maker of Heaven and Earth: A Study of the Christian Doctrine of Creation*. Garden City, NY: Doubleday, 1959.

Gunton, Colin. *The Doctrine of Creation: Essays in Dogmatics, History, and Philosophy*. Edinburgh: T. & T. Clark, 1997.

Hayes, Zachary. *Gift of Being: A Theology of Creation*. Collegeville, MN: Liturgical Press, 2001.

Moltmann, Jürgen. *God in Creation: A New Theology of Creation and the Spirit of God*. New York: HarperCollins, 1991.

Prenter, Regin. *Creation and Redemption*. Philadelphia: Fortress Press, 1967.

Ruether, Rosemary R. *Gaia and God: An Eco-feminist Theology of Earth Healing*. San Francisco: HarperSanFrancisco, 1994.

Schwarz, Hans. *Creation*. Grand Rapids: Wm. B. Eerdmans Publishing Co., 2002.

Staniloae, Dimitru. *The World: Creation and Deification*, vol. 2 of *The Experience of God: Orthodox Dogmatic Theology*. Ed. and trans. Ioan Ionita and Robert Barringer. Brookline, MA: Holy Cross Orthodox Press, 2005.

Books on the Topic of Origins

Craig, William L. *Theism, Atheism and Big Bang Cosmology*. Oxford: Oxford University Press, 1983.

Dales, Richard C. *Medieval Discussions of the Eternity of the World*. Leiden: E. J. Brill, 1990.

Davies, Paul. *God and the New Physics*. New York: Penguin, 1990.
Drees, Willem B. *Beyond the Big Bang: Quantum Cosmologies and God*. LaSalle, IL: Open Court, 1990.
Keller, Catherine. *Face of the Deep: A Theology of Becoming*. New York: Routledge, 2000.
May, Gerhard. *Creatio ex Nihilo: The Doctrine of Creation Out of Nothing in Early Christian Thought*. Trans. A. S. Worrall. Edinburgh: T. & T. Clark, 1994.
Stannard, Russell. *Doing Away with God? Creation and the Big Bang*. London: Faber & Faber, 1993.
Welker, Michael. *Creation and Reality*. Minneapolis: Augsburg Fortress, 1999.
Worthing, Mark W. *God, Creation and Contemporary Physics*. Minneapolis: Augsburg Fortress, 1995.

Books on Theological Anthropology
Balthasar, Hans Urs von. *A Theological Anthropology*. New York: Sheed & Ward, 1967.
Brunner, Emil. *Man in Revolt: A Christian Anthropology*. Trans. Olive Wyon. London: Lutterworth, 1939.
Gonzalez, Michelle A. *Created in God's Image: An Introduction to Feminist Theological Anthropology*. Maryknoll, NY: Orbis, 2007.
Hall, Douglas John. *Imaging God: Dominion as Stewardship*. Grand Rapids: Wm. B. Eerdmans Publishing Co., 1986.
Hefner, Philip. *The Human Factor: Evolution, Culture, Religion*. Minneapolis: Fortress Press, 1993.
Hopkins, Dwight N. *Being Human: Race, Culture, and Religion*. Minneapolis: Fortress Press, 2005.
McFadyen, Alistair. *The Call to Personhood: A Christian Theory of the Individual in Social Relationships*. Cambridge: Cambridge University Press, 1990.
McFarland, Ian. *Difference and Identity: A Theological Anthropology*. Cleveland: Pilgrim Press, 2001.
Nellas, Panayiotis. *Deification in Christ: The Nature of the Human Person*. Crestwood, NY: St. Vladimir's Seminary Press, 1997.
Niebuhr, Reinhold. *The Nature and Destiny of Man: A Christian Interpretation*. 2 vols. London: Nisbet, 1941–1943.
Pannenberg, Wolfhart. *Anthropology in Theological Perspective*. Trans. Geoffrey W. Bromiley. Edinburgh: T. & T. Clark, 1985.

Books on the Problem of Evil and Sin
Adams, Marilyn McCord. *Horrendous Evils and the Goodness of God*. Ithaca, NY: Cornell University Press, 1999.

Farley, Wendy. *Tragic Vision and Divine Compassion: A Contemporary Theodicy*. Louisville, KY: Westminster John Knox Press, 1990.
Griffin, David Ray. *God, Power, and Evil: A Process Theodicy*. Philadelphia: Westminster Press, 1976.
McFadyen, Alistair. *Bound to Sin: Abuse, Holocaust, and the Christian Doctrine of Sin*. Cambridge: Cambridge University Press, 2000.
Plaskow, Judith. *Sex, Sin and Grace: Women's Experience and the Theologies of Reinhold Niebuhr and Paul Tillich*. Lanham, MD: University Press of America, 1980.
Ray, Stephen G. *Do No Harm: Social Sin and Christian Responsibility*. Minneapolis: Fortress Press, 2003.
Schwarz, Hans. *Evil: A Historical and Theological Perspective*. Trans. Mark Worthing. Minneapolis: Fortress Press, 1995.
Suchocki, Marjorie Hewitt. *The Fall to Violence: Original Sin in Relational Theology*. New York: Continuum, 1994.
Wiley, Tatha. *Original Sin: Origins, Developments, Contemporary Meaning*. New York: Paulist Press, 2002.

Books on Providence and Divine Action
Berkouwer, G. C. *The Providence of God*. Trans. Lewis B. Smedes. Grand Rapids: Wm. B. Eerdmans Publishing Co., 1952.
Burrell, David. *Aquinas: God and Action*. Notre Dame, IN: University of Notre Dame Press, 1979.
Gwynne, Paul D. *Special Divine Action: Key Issues in the Contemporary Debate (1965–1995)*. Rome: Gregorian University Press, 1996.
McFague, Sallie. *The Body of God: An Ecological Theology*. Minneapolis: Fortress Press, 1993.
Overman, Richard H. *Evolution and the Christian Doctrine of Creation: A Whiteheadian Interpretation*. Philadelphia: Westminster Press, 1967.
Page, Ruth. *God and the Web of Creation*. London: SCM, 1996.
Peters, Ted. *Evolution from Creation to New Creation: Conflict, Conversation, and Convergence*. Nashville: Abingdon Press, 2003.
Polkinghorne, John. *Science and Providence: God's Interaction with the World*. London: SPCK, 1989.
Santmire, Paul. *Nature Reborn: The Ecological and Cosmic Promise of Christian Theology*. Minneapolis: Fortress Press, 2000.
Saunders, Nicholas. *Divine Action and Modern Science*. Cambridge: Cambridge University Press, 2002.
Tanner, Kathryn. *God and Creation in Christian Theology: Tyranny or Empowerment?* Oxford: Basil Blackwell, 1988.

Tracy, Thomas F., ed. *The God Who Acts: Philosophical and Theological Explorations*. College Station: Pennsylvania State University, 1994.
Ward, Keith. *God, Chance and Necessity*. Oxford: Oxford University Press, 1996.

Index

Ambrose, 260n42
Anselm, 35, 48–49
Anselm of Laon, 235n5
Aquinas, Thomas, 16, 56, 265
 on the creature, 129–37
 on evil and sin, 215–30
 on God as creator, 24–30
 on providence, 353–62, 390n29
Arendt, Hannah, 302
Aristophanes, 171n21
Aristotle, 17, 24-25, 27, 34, 56, 217, 220-21, 225-26, 354
Armour, Ellen, 179n16, 188
Athanasius, 93–94
 on evil and sin, 200–204
Augustine of Hippo, 17, 19, 24, 130–34 passim, 136, 328, 338, 357
 on evil and sin, 204–17, 222, 224–27, 231, 233, 235–36, 237n9, 239, 259n40, 260n43, 261n49l, 356
 on God as creator, 9-16, 35n12, 37, 53, 61–62, 66
 on providence, 344–53, 358–59, 361, 369n3
Austin, J. L., 50, 64
Averroes, 225

Balthasar, Hans Urs von, on the creature, 148–55
Barth, Karl, 67n6, 151, 313
 on the creature, 138–47
 on evil and sin, 269–81
 on providence, 391–99
Basil the Great (Basil of Caesarea), 28, 88–90, 104-5
Bechtel, Lynn, 80
Bede, 224
Belsey, Catherine, 177n10
Benedict, Ruth, 291–92
Benjamin, W., 71n10
Bergson, Henri, 399
Bernard of Clairvaux, 221, 232
Bethune-Baker, J. F., 235n5
Bloch, Ernst, 71, 314
Boehme, Jakob, 84, 284n4, 418

Boethius, 130-31, 359-61
Bonaventure, 56
 on God as creator, 16–24
Bonhoeffer, Dietrich, 326, 328, 332
Brightman, E. S., 323n41
Brunner, Emil, 67
Buddeus, Johann Franz, 390n29
Bultmann, Rudolf, 39n1
Bunyan, John, 266
Butler, Judith, 83, 179–81, 186

Calvin, John, 32, 328
 on evil and sin, 230–39
 on providence, 367–74
Childs, Brevard, 58n7
Churchland, Patricia S., 433
Cicero, 254n27, 357
Clarke, Samuel, 426
Clément, Olivier, 89n4
Cobb, John R., Jr., 80, 315
 on providence, 406–11
Coelestius, 233n3
Cohen, Arthur A., xxiiin7
Comstock, Gary David, 332n6
Cone, James H., on evil and sin, 304–15
Coward, Rosalind, 177n10
Cyprian of Carthage, 204
Cyril of Alexandria, 166

Daly, Mary, 185
Damian, Peter, 155n7
Dante, 68
Danto, Arthur, 412n1, 413
Dawkins, Richard, xxxi
de Beauvoir, Simone, 175
Deleluze, Gilles, 79
de Leon, Moses, 81
Democritus, 354, 356
Derrida, Jacques, 178n12
Descartes, René, 420
de Staël, Anne Louise Germaine, 297
Deutsch, Helene, 293, 301n15
Dionysius the Areopagite, 92, 128, 130–31, 216, 218, 220–22, 226, 359, 362
Donovan, Josephine, 175n7

Eckhart, Meister, 74, 84n38
Eichrodt, Walther, 74n4, 75, 76n14
Einstein, Albert, 53
Eisenstein, Hester, 175n7
El Greco, 79
Ely, Stephen, 317-19
Engels, Frederick, 175n6
Ephrem the Syrian, 155
Euripides, 171n21
Evans, Donald, 49-50, 54

Fabre, Jean Henri, 263
Fairweather, E. R., 235n5
Faraday, Michael, 425
Farnham, Marynia F., 298n13
Farrer, Austin, xxx, 64n17, 432
Fewell, Danna, 74-75
Foucault, Michel, 179n15, 180
Freud, Sigmund, 249n5
Fromm, Erich, 293
Fulgentius, 218
Fulkerson, Mary McClintock, 81n28
  on the creature, 173-89

Gage, Frances, 137
Garrison, William Lloyd, 137
Gerhard, Johann, 391n33
Gilkey, Langdon, xxvn8
Gilson, Etienne, 51n2
Glennon, Lynda M., 160n3
Grant, Jacquelyn, 332
Greggs, Gil, 186n29
Gregory of Nazianzus, 104, 123, 124n1
Gregory of Nyssa, 88, 124nn2, 3; 125n8, 161, 163n2, 358
  on the creature, 104-18
Gregory the Great, 132, 357
Griffin, David Ray
  on evil and sin, 315-25
  on providence, 406-11
Guattari, Pierre-Felix, 79
Gunn, David, 74-75
Gunton, Colin E., 327n4

Haldane, J. B. S., 401
Hamann, J. G., 67
Haraway, Donna, 174-75, 187-89
Hare, Peter, 317, 318, 323n41
Hartmann, Heidi, 175n6
Hegel, G. W. F., 84, 327n1
Hesiod, 4, 6
Hilary of Poitiers, 35, 131

Hippolytus, 36n16
Hodge, C., 235n5
Huxley, Julian, 401
Hystaspes, 3

Ibn Ezra, Abraham, 75, 76n13, 77
Innocent VIII, 265
Irenaeus, 60, 105, 193
  on the creature, 97-104
  on providence, 341-44
Irigaray, Luce, 73
Isidore of Seville, 224

Jaggar, Alison, 175n7
Jakobson, Roman, 184
Jameson, Frederic, 185
Jantzen, Grace M., 83n33
  on providence, 411-19, 429
Jastrow, Robert, 62n14
Jeans, James, 399, 405
Jerome, 8, 226
John Chrysostom, on the creature, 118-23
John of Damascus, 36n17
Johnson, Elizabeth, 332
Julian of Norwich, on providence, 362-66
Jung, C. J., 158n1
Justin Martyr, 4, 57, 59, 343
  on God as creator, 3-4, 11n1

Kant, Immanuel, 426
Keller, Catherine, xvi
  on God as creator, 72-86
Kelsey, David, on God as creator, 47-65
Kenny, Anthony, 412-13
Kierkegaard, Søren, 282-84

Lactantius, 369n3
Langton, Stephen, 237n9
Latour, Bruno, 78-79
Leibniz, Gottfried, 426
Leo I, 166
Lombard, Peter, 17, 215n2, 237
Lossky, Vladimir, 93
Lundberg, Ferndinand, 298n13
Luria, Isaac, 66
Luther, Martin, xiv, 31n2, 32, 260n41, 265, 328, 394
  on creation, 36n13

Madden, Edward, 317-18, 323n41
Marcion, 39n1
Martineau, James, 285n5

Matt, Daniel Chanan, 82n29
Maximus the Confessor, 88n1, 92, 161, 163n2, 168n11, 170nn17, 18; 171n23
　on the creature, 123-29
McFague, Sallie, 160n4
McGlone, Jeannette, 158n2
McMullin, Ernan, 53n3, 62-63
Mead, Lawrence, 329-30
Mead, Margaret, 292-93, 295n9, 297, 299
Melanchthon, Philipp, 251n14
Menander, 3
Mitchell, Julie, 175n6
Moltmann, Jürgen, 80, 419
　on God as creator, 65-72
Montagu, Ashley, 293
Moore, Stephen, 78n19
Morris, Simon Conway, xxxi
Morus, Friedrich Nathanael, 38n23, 382n11, 383n13, 390n28, 390n30
Mosheim, Johannes Laurentius, 387, 388n24
Mowinckel, Sigmund, 42nn3, 6

Nachmanides, 77, 85
Newton, Isaac, 53, 420, 426
Nicholas of Cusa, 67
Nicholas of Lyra, 260n41
Niebuhr, Reinhold, 296, 326-28, 332
　on evil and sin, 281-90
Nygren, Anders, 289

Oetinger, Friedrich, 67
Origen of Alexandria, 31, 37, 92, 424
　on evil and sin, 193-200, 261n45
　on God as creator, 7-9

Pannenberg, Wolfhart, 80
　on providence, 419-29
Parsons, Talcott, 293
Pascal, Blaise, 287
Paul, Nathaniel, 312-13
Payne, Daniel, 312
Peacocke, Arthur, on providence, 429-35
Pedersen, Johannes, 40n2, 42n5
Pelagius, 233
Pelikan, Jaroslav, 53n3, 61
Penelhum, Terence, 413
Philo, 33
Pius XII, 62n14, 94n12
Plantinga, Cornelius, 326-28, 331-32
Plaskow, Judith, 83n33
Plato, 3, 4, 11n1, 88, 93, 316, 358, 407-8, 439
Plotinus, 426-27

Prenter, Regin, on God as creator, 39-47
Prigogine, Ilya, 78n18
Przywara, E., 151n3

Quenstedt, Johann Andrea, 380n7, 382n12, 389n27
Quick, Paddy, 175n6

Rashi, 76
Rauschenbusch, Walter, on evil and sin, 262-69, 281-82
Ray, Stephen G., Jr., on evil and sin, 325-34
Reik, Theodore, 293
Reinhard, Franz Volkmar, 388n25, 390n30
Riesman, David, 302
Rubenstein, Richard L., xxiiin7
Rudavshy, Tamar, 77n16
Ruether, Rosemary Radford, 173, 181-83, 185, 188
　on the creature, 156-61
Russell, Bertrand, 284n3

Saiving, Valerie, on evil and sin, 289-304, 325
Samuelson, Norbert, 75n10, 77-78, 80
Santmire, H. Paul, xxn6
Saussure, Ferdinand de, 177-78, 183, 185
Schelling, Friedrich Wilhelm Joseph von, 67, 83-84, 284n4
Schleiermacher, Friedrich, 47
　on evil and sin, 247-61, 262
　on God as creator, 30-39
　on providence, 374-91
Schonberg, Arnold, 77
Schwöbel, Christoph, 327n3
Sejnowski, T. J., 433
Serres, Michel, 73, 78-81
Sibyl, the, 3
Singer, Isaac Bashevis, 66n2
Socrates, 380n9
Speiser, E. A., 58, 80n23
Spelman, Elizabeth, 176
Speyr, Adrienne von, 148
Spinoza, Baruch, 426
Staniloae, Dumitru, on God as creator, 85-94
Stock, K., 72n11
Storr, Gottlob Christian, 386n18, 389n25
Strindberg, August, 149n2
Swinburne, Richard, 413-14

Tanner, Kathryn, on providence, 435-50

Teilhard de Chardin, Pierre, xxxi, 169n12
  on providence, 399–406, 411
Teresa of Avila, on evil and sin, 239–47
Themistius, 225
Theophilus of Antioch, 59, 61, 97
  on God as creator, 4–7
Tillich, Paul, 418n6
Tompkins, Jane, 178–79
Tong, Rosemarie, 175n7
Trembelas, P., 170n17
Trilling, Lionel, 302–3
Truth, Sojourner, on the creature, 137–38
Tully, 357

Victor, Vincentius, 235n5
von Oettingen, A., 67
von Rad, Gerhard, 58n7, 75n9

Waskwo, Arthur, 84n36
Weedon, Chris, 177n10
Wehram, Gordon, 74n5
White, Lynn, Jr., xxn6
Whitehead, Alfred North, xviii, 85, 316–23, 407–10
Wilken, Robert, 60n11
Williams, Rowan, on evil and sin, 334–38
Wittig, Monique, 179n16
Wolfson, Elliott, 83
Woolf, Virginia, 301

Zizioulas, John, on the creature, 161–73
Zornberg, Avivah Gottleib, 76
Zozimus, 233n3

green press
INITIATIVE

Presbyterian Publishing is committed to preserving ancient forests and natural resources. We elected to print this title on 30% post consumer recycled paper, processed chlorine free. As a result, for this printing, we have saved:

14 Trees (40' tall and 6-8" diameter)
6 Million BTUs of Total Energy
102 Pounds of Greenhouse Gases
6,454 Gallons of Wastewater
218 Pounds of Solid Waste

Presbyterian Publishing made this paper choice because our printer, Thomson-Shore, Inc., is a member of Green Press Initiative, a nonprofit program dedicated to supporting authors, publishers, and suppliers in their efforts to reduce their use of fiber obtained from endangered forests.

For more information, visit www.greenpressinitiative.org

Environmental impact estimates were made using the Environmental Defense Paper Calculator. For more information visit: www.edf.org/papercalculator

www.ingramcontent.com/pod-product-compliance
Lightning Source LLC
Chambersburg PA
CBHW031359290426
44110CB00011B/215